JEWISH LAW | HISTORY, SOURCES, PRINCIPLES | *Ha-Mishpat Ha-Ivri*

VOLUME I

PART ONE

The History and Elements of Jewish Law

and

PART TWO

The Legal Sources of Jewish Law

SECTION 1

Exegesis and Interpretation

VOLUME II

PART TWO (*continued*)

The Legal Sources of Jewish Law

SECTION 2

Legislation, Custom, Precedent, and Legal Reasoning

VOLUME III

PART THREE

The Literary Sources of Jewish Law

VOLUME IV

PART FOUR

Jewish Law in the State of Israel

and

Appendixes, Glossary, Bibliography, Indexes

A PHILIP AND MURIEL BERMAN EDITION

MENACHEM ELON

DEPUTY PRESIDENT, SUPREME COURT OF ISRAEL

JEWISH LAW

HISTORY, SOURCES, PRINCIPLES

Ha-Mishpat Ha-Ivri VOLUME III

Translated from the Hebrew
by Bernard Auerbach
and Melvin J. Sykes

THE JEWISH PUBLICATION SOCIETY Philadelphia Jerusalem 5754 / 1994

Originally published in Hebrew under the title
Ha-Mishpat Ha-Ivri
by the Magnes Press, The Hebrew University, Jerusalem

Manufactured in the United States of America

The author and publisher gratefully acknowledge the support of the Philip and Muriel Berman Book Fund of The Jewish Publication Society, sponsored by Mr. and Mrs. Philip I. Berman, Allentown, Pennsylvania, in the publication of this book.

Library of Congress Cataloging-in-Publication Data

Elon, Menachem.
[Mishpaṭ ha-ʻIvri. English]
Jewish law : history, sources, principles / Menachem Elon ; translated from the Hebrew by Bernard Auerbach and Melvin J. Sykes.
p. cm.
Includes bibliographical references and index.
Volume I, ISBN 0–8276–0385–1
Volume II, ISBN 0-8276-0386-X
Volume III, ISBN 0-8276-0387-8
Volume IV, ISBN 0-8276-0388-6
Four-volume set, ISBN 0-8276-0389–4
1. Jewish law—History. 2. Rabbinical literature—History and criticism. 3. Law—Israel—Jewish influences. I. Title.
BM520.5.E4313 1993
296.1′8′09—dc20 93–9278
CIP

Designed by Arlene Putterman

Typeset in Meridien and Perpetua by Graphic Composition, Inc.
Printed by Hamilton Printing Company

Philip and Muriel Berman Edition

The Author

JUSTICE MENACHEM ELON was first appointed to the Supreme Court of Israel in 1977 and was named Deputy President of the Court in 1988. A legal scholar and teacher, he was awarded the Israel Prize in 1979 for *Ha-Mishpat Ha-Ivri*.

Justice Elon has published many works on the history and nature of Jewish law and the relation between it and the modern State of Israel, including *The Freedom of the Person of the Debtor in Jewish Law* (1964) and *Religious Legislation in the Laws of the State of Israel and Within the Jurisdiction of the Civil and Rabbinical Courts* (1968). From 1968 to 1971 he was editor of the Jewish Law section of the *Encyclopaedia Judaica*, which was subsequently collected in his *Principles of Jewish Law* (1975). By 1984 he had edited 10 volumes of *The Annual of the Institute for Research in Jewish Law of The Hebrew University of Jerusalem* and was also editing a digest of the responsa of the medieval authorities. He has been a member of government committees for the preparation of various bills of the Israeli Civil Law Coordination.

An ordained rabbi, Justice Elon earned his diploma from the Tel Aviv School of Law and Economics in 1948, received a master's degree in humanities, and was awarded a doctor of laws degree *cum laude* from The Hebrew University of Jerusalem. He began his affiliation with The Hebrew University in 1954 as an instructor of law and was subsequently appointed teaching associate, senior lecturer, associate professor, and, in 1972, Professor of Jewish Law.

Translators

BERNARD AUERBACH, Professor of Law, University of Maryland School of Law (retired, 1992). B.A. (Yeshiva University), J.D. (New York University), LL.M. (Yale University), Rabbinic Ordination (Rabbi Isaac Elchanan Theological Seminary, Yeshiva University), Sterling Fellow, (Yale University). *Consultant:* Court of Appeals of Maryland Standing Committee on Rules of Practice and Procedure (1965–1980). *Reporter:* Maryland Judicial Conference (1967–1970). *Recipient:* Bernard Revel Memorial Award for Arts and Sciences, Yeshiva College Alumni Association. *Member:* Jewish Law Association; American Bar Association.

MELVIN J. SYKES, A.B. (Johns Hopkins University), LL.B. (Harvard University), Diplomate, Baltimore Hebrew College. *Fellow:* American College of Trial Lawyers, American College of Trust and Estate Counsel, American Bar Foundation, Maryland Bar Foundation (former president). *Member:* American Law Institute, Court of Appeals of Maryland Standing Committee on Rules of Practice and Procedure; American and Maryland State Bar Associations, Bar Association of Baltimore City. *Sole Practitioner, Baltimore, Maryland:* General practice, trial and appellate litigation, probate and trusts. *Adjunct Faculty Member:* University of Maryland School of Law.

Editorial Consultant

DANIEL D. CHAZIN, *Member:* New Jersey and New York Bars. B.A. (Yeshiva University), J.D. (New York University). *Member:* American Bar Association, New Jersey and New York State Bar Associations. Gruss Fellow, 1989–90, New York University School of Law.

Assistant Editorial Consultant

NORMAN MENACHEM FEDER, A.B., M.A. (Columbia University), J.D. (New York University). Editor-in-Chief, N.Y.U. Journal of International Law & Politics (1986–1987). Luce Scholar (1987–1988). Law Clerk to Judge Roger J. Miner, United States Court of Appeals for the Second Circuit (1988–1989). Law Clerk to Deputy President Menachem Elon, Supreme Court of Israel (1989–1990). Associate, Cleary, Gottlieb, Steen & Hamilton, New York.

SUMMARY OF CONTENTS

	BIBLIOGRAPHICAL ABBREVIATIONS OF BOOKS AND ARTICLES FREQUENTLY CITED	xxv
	ABBREVIATIONS USED IN CITING RABBINIC WORKS AND SCHOLARLY LITERATURE	xxix
	ABBREVIATIONS USED IN CITING MODERN LEGAL MATERIALS	xxxi
	ACRONYMS AND APPELLATIONS OF HALAKHIC AUTHORITIES	xxxiii
	TRANSLITERATION GUIDE	xxxvii

VOLUME I

PART ONE
The History and Elements of Jewish Law

Chapter 1	THE HISTORY OF JEWISH LAW	1
Chapter 2	THE DEVELOPMENT OF JEWISH LAW: SOME IMPORTANT FACTORS	46
Chapter 3	THE SCIENTIFIC STUDY OF JEWISH LAW	75
Chapter 4	*MISHPAT IVRI:* DEFINITION AND NATURE	92
Chapter 5	THE ORAL LAW: DEFINITION AND GENERAL PRINCIPLES	190
Chapter 6	THE BASIC NORM AND THE SOURCES OF JEWISH LAW	228
Chapter 7	THE PREROGATIVES OF THE HALAKHIC AUTHORITIES	240

PART TWO
The Legal Sources of Jewish Law
SECTION 1 *Exegesis and Interpretation*

Chapter 8	EXEGESIS AND INTERPRETATION (MIDRASH AND *PARSHANUT*): INTRODUCTION	275
Chapter 9	EXEGETICAL INTERPRETATION OF THE TORAH	281
Chapter 10	INTERPRETATION OF THE *HALAKHAH*	400
Chapter 11	INTERPRETATION OF DOCUMENTS	422
Chapter 12	INTERPRETATION OF COMMUNAL ENACTMENTS	444

GLOSSARY G•1

VOLUME II

PART TWO *(continued)*
The Legal Sources of Jewish Law
SECTION 2 *Legislation, Custom, Precedent, and Legal Reasoning*

Chapter 13	LEGISLATION: INTRODUCTION	477
Chapter 14	LEGISLATION: NATURE, OBJECTIVES, AND PRINCIPLES OF LEGISLATION BY THE HALAKHIC AUTHORITIES	494
Chapter 15	LEGISLATION: ENACTMENTS THROUGH THE END OF THE TANNAITIC PERIOD	545
Chapter 16	LEGISLATION IN THE AMORAIC PERIOD	622
Chapter 17	LEGISLATION IN THE GEONIC PERIOD	643
Chapter 18	POST-GEONIC LEGISLATION: INTRODUCTION	666
Chapter 19	COMMUNAL ENACTMENTS	678
Chapter 20	SURVEY OF LEGISLATION FROM THE TENTH CENTURY C.E. TO THE PRESENT	780
Chapter 21	CUSTOM *(MINHAG)*: ITS NATURE AND THE SOURCE OF ITS BINDING FORCE	880
Chapter 22	CUSTOM: OPERATION AND CATEGORIES	895
Chapter 23	*MA'ASEH* AND PRECEDENT	945
Chapter 24	LEGAL REASONING *(SEVARAH)*	987
	GLOSSARY	G•1

VOLUME III

PART THREE
The Literary Sources of Jewish Law

Chapter 25	THE LITERARY SOURCES OF JEWISH LAW: NATURE AND DEFINITION	1017
Chapter 26	THE LITERARY SOURCES FROM THE SINAITIC REVELATION UNTIL THE *TANNAIM*	1020
Chapter 27	THE LITERARY SOURCES FROM THE TANNAITIC PERIOD UNTIL THE REDACTION OF THE TALMUD: INTRODUCTION	1038
Chapter 28	THE LITERARY SOURCES IN THE TANNAITIC PERIOD	1041
Chapter 29	THE LITERARY SOURCES IN THE AMORAIC PERIOD	1083
Chapter 30	THE LITERARY SOURCES AND OTHER HALAKHIC	

	LITERATURE IN THE POST-TALMUDIC PERIOD: INTRODUCTION	1101
Chapter 31	COMMENTARIES AND NOVELLAE	1104
Chapter 32	THE CODIFICATORY LITERATURE: NATURE AND STRUCTURE; THE PROBLEM OF CODIFICATION	1138
Chapter 33	THE CODIFICATORY LITERATURE: FROM THE GEONIC PERIOD UNTIL MAIMONIDES' *MISHNEH TORAH*	1149
Chapter 34	THE CODIFICATORY LITERATURE: MAIMONIDES' *MISHNEH TORAH*	1180
Chapter 35	THE CODIFICATORY LITERATURE: FROM MAIMONIDES UNTIL THE *SHULḤAN ARUKH;* THE *SEFER HA-TURIM*	1236
Chapter 36	THE CODIFICATORY LITERATURE: THE WORKS OF JOSEPH CARO AND MOSES ISSERLES	1309
Chapter 37	THE CODIFICATORY LITERATURE: REACTIONS TO THE *SHULḤAN ARUKH,* AND ITS FINAL ACCEPTANCE	1367
Chapter 38	THE CODIFICATORY LITERATURE: COMMENTARIES ON AND CODIFICATION AFTER THE *SHULḤAN ARUKH*	1423
Chapter 39	THE RESPONSA LITERATURE	1453
Chapter 40	LITERATURE FACILITATING RESEARCH IN JEWISH LAW: COMPILATIONS OF LEGAL DOCUMENTS, REFERENCE WORKS	1529
	GLOSSARY	G•1

VOLUME IV

PART FOUR
Jewish Law in the State of Israel

Chapter 41	INTRODUCTION: JEWISH LAW FROM THE ABROGATION OF JEWISH JURIDICAL AUTONOMY TO THE ESTABLISHMENT OF THE STATE OF ISRAEL	1575
Chapter 42	JEWISH LAW IN THE GENERAL LEGAL SYSTEM OF THE STATE OF ISRAEL	1619
Chapter 43	THE LAW OF PERSONAL STATUS IN THE RABBINICAL AND GENERAL COURTS: ADDITIONAL ASPECTS OF THE PROBLEM OF THE STATUS OF JEWISH LAW IN THE LAW OF THE STATE OF ISRAEL	1752
Chapter 44	THE FOUNDATIONS OF LAW ACT, 1980	1827
Chapter 45	THE RELIGIOUS AND CULTURAL ASPECTS OF THE QUESTION OF THE STATUS OF JEWISH LAW IN THE JEWISH STATE	1898

Appendixes, Glossary, Bibliography, Indexes

Appendix A	CROSS-REFERENCE TABLE—THE *MISHNEH TORAH* AND THE *SHULḤAN ARUKH*	1949

Appendix B	ADDITIONAL COMPARISONS OF THE LANGUAGE AND STYLE OF THE *MISHNEH TORAH,* THE *TURIM,* AND THE *SHULḤAN ARUKH*	1979
Appendix C	A LISTING OF THE MOST WIDELY KNOWN COMPILATIONS OF RESPONSA	1989
	GLOSSARY	2009
	BIBLIOGRAPHY	2025
	INDEX OF SOURCES	2063
	SUBJECT INDEX	2129

CONTENTS

BIBLIOGRAPHICAL ABBREVIATIONS OF BOOKS AND ARTICLES FREQUENTLY CITED xxv

ABBREVIATIONS USED IN CITING RABBINIC WORKS AND SCHOLARLY LITERATURE xxix

ABBREVIATIONS USED IN CITING MODERN LEGAL MATERIALS xxxi

ACRONYMS AND APPELLATIONS OF HALAKHIC AUTHORITIES xxxiii

TRANSLITERATION GUIDE xxxvii

VOLUME III

PART THREE
The Literary Sources of Jewish Law

Chapter 25 THE LITERARY SOURCES OF JEWISH LAW: NATURE AND DEFINITION 1017

I. The Literary Sources of Law, 1017
A. In General, 1017
B. Official Publications, 1017
C. Legal Literature and General Literature, 1018
II. The Literary Sources of Jewish Law, 1019

Chapter 26 THE LITERARY SOURCES FROM THE SINAITIC REVELATION UNTIL THE *TANNAIM* 1020

I. The Written Law, 1020
II. The Prophets and the Hagiographa, 1021
A. The Laws of the Sabbath, 1021
B. Modes of Acquisition, 1022
C. The King's Law, 1024
D. "A Person Shall Be Put to Death Only for His Own Crime", 1025
E. The Law of Suretyship, 1026

III. Legal and General Literature, 1027
A. Introduction, 1027
B. The Papyri, 1028
C. The Septuagint, 1029
D. Philo of Alexandria, 1030
E. Flavius Josephus, 1031
F. The Apocrypha, 1033
IV. Summary, 1037

Chapter 27 **THE LITERARY SOURCES FROM THE TANNAITIC PERIOD TO THE REDACTION OF THE TALMUD: INTRODUCTION** **1038**
I. Form and Substance of Talmudic Halakhic Literature, 1038
II. The Types of Literary Sources, 1039

Chapter 28 **THE LITERARY SOURCES IN THE TANNAITIC PERIOD** **1041**
I. The Term *Tanna*, 1042
II. The Generations of the *Zugot* and the Major *Tannaim*, 1043
III. Aramaic Translations of Scripture, 1045
IV. Compilations of Halakhic *Midrashim*, 1047
A. From the School of R. Ishmael, 1048
B. From the School of R. Akiva, 1048
V. The Mishnah—in General, 1049
A. The Literary Form of the *Halakhah* in the Mishnah as Compared with That in the Halakhic *Midrashim*, 1049
B. The Development and Redaction of the Mishnah, 1050
VI. The Literary Structure of the Mishnah, 1052
A. Etymology of the Term *Mishnah*, 1052
B. The Divisions of the Mishnah and Their Contents, 1053
C. The Arrangement of the Laws in the Mishnah, 1055
VII. The Codificatory Nature of the Mishnah, 1057
A. The Content of the Mishnah, 1057
1. Comparison Between the Law as Set Forth in the Mishnah and the Law in Cognate Sources, 1058
2. Statement of the Law without Attribution to a Source, or by Attribution to "the Sages", 1060
3. The Amoraic View of the Authoritative Character of the Mishnah, 1061
4. Diversity and Uniformity in Jewish Law, 1061
5. Multiplicity of Opinions in the Mishnah, 1070
B. The Legal Style of the Mishnah, 1072
1. The Casuistic Style, 1073
2. The Hybrid Casuistic-Normative Style, 1074
a. Possession of Real Property for Three Years as Proof of Ownership, 1075
b. Division of Property Owned in Common, 1075
3. The Normative Style, 1076
C. The Literary Style of the Mishnah, 1078
VIII. The *Tosefta*, 1078
IX. Summary, 1082

Chapter 29 **THE LITERARY SOURCES IN THE AMORAIC PERIOD** **1083**

I. Introduction, 1083
A. The Two Talmuds, 1083
B. Some Preliminary Definitions, 1083
1. *Amora*, 1083
2. Talmud, 1084
3. *Gemara*, 1084
II. The Leading *Amoraim* Listed by Generations, 1085
III. The Babylonian Talmud, 1087
A. The Babylonian Diaspora, 1087
B. The Teachings of the Babylonian *Amoraim* and the Contents of the Babylonian Talmud, 1088
C. The Redaction and Completion of the Babylonian Talmud, 1091
D. The *Savoraim*, 1093
E. Compilation of the Talmud on Only Part of the Mishnah, 1094
IV. The Jerusalem Talmud, 1095
A. Contents of the Jerusalem Talmud; Differences from the Babylonian Talmud, 1095
B. The Redaction of the Jerusalem Talmud, 1097
V. The Literary-Legal Nature of the Talmud and the Place of the Talmud in the Jewish Legal System, 1098

Chapter 30 **THE LITERARY SOURCES AND OTHER HALAKHIC LITERATURE IN THE POST-TALMUDIC PERIOD: INTRODUCTION** **1101**

I. *Geonim, Rishonim*, and *Aḥaronim*, 1101
II. The Three Major Types of Literary Sources of the *Halakhah*; the Various Kinds of Other Halakhic Legal Literature, 1102

Chapter 31 **COMMENTARIES AND NOVELLAE** **1104**

I. The Nature of Commentaries and Novellae, 1105
II. Commentaries and Novellae on the Mishnah, 1106
A. The Geonic Period, 1106
B. Maimonides' Commentary, 1106
C. Obadiah of Bertinoro's Commentary, 1108
D. *Tosafot Yom Tov* by Yom Tov Lipmann Heller, 1108
E. *Melekhet Shelomo* by Solomon Adeni, 1109
F. *Tiferet Yisra'el* by Israel Lipschutz, 1109
G. Ḥanokh Albeck's Commentary, 1110
III. Commentaries and Novellae on Halakhic *Midrashim* and the *Tosefta*, 1110
A. Halakhic *Midrashim*, 1110
1. Rabad's Commentary on the *Sifra*, 1110
2. Rabbenu Hillel's Commentary on the *Sifra* and the *Sifrei*, 1111
B. The *Tosefta*, 1111
1. *Ḥasdei David* by David Pardo, 1112
2. *Tosefta ki-Feshutah* by Saul Lieberman, 1112

IV. Commentaries on the Babylonian Talmud, 1113
A. The Geonic Period, 1113
B. Rabbenu Hananel's Commentary, 1114
C. Rabbenu Gershom Me'or Ha-Golah and His Students, 1115
D. Rashi's Commentary on the Talmud, 1116
V. Novellae on the Babylonian Talmud, 1118
A. The Ashkenazic Novellae; the Tosafists, 1118
1. In General, 1118
2. How the Novellae of the Tosafists Were Created, 1119
3. The Leading Tosafists, 1120
a. Samuel b. Meir (Rashbam), 1120
b. Jacob b. Meir (Rabbenu Tam), 1120
c. Isaac b. Samuel (Ri), 1120
d. Samson b. Abraham (Rash) of Sens, 1121
e. Meir b. Baruch (Maharam) of Rothenburg, 1121
4. Decisions and Responsa in the *Tosafot*, 1122
B. The Sephardic Novellae/Commentaries, 1123
1. Joseph ibn Migash (Ri Migash), 1123
2. Abraham b. David (Rabad) of Posquières, 1123
3. Meir Abulafia (Ramah), 1124
4. Naḥmanides (Ramban), 1124
5. Solomon b. Abraham Adret (Rashba), 1124
6. Yom Tov Ishbili (Ritba), 1125
7. Nissim Gerondi (Ran), 1125
8. Menahem Meiri, 1126
9. Beẓalel Ashkenazi, 1126
C. Novellae in the Period of the *Aḥaronim*, 1127
1. *Ḥiddushei Halakhot* by Samuel Eliezer Edels (Maharsha), 1128
2. *Penei Yehoshu'a* by Jacob Joshua Falk, 1129
VI. Commentaries and Novellae on the Jerusalem Talmud, 1130
A. The Jerusalem Talmud—Its Study and Use as a Basis for Legal Decisions, 1130
B. Solomon Sirillo's Commentary, 1132
C. *Sedeh Yehoshu'a* by Joshua Benveniste, 1134
D. Elijah of Fulda's Commentary and Novellae, 1134
E. David Fraenkel's Commentary and Novellae, 1135
F. Moses Margoliot's Commentary and Novellae, 1135
G. The Gaon of Vilna's Commentary, 1136

Chapter 32 **THE CODIFICATORY LITERATURE: NATURE AND STRUCTURE; THE PROBLEM OF CODIFICATION** **1138**
I. The Relationship of Codificatory Literature to Commentaries, Novellae, and the Responsa Literature, 1138
II. The Two Basic Types of Codes, 1139
III. Codification in Other Legal Systems, 1140
A. The Term "Codification", 1140
B. Codification in Continental Europe, 1141
C. Codification in Common-Law Countries, 1142
IV. The Nature and Problem of Codification in Jewish Law, 1144

Chapter 33 **THE CODIFICATORY LITERATURE FROM THE GEONIC PERIOD UNTIL MAIMONIDES' *MISHNEH TORAH*** **1149**

I. Codificatory Works in the Geonic Period, 1150
 A. *Sefer ha-She'iltot* by Aḥa of Shabḥa, 1150
 B. *Halakhot Pesukot* by Yehudai Gaon, 1153
 C. *Halakhot Gedolot*, 1155
 D. Motivating Factors for and against Codification in the Geonic Period, 1156
 E. Halakhic Monographs, 1158
  1. Saadiah Gaon, 1159
  2. Samuel b. Ḥophni Gaon, 1161
  3. Hai Gaon, 1164
  4. The Objectives of Halakhic Monographs, 1166
II. *Sefer ha-Halakhot* by Isaac Alfasi (Rif), 1167
 A. The Nature and Content of *Sefer ha-Halakhot*, 1167
 B. Commentaries on *Sefer ha-Halakhot*, 1173
  1. Zeraḥiah ha-Levi Gerondi (Rezah), 1173
  2. Abraham b. David (Rabad) of Posquières, 1173
  3. Naḥmanides (Ramban), 1174
  4. Jonathan of Lunel, 1175
  5. Nissim Gerondi (Ran), 1175
  6. Joseph Ḥabiba, 1176
  7. Joshua Boaz b. Simon Baruch, 1176
  8. Other Commentators, 1176
III. Codificatory Works from Alfasi to Maimonides, 1177
 A. Spain, 1177
  1. Isaac ibn Ghayyat (Riẓag), 1177
  2. Judah al-Bargeloni, 1177
 B. France and Germany, 1178
  1. The School of Rashi, 1178
  2. Eliezer b. Nathan (Raban), 1179

Chapter 34 **THE CODIFICATORY LITERATURE: MAIMONIDES' MISHNEH TORAH** **1180**

I. Strengthening of the Tendency toward Codification at the Beginning of the Rabbinic Period, 1181
II. Maimonides and his Codificatory Work, 1184
 A. Goals, 1184
 B. Compiling and Reworking the Halakhic Material, 1186
 C. Topical Arrangement and Classification, 1195
 D. Categorical Statement of Legal Rules with No Reference to Sources or Contrary Opinions, 1203
 E. Style and Draftsmanship of the *Mishneh Torah*, 1206
 F. Factual-Casuistic Formulation, 1211
 G. A Legal Code for the People, 1214
III. Critical Reaction to Maimonides' Codificatory Methodology, 1215
 A. Correspondence with *Dayyan* (Judge) Phinehas b. Meshullam of Alexandria, 1216
 B. Correspondence with Joseph ibn Aknin; Rendering Decisions on the Basis of the *Mishneh Torah*, 1222

C. Rabad's Critical Glosses, 1223
D. Asheri's Reaction, 1226
E. Interim Summary of the Stages of Codification of Jewish Law, 1229
IV. Commentaries on the *Mishneh Torah*, 1231
A. *Migdal Oz* by Shem Tov ibn Gaon, 1232
B. *Maggid Mishneh* by Vidal of Tolosa, 1232
C. *Kesef Mishneh* by Joseph Caro, 1233
D. *Yekar Tiferet* by David ibn Zimra (Radbaz), 1233
E. *Leḥem Mishneh* by Abraham di Boton, 1233
F. *Mishneh la-Melekh* by Judah Rosanes, 1234
G. *Haggahot Maimuniyyot* by Meir ha-Kohen of Rothenburg, 1234
V. The Ultimate Achievement of the *Mishneh Torah*, 1235

Chapter 35 **THE CODIFICATORY LITERATURE: FROM MAIMONIDES UNTIL THE *SHULḤAN ARUKH;* THE *SEFER HA-TURIM*** **1236**

I. Codificatory Literature Until the *Sefer ha-Turim*, 1237
A. Books Following the Order of the Talmud, and/or Organized in Whole or in Part According to Topic, 1238
1. *Sefer Avi ha-Ezri* and *Sefer Avi'asaf* by Eliezer b. Joel ha-Levi (Raviah), 1238
2. *Sefer ha-Roke'aḥ* by Eleazar b. Judah, 1239
3. *Sefer ha-Terumah* by Baruch b. Isaac, 1239
4. *Sefer ha-Manhig* by Abraham b. Nathan ha-Yarḥi, 1240
5. *Or Zaru'a* by Isaac b. Moses (Riaz), 1241
6. Codificatory Works by Naḥmanides (Ramban), 1242
7. *Sefer ha-Hashlamah* by Meshullam b. Moses of Beziers, 1243
8. *Sefer ha-Terumot* by Samuel Sardi, 1244
9. *Sefer Shibbolei ha-Leket* by Zedekiah b. Abraham ha-Rofe, 1247
10. *Sefer ha-Tanya*, 1248
11. *Sefer ha-Neyar*, 1248
12. *Sha'arei Dura* by Isaac b. Meir of Düren, 1248
13. *Sefer ha-Mordekhai* by Mordecai b. Hillel ha-Kohen, 1249
14. *Piskei ha-Rosh* by Asheri, and Its Commentaries, 1251
a. *Piskei ha-Rosh*, 1251
b. Commentaries on *Piskei ha-Rosh*, 1253
(1) *Haggahot Asheri* by Israel of Krems, 1253
(2) *Peri Megadim et al. by* Yom Tov Lipmann Heller, 1254
(3) *Korban Netanel* by Nethanel Weil, 1255
15. *Sefer ha-Tashbeẓ* by Samson b. Ẓadok and *Sefer ha-Parnas* by Moses Parnas of Rothenburg, 1255
16. *Sefer Eẓ Ḥayyim* by Jacob b. Judah Ḥazzan, 1255
17. *Sefer Orḥot Ḥayyim* by Aaron b. Jacob ha-Kohen, 1257
18. *Sefer Kol Bo*, 1258
B. Books Organized on the Basis of an Enumeration of the Biblical Commandments, 1259
1. *Sefer Yere'im* by Eliezer b. Samuel (Re'em), 1259

2. *Sefer Mizvot Gadol* (*Semag*) by Moses of Coucy, 1261
3. *Sefer Mizvot Katan* (*Semak*) by Isaac of Corbeil, 1263
4. *Sefer ha-Ḥinnukh*, 1265
C. Books Organized According to Idiosyncratic Criteria, 1267
1. *Sefer ha-Ittur* by Isaac of Marseilles, 1267
2. *Sefer Meisharim* and *Toledot Adam ve-Ḥavvah* by Rabbenu Jeroham b. Meshullam, 1269
D. The Codificatory Methodology of Solomon b. Abraham Adret (Rashba), 1273
1. *Torat ha-Bayit ha-Arokh, Torah ha-Bayit ha-Kaẓer,* and Other Codificatory Works by Rashba, 1273
2. *Bedek ha-Bayit* and *Mishmeret ha-Bayit*, 1276
II. *Sefer ha-Turim* by Jacob b. Asher, 1277
A. Jacob b. Asher's Codificatory Methodology, 1277
B. The Structure and Organization of *Sefer ha-Turim*, 1287
III. Commentaries on *Sefer ha-Turim*, 1302
A. *Bet Yosef* by Joseph Caro and *Darkhei Moshe* by Moses Isserles (Rema), 1303
B. *Bet Yisra'el* by Joshua Falk, 1303
C. *Bayit Ḥadash* (*Baḥ*) by Joel Sirkes, 1303
D. Compilations of Responsa Arranged According to the Organization of *Sefer ha-Turim*, 1304
IV. Codificatory Literature from *Sefer ha-Turim* to the *Shulḥan Arukh*, 1304

Chapter 36 **THE CODIFICATORY LITERATURE: THE WORKS OF JOSEPH CARO AND MOSES ISSERLES** **1309**

I. Joseph Caro and His Codificatory Achievement, 1309
A. Historical and Halakhic Circumstances, 1309
B. A Two-Part Code: A Book of *Halakhot* and a Book of *Pesakim*, 1312
C. *Bet Yosef*, 1313
1. Compendious Presentation of All the Halakhic Material, 1313
2. Methodology of Determining the Law, 1316
D. The *Shulḥan Arukh*, 1319
1. Codificatory Approach, 1319
2. Structure and Arrangement, 1323
3. Language and Style As Compared to the *Turim* and the *Mishneh Torah*, 1327
E. The Crystallization of the Methodology for Codifying Jewish Law, 1341
II. Moses Isserles (Rema) and His Contribution to the Codificatory Literature, 1345
A. The Polish Jewish Community, 1345
B. Jacob Pollack and Shalom Shakhna, and Their Attitude toward Codification, 1345
C. Moses Isserles (Rema), 1349
D. *Darkhei Moshe:* Its Purpose and Methodology, 1350
E. *Torat Ḥattat* and Its Methodology, 1357
F. Glosses to the *Shulḥan Arukh:* The *Mappah*—Its Objectives and Methodology, 1359

G. The *Shulḥan Arukh* as the Authoritative Code of Jewish Law, 1365

Chapter 37 **THE CODIFICATORY LITERATURE: REACTIONS TO THE *SHULḤAN ARUKH,* AND ITS FINAL ACCEPTANCE** **1367**

I. Introduction, 1368
II. The Eastern Countries, 1368
A. Joseph ibn Lev (Maharibal), 1368
B. The Agreement of Two Hundred Rabbis to Caro's Principle of Decision Making, 1369
C. Critiques of Specific Laws in the *Shulḥan Arukh,* 1370
1. Jacob Castro (Maharikash), 1371
2. Samuel Aboab, 1371
3. Yom Tov Ẓahalon (Maharitaẓ), 1372
D. The Acceptance of the *Shulḥan Arukh,* 1373
III. The Western Countries, 1374
A. Opposition to the *Shulḥan Arukh* without Proposing Any Alternative Type of Code, 1375
1. Ḥayyim b. Beẓalel, 1375
2. Judah Loew b. Beẓalel (Maharal of Prague), 1379
3. Samuel Eliezer Edels (Maharsha) and Meir b. Gedaliah (Maharam of Lublin), 1383
B. Opposition to the *Shulḥan Arukh* as Manifested by the Composition of Alternative Types of Codes, 1385
1. Solomon Luria (Maharshal), 1385
2. Mordecai Jaffe, 1394
3. Yom Tov Lipmann Heller, 1403
C. Opposition to the *Shulḥan Arukh* as the Sole Basis for Legal Decisions; Commentaries on the *Shulḥan Arukh,* 1407
1. Joshua Falk, 1408
2. Joel Sirkes, 1415
IV. The Acceptance of the *Shulḥan Arukh* as the Definitive and Authoritative Code of Jewish Law, 1417
A. The Completion of the Codificatory Structure of the *Shulḥan Arukh* by Its Commentaries, 1417
B. Historical Circumstances as a Factor in the Acceptance of the *Shulḥan Arukh,* 1419

Chapter 38 **THE CODIFICATORY LITERATURE: COMMENTARIES ON AND CODIFICATION AFTER THE *SHULḤAN ARUKH*** **1423**

I. Introduction, 1424
II. Commentaries on *Ḥoshen Mishpat,* 1424
A. *Sefer Me'irat Einayim* (*Sema*) by Joshua Falk, 1424
B. *Turei Zahav* (*Taz*) by David b. Samuel ha-Levi, 1425
C. *Siftei Kohen* (*Shakh*) by Shabbetai b. Meir ha-Kohen, 1425
D. *Be'er ha-Golah* by Moses Rivkes, 1426
E. *Urim ve-Thummim* by Jonathan Eybeschütz, 1426
F. *Be'ur ha-Gra* by Elijah, Gaon of Vilna, 1427
G. *Keẓot ha-Ḥoshen* by Aryeh Leib Heller, 1428
H. *Netivot ha-Mishpat* by Jacob Lorbeerbaum, 1429

III. Commentaries on *Even ha-Ezer*, 1429
A. *Turei Zahav* (*Taz*) by David b. Samuel ha-Levi, 1429
B. *Ḥelkat Meḥokek* by Moses Lima, 1429
C. *Bet Shemu'el* by Samuel Phoebus, 1430
D. *Be'er ha-Golah* by Moses Rivkes, 1430
E. *Be'ur ha-Gra* by Elijah, Gaon of Vilna, 1430
F. *Avnei Millu'im* by Aryeh Leib Heller, 1431
IV. Commentaries on *Oraḥ Ḥayyim* and *Yoreh De'ah*, 1431
V. Responsa Compilations Arranged in the Topical Sequence of the *Shulḥan Arukh*, 1432
A. *Panim Ḥadashot* by Isaac Jesurun, 1433
B. *Keneset ha-Gedolah* by Ḥayyim Benveniste, 1434
C. *Be'er Heitev* by Judah Ashkenazi and Zechariah Mendel b. Aryeh Leib, 1437
D. *Leket ha-Kemaḥ* by Moses Ḥagiz, 1437
E. *Yad Aharon* by Aaron Alfandari, 1438
F. *Birkei Yosef* by Ḥayyim Joseph David Azulai (Ḥida), 1439
G. *Matteh Shim'on* by Simon Mordecai Bekemoharar, 1439
H. *Sha'arei Teshuvah* by Ḥayyim Mordecai Margolioth, 1440
I. *Pitḥei Teshuvah* by Abraham Eisenstadt, 1441
J. *Oraḥ Mishpat* by Raḥamim Elijah Ḥazzan, 1442
K. *Darkhei Teshuvah* by Ẓevi Hirsch Shapira and His Son Ḥayyim Eleazar Shapira, 1442
L. *Oẓar ha-Posekim*, 1442
M. *Halakhah Pesukah*, 1443
VI. Codificatory Literature after the *Shulḥan Arukh*, 1443
A. In General, 1443
B. Compilations of Tax Laws, 1444
1. *Massa Melekh* by Joseph ibn Ezra, 1445
2. *Avodat Massa* by Joshua Abraham Judah, 1446
3. *Massa Ḥayyim* by Ḥayyim Palache, 1447
C. Codificatory Literature Devoted Mainly to Religious Law, 1447
D. *Arukh ha-Shulḥan* by Jehiel Michal Epstein, 1448
E. Causes of the Decline of Codificatory Authority and Activity, 1450
F. The Problem of Codification at the Present Time, 1451

Chapter 39 **THE RESPONSA LITERATURE** **1453**
I. Introduction, 1454
II. Responsa in the Talmudic Literature, 1454
III. The Nature and Content of the Responsa Literature, 1456
A. The Distinctiveness of the Responsa Literature as Compared with the Other Types of Post-Talmudic Halakhic Literature, 1456
B. The Special Significance and Weight of the Rulings in the Responsa, 1457
C. The Respondent as a Supreme Judicial Tribunal, 1460
D. Responsa and the Development of Jewish Law, 1461
E. Matters of *Mishpat Ivri* as the Major Subjects of the Responsa, 1461
F. The Magnitude of the Responsa Literature, 1462
G. Responsa as a Source for Knowledge of Enactments,

Customs, Legal Documents, and Non-Jewish Law, 1463
H. Responsa on Questions of Textual Interpretation, Philosophy, and Religious Beliefs, 1464
I. Responsa as a Source for the History of Halakhic Literature, 1464
J. Responsa as a Historical Source, 1465
K. Responsa and Parallels in Other Legal Systems, 1466
IV. The Different Periods of the Responsa Literature, 1468
A. The Geonic Period, 1468
B. The Period of the *Rishonim* (Early Authorities), 1473
1. The Nature and Content of the Responsa in the Period of the *Rishonim*, 1473
2. The Twelfth to Fourteenth Centuries, 1477
3. The Fifteenth Century, 1479
4. Summary, 1480
C. The Period of the *Aḥaronim* (Later Authorities) up to the End of the Eighteenth Century, 1482
1. The Nature and Content of the Responsa in the Period of the *Aḥaronim*, 1482
2. The Sixteenth Century, 1486
3. The Seventeenth Century, 1488
4. The Eighteenth Century, 1489
D. The Period of the Emancipation—the Nineteenth Century, 1491
1. Nature and Content of the Responsa of the Nineteenth Century and Thereafter, 1491
2. The Responsa in Different Jewish Centers, 1495
E. The Period of National Awakening, the Holocaust, and the Establishment of the Jewish State—the Twentieth Century, 1496
1. The Responsa Literature until the 1940s, 1496
2. The Responsa Literature in the 1940s and Thereafter, 1497
F. Summary, 1499
V. General Overview of the Methodology, Structure, and Form of the Responsa, 1501
A. The Questioners; Submission of Questions, 1501
B. The Structure, Form, Style, Transmittal, and Copying of the Question and Response, 1507
C. Fictitious Names of Persons and Places in the Responsa, 1512
D. Hypothetical Responsa; *Terumat ha-Deshen*, 1516
VI. Compilations of Responsa—Redaction and Organization, 1517
VII. Research in the Responsa; Digest of the Responsa Literature, 1523

Chapter 40 **LITERATURE FACILITATING RESEARCH IN JEWISH LAW: COMPILATIONS OF LEGAL DOCUMENTS, REFERENCE WORKS** **1529**

I. Introduction, 1530
II. Compilations of Legal Documents, 1531

A. Enactments, 1531
B. Legal Instruments (*Shetarot*), 1533
1. *Sefer ha-Shetarot* [The Book of Legal Instruments] by Saadiah Gaon, 1535
2. *Sefer ha-Shetarot* by Hai Gaon, 1536
3. *Sefer ha-Shetarot* of Lucena, Spain, 1536
4. *Sefer ha-Shetarot* by Judah al-Bargeloni, 1536
5. Compilation of Legal Instruments in *Maḥzor Vitry*, 1537
6. Compilations in *Sefer ha-Ittur* and *Yad Ramah*, 1537
7. Compilations of Legal Instruments Used by English Jews in the Eleventh to Thirteenth Centuries, 1537
8. Legal Instruments Used in Christian Spain in the Twelfth to Fifteenth Centuries, 1538
9. *Tikkun Soferim* [The Scribe's Handbook] by Solomon b. Simeon Duran (Rashbash), 1538
10. *Tikkun Soferim* by Moses Almosnino and Samuel Jaffe, 1538
11. *Tikkun Shetarot* by Eliezer Milli, 1538
12. The Compilation in *Naḥalat Shiv'ah* by Samuel ha-Levi, 1539
13. *Et Sofer* [The Scribe's Quill] by Jacob ibn Ẓur, 1539
14. *Oẓar ha-Shetarot* [A Treasury of Legal Instruments] by Asher Gulak, 1539
15. Legal Instruments Used in Spain and North Africa in the Eleventh to Fifteenth Centuries, 1540

III. Reference Works, 1540
A. Guidebooks, 1541
1. *Seder Tannaim va-Amoraim* [Chronicles of the *Tannaim* and *Amoraim*], 1541
2. *Iggeret Rav Sherira Gaon* [The Epistle of Rabbi Sherira Gaon], 1542
3. *Mevo ha-Talmud* [Introduction to the Talmud] by Samuel ha-Nagid of Egypt, Attributed to Samuel ha-Nagid of Spain, 1543
4. Maimonides' Introduction to His *Commentary on the Mishnah;* The Introductions of Menahem Meiri to *Bet ha-Beḥirah*, 1543
5. *Sefer Keritut* by Samson of Chinon, 1544
6. *Halikhot Olam* by Joshua ha-Levi, 1545
7. *She'erit Yosef* by Joseph ibn Verga, 1545
8. *Kelalei ha-Gemara* [Principles of the *Gemara*] by Joseph Caro, 1545
9. *Kelalei ha-Talmud* [Principles of the Talmud] by Beẓalel Ashkenazi, 1547
10. *Yavin Shemu'ah* by Solomon Algazi, 1547
11. *Yad Malakhi* by Malachi ha-Kohen, 1547
12. Guidebooks from the Nineteenth Century and Thereafter, 1548

B. Encyclopedias, 1551
1. *Paḥad Yiẓḥak* by Isaac Lampronti, 1551
2. *Sedei Ḥemed* by Ḥayyim Hezekiah Medini, 1552
3. *Die Exegetische Terminologie der Jüdischen*

Traditionsliteratur [The Exegetical Terminology of the Literature of the Jewish Tradition] by Wilhelm Bacher, 1553
4. *Mafte'aḥ ha-Talmud* [Key to the Talmud] by Jehiel Michal Guttmann, 1553
5. *Enẓiklopedyah Talmudit* [Talmudic Encyclopedia], 1554
6. Halakhic Works Arranged Alphabetically, 1554
7. *Mishpat Ivri* Alphabetically Arranged by Subject, 1554

C. Biographies of Halakhic Authorities, 1556
1. Biographies According to Historical Periods, 1557
2. Biographies According to Geographical Areas, 1558
3. Biographies of Individual Authorities, 1559
4. Encyclopedias with Biographical Articles, 1560

D. Bibliographies, 1560
1. General Bibliographies, 1561
2. Bibliographies According to Type of Halakhic Literature, 1562
3. Bibliographies of Scholarly Literature on *Mishpat Ivri*, 1562

E. Lexicons, 1564
F. Books Explaining Abbreviations, 1566
G. Textual Variants, 1567
H. Concordances, 1568
I. Source References, Sayings, and Aphorisms, 1568
J. Scholarly Research in *Mishpat Ivri*, 1569
K. Journals and Periodicals on *Mishpat Ivri*, 1570

GLOSSARY **G•1**

BIBLIOGRAPHICAL ABBREVIATIONS OF BOOKS AND ARTICLES FREQUENTLY CITED

H. Albeck, *Mavo la-Mishnah* [Introduction to the Mishnah], Jerusalem, 1959 = Albeck, *Mavo*.

G. Alon (or Allon), *Meḥkarim be-Toledot Yisra'el bi-Mei Bayit Sheni u-vi-Tekufat ha-Mishnah ve-ha-Talmud* [Studies in Jewish History in the Days of the Second Temple and in the Mishnaic and Talmudic Period], 2 vols., Tel-Aviv, 1957–1958 = Alon, *Meḥkarim*. (For an English version, *see Jews, Judaism and the Classical World: Studies in Jewish History in the Times of the Second Temple and Talmud*, I. Abrahams and A. Oshery trans., Jerusalem, 1977.)

——— *Toledot ha-Yehudim be-Ereẓ Yisra'el bi-Tekufat ha-Mishnah ve-ha-Talmud* [History of the Jews in the Land of Israel in the Mishnaic and Talmudic Period], 3rd ed., Tel-Aviv, 1959 = Alon, *Toledot*. (For an English version, *see The Jews in Their Land in the Talmudic Age*, G. Levi trans. and ed., Jerusalem, 1 vol., Magnes Press, 1980–1984; reprinted, Harvard University Press, 1989.)

S. Assaf, *Battei ha-Din ve-Sidreihem Aḥarei Ḥatimat ha-Talmud* [Jewish Courts and Their Procedures after the Completion of the Talmud], Jerusalem, 1924 = Assaf, *Battei Din*.

——— *Ha-Onshin Aḥarei Ḥatimat ha-Talmud* [Penal Law After the Completion of the Talmud], Jerusalem, 1922 = Assaf, *Onshin*.

——— *Tekufat ha-Geonim ve-Sifrutah* [The Geonic Period and Its Literature], Jerusalem, 1956 = Assaf, *Geonim*.

Y. Baer, *Toledot Ha-Yehudim bi-Sefarad ha-Noẓrit* [A History of the Jews of Christian Spain], 2nd ed., Tel Aviv, 1965. An English translation, *A History of the Jews in Christian Spain*, JPS, 2 vols., 1961–1966 = Baer, *Spain*.

S.W. Baron, *A Social and Religious History of the Jews*, JPS-Columbia, 18 vols. 1952–1983 = Baron, *History*.

M.A. Bloch, *Sha'arei Torat ha-Takkanot* [On Legislative Enactments], Vienna *et al.*, 7 vols., 1879–1906 = Bloch, *Sha'arei*.

P. Dykan (Dikstein), *Toledot Mishpat ha-Shalom ha-Ivri* [History of the Jewish Court of Arbitration], Tel Aviv, 1964 = Dykan, *Toledot.*

M. Elon, *Ḥakikah Datit be-Ḥukkei Medinat Yisra'el u-va-Shefitah Shel Battei ha-Mishpat u-Vattei ha-Din ha-Rabbaniyyim* [Religious Legislation in the Statutes of the State of Israel and in the Decisions of the General and Rabbinical Courts], Tel Aviv, 1968 = Elon, *Ḥakikah.*

——— "Ha-Ma'asar ba-Mishpat ha-Ivri" [Imprisonment in Jewish Law], *Jubilee Volume for Pinḥas Rosen,* Jerusalem, 1962, pp. 171–201 = Elon, *Ma'asar.*

——— *Ḥerut ha-Perat be-Darkhei Geviyyat Ḥov ba-Mishpat ha-Ivri* [Individual Freedom and the Methods of Enforcing Payment of Debts in Jewish Law], Jerusalem, 1964 = Elon, *Ḥerut.*

——— (ed.) *Principles of Jewish Law,* Jerusalem, 1975 = *Principles.*

——— "Samkhut ve-Oẓmah ba-Kehillah ha-Yehudit, Perek be-Mishpat ha-Ẓibbur ha-Ivri" [Authority and Power in the Jewish Community, A Chapter in Jewish Public Law], in *Shenaton ha-Mishpat ha-Ivri* [Annual of the Institute for Research in Jewish Law], Hebrew University of Jerusalem, III–IV (1976–1977), pp. 7ff. = Elon, *Samkhut ve-Oẓmah.* (For an English translation, *see* "Power and Authority—Halachic Stance of the Traditional Community and Its Contemporary Implications," in *Kinship and Consent, The Jewish Political Tradition and Its Contemporary Uses,* D. Elazar ed., Turtledove Publishing, 1981, pp. 183–213).

——— "Yiḥudah Shel Halakhah ve-Ḥevrah be-Yahadut Ẓefon Afrikah mi-le-aḥar Gerush Sefarad ve-ad Yameinu" [The Exceptional Character of *Halakhah* and Society in North African Jewry from the Spanish Expulsion to the Present], in *Halakhah u-Fetiḥut, Ḥakhmei Morokko ke-Fosekim le-Doreinu* [Halakhah and Open-Mindedness: The Halakhic Authorities of Morocco as Authorities for Our Own Time], 1945, pp. 15ff. = Elon, *Yiḥudah Shel Halakhah.*

J.N. Epstein, *Mavo le-Nusaḥ ha-Mishnah* [Introduction to the Text of the Mishnah], 2nd ed., Jerusalem, 1964 = Epstein, *Mavo.*

——— *Mevo'ot le-Sifrut ha-Tannaim,* [Introduction to Tannaitic Literature], Jerusalem, 1957 = Epstein, *Tannaim.*

——— *Mevo'ot le-Sifrut ha-Amoraim,* [Introduction to Amoraic Literature], Jerusalem, 1963 = Epstein, *Amoraim.*

L. Finkelstein, *Jewish Self-Government in the Middle Ages,* New York 1924 (second printing, New York, 1964) = Finkelstein, *Self-Government.*

Z. Frankel, *Darkhei ha-Mishnah* [The Methodology of the Mishnah], Leipzig, 1859 (facsimile ed., Tel Aviv, 1969) = Frankel, *Mishnah.*

——— *Mevo ha-Yerushalmi* [Introduction to the Jerusalem Talmud], Breslau, 1870 (facsimile ed., Jerusalem, 1967) = Frankel, *Mevo.*

A.H. Freimann, *Seder Kiddushin ve-Nissu'in Aḥarei Ḥatimat ha-Talmud, Meḥkar Histori-Dogmati be-Dinei Yisra'el* [Law of Betrothal and Marriage after the Completion of the Talmud: A Historical-Dogmatic Study in Jewish Law], Mosad ha-Rav Kook, Jerusalem, 1945 = Freimann, *Kiddushin ve-Nissu'in.*

L. Ginzberg, *Perushim ve-Ḥiddushim ba-Yerushalmi* [A Commentary on the Palestine Talmud] (English title by Prof. Ginzberg), New York, 1941 (facsimile ed., New York, 1971) = Ginzberg, *Perushim.*

A. Gulak, *Yesodei ha-Mishpat ha-Ivri* [The Foundations of Jewish Law], Jerusalem, 1923 (facsimile ed., Tel Aviv, 1967) = Gulak, *Yesodei.*

I. Halevy, *Dorot ha-Rishonim* [The Early Generations—A History of the Oral Law to the *Geonim*], Frankfort, 1897–1906 (facsimile ed., Jerusalem, 1957) = Halevy, *Dorot.*

I. Herzog, *The Main Institutions of Jewish Law,* 2nd ed., London, 2 vols., 1965–1967 = Herzog, *Institutions.*

D.Z. Hoffmann, *Das Buch Deuteronomium Übersetzt und Erklärt* [The Book of Deuteronomy: Translation and Commentary] = Hoffmann, *Commentary on Deuteronomy.*

Kovez̧ Teshuvot ha-Rambam ve-Iggerotav [Compilation of Responsa and Epistles of Maimonides], Leipzig, 1859 = *Kovez̧ ha-Rambam.*

J. Levy, *Wörterbuch über die Talmudim und Midraschim* [Talmudic and Midrashic Dictionary], 2nd ed., Berlin, 1924 = Levy, *Wörterbuch.*

S. Lieberman, *Greek in Jewish Palestine* = Lieberman, *Greek.*

——— *Hellenism in Jewish Palestine* = Lieberman, *Hellenism.*

A. Neubauer, *Seder ha-Ḥakhamim ve-Korot ha-Yamim* [Medieval Jewish Chronicles], Oxford, 1895 (facsimile ed., Jerusalem, 1967) = Neubauer, *Seder ha-Ḥakhamim.*

J.W. Salmond, *On Jurisprudence,* 12th ed., London, 1966 = Salmond.

Shenaton ha-Mishpat ha-Ivri [Annual of the Institute for Research in Jewish Law, Hebrew University of Jerusalem] = *Shenaton.*

M. Silberg, *Ha-Ma'amad ha-Ishi be-Yisra'el* [Personal Status in Israel], 4th ed., Jerusalem, 1965 = Silberg, *Ha-Ma'amad.*

H. Tykocinski, *Takkanot ha-Geonim* [Geonic Enactments], Jerusalem, 1960 = Tykocinski, *Takkanot.*

E.E. Urbach, *Ḥazal, Pirkei Emunot ve-De'ot* [The Sages: Doctrines and Beliefs], rev. ed., Jerusalem, 1971 = Urbach, *The Sages.* (For an English version *see The Sages, Their Concepts and Beliefs,* I. Abrahams trans., Magnes Press, 2 vols., Jerusalem, 1975.)

——— *Ba'alei ha-Tosafot, Toledoteihem, Ḥibbureihem ve-Shittatam* [The Tosafists, Their History, Writings and Methodology], 2nd ed, Jerusalem, 1968 = Urbach, *Tosafot.*

Z. Warhaftig, (ed.); *Osef Piskei ha-Din Shel ha-Rabbanut ha-Rashit le-Erez̧ Yis-*

ra'el [A Compilation of the Rulings of the Chief Rabbinate of the Land of Israel], 1950, = *Osef Piskei ha-Din.*

I.H. Weiss, *Dor Dor ve-Doreshav* [The Generations and Their Interpreters—A History of the Oral Law], 6th ed., Vilna, 1915 = Weiss, *Dor Dor ve-Doreshav.*

ABBREVIATIONS USED IN CITING RABBINIC WORKS AND SCHOLARLY LITERATURE

ad loc.	*ad locum*, "at the place," used after a citation to designate commentary on the passage cited
A.M.	*anno mundi*, "in the year [from the creation] of the world"
b.	ben, bar, "son of"—as in Simeon b. Gamaliel
Baḥ	*Bayit Ḥadash*, a commentary on *Tur* by Joel Sirkes.
B.C.E.	before the common era, equivalent of B.C.
ca.	*circa*, "approximately"
C.E.	common era, equivalent of A.D.
cf.	*confer*, "compare"
EH	*Even ha-Ezer*, part of the *Shulḥan Arukh*
EJ	Encyclopaedia Judaica
ET	*Enẓiklopedyah Talmudit* [Talmudic Encyclopedia]
ḤM	*Ḥoshen Mishpat*, part of the *Shulḥan Arukh*
HUCA	*Hebrew Union College Annual*
ibn	"son of," equivalent of "b." (which *see*)
id.	*idem*, "the same," used instead of repeating the immediately preceding citation
JJGL	*Jahrbuch für jüdische Geschichte und Literatur* [Jewish History and Literature Annual]
JJLG	*Jahrbuch der jüdisch-literarischen* Gesellschaft [Jewish Literary Society Annual]
JPS	The Jewish Publication Society
JQR	*Jewish Quarterly Review*
lit.	literally
loc. cit.	*loco citato*, "in the place [previously] cited"
M	Mishnah, used to designate a Mishnaic tractate
MGWJ	*Monatsschrift für Geschichte und Wissenschaft des Judenthums* [Monthly for the History and Science of Judaism]
ms., mss.	manuscript(s)
MT	*Mishneh Torah* (Maimonides' code)

n.	note
nn.	notes
OḤ	*Oraḥ Ḥayyim,* part of the *Shulḥan Arukh*
op. cit.	*opere citato,* "in the work [previously] cited"
R.	Rabbi, Rav, or Rabban, used in the present work for the Talmudic Sages
Resp.	Responsa
Sema	*Sefer Me'irat Einayim* by Joshua Falk
Semag	*Sefer Miẓvot Gadol* by Moses of Coucy
Semak	*Sefer Miẓvot Katan* by Isaac of Corbeil
Shakh	*Siftei Kohen* by Shabbetai b. Meir ha-Kohen
Sh. Ar.	*Shulḥan Arukh*
"Shum"	Hebrew acrostic for the communities of Speyer, Worms, and Mainz
s.v.	*sub verbo, sub voce,* "under the word," designating the word or expression to which commentary is appended. Equivalent of Hebrew "d.h." (*dibbur ha-matḥil*)
Taz	*Turei Zahav* by David b. Samuel ha-Levi
TB	Talmud Bavli [Babylonian Talmud]
TJ	Talmud Yerushalmi [Jerusalem Talmud, sometimes called Palestine Talmud]
Tur	*Sefer ha-Turim* by Jacob b. Asher
v.l.	*varia lectio,* pl. *variae lectiones,* "variant reading(s)"
YD	*Yoreh De'ah,* part of the *Shulḥan Arukh*

ABBREVIATIONS USED IN CITING MODERN LEGAL MATERIALS

A.2d	Atlantic Reports, Second Series (U.S.)
A.B.A.J.	*American Bar Association Journal*
A.C.	Law Reports Appeal Cases (Eng.)
All E.R.	All England Law Reports, formerly All England Law Reports Annotated
Atk.	Atkyns English Chancery Reports (1736–1755)
Ch.	Chancery (Eng.)
C.L.R.	Current Law Reports (cases decided during the British Mandate)
Colum. L. Rev.	*Columbia Law Review*
D.C. App.	District of Columbia Court of Appeals
DK	*Divrei ha-Keneset* [The Knesset Record]
E.R., Eng. Rep.	English Reports, Full Reprint (1220–1865)
Ex.	Court of Exchequer (Eng.)
Harv. L. Rev.	*Harvard Law Review*
H.L.C.	Clark's House of Lords Cases (Eng.)
I.C.L.Q.	*International and Comparative Law Quarterly*
I.S.C.J.	Israel Supreme Court Judgments
Jur.	Jurist Reports (Eng., 18 vols.)
K.B.	King's Bench (Eng.)
L.J.	Law Journal
L.J.Q.B.	Law Journal Reports, New Series, Queen's Bench (Eng.)
L.Q.	Law Quarterly
L. Rev.	Law Review
Md. L. Rev.	*Maryland Law Review*
Minn. L. Rev.	*Minnesota Law Review*
Mod.	Modern Reports, 1669–1732 (Eng.)
N.E.2d	Northeastern Reporter, Second Series (U.S.)
Ohio App.	Ohio (Intermediate) Appellate Court reports

Osef Piskei ha-Din	a collection of rabbinical court decisions compiled by Zeraḥ Warhaftig
P.D.	*Piskei Din,* Israel Supreme Court Reports
P.D.R.	*Piskei Din Rabbaniyyim,* Israel Rabbinical Court Reports
P.L.R.	Palestine Law Reports (Court Decisions during the British Mandate)
P.M.	*Pesakim Meḥoziyyim,* Israel District Court Reports
Q.B.	Queen's Bench (Eng.)
SCJ	Supreme Court Judgments Annotated (Reports of cases in the Supreme Court of the Land of Israel during the British Mandate)
Vand. L. Rev.	*Vanderbilt Law Review*
Wis. L. Rev.	*Wisconsin Law Review*
W.L.R.	Weekly Law Reports (Eng.)

ACRONYMS AND APPELLATIONS OF HALAKHIC AUTHORITIES

Alfasi	Isaac b. Jacob ha-Kohen of Fez, Rif
Asheri	Asher b. Jehiel, Rosh
Ba'al ha-Roke'aḥ	Eliezer b. Judah
Ba'al ha-Turim	Jacob b. Asher
Baḥ	Joel Sirkes
Ḥafeẓ Ḥayyim	Israel Meir ha-Kohen
Ha-Gra	Elijah b. Solomon Zalman (Gaon of Vilna)
Ha-Kala'i	Alfasi
Ḥakham Zevi	Zevi Hirsch b. Jacob Ashkenazi
Ḥatam Sofer	Moses Sofer
Ḥayyim Or Zaru'a	Hayyim b. Isaac
Ḥazon Ish	Abraham Isaiah Karelitz
Ḥida	Ḥayyim Joseph David Azulai
Mabit	Moses b. Joseph Trani
Maharaḥ	Ḥayyim b. Isaac, also known as Ḥayyim Or Zaru'a
Maharai	Israel Isserlein
Maharal of Prague	Judah Loew b. Beẓalel
Maharalbaḥ	Levi b. Ḥabib
Maharam Alashkar	Moses b. Isaac Alashkar
Maharam Alshekh	Moses b. Ḥayyim Alshekh
Maharam of Lublin	Meir b. Gedaliah of Lublin
Maharam Mintz	Moses b. Isaac Mintz
Maharam of Padua	Meir Katzenellenbogen
Maharam of Rothenburg	Meir b. Baruch of Rothenburg
Maharash Kastilaẓ	Simeon Kastilaẓ
Maharashdam	Samuel b. Moses Medina
Maharaẓ Chajes	Ẓevi Hirsch Chajes
Mahardakh	David ha-Kohen of Corfu
Maharḥash	Ḥayyim Shabbetai of Salonika

Mahari Bruna	Israel b. Ḥayyim Bruna
Mahari Caro	Joseph Caro, also known as Maran
Mahari Minẓ	Judah Minẓ
Mahari Weil	Jacob b. Judah Weil, also known as Maharyu
Maharibal	Joseph ibn Lev
Maharif	Jacob Faraji
Maharik	Joseph b. Solomon Colon
Maharikash	Jacob b. Abraham Castro
Maharil	Jacob b. Moses Moellin
Maharit	Joseph b. Moses Trani
Maharit Algazi	Yom Tov b. Israel Jacob Algazi
Maharitaẓ	Yom Tov b. Akiva Ẓahalon
Mahariẓ	Yeḥaiah (Yaḥya, Yiḥye) b. Joseph Ẓalaḥ (Saliḥ)
Maharsha	Samuel Eliezer b. Judah ha-Levi Edels
Maharshak	Samson b. Isaac of Chinon
Maharshakh	Solomon b. Abraham
Maharshal	Solomon b. Jehiel Luria
Maharsham	Shalom Mordecai b. Moses Schwadron
Maharyu	Jacob b. Judah Weil, also known as Mahari Weil
Malbim	Meir Leib b. Jehiel Michael
Maran	Joseph Caro, also known as Mahari Caro
Neẓiv (Naẓiv)	Naphtali Ẓevi Judah Berlin
Noda bi-Yehudah	Ezekiel b. Judah ha-Levi Landau
Rabad (Rabad I)	Abraham b. David (ibn Daud) of Posquières
Rabad (Rabad II)	Abraham b. David (ibn Daud) ha-Levi
Raban	Eliezer b. Nathan of Mainz
Rabi	Abraham b. Isaac of Narbonne
Radbaz	David ibn Zimra
Ralbag	Levi b. Gershom, Gersonides
Ralbaḥ	Levi ibn Ḥabib
Ramah	Meir Abulafia
Rambam	Moses b. Maimon, Maimonides
Ramban	Moses b. Naḥman, Naḥmanides
Ran	Nissim of Gerona (Gerondi)
Ranaḥ	Elijah b. Ḥayyim
Rash	Samson b. Abraham of Sens

Rashba	Solomon b. Abraham Adret
Rashbam	Samuel b. Meir
Rashbash	Solomon b. Simeon Duran
Rashbeẓ (Rashbaẓ)	Simeon b. Ẓemaḥ Duran
Rashi	Solomon b. Isaac of Troyes
Rav Za'ir	Chaim Tchernowitz
Raviah	Eliezer b. Joel ha-Levi
Redak (Radak)	David Kimḥi
Re'em	Elijah b. Abraham Mizraḥi; Eliezer b. Samuel of Metz
Re'iyah	Abraham Isaac ha-Kohen Kook
Rema	Moses Isserles
Remakh	Moses ha-Kohen of Lunel
Reshakh	Solomon b. Abraham, Maharshakh
Rezah	Zeraḥia ha-Levi Gerondi
Ri	Isaac b. Samuel, also known as Isaac the Elder
Ri Migash	Joseph ibn Migash
Riaz	Isaac b. Moses of Vienna; Isaiah b. Elijah of Trani
Ribash	Isaac b. Sheshet Perfet
Rid	Isaiah b. Mali di Trani the Elder
Rif	Isaac b. Jacob ha-Kohen, Alfasi
Ritba	Yom Tov b. Abraham Ishbili
Riẓag	Isaac ibn Ghayyat
Rogachover	Joseph Rozin (Rosen)
Rosh	Asher b. Jehiel, Asheri
Shadal (Shedal)	Samuel David Luzzatto
Tashbaẓ (Tashbeẓ)	Samson b. Ẓadok
Tukh	Eliezer of Touques
Yaveẓ	Jacob Emden
Yaveẓ of North Africa	Jacob ibn Ẓur of Morocco

TRANSLITERATION GUIDE

LETTERS

NAME OF LETTER	SYMBOL	TRANSLITERATION	SOUND	REMARKS
aleph	א	not transliterated		
bet	בּ	b	as in *b*oy	
vet	ב	v	as in *v*alue	
gimmel	גּ, ג	g	as in *g*ate	no distinction between gimmel with *dagesh lene* and *gimmel* without *dagesh*
dalet	דּ, ד	d	as in *d*ance	no distinction between *dalet* with *dagesh lene* and *dalet* without a *dagesh*
he	ה	h	as in *h*ome	
vav	ו	v	as in *v*alve	when used as a vowel, transliterated as "o" or "u"
zayin	ז	z	as in Zion	
ḥet	ח	ḥ	ch as in German *Achtung*	no English equivalent
tet	ט	t	t as in *t*ag	
yod	י	y or i	y as in *y*es or when i, like ee in sh*ee*n	y except when vowel, and then "i"
kaf	כּ	k	k as in *k*ing or c as in *c*ome	English has no equivalent for the difference between *ḥet* and *khaf* in Hebrew
khaf	כ,ך	kh	like ch as in *Achtung*	

LETTERS (*continued*)

NAME OF LETTER	SYMBOL	TRANSLITERATION	SOUND	REMARKS
lamed	ל	l	l as in *l*ean	
mem	מ,ם	m	m as in *m*other	
nun	נ,ן	n	n as in *n*o	
samekh	ס	s	s as in *s*ing	
ayin	ע	not transliterated		indicated by apostrophe
pe	פּ	p	p as in *p*ost	
fe	פ,ף	f	f as in *f*ine	
ẓade sade tsade	צ,ץ	z	like ts in fi*ts*	
kof	ק	k	like ck as in lo*ck*	
resh	ר	r	r as in *r*ain	may be rolled
shin	שׁ	sh	sh as in *sh*ine	
sin	שׂ	s	s as in *s*ong	
tav taw	תּ ת	t	t as in *t*ame	no distinction between *tav* with *dagesh lene* and *tav* without a *dagesh*

VOWELS

NAME OF VOWEL	SYMBOL (PLACED BELOW LETTER)	TRANSLITERATION	SOUND	REMARKS
kamatz kameẓ kamaẓ	ָ	a o	like a in f*a*ther like aw in l*aw*	if "long" kamaẓ if "short" kamaẓ
pataḥ	ַ	a	like a in f*a*ther	
ḥataf-pataḥ	ֲ	a	like a in *a*lignment	but no precise English equivalent

VOWELS ***(continued)***

NAME OF VOWEL	SYMBOL (PLACED BELOW LETTER)	TRANSLITERATION	SOUND	REMARKS
ẓere tsere	..	e or ei	like *ai* as in pl*ai*n, ei as in "v*ei*n"	except *bet* not *beit*
segol	∴	e	like e in l*e*d	
ḥataf-segol	∵:	e	like second e in heg*e*mony	
sheva	:	e	like e in sh*e*nanigan	*sheva na* is transliterated, *sheva naḥ* is not
ḥirek ḥireq	.	i	between ee in sh*ee*n and i in p*i*n	
holam	וֹ, ˙	o	o as in h*o*me	dot placed above letter
kubbuẓ kibbuẓ	וּ, ⋱	u	u as in bl*ue*	

Notes

1. *Dagesh forte* is represented by doubling the letter, except that the letter *shin* is not doubled.

2. The definite article "ha" is followed by a hyphen, but although the following letter always has a *dagesh forte* in the Hebrew, it is not doubled in the transliteration. The transliteration of the definite article starts with a small "h" except in the name of Rabbi Judah Ha-Nasi, Rosh Ha-Shanah (the holiday) and the beginning of a sentence or title.

3. An apostrophe between vowels indicates that the vowels do not constitute a diphthong, but each is to have its separate pronunciation.

PART THREE

The Literary Sources of Jewish Law

Chapter 25

THE LITERARY SOURCES OF JEWISH LAW: NATURE AND DEFINITION

I. The Literary Sources of Law
  A. In General
  B. Official Publications
  C. Legal Literature and General Literature
II. The Literary Sources of Jewish Law

I. THE LITERARY SOURCES OF LAW[1]

A. In General

Up to this point, our discussion of the sources of Jewish law has focused on the legal sources, namely, those sources that Jewish law recognizes as the processes and instruments of its ongoing creative development. On occasion, reference also has been made to the historical sources of Jewish law, *i.e.,* those sources that historically gave rise to particular halakhic rules. In addition, there is a third category of sources of law—the literary sources. Literary sources of the law are of three types: official publications, legal literature, and general literature.

B. Official Publications

In its narrow sense, "literary sources of law" refers to the official publications that are the authoritative and recognized repositories of the various rules of a legal system, *i.e.,* the sources from which the norms of the system

1. In the Hebrew editions of the present work, the term *mekorot rishumiyyim* was coined as the Hebrew for "literary sources." In German, such sources are called *Erkenntnisquellen des Rechts.* For a fuller discussion of this terminology, *see supra* p. 235 n. 25.

may be ascertained.[2] For example, in all legal systems, official statute books are the sources for the authentic text of legislation.

C. Legal Literature and General Literature

In its broad sense, "literary sources of law" includes two additional types of writings. The first is legal literature, which discusses and explains the law but is neither authoritative nor recognized as an official source for ascertaining the content of binding legal norms. Legal literature includes articles and books by jurists on legal subjects. Such literature is not part of the *corpus juris* of the legal system, although its contents enrich our knowledge of the norms that are part of the *corpus juris*.[3]

The second type of literary source of law in the broad sense is general literature, which is not without importance for the study and understanding of a legal system. Literature describing or discussing historical or economic conditions may incidentally contain many legal references that can add to our knowledge of the nature and content of the legal system of a particular place and time. For instance, if in the course of a discussion of an economic situation, the author quotes a report on the number of bankruptcies and the subsequent imprisonment of debtors, we may conclude that, in the period under review, imprisonment was a sanction employed for nonpayment of debts. Thus, even books not dealing directly with a legal subject may shed light on the existence of particular legal institutions or practices.

Sometimes, legal literature and general literature are the major sources for understanding the nature and contents of a legal system, especially in the system's early stages. At that time, there are generally few authoritative literary sources such as statute books; and the researcher must look to the unofficial, nonauthoritative legal literature and to general literature. However, one must be extremely cautious and use great care in investigating how accurately the facts and legal norms are depicted; in regard to literature that is not an authoritative legal repository (especially descriptive historical literature and the like), there may be reasonable ground to suspect

2. *See supra* p. 228.

3. *See* Salmond, p. 112 note c: "In addition to the historical and legal sources of the law, it is necessary to note and distinguish what may be termed its literary sources. . . . The literary sources are the sources of our knowledge of the law, or rather the original and authoritative sources of such knowledge, as opposed to later commentary or literature. The sources of Roman law are in this sense the compilations of the Emperor Justinian, as contrasted with the works of commentators. So the sources of English law are the statute book, the reports, and the older and authoritative text-books, such as Littleton. The literature, as opposed to the sources of our law, comprises all modern text-books and commentaries."

that the author had some ulterior purpose and that his descriptions may not reflect the facts so much as what he wished the facts to be.

II. THE LITERARY SOURCES OF JEWISH LAW

The distinction between authoritative literary sources of the law, on the one hand, and nonauthoritative legal and general literature, on the other, also exists in Jewish law. A substantial part of our knowledge of the pre-tannaitic *Halakhah* is derived not from authoritative sources such as the Torah, the Prophets, and the Hagiographa but, as more fully appears later, from an extensive general literature that includes the Apocrypha, the Septuagint, Josephus, and Philo. However, this general literature, with its considerable halakhic information, is not recognized by the halakhic authorities as an authoritative source for ascertaining the law; and the general character of this literature, which had its own particular religious and historical agenda, calls for great caution in drawing conclusions with regard to the law during the period to which the literature relates.

The following chapters divide the discussion of the literary sources of Jewish law into three historical periods: (1) from the Sinaitic Revelation until the *tannaim,* (2) the Talmudic period, and (3) the post-Talmudic period.

Since a considerable portion of our knowledge of Jewish law in its initial period is drawn from legal and general literature, the major exemplars of those types of sources will be reviewed. In the Talmudic period, too, there are sources from the legal and general literature, and any research must take account of them. However, since our knowledge of almost the entire content of the Jewish law of the Talmudic period is derived from extensive authoritative literary sources, only those sources will be reviewed. In the post-Talmudic period also, much information about Jewish law can be obtained from legal and general literature. However, this period is extremely rich in authoritative literary sources and in guidebooks to these sources, and the review here is therefore confined to authoritative sources and guidebooks.

Chapter 26

THE LITERARY SOURCES FROM THE SINAITIC REVELATION UNTIL THE *TANNAIM*

I. The Written Law
II. The Prophets and the Hagiographa
   A. The Laws of the Sabbath
   B. Modes of Acquisition
   C. The King's Law
   D. "A Person Shall Be Put to Death Only for His Own Crime"
   E. The Law of Suretyship
III. Legal and General Literature
   A. Introduction
   B. The Papyri
   C. The Septuagint
   D. Philo of Alexandria
   E. Flavius Josephus
   F. The Apocrypha
IV. Summary

I. THE WRITTEN LAW

The Written Law (*Torah she-bi-khetav*), contained in the Pentateuch, is the first and foremost literary source of Jewish law—the source upon which the Prophets, the Hagiographa, and the Oral Law all rest. It was the source from which Jewish law was derived in actual practice and in accordance with which day-to-day judicial determinations were made.[1] Every section, verse, and letter—indeed even every ornamentation on the letters—of the Torah has been recognized as an authoritative source of Jewish law.

1. For a discussion of some of the legal institutions of the Written Law, *see supra* pp. 194–203. The books and chapters of the Pentateuch with a particularly "legal" content are: Exodus 20–23; Leviticus 5, 18–21, 24, 25, 27; Numbers 27, 35, 36; Deuteronomy 1, 4, 5, 16–17, 19–25.

II. THE PROPHETS AND THE HAGIOGRAPHA

Little information is available as to the substance of the *Halakhah* before the beginning of the Second Temple period in the fifth century B.C.E. The authoritative literary sources dating from after the Written Law to the beginning of the Second Temple period are the Prophets (*Nevi'im*) and the Hagiographa (*Ketuvim*). Despite the paucity of halakhic material in the Prophets and the Hagiographa, these books provide a basis for conclusions as to the existence of various laws and legal institutions not mentioned in the Written Law.

The lack of extensive legal material in these books is readily understandable:[2] the prophets and chroniclers who wrote the books were primarily concerned with the frequent internal strife and foreign wars, with ethical, social, and religious problems, and with polemics. They did not, therefore, dwell particularly on matters of contemporary legal interest. However, it would be incorrect to conclude from this silence, which encompasses most fields of law, that a Jewish legal system did not then exist, since there can be no doubt that every functioning society must be based upon a legal order.[3]

The following are a few examples of laws and legal institutions for which there is evidence in the Prophets and the Hagiographa.

A. The Laws of the Sabbath

The previous discussion of the Oral Law[4] has shown that unwritten laws explaining and complementing the Written Law necessarily had to exist. One example cited was the prohibition of labor on the sabbath, as to which only a few details are specified in the Torah. Some additional details are spelled out in the Prophets and the Hagiographa. The Book of Isaiah states:[5]

> If you refrain from trampling the sabbath, from pursuing your affairs on My holy day; if you call the sabbath "delight," the Lord's holy day "honored"; and if you honor it and go not your ways nor look to your affairs, nor strike bargains. . . .

2. *See* Z. Frankel, *Der Gerichtliche Beweis* [Forensic Proof], p. 34; *id.*, *Mishnah*, p. 2.
3. The Sages refer to the Prophets and the Hagiographa as *divrei kabbalah*, matters—or words—of tradition. For an explanation of this term, and for the derivation of halakhic principles from such sources, *see supra* pp. 203–204.
4. *Supra* pp. 200–203.
5. Isaiah 58:13

The Book of Jeremiah focuses on the prohibition of carrying from one domain to another:[6]

> Thus said the Lord: Guard yourselves for your own sake against carrying burdens on the sabbath day, and bringing them through the gates of Jerusalem. Nor shall you carry out burdens from your houses on the sabbath day, or do any work, but you shall hallow the sabbath day, as I commanded your fathers.

The Book of Nehemiah refers to the observance of the prohibition of commerce on the sabbath as a well-known practice:[7]

> The peoples of the land who bring their wares and all sorts of foodstuff for sale on the sabbath day—we will not buy from them on the sabbath or a holy day.[8]

B. Modes of Acquisition

The books of Ruth and Jeremiah shed light on another area of the law, namely, the acquisition of property. The Book of Ruth states:[9]

> Now this was formerly done in Israel in cases of redemption or exchange:[10] to validate any transaction, one man would take off his sandal and hand it to the other. Such was the practice in Israel.

Thus, acquisition by the symbolic act of taking off one's shoe and handing it to the other party was an ancient practice antedating the Book of Ruth. The Book of Jeremiah describes how the prophet bought a field from his cousin, Hanamel ben Shallum:[11]

6. Jeremiah 17:21–22.

7. Nehemiah 10:32.

8. *See also* Nehemiah 13:15–19; Amos 8:5 ("If only the New Moon were over, so that we could sell grain; the sabbath, so that we could offer wheat for sale"). The term "sabbath" in Amos has been variously interpreted as referring to the sabbatical year, a week, or the sabbath of creation, *i.e.*, the seventh day of the week; *see* the Targum, and commentaries of Rashi, Redak (David Kimḥi), and M.Z. Segal, on Amos, *ad loc.* The discussion of whether the halakhic prohibition of commerce on the sabbath is Biblical (*de-oraita*) or rabbinic (*de-rabbanan*) is largely based on the verses in Nehemiah and Isaiah. *See Mekhilta de-R. Ishmael,* Ki Tissa, Tractate De-Shabbata (ed. Horowitz-Rabin, p. 341); Rashi, Shabbat 113b, s.v. She-lo; Rashi, Beẓah 27b, s.v. Ein posekin; *id.*, 37a, s.v. Mishum mikaḥ u-mimkar; Maimonides, *MT,* Shabbat 23:12, Mekhirah 30:7; Naḥmanides, *Commentary on Leviticus* 23:24; *see also Sedeh Ḥemed,* Divrei Ḥakhamim #81 (V, p. 404) for further sources.

9. Ruth 4:7.

10. Scholars have offered many opinions as to the explanation of the terms *ge'ulah* ("redemption") and *temurah* ("exchange"). TB Bava Meẓi'a 47a interprets "redemption" as meaning "sale," and "exchange" as meaning "barter."

11. Jeremiah 32:9–12.

> So I bought the land in Anathoth from my cousin Hanamel. I weighed out the money to him, seventeen shekels of silver. I wrote a deed, sealed it, and had it witnessed; and I weighed out the silver on a balance. I took the deed of purchase, the sealed text and the open one according to rule and law, and gave the deed to Baruch son of Neriah son of Mahseiah in the presence of my kinsman Hanamel, of the witnesses who were named in the deed, and all the Judeans who were sitting in the prison compound.

Jeremiah went on to say:[12]

> Fields shall be purchased, and deeds written and sealed, and witnesses called.

These verses are a detailed account of a property transaction: writing a deed of purchase, sealing it, weighing out the money and handing it over, delivering the deed, and many more details of the laws of acquisition. Jeremiah's description is quite different from that in Ruth, which tells us that formerly, in order "to validate any transaction" it was customary to take off a sandal. In Jeremiah's time, however, we are told of weighing money and writing and sealing a document called "a deed of purchase," which consisted of two parts, known as "the sealed" and "the open." The difference between these two sources shows the extent to which the modes of acquisition had developed between the dates of the two books.

However, the transactions described in the two texts do have a common feature; both transactions are open and notorious. Boaz turned to "the elders and to the rest of the people" and said, "You are witnesses today that I am acquiring from Naomi all that belonged to Elimelech";[13] and Jeremiah gave the deed of purchase to Baruch "in the presence of my kinsman Hanamel, of the witnesses who were named in the deed, and all the Judeans who were sitting in the prison compound."[14]

The Sages took note of the development that had occurred:[15]

> Originally, they would acquire by taking off the sandal, as it is written, "Now this was formerly done in Israel in cases of redemption or exchange: . . . one man would take off his sandal. . . . "
>
> They then used a mode of acquisition called *kezazah*. What is *kezazah*? When a man would sell a field of his ancestral holding, his kinsmen would bring jars and fill them with parched corn and nuts and break the jars in the presence of children, and the children would gather [the corn and the nuts]

12. *Id.* 32:44.

13. Ruth 4:9.

14. Jeremiah 32:12. Abraham's purchase of the Machpelah cave similarly took place in public. *See* Genesis 23:16–18. *See supra* pp. 195–196 for details of the laws of acquisition of property that the Sages connected to the account of the Machpelah transaction.

15. TJ Kiddushin 1:5, 16a (1:5, 60c).

> and proclaim, "So-and-so has been cut off [*nikẓaẓ*] from his ancestral property." When he [the seller] would repurchase his property, they would do the same and [the children would] proclaim, "So-and-so has returned to his property. . . ."[16]
>
> Later, they effected acquisition by handing over money, by deed of conveyance, or by *ḥazakah* [performing an act of dominion usually done by an owner, such as locking the premises, putting up a fence, or opening a gateway].
>
> Handing over money, as it is written, "Fields shall be purchased"—this refers to [acquisition by payment of] money. "And deeds written and sealed"—this refers to the witnesses on the document. "And witnesses called"—these are the witnesses to the act of *ḥazakah*.[17]

We have here an interesting example of developments in an important legal institution in a period about which, generally speaking, little information is available; and the conclusion to be drawn is broader than the particular example, since other legal institutions undoubtedly existed that also passed through various stages of development in the pre-tannaitic period.[18]

C. The King's Law

The section in Deuteronomy on the king's law deals mainly with the way the king is expected to conduct himself. This expectation is epitomized in his obligation to write for himself a Torah scroll and read it all the days of his life, so that "he will not act haughtily toward his fellows or deviate from the Instruction [*miẓvah*, lit. "commandment"] either to the right or to the left."[19] The Book of Samuel states in detail the king's prerogatives vis-à-vis the people and the people's duties toward him:[20]

16. Here too, the element of publicity is preserved ("his kinsmen would bring . . . "), albeit in a more limited fashion. TJ stresses the interest of the kinsmen in keeping the property in the family; *cf.* Ruth 3:12, 4:4 and Jeremiah 32:7, where the sale is to a "redeemer" who is a relative.

17. *Cf.* TB Bava Batra 160a. *Midrash Ruth Rabbah* 7:11 presents a different version of the development of the law of acquisition. *See supra* pp. 297–298, 510–511, 580–587, 913–920, for details as to the modes of acquisition in Jewish law.

18. For additional legal principles for which the Book of Ruth provides evidence, *see* M.Z. Segal, *Sefer Ha-Zikkaron le-A. Gulak u-le S. Klein* [Memorial Volume for A. Gulak and S. Klein], Jerusalem, 1942, pp. 124ff.

19. Deuteronomy 17:14–20. For general legal principles derived from this section, *see also supra* pp. 55–57.

20. I Samuel 8:11–17. In TB Sanhedrin 20b, Rav and Samuel disagree as to whether the statement in the Book of Samuel describes the king's rights or whether the prophet was merely trying to frighten the populace against having a king; *see supra* p. 66 n. 53.

> This will be the practice of the king who will rule over you: He will take your sons and appoint them as his charioteers and horsemen, and they will serve as outrunners for his chariots. He will appoint them as his chiefs of thousands and of fifties; or they will have to plow his fields, reap his harvest, and make his weapons and the equipment for his chariots. He will take your daughters as perfumers, cooks, and bakers. He will seize your choice fields, vineyards, and olive groves, and give them to his courtiers. He will take a tenth part of your grain and vintage and give it to his eunuchs and courtiers. He will take your male and female slaves, your choice young men, and your asses, and put them to work for him. He will take a tenth part of your flocks, and you shall become his slaves.

The incident involving King Ahab and Naboth the Jezreelite[21] indicates that notwithstanding the far-reaching prerogatives of the king, his right to expropriate property of his subjects was limited. The Book of Kings relates that Naboth refused to give up his land to the king ("The Lord forbid that I should give up to you what I have inherited from my fathers!"[22]); and Ahab was unable to take it unless Naboth agreed to exchange or sell the vineyard to him.[23] Consequently, the queen, Jezebel, fabricated the accusation that "Naboth has reviled God and king,"[24] in order to justify executing him and confiscating his property.

The account of the incident also discloses another norm of the king's law, namely, that the property of a person executed for an offense against the king reverted to the king:

> As soon as Jezebel heard that Naboth had been stoned to death, she said to Ahab, "Go and take possession of the vineyard which Naboth the Jezreelite refused to sell you for money; for Naboth is no longer alive, he is dead." When Ahab heard that Naboth was dead, Ahab set out for the vineyard of Naboth the Jezreelite to take possession of it.[25]

D. "A Person Shall Be Put to Death Only for His Own Crime"

The Book of Kings recounts that King Amaziah executed the conspirators who had killed his father, King Joash, but "he did not put to death the children of the assassins, in accordance with what is written in the Book of

21. I Kings ch. 21.

22. *Id.* 21:3.

23. *Id.* 21:2, and *see* Redak's commentary on verse 10.

24. *Id.* 21:13. The Hebrew *berakh,* translated as "reviled," is a euphemism. Its literal meaning is "blessed." *See* commentators, *ad loc.*

25. *Id.* 21:15–16; *see also* verse 18. The Sages derived the norm as to reversion of property to the king from this Biblical account. *See* TB Sanhedrin 48b. For a detailed discussion of the king's law, *see supra* pp. 55–57.

the Torah of Moses, where the Lord commanded, 'Parents shall not be put to death on account of children, nor children put to death on account of parents; a person shall be put to death only for his own crime.'"[26] This indicates that Amaziah, even though king, followed the law of the Torah that each person is responsible only for his own transgression and no one should be killed for the transgression of another.[27] Thus, even a king punishing conspirators against his throne was bound to observe the basic principles of Jewish law, from which his rank gave him no privilege to deviate.

E. The Law of Suretyship

The Torah does not mention suretyship except for Judah's promise to Jacob regarding Benjamin's journey to Egypt: "I myself will be surety for him; you may hold me responsible: If I do not bring him back to you and set him before you, I shall stand guilty before you forever."[28] However, this does not constitute the accepted legal commitment of a surety, since the required "triangle"—creditor, debtor, and surety—is lacking; Judah was both the "debtor" and the "surety."[29]

The Hagiographa, however, supplies important details of the laws of suretyship. The Book of Proverbs gives a detailed description of the legal and social aspects of the surety's obligation:

> My son, if you have stood surety for your fellow, given your hand for another, you have been trapped by the words of your mouth, snared by the words of your mouth. Do this, then, my son, to extricate yourself, for you have come into the power [lit. "hand"] of your fellow: Go grovel—and badger your fellow; give your eyes no sleep, your pupils no slumber. Save yourself like a deer out of the hand [of a hunter], like a bird out of the hand of a fowler.[30]

These verses reveal two important points about how the obligation of suretyship was created:

1. A handshake between the creditor and the surety (" . . . given your hand . . . ," "you have come into the hand of your fellow") is effective to create the obligation.

26. II Kings 14:6.

27. Deuteronomy 24:16. *See also supra* p. 73 and n. 84, and pp. 303–304.

28. Genesis 43:9. The term *eravon* (pledge) is found in the Torah (Genesis 38:17–18, 20), but there it means a chattel given as collateral security, not a personal undertaking to be responsible for the performance of another's obligation. *Cf.* Nehemiah 5:3.

29. *See* TB Bava Batra 173b as per the reading in *She'iltot* (ed. Mirsky), Mikeẓ, *she'ilta* #33.

30. Proverbs 6:1–5.

2. Creation of suretyship does not require a writing ("you have been trapped by the words of your mouth").

It is clear that the Book of Proverbs takes an altogether negative view of suretyship, describing it as a snare and a trap to be assiduously avoided.

Other verses in Proverbs not only corroborate that the creation of a suretyship requires no greater formality than a handshake but also express the same negative attitude to the whole institution: "Harm awaits him who stands surety for another; he who spurns pledging [Hebrew: *toke'im,* lit. "handshakers"] shall be secure";[31] "Seize his garment, for he stood surety for another; take it as a pledge, [for he stood surety] for an unfamiliar woman."[32] The second of these verses indicates that remedies against a defaulting surety were limited to execution against the surety's property and did not extend to his person.[33] The most serious deterrent invoked against becoming a surety was that the creditor might take the surety's clothing and bed.[34] Had the creditor been able to enslave the person of the surety,[35] the Book of Proverbs would certainly have warned of that possibility as a reason to avoid undertaking to answer for the obligation of another.[36]

III. LEGAL AND GENERAL LITERATURE

A. Introduction

There is no extant authoritative literary source of Jewish law composed during the period from Ezra and Nehemiah to the end of the Second Temple. However, the authoritative literary collections composed afterward during the period of the *tannaim* contain a great number of laws that originated in this earlier period, and a rather rich legal and general literature

31. *Id.* 11:15.

32. *Id.* 20:16. *See also id.* 17:18 ("Devoid of sense is he who gives his hand to stand surety for his fellow"), and sources *infra* n. 33.

33. *Id.* 22:26–27 is to similar effect. *See also id.* 27:13.

34. *Id.* 22:26–27.

35. *See* Elon, *Ḥerut,* p. 8 and n. 54. For suretyship in the Hagiographa, *see also* Job 17:3. The subject is also mentioned in the Apocrypha, *see infra* p. 1035. It should be pointed out that the handshake is not mentioned in the Talmud as a method of creating either suretyship or any other obligation. However, it does reappear in later periods in connection with suretyship (*see* Rema to Sh. Ar. ḤM 129:5) and as a mode of acquisition generally (Sh. Ar. ḤM 201:2 and commentaries, *ad loc.*). *See supra* p. 916 and n. 71.

36. For another example of a new legal institution in the Prophets and the Hagiographa, *see* I Samuel 30:24–25 and *supra* p. 554. For legal practices not in accordance with the law of the Torah that became widespread and are noted in the Prophets and Hagiographa, *see* Elon, *Ḥerut,* pp. 8–10, and *supra* pp. 199–200.

from the earlier period contains a great deal of information shedding light on various legal subjects.

This legal and general literature contains laws that are sometimes consonant and sometimes in conflict with laws in the Talmud. There are several possible explanations for the conflicts: (1) laws may have changed in the course of their development, as in the instance noted above;[37] (2) this literature does not always give a fully accurate description of the law, since not all the authors were knowledgeable in the law; (3) occasionally, the author represented a small sect that deviated from the accepted *Halakhah*; (4) most of the literature of the period under discussion has reached us not in its original form but in translation, which may not be entirely accurate; and (5) the Talmudic *Halakhah* we have is neither complete nor exhaustive, and many laws and sources have not survived.

We discuss here some of the main aspects of this body of literature.

B. The Papyri

An examination of papyri on general subjects, as well as papyri of a more distinctly legal character, sheds light on various ancient legal matters. The Elephantine papyri are perhaps the best known. In the ruins of the town of Elephantine (known as *Yev* in Hebrew) in southern Egypt, documents were discovered dating from the beginning of the Second Temple period (fifth century B.C.E.). The documents are in Aramaic (and hence also known as the Aramaic Papyri of Elephantine), and they shed light on the life of the Jewish military post then at Elephantine. The documents contain a great deal of important legal material. Most of them deal with civil-law matters, marriage and divorce, and succession; and they indicate that various laws later recorded in the Talmud were known and followed by Jews in the fifth century B.C.E.[38]

Also extant are documents from the later period of the Egyptian Ptolemies (323–30 B.C.E.),[39] and scholarly studies have dealt with the relationship between Jewish law and the legal materials in these documents.[40]

37. *See supra* pp. 1022–1024 regarding changes in the modes of acquisition.

38. *E.g.*, laws of succession, some of which correspond to Talmudic law and some of which do not. *See* R. Yaron, *Ha-Mishpat Shel Mismekhei Yev* [Law in the Elephantine Papyri], pp. 82ff., 176ff.

39. These documents have been collected in *Corpus Papyrorum Judaicorum* by V.A. Tcherikover and A. Fuchs, vols I–III, 1957–1964.

40. *Id.*, I, pp. 34–36. *See also supra* p. 424 n. 8; A. Gulak, *Das Urkendenwesen im Talmud* [The Nature of Legal Instruments in the Talmud], Jerusalem, 1935.

C. The Septuagint

A further source of information regarding the norms of Jewish law in the pre-tannaitic period is the Septuagint, a translation of the Torah into Greek, which was completed, at the latest, in 222 B.C.E. during the reign of King Ptolemy IV.[41] The Septuagint is an important source of information about Jewish law in that period, because it is not always a literal translation but frequently translates according to the contemporary consensus as to the meaning of various concepts contained in the Torah. The Septuagint thus provides information about a number of legal rules, some similar to those recorded in Talmudic literature and others not. The following are examples:

1. The verse in Deuteronomy[42] regarding the punishment to be meted out to a man who slanders his newly taken wife—"The elders of that town shall then take the man and punish (*ve-yisru*) him"—is translated in the Septuagint as "and flog him." Talmudic literature also interprets the term *ve-yisru* as referring to flogging.[43]
2. The law of levirate marriage as presented in the Torah is: "When brothers dwell together and one of them dies and leaves no son (*ben*). . . . "[44] The Septuagint translates *ben* as "offspring," *i.e.*, even if the deceased left no son but did leave a daughter or grandchildren, his widow is exempt from the requirement of levirate marriage. This, too, is the law in Talmudic literature.[45]
3. An example where the Septuagint does not correspond to Talmudic *Halakhah* involves the law of bailments. The Torah states:[46] "If the thief is not caught, the owner of the house [*i.e.*, the bailee] shall come near to *elohim* if he has not laid hands on his neighbor's property." The verse is translated in the Septuagint as requiring an oath before God; Talmudic literature also interprets "come near" as meaning "swear an oath,"[47] but interprets *elohim* as referring to a judge, not God,[48] so that the halakhic meaning is that the bailee takes an oath in court.

41. *See* Epstein, *Tannaim*, p. 516 n. 1.

42. Deuteronomy 22:18.

43. *Sifrei*, Deuteronomy, sec. 238 (ed. Finkelstein, p. 270); TB Ketubbot 46a; and *see id.* 45b.

44. Deuteronomy 25:5.

45. *Midrash Tannaim*, Devarim, p. 165; *Sifrei*, Deuteronomy, sec. 288 (ed. Finkelstein, p. 306); TB Bava Batra 109a. *See also* Rashbam, *ad loc.*, s.v. Ben u-vat ki hadadi ninhu.

46. Exodus 22:7.

47. *Mekhilta*, Mishpatim, sec. 15 (ed. Horowitz-Rabin, p. 300). The 1985 JPS *Tanakh* translates Exodus 22:7: "If the thief is not caught, the owner of the house shall depose before God that he has not laid hands on the other's property."

48. *Mekhilta*, *supra* n. 47: "Should I understand from this that one should consult the *Urim* and *Thummin* [so as to divine the will of God]? Therefore, Scripture states [Exodus

D. Philo of Alexandria

Philo was a Jewish philosopher who lived in Alexandria, Egypt, in the first half of the first century C.E. Most of his works are commentaries on the Torah. His books, particularly *De Specialibus Legibus* [On Special Laws], contain a great deal of legal material which, like that in the Septuagint, is sometimes consistent with Talmudic law and sometimes not.

An example of a commentary consistent with Talmudic law deals with the punishment for the rape of a woman betrothed to another man. A critical factor, according to the Torah, is the place where the offense is committed:[49] If the incident takes place in a town, the woman is culpable, but if she is raped in the open country she is not liable to punishment. The rationale is that in the open country she is presumed to have shouted for help without having been heard; in a town, however, if she had shouted she would have been heard and rescued, so the conclusion is that she did not cry out or resist. In his discussion of the relevant verses, Philo wrote:[50]

> The judge must examine the matter of the woman's culpability carefully and not rule on the basis of the locality [of the offense], because she may very well have been raped in a street in the town, just as she may have been a willing participant in the country. Therefore, the Torah was very careful to say [Deuteronomy 22:27], when it acquitted a maiden who was raped in a field, "though the betrothed girl cried for help, there was no one to save her." This means that if she did not cry for help or try to defend herself but gave herself to him of her own free will, she is certainly guilty, because she is cunningly using the location of the act as a proof that she was raped.
>
> The converse is also true if the forbidden intercourse took place in a town. What can a woman who is prepared to sacrifice everything for her honor do if she is unable to defend herself against a man who is bent on illicit intercourse and is stronger than she is? For such a woman, a rape in a town may be no different than rape in a deserted locality, because in fact no rescuer was available in either place. But the other woman who gave herself freely even in a deserted locality is like a woman in a town.

According to Philo, the woman is not to be judged on the basis of the location where the forbidden intercourse takes place. The critical question is the volition of the woman, because rape is possible not only in the coun-

---

22:8]: 'He whom *elohim* declares guilty [shall pay double to the other].' The only *elohim* to which the verse refers is such *elohim* as find a man guilty [*i.e.*, judges]." *See also id.* at 302.

49. Deuteronomy 22:23–27.

50. Philo, *De Specialibus Legibus*, III, pp. 77–78 (Loeb Classical Library, vol. VII, translated by F.M. Colson, pp. 77–78 [with stylistic changes]). *See* Epstein, *Tannaim*, p. 517.

try but also in a town, and consent is possible not only in a town but also in the country.

The *Sifrei*[51] gives the same interpretation:

> "For he came upon her in the open." Shall we take this to mean that she is guilty [if the incident occurred] in the city, but is innocent [if it occurred] in the open country? But does not Scripture state: "Though the betrothed girl cried for help, there was no one to save her"? This implies that if there was someone there to save her, whether in the city or in the open country, she is guilty, and that if there was no one to save her, whether in the city or in the open country, she is innocent.[52]

Thus, the law recorded in the *Sifrei* was known to Philo.

E. Flavius Josephus

The works of Flavius Josephus, especially *The Antiquities of the Jews*, contain much material on Jewish law in the period of the destruction of the Second Temple.

For example, among the laws of the Torah regarding bondmen, it is stated that if a Hebrew slave marries and has children and does not want to go free at the end of his six years of service, "his master shall pierce his ear with an awl, and he shall then remain his slave for life" (*le-olam*, lit. "forever").[53] Josephus wrote:

> [I]f he have a son by a woman servant in his purchaser's house, and if, on account of his good will to his master, and his natural affection to his wife and children, he will be his servant still, let him be set free only at the coming of the year of jubilee, which is the fiftieth year.[54]

Josephus thus interprets "forever" as meaning "until the jubilee year," which is the interpretation given in the Talmud:

> "And he shall then remain his slave forever." Rabbi [Judah Ha-Nasi] said, "Come and see that 'forever' means only fifty years, since it [Scripture] states, 'he shall then remain his slave forever'—[but he remains in service only] until the jubilee year."[55]

51. *Sifrei*, Deuteronomy, Ki Teẓe, sec. 243 (ed. Finkelstein, p. 273).
52. For further discussion, *see supra* pp. 339–340.
53. Exodus 21:6.
54. *Antiquities*, Book IV, 8:28 (Whiston trans.). For another English version of the *Antiquities*, *see* Loeb Classical Library, ed. Thackery, 1930.
55. *Mekhilta*, Mishpatim, sec. 2 (ed. Horowitz-Rabin, p. 254); *see also* TB Kiddushin 15a: "'*le-olam*'—to the *olam* of the jubilee [*i.e.*, until the next jubilee]."

Occasionally, Josephus manifests a pronounced tendentiousness both in his historical accounts and in his descriptions of specific aspects of legal rules. Indeed, before his treatment of Jewish law, he states:[56]

> I shall now first describe this form of government which was agreeable to the dignity and virtue of Moses; and shall thereby inform those that read these Antiquities, what our original settlements [the nature of our laws from ancient times] were, and shall then proceed to the remaining histories. Now those settlements are all still in writing, as he [Moses] left them; and we shall add nothing by way of ornament, nor any thing besides what Moses left us.

However, as can be seen from many passages in Josephus, there was very little in his statement of intention that was accurate. "The sole purpose of this statement of Josephus was to impress his Hellenistic-Roman readers. . . . In fact, in many places [in his discussion], he follows other traditions outside the Torah and both adds to and subtracts from Scripture."[57]

Examples of Josephus's tendentious approach can be found throughout his works. In one instance, he wrote that among the laws promulgated by Moses in God's name was the following:

> Let no one of the Israelites keep any poison that may cause death, or any other harm; but if he be caught with it, let him be put to death, and suffer the very same mischief that he would have brought upon them for whom the poison was prepared.[58]

In neither the Torah nor the Talmud is there any mention of the death penalty for possessing a lethal poison in one's home; what Josephus was doing was tailoring his statement of Jewish law in light of notions current among the Romans. "In imperial Rome the compounding of lethal poisons and other injurious drugs was very widespread; physicians and others were so occupied in this industry that it became necessary to invent antidotes."[59]

Zacharias Frankel[60] evaluated Josephus's literary work as follows:

> He wrote some of his books to be read by Roman readers, and in these he frequently deviated from the Biblical stories and did not address himself to the truth but rather to his readers, to curry favor in their eyes. Furthermore, in passages where he tries to clear himself of the accusations aimed at him—he had, after all, betrayed his people during the war and collaborated with the Romans—the reader must carefully scrutinize Josephus's statements be-

56. *Antiquities,* Book IV, 8:4 (Whiston trans.).

57. *Antiquities,* Book II (ed. Schalit, Hebrew), p. 82 n. 108; *see also id.*, n. 117.

58. *Antiquities,* Book IV, 8:34 (Whiston trans.).

59. Shur, *Kadmoniyyot ha-Yehudim* [Antiquities of the Jews], I, p. 209 n. 3, in the name of Friedlander.

60. Frankel, *Mishnah,* p. 334.

cause he wraps himself in a cloak of deceit in order to remove this great burden from himself and place it on the shoulders of his adversaries. However, in passages where he stands to gain nothing from perverting the truth, he can be relied upon.

F. The Apocrypha

Another source of information on Jewish law in the pre-Mishnaic period is the Apocrypha. This is a collection of books that the Sages excluded from the canon of the Bible and "put away"—hence the Hebrew name *ḥiẓonim* (external) and the Greek name *apocrypha* (hidden) for these writings. Some of the books of the Apocrypha were originally written in Hebrew or Aramaic, but most of these have not reached us in the original language; others were written in other languages, mainly Greek.

The books of the Apocrypha were apparently composed between the fourth century B.C.E. and 200 C.E., but scholars do not agree on the dating of each individual book. The Apocrypha include historical works, wisdom literature, and books of ethics and poetry, as well as collections of stories, legends, and prophetic visions. From these works, one can learn the history of the Jews, their customs and outlook, and their legal norms and practices in the post-Biblical period—some of which were consistent and some in conflict with Talmudic law. The inconsistencies were sometimes due to differences of opinion not resolved until later and sometimes due to the fact that laws described in the Apocrypha were not generally accepted but represented the practice of particular religious sects. The following are a few examples:

1. The Book of Jubilees[61] (composed in the third or second century B.C.E.) deals with many subjects in various areas of law. For instance, the Mishnah states:[62] "[This is] the mandate for those to be beheaded; they would cut off the head with a sword, just as the government does," *i.e.*, those criminals sentenced to death by *hereg*, such as murderers,[63] are to be executed by decapitation with a sword.

The account of the story of Cain and Abel in the Book of Jubilees states:[64]

> At the end of this jubilee, Cain was killed one year after him [Abel]. His house collapsed on him and he died inside it, having been killed by its stones; for

61. Hebrew, *Sefer ha-Yovelot*, also called *Sefer ha-Yovelim; see* A. Kahana, *Ha-Sefarim ha-Ḥiẓonim*, I, Introduction to *Sefer ha-Yovelim*.

62. M Sanhedrin 7:3.

63. *Id.* 9:1.

64. Jubilees 4:31–32 (ed. Kahana, p. 34).

> he had killed Abel with a stone and so he was killed by a stone, in just retribution. Therefore, it was established in the Tablets of Heaven: by whatever instrument a man uses to kill his fellow, he too shall be killed; as he injures [his fellow], so he too shall be injured.

Thus, according to the Book of Jubilees, a murderer is to be executed by the same means he used to kill his victim. Indeed, the Jerusalem Talmud[65] records a discussion on this very point:

> R. Johanan said: "[As to the law stated in the Mishnah that the execution of those condemned to die by *hereg* is always decapitation by sword,] we have also learned this in a *baraita*: '"The manslayer shall be killed."[66] Is it by the same means whereby he killed? Can it be that if he killed [his victim] with a sword, they should kill him with a sword, and if with a stick, they should kill him with a stick? [No]. The term "vengeance" is used here [in connection with murder],[67] and the term "vengeance" is used later:[68] "I will bring a sword against you to wreak vengeance for the covenant." Just as "vengeance" there means with a sword, so too "vengeance" here means death by sword.'"

Thus, the possibility was considered that the punishment should be by means of the same type of weapon that was used to commit the crime; but the Sages, by use of the canon of *gezerah shavah* (inference from the similarity of words or phrases), analogizing from the use of the term "vengeance" in one instance as referring to a sword, ruled that execution for murder is always by the sword.[69]

2. The Book of Tobit (composed not later than the third century B.C.E.) describes several legal practices relating to marriage and the *ketubbah*. In the detailed description of Tobit's marriage to Reuel's daughter Sarah,[70] the book states that he took her as his wife according to the law of Moses, and that they recited the benedictions and wrote a *ketubbah*—details that bring to mind the marriage laws of the Talmud.

3. The Book of Ben Sira (composed in the middle of the third century B.C.E.), mainly a work of wisdom literature and ethical instruction, also contains or allusively refers to legal rules. For example, in the beginning of

65. TJ Sanhedrin 7:3, 31b (7:3, 24b).

66. Numbers 35:30: "If anyone kills a person, the manslayer may [lit. "shall"] be executed [lit. "killed"] only on the evidence of witnesses; the testimony of a single witness against a person shall not suffice for a sentence of death."

67. Exodus 21:20: "When a man strikes his slave, male or female, with a rod, and he [or she] dies there and then, he [or she] must be avenged."

68. Leviticus 26:25.

69. *See* H. Albeck, *Das Buch der Jubiläen und die Halacha* [The Book of Jubilees and the *Halakhah*], pp. 25–26 and n. 179; *id.*, *Commentary on M Nezikin,* Hashlamot, p. 453.

70. Tobit 7:12ff. (ed. Kahana, II, p. 331).

chapter 42, Ben Sira states: "But of these be not ashamed and do not show partiality and thus sin," and in the list of things about which scrupulous care must be taken he includes:[71] "also the fine dust on scales and balances and the dust on the weights *ephah* and *even*," *i.e.*, a merchant must clean the dust from the balance scales he uses to weigh his merchandise and must clean his weights and measures so that the purchaser does not lose by having the weight of the dust included in the weight of the purchase.

The same matter is treated in the Mishnah:[72]

> A wholesaler must clean his measures once every thirty days, and a householder once every twelve months. Rabban Simeon b. Gamaliel says: "The reverse is the case."
>
> A shopkeeper must clean his measures twice a week, rub up his weights once a week, and clean his scales each time he uses them for weighing.

Another legal topic mentioned by Ben Sira is suretyship: "A good man will stand surety for a neighbor."[73] At the same time, he advises: "Stand surety for your neighbor as well as you can, but watch yourself lest you fall,"[74] *i.e.*, stand surety for as much as you can afford to pay, so that you will not suffer if you are required to make good on your guaranty.[75]

4. The legal matter in the Book of Maccabees[76] reveals the development of the laws of waging war on the sabbath. I Maccabees[77] cites an earlier law according to which waging war on the sabbath, even in self-defense, was forbidden. The existence of this law is corroborated by statements in another source that the enemy, knowing that Jews would not fight on the sabbath, deliberately chose that day for military attack. Josephus quotes the testimony of a Greek author, Agatharchides, that the Jews did not even defend Jerusalem on the sabbath and thus allowed Ptolemy Lagos (ca. 300 B.C.E.) to conquer the city without a battle.[78] From the Books of the Maccabees and from Josephus it is clear that even as late as the time of Mattathias the Hasmonean, the Jews did not defend themselves on the sabbath.

71. Ben Sira 42:4 (ed. Kahana, II, p. 515).

72. M Bava Batra 5:10.

73. Ben Sira 29:17 (ed. Segal; ed. Kahana 29:14).

74. *Id.* 29:23 (ed. Segal; ed. Kahana 29:20 with a textual variation). *See also* 29:18–22 and 8:16–17 (ed. Segal; ed. Kahana 29:15–19, 8:12–13). The attitude to suretyship is not negative in Ben Sira as it is in Proverbs (*see supra* pp. 1026–1027); the surety is merely warned not to be surety for more than he can pay.

75. *See supra* pp. 1026–1027 for the Scriptural laws of suretyship.

76. In a later period, the book was called "The Book of the Hasmoneans." *See* Kahana, *supra* n. 61, II, p. 81.

77. I Maccabees 2:32ff. (ed. Kahana, II, p. 107).

78. *Antiquities*, Book XII, 1:1; *Contra Apionem*, I, sec. 22 (end).

However, when Mattathias and his men realized that this practice might lead to the total destruction of the Jewish people, they instructed their forces to fight in self-defense on the sabbath, and since then "and until this day it has been our practice to fight even on the sabbath whenever there is a need to do so."[79] This dispensation was extended, in certain circumstances, even to offensive warfare, as the *Tosefta* states:[80]

> If a camp [*i.e.*, army] goes out to a voluntary war [*milḥemet reshut,* as opposed to a *milḥemet mizvah,* a war required for the defense of the Jewish people or of the Land of Israel], they may not lay siege to a gentile city less than three days before the sabbath; but once they start, they do not interrupt it even on the sabbath. Thus did Shammai the Elder[81] interpret: "'Until it has been reduced'[82]—even on the sabbath."[83]

Of the rest of the Apocrypha, we mention here only the Letter of Aristeas. This work describes how the Septuagint came into being and refers to the commandments of *mezuzah* and phylacteries as follows: "So did He command us to affix these sections [of the Torah] to the gates and the doors to keep us mindful of God's presence, and He also commanded in clear words to bind the sign [*i.e.*, the Torah sections contained in the phylacteries] around the arm,"[84] which is the same interpretation that the Talmud gives to those precepts.[85]

79. *Antiquities,* Book XII, 6:2 (ed. Schalit, III, p. 58).

80. *Tosefta* Eruvin 4:7 (ed. Lieberman 3:7, p. 100); similarly, *Sifrei,* Deuteronomy, secs. 203 (ed. Finkelstein, p. 238), 204 (ed. Finkelstein, p. 240), and a *baraita* quoted at TB Shabbat 19a (with slight textual variation). *See* Lieberman, *Tosefta ki-Feshutah,* Eruvin, pp. 342–343.

81. In *Tosefta,* ed. Zuckermandel: "Hillel the Elder"; in ed. Lieberman: "Shammai the Elder"; in the *baraita,* TB Shabbat 19a: "Shammai used to say."

82. Deuteronomy 20:20.

83. *See* S. Goren, "Leḥimah be-Shabbat le-Or ha-Mekorot" [Warfare on the Sabbath in Light of the Sources], *Sinai,* Jubilee Volume, Jerusalem, 1958, pp. 149ff.; M.D. Herr, "Le-Va'ayat Hilkhot Milḥamah be-Shabbat bi-Mei Bayit Sheni u-vi-Tekufat ha-Mishnah ve-ha-Talmud" [On the Question of the Laws of War on the Sabbath in the Second Commonwealth and the Mishnaic and Talmudic Periods], *Tarbiz,* XXX, pp. 242ff., 341ff.

84. Letter of Aristeas 158–159 (ed. Kahana, II, p. 49).

85. As to additional Apocryphal literature, *see Enziklopedyah Mikra'it,* V, pp. 1103–1121. Important legal material is being discovered in the Dead Sea Scrolls and in legal documents from the Bar Kokhba period. *See id.*, IV, pp. 639–671 and bibliography, *ad loc. See also Yedi'ot be-Ḥakirat Erez Yisra'el ve-Atikotehah* [Recent Developments in the Archeology of Ancient Israel], 1962, containing articles by Y. Yadin ("Maḥaneh D—Me'arat ha-Iggerot" [Camp D—The Cave of the Documents], pp. 204–236) and I. Polotzki ("Ha-Te'udot ha-Yevaniyyot mi-Me'arat ha-Iggerot" [Greek Documents from the Cave of the Documents], pp. 237–241); *Maḥanayim,* LIX (1961), p. 36 (concerning a contract of sale from the Bar Kokhba cave); Y. Yadin, *Ha-Ḥippusim Aḥar Bar Kokhba* [In Search of Bar Kokhba], 1971, pp. 175ff., 229ff.

IV. SUMMARY

This brief review of the legal and general literature of the period from Ezra and Nehemiah to the *tannaim* has shown that this literature can supply important information as to Jewish law during that period. As noted above, the literature contains some laws that are identical and some that are inconsistent with the Talmud. These inconsistencies may be explained in various ways, *e.g.*, as representing a particular stage in the development of a law, or as reflecting a minority opinion or a sectarian practice.

However, extreme caution must be exercised in drawing conclusions regarding the state of Jewish law in this period. The tendentious bias in some of Josephus's writings has already been noted. In addition, even the laws described in the texts that do not show such obvious bias may not have been generally accepted and followed at the time. For example, not everything in the Elephantine documents necessarily reflects Jewish law as it was then practiced. It is a reasonable assumption that the Jewish outpost in Elephantine was influenced by the surrounding Egyptian legal system, and it is possible that a particular legal norm stated in a papyrus may not have been a Jewish law at all, but one adopted from the neighboring system. The same is true with regard to the Septuagint. As indicated, the translation is not literal, nor is it always scrupulously faithful even to the spirit of the original. One therefore can never be sure that elements from a foreign legal system have not been introduced into the translation.[86] The same caution is also required as regards Philo. He was not well versed in Judaism; what he did know he learned from Greek translations and not from the original Hebrew sources. This fact alone requires that his statements be treated with considerable reserve.[87]

In short, the scholar investigating the pre-tannaitic period in the history of Jewish law has available a wealth of important literary material to which he must direct his attention. He must, however, be extremely careful in making judgments and drawing conclusions on the basis of this material.[88]

86. *See* Tractate *Soferim* 1:7 (ed. Higger, pp. 100–105), commenting on the translation of the Torah: "That day was as difficult for Israel as the day they made the golden calf, because the Torah could not be translated as well as it needed to be"; *id.*, "They changed thirteen things in it. . . . "

87. *See* I. Heinemann, *Philons Griechische und Jüdische Bildung* [Philo's Greek and Jewish Education], 1932, pp. 523ff. and particularly p. 527; H. Albeck, *supra* n. 69, Introduction; and *cf.* G. Alon, "On Philo's Halakhah," in *Jews, Judaism and the Classical World*, Jerusalem, 1977, pp. 89–137. *But see* S. Belkin, *Philo and the Oral Law* (1940).

88. *See also* Frankel, supra n. 2 at 102 and n. 3; I. Herzog, "Mashehu al Yosef ben Mattityahu" [A Note on Josephus], *Sinai*, XXV, pp. 8–11; L. Ginzberg, "Al ha-Shittah ha-Madda'it be-Ḥakirat ha-Mishpat ha-Ivri" [On the Scientific Method of Research in Jewish Law], *Ha-Mishpat ha-Ivri*, IV, pp. 209–210; Z. Falk, *Introduction to Jewish Law of the Second Commonwealth*, Leiden, 1972.

Chapter 27

THE LITERARY SOURCES FROM THE TANNAITIC PERIOD TO THE REDACTION OF THE TALMUD: INTRODUCTION

I. Form and Substance of Talmudic Halakhic Literature
II. The Types of Literary Sources

I. FORM AND SUBSTANCE OF TALMUDIC HALAKHIC LITERATURE

In examining the extensive Talmudic literature, it is important at the outset to clarify two points. The first is formal; the second, substantive.

First, the form of Talmudic halakhic literature is totally different from the form of legal literature today. On turning to any page of the Talmud, one finds oneself immersed in debate, in thrust and counterthrust, in question and response. One will search in vain for a general introduction to the subject under discussion or for definitions of the halakhic-legal terms employed in the argument.[1]

This is the consequence of the nature of the Oral Law and the method by which it was studied. The Oral Law is what its name indicates: it was meant to be the product of discourse and to be transmitted orally. Although some Sages did put certain halakhic material in writing, these writings were only mnemonic aids for their own personal use, not finished works to be used by others.[2] The Sages therefore studied and taught in the manner most appropriate for oral study, memorization, and transmission of the *Halakhah* from person to person and from generation to generation.

Moreover, the Oral Law was taught and developed through debate,

1. In the post-Talmudic period, introductions to the Talmud, as well as reference works and guidebooks, were written. *See infra* pp. 1540ff.

2. *See supra* p. 224.

resolution of real-life problems, and close analysis of problems raised in the study hall. Each succeeding generation wove its own argumentation into the warp and woof of the deliberations of previous generations. After the entire Talmudic *Halakhah* was reduced to writing, it still retained the style that characterized it when it was studied and taught by means of oral discussion and deliberation.

As to the substance of Talmudic halakhic literature, the Talmud as redacted at the end of the fifth century C.E. includes laws handed down by oral tradition from generation to generation, as well as laws developed out of the ongoing life of the people. A considerable portion of such laws was transmitted anonymously; and even when a particular legal rule is attributed to a particular Sage (the Sages took great care to identify the transmitters of the law), there is no certainty that the Sage to whom a rule is attributed actually originated it. He could have been transmitting an ancient and anonymous tradition that he possessed, without in any way indicating that it did not originate with him. Such a practice is a natural result of the methods and objectives of the Sages for studying and developing the law. They viewed the entire corpus of the *Halakhah* as a single continuum and therefore had no interest in identifying the historical boundaries of the various stages in its development. Their interest was in a pattern of conduct for this life and for life eternal: they sought to be part of the long chain of the *Halakhah* and had no desire to separate the chain into individual links according to eras and generations.

Because of these basic characteristics of Talmudic halakhic literature, the study of Talmudic law requires balanced judgment and the exercise of great care not to go astray. One must systematize this vast literature, consider how to approach it, master its definitions and principles, and penetrate its deepest recesses. One must scrutinize the historical and social background of each tier of its massive structure, as well as the language and style characteristic of its different elements. In addition, one must thoroughly comprehend the content of the halakhic rules themselves, the Sages' unique and incisive mode of legal thought, and their profound faith and spirit. The task requires historical-philological research as well as mastery of halakhic doctrines.[3]

II. THE TYPES OF LITERARY SOURCES

The literary sources of Jewish law from the tannaitic period to the redaction of the Talmud include, in chronological order: (a) the tannaitic period—the

3. *See further supra* pp. 75–91.

Aramaic *Targumim* (translations of Scripture), collections of halakhic *midrashim*, the Mishnah, and the *Tosefta*, and (b) the amoraic period—the Jerusalem and Babylonian Talmuds.

These are the extant systematic and organized compilations. As is discussed later, there are additional sources, such as the *baraitot* from the tannaitic period, which are quoted by the *amoraim* in the two Talmuds. These *baraitot* are unquestionably an authoritative source of great value;[4] but they do not appear in a distinct, complete literary work and are therefore discussed in conjunction with the other literary sources[5] rather than separately.

4. For a detailed discussion of the *baraitot*, see H. Albeck, *Mavo la-Talmudim*, pp. 19–50. The *baraitot* scattered through the two Talmuds were collected and organized by M. Higger in his ten-volume work, *Ozar ha-Baraitot* [A Treasury of the *Baraitot*].

5. Among the sources, specific mention should be made of *Megillat Ta'anit* [The Scroll of Fasts], which contains halakhic-legal material in addition to descriptions of military and political events. For a detailed discussion of the contents of *Megillat Ta'anit* and the date of its composition, *see* H. Lichtenstein, "Die Fastenrolle, Eine Untersuchung zur Jüdisch-hellenistischen Geschichte" [The Scroll of Fasts—An Inquiry in Jewish-Hellenistic History], *HUCA*, VIII–IX (1931–1932), pp. 257–317. Lichtenstein presents a scientific edition of *Megillat Ta'anit* based on manuscripts and ancient printed editions (pp. 318–351) and a bibliography (pp. 308ff.). *See also* B.Z. Luria, *Megillat Ta'anit*, Jerusalem, 1964.

The following is an example of material of legal interest contained in *Megillat Ta'anit*: "On the twenty-fourth [of the month of Av] we reverted to our laws. When the Greeks ruled, they judged by the laws of the gentiles, but when the Hasmonean dynasty came into power, they canceled them [*i.e.*, the gentiles' laws] and reverted to adjudication pursuant to Jewish law. The day they canceled them they declared a holiday." (Lichtenstein, *supra* at 278–279, 319, 334). *See also supra* p. 515 n. 94.

Chapter 28

THE LITERARY SOURCES IN THE TANNAITIC PERIOD

I. The Term *Tanna*
II. The Generations of the *Zugot* and the Major *Tannaim*
III. Aramaic Translations of Scripture
IV. Compilations of Halakhic *Midrashim*
    A. From the School of R. Ishmael
    B. From the School of R. Akiva
V. The Mishnah—in General
    A. The Literary Form of the *Halakhah* in the Mishnah as Compared with That in the Halakhic *Midrashim*
    B. The Development and Redaction of the Mishnah
VI. The Literary Structure of the Mishnah
    A. Etymology of the Term *Mishnah*
    B. The Divisions of the Mishnah and Their Contents
    C. The Arrangement of the Laws in the Mishnah
VII. The Codificatory Nature of the Mishnah
    A. The Content of the Mishnah
        1. Comparison Between the Law as Set Forth in the Mishnah and the Law in Cognate Sources
        2. Statement of the Law without Attribution to a Source, or by Attribution to "the Sages"
        3. The Amoraic View of the Authoritative Character of the Mishnah
        4. Diversity and Uniformity in Jewish Law
        5. Multiplicity of Opinions in the Mishnah
    B. The Legal Style of the Mishnah
        1. The Casuistic Style
        2. The Hybrid Casuistic-Normative Style
            a. Possession of Real Property for Three Years as Proof of Ownership
            b. Division of Property Owned in Common
        3. The Normative Style
    C. The Literary Style of the Mishnah
VIII. The *Tosefta*
IX. Summary

I. THE TERM *TANNA*

Tanna (plural, *tannaim*) is an Aramaic word meaning "one who repeats" (*i.e.*, learns by rote) or "one who studies." The term has come to be used in either of two senses:[1]

1. *As indicating a Sage who lived in the tannaitic period (first century* C.E. *to 220* C.E.). The statements of such a Sage are generally recorded in the literary sources of that period, *i.e.*, collections of halakhic *midrashim*, the Mishnah, the *Tosefta*, and the *baraitot*.
2. *As indicating a person whose function was to learn mishnayot and baraitot by heart and to repeat them on request.* Such a person served a reference function as a "walking encyclopedia" for his teacher, his colleagues, and the students at the academy. Such functionaries were essential, since the *Halakhah* was studied orally[2] and students needed the help of scholars with special ability to memorize with perfect fidelity the laws whose number continually increased over the course of time. Every academy had its own *tanna* in this sense of the term, and such *tannaim* continued to exist in the periods of the *amoraim* and the *geonim* after there were no longer any *tannaim* in the first sense of the term. The Sages did not always treat these functionaries with great respect, because some of these *tannaim* merely parroted the texts without understanding them. In one source, such *tannaim* are described as "wreaking havoc in the world,"[3] because they made legal rulings by woodenly applying the language of the Mishnah as they remembered it, without correctly understanding the underlying rationale of the law.

Except when otherwise expressly stated, the term *tanna* or *tannaim* is used in this work in its first sense and refers to halakhic Sages who lived in the tannaitic period.

1. *See* W. Bacher, *Erkhei Midrash*, II, p. 319; Epstein, *Mavo*, pp. 673ff.
2. *See supra* pp. 224–226.
3. TB Sotah 22a. TB Megillah 28b describes such a *tanna* as "a basket full of books." *See* Rashi, *ad loc.*

II. THE GENERATIONS OF THE *ZUGOT* AND THE MAJOR *TANNAIM*

Before discussing the literary sources of Jewish law in the tannaitic period, it will be helpful to review briefly the generations of the Sages until the end of that period.

The first part of Tractate *Avot* records the chain of tradition of the Oral Law and describes Simeon the Just as being "of the remnants of the Great Assembly (*ha-Keneset ha-Gedolah*)." He was the first of the Sages in the post-Biblical period known to us by name. Antigonus of Sokho,[4] in whose name only one statement has survived,[5] received the tradition from him. After them, the Mishnah lists five *Zugot* ("pairs") (who are also mentioned in Tractate *Ḥagigah*):[6]

1. Yose b. Joezer and Yose b. Johanan.[7]
2. Joshua b. Peraḥyah and Nittai ha-Arbeli.
3. Judah b. Tabbai and Simeon b. Shataḥ.[8]
4. Shemaiah and Avtalyon.[9]
5. Hillel and Menahem,[10] Shammai.[11]

The first Sage listed in each pair was usually the patriarch (*nasi*), *i.e.*, the titular leader of the Jewish people; and the second was the president of the court (*av bet din*).[12] Simeon b. Shataḥ, who is listed second in his pair, was later appointed patriarch.

Hillel was patriarch and was succeeded by his son Simeon, who, in turn, was succeeded by his son Rabban Gamaliel the Elder. Among the leading *tannaim* of the generation of Rabban Gamaliel the Elder, mention

4. A resident of the town of Sokho in Judea, where there were two towns of this name, one in the plains and one in the mountains. *See* Joshua 15:35,48 and I Samuel 17:11.

5. M Avot 1:3. For the chronology of Simeon the Just and Antigonus of Sokho, *see* Albeck, *Mavo*, p. 25.

6. M Avot 1:4–15; M Ḥagigah 2:2.

7. They lived in the period of Antiochus Epiphanes' decrees, which led to the Hasmonean revolt.

8. These Sages fled Jerusalem because of Alexander Jannai and returned when Salome Alexandra succeeded to the throne.

9. These two Sages were described by Hillel as "great exegetes" (TB Pesaḥim 70b), *i.e.*, they were experts in Biblical exegesis. *See supra* pp. 314–315.

10. Menahem served for a short time and was succeeded by Shammai: "Menahem departed and Shammai entered" (M Ḥagigah 2:2).

11. The Hebrew spelling of the name Shammai is not uniform in the various sources. In I Chronicles 2:28 it occurs without the letter *aleph*. It also appears in the same form in various tannaitic sources; *see*, *e.g.*, *Tosefta* Yevamot (ed. Lieberman) 1:8–10; however, in ed. Zuckermandel it appears with the *aleph*. In *Sifrei* (ed. Finkelstein), Ki Teẓe, sec. 269, it appears without the *aleph* and with two *yods*.

12. M Ḥagigah 2:2. As to the *Zugot* and the titles *nasi* and *av bet din*, *see* H.D. Mantel, *Studies in the History of the Sanhedrin*, pp. 2ff., 13ff., 102ff.

should be made of Akavyah b. Mahalalel, and R. Ḥanina Segan ha-Kohanim. The traditionally accepted number of the generations of *tannaim* following that of Rabban Gamaliel the Elder is five. The chief *tannaim* of each of these five generations were:

1. First generation:[13] Rabban Simeon b. Gamaliel, patriarch; R. Johanan b. Zakkai; R. Ḥanina b. Dosa; R. Ẓadok.
2. Second generation:[14] Rabban Gamaliel of Yavneh (grandson of Rabban Gamaliel the Elder), also known as Rabban Gamaliel II, patriarch; R. Judah b. Bathyra; the disciples of R. Johanan b. Zakkai (R. Eliezer b. Hyrcanus, R. Joshua b. Hananiah, *et al.*); R. Neḥunya b. ha-Kanah;[15] and Nahum of Gimzo.[16]
3. Third generation:[17] R. Tarfon, R. Akiva b. Joseph, R. Ishmael b. Elisha, R. Yose ha-Gelili (the Galilean), Simeon b. Zoma, and Simeon b. Azzai.
4. Fourth generation:[18] Rabban Simeon b. Gamaliel II, patriarch; and the disciples of R. Akiva, namely, R. Johanan ha-Sandelar, R. Meir, R. Judah b. Ilai, R. Simeon b. Yoḥai, R. Yose b. Ḥalafta, and R. Nehemiah.
5. Fifth generation:[19] R. Judah Ha-Nasi, patriarch, the redactor of the Mishnah (also called "Rabbenu Ha-Kadosh" ["Our Sainted Master"] and "Rabbi"); Symmachus b. Joseph; and Simeon b. Eleazar.

After these five generations, there was a transitional generation between the tannaitic and amoraic periods.[20] The patriarch in that generation was Rabban Gamaliel b. R. Judah Ha-Nasi, also known as Rabban Gamaliel III; and his chief colleagues were R. Ḥiyya Rabbah (R. Ḥiyya "the Great") and R. Oshaiah.[21]

The foregoing list includes only the leading Sages of their respective generations in the tannaitic period.[22] We now turn to the literary sources of this period that are recognized by Jewish law as authoritative.

13. 40–80 C.E. (thirty years before until ten years after the destruction of the Temple).

14. 80–120 C.E.

15. A resident of the village Kanah in lower Galilee.

16. Gimzo is the name of a town near Lydda; *see* II Chronicles 28:18. According to an aggadic legend, Nahum was called *gam zo* ("this too") because he would remark frequently, "This too is for good [*i.e.*, for the best]"; *see* TB Ta'anit 21a.

17. 120–140 C.E.

18. 140–170 C.E.

19. 170–200 C.E.

20. 200–220 C.E.

21. For the origin of the name Oshaiah, *see* A. Hyman, *Toledot Tannaim va-Amoraim* [History of the *Tannaim* and *Amoraim*], I, p. 110; H. Albeck, *Mavo la-Talmudim* [Introduction to the Talmuds], p. 163.

22. *See further* Frankel, *Mishnah*, pp. 30ff.; Albeck, *Mavo*, pp. 216ff.; *id.*, *Mavo la-Talmudim*, pp. 144–170.

III. ARAMAIC TRANSLATIONS OF SCRIPTURE

Chronologically, the first literary sources of the tannaitic period are the Aramaic translations of the Bible. In the Second Temple period, Aramaic in its various dialects was the vernacular in both Babylonia and the Land of Israel; therefore the Torah, Prophets, and Hagiographa were translated into that language. The main translations are Onkelos's translation of the Torah[23] and Jonathan b. Uzziel's translation of the Prophets.[24] Both translations were composed before the destruction of the Temple, which took place in the middle of the first century C.E.

Two Aramaic translations of the Torah besides that of Onkelos have long been known to be extant: *Targum Yonatan* [Jonathan's Translation], attributed to Jonathan b. Uzziel, referred to above, and another called *Targum Yerushalmi* [The Jerusalem Translation]. However, as several scholars have demonstrated, the translation attributed to Jonathan is, in fact, the Jerusalem Translation, and the one called the *Targum Yerushalmi* is another version of that same translation,[25] dating from a much later period.[26] A third Targum, called *Neofiti I*, which covers the entire Pentateuch, was discovered in 1956.

The Aramaic translations include important halakhic material recognized as authoritative. The most important such translation is that of Onkelos, which contains "many substantive laws that are not written and explained in our sacred Torah, but were transmitted to Moses orally, and by

23. "[As to] the [Aramaic] translation (*targum*) of the Torah, Onkelos the Proselyte said [*i.e.*, composed] it." TB Megillah 3a. On *Targum Onkelos, see* A. Berliner, *Targum Onkelos*, Berlin, 1884, 2 vols. The first volume presents Onkelos's translation of the Torah according to the printed version of Sabbioneta, 1557; the second contains a detailed discussion of the style, methodology, and content of the translation. *See also* S.D. Luzzatto, *Ohev Ger*, 2nd ed., Cracow, 1895; N.M. Adler, *Netinah la-Ger* (a commentary on *Targum Onkelos*).

24. "[As to] *Targum* of the Prophets, Jonathan b. Uzziel said [*i.e.*, composed] it." TB Megillah 3a.

25. J.L. Zunz, *Ha-Derashot be-Yisra'el ve-Hishtalshelutan ha-Historit* [Midrashic Literature and Its Historical Evolution] (a Hebrew version of the original German, *Die Gottesdienstliche Vorträge der Juden*), ed. H. Albeck, pp. 37–38. *See also* M. Ginzburger, *Targum Yerushalmi la-Torah Ne'etak mi-Khetav Yad Paris* [The Jerusalem Translation of the Torah, Copied from the Paris Manuscript], Berlin, 1899 (reprinted 1969); *id., Targum Yonatan ben Uzziel al ha-Torah, Ne'etak mi-Khetav Yad London* [Jonathan b. Uzziel's Translation of the Torah, Copied from the London Manuscript], Berlin, 1903. Both of Ginzburger's works contain introductions in German.

26. Zunz, *supra* n. 25 at 38, and *see* Ginzburger, *supra* n. 25, Introduction. A scientific edition of the major Aramaic translations has been published—A. Sperber, *Kitvei ha-Kodesh be-Aramit al Yesod Kitvei Yad u-Sefarim Atikim* [The Holy Scriptures in Aramaic on the Basis of Manuscripts and Ancient Books], 4 vols., 1959–1968. It contains Onkelos's translation, *Targum Yonatan* of the First and Latter Prophets, and a *targum* of the Hagiographa.

him, from generation to generation, to the Sages of the Mishnah, of blessed memory. Onkelos . . . included them in his translation."[27]

Onkelos is cited in halakhic sources and even in the codificatory literature.[28] Various laws are incorporated into his translation. For example, Onkelos translates the verse "And they shall be for frontlets between your eyes"[29] as "And they shall be for phylacteries (*tefillin*) between your eyes"; and the verse "Inscribe them on the doorposts of your house"[30] as "Write them on *mezuzin* [Aramaic, plural of *mezuzah*] and affix them to the doorposts of your house," *i.e.*, as the source of the obligation to affix a *mezuzah* to the doorposts of living quarters. Similarly, the verse "Do not bring death on those who are innocent and in the right"[31] is translated "You shall not kill the innocent or one who has been acquitted[32] in legal proceedings," *i.e.*, neither a person found guilty but in whose favor new exculpatory evidence is discovered nor a person previously acquitted but against whom new inculpatory evidence is discovered is to be executed. The interpretation of the last-quoted verse in the *Mekhilta*[33] is to the same effect:

> "Do not bring death on those who are innocent." If a person has been found guilty and exculpatory evidence is later discovered, should I understand that he is to be executed? Scripture therefore says, "Do not bring death on those who are innocent."
>
> "Do not bring death on . . . those who are in the right." If a person has been acquitted and inculpatory evidence is later discovered, should I understand that he is to be found guilty? Scripture therefore says, "Do not bring death . . . on those who are [*i.e.*, who have been judged to be] in the right."[34]

27. N.M. Adler, Introduction to *Netinah la-Ger* (on *Targum Onkelos*).

28. *See* Maimonides, *MT*, Issurei Bi'ah 12:13: "For Onkelos the translator included intercourse with a male or female slave within the prohibition of 'No Israelite man shall be a cult prostitute (*kadesh*), nor shall any Israelite woman be a cult prostitute (*kedeshah*)' [*see* Deuteronomy 23:18]." *See also* Adler, *Netinah la-Ger, ad loc.*; Frankel, *Mishnah*, p. 332; Berliner, *supra* n. 23 at II, 224–245.

29. Deuteronomy 6:8. *Cf. also* Exodus 13:16; Deuteronomy 11:18.

30. Deuteronomy 6:9, 11:20.

31. Exodus 23:7.

32. For variant readings of the Aramaic word for "acquitted," *see* Berliner, *supra* n. 23 at II, 26–27.

33. *Mekhilta*, Mishpatim, sec. 20 (ed. Horowitz-Rabin, p. 328); *see also* TB Sanhedrin 33b.

34. The verse is explained in the same way in the *Targum* attributed to Jonathan b. Uzziel: "Whenever anyone has been acquitted and inculpatory evidence is later found, or anyone has been convicted and exculpatory evidence is later found, you shall not put that person to death."

IV. COMPILATIONS OF HALAKHIC *MIDRASHIM*

The earliest literary form of halakhic study was oriented to verses of the Torah. When the Sages studied the *Halakhah* and taught it to the people, they would connect the laws to the appropriate sections of the Torah. They taught the laws pertaining to the sabbath, for example, in conjunction with the verses commanding sabbath observance; they taught the laws relating to damage caused by an ox, a pit, or a fire in conjunction with the verses of Exodus 21 and 22; and they taught the laws relating to the liabilities of bailees in conjunction with the verses on that subject in Exodus 22. This is the method of midrash.

Midrash was convenient and effective for two reasons: (1) as has been seen,[35] Biblical interpretation was the legal source of a significant number of laws, and, naturally, such laws were studied and recited together with the verses from which they were derived; and (2) the midrashic method made it easier to memorize and study the laws, which in much of the period under discussion were taught and studied orally and not from a written text. This mnemonic feature was the reason that even laws not derived through interpretation but originating in one of the other legal sources of the law[36] were also connected to Scriptural verses. Thus, in his famous epistle describing the development of the Oral Law, Sherira Gaon, one of the great Babylonian *geonim* of the tenth century C.E., wrote:

> *Sifra* and *Sifrei* [compilations of halakhic *midrashim*] are expositions of verses and [indicate] where the laws are hinted at in the verse. This [*i.e.*, midrash] was their method of study from the beginning of the Second Temple [period] in the days of the early masters (*rishonim*).[37]

The midrashic method of halakhic study continued until the end of the tannaitic and, to some degree, even into the amoraic period. For generations it was the only method of study, until in a later period another method, the "halakhic method," centering on the Mishnah, came to be used.

The midrashic method, both as a method of study and as a legal source of the law, reached its peak at the time of R. Ishmael and R. Akiva, the

35. *See supra* pp. 286–290.

36. *I.e.*, where the *midrash* is integrative rather than creative. *See supra* pp. 297–300.

37. *Iggeret Rav Sherira Gaon* [Epistle of Rabbi Sherira Gaon], ed. B.M. Lewin, p. 39, French recension. The Spanish recension has "in the days of the early Sages (*be-yomai de-rabbanan kamma'i*)." For an example of this method of study, *see Tosefta* Shevu'ot 3:8 on Leviticus 5:1, regarding the criteria for competency of witnesses. *See supra* pp. 283–284 for additional discussion.

respective founders of two schools—in effect two different methodological systems—of Biblical exegesis.[38] Still extant from those schools are compilations of halakhic *midrashim, i.e.*, compilations of laws and rules taught by the midrashic method. The following are some of the more important midrashic compilations.

A. From the School of R. Ishmael

Mekhilta de-R. Ishmael to Exodus (beginning at chapter 12) collects the *midrashim* of R. Ishmael's school on the Book of Exodus.[39]

Sifrei to Numbers collects the *midrashim* on the Book of Numbers.

Sifrei to Deuteronomy collects the *midrashim* on the Book of Deuteronomy up to 11:28.

Baraita de-R. Ishmael discusses the thirteen canons of Biblical interpretation and is quoted at the beginning of the *Sifra*.[40]

B. From the School of R. Akiva

Mekhilta de-R. Simeon b. Yoḥai to Exodus.

Sifra (also known as *Torat Kohanim*) to Leviticus.

Sifrei Zuta to Numbers.

Sifrei to Deuteronomy, from 11:28.

Some compilations of halakhic *midrashim* have not survived except for excerpts preserved in the Babylonian and Jerusalem Talmuds.[41]

The contents of the various compilations of halakhic *midrashim* date from different historical periods—occasionally from very ancient times—and it is not always possible to determine when a specific law originated:

> Through our methodology we have come to realize that the *midrashim* that are set forth in the halakhic *midrashim* without attribution of source, and even such as are reported in the name of later *tannaim*, can be very ancient; those to whom they were attributed are *tannaim* who [merely] repeated and transmitted them.[42]

38. *See supra* pp. 316–317.

39. For the meaning of *Mekhilta, see* M. Ish-Shalom, *Mekhilta de-R. Ishmael*, Introduction, pp. 30ff.; Epstein, *Tannaim*, pp. 545–546; H. Albeck, *supra* n. 21 at 80.

40. *Midrash Tannaim* to Deuteronomy also belongs to R. Ishmael's school. It was published by D.Z. Hoffmann on the basis of excerpts and manuscript fragments.

41. The halakhic *midrashim* in TB were collected and arranged by E.Z. Melamed, *Midreshei Halakhah Shel ha-Tannaim ba-Talmud ha-Bavli* [The Halakhic *Midrashim* of the *Tannaim* in the Babylonian Talmud], Jerusalem, 1943.

42. Epstein, *Tannaim*, p. 513. "*Tannaim*" is used here in the second sense described *supra* p. 1042.

The compilations are thought to have been redacted in the same period as the Mishnah or a generation later, and it is generally accepted that the redaction was done by various editors. As noted above, halakhic *midrashim* were compiled for four of the five books of the Pentateuch; the only *midrashim* on Genesis are aggadic, since that book contains almost no halakhic material.[43]

V. THE MISHNAH—IN GENERAL

A. The Literary Form of the *Halakhah* in the Mishnah as Compared with That in the Halakhic *Midrashim*

The most important literary source of the *Halakhah* from the tannaitic period is the Mishnah, which was redacted at the end of the second century C.E. by R. Judah Ha-Nasi, approximately 120 years after the destruction of the Temple. The literary form of the Mishnah is distinct from that of the halakhic *midrashim* in two characteristic respects:

1. The Mishnah records the rules of the Oral Law as abstract, self-contained legal propositions with no connection or reference to Scriptural verses, in a style known as the "halakhic" or the "mishnaic" style, as opposed to the "midrashic" style characteristic of the compilations of the halakhic *midrashim.*
2. The Mishnah, as a general rule, is arranged according to subjects and issues.

As stated above, at some point the *Halakhah* began to be studied in abstract form independent of Scriptural texts. It is difficult to date precisely when this development occurred. As early as the time of the first "pair,"[44] however, Yose b. Joezer transmitted several laws in the form of abstract independent propositions in the "halakhic" style.[45]

Scholars have assigned two main reasons for the change from the midrashic to the mishnaic method of halakhic study:

43. The halakhic *midrashim* also contain passages in which nonlegal sections of the Torah are interpreted in an aggadic manner. On the halakhic *midrashim, see* Epstein, *Tannaim,* pp. 501–746; H. Albeck, *supra* n. 21 at 79–143. *See also id.* at 79–84 for a full list of all editions, including recent scientific editions, of halakhic *midrashim.*

44. *See supra* p. 1043.

45. M Eduyyot 8:4. Study of *Halakhah* in the form of abstract legal propositions means that the legal rule being studied is considered independently, without being connected to a Biblical text. The style, however, is usually casuistic (expressed in concrete examples) rather than normative (expressed in terms of prescriptive generalizations). For detailed discussion of the distinction between the casuistic and normative style, *see infra* pp. 1072–1078.

1. The Torah often treats the same subject in different sections and books. For example, the Torah deals with the sabbath in more than ten different places, and under the midrashic method various laws relating to the sabbath are connected to verses in each place. As a result, the sabbath laws in the midrashic literature were scattered throughout many different places, depending upon the location of the particular verse to which a given law was connected. This substantially increased the difficulty of finding and learning the law. The need to collect in one place all the laws on a given subject naturally led to their being studied independently of the scattered Biblical verses.
2. During the course of time, the *corpus juris* of Jewish law was augmented by a substantial number of laws stemming from legal sources other than interpretation. These new laws, which originated in legislation, custom, *ma'aseh,* or legal reasoning, could not always be easily connected to a Scriptural text, and were necessarily dealt with as abstract, self-contained legal propositions.[46]

B. The Development and Redaction of the Mishnah

The mishnaic method of halakhic study achieved widespread acceptance; in the course of time, abstract statements of the law in the form of *mishnayot* began to be systematically compiled. According to most scholars, the redaction of such compilations began as early as the Second Temple period. It can be concluded from many sources—both Talmudic and extra-Talmudic—that there was "a fixed and known tradition that several compilations of laws had existed from ancient times."[47] The arrangement of those laws in the Mishnah and *Tosefta* that are designated as "early Mishnah" (*mishnah rishonah*) should also be attributed to the end of the Second Temple period.[48] In Talmudic sources, even entire tractates are attributed to *tannaim* who lived in that period: "Who taught [Tractate] *Middot*? R. Eliezer b. Jacob";[49] "Who taught Tractate *Yoma*? R. Simeon of Mizpeh."[50]

46. Sometimes, these laws are stated in the Mishnah in their original form—as a *takkanah, ma'aseh,* custom, etc.—and sometimes in abstract form as a halakhic rule. However, in the latter case, a comparison of parallels in the Mishnah itself or in outside sources such as the *Tosefta* reveals the actual legal source of the rule. *See, e.g., supra* pp. 950–957 as to laws originating in *ma'aseh.*

47. Epstein, *Tannaim,* p. 18. *See also id.* at 15ff. and bibliography.

48. *Id.* at 21–24. *See also* D.Z. Hoffmann, *Die Erste Mischna und die Controversen der Tannaim* [The Early Mishnah and the Tannaitic Disputes] (translated into Hebrew as *Ha-Mishnah ha-Rishonah u-Felugta de-Tanna'i* by S. Greenberg, Berlin, 1914).

49. TB Yoma 16a. The first R. Eliezer b. Jacob lived in the Second Temple period; *see* Albeck, *Mavo,* p. 220.

50. TB Yoma 14b. R. Simeon of Mizpeh lived in the Second Temple period; *see* M Pe'ah 2:6. *See also* Epstein, *Tannaim,* pp. 25ff. According to Albeck, the sources indicate the

The process of editing compilations of *mishnayot* was strongly stimulated by R. Akiva. In addition to his outstanding activity in Biblical exegesis, which resulted in compilations of halakhic *midrashim,*[51] he was one of the Sages who established the pattern for mishnaic compilations. This enormous literary contribution of R. Akiva was described in a Talmudic source[52] as follows:

> To what can R. Akiva be compared? To a laborer who takes his basket and goes forth. When he finds wheat, he puts it there [in his basket]; barley, he puts it there; spelt, he puts it there; lentils, he puts them there. When he returns to his home, he separates the wheat, the barley, the beans,[53] and the lentils, each by itself. So did R. Akiva, and he made the Torah into [a series] of rings.

According to another source, R. Akiva made "the entire Torah into [separate] coins. He separated and arranged the *midrashim* of *Sifrei* and *Sifra* and taught them separately to his disciples, also *halakhot* separately and *aggadot* separately."[54] R. Akiva thus redacted various compilations: halakhic *midrashim, aggadot,* and *halakhot, i.e., mishnayot.*

R. Akiva's most important disciples—R. Meir, R. Judah, R. Yose, R. Simeon, and R. Nehemiah—redacted, on the basis of R. Akiva's compilation, other collections of *mishnayot* that reflected the halakhic discussions in the various academies. Proliferation of such collections led once again to uncertainty and lack of uniformity in the law. R. Judah Ha-Nasi, a disciple of R. Akiva's disciples, edited and arranged a compilation of *mishnayot* based on the existing compilations, particularly that of R. Jacob b. Korshai (the "*tanna*"[55] of the patriarchate), which was the "official" Mishnah of the pa-

---

existence of ancient mishnaic laws but not that the laws were arranged or redacted. In his opinion, the foundation for the redaction of the Mishnah was laid by the Sages in Yavneh after the destruction of the Temple, when they arranged Tractate *Eduyyot. See* Albeck, *Mavo,* p. 83, and *in extenso* pp. 63–87.

51. *See supra* pp. 316–317.

52. *Avot de-R. Nathan,* 1st version, ch. 18 (ed. Schechter, p. 34a).

53. *See id.* at 73a, in which "beans" appears also in the first part of the comparison instead of "spelt"; *see also* Rashi, Gittin 67a, s.v. Oẓar balum, where the reading is "beans" in the first part.

54. Rashi, Gittin 67a, in his explanation of the *baraita* from *Avot de-R. Nathan. See also* TJ Shekalim 5:1, 21a (5:1, 48c): "R. Akiva, who arranged (*hitkin*) *midrash, halakhot, ve-haggadot*" (so in ed. Venice; ed. Vilna: *"midrash ha-halakhot"; see Mar'eh Panim, ad loc.*). In *Tosefta* Zavim 1:5, the reading is "He would arrange *halakhot* for his disciples." *See* Lieberman, *Hellenism,* pp. 91ff.

55. In the sense of a scholar who repeated the *mishnayot* by heart in the academy. R. Jacob b. Korshai was the *"tanna"* of R. Judah Ha-Nasi's father, Rabban Simeon b. Gamaliel the Patriarch, and was one of R. Judah Ha-Nasi's teachers.

triarch and his court. The "official" Mishnah contained selections from the *mishnayot* of R. Akiva's disciples, particularly those of R. Meir.[56]

J. N. Epstein has described the method of R. Judah Ha-Nasi as follows:

> Rabbi [R. Judah Ha-Nasi] changed, added and deleted, examined, and scrutinized the *mishnayot* before him. . . . He combined sources and *mishnayot* of R. Meir, R. Judah, R. Yose, R. Simeon, and R. Eleazar; he created pairs (*i.e.*, "R. Meir and R. Judah said," "R. Yose and R. Simeon said," "R. Eleazar and R. Simeon said"); he added statements of the disciples of R. Akiva's disciples to the existing *mishnayot*; he added and inserted, without attribution, statements of his great colleagues such as R. Menahem b. R. Yose, R. Yose b. R. Judah, R. Eleazar b. R. Simeon, R. Yose b. ha-Meshullam, and others.[57]

The Sages of the generation following R. Judah Ha-Nasi supplemented his Mishnah with several additions, including his own statements and enactments, and the Mishnah was completed at that time.[58]

R. Judah Ha-Nasi's Mishnah became "The Mishnah," or "Our Mishnah" (*matnitin* in Aramaic); and all other mishnaic collections—both those edited before him and those edited in his own and the following generation—were displaced and became "outside (*baraita*) Mishnah," or simply *baraita* (plural, *baraitot*). Some of the *baraitot* have been preserved in the discussions aimed at clarifying the Mishnah; in the main, they have survived as a result of their inclusion by the *amoraim* in the Talmud.[59]

VI. THE LITERARY STRUCTURE OF THE MISHNAH

A. Etymology of the Term *Mishnah*

Some scholars believe that the word *mishnah* is derived from the Hebrew root *shanoh*, which means to repeat, and hence to learn or to teach. Other

56. *See* Epstein, *Tannaim*, pp. 96, 186–188, 204, 224. TB Sanhedrin 86a reads: "An anonymous *mishnah* [reflects the view of] R. Meir . . . reflecting the view of R. Akiva." *See also* TJ Yevamot 4:11, 28a (4:11, 6b): "Most anonymous *mishnayot* are those of R. Meir."

57. Epstein, *Tannaim*, p. 224. *See* H. Albeck's contrary opinion, *Mavo*, pp. 102–109. *See further* Epstein, *Mavo*, pp. 7ff.; Frankel, *Mishnah*, pp. 209ff.; Lieberman, *Hellenism*, pp. 96ff.

58. Epstein, *Tannaim*, pp. 227ff.; *see, e.g.*, M Makkot 3:15, M Avot 2:2. The Mishnah even contains statements by R. Judah Nesi'ah, R. Judah Ha-Nasi's grandson; *see* M Avodah Zarah 2:6 and *Tosafot*, Avodah Zarah 36a, s.v. Asher.

59. The one compilation of *baraitot* that has survived intact is the *Tosefta*; *see infra* pp. 1078–1081.

scholars are of the opinion that the root is *sheni* ("second"): R. Judah Ha-Nasi's intention was that his Mishnah should be second to the Torah.[60]

"Mishnah" can have various meanings depending on the context. The two that are material here are:

1. The complete collection of laws redacted by R. Judah Ha-Nasi. In the present work, when used in this sense, the term is printed in Roman type and capitalized—"Mishnah."
2. A paragraph or section from a chapter of a specific tractate. When used in this sense, the term is italicized and not capitalized—"*mishnah*" (plural, "*mishnayot*").[61]

B. The Divisions of the Mishnah and Their Contents

The Mishnah is divided into six "Orders" (Hebrew *sedarim*, singular *seder*)[62] as follows:

1. *Zera'im*—mainly agricultural and cognate laws that apply in the Land of Israel, such as *pe'ah* (concerning the obligation to leave the corners of a harvested field for the poor), tithes, the sabbatical (seventh) year, first-fruits, and the like.[63]
2. *Mo'ed*—laws relating to the sabbath and festivals.
3. *Nashim*—family law.
4. *Nezikin*—civil and criminal law, including evidence and judicial procedure.[64]

60. *See* W. Bacher, *Erkhei Midrash*, Tanna'im, p. 84, s.v. Mishnah; Albeck, *Mavo*, p. 1; H. Strack, *Introduction to the Talmud and Midrash*, Athenaeum, 1974, p. 3; Levy, *Wörterbuch*, III, p. 286, s.v. Mishnah.

61. For the purpose of citation, "M Ketubbot 4:6" refers to the sixth paragraph (or *mishnah*) of the fourth chapter of Tractate Ketubbot.

62. Hence the Hebrew abbreviation *shas* (**sh***ishah* **s***edarim*, "six Orders"). *See* TB Ketubbot 103b and Bava Meẓi'a 85b: *shita sidrei* (Aramaic for "six Orders"). *Song of Songs Rabbah* 6:10 has: "Six *erkhei* (Orders of) Mishnah." *See also* TB Shabbat 31a for Resh Lakish's remarks on the six Orders. In present-day usage, *shas* refers to the entire Talmud and not just the Mishnah.

63. *Berakhot*, the first tractate in this Order, deals with benedictions and prayers. According to Maimonides, *Commentary on the Mishnah*, Introduction (ed. Rambam la-Am, Mosad ha-Rav Kook, XVIII, pp. 43–46), this is because the produce of the earth, which is necessary to sustain life, may not be eaten unless the proper benediction is first pronounced. The first law of agriculture is that the earth is the Lord's.

64. *See* Herzog, *Institutions*, I, p. 34, asking why the name of the Order is *Nezikin* ("Injuries," or "Damages") when most of its contents have no connection with the law of torts, and suggesting that it should better have been named *Mishpatim*. There seem to be two answers to Herzog's query. The term *mishpatim* in Jewish law does not refer exclusively to laws governing relationships among people but also includes laws on matters between

5. *Kodashim*—laws pertaining to ritual slaughter, dietary laws, and Temple sacrifices.
6. *Tohorot*—laws of ritual purity and impurity.[65]

Each Order is divided into "tractates" (Hebrew *massekhtot,* singular *massekhet*).[66] The six Orders originally contained a total of sixty tractates. Today there are 63, since Tractate *Nezikin* was divided because of its length into three tractates—*Bava Kamma* [First Gate], *Bava Meẓi'a* [Middle Gate], and *Bava Batra* [Last Gate]—and Tractates *Sanhedrin* and *Makkot,* which were originally one tractate, became two. Each tractate is divided into chapters, and each chapter into paragraphs (*mishnayot*), which are also called *halakhot* (the term used in the Jerusalem Talmud). When an individual *mishnah* is long, it is subdivided into *bavot* (singular *bava,* lit. "gate"). Some are divided into two *bavot,* the *reisha* (beginning) and the *seifa* (end), and others into three—*reisha, meẓi'ata* (middle), and *seifa.*

The Mishnah encompasses not only the legal but also all other aspects of Judaism. It contains philosophical material, ethical precepts, and moral exhortations. There is even an entire tractate in the Order of *Nezikin*—Tractate *Avot*—which describes the chain of tradition of the Oral Law[67] and consists essentially of moral and philosophical sayings of Sages of various periods.[68]

---

people and God (*see supra* p. 107). Furthermore, the Order was called *Nezikin* because of the initial subject of its first tractate, namely, Tractate *Nezikin* (as it was called before its division into three tractates, *see infra*), which begins with a discussion of the four primary causes of tortious injury (*avot nezikin*).

65. A mnemonic for all six Orders is *ZeMaN NaKaT,* which means "it takes time." In the mnemonic, each capitalized letter is the first letter of the title of the appropriate Order, and the sequence of these letters is the same as the sequence of the Orders to which the letters allude.

66. *See* TB Shabbat 3b *et al.; Song of Songs Rabbah* 6:14, where the reading is: "sixty tractates (*massekhtot*) of laws (*halakhot*)." The word *massekhet* is from a root meaning "to weave" and refers to the threads of a cloth. *See* M Kelim 21:1, M Oholot 8:4; and *cf.* Judges 16:13: "If you weave seven locks of my head into the web (*ha-massakhet*)." *See also* commentators and Y. Kaufmann, *Commentary on the Book of Judges,* 1962, *ad loc.* The term has been extended metaphorically to intellectual or academic matter woven together and gathered into a unit, and thus its use for "tractate." *See* Levy, *Wörterbuch,* s.vv. Massekhet, Massekhta.

67. The term *avot* (lit. "fathers") is a common appellation for the nation's great Sages; *see, e.g.,* M Eduyyot 1:4: "The fathers of the world." *Cf.* the frequent reference to the "Founding Fathers" in American history and constitutional jurisprudence.

68. For the logic of the sequential order of the tractates, their number, and their division into chapters, *see* Maimonides, *supra* n. 63. Maimonides' explanation (*id.* at 54, 57) of the sequence of *Sanhedrin, Avot,* and *Horayot* in the Order of *Nezikin* is of particular interest. *Sanhedrin* deals with judges and judicial procedure, while *Avot* deals with morality, ethics, and proper human behavior. According to Maimonides, *Avot* follows immediately after *Sanhedrin* because:

The name of each tractate generally describes the tractate's main content,[69] although some tractates have names, taken from their opening phrases, that do not indicate the nature of the contents;[70] and the names of the tractates, like the text of the Mishnah itself, are in Hebrew. There are a few exceptions: the names *Bava Kamma, Bava Meẓi'a,* and *Bava Batra* have no connection with the contents of the tractates they designate; they are not derived from the opening phrases of the tractates and are not Hebrew but Aramaic. As stated above, these three tractates were given their present names after the original tractate was subdivided; and because that occurred in Babylonia, the names they were given were Aramaic.[71]

C. The Arrangement of the Laws in the Mishnah

As has been pointed out, one of the main purposes of the Mishnah was to arrange the various laws according to their content and subject matter.[72] For the most part, the Mishnah achieved this aim, but occasionally the pattern is disturbed because of various contextual and external factors. For example, Tractate *Kiddushin,* as its name indicates, treats matters pertaining to marriage—the ceremony, its validity, and related legal problems. The first *mishnah* of that tractate deals with the "modes of acquisition" by which marriage may be effected. However, *mishnayot* two to six discuss modes of acquisition applicable to areas of the law other than marriage. The common denominator of this cluster of laws is that each *mishnah* deals with acquisition, with the object of the acquisition varying from *mishnah* to *mishnah.*

> No one needs such exhortation more than judges. If ordinary people are not ethical, there is no injury to the general public but only to themselves. However, a judge who is unethical and pretentious harms not only himself but also society as a whole. Therefore, the beginning of *Avot* treats the ethics [required] of judges.

Tractate *Horayot*—which deals with laws pertaining to a court that has erred—follows *Avot* because:

> When the discussion of judges' ethics was completed, [the Mishnah] embarked on an explanation of their mistakes, for it is impossible that mortals will not err and sin. Therefore, *Horayot* follows *Avot.*

69. *E.g.,* Tractate *Gittin* [Divorces] deals mainly with divorce.

70. *E.g.,* Tractate *Yom Tov,* which deals with the festivals, is also called *Beẓah* [Egg], after its opening sentence, "An egg (*beẓah*) that is laid on a festival. . . . "

71. *Bava Kamma*—the first gate, *i.e.,* the first part of Tractate *Nezikin; Bava Meẓi'a*—the middle gate; *Bava Batra*—the last gate. *See* Maimonides, *supra* n. 63 at 51. Another tractate that does not bear a Hebrew name is *Yoma* in the Order of *Mo'ed. See* H. Albeck's Introduction to his commentary on that tractate, *Seder Mo'ed,* at 217. *Yoma* was not the tractate's original name, which was *Kippurim* or *Yom ha-Kippurim.*

72. Josephus, *Antiquities,* IV, 8:4, claims that Josephus innovated this type of organization in his discussion of the laws of the Torah "which we arranged, each according to its classification." However, Philo's *De Specialibus Legibus,* which antedated Josephus, also has a topical arrangement. *See supra* pp. 1030–1031.

Occasionally, the connection is more external. M Gittin 4:2, for example, discusses two enactments of Rabban Gamaliel the Elder, one regarding the revocation of a *get* (bill of divorcement) by the husband, and the other concerning the procedure for writing the *get*. Both enactments were adopted, as the *mishnah* put it, "to promote the public welfare" (*tikkun ha-olam*). After this *mishnah,* for the rest of chapter four and into chapter five, a long series of *mishnayot* is set forth containing enactments in a variety of areas, including the collection by a widow of the amount of her *ketubbah* from her husband's estate, *prosbul* (whereby cancellation of debts in the sabbatical year may be avoided), redemption of captives, claims for maintenance, and return of lost property. The only common feature of all these subjects, which led to their being linked in consecutive order in the Mishnah, is that they are all enactments adopted to promote the public welfare.[73]

Sometimes, the sequence of *mishnayot* is based on historical circumstance. For example, chapter four of Tractate *Yadayim* in the Order of *Tohorot,* which treats matters of ritual purity, records a dispute between the Pharisees and Sadducees concerning the question of impurity of hands (M Yadayim 4:6). The next *mishnah* treats another dispute between the same factions involving a master's liability for damage caused by his slave, and the following *mishnah* reviews yet another difference between them concerning how a bill of divorcement should be dated. The only common feature of these *mishnayot* is the historical fact that their subjects were matters of dispute between the Pharisees and Sadducees.[74]

Apparently, R. Judah Ha-Nasi's incorporation in the Mishnah of preexisting compilations in their original arrangement, and his desire to maintain their integrity and preserve their original form led, occasionally, to exceptions to his characteristic pattern of organization. However, such exceptions do not detract from the overall achievement of the Mishnah in compiling the *corpus juris* of Jewish law and arranging the laws topically according to their subject matter.

73. Another example is M Gittin 5:8–9, which presents a series of laws on different legal subjects that have in common only the fact that they are all "to promote peace and tranquillity."

74. Occasionally, laws on different subjects are strung together because of a common terminological feature, such as " . . . differs from . . . only in that . . . " (M Megillah 1:4–11), or because they all contain a common number (*e.g.*, M Bava Meẓi'a 4:7–8, M Shevu'ot 1:1). *Cf.* TJ Shekalim 5:1, 21a (5:1, 48d): "[They were called] *soferim* [scribes, lit. "counters"] because they set forth the Torah by means of numbers, [such as] 'Five persons may not set aside *terumah,*' 'Five things are required with regard to *ḥallah,*' 'Fifteen women free their co-wives.'" For further examples, *see* Albeck, *Mavo,* pp. 88–89.

VII. THE CODIFICATORY NATURE OF THE MISHNAH

A. The Content of the Mishnah

A question of primary importance for the *Halakhah* in general and for codification in particular is: What was R. Judah Ha-Nasi's purpose in arranging and redacting the Mishnah? Was his intention simply to compile the laws of his time and arrange them topically in coherent fashion in order to make it easier and more convenient to find them? Or did he aim to do more, *i.e.*, to create a legal code that would set forth authoritatively the law by which decisions and rulings were to be governed? In other words, was his goal limited to producing an encyclopedia of Jewish law—as Albeck[75] put it, "a compendium of the Oral Law"—without any intention of establishing normative law, or did he intend to create a code—as Blau[76] put it, a "*Corpus Juris*" of Jewish law, similar to the *Corpus Juris Civilis*, the Justinian code of Roman law? The question is extremely important not only because it relates to the nature of the Mishnah itself but also because of its relevance in a number of important respects to the problem of codification in Jewish law generally.

Scholars disagree as to the answer to this question. Some believe that R. Judah Ha-Nasi's aim was to assemble the then-existing rules of the *Halakhah* into a single compilation without any intention of authoritatively determining the law himself.[77] Most scholars, however, are of the opinion that his purpose was to create an authoritative code.[78]

The essential difficulty in ascertaining R. Judah Ha-Nasi's purpose stems from the fact—evident from even the most cursory examination of the Mishnah—that the Mishnah generally does not set forth a single, clear-cut statement of the law; a very significant portion of the six Orders includes differing opinions as to the law on the subject under discussion. In some cases, there is a dispute between individual *tannaim*; in others, an individual dissents from the view of the other Sages. Occasionally, more than two views are recorded, with no explicit statement as to which view is determined to be the law. However, it does not necessarily follow that the Mishnah was intended to be less than a code that authoritatively sets forth

75. Albeck, *Mavo*, p. 109.

76. L. Blau, "Das Gesetzbuch des Maimonides Historisch Betrachtet" [A Historical View of Maimonides' Code], in *Moses Ben Maimon, Sein Leben, Seine Werke und Sein Einfluss* [Maimonides: His Life, Works, and Influence], Leipzig, 1914, II, p. 332.

77. Weiss, *Dor Dor ve-Doreshav*, II, p. 186; Albeck, *Mavo*, pp. 105–111.

78. Frankel, *Mishnah*, pp. 226, 284 (ch. 4, rule 2); Blau, *supra* n. 76; Epstein, *Tannaim*, pp. 225–226; J. Bassfreund, "Zur Redaktion der Mischna" [On the Redaction of the Mishnah], *MGWJ*, LI (1907), p. 429ff.

the law to govern actual cases. Careful examination of the Mishnah and the amoraic sources, as well as consideration of the nature of Jewish law in general, indicates that R. Judah Ha-Nasi's goal was indeed to create an authoritative code of laws, and that the Mishnah was accepted as such by the Sages of the Talmud. The following sections review the evidence for this conclusion.

1. COMPARISON BETWEEN THE LAW AS SET FORTH IN THE MISHNAH AND THE LAW IN COGNATE SOURCES

In the *baraitot* and in the *Tosefta,* various laws are recorded about which *tannaim* disagreed, and we are there told that R. Judah Ha-Nasi either decided "like both," *i.e.,* agreed in part with the opinion of each ("A is correct with regard to . . . and B is correct insofar as . . . ") or that he agreed with the view of one of them ("Rabbi [Judah Ha-Nasi] responded . . . "); and the rule as he determined it is set forth in the Mishnah as the law.[79]

For example, the Mishnah states:[80]

> The sabbatical year cancels any loan, whether pursuant to a written instrument (*shetar*) or an oral transaction. It does not cancel debts due to a shopkeeper [for purchases] on a running account, but if the shopkeeper carries the credit as a loan, the sabbatical year cancels it.

The *Tosefta* states:[81]

> [The sabbatical year] does not cancel debts due to a shopkeeper on a running account—this is the opinion of R. Judah. The Sages say: "It does cancel." Rabbi [R. Judah Ha-Nasi] said: "R. Judah's opinion is correct when the document specifies fruit [*i.e.,* the particular commodity purchased], and the Sages' opinion [is correct] when the document specifies money."

This *Tosefta* reveals that there was a difference of opinion between R. Judah and the other Sages, and that R. Judah Ha-Nasi decided that if the credit was transformed into a loan, *i.e.,* by specifying money in the document, it is canceled by the sabbatical year. The rule in the Mishnah is thus formulated according to his resolution of the dispute as revealed by the *Tosefta.*[82]

Occasionally, a comparison of the Mishnah's formulation of a law with that of a *baraita* reveals that the law was disputed in whole or in part and

79. In one place, R. Judah Ha-Nasi's decision is contained in the *mishnah* itself, M Arakhin 8:5; *but see* Epstein, *Tannaim,* p. 211.

80. M Shevi'it 10:1; and *see supra* pp. 511–513.

81. *Tosefta* Shevi'it 8:3.

82. Epstein, *Tannaim,* p. 209. For another example, *see id.* at 210 on M Ḥullin 8:3 and *Tosefta* Ḥullin 8:6.

that R. Judah Ha-Nasi did not mention one of the views but set forth in the Mishnah only the opinion with which he agreed. For example, the Mishnah states:[83]

> From what time may one recite the *Shema* in the evening? From the time the priests [who were impure and have performed ritual immersion to purify themselves] enter to eat their *terumah* [a time which is after sunset].[84]

This *mishnah* thus establishes that the time the priests enter to eat their *terumah* is also the earliest time for the evening recitation of the *Shema*.[85] However, the *Tosefta*[86] states the law differently:

> From what time may one recite the *Shema* in the evening? From the time when people sit down [lit. "enter"] to eat their meal on the eve of the sabbath [*i.e.*, earlier than sunset]—this is R. Meir's opinion; but the Sages say: "From the time when the priests are permitted to eat their *terumah*, that time being when the stars first appear."

The *Tosefta* demonstrates that R. Meir and the other Sages disagreed on the earliest time when the *Shema* could be recited in the evening. Since R. Judah Ha-Nasi determined that the law accords with the view of the Sages, his statement of the law in the Mishnah ignored R. Meir's opinion and set forth the view of the Sages without indicating the existence of a difference of opinion and without indicating upon whose opinion the law stated in the Mishnah was based.[87]

83. M Berakhot 1:1.

84. *See* Leviticus 22:7: "As soon as the sun sets, he shall be clean; and afterward he may eat of the sacred donations."

85. *See* Rashi, Berakhot 2a and Bertinoro, *Commentary on the Mishnah, ad loc.* Some commentators say that all the priests, even if not impure, would perform ritual immersion. *See also* Albeck, *Commentary on the Mishnah, ad loc.* and in his Hashlamot; Lieberman, *Tosefta ki-Feshutah*, Berakhot, p. 1.

86. *Tosefta* Berakhot 1:1 and TB Berakhot 2b.

87. Epstein, *Tannaim*, pp. 219–224. M Bava Kamma 3:6 provides a further example:

> If two men were going along in the public domain, one running and the other walking, or both of them were running, and they injured each other, neither is liable.

Tosefta Bava Kamma 2:11 adds:

> . . . because both were proceeding rightfully. Issi the Babylonian [a contemporary of R. Judah Ha-Nasi] says: "The one who was running is liable because he was acting in an unusual manner." But Issi the Babylonian agrees that if it was Friday near dark, he is not liable [since running under those circumstances is not unusual].

A comparison of the *mishnah* and *baraita* reveals that R. Judah Ha-Nasi sets forth one opinion as the law, completely ignores Issi's opinion, and hence omits the qualification of the rule based on the special circumstances on the eve of the sabbath. *See* TB Bava Kamma 32a: "The *mishnah* does not accord with Issi b. Judah, as we have learned in a *baraita*. . . . " *See also* Rashi, Bava Kamma 48b, s.v. Ḥayyavim; *Tosafot, ad loc.*, s.v. U-sheneihem.

2. STATEMENT OF THE LAW WITHOUT ATTRIBUTION TO A SOURCE, OR BY ATTRIBUTION TO "THE SAGES"

An examination of the text of the Mishnah as compared to cognate sources reveals that even when R. Judah Ha-Nasi cited more than one opinion as to the law on a question, he indicated in a particular manner his own conclusion as to which view of the law should be accepted: he stated that view in "anonymous" form, *i.e.*, without attribution to a source and without naming the *tanna* who stated that view. The view stated without attribution to a source represents the accepted law, while the differing view recorded in the name of a specified *tanna* is not accepted as law. That this was indeed R. Judah Ha-Nasi's method of indicating his determination of the law is attested by the leading *amora* of the Land of Israel, R. Johanan, who actually saw R. Judah Ha-Nasi and studied under his disciples. The Talmud states:[88]

> R. Ḥiyya b. Abba said in the name of R. Johanan: "Rabbi [R. Judah Ha-Nasi] agreed with R. Meir in the matter of the slaughter of an animal and its young on the same day, and recorded [that opinion] as being the view of 'the Sages.' [He accepted] R. Simeon's opinion as to the law concerning the covering of the blood of a slaughtered animal, and recorded [that opinion] as being the view of 'the Sages.'"[89]

Thus, R. Judah Ha-Nasi determined the law in these two matters of ritual slaughter by setting forth the opinions of individual *tannaim* with whom he concurred as the view of "the Sages" generally.[90]

88. TB Ḥullin 85a, and *see Dikdukei Soferim, ad loc.*, nn. (a) and (b).

89. R. Judah Ha-Nasi also used other forms of "anonymous" (unattributed) statements of the law, as in the following two examples. M Berakhot 1:2 states:

> From what time may one recite the *Shema* in the morning? When one can distinguish [because it is light enough] between [the] blue and white [threads of the *ẓiẓit*]. R. Eliezer says: "Between blue and [the] green [of a leek, the color of which is very similar to blue]."

The first opinion, which is apparently that of R. Joshua, is not set forth in his name but is stated anonymously—a form of statement by which R. Judah Ha-Nasi intended to indicate its status as the law—in contrast to the other opinion, which is set forth in the name of the *tanna* who held it. In this case, R. Judah Ha-Nasi stated first and anonymously the opinion that he favored. Occasionally, however, the favored opinion is stated last and is identified by the formula "But the Sages say. . . . " For example, M Berakhot 1:1, quoted in part above, reads:

> From what time may one recite the *Shema* in the evening? From the time the priests enter to eat their *terumah* until the end of the first watch [*i.e.*, one-third of the night]; this is the opinion of R. Eliezer. But the Sages say: "Until midnight [*i.e.*, one-half of the night]."

In this dispute, which was also apparently between R. Eliezer and R. Joshua, R. Eliezer's opinion is stated first and in his name, whereas R. Joshua's opinion, which R. Judah Ha-Nasi favored, is stated last and attributed to "the Sages." *Cf.* TB Ḥullin 85a, quoted *supra*.

90. Yet another method of determining the law from a *mishnah*, notwithstanding that different opinions are expressed in it, was by the rules of decision making that determine

3. THE AMORAIC VIEW OF THE AUTHORITATIVE CHARACTER OF THE MISHNAH

The foregoing evidence that R. Judah Ha-Nasi intended to determine and declare the law comes from the Mishnah itself. The *amoraim,* who were the interpreters and explicators of the Mishnah, provide further significant evidence of this intention. The *amoraim* close to the time of the tannaitic period, as well as those of later generations, clearly expressed the view that R. Judah Ha-Nasi decided between differing views of the law and set forth his rulings in the Mishnah. As previously noted, R. Johanan stated that R. Judah Ha-Nasi recorded as the view of "the Sages" individual opinions of R. Meir and R. Simeon that he accepted as correct. R. Yose[91] similarly declared: "Rabbi [Judah Ha-Nasi] agreed with R. Eleazar b. R. Simeon and taught accordingly";[92] and the Babylonian *amoraim* R. Joseph, R. Kahana, and R. Ashi also concurred in the view that the Mishnah expresses as normative those disputed legal propositions with which R. Judah Ha-Nasi agreed.[93]

4. DIVERSITY AND UNIFORMITY IN JEWISH LAW

The conclusion that R. Judah Ha-Nasi intended his Mishnah to be the *Corpus Juris* of Jewish law is buttressed by an examination of one of the most important characteristics of Jewish law, namely, that it is at once both diverse and of one piece. The diversity within Jewish law is manifested by the existence of differences of opinion. The pressure for uniformity stems from the need for decisive rulings. The tension between diversity and uniformity is of crucial importance for the continued development and creativity of Jewish law; and throughout the long history of the Jewish legal system, halakhic authorities have adopted differing approaches to the res-

---

whose view prevails in disputes between the schools of Shammai and Hillel, between R. Meir and R. Judah, etc. Most of these rules had already crystallized by the time of R. Judah Ha-Nasi. *See* Epstein, *Tannaim,* p. 226.

91. Of the fourth generation of *amoraim* in the Land of Israel.

92. TJ Sotah 3:6, 17b (3:6, 19b).

93. TB Shevu'ot 4a:

> R. Joseph said: "It is the view of Rabbi [Judah Ha-Nasi], who followed the views of [other] *tannaim.* In the matter of knowledge of impurity, he followed the view of R. Ishmael, while in regard to oaths, he followed the view of R. Akiva." R. Ashi said: "I repeated this statement to R. Kahana, and he said to me: 'Do not say that Rabbi merely followed the views of [other] *tannaim* while not agreeing with them. Rabbi's exposition reflected his own view as to the correct legal principles.'"

See also R. Abbahu's statement, TB Yevamot 42b–43a, and Rashi, *ad loc.*, regarding anonymous *mishnayot* and disputes in *baraitot.* To the same effect is TJ Yevamot 4:11, 28a (4:11, 6b). *See also* Epstein, *Tannaim,* pp. 225–226; Albeck, *Mavo,* pp. 270–283.

olution of this tension.[94] At this point, we consider how this dual character of Jewish law manifested itself in the period under discussion.

The ancient *Halakhah*, as it has come down to us, is notable for its anonymity[95] and uniformity. In the time of the first "pair," Yose b. Joezer and Yose b. Johanan, only one law is known to have been in dispute—the question of whether the ceremony of "laying on of hands" on the head of a sacrificial animal was to be performed on a festival,[96] a dispute that was not finally resolved until much later, in the time of the schools of Shammai and Hillel.[97] As late as the time of the last "pair," Hillel and Shammai, only four laws were in dispute:[98]

> Originally, the only legal issue on which authorities in Israel disagreed was the "laying on of hands"; then Shammai and Hillel arose and made them [the disputed laws] into four.[99]

The reason for this virtually monolithic character of the law in that period is that all issues were authoritatively decided by the Sanhedrin, the nation's legal institution of last resort, possessing both legislative and judicial power, and final authority in regard to both. It is for this reason that the laws of this early period are generally recorded anonymously; the Sanhedrin determined the law by majority vote, and it was pointless and unnecessary to specify which member had voted a particular way.

When the period of the "pairs" ended, differences of opinion proliferated in all areas of the *Halakhah*. As demonstrated below, these differences, concerning fundamental issues in all areas of the law, were not merely theoretical; each school actually followed the law as it determined the law to be. This significant turning point in the character of Jewish law resulted from the Sanhedrin's general decline and particularly from its diminishing ability to act as the final authoritative decisionmaker. Both external political developments and internal factors in the half-century before the destruction of the Second Temple were instrumental in depriving the halakhic system of its principal authoritative institution and its capacity to make final decisions. The internal factors, which operated for a considerable time, included

94. *See infra* pp. 1222–1229, 1273–1287, 1311–1319, 1378–1379, 1451–1452, *et al.* As to pluralism in *Halakhah* and *Aggadah, see* A.I. Kook, *Eder ha-Yekar,* pp. 13ff.

95. Only rarely is a halakhic discussion attributed to a specific person, *e.g.*, "The prophet Haggai considered the matter and said three things" (TB Yevamot 16a).

96. M Ḥagigah 2:2.

97. *Tosefta* Ḥagigah 2:11; TJ Ḥagigah 2:3, 12a (2:3, 78a); TB Beẓah 20a. The sources present minor v.l.

98. M Eduyyot 1:1–3; TB Shabbat 15a; TJ Ḥagigah 2:2, 10b (2:2, 77d).

99. TJ *id.*

the growth of sectarianism in Jewry (Pharisees versus Sadducees) and the substantive differences of opinion within the Pharisaic movement itself (the schools of Shammai and Hillel). Only rarely, in exceptional circumstances, were disputed matters effectively resolved.[100]

R. Yose has provided an instructive description of this historical development:[101]

> R. Yose said: "At first, there were no disputes [about legal issues] in Israel.[102] There was a court of seventy-one [judges] which sat in the Chamber of Hewn Stone [in the Temple compound] and two courts of twenty-three [judges] each, one sitting at the entrance to the Temple Mount and the other at the entrance to the Temple courtyard; and other courts of twenty-three judges were located in all the towns of Israel.
>
> "When a question arose, it was asked of the local court. If they [the judges] had heard [*i.e.*, had a tradition as to how to determine the question], they told it to them [the litigants]; if not, they went to the court near their town. If they [the judges there] had heard, they told them, and if not, they came to the court at the entrance to the Temple Mount. If they had heard, they told them, and if not, they proceeded to the court at the entrance to the Temple courtyard.
>
> "He [*i.e.*, one of the judges] would say, 'This is my interpretation and this is the interpretation of my colleagues. This is what I taught and this is what my colleagues taught.' If they had heard, they told them, and if not, they all proceeded to the Chamber of Hewn Stone. . . . The question was posed before them [the judges of the Sanhedrin]. If they had heard, they told them, and if not, they took a vote. If those for a judgment of 'impure' were in the majority, it was declared impure; if those who considered it 'pure' were in the majority, it was declared pure. From there, the *Halakhah* would go forth and spread throughout Israel."[103]

R. Yose here presents a description of a judicial hierarchy. If the inferior courts—starting with the local courts and proceeding up to the court at the entrance to the Temple courtyard—were not certain of the law and had no tradition regarding it, the matter was settled in the highest court, the Sanhedrin, if necessary by a vote. Thus, almost total uniformity was preserved. What changed this state of affairs? The *baraita* concludes:

100. *See* M Shabbat 1:4; *Tosefta* Shabbat 1:16; TB Shabbat 15a; TJ Shabbat 1:4, 9a (1:8, 3c). *See also* Albeck, *Mavo,* pp. 61–62.

101. *Tosefta* Ḥagigah 2:9, Sanhedrin 7:1; TB Sanhedrin 88b; TJ Sanhedrin 1:4, 8b (1:4, 19c). *See further supra* pp. 287–288.

102. In TB Sanhedrin 88b the reading is: "At first, there were few disputes in Israel." Ms. Munich follows the *Tosefta. See Dikdukei Soferim,* Sanhedrin, *ad loc.*, Letter *ḥet.* In TJ the reading is: "At first, there was no dispute in Israel."

103. The last sentence is absent in TB. The entire *baraita* is quoted in the various sources with minor v.l.

> From the time when there was an increase in the number of students of Shammai and Hillel who did not serve [their teachers] sufficiently [*i.e.*, did not follow a sufficiently long course of apprenticeship, or, did not study enough],[104] disputes in Israel multiplied and the Torah became as two Torahs.[105]

These disputes introduced for the first time the phenomenon of pluralism with regard to the law applied in practical life; and the students of the schools of Shammai and Hillel "separated into two sects."[106] The following rules were then established to govern actual conduct:[107]

> Whoever wishes to be strict with himself and follow [the stringencies of] both the School of Shammai and the School of Hillel is described by the saying "A fool will walk in darkness" [*cf.* Ecclesiastes 2:14].[108] Whoever adopts the lenient rulings of the School of Shammai and the lenient rulings of the School of Hillel is a wicked man. Therefore, if one follows the School of Shammai, [one should follow] both their lenient rulings and their stringent rulings; if one follows the School of Hillel, [one should follow] both their lenient rulings and their stringent rulings.[109]

Various Talmudic sources reveal that while some of the Sages conducted themselves in accordance with the rulings of the School of Shammai,[110] the practice of many others followed the School of Hillel.

104. In TJ Sanhedrin the reading is: "who did not serve their teachers as they should have."

105. This *baraita* appears in the sources cited *supra* n. 101, with certain v.l. *Cf. Tosefta* Sotah 14:9 (and TB Sotah 47b):

> When haughty students [*zihurei ha-lev;* printed versions of TB read *zeḥoḥei ha-lev*] increased, disputes in Israel multiplied, and two Torahs were created. From the time when there was an increase in the number of students of Shammai and Hillel who did not serve [their teachers] sufficiently, disputes in Israel multiplied and two Torahs were created.

See also Rashi, Sotah, *ad loc.*, s.v. Zeḥoḥei ha-lev. The *baraita* concludes that they would send emissaries to all the towns in the Land of Israel to find candidates of suitable wisdom, personality, and character to serve as judges. That addition clarifies the clause "who did not serve sufficiently," *i.e.*, sufficiently to fulfill their function properly, since great care was taken to appoint as judges only those possessed of all the necessary personal qualities.

106. TJ Ḥagigah 2:2, 10b (2:2, 77d).

107. *Tosefta* Yevamot 1:13; TJ Yevamot 1:6, 9a (1:6, 3b); TB Eruvin 6b; and parallel sources.

108. The reading "will walk (*yelekh*)" appears in the *Tosefta*, ed. Lieberman. The verse in Ecclesiastes reads "walks (*holekh*)," which likewise appears in v.l. in *Tosefta, ad loc.*

109. The beginning of this *baraita* in the *Tosefta* and TB states: "The law always accords with the view of the School of Hillel." That rule, however, was established in a later period, as hereinafter shown. *See also* TB and TJ, *supra* n. 107.

110. *E.g.*, R. Tarfon (M Berakhot 1:3; *Tosefta* Yevamot 1:10; TB Yevamot 15a); R. Eleazar (TB Berakhot 11a); Rabban Gamaliel (M Beẓah 2:6). Similarly, TB Yevamot 16a concludes that the adherents of the School of Shammai applied their opinions in practice.

In the beginning, and for some time, the existence of two divergent trends within the *Halakhah* was tolerable, as the *Tosefta* indicates:[111]

> Although the School of Shammai disagreed with the School of Hillel regarding [the laws of levirate marriage of] co-wives, sisters, and women whose status as wives was doubtful, [the validity of] a predated *get* (bill of divorcement) and of a marriage effected by [giving to the bride] property worth only a *perutah*, and the status of a divorced woman who spends the night with her former husband in the same inn,[112] [the adherents of] the School of Shammai did not refrain from marrying women from [families of] the School of Hillel; nor did [the adherents of] the School of Hillel refrain from [marrying women from families of] the School of Shammai. Rather, they behaved toward each other honestly and amicably, as it is written [Zechariah 8:19], "You must love truth and peace."[113] And although one school prohibited what the other permitted, that did not prevent the adherents of either from using utensils that belonged to the other to prepare food that was ritually pure, thus fulfilling the verse "All the ways of a man seem right to him, but the Lord probes the mind."[114]

The *amoraim* of the Land of Israel and of Babylonia debated at length how adherents of one school could permit themselves to marry into families of the other in the face of conflicting rulings of the two schools as to whether certain marriages were permissible or prohibited, particularly when the punishment for a prohibited marriage was *karet* (divine punishment of premature death) and the issue of such a marriage were *mamzerim*.[115] As the Jerusalem Talmud puts it, "their dispute concerns whether children are

---

See L. Ginzberg, *Perushim,* Berakhot, I, pp. 81–85, 88–92, 149–150; H. Albeck, *Commentary on the Mishnah,* Nashim, pp. 332–333; S. Lieberman, *Tosefta ki-Feshutah,* Yevamot, pp. 7–9.

111. *Tosefta* Yevamot 1:10–11; the same basic idea is also expressed in M Yevamot 1:4 and M Eduyyot 4:8.

112. For elucidation of these various disputes between the schools of Shammai and Hillel, *see* commentators to the *Tosefta,* and Lieberman, *supra* n. 110 at 7.

113. TB Yevamot 14b reads: "to teach you that they behaved toward each other with love and friendship in order to fulfill that which is written [Zechariah 8:19], 'You must love truth and peace (*ha-emet ve-ha-shalom*).'" The Biblical text we have is slightly different: *ve-ha-emet ve-ha-shalom.* The 1985 JPS *Tanakh* translates *shalom* as "integrity" rather than "peace."

114. *See* Proverbs 16:2, 21:2. The quotation in the *Tosefta* does not precisely track either of those verses, but is a combination of the two. *See* Lieberman, *supra* n. 110 at 8.

115. *E.g.,* if a man who has two wives dies childless, children born as a result of levirate marriage to one of the widows when the *levir*'s union with the other widow would have been incestuous have no taint according to the School of Shammai, but according to the School of Hillel such children are *mamzerim.* The view of the School of Hillel was that in these circumstances a levirate marriage is not required and therefore the general prohibition of marriage to a brother's wife, which carries the penalty of *karet,* applies. *See* TB Yevamot 14a and Rashi, *ad loc.*, s.v. Ḥayyavei keritut.

mamzerim, and you still maintain [that the adherents of one school would marry women from families of the other school]?"[116]

The Babylonian *amoraim* explained that neither school had a general policy against marriage with the other's adherents, but each school informed the other of any occurrences in a family that could result in a marriage prohibited by the other school, whose members would then not marry into that particular family.[117] The answer of the *amoraim* of the Land of Israel was different: "The Almighty watched over them and such a case never happened."[118]

However, this "pluralism" with regard to rules governing practical conduct could not possibly continue. The fear increased that families would be off-limits to each other for marriage. At first, the Sages attempted to solve the problem by legislation, but without success.[119] The controversies between Shammai and Hillel themselves—and, for a time, between their schools—which at first were pointed to as prime examples of dispute "for the sake of Heaven,"[120] turned acrimonious and bitter, to the point that swords were thrust in the study hall[121] and Shammaites attempted to kill Hillelites.[122] That was said to be as sad a day for the Jewish people as "the day on which they made the golden calf,"[123] when brother killed brother.

The schism in the *Halakhah*—and consequently in Judaism—became increasingly wider, and the consequences were particularly severe in that period of draconian Roman decrees and the destruction of the Temple. The former center of Jewish law was displaced, and the Sages and their courts—as many as survived the war—wandered from place to place, while the nation was threatened from within with spiritual disintegration.

A generation after the destruction of the Temple, at the beginning of the second century C.E., uniformity of halakhic practice was restored with the establishment of the new center at Yavneh under the patriarchate of

116. TJ Yevamot 1:6, 9a (1:6, 3b).

117. TB Yevamot 14a: "They would inform them, and they refrained"; *see* Rashi, *ad loc.*, s.v. De-modai le-hu.

118. TJ Yevamot 1:6, 9a (1:6, 3b).

119. *Tosefta* Yevamot 1:9–10, statements of R. Johanan b. Nuri and Rabban Gamaliel. *See also* Rashi, Yevamot 15a, s.v. Mah na'aseh; TB Yevamot 14b (end).

120. M Avot 5:17.

121. TB Shabbat 17a.

122. TJ Shabbat 1:4, 9a (1:8, 3c). *See also Tosafot,* Gittin 36b, s.v. Ella.

123. TB Shabbat 17a; TJ Shabbat 1:4, 9a (1:8, 3c); *Tosefta* Shabbat 1:16. *See also* Lieberman, *Tosefta ki-Feshutah,* Shabbat, p. 15, for clarification of the statement in TB Shabbat, "On that day Hillel sat bent over [*i.e.,* subservient] before Shammai," which implies that even in the days of Shammai and Hillel themselves, relations between them were difficult. This statement does not appear in the other sources. *See Tosafot,* Shabbat 14b, s.v. Veillu Shammai ve-Hillel; S. Lieberman, *Yerushalmi ki-Feshuto,* pp. 38, 52.

Rabban Gamaliel II. An important piece of historical evidence[124] reflects the change:

> When the Sages gathered in the "vineyard" at Yavneh, they said: "A time will come when someone will seek to learn what the Torah says on a particular question but will not find it, and what the Sages say but will not find it, as it is written,[125] 'A time is coming—declares my Lord God—when I will send a famine upon the land: not a hunger for bread or a thirst for water, but for hearing the words of the Lord. Men shall wander from sea to sea and from north to east to seek the word of the Lord, but they shall not find it' . . . because no statement about what the Torah says will be like any other." They said, "Let us begin with Hillel and Shammai."[126]

It was essential to have an authoritative declaration of the law to be applied in practice, and the most pressing need in this regard arose out of the conflicting views of the schools of Hillel and Shammai. The Jerusalem Talmud records that in Yavneh, "A voice from heaven emerged and declared: 'The words of both are the words of the living God, but the law is in accordance with the School of Hillel!'"[127] However, while it was thus unequivocally determined that the *Halakhah* could not tolerate pluralism in practice, the important principle was also established that in the realm of ideas, for the purpose of debate and study, "the words of both are the words of the living God." In regard to practical application, "Why did the School of Hillel merit having the law established in accordance with their opinions? Because they were pleasant and tolerant."[128]

124. *Tosefta* Eduyyot 1:1.

125. Amos 8:11–12. Our Hebrew version is slightly different from that quoted in the *Tosefta*.

126. *See Sifrei*, Deuteronomy, Ekev, sec. 48 (ed. Finkelstein, p. 113) for an interpretation of Amos 8:11–12. *Sifrei* interprets:

> R. Simeon b. Yoḥai says: "Can it mean that the Torah will be forgotten in the future? Has it not already been said [Deuteronomy 31:21], 'It will never be lost [lit. "forgotten"] from the mouth of their offspring'? Rather, [it means] that one will prohibit and another will permit; one will declare [a thing] to be impure and another [declare it] to be pure, and people will not find a clear answer."

See also TB Shabbat 138b, where both *baraitot*—the one in the *Tosefta* and the one in the *Sifrei*—are quoted.

127. TJ Berakhot 1:4, 9a (1:4, 3b/c); Yevamot 1:6, 9a (1:6, 3b), where the text reads: "The law is always in accordance with the School of Hillel." In order to emphasize the categorical nature of this rule, the Talmud adds: "And any person who transgresses the rulings of the School of Hillel is liable to the death penalty"; TJ, *loc. cit.*

128. TB Eruvin 13b. *See* TB Ḥagigah 3b ("The *'ba'alei asufot'* [lit. "masters of assemblies"] are scholars who sit . . . and occupy themselves with Torah; some declare 'impure' while others declare 'pure' . . . , [yet] all [opinions] have been given from the same Shepherd"); and Rashi, *ad loc.*, s.v. Kullon el eḥad amaran. Approval of pluralism in regard to theory, and rejection of pluralism in regard to practice became an established legal principle in the law of the rebellious elder (M Sanhedrin 11:2):

A dramatic description of the end of the era of pluralistic halakhic practice is to be found in the account of the confrontation between R. Eliezer b. Hyrcanus, a disciple of the School of Shammai, and R. Joshua and his colleagues over a matter of ritual purity—the case of the oven of Akhnai, previously discussed.[129] A voice from heaven itself sided with R. Eliezer b. Hyrcanus, proclaiming that the law always follows his opinion, but the majority view as expressed by R. Joshua was accepted as law: "We pay no attention to a heavenly voice because You [God] have already written in the Torah at Mt. Sinai, 'Follow the majority [Exodus 23:2].'"[130] The heavenly voice at Yavneh that proclaimed that the *Halakhah* accords with the view of the School of Hillel prevailed over the heavenly voice that declared that the *Halakhah* follows the view of R. Eliezer (the Shammaite) in every instance.[131]

Whereas, at the beginning of the period of disputes between the two schools, "although one school prohibited what the other permitted, that did not prevent the adherents of either from using utensils that belonged to the other to prepare food that was ritually pure,"[132] by the time that period ended, the Sages realized that pluralism in practice was not viable. "On that day they brought all the things R. Eliezer had declared pure and burned them, and they took a vote concerning him [R. Eliezer] and put him under a ban."[133] The decision was difficult and painful, but the Sages of that generation, led by the patriarch Rabban Gamaliel II, saw it as part of their duty to safeguard the continued viability of Jewish law.[134] The Talmud concludes its account of R. Eliezer's confrontation with his colleagues as follows:

> When he returns to his town, if he merely continues to teach in the same way that he previously taught [before the Sanhedrin had decided otherwise], he is innocent; but if he instructs that his ruling be applied in actual practice [in accordance with his previous ruling rejected by the Sanhedrin], he is guilty, as is stated: "Should a man act presumptuously . . . " [Deuteronomy 17:12]. He is not guilty unless he instructs that his view of the law be carried out in practice.

For further discussion, *see supra* pp. 240ff. and 1061–1063 and sources cited in n. 94.

129. *Supra* pp. 261–263.

130. TB Bava Meẓi'a 59b, and *see supra* p. 262.

131. *See Tosafot,* Bava Meẓi'a 59b, s.v. Lo va-shamayim hi. As to the different approaches to the question of suprahuman intervention in halakhic decisions, *see supra* pp. 264–265.

132. M Yevamot 1:4; M Eduyyot 4:8; and *cf. Tosefta* Yevamot 1:11.

133. TB Bava Meẓi'a 59b; *see id.* as to the difficulties the Sages had regarding how R. Eliezer should be informed of the ban against him.

134. Jewish law recognizes a measure of pluralism in practice, by way of custom and local enactments (*see supra* pp. 486–490, 666–677, 932–936); such recognition is reflected in the rules relating to conflict of laws.

> At that time, Rabban Gamaliel [II] was traveling on a ship and a storm threatened to engulf him. He said, "It seems to me that this can be happening only on account of R. Eliezer b. Hyrcanus." He stood up and proclaimed, "Lord of the universe! You must surely know that it was not for my honor or for the honor of my father's house that I acted, but for Your honor, so that controversy should not proliferate in Israel." The sea's rage thereupon was calmed.[135]

An essential step toward restoring uniformity to the *Halakhah* was the collection and arrangement of its legal rules. At that time in Yavneh, various Sages testified to the tradition of numerous laws; these were then collected and arranged in Tractate *Eduyyot*.[136] The expansion and development of the law in the schools of R. Akiva, R. Ishmael, and their contemporaries intensified the need to redact the various compilations.[137] In the following generation—that of R. Akiva's disciples (R. Meir, R. Judah, R. Simeon, R. Yose, *et al.*)—there were increasing disagreements as to the substance of many laws, and "new troubles came all the time; the Roman Empire expanded and became stronger, and Israel was tossed about and fragmented."[138]

This state of affairs, like that at the time of the destruction of the Temple, before the establishment of the academy at Yavneh, resulted in a lack of certainty in halakhic matters. The Sages were once again faced with the urgent need to crystallize and summarize an enormous amount of halakhic material, to determine the law where it was disputed, and to reduce it to clear and uniform rules to govern conduct. The great challenge facing R. Judah Ha-Nasi, a disciple of R. Akiva's disciples, was, therefore, not only to bring together the laws already collected in the various compilations available to him, but also, and much more importantly, to decide between the opposing opinions and thus to restore the *Halakhah* as a uniform and certain guide to practical conduct.

The foregoing historical survey reinforces the conclusion reached as a result of our examination of the Mishnah and of the statements of the *amoraim*: In redacting the Mishnah, R. Judah Ha-Nasi's objective was the same as that of his grandfather Rabban Gamaliel II before him—to forestall the

135. TB Bava Meẓi'a 59b.

136. *See Tosefta* Eduyyot 1:1: "When the Sages gathered in the 'vineyard' at Yavneh . . . they said, 'Let us begin with Hillel and Shammai. Shammai says [that *ḥallah* must be separated] from a *kab* of dough, whereas Hillel says [that the minimum measure is] two *kabim*'"; and they proceeded according to the order in M Eduyyot. *See also* Epstein, *Tannaim*, pp. 422–429.

137. *See supra* pp. 1051–1052.

138. Maimonides, *MT*, Introduction. Maimonides gives this as a reason that motivated R. Judah Ha-Nasi to redact the Mishnah.

danger to the uniformity of the *Halakhah* and, consequently, to the unity of the nation, from the proliferation of conflicting opinions as to the law to be applied in practice. To this end, he redacted the Mishnah so that it did not merely set out legal rules in an orderly arrangement but indicated the binding rules to be applied in practice.

5. MULTIPLICITY OF OPINIONS IN THE MISHNAH

We now return to the point raised at the beginning of our discussion of R. Judah Ha-Nasi's objectives in redacting the Mishnah. If his purpose was to compile an authoritative code of laws, why did he employ such indirect methods as setting forth in anonymous form the view he determined to be the law (without naming the *tanna* who stated that view), attributing the opinion he favored to "the Sages," and relying on the application of rules for decision making when there were conflicting opinions?[139] Why did he not simply set forth a single normative, categorical statement of each law, without attribution to any individual Sage? If the Mishnah is indeed a code, why is it full of conflicting opinions cited in the names of their authors and transmitters, and why did R. Judah Ha-Nasi indicate only indirectly what view he had determined to be the normative *Halakhah*?

There are two answers, which really boil down to one, and they are implicit in the very nature of Jewish law. The reason for the binding character of the *Halakhah* is that it has been continuously transmitted from person to person throughout the generations. The force and vitality of any norm that is added to the *corpus juris* of Jewish law by means of any of the creative sources of the law[140] ultimately derives from the highest level, the primary legislation of the system, *i.e.*, the written Torah, and from the chain of tradition. The continuity of the *Halakhah* is expressed in teachings transmitted from one Sage to the next in formulations that have been accepted throughout the generations. Thus, a bare statement of law without attribution to its source or to the Sage who transmitted it would constitute a break in the continuity of the *Halakhah*, if only from the point of view of its form. Such a formulation would detach the law from its *fons vitae*. As Nachman Krochmal put it:[141]

> The Oral Law, which includes the ancestral heritage and ancient traditions, strongly requires a special style. It must be unique and very recognizable, not only in citing the names of those who received it, but also, more importantly,

139. *See supra* n. 90.

140. *I.e.*, the legal sources—tradition, interpretation, legislation, custom, *ma'aseh*, and *sevarah*. *See supra* pp. 228–239, 275–280.

141. N. Krochmal, *Moreh Nevukhei ha-Zeman* [Guide for the Perplexed of the Time], ed. S. Rawidowicz, Berlin, 1924, Sha'ar 13 (end), p. 232.

> in its pristine literary style and language and its description of the manner of this transmission. All these aspects are the clear sign that it is, in the main, the tradition faithfully transmitted from father to son. Therefore, in formulating a single comprehensive Mishnah, the Sages chose to indicate their connection with their predecessors by using the same style and language as in former times, and, within that framework, to give their work the greatest possible measure of uniformity, clarity, order, and value.

In other words, R. Judah Ha-Nasi, notwithstanding his desire to present the authoritatively determined law, was duty bound to cite the sources of the laws and to indicate the manner of their transmission by the Sages, identifying them and their views, and retaining the original style and language, in order to underscore the continuity of the chain of tradition reflected in the Mishnah.

The second answer to the question as to why the Mishnah was written as it was is a corollary to the first. The Mishnah's editorial method of citing conflicting opinions is a natural consequence of the pluralism characteristic of Jewish law, which has already been discussed and is further discussed below.[142] As necessary as it is that the law be clear and uniform in its practical application, it is equally vital that, on the theoretical and academic level, it express the plurality of opinions and possible approaches.

As previously noted, when it was determined that the law follows the views of the School of Hillel, it was also determined that all the various shades in the spectrum of halakhic opinion are "the words of the living God." This dual nature of the halakhic system—uniformity in practice but pluralism in theory—is not self-contradictory; it actually tends to perfect the law. The multitude of opinions considered in the study of a legal point increases the likelihood that the solution ultimately arrived at as the uniform guide to practical conduct will be correct.[143] The dual nature of Jewish law thus dictated that the Mishnah not only set forth the final decision but also cite the whole range of opinions expressed in the course of the discussion of the legal rule or principle involved.

Ever since the Mishnah, all codifiers of Jewish law have struggled to meet the demands resulting from this dual nature of the halakhic system.[144] The problem is especially evident in the case of Maimonides, the greatest of the codifiers, approximately a millennium after the redaction of the Mishnah. Maimonides' *Mishneh Torah* is a legal code, a *Corpus Juris* of Jewish law in the fullest sense of that term. In a remarkably lucid and uniform

142. *See supra* pp. 240–272 and 1061–1063, and references in n. 94.

143. *See* M Eduyyot 1:5–6 and sources referred to *supra* n. 142. *See also supra* p. 541 and n. 195.

144. *See supra* n. 142.

Hebrew style, Maimonides formulated clear and unequivocal prescriptive rules without attribution to source.[145] However, it was precisely this formulation that aroused the opposition to Maimonides' code by the overwhelming majority of halakhic authorities. They argued that Maimonides' code severed the law from its sources and impoverished it by omitting reference to the range of differing opinions.[146] It was not until four centuries after Maimonides—until the *Shulḥan Arukh* of Joseph Caro—that a code was produced whose form and methodology were compatible with the nature and spirit of Jewish law.[147]

B. The Legal Style of the Mishnah

In order to understand the nature of the Mishnah as a code, it is necessary to consider an additional aspect of mishnaic draftsmanship that also left its imprint on all subsequent attempts to codify Jewish law. A legal rule can be formulated in either of two ways: casuistically, by specific instances, or normatively, by prescriptive generalization. Casuistic formulation sets forth the law by describing specific cases detailing the concrete factual circumstances to which a given law is applicable. The normative style, on the other hand, states the norm, the abstract legal principle, without reference to any concrete factual situation.

Contemporary statute books are generally drafted in the normative style and set forth legal principles without casuistic examples. By contrast,

145. *See infra* pp. 1184ff.

146. *See infra* pp. 1223–1229.

147. *See infra* pp. 1319ff. As we conclude our discussion as to whether R. Judah Ha-Nasi's purpose in redacting the Mishnah was to determine the law authoritatively, it is appropriate to consider an argument not previously noted, made by H. Albeck, in support of his position that R. Judah Ha-Nasi did not have such a purpose in mind (*see supra* p. 1057). Albeck argues (*Mavo*, p. 106):

> We frequently find that amoraic rulings are contrary to the law stated in anonymous form in a *mishnah* if the *amoraim* believed that the *mishnah* represented an individual opinion. They did not say, "Since Rabbi [R. Judah Ha-Nasi] states the law without attribution of source [it states his opinion, and consequently], since he and his court are the majority, the law must follow the majority." [They did not say this because] they knew that Rabbi did not use "anonymous" *mishnayot* in this way [*i.e.*, for this purpose].

There are several objections to this argument. R. Judah Ha-Nasi's Mishnah did not always include the *mishnayot* that contradicted his own opinion (Albeck, *Mavo*, pp. 110–111); and therefore when *amoraim* said, "This *mishnah* represents an individual opinion," they may have been relying on other *mishnayot* of which R. Judah Ha-Nasi was not aware, and therefore they did not rule as he did. Furthermore, it is entirely possible that not all the *amoraim* acknowledged that his purpose was to determine the law; and even if they did all acknowledge that this was his purpose, they were still free to prove that he had followed a minority opinion and on that ground they could legitimately reject his decision.

the Mishnah is for the most part drafted casuistically; indeed, the casuistic style is typical of Jewish law from its beginnings in the Written Law until the present day. Jewish law developed and grew out of life's circumstances, which, in turn, affected the way the law was determined and handed down from generation to generation. This does not mean, however, that there are not occasionally paragraphs in the Mishnah combining the casuistic and the normative styles, or even passages that are couched in a purely normative manner. The following examples are illustrative.

1. THE CASUISTIC STYLE

The Mishnah states:[148]

> No person may dig a pit near the pit of his neighbor; nor may he dig a ditch, a cave, a water-channel, or a washpool unless he separates it by three handbreadths[149] from his neighbor's wall [*i.e.*, the wall of his neighbor's pit] and plasters it with lime.

This *mishnah* lays down a substantive principle in the law of torts, according to which a person performing an act on his own property is obligated to take care not to cause damage to his neighbor. He is, therefore, required to distance the various kinds of excavations—even if they are on his own property—by at least three handbreadths from the wall of his neighbor's pit; and he must plaster the walls of his pit with lime to prevent damage from percolation into his neighbor's pit.

This *mishnah* continues:

> Olive-refuse, manure, salt, lime, and stones must be kept at a distance of three handbreadths from his neighbor's wall, and [the place where they are kept] must be plastered with lime. Seeds [which cause rotting], a plow [which can weaken a wall's foundation], and urine [which weakens cement or mortar or unburnt bricks] must be kept at a distance of three handbreadths from the wall [of one's neighbor, so as not to undermine the wall]. A handmill must be kept at a distance of three [handbreadths measured] from the lower millstone [the broader millstone (fixed to the floor) on which the concave upper millstone moves]; this is the equivalent of four [handbreadths measured] from the upper millstone. An oven must be kept at a distance of three [handbreadths measured] from the belly [of the oven], which is the

148. M Bava Batra 2:1.

149. A handbreadth is approximately eight centimeters (a little more than three inches). For a discussion of weights and measures in the Talmud, *see* H.J. Sheftel, *Erekh Millin, le-Shi'urei Torah she-bi-Khetav ve-she-be-al Peh, le-Matbe'ot, Middot* . . . [On Units of Measurement in the Written and the Oral Law for Coins, Measures, etc.], 1904 (reprint: 1969); D. Sperber, EJ, XVI, p. 388, s.v. Weights and measures. *See also* H. Albeck, *Commentary on M Bava Batra* 1:1.

> equivalent of four [handbreadths measured] from the rim. [These distances assure that the milling or baking will not damage the neighbor's wall.]

This *mishnah* is a classic example of the casuistic style of legal drafting. The legal norm implicit in the many concrete, real-life examples in the *mishnah* is that a person is forbidden to create a situation—even on his own property—that tends to cause damage to his neighbor, and that he is obligated to keep the possibly harmful substance as far away from his neighbor's property as is necessary to avoid causing damage. The idea implicit in all the actual instances mentioned in the *mishnah* could have been expressed by stating it as an abstract legal norm without examples.[150] The *mishnah*, however, expressed it in a series of illustrative everyday examples, some possibly based on decisions of actual cases, and others on hypothetical situations.[151]

2. THE HYBRID CASUISTIC-NORMATIVE STYLE

The Mishnah sometimes adopts a combination of the casuistic and normative styles; the norm summarizes and states explicitly the legal conclusion to be drawn from the instances set forth. Here are two examples of this hybrid style:

150. *See, e.g.*, Civil Wrongs Ordinance (New Version), 1968, sec. 44:

> (A) Personal conduct or operation of a business or use of real estate under one's control constitutes a private nuisance if it is such as to cause serious interference to another's reasonable use or enjoyment of his property, giving due consideration to the nature and location of the properties involved; but no damages for a private nuisance shall be payable except for actual harm caused thereby.

151. *See* Y. Baer's interesting discussion of the substance and dating of the *mishnayot* in chapters 1 and 2 of M Bava Batra (Y. Baer, "Ha-Yesodot ha-Historiyyim Shel ha-Halakhah" [The Historical Foundations of the *Halakhah*], *Zion*, XVII, pp. 24–27). He attributes the rules contained in those *mishnayot* to the third century B.C.E. and points to parallels in other ancient legal systems but reaches no conclusion as to whether the parallels are the result of reciprocal influence or are simply parallel developments due to similar economic and social conditions. He summarizes his point as follows:

> The above-mentioned laws of the Mishnah are not the creations of academies, courts, legislative authorities, or later Sages, but are rather taken from a living historical and social reality. Such provisions were adopted by the residents of towns and villages who at some time decided to establish regulations for the mutual benefit of all the townspeople.

If this theory is correct, as it may well be, these laws constitute another example of communal legislation, in addition to those listed in *Tosefta* Bava Meẓi'a 11:23 and TB Bava Batra 8b. For detailed discussion, *see supra* pp. 487–488, 679–681. However, it is equally possible that these rules are enactments adopted by courts or authorized halakhic authorities. In any event, the extant records explicitly referring to communal legislation relate only to food prices, weights and measures, laborers' wages, and internal municipal services and regulations. *See Tosefta* and TB, *supra*. *See also supra* pp. 679–681.

a. POSSESSION OF REAL PROPERTY FOR THREE YEARS AS PROOF OF OWNERSHIP

The Mishnah states:[152]

> [The period of] possession [needed to prove ownership] of: houses; pits, ditches, and caves [used as receptacles for water]; dovecotes; bathhouses; olive presses; irrigated fields; slaves; and anything that is continually productive—is three years from day to day [*i.e.*, possession by the occupier for three complete years is sufficient to constitute proof that the property belongs to him]. In the case of a field not under irrigation, [the period of] possession is three years, which need not be from day to day.

This *mishnah* establishes two periods of possession sufficient to constitute proof of ownership. For property that is continually productive throughout the year, the period is three complete and uninterrupted years, whereas for property that is productive only once a year, such as a field not under irrigation, the period is also three years, but the field need not be worked for each entire year, since it produces a crop only once a year. The *mishnah* itself explicitly states this principle; but, not content with the bare statement of the principle, it begins by setting forth a number of illustrative concrete examples.

b. DIVISION OF PROPERTY OWNED IN COMMON

The Mishnah states:[153]

> A courtyard may not be divided [*i.e.*, one co-owner may not compel another co-owner to divide up a courtyard] unless there is [enough] space to provide four [square] cubits to each.
>
> Nor [may] a field [be divided] unless there is [sufficient ground to plant] nine *kabim* [a *kab* is approximately a peck, or 2.2 liters] for each co-owner. R. Judah says: "Unless there is [sufficient ground to plant] nine half-*kabim* for each."
>
> Nor [may] a garden [be divided] unless there is [sufficient ground to plant] a half-*kab* for each. R. Akiva says: "A quarter-*kab* [for each]."
>
> Nor [may] a dining hall, a watchtower, a dovecote, a cloak, a bathhouse, or an olive-press [be divided] unless there is a portion sufficient for each [co-owner].
>
> This is the general principle: Whatever when divided can still be called by the same name [*i.e.*, whatever retains its identity after the division] may be divided; otherwise it may not be divided.

152. M Bava Batra 3:1. This *mishnah* has already been discussed in connection with legal reasoning (*sevarah*) as a legal source of law, *supra* pp. 1007–1014. *See also infra* pp. 1331–1335.

153. M Bava Batra 1:6.

This is another example of a combination of the casuistic and the normative styles. The *mishnah* opens with a list of concrete examples and establishes for each one the specific criterion that allows one co-owner to require the other to divide property owned in common. The underlying principle is that a division cannot be compelled over the objection of a co-owner unless the portion that each co-owner will receive as a result of the division is fit for the same use as it was before it was divided. The *amoraim* established that there was no real conflict between the first *tanna,* who requires that at least enough land be left to each to sow nine *kabim,* and R. Judah, according to whom nine half-*kabim* suffice. The *amoraim* explained that "each was referring to his own locality," *i.e.,* each fixed the minimum size of a field according to the criteria accepted in his own place of residence.[154] At the end of the *mishnah,* the principle implicit in all the examples is stated as a general norm: "Whatever when divided can still be called by the same name [*i.e.,* retains its identity] may be divided." This norm, without more, would have covered all the specific instances mentioned earlier in the *mishnah.*[155]

3. THE NORMATIVE STYLE

Very occasionally, the Mishnah states a legal rule in a purely normative manner, without any element of the casuistic style. The following is an example:[156]

> If I am responsible for the care of anything, I [am held to have] render[ed] possible the damage that it causes. If I am the immediate cause of that damage, I am as responsible for that damage as if I had been the sole cause.

This *mishnah,* as interpreted in a *baraita* and by the *amoraim,* establishes two principles in tort law: (1) if anything that a person is responsible to take care of causes damage because of his failure to take proper care, he is liable for the damage, and (2) if a person is the immediate cause of the damage, even though not the sole cause, he is responsible to pay for the damage as if he were the sole cause. For example, one who digs a pit in the public domain into which an ox falls and dies is liable in damages for the death of the ox. The Talmud lays down the general rule that for the digger to be liable for the death of the ox, the pit must be at least ten handbreadths deep.[157] The theory is that a fall into a shallower pit, while likely

154. TB Bava Batra 12a.

155. For an additional example, *see* M Gittin 2:5–6, which also begins with a number of concrete instances and concludes: "This is the general rule: If at the beginning and at the end an act is performed with full understanding, it is valid."

156. M Bava Kamma 1:2.

157. *See supra* n. 149.

to injure the animal, is not likely to be fatal; the shallower pit therefore is not considered to be the cause of the death. The second principle of the *mishnah* establishes that one who excavates only an additional handbreadth in a pit that is already nine handbreadths deep is liable for the entire damage if an ox falls into the pit and dies.

The *mishnah* contains no casuistic formulations, but presents two legal principles as normative propositions on the basis of which a ruling may be arrived at in every case. Indeed, the Talmud[158] cites several concrete cases for which the second principle provides the basis of decision. For example, if A starts a fire in his own field in such a manner that it will not spread to any neighboring property, and B adds to the fire and as a result it spreads to C's field, then B is liable for any resulting damage to C. Similarly, if five people have been sitting on a bench without damaging it, and the bench breaks when a sixth person sits on it, the sixth person is liable for the damage. If ten people successively strike the same person, and the victim is alive after the ninth assault but dies after the tenth, then the tenth attacker, according to R. Judah b. Bathyra, is liable for the death. In all these examples, it is the last person who was "the immediate cause" of the damage.

The examples cited thus illustrate three Mishnaic styles:

1. The most common, used in the majority of *mishnayot*—exclusively casuistic.
2. The form used in a number of *mishnayot*—a combination of the casuistic and normative styles; generally, the normative statement sets forth the principle arising out of the casuistic formulations.
3. The style only rarely encountered—exclusively normative.[159]

The casuistic style of the Mishnah, the first code of Jewish law after the Torah, left its mark on all subsequent Jewish legal codes. The accepted style was, and remains, casuistic; even Maimonides, who brought the codification of Jewish law to its zenith by categorically stating the law without attribution to sources, continued, by and large, to employ casuistic formulations in his *Mishneh Torah,* although he made frequent use of the combined casuistic-normative style.[160]

The question of style is not merely a matter of outward form; it is an expression of the methodology of Jewish law that gives that law its capacity for continued development. By concentrating on actual problems and particular issues, and by formulating the solution to concrete cases, Jewish law achieved great flexibility in solving new problems. New problems were

158. TB Bava Kamma 10a/b.

159. For other examples of pure normative style, *see* the continuation of the *mishnah* in Bava Kamma, ch. 1, and several *mishnayot* in Kiddushin, ch. 1.

160. *See infra* pp. 1211–1214.

solved by comparing them to problems already solved, and the applicability of the prior solution depended on the actual facts of each case and on reasoned judgment as to whether to limit or extend the existing law in light of the inner logic of the law and the needs of the time and place. This broad flexibility is more achievable with casuistic formulation, which lays down rules case by case, than it is with normatively stated law, which broadly declares general legal principles in the form of obligatory norms.[161]

C. The Literary Style of the Mishnah

Another characteristic of the Mishnah, which sets it apart as a book of laws, is its literary style. On the one hand, it is terse—*multum in parvo*—and on the other, it is simple and lucid. Brevity and clarity are the two basic requisites of all legal draftsmanship, and the Mishnah exemplifies them *par excellence*. Indeed, the literary style of the Mishnah still serves as a model for the Hebrew language generally and for *mishpat ivri* in particular.

Maimonides, describing how he decided to use the style of the Mishnah for his own code, stated:

> I also found it advisable not to compose it in the style of Scripture, since that sacred tongue is too limited for us now to express the laws in all their complexity. I also will not compose it in the language of the Talmud [Aramaic], because only a few of our people now understand it [Aramaic], and even those who are expert in the Talmud find many of its words strange and difficult. Instead, I will compose it in the style of the Mishnah, so that it will be easily understood by most people.[162]

VIII. THE *TOSEFTA*

An additional literary source of the *Halakhah* dating from the tannaitic period is the *Tosefta*. As previously mentioned, in addition to the Mishnah of R. Judah Ha-Nasi, there were other compilations of *mishnayot* that were

161. In Jabotinski v. Weizmann, 5 *P.D.* 801, 811 (1951), the President of the Court, Justice Zamora, stated:

> The power of statutory law, which speaks in normative rather than casuistic form, is that it creates vessels which can be filled with content that was not even in existence when the law was enacted.

Jewish law, however, preferred not to solve every new problem *a priori* but rather to seek the solution after the problem arises, since only then is it possible to perceive, after due and fair deliberation, both the general demands of the law and the requirements of the special circumstances of the specific case. *See also supra* pp. 950–957, 960–966.

162. *Sefer ha-Mizvot,* Introduction (ed. Rambam la-Am, Mosad ha-Rav Kook, Jerusalem, 1958, pp. i–ii). *See infra* pp. 1207–1210.

composed by Sages of his generation and the generations immediately preceding and following. Of all those compilations (some of which were still available during a portion of the amoraic period), the only one that has survived intact is the *Tosefta*. Parts of the other compilations have survived only to the extent that they are quoted in the Babylonian and Jerusalem Talmuds. Apparently, the *Tosefta* survived intact by virtue of its close connection with the Mishnah of R. Judah Ha-Nasi; as its name implies (*Tosefta* means "addition"), the *Tosefta* is an addition and supplement to the Mishnah.

Sometimes, the *Tosefta* explains a *mishnah* by quoting it, excerpt by excerpt, and explaining each quotation; and sometimes it gives reasons, by way of additional arguments or clarification, for the statements in a *mishnah*. Thus, a *mishnah* states:[163]

> Assessment [of damages] in money or the equivalent of money [must be made] before a court of law on the testimony of witnesses who are freemen and of the Jewish faith [lit. "sons of the Covenant"]. Women may sue and be sued for tortious injury. And the victim and the tortfeasor [must in certain cases] share the [burden of the] damages.

This short *mishnah* cryptically sets forth certain general rules of the law of torts upon which the *Tosefta* elaborates as follows:[164]

> "Assessment [of damages] in money":[165] We do not say, "Let the cow be taken as compensation for the cloak [which the cow damaged]" or "Let the cloak be taken as compensation for the cow [which tripped over the cloak and suffered injury]," but we make a monetary assessment of the damages.
>
> "Or the equivalent of money": This teaches that the court assesses only against real property [which is the security for the tortfeasor's obligation and is thus equal to money]; however, if the injured party seized [items of] personal property [of the tortfeasor], they are assessed for him in the presence of the court.
>
> "Before a court of law": This teaches that he [the tortfeasor] is not responsible [to pay for the damage] until he has been found liable by a court.
>
> "On the testimony of witnesses": This teaches that anything in the category of *kenas* [penalty] is not paid on [the basis of the defendant's] admission [of liability, but only on the evidence of witnesses].
>
> "Freemen and sons of the Covenant": This excludes gentiles, slaves, and persons ineligible to be witnesses.
>
> "Women may sue and be sued for tortious injury": Although Scripture uses the male gender in stating the law, females are also included [and have

163. M Bava Kamma 1:3.
164. *Tosefta* Bava Kamma 1:2–3.
165. The text quoted follows v.l. in *Tosefta*, ed. Zuckermandel.

the same legal rights and obligations as males in regard to torts committed by or against them].

"The victim and the tortfeasor [must in certain cases] share the [burden of the] damages": When half damages are paid. [In the case of an "innocuous" ox (*i.e.*, an ox that has not previously gored to an extent that the owner is on notice of its dangerousness) that gores, the owner of the goring ox is liable to pay only one-half of the damages, and thus the injured party suffers half the loss.]

This *Tosefta* illustrates the style of quoting phrases from a *mishnah* and explaining each one.[166]

Sometimes, as noted in the previous discussion of the Mishnah as a code,[167] the *Tosefta* sheds light on R. Judah Ha-Nasi's codificatory purpose by recording conflicting opinions as to laws that the Mishnah sets forth categorically, or by setting forth only an opinion contrary to the rule stated in the Mishnah.[168]

Sometimes, the *Tosefta* supplements the Mishnah with additional laws and even with entirely new subjects not contained in the Mishnah. Thus, a *mishnah* states:[169]

If one leaves produce in his fellow's charge, he [the bailee] may not touch it [*i.e.*, sell it] even if it spoils. Rabban Simeon b. Gamaliel says: "He may sell it under the supervision of a court because [in so doing] he is like one who restores lost property to its owner."

The *Tosefta*[170] states this rule and adds another:

If one leaves produce in his fellow's charge, he [the bailee] may not touch it even if it spoils. Therefore, the owner of the produce may declare it to be *terumah* and tithes for [produce he has in] another place.

Rabban Simeon b. Gamaliel says: "In the case of spoilage, he should sell it under the supervision of a court because [in so doing] he is like one who restores lost property to its owner."

In the succeeding paragraph in the *Tosefta*,[171] the same law is set forth in a different formulation with yet a further addition:

166. *See* Epstein, *Tannaim*, pp. 246, 248–249; H. Albeck, *Meḥkarim ba-Baraita u-va-Tosefta* [Studies in *Baraita* and *Tosefta*], p. 139.

167. *Supra* pp. 1058–1059.

168. *See, e.g.*, M Bava Batra 6:3 and *Tosefta* Bava Batra 6:5; *see also* Albeck, *supra* n. 166 at 160.

169. M Bava Meẓi'a 3:6.

170. *Tosefta* Bava Meẓi'a 3:7.

171. *Id.* 3:8.

> If one leaves produce in his fellow's charge and it rots, or wine and it goes sour, or oil and it becomes rancid, then even if they spoil, he [the bailee] may not touch them; this is the opinion of R. Meir. The Sages say: "They are to be converted into money under the supervision of a court; he is to sell them to others, but he may not sell them to himself [since he might then fix an unfairly low price]."

The last part of the paragraph is an addition to the *mishnah,* and the example as a whole reveals that at times the law of the Mishnah is quoted in the *Tosefta* in a slightly different form. Thus, where the Mishnah states: "even if it spoils," the *Tosefta* states: "produce . . . and it rots, or wine and it goes sour, or oil and it becomes rancid." Apparently, the law in the *Tosefta* came from a different source, *i.e.,* from a compilation of *mishnayot* of a different academy.

The *Tosefta* also contains laws that are not in the Mishnah at all. For example, the Mishnah[172] contains an interpretation of the text of the *ketubbah,* whereas the *Tosefta*[173] sets forth additional tannaitic interpretations of the *ketubbah* as well as of various other documents, such as pledge agreements.[174]

The *Tosefta* and the Mishnah also sometimes differ in sequence and arrangement. Occasionally, the chapters in a tractate of the *Tosefta* are not congruent with the chapters in the same tractate of the Mishnah. Sometimes, corresponding chapters or tractates do not set forth the laws in the same sequence. The reason for these differences is that the editor of the extant version of the *Tosefta* utilized an earlier compilation of the *Tosefta,* edited by R. Nehemiah, which was coordinated with a mishnaic compilation that predated the Mishnah of R. Judah Ha-Nasi.[175]

The redaction of the *Tosefta* should probably be dated to the generation immediately following R. Judah Ha-Nasi, *i.e.,* the transitional generation between the *tannaim* and the *amoraim*. Scholars do not agree on the identity of the redactor of the extant version of the *Tosefta.*[176]

172. M Ketubbot 4:6.

173. *Tosefta* Ketubbot 4:9–13.

174. *See* Albeck, *supra* n. 166 at 140–141.

175. Epstein, *Tannaim,* p. 242.

176. Some attribute the redaction of the *Tosefta* to R. Ḥiyya; *see* Epstein, *Tannaim,* pp. 242–246, 250–262. For details on the *Tosefta*—its compilation, its relation to the Mishnah, and the attitude of the two Talmuds to it—*see* Albeck, *supra* n. 21 at 51–78, 604–608. As to reliance on the *Tosefta* for determining the law to be applied in practice, *see* L. Ginzberg, *Geonica,* II, p. 328: "With regard to your question whether the *Tosefta* can properly be relied on, there is no overall answer because the *Tosefta, Torat Kohanim,* and *Sifrei,* [which] are designated in the Talmud as *baraitot,* sometimes state the accepted law and sometimes do not."

IX. SUMMARY

When the literary sources of Jewish law in the tannaitic period—particularly the Mishnah of R. Judah Ha-Nasi—were redacted, they became the authoritative source for the study of *Halakhah* and for the determination of the legal rules to be applied in practice. From that time onward, legal decisions were no longer reached on the basis of the Written Law of the Torah but rather on the basis of the law in the tannaitic sources—primarily the Mishnah, which became the authoritative code of Jewish law. The Written Law had been, and remained, the primary source of law from the standpoint of both importance and chronology, but only in the sense that the Written Law constituted the highest level of the legal system. For practical purposes, the literary sources of the tannaitic period were the sources used to ascertain and apply the law. Foremost among these sources was the Mishnah of R. Judah Ha-Nasi, which became the *Corpus Juris* of the *Halakhah*.[177]

177. While it is true that Biblical exegesis continued to develop in the amoraic period and that the *amoraim* considered themselves authorized to interpret the Written Law, interpretation in that period was actually not creative but integrative. *See supra* pp. 383–384.

Chapter 29

THE LITERARY SOURCES IN THE AMORAIC PERIOD

I. Introduction
   A. The Two Talmuds
   B. Some Preliminary Definitions
      1. *Amora*
      2. Talmud
      3. *Gemara*
II. The Leading *Amoraim* Listed by Generations
III. The Babylonian Talmud
   A. The Babylonian Diaspora
   B. The Teachings of the Babylonian *Amoraim* and the Contents of the Babylonian Talmud
   C. The Redaction and Completion of the Babylonian Talmud
   D. The *Savoraim*
   E. Compilation of the Talmud on Only Part of the Mishnah
IV. The Jerusalem Talmud
   A. Contents of the Jerusalem Talmud; Differences from the Babylonian Talmud
   B. The Redaction of the Jerusalem Talmud
V. The Literary-Legal Nature of the Talmud and the Place of the Talmud in the Jewish Legal System

I. INTRODUCTION

A. The Two Talmuds

The literary sources of Jewish law in the post-tannaitic period are the two Talmuds: the Jerusalem and the Babylonian. These two sources—and particularly the latter—which mainly contain the teachings of the *amoraim,* are to this day the most authoritative and important literary sources of Jewish law.

B. Some Preliminary Definitions

1. *AMORA*

The source of the name *amora* is the root *amor,* which means "to speak" and (in Aramaic) also means "to interpret" or "to translate." The

Sages who lived after the redaction of the Mishnah, beginning with the third century C.E., are called *amoraim* because they devoted themselves to interpreting and explicating the Mishnah.[1] The name *amora* also designates the *meturgeman*—one who stood beside the Sage at public lectures (known as *pirka*) and repeated the Sage's words to make them audible to the audience.[2]

2. TALMUD

"Talmud" has several meanings. Sometimes, it means "study," in contradistinction to conduct or action;[3] sometimes, it signifies the colloquy between *tannaim* on a specific law;[4] and it also has other meanings.[5] In the present discussion, the term is used in two of its senses: (1) the discussions of the Mishnah by the *amoraim* (in which case the word is written *"talmud"*—italicized and not capitalized), and (2) the name of the work that includes both the Mishnah and the amoraic discussions of the Mishnah (in which case it is written "Talmud"—capitalized but not italicized—as in "Jerusalem Talmud" and "Babylonian Talmud"). The second meaning is the generally recognized sense of "Talmud" in contemporary Hebrew.

1. *Arukh ha-Shalem,* I, p. 128, s.v. Amar; I.M. Guttmann, *Mafte'aḥ ha-Talmud,* III, p. 184, s.v. Amora.

2. *Arukh ha-Shalem, supra* n. 1; Guttmann, *supra* n. 1 at 182. Occasionally, more than one *meturgeman* was utilized if the audience was large. *See, e.g.,* TB Ketubbot 106a: "R. Huna would lecture with thirteen *amoraim,*" and Rashi, *ad loc.:* " . . . who would listen to him and make [his words] audible to the multitude, one on each side, and in the front and in the rear; they deployed themselves in many places because there were a great many people."

3. "Is *talmud* [*i.e.,* study] greater or is action greater?" *Sifrei,* Deuteronomy, Ekev, sec. 41 (ed. Finkelstein, pp. 84–86); TB Kiddushin 40b.

4. This is the sense of *talmud* in M Avot 4:13 ("R. Judah says: 'Be cautious in *talmud,* for an error in *talmud* is accounted as a deliberate transgression'") and *id.* 5:21 ("Fifteen [is the age] for *talmud*"). For examples of the *talmud* of the *tannaim, see* M Bava Kamma 2:5 (the colloquy between R. Tarfon and the Sages) and M Yadayim 4:3 (the colloquy among several *tannaim*).

5. Some scholars believe that midrash is also sometimes called *talmud;* W. Bacher, *Erkhei Midrash* [A Midrashic Dictionary], Tannaim, p. 136. *But see* H. Albeck, *Mavo la-Talmudim,* p. 3 n. 2, and pp. 3–7.

3. *GEMARA*

Scholars differ as to the etymology of the term *Gemara.* Some believe that it derives from the root *gamor* and signifies "completion," whereas others are of the opinion that it means "study." Still others believe that it means "tradition."[6] In the well-known incident of the Patriarch Hillel and the gentile who wanted to learn the whole Torah while standing on one leg, Hillel told him: "That which is hateful to you, do not do to your fellow. That is the whole Torah; the rest is commentary. Go and *gemor* [*i.e.,* study (or, complete) it]."[7] In current Hebrew, the *Gemara* denotes the studies, debates, and statements of the *amoraim.*

II. THE LEADING *AMORAIM* LISTED BY GENERATIONS

Before discussing the literary sources of the amoraic period, it is appropriate to list briefly by generation the halakhic Sages of this period.

The amoraic period in Babylonia lasted some three hundred years, from about 220 to 500 C.E. The amoraic period in the Land of Israel was shorter, lasting some two hundred years, from about 220 to 400 C.E.[8] The Babylonian period is usually divided into seven generations, and the period in the Land of Israel into five. The table on the following page lists some of the leading *amoraim* in each generation in the Land of Israel and in Babylonia.[9]

6. *See* H. Strack, *Introduction to the Talmud and Midrash,* Atheneum, New York, 1974, p. 5. According to some scholars, the term *gemara,* as referring to the discussion of the Mishnah by the *amoraim,* already appears in TB: "You have fixed it in *gemara*" (Eruvin 32b). *But see* Albeck, *supra* n. 5 at 577. In any event, the *geonim* used the term in that sense, such as in the phrase "the *Gemara* of the Land of Israel." *See* Strack, *supra;* Bacher, *Erkhei Midrash,* Amoraim, pp. 163–166; Albeck, *supra* n. 5 at 4–7, 599–601.

7. TB Shabbat 31a.

8. The shortness of the period in the Land of Israel was due to the difficult political and economic conditions there; *see* the discussion regarding TJ, *infra* pp. 1095–1098.

9. According to Albeck, *supra* n. 5 at 144–151. *See id.* at 669–681 for an alphabetical index of names of *amoraim.*

Leading *Amoraim,* 220 to 500 C.E.

	THE LAND OF ISRAEL	BABYLONIA
First Generation	R. Ḥanina b. Ḥama, R. Yannai, R. Hoshaiah (Oshaiah), R. Judah Nesi'a and Hillel (both grandchildren of R. Judah Ha-Nasi), R. Joshua b. Levi[10]	Rav, Samuel, Abuha de Samuel, Mar Ukva (exilarch), R. Assi, R. Kahana
Second Generation	R. Johanan, R. Simeon b. Lakish (Resh Lakish), R. Yose b. Ḥanina	R. Huna, R. Judah b. Ezekiel, R. Jeremiah b. Abba, R. Kahana II,[11] R. Hamnuna
Third Generation	R. Abbahu, R. Eleazar b. Pedat, R. Ammi, R. Assi, R. Zeira (Ze'eira), R. Samuel b. Naḥmani	R. Hamnuna, R. Zevid, R. Ḥisda, R. Zeira, Rabbah b. Naḥmani, R. Joseph, R. Naḥman b. Jacob, R. Sheshet, R. Jeremiah b. Abba, R. Safra, Ulla, Rabbah b.b. Ḥana, Rabbah b. R. Huna
Fourth Generation	R. Jeremiah, R. Jonah, R. Yose (Josah), R. Aḥa, R. Ḥaggai (Ḥagga), R. Yose b. Avin (b. R. Bun)	Abbaye, Rava, Rami b. Ḥama, R. Naḥman b. Isaac, R. Ada b. Ahavah, R. Dimmi, Ravin
Fifth Generation	R. Mana, R. Yose b. Avin, R. Hezekiah	R. Papa, R. Papi, R. Huna b. R. Joshua, Ravina
Sixth Generation		Ameimar, Mar Zutra, R. Ashi (redactor of the Talmud), R. Yeimar
Seventh Generation		R. Aḥa mi-Difti, Mar b. R. Ashi, Mereimar

The seventh generation is followed by a transitional period between the *amoraim* and the *savoraim.* At the beginning of that period, Ravina II, a disciple of Mereimar, completed the redaction of the Babylonian Talmud. At the end of the transitional period, R. Yose was one of the last to put the finishing touches on the compilation of the Talmud and was also one of the first *savoraim.*[12]

10. *See also supra* p. 1044 with regard to the transitional generation between the *tannaim* and *amoraim.*

11. In several generations in Babylonia, there were *amoraim* named R. Kahana.

12. *See infra* pp. 1093–1094.

III. THE BABYLONIAN TALMUD

A. The Babylonian Diaspora

The expulsions from Judea brought masses of Jews to Babylonia; some remained for generations, and others returned at various times to the Land of Israel. The Jewish settlement in Babylonia became known as the *golah* ("exile," "diaspora"),[13] and it appears that during most of that period there were more Jews in Babylonia than in any other country in the diaspora. There was a large Jewish settlement in Babylonia at about the time the Second Temple was destroyed,[14] and there is evidence that in some cities Jews constituted a significant portion of the population.[15] Knowledge of Torah was widespread in Babylonia from ancient times. A Talmudic tradition relates:[16]

> At the beginning, when the Torah had been forgotten in Israel, Ezra went up [to the Land of Israel] from Babylonia and established it; when it was again forgotten, Hillel went up from Babylonia and established it; when it was again forgotten, R. Ḥiyya and his sons went up and established it.

In addition to Hillel, who immigrated to the Land of Israel from Babylonia and presided over the Sanhedrin, there were other Babylonian Sages active in the Land of Israel, such as Nahum the Mede, who was a judge in Jerusalem.[17] In the period after the destruction of the Second Temple, there are references to a court esteemed as a "distinguished court"[18] in Nezivin, presided over by R. Judah b. Bathyra, as well as to R. Nathan, who brought *mishnayot* with him from Babylonia.[19] However, up to the beginning of the third century C.E., the major center of learning was in the Land of Israel. At that point, a severe political and economic crisis struck the Jews there; and the tax burden became oppressive, making the study and teaching of Torah

13. This name for the Jewish settlement in Babylonia appears in Jeremiah 29:4, 31; Ezekiel 1:1, 3:11, 15; and *Iggeret Rav Sherira Gaon* [Epistle of R. Sherira Gaon], ed. B.M. Lewin, p. 40, based on TB Rosh ha-Shanah 23b.

14. Josephus, *Antiquities*, XI, 5:2; XV, 3:1 (World Library, rev. ed., vol. IV, p. 159, vol. V, p. 488; Hebrew trans., ed. Schalit, pp. 14, 166).

15. *E.g.*, Maḥoza, *see* TB Yoma 11a and Rashi, *ad loc.*; TB Eruvin 6b.

16. TB Sukkah 20a, and *see* Rashi, *ad loc.* The transmitter of this tradition was R. Simeon b. Lakish (Resh Lakish), one of the greatest of the *amoraim* of the Land of Israel.

17. *Tosefta* Bava Batra 9:1; TB Ketubbot 105a; TJ Ketubbot 13:1, 68a. *See also* M Nazir 5:4; TB Avodah Zarah 7b; Albeck, *supra* n. 5 at 8–12.

18. TB Sanhedrin 32b.

19. *Iggeret Rav Sherira Gaon*, *supra* n. 13 at 41.

more difficult.[20] After Rav and Samuel (disciples of R. Judah Ha-Nasi)[21] returned to Babylonia, where the Jews fared better, Babylonia became the center of Jewish learning.

Rav and Samuel, who were among the first Babylonian *amoraim,* headed the two central Babylonian *yeshivot* (academies), Rav in Sura and Samuel in Nehardea. They brought about a complete metamorphosis in the status of Babylonia as a halakhic center—a center which, over a period of three hundred years, developed and created the Babylonian Talmud, the major and paramount literary source of Jewish law. In the course of time, the *yeshivah* of Sura moved to nearby Mata Meḥasya; and in the fourth generation of *amoraim,* in the time of Rava, it moved to Maḥoza, and after his death, to Naresh. After Samuel's death, the *yeshivah* of Nehardea moved to Pumbedita. The leading *amoraim* headed these *yeshivot,* which became the primary center for the study and teaching of Torah and *Halakhah,* first for the Babylonian Jews, and then for the Jews of other lands as well.

B. The Teachings of the Babylonian *Amoraim* and the Contents of the Babylonian Talmud

Rav and Samuel brought with them to Babylonia the Mishnah of their teacher R. Judah Ha-Nasi,[22] which became "Our Mishnah" (*matnitin*) to the Babylonian *amoraim.* This Mishnah became the code of Jewish law,[23] which the halakhic scholars studied, and it took precedence over all of the other *mishnayot,* which became *baraitot* (external material). The *amoraim* began to elucidate the Mishnah, explain its content and terminology, and reconcile and harmonize inconsistencies between various laws in the Mishnah, and between laws in the Mishnah and those in the *baraitot* and the *Tosefta.* The analytical depth of amoraic study and teaching, coupled with new problems arising in daily life, led to the expansion and development of the law and to the creation of new *memrot* (lit. "statements")—the term for laws originated by the *amoraim.*[24]

20. *See* Alon, *Toledot,* II, pp. 182ff., 254ff.; M. Avi-Yonah, *The Jews under Roman and Byzantine Rule,* Magnes Press, 1984, pp. 89ff.

21. Epstein, *Mavo,* pp. 166, 212. *See also* A. Hyman, *Toledot Tannaim va-Amoraim* [History of the *Tannaim* and *Amoraim*], p. 1123.

22. *See Kerem Ḥemed,* VII, Letter *tet,* pp. 158ff.; *but see* Albeck, *supra* n. 5 at 171.

23. *See supra* pp. 1057–1058. Although Rav, Samuel, and other *amoraim* occasionally relied on other traditions and in those instances did not rule in accordance with the Mishnah (*see* Epstein, *Mavo,* pp. 349ff.), they still considered the Mishnah as the *Corpus Juris* of the *Halakhah.*

24. " . . . *amoraim,* who are the authors of *memrot,*" *Arukh ha-Shalem,* s.v. Amar (I, p. 128). Some of the amoraic discussion is devoted to harmonizing *memrot* of *amoraim* with laws in the Mishnah.

The creative development of the *Halakhah* in the amoraic period was accomplished for the most part by the same method as in the tannaitic period, namely, through midrash—interpretation. The attitude of the *amoraim* to the authoritative nature and finality of the law as stated in the Mishnah was similar to the attitude of the *tannaim* to the unchallengeable authority of the Torah. Just as the *tannaim* developed the law by seeking out the inner meaning of the verses and passages of the Torah, so the *amoraim,* using the same principles and canons of interpretation, derived new laws by searching beneath the surface of the laws stated in the Mishnah.[25] In addition, like the earlier Sages, the *amoraim* continued to develop the halakhic system through legislation.[26] The Talmud, to a much greater extent than the Mishnah, also developed new principles and rules from "cases" and actual decisions rendered by the *amoraim.*[27] Many Talmudic laws were stated in the form of responsa, *i.e.,* a question was transmitted—sometimes in writing—from one place to another in Babylonia or even from the Land of Israel to Babylonia and vice versa, and the responsum was conveyed in reply.[28]

An additional literary-halakhic aspect of the Talmud is the inclusion of rules for decision making,[29] *i.e.,* principles governing how to determine the law when the Sages do not agree. Thus, "when R. Meir and R. Judah disagree, the law is in accordance with the view of R. Judah";[30] "when R. Judah and R. Yose disagree, the law is in accordance with the view of R. Yose";[31] "when R. Judah and R. Simeon disagree, the law is in accordance with the view of R. Judah";[32] and so forth.[33] The Talmud also includes many principles of interpretation and explication developed by the *amoraim* in the course of their interpretation of the *Halakhah* they had received.[34]

25. *See supra* pp. 407–414.

26. *See supra* pp. 622–642.

27. *See supra* pp. 954–957, 959–960, 964–966. *Ma'aseh* in both senses of the term (also called *uvda*) was an important legal source in the amoraic period: (1) as a ruling delivered in an actual case, and (2) as an incident involving the conduct of a recognized halakhic authority. In several places, the Talmud contains compilations of judicial decisions. *See, e.g.,* TB Bava Batra 29b–31a, 32b–34b; Ketubbot 84b–86a.

28. *See infra* pp. 1454–1456.

29. Such rules are also set forth in the Mishnah (*e.g.,* M Eduyyot 1:5), but for the most part they are contained in the Talmud. *See supra* p. 1060 n. 90.

30. TB Eruvin 46b.

31. *Id.*

32. *Id.*

33. A considerable number of the rules for decision making had already been established by the time of R. Judah Ha-Nasi; and, although it may not always be evident from the Mishnah itself, he relied on them in determining the normative law stated in the Mishnah. *See supra* p. 1060 and n. 90.

34. For further details, *see supra* pp. 407–408 and n. 23.

The Babylonian Talmud contains many teachings of the *amoraim* of the Land of Israel, just as many teachings of the Babylonian *amoraim* are recorded in the Jerusalem Talmud. *Amoraim* of each center went to the other to study, and returned bringing with them the doctrines of their teachers and colleagues.[35] This cross-fertilization is reflected not only in responsa from "here to there" and from "there to here" and in statements in the Babylonian Talmud of the views of Sages of the Land of Israel, and vice versa, but also in the large number of discussions of Babylonian *amoraim* focusing on statements of the *amoraim* of the Land of Israel (such as R. Johanan and Resh Lakish) and in the extensive deliberations of the *amoraim* in the Land of Israel focusing on statements of Babylonian *amoraim* (such as Rav, Samuel, R. Kahana, and R. Huna).[36]

The amoraic method of halakhic debate and deliberation (*havayot*),[37] and the comparison, consolidation, and harmonization of the various laws in the Mishnah, the *baraitot*, and the *Tosefta*, brought about a significant approach—both literary and substantive—that profoundly influenced the development of halakhic institutions and the methods of halakhic thought and reasoning. Our previous discussion has already referred to the rationalistic approach of the *amoraim* and to their endeavor to crystallize general principles concerning the legal sources of Jewish law, such as principles relating to legislative methodology, the legal effect of *ma'aseh*, and the creative power of legal reasoning.[38] This approach also found expression in the tendency to establish broad legal principles and formulate abstract theoretical concepts underlying related legal decisions and rules. The *amoraim* formulated many such principles and concepts, which generalize and explain numerous concrete-casuistic rules taught in the tannaitic period.[39]

35. *See, e.g.*, Albeck, *supra* n. 5 at 302 (Ulla), 352 (Ravin), and 358 (R. Dimmi). Because they were in the habit of leaving the Land of Israel to go to Babylonia, they were known as *neḥotei* ("those who go down").

36. Occasionally, the views of the *amoraim* of the Land of Israel were stated differently in TB than in TJ, and vice versa. *Compare, e.g.*, the statement of Rabbah b.b. Ḥana in the name of R. Johanan in TB Bava Batra 173b *with* that of R. Abbahu in the name of R. Johanan in TJ Bava Batra 10:8, 33a (10:14, 17d). For further details, *see* M. Elon, "He-Arev, ha-Ḥayyav ha-Ikkari ve-Ekron Ḥofesh ha-Hatna'ah be-Dinei Arvut ba-Mishpat ha-Ivri" [The Surety, the Principal Debtor, and the Principle of Freedom of Contract in the Jewish Law of Suretyship], *Proceedings of the Fourth International Congress of Jewish Studies*, 1967, I, pp. 197ff.

37. *See* TB Berakhot 20a ("the debates [*havayot*] of Rav and Samuel"); TB Sukkah 28a, Bava Batra 134a ("the debates [*havayot*] of Abbaye and Rava"). This phrase is the source of a common verb used to introduce discussions in the Talmud: *havi bah* ([so-and-so] discussed it); *havinan bah* (we discussed it). *See* Bacher, *supra* n. 6 at 178.

38. *Supra* pp. 505–533, 622–642, 960–964, 998–999.

39. *See* B. De Vries, *Toledot ha-Halakhah ha-Talmudit* [History of Talmudic *Halakhah*], pp. 142–156.

Examples of such principles and concepts include: *bererah* (that an event which has not yet occurred at the time of a transaction but does occur later can retroactively apply to the transaction); *asmakhta* (indication of the absence of a deliberate and unqualified intention to enter into a transaction); and *hazmanah milta* ("the dedication of an object is decisive," *e.g.*, the preparation of a shroud for a particular corpse prohibits the use of the shroud for any other purpose). The establishment of these abstract principles generated a reasoned jurisprudential analysis of the rules of Jewish law, and paved the way for methodologies of halakhic classification and nomenclature.

The Babylonian Talmud thus includes (besides *Aggadah*, ethics, and philosophical meditations) a vast and variegated mass of legal material: commentaries on and explanations of the Mishnah and tannaitic *Halakhah*, *memrot*, legislative enactments, customs, *ma'asim*, responsa, rules for decision making, canons of interpretation, and general legal principles distilled from various laws relating to a particular subject. In addition, the Talmud preserves a large part of the teachings and the laws of the previous periods: *baraitot*, statements, enactments, and *ma'asim*—all of which were transmitted by the *amoraim* and integrated into their debates and deliberations.

C. The Redaction and Completion of the Babylonian Talmud

The massive material in the Babylonian Talmud was not edited all at once; a careful analysis of its contents reveals that it is a collage of "many sources, strata from different periods and generations, different authors and editors and different *yeshivot* (academies)."[40] Each *yeshivah* taught the Talmud according to its own individual approach and style: "In Sura it was taught one way; in Nehardea another way."[41] Most scholars believe that the editing of the material in the Babylonian Talmud began at the height of the amoraic period:

> When we probe deeply into how R. Ashi and his successors edited the Talmud and we bear in mind that it was impossible for them to have remembered all the statements made by the previous Sages as well as the questions and answers, the problems and solutions, etc., of their predecessors, it becomes obvious that some topics had already been fully developed in the study halls. Thus, the students were completely familiar with any given statement by a particular *amora*. [They were] also [familiar with] any difference of opinion between *amoraim*, and [with] the questions and the answers provided in the previous generation; and these were associated by the students with the state-

40. Epstein, *Amoraim*, p. 12.
41. TB Gittin 35a.

ment itself, so that when they reviewed the statement, they also reviewed the entire manner in which the subject had previously been dealt with.[42]

The major redaction was done by R. Ashi and Ravina, who constituted "the end of instruction" (*sof hora'ah*).[43] Rashi explained:[44]

> Until their time, there was no orderly arrangement of the *Gemara;* rather, when a question was asked in the study hall concerning the rationale of a *mishnah* or concerning a case involving civil or religious law, everyone would give his own explanation. R. Ashi and Ravina arranged the amoraic statements handed down to them, put them in a set order according to the sequence of the tractates, each one near the appropriate and relevant *mishnah,* . . . and set it all down in the *Gemara.*

The redaction of the Talmud was accomplished by compiling and arranging the material studied in the *yeshivot* according to the sequence of the tractates of R. Judah Ha-Nasi's Mishnah. All the material relevant to each *mishnah,* including the debates and deliberations in the *yeshivot* and the pertinent *ma'asim* and *memrot,* was placed after the *mishnah* to which it pertained.

Maimonides summarized R. Ashi's role in editing the Babylonian Talmud as follows:[45]

> R. Ashi devoted himself to assembling them [the teachings of the Talmudic Sages]. He decided to arrange the statements of all those who lived after our saintly Master [R. Judah Ha-Nasi] in the same manner that our saintly Master had arranged the statements of all those who lived after Moses. He collected, clarified, and collated all the amoraic traditions, the names of their authors, and the pertinent analyses, explanations, and comments. His total knowledge [of the material] was made possible by his God-given qualities of patience, perseverance, and love of learning; and thus he redacted the Talmud.
>
> He set himself four goals:
>
> First and foremost, to explicate the Mishnah and all the different commentaries on those portions of the Mishnah that were not entirely definitive,

42. Frankel, *Mevo,* p. 47a, and *see also* Halevy, *Dorot,* II, pp. 480–482, 552; Albeck, *supra* n. 5 at 557–596, particularly 580 n. 6; A. Weiss, *Hithavut ha-Talmud bi-Shelemuto* [The Formulation of the Full Text of the Talmud], 1947; *id., Le-Ḥeker ha-Talmud* [Researching the Talmud], 1955 (various chapters); J. Kaplan, *The Redaction of the Babylonian Talmud,* 1933, p. 336.

43. TB Bava Meẓi'a 86a.

44. *Ad loc.,* s.v. Sof hora'ah.

45. *Commentary on the Mishnah,* Introduction, according to the Hebrew translation of J. Kafaḥ, *Mishnah im Perush Rabbenu Moshe ben Maimon, Seder Zera'im* [Mishnah with Maimonides' Commentary, Order of *Zera'im*], Jerusalem, 1963, pp. 34–35 (p. 19 in ed. without Arabic text).

> together with the points made by each commentator about the views of the others, and to determine which view is correct.
>
> Second, to decide which opinion in a *mishnah* recording conflicting opinions, or which opinion regarding the meaning of the *mishnah*, its implications, or the analogies to be properly drawn from it, is to be accepted as law.
>
> Third, [to compile] the new interpretations that the Sages of each generation had based on the Mishnah; to clarify the principles and implications which they had derived from these interpretations; to support the interpretations by the statements of the *tannaim* in the Mishnah on the basis of which the interpretations were derived . . . ; and [to include] the *gezerot* and *takkanot* enacted between R. Judah Ha-Nasi's time and his own.
>
> Fourth, [to offer] interpretations relevant to the subject matter of each point as appropriate.

According to some scholars, the Talmud was completed by Ravina II. An epistle of Sherira Gaon provides support for this view:[46]

> On Wednesday, the thirteenth day of Kislev in the year 811 [of the Seleucid era = 4260 A.M. = 499 C.E.],[47] Rabbana Avina b. R. Huna, known as Ravina, died; and with him came "the end of instruction (*sof hora'ah*)."

With the death of Ravina II, the amoraic period came to an end.[48]

D. The *Savoraim*

Even after the completion of the Talmud, various supplements and additions were inserted by the *savoraim*. The members of the generation following Ravina II, such as R. Raḥumi, R. Yose, and R. Aḥai of Bei-Ḥittim, constituted the first generation of *savoraim*; and their statements were recorded in the Talmud.[49]

The length of the savoraic period is a subject of dispute. Some scholars

46. *Iggeret Rav Sherira Gaon*, ed. B.M. Lewin, 1921 (Spanish recension), p. 95.

47. As to the accuracy of this date, *see id.*, ed.'s n. 5, and B.M. Lewin, "Rabbanan Savora'i ve-Talmudam" [The Savoraic Rabbis and Their Talmud], *Rabbi Kook Memorial Volume*, IV, pp. 148ff.

48. According to other scholars, the Talmud was completed by R. Yose, one of the last *amoraim* and of the first *savoraim*, who was the head of the *yeshivah* at Pumbedita and lived after Ravina. This opinion rests on another passage in *Iggeret Rav Sherira Gaon*, *supra* n. 46 at 97: "After him, R. Yose ruled, and his day witnessed the end of instruction and the Talmud was completed." *See also* S. Albeck, "Sof ha-Hora'ah ve-Aḥaronei ha-Amoraim" [The End of Instruction and the Last *Amoraim*], *Sinai*, Jubilee Volume, pp. 57–73; H. Albeck, "Sof ha-Hora'ah ve-Siyyum ha-Talmud" [The End of Instruction and the Completion of the Talmud], *Sinai*, *supra* at 73–79.

49. *Iggeret Rav Sherira Gaon*, *supra* n. 46 at 70, and *see id.*, ed.'s n. 1.

are of the opinion that R. Eina and R. Simona, who headed the *yeshivot* in Sura and Pumbedita, respectively, were the last of the *savoraim*, and that their death, approximately in the middle of the sixth century C.E., marks the end of the period.[50] Others believe that the savoraic period lasted to the end of the sixth century C.E.[51] Rabad,[52] author of *Sefer ha-Kabbalah* [The Book of Tradition], states that the savoraic period extended beyond the middle of the seventh century.[53]

The major literary activity of the *savoraim* consisted of supplementing the Babylonian Talmud. A number of Talmudic statements are explicitly attributed to various *savoraim*, especially of the first generation. Thus, Sherira Gaon states: "A number of the logical deductions included in the *Gemara* are those of the later authorities, such as R. Eina and R. Simona,"[54] and "they explained whatever had been left unclear."[55] These savoraic decisions and explanations were incorporated into the text of the Talmud. Also, a number of editorial refinements and rules for decision making are attributed to the *savoraim*.[56] Some scholars credit the *savoraim* with reducing the Mishnah and the Talmud to writing.[57] As late as the beginning of the geonic period, technical changes and additions were inserted into the Babylonian Talmud,[58] thus completing the final text.

E. Compilation of the Talmud on Only Part of the Mishnah

The Babylonian Talmud covers only thirty-six of the Mishnah's sixty-three tractates.[59] There is no Babylonian Talmud for the Order of *Zera'im* (except

50. H. Graetz, *History of the Jews*, JPS, 1894, III, pp. 5–7; Weiss, *Dor Dor ve-Doreshav*, IV, p. 5.

51. Halevy, *Dorot*, III, pp. 30–33; *see also id.* at 27ff.; Kaplan, *supra* n. 42 at 336.

52. Abraham ibn Daud ha-Levi (ca. 1110–1180), a Spanish scholar known as "the first Rabad."

53. "R. Mesharshia bar Taḥlifa passed away in 4449 [689 C.E.], and he was the last of the saboraic rabbis. Thus, there were five generations of saboraic rabbis over a period of 187 years." *Sefer ha-Qabbalah*, trans. and ed. G. Cohen, JPS, 1967, p. 45. *See also* Kaplan, *supra* n. 42 at 309, 335ff., for a discussion of the various sources and the accuracy of the dates.

54. *Iggeret Rav Sherira Gaon*, *supra* n. 46 at 71, citing the discussion at the beginning of TB Kiddushin as an example.

55. *Id.* at 69–70. *See also* Lewin, *supra* n. 47 at 186ff. (as published separately, pp. 42ff.).

56. *See* Halevy, *Dorot*, III, pp. 36ff.

57. *See supra* p. 227.

58. Frankel, *Mevo*, p. 47a: "The redaction [of the Talmud] continued all through the period of the Talmudic Sages who lived after R. Ashi, the period of the savoraic rabbis, and the first part of the geonic period." *See also id.* at 48b and, in greater detail, Lewin, *supra* n. 47.

59. Plus four of the seven chapters of Tractate *Tamid*. As to the reasons for this and as to why TB included parts of the Order of *Kodashim*, *see supra* p. 52 and n. 10.

for Tractate *Berakhot*), for the Order of *Tohorot* (except for Tractate *Niddah*), for some tractates in the Order of *Kodashim* (*Middot, Kinnim,* and part of *Tamid*), and for scattered tractates in other Orders. This selectivity is a striking demonstration of the close correlation between law in the books and law in action. The Order of *Zera'im,* for example, which, except for Tractate *Berakhot,* deals with laws relating to such matters as *pe'ah* (the corners of the fields to be left for the poor), *shevi'it* (the sabbatical year), *terumah* (the priestly tithe), other tithes, and firstfruits, was studied in Babylonia as an academic exercise, inasmuch as those laws have practical relevance only in the Land of Israel. Because the laws relating to these subjects were not applicable in the diaspora, they were not compiled in a final and definitive form.[60]

The same pattern even more strikingly characterizes the overwhelming majority of codificatory works after the completion of the Talmud. Alfasi, Asheri, and the authors of the *Turim* and *Shulḥan Arukh*[61] limited the scope of their codificatory writings to "the laws that apply at this time," *i.e.*, mainly to the laws in the Orders of *Mo'ed, Nashim,* and *Nezikin,* which constitute approximately half of the halakhic material covered by the Mishnah of R. Judah Ha-Nasi, and considerably less than the material included in the Babylonian Talmud. Maimonides aspired to restore the scope of the *Halakhah* to its ancient glory—as in the Mishnah—and included in his code (the *Mishneh Torah*) the entire *corpus juris* of Jewish law. His work, however, remains an isolated effort; both before and after him, codification has been limited to the portions of the law that have practical relevance.[62]

IV. THE JERUSALEM TALMUD

A. Contents of the Jerusalem Talmud; Differences from the Babylonian Talmud

Even after the redaction of the Mishnah of R. Judah Ha-Nasi, the compilation and editing of tannaitic teachings and laws continued in the Land of Israel for some time. R. Judah Ha-Nasi's contemporaries, as well as the members of the succeeding generation, and especially his leading disciples,

60. As to the coverage of *Kodashim* in TB, *see supra* n. 59. Later codificatory works did not generally cover *Kodashim, see infra. See also infra* p. 1098, as to the redaction of TJ.

61. Although Joseph Caro, the author of the *Shulḥan Arukh,* lived in the Land of Israel, he followed the example of most of the prior codifiers and did not codify the laws in the Order of *Zera'im,* even though halakhic literature was then beginning to deal once again with these laws. *See infra* pp. 1132–1133.

62. *See infra* pp. 1447–1451, 1491–1492, as to the further constriction of the legal areas dealt with in codes and responsa after the Emancipation.

edited compilations of different *mishnayot* (*e.g.*, the compilations of R. Oshaiah ha-Gadol, R. Ḥiyya, and Levi). However, the *amoraim* in the Land of Israel, like those in Babylonia, focused primarily on the study of R. Judah Ha-Nasi's Mishnah, which became the authoritative code of Jewish law. Like the Babylonian *amoraim*, the *amoraim* of the Land of Israel used the other mishnaic collections to clarify, explain, and interpret the Mishnah of R. Judah Ha-Nasi.

In the same manner that the Babylonian *amoraim* created and developed the Babylonian Talmud, the *amoraim* of the Land of Israel created and developed the Jerusalem Talmud, which includes all the literary categories contained in the Babylonian Talmud: interpretations and explanations of the Mishnah, *memrot*, *ma'asim*, responsa, legislative enactments, customs, rules for decision making, and canons of interpretation. It also contains many teachings and laws of previous periods quoted in the halakhic discussions of the *amoraim* of the Land of Israel. *Yeshivot* were established in various places in the Land of Israel, the major ones being in Tiberias, Sepphoris, Caesaria, and Lydda. As previously mentioned, the communication between the *amoraim* of Babylonia and those of the Land of Israel resulted in the introduction of many of the teachings of the Babylonian *amoraim* into the Jerusalem Talmud.

The literary and substantive differences between the Jerusalem and Babylonian Talmuds have been extensively studied by scholars. The literary differences are reflected particularly in the scope of the debates (which are much briefer in the Jerusalem Talmud) and in the language used (the Aramaic of the Jerusalem Talmud is different from that of the Babylonian Talmud). There are also important substantive differences in parallel passages of the two Talmuds. The texts of the same tannaitic and amoraic laws vary, and many discussions on the same subject follow different approaches and reach different conclusions. Sometimes, one of the Talmuds specifically points out the differences in text, interpretation, or conclusion between itself and the other Talmud.[63] These differences of approach also shed light

63. *See, e.g.*, TB Bava Kamma 27b with regard to the care a person must exercise in the public domain. The rule in TB is, "He should have looked where he was going"; but "this is what they say in the west [the Land of Israel]: 'People do not usually examine the road [while walking]'" (*see supra* pp. 411–413). Another example: TB limits the freedom of contract between surety and creditor, since it sees in an ordinary suretyship the taint of *asmakhta* (the absence of an unqualified intention on the part of the surety to pay, since the surety expects the debtor to pay the debt), and it therefore recognizes a special form of suretyship—the *arev kabbelan*, where the surety states to the creditor: "Give to him [the principal debtor] and I shall give to you"—pursuant to which the creditor may proceed against the surety directly without first exhausting his remedies against the principal debtor. TJ, however, treats every suretyship agreement like any other agreement, because it does not consider *asmakhta* to be a problem in a suretyship transaction. (There is no parallel in

on the historical, political, and social factors that influenced the development of various legal principles in the two centers.[64]

B. The Redaction of the Jerusalem Talmud

The Jerusalem Talmud, too, apparently underwent successive stages of composition. In Lieberman's view, Tractates *Bava Kamma, Bava Meẓi'a,* and *Bava Batra* were redacted in Caesaria,[65] approximately two generations before the other Orders and tractates.[66] Most of the Jerusalem Talmud was redacted in Tiberias. In the view of most scholars, the redaction took place at the beginning of the fifth century C.E., about two or three generations before the redaction of the Babylonian Talmud by R. Ashi.

The redaction of the Jerusalem Talmud is much inferior to that of the Babylonian Talmud. The difficult political conditions in the Land of Israel in the fifth century C.E. made it impossible for the Sages there to achieve an orderly and definitive redaction:

> Some of the statements, questions and answers, etc., were completely familiar to the students of the *yeshivah,* and the editors [fully] recorded them. Others were taken from notes that scholars and students had written down in an extremely terse kind of shorthand. . . . But the times were extremely harsh . . . , and who cannot recognize and understand that at such a grim period there is no time for arranging passage after passage properly . . . , each one in its appropriate place, and in particular [no time] for penetrating deeply into what the scholars and students only hinted at in their notes, or for expanding on what they had written very briefly solely for mnemonic purposes? It should not be surprising . . . that [the Jerusalem Talmud] is often so laconic that the greatest commentators labor in vain to discover its meaning.[67]

The character of the redaction, the political conditions, and factors internal to the Jewish community all worked against the widespread study of the

---

TJ to the concept of *asmakhta* in TB.) TJ therefore does not recognize the *arev kabbelan,* since TJ has no need for it; because TJ allows full freedom of contract, the creditor can stipulate with *any* surety that the debt may be collected directly from the surety without first proceeding against the principal debtor. *See* TB Bava Batra 173b; TJ Bava Batra 10:8, 33a (10:14, 17d). For further details, *see* Elon, *supra* n. 36 at 197ff.

64. *See, e.g.,* the doctrine of *dina de-malkhuta dina* ("the law of the land is law"), which originated and was operative in Babylonia and is entirely absent in TJ. For detailed discussion, *see supra* pp. 64–74. *See also infra* p. 1137 n. 129.

65. S. Lieberman, *Talmudah Shel Keisarin* [The Talmud of Caesaria], Jerusalem, 1931, (published in *Tarbiẓ* [supplement], II, book 4, pp. 9ff.).

66. *Id.* at 18ff.

67. Frankel, *Mevo,* p. 48a.

Jerusalem Talmud, which was considered less authoritative than the Babylonian Talmud. Pursuant to a principle established in a later period, Talmudic law may be ascertained from both the Babylonian and Jerusalem Talmuds, but in case of a conflict between them, the Babylonian Talmud is determinative.[68]

The Jerusalem Talmud was compiled on the first four Orders of the Mishnah—*Zera'im, Mo'ed, Nashim,* and *Nezikin*—and on the initial chapters of Tractate *Niddah.* As previously noted, there was no Babylonian Talmud compiled on *Zera'im,* most of which deals with laws applicable only in the Land of Israel. This Order, however, is covered in the Jerusalem Talmud because these laws had great practical relevance for life in the Land of Israel. The number of tractates covered by the Jerusalem Talmud is thirty-nine—three more than are covered by the Babylonian Talmud. Nevertheless, the Jerusalem Talmud, because of its terse style and its scant summaries of the halakhic debates, is only one-third the size of the Babylonian Talmud.

V. THE LITERARY-LEGAL NATURE OF THE TALMUD AND THE PLACE OF THE TALMUD IN THE JEWISH LEGAL SYSTEM

Scholars have raised a question with regard to the literary-legal nature of the Talmud that is similar to the question raised in connection with the Mishnah: Was the Talmud, in addition to being the authoritative expositor of the Mishnah, also intended to serve as a code of Jewish law?

At first glance, it is difficult to conceive of the Talmud as a code, if only on account of its unique arrangement and content. It consists mainly of questions, opinions, debates, *ma'asim,* and precedents. Only occasionally does it set forth categorical legal principles or rules for decision making. However, some scholars believe that although the Talmud may not have the appearance of a code in the contemporary sense of the term, it was in-

68. *See* Hai Gaon in *Teshuvot ha-Geonim* [Responsa of the *Geonim*], ed. S. Assaf, 1929, pp. 125–126; *Teshuvot ha-Geonim,* ed. Lyck, #46; Sherira Gaon in *Teshuvot ha-Geonim,* ed. Harkavy, #349, #434; Alfasi, Eruvin, end of #687; *Resp. Alfasi,* ed. Leiter, #14; *Resp. Rabbenu Tam, Sefer ha-Yashar,* ed. Rosenthal, #101, p. 210.

As to the actions taken by the Babylonian *geonim* to endow TB with binding authority, *see* Frankel, *Mevo,* pp. 46–47; L. Ginzberg, *Perushim,* I, Introduction, pp. 83ff.; M. Margaliot, *Ha-Ḥillukim she-bein Anshei Mizraḥ u-Venei Ereẓ Yisra'el* [The Differences between the People of the East and the Residents of the Land of Israel], 1938, Introduction. *See also supra* p. 42 and *infra* pp. 1130–1132.

tended to be a code from the very beginning and was actually used as such in its time. In the same way that the Mishnah came to be used as the binding code, so, according to Blau,[69] did the Talmud become the code that was meant to replace the Mishnah; and the *amoraim*, *savoraim*, and *geonim* were well versed in it. According to this view, the Mishnah remained the basis for the Talmud, but cases could be decided only on the basis of the laws set forth by the *amoraim* and not directly on the basis of the law as stated in the Mishnah. In contrast to this view, Ginzberg was of the opinion[70] that the Talmud was not originally meant to be a code; the Mishnah is the code, and the *Gemara* consists of texts and commentaries on the Mishnah.

Whether the Talmud was originally an independent book of laws or only a commentary, all agree that it was accepted as the sole authoritative source for the entire *corpus juris* of Jewish law. The major accomplishment of the *geonim* was to transform the Babylonian Talmud "from a book of texts and commentaries into the book of laws"[71] for the Jewish nation:

> The Talmud was the basis for all the answers to all the questions that were submitted to the *geonim* for decision in actual cases; it was the source for every legal decision and, through analogical reasoning from it, the answers to all life's problems were found in it.[72]

The completion of the Babylonian Talmud provided Jewish law with its most authoritative and essential source; all of the rules, principles, opinions, and statements included in it were given full and binding force.

Maimonides' Introduction to the *Mishneh Torah* states:[73]

> Everything in the Babylonian Talmud is binding on all Israel. Every town and country must follow the customs, obey the decrees, and carry out the enactments of the Talmudic Sages, because the entire Jewish people accepted everything contained in the Talmud. The Sages who adopted the enactments and decrees, instituted the practices, rendered the decisions, and derived the laws, constituted all or most of the Sages of Israel. It is they who received the tradition of the fundamentals of the entire Torah in unbroken succession going back to Moses, our teacher.

69. L. Blau, "Das Gesetzbuch des Maimonides Historisch Betrachtet" [A Historical View of Maimonides' Code], in *Moses Ben Maimon, Sein Leben, Seine Werke und Sein Einfluss* [Maimonides: His Life, Works, and Influence], Leipzig, 1914, II, pp. 334–335.

70. L. Ginzberg, *Geonica*, I, p. 73.

71. *Id.*

72. Assaf, *Geonim*, p. 147. *See also* references cited *supra* n. 68.

73. *Sefer ha-Madda*, ed. Rambam la-Am, Mosad ha-Rav Kook, 1957, p. 13. *See also Kesef Mishneh* to *MT*, Mamrim 2:1; *supra* pp. 267–271.

The law contained in the Talmud is the crystallization of the Oral Law; it became, together with the Written Law, part and parcel of a single integrated *corpus juris*:

> It [the Babylonian Talmud] spread throughout the entire Jewish people, who took it upon themselves to abide by it; the scholars of every generation publicly taught it, and the entire Jewish people accepted it. There may be neither additions to it nor subtractions from it.[74]

Just as there may be no addition to or subtraction from the Written Law,[75] so the accepted law of the Talmud is subject to neither addition nor subtraction. And just as Jewish law developed subsequent to the Written Law through interpretation, *ma'aseh,* and *sevarah,* which sought the inner meaning of the Written Law, and through legislation (either overtly by *takkanot* and *gezerot* or covertly by custom), so the continued development of post-Talmudic law—vast, dynamic, and comprehensive as it was—also took the path of revealing the innermost recesses of Talmudic law, as well as the path of legislation. The Talmud became the basis for all study and debate in all the areas of Jewish law. It is the starting point and the wellspring for the halakhic patterns of thought, modes of logical reasoning, forms of expression, building blocks, and creative methods during all subsequent periods.[76]

74. Abraham ibn Daud, *Sefer ha-Kabbalah,* in Neubauer, *Seder ha-Ḥakhamim,* p. 59. Maimonides, *Commentary on the Mishnah,* Introduction (Heb. trans., J. Kafaḥ, p. 25 in ed. of only Hebrew; p. 46 in ed. containing Arabic) similarly states: "There may be neither addition to it nor subtraction from it." *See* A.H. Freimann, "Darkhei ha-Ḥakikah be-Yisra'el" [The Methodology of Jewish Legislation], *Yavneh,* I (1946), 2–3, p. 41, for his conclusions as to the views of Rabad and Maimonides in regard to acceptance by the people. As to the concept of acceptance by the entire people, *see* Chief Rabbi A.I. Kook, *Eder ha-Yekar,* pp. 31ff.

75. Deuteronomy 4:2, 13:1. *See supra* pp. 496–502.

76. *See further supra* pp. 42, 1038–1039, and *infra* pp. 1157–1158, 1226–1229, 1387–1388, 1427 *et al.* For general discussion in English of the methodology and scope of the Talmud, *see* EJ, XV, pp. 750–779, and bibliography there.

Chapter 30

THE LITERARY SOURCES AND OTHER HALAKHIC LITERATURE IN THE POST-TALMUDIC PERIOD: INTRODUCTION

I. *Geonim, Rishonim,* and *Aḥaronim*
II. The Three Major Types of Literary Sources of the *Halakhah*; the Various Kinds of Other Halakhic Legal Literature

I. *GEONIM, RISHONIM,* AND *AḤARONIM*

As previously discussed,[1] the generally accepted subdivisions of the post-Talmudic period are: (1) the geonic period, which extended from the seventh century C.E. until the middle of the eleventh century, and (2) the rabbinic period, which is further subdivided into (a) the period of the *rishonim* (the early authorities—from the middle of the eleventh century to the sixteenth century), and (b) the period of the *aḥaronim* (the later authorities—sixteenth century and thereafter).[2] As has been noted,[3] all periods of Jewish law have distinguished between *rishonim* and *aḥaronim*. The distinction expresses one of the characteristics of the halakhic system: the earlier a scholar is in time, the higher is his status and the more he is venerated.[4] However, for quite some time now, these two terms have been used almost exclusively with reference to the halakhic authorities of the rabbinic period.

---

1. *Supra* pp. 42–44.

2. *See supra* p. 44, where the period starting at the end of the eighteenth century, *i.e.,* the beginning of the Emancipation, was classified as a separate period, in which Jewish juridical autonomy came to an end. As is pointed out there, that period itself consists of three subperiods. Distinguishing between these subperiods is significant not only for the history of *mishpat ivri* but also for the study of its literary sources. *See infra* pp. 1447–1452, 1491–1499.

3. *Supra* pp. 267–268.

4. This great veneration for earlier authorities did not prevent the establishment of the rule that "the law is in accordance with the views of the later authorities." *See* the detailed discussion, *supra* pp. 267–272.

II. THE THREE MAJOR TYPES OF LITERARY SOURCES OF THE *HALAKHAH;* THE VARIOUS KINDS OF OTHER HALAKHIC LEGAL LITERATURE

From the geonic period and throughout the rabbinic period to the present day, there have been three major types of literary sources of Jewish law:

1. Commentaries and novellae on the Mishnah and the Talmud[5] (and on the rest of Talmudic literature).[6]
2. Codificatory works.
3. Responsa.

Our present work focuses on these three major literary sources of the post-Talmudic period, but two additional types of literary sources and various types of reference works should also be mentioned. The additional literary sources are:

1. Collections of legal instruments—forms of documents that set out the relationships between the parties in various legal situations. Such instruments include bills of sale, promissory notes, leases, marriage contracts, receipts for payment of the *ketubbah,* etc.
2. Collections of *takkanot*—compilations of legislative enactments, particularly communal enactments, *i.e.,* legislation enacted by the representatives of the public rather than by the halakhic authorities.[7]

The types of reference works written in the post-Talmudic period are:

1. Guidebooks to the Talmud and to the *Halakhah* in general.
2. Encyclopedias.
3. Biographies of halakhic authorities.
4. Bibliographies.
5. Lexicons.
6. Books explaining abbreviations.
7. Textual variants.
8. Concordances.

5. There are also commentaries and novellae composed on other post-Talmudic commentaries and novellae, *e.g.,* on Rashi and *Tosafot; see infra* pp. 1127–1129.

6. The Biblical commentaries by the great *rishonim* and *aḥaronim*—such as Rashi, Naḥmanides, Rashbam, Mizraḥi, and (closer to our own day) commentaries such as *Ha'amek Davar* by Neẓiv—deserve mention among the post-Talmudic literary sources. The present work has from time to time made reference to such commentaries (*see, e.g.,* pp. 13 n. 36, 14 n. 38, 244–245, 610 n. 272), as well as to philosophical works, such as Judah Halevi's *Sefer ha-Kuzari,* Maimonides' *Guide for the Perplexed* and Albo's *Sefer ha-Ikkarim* [The Book of Basic Principles], which contain material relevant to the consideration of halakhic questions (*see, e.g.,* pp. 241, 1190 n. 28, 1230 n. 139). However, this part of our study treats only the literature directly dealing with Jewish law and halakhic research.

7. *See supra* pp. 679ff.

9. Source references, sayings, and aphorisms.
10. Scholarly research in *mishpat ivri.*

It should be emphasized that this division of post-Talmudic literature into three major types of literary sources on the one hand, and all the other types of literature on the other, is not necessarily congruent with the extent to which, under the criteria outlined at the beginning of this discussion of the literary sources of the Jewish law,[8] these various sources are recognized as authoritative. Thus, for example, the legal material found in certain compilations of enactments[9] and legal instruments[10] is recognized in the halakhic system as authoritative and binding, and material in various reference works has achieved a similar status.[11]

Nevertheless, the distinction made here between the major literary sources of the law and the other types of halakhic-legal literature commends itself as both useful and sound on two grounds: (a) unlike the three major types of literary sources, a considerable part of the other literature did not achieve recognition as an authoritative source within the halakhic system; and (b) these three major types of literary sources encompass the overwhelming majority of the post-Talmudic legal material recognized as authoritative, and constitute the direct continuation of the halakhic-legal creativity of earlier periods.

Even today, the Talmud remains the foremost literary source of Jewish law, as it has been throughout the post-Talmudic era. Around the Talmud, and as a continuation of it, a vast and rich literature was generated in each of the three major types of literary source. Each branch of this literature is reviewed in depth in the remaining chapters of this volume.

8. *Supra* pp. 1017–1019.

9. *E.g., The Book of Takkanot of the Community of the Exiles [from Castile] in Fez; see supra* pp. 806–809.

10. *E.g.,* forms of legal instruments written by Hai Gaon and Judah al-Bargeloni, etc. *See infra* pp. 1533–1540.

11. *E.g., Seder Tannaim va-Amoraim* [Chronicles of the *Tannaim* and *Amoraim*]; *Iggeret Rav Sherira Gaon* [Epistle of R. Sherira Gaon]; *Sefer Keritut* by Samson b. Isaac of Chinon (*see infra* pp. 1544–1545.); *Sefer ha-Kabbalah* [The Book of Tradition] by Rabad (*see infra* p. 1557); *He-Arukh* by Nathan b. Jehiel of Rome (*see infra* pp. 1564–1565).

Chapter 31

COMMENTARIES AND NOVELLAE

I. The Nature of Commentaries and Novellae
II. Commentaries and Novellae on the Mishnah
  A. The Geonic Period
  B. Maimonides' Commentary
  C. Obadiah of Bertinoro's Commentary
  D. *Tosafot Yom Tov* by Yom Tov Lipmann Heller
  E. *Melekhet Shelomo* by Solomon Adeni
  F. *Tiferet Yisra'el* by Israel Lipschutz
  G. Ḥanokh Albeck's Commentary
III. Commentaries and Novellae on Halakhic *Midrashim* and the *Tosefta*
  A. Halakhic *Midrashim*
    1. Rabad's Commentary on the *Sifra*
    2. Rabbenu Hillel's Commentary on the *Sifra* and the *Sifrei*
  B. The *Tosefta*
    1. *Ḥasdei David* by David Pardo
    2. *Tosefta ki-Feshutah* by Saul Lieberman
IV. Commentaries on the Babylonian Talmud
  A. The Geonic Period
  B. Rabbenu Hananel's Commentary
  C. Rabbenu Gershom Me'or Ha-Golah and His Students
  D. Rashi's Commentary on the Talmud
V. Novellae on the Babylonian Talmud
  A. The Ashkenazic Novellae; the Tosafists
    1. In General
    2. How the Novellae of the Tosafists Were Created
    3. The Leading Tosafists
      a. Samuel b. Meir (Rashbam)
      b. Jacob b. Meir (Rabbenu Tam)
      c. Isaac b. Samuel (Ri)
      d. Samson b. Abraham (Rash) of Sens
      e. Meir b. Baruch (Maharam) of Rothenburg
    4. Decisions and Responsa in the *Tosafot*
  B. The Sephardic Novellae/Commentaries
    1. Joseph ibn Migash (Ri Migash)
    2. Abraham b. David (Rabad) of Posquières
    3. Meir Abulafia (Ramah)
    4. Naḥmanides (Ramban)
    5. Solomon b. Abraham Adret (Rashba)
    6. Yom Tov Ishbili (Ritba)
    7. Nissim Gerondi (Ran)
    8. Menahem Meiri
    9. Beẓalel Ashkenazi
  C. Novellae in the Period of the *Aḥaronim*
    1. *Ḥiddushei Halakhot* by Samuel Eliezer Edels (Maharsha)
    2. *Penei Yehoshu'a* by Jacob Joshua Falk

VI. Commentaries and Novellae on the Jerusalem Talmud
A. The Jerusalem Talmud—Its Study and Use as a Basis for Legal Decisions
B. Solomon Sirillo's Commentary
C. *Sedeh Yehoshu'a* by Joshua Benveniste
D. Elijah of Fulda's Commentary and Novellae
E. David Fraenkel's Commentary and Novellae
F. Moses Margoliot's Commentary and Novellae
G. The Gaon of Vilna's Commentary

I. THE NATURE OF COMMENTARIES AND NOVELLAE

Commentaries and novellae are what their names indicate. Commentaries explain the Mishnah, the two Talmuds, and the other sources from the Talmudic period so as to facilitate their comprehension and study. Novellae trace the fundamental principles implicit in the Talmud and the other sources, reconcile inconsistencies posed by a comparison of the different sources, and, in the process, derive new interpretations and laws.[1]

It is not always possible to delineate clear boundaries between commentaries and novellae or to determine precisely the extent to which a particular work constitutes commentary or novellae. The other two major types of post-Talmudic literary sources—codes[2] and responsa[3]—also contain some commentary and novellae, which, however, are generally incidental to the declared and major objective of determining the law or responding to a specific request for a decision on a legal point. Works categorized as commentaries and novellae are primarily devoted to explanation and novel insights and interpretations.

Chronologically, the commentaries and novellae did not appear simultaneously. Commentaries came first, reaching their zenith in the eleventh century C.E.; novellae appeared subsequently and have continued to the present.

1. There are also commentaries and novellae written on commentaries and novellae of the post-Talmudic period; *see supra* p. 1102 n. 5. A commentary on a commentary is sometimes termed a supercommentary.

2. For the difference between two types of codes—books of *pesakim* and books of *halakhot*—*see infra* pp. 1139–1140. A substantial amount of commentary and novellae on the Talmud can be found in the commentaries on the codes; *see infra* pp. 1173ff. for details of the commentaries on the various codes. Some such works are essentially novellae, such as *Keẓot ha-Ḥoshen* and *Netivot ha-Mishpat* on Sh. Ar. ḤM; *see infra* pp. 1428–1429.

3. *See infra* pp. 1470, 1474, 1480, 1485, 1492.

II. COMMENTARIES AND NOVELLAE ON THE MISHNAH

A. The Geonic Period

As early as the geonic period, commentaries were written on all or part of the six Orders of the Mishnah, but only a few have survived.[4] Of those that are extant, one deserving special mention is the commentary on the Order of *Tohorot,* ascribed to Hai Gaon.[5]

B. Maimonides' Commentary

Maimonides wrote a commentary on all six Orders of the Mishnah, which he began at the age of twenty-three and completed when he was thirty.[6] The commentary was written in Arabic. It is known as *Sefer ha-Ma'or,*[7] and its various parts have been translated into Hebrew by several different translators.[8] In his Introduction,[9] Maimonides explained his purpose as follows:

> It [the commentary] will be highly valuable in four respects:
>
> First—we will clarify the correct interpretation of the Mishnah and the meaning of its language. [This is necessary] because if you ask even one of the greatest learned authorities for an explanation of a law in the Mishnah, he will not be able to tell you anything about it unless he remembers by heart [what] the Talmud [says] concerning that law, or he will tell you [to wait] "until we examine what they said in the Talmud about it"; and no one can remember the whole Talmud by heart. This is particularly so in the case of a

4. *See* Frankel, *Mishnah,* pp. 336–339; Albeck, *Mavo,* pp. 237–238.

5. The commentary was published, with glosses and notes, by J.N. Epstein, Berlin, 1924. *See also id.,* "Tashlum Perush ha-Geonim le-Tohorot" [Supplement to the Geonic Commentary on *Tohorot*], *Tarbiz,* XVI, pp. 71–134. In 1956, a commentary on the entire Mishnah by Rabbenu Nathan Av ha-Yeshivah ("Head of the Yeshivah" [in the Land of Israel]) was published from mss. (El ha-Mekorot, 13 vols.; the commentary is printed at the end of each volume of the Mishnah.) Rabbenu Nathan lived in the eleventh century, and his commentary is the earliest extant on all six Orders of the Mishnah. It was translated from the original Arabic into Hebrew by J. Kafaḥ, who wrote an introduction and added the notes of M.J.L. Zachs.

6. *See* the conclusion of his commentary on Tractate *Ukzin.*

7. *See* J. Kafaḥ, *Targum Perush ha-Mishnah la-Rambam* [Translation of Maimonides' *Commentary on the Mishnah*], *Zera'im,* Introduction, p. 20. The name *Sefer ha-Ma'or* was given to the work in a later period and is not mentioned in Maimonides' works or in ancient mss.

8. *See* Kafaḥ, *supra* n. 7, Introduction at 8ff.; Frankel, *Mishnah,* pp. 351–352. The most recent translation is that of Kafaḥ (Jerusalem, 1963 *et seq.*). The quotations below are from that translation, and the page citations are to the Hebrew edition.

9. Kafaḥ, *supra* n. 7 at 25–26.

> law of the Mishnah that the Talmud takes four or five pages to explain, because they [the Sages of the Talmud] go from subject to subject and multiply proofs, questions, and answers to such an extent that only an expert in the study [of Talmud] is able to summarize the real explanation of the *mishnah*. Even all this [will be the end of the difficulty] only if the law in question is not one of those for which the full explanation can be ascertained only by reviewing two or [even] three tractates.[10]
>
> Second—the legal rulings. Alongside of the explanation of each law, I inform you as to which opinion states the rule that must be followed in practice.[11]
>
> Third—it will serve as an introduction for the beginning student, who will learn from it how to analyze matters precisely and understand them. He will thus be as one who has encompassed the whole Talmud, which will help him greatly with whatever in the Talmud [he is studying].
>
> Fourth—it will serve to refresh the memory of one who has already studied, so that everything he has learned will be constantly accessible to him, and his studies will be fully organized.

In order to achieve these four objectives, Maimonides recognized the importance of conciseness:

> I will try to be as brief as possible without sacrificing clarity and accuracy, for our work is not intended to explain to stones, but rather to explain to intelligent [readers].[12]

Maimonides preceded his commentary with a detailed introduction that set out the history and sources of the *Halakhah*, at the end of which he devoted ten chapters to various matters related to the *tannaim* mentioned in the Mishnah.[13] In addition to the general introduction, Maimonides' commentary also includes introductions to various Orders and tractates.[14]

10. Occasionally, Maimonides interprets a *mishnah* differently than does the Talmud; *see* Frankel, *Mishnah*, pp. 343–345; Albeck, *Mavo*, p. 244 and the examples in n. 7, *ad loc. See also Tosafot Yom Tov*, M Shevi'it 4:10, and M Nazir 5:5, as quoted by Albeck, *supra*. However, when Maimonides' interpretation would lead to a different halakhic conclusion, as in M Shevi'it 4:10, his actual ruling follows the Talmud's interpretation.

11. Maimonides wrote a second edition of his commentary, which accounts for the occasional inconsistencies between his rulings in his commentary as we have it and those in his *Mishneh Torah*, which follows the later edition. Many inconsistencies and other difficulties are the result of errors in copying and translating. *See* Frankel, *Mishnah*, pp. 346–348; S. Lieberman, *Hilkhot ha-Yerushalmi le-Rabbenu Moshe ben Maimon* [Laws of TJ According to Maimonides], 1948, Introduction, pp. 5–15; Albeck, *Mavo*, pp. 244–245; Kafaḥ, *supra* n. 7, Introduction at 6, 15–16.

12. Kafaḥ, *supra* n. 7 at 26a.

13. For a précis of the Introduction, *see* Albeck, *Mavo*, pp. 243–244.

14. *See* Frankel, *Mishnah*, pp. 340–341; Albeck, *Mavo*, pp. 243–244.

C. Obadiah of Bertinoro's Commentary

The most widely accepted commentary on all six Orders of the Mishnah[15] is that of Obadiah, of the town of Bertinoro in Italy.[16] This commentary is printed in nearly all editions of the Mishnah. Obadiah of Bertinoro (Ra'ab or Rab, also known as Bartenura) based his commentary primarily on Rashi's commentary on the Mishnah as it appears in the Babylonian Talmud, and, for those tractates on which there is no Babylonian Talmud, on commentaries on the Mishnah by other *rishonim.* Occasionally, he also included explanations that he heard from his teacher or originated himself. His commentary explains clearly and simply every statement in the Mishnah that he felt needed clarification and, like the commentary of Maimonides, states the rule that is to be followed in practice.

D. *Tosafot Yom Tov* by Yom Tov Lipmann Heller

More than a century after Obadiah of Bertinoro, Yom Tov Lipmann Heller[17] composed "additions" (*tosafot*) to Obadiah's commentary,[18] and entitled them *Tosafot Yom Tov.* Heller's purpose was to compose a unique commentary on the Mishnah following the educational and dialectical methodology of his teacher, Judah Loew of Prague (Maharal), who rejected the method of Talmudic study prevalent in his time and taught his students to examine the text of the Mishnah thoroughly before embarking on the study of the Talmud and its commentaries. To this end, Maharal established "many groups who . . . study a chapter of the Mishnah daily and review it over and over again. [It is as though] this is [a command] from God, a law that must not be broken. Not only in Prague, from which Maharal sent forth his teaching, but also in other holy communities, both near and far, have the people taken it upon themselves to study [chapters of the Mishnah]."[19] To facilitate profound study of the Mishnah, a comprehensive and detailed commentary was required. As Heller put it:

> Indeed, this is my task: to examine the Mishnah meticulously [in order to discover] whether there is anything requiring clarification that Rabbi Oba-

15. For other commentaries on the Mishnah prior to Obadiah of Bertinoro, *see* Frankel, *Mishnah,* pp. 352–362; Albeck, *Mavo,* pp. 245–249.

16. 1445 (Italy)–ca. 1510 (Jerusalem). In 1486, he moved to the Land of Israel and settled in Jerusalem, where he served as rabbi of the city until his death. He did a great deal for the betterment of the internal conditions of the Jewish community there.

17. 1579 (Wallerstein, Bavaria)–1654 (Cracow). He served as rabbi in various communities in Bohemia, Austria, Russia, and Poland, and was one of the leaders of the Council of the Four Lands.

18. *See* the end of his Introduction to his commentary.

19. Introduction to Heller's commentary (beginning); *see also infra* pp. 1379–1382, 1403–1407, for a detailed description of the methodology of Maharal and Heller.

diah did not explain, or whether there is an inconsistency with a *mishnah* in another place upon which he did not comment . . . , or whether he himself is internally inconsistent or, even worse, inconsistent with a *mishnah*. I return to the *Gemara* and its commentary [*i.e.*, Rashi] and to *Tosafot* and the codificatory literature and their commentaries [to ascertain] whether I can find another interpretation or a solution to the inconsistency. I content myself with one interpretation and I will not prolong [my commentary] by citing various interpretations.[20]

Heller's intention was thus not just to explain the Mishnah, but to use an innovative comparative-critical method, in the manner of the Tosafists' novellae on the Talmud.[21] His commentary is, therefore, in the nature of novellae.[22] Using various editions of the Mishnah and the Talmud, Heller prepared a more accurate text of the Mishnah, which served as the basis for subsequent editions of the Mishnah.[23]

E. *Melekhet Shelomo* by Solomon Adeni

Another commentary of great importance is *Melekhet Shelomo* [The Work of Solomon], composed by Solomon Adeni.[24] He, too, examined all the extant commentaries and supplemented Obadiah of Bertinoro's work, occasionally disagreeing with Obadiah. In addition, he provided references to the Babylonian and Jerusalem Talmuds, to Maimonides, to the *Turim*, and to the works of *rishonim* who cited the Mishnah. He also made valuable comments on the text of the Mishnah based on various manuscripts to which he had access and on the glosses of earlier authorities, particularly Joseph Ashkenazi.[25]

F. *Tiferet Yisra'el* by Israel Lipschutz

Another important commentary on the Mishnah is *Tiferet Yisra'el* [The Glory of Israel], written by Israel Lipschutz.[26] Lipschutz devoted a great part

20. Introduction to Heller's commentary (toward the end).
21. *See infra* pp. 1118–1123.
22. His system of arriving at halakhic decisions also influenced the methodology of his interpretation of the Mishnah. *See infra* p. 1404.
23. *See* Epstein, *Mavo*, pp. 1281–1284; Albeck, *Mavo*, pp. 124–125.
24. 1567–ca. 1624. Adeni came to the Land of Israel from Yemen in his childhood and settled in Hebron. He was a disciple of Beẓalel Ashkenazi, the author of *Shittah Mekubbeẓet*. *See infra* pp. 1126–1127.
25. *See* Epstein, *Mavo*, pp. 1284, 1290; Albeck, *Mavo*, p. 252.
26. 1782–1861. He lived in Germany, in Dessau and Danzig.

of his commentary to explaining the language of the Mishnah and its difficult terms. For laws still applicable in practice, he indicated the accepted view, following the *Shulḥan Arukh* and its commentators. *Tiferet Yisra'el* includes introductory essays on individual Orders and on various tractates.[27]

G. Ḥanokh Albeck's Commentary

Of the comprehensive commentaries written in the twentieth century, particular mention should be made of that of Professor Ḥanokh Albeck.[28] It includes forewords to each of the Orders and introductions to all the tractates. In addition to a brief explanation of the text of the Mishnah, Albeck's commentary contains supplements (*hashlamot*) and addenda (*tosafot*) clarifying and explaining various laws discussed in the Mishnah.[29]

III. COMMENTARIES AND NOVELLAE ON HALAKHIC *MIDRASHIM* AND THE *TOSEFTA*

A. Halakhic *Midrashim*

Several *rishonim* composed commentaries on the *Mekhilta*, the *Sifra*, and the *Sifrei*; however, a large portion of these commentaries either have not survived or have not appeared in print. Our only knowledge of their existence is from quotations and references in various halakhic works.[30] The following are two early commentaries that are extant:

1. RABAD'S COMMENTARY ON THE *SIFRA*

Abraham b. David of Posquières (Rabad), the author of the critical glosses on Maimonides' *Mishneh Torah*,[31] was one of the greatest halakhic

27. For additional details on *Tiferet Yisra'el* and for other commentators on the Mishnah, *see* Frankel, *Mishnah*, p. 363; Albeck, *Mavo*, p. 253. For a comprehensive list of commentaries on the Mishnah, *see* Pinḥas ha-Kohen, *Oẓar ha-Be'urim ve-ha-Perushim* [A Thesaurus of Explanations and Commentaries], London, 1952, pp. 1–12. A helpful and widely used modern commentary is P. Kahati, *Mishnayot Mevo'arot*, 2nd ed., 12 vols., Heichal Shelomo, Tel Aviv, 1970.

28. Published in various editions since 1952. The vowel points to the text were done by H. Yalon according to various oral traditions, mss., and printed editions; the vowel points greatly facilitate the understanding of the text.

29. Detailed introductions to several tractates can also be found in Epstein, *Tannaim*, pp. 269–488. In recent times, the Mishnah has been translated into various languages, including German (by D.Z. Hoffmann *et al.*, Wiesbaden/Berlin, 1924–1933) and English (by H. Danby, Oxford, 1933, and P. Blackman, London, 1951–1956).

30. *See* S. Lieberman, *Tosefta ki-Feshutah, Zera'im*, Introduction, p. 14, nn. 2–4 and sources cited there.

31. Ca. 1120 (Narbonne)–1198. *See infra* pp. 1223–1225.

authorities. He composed many significant works in all categories of halakhic literature.[32] His commentary on the *Sifra* is the most important and comprehensive work on that halakhic *midrash*.[33]

2. RABBENU HILLEL'S COMMENTARY ON THE *SIFRA* AND THE *SIFREI*

Rabbenu Hillel b. Eliakim, who is known as Rabbi Hillel of Greece or Rabbenu Hillel of Rumania,[34] composed a detailed, comprehensive commentary on the *Sifra* and the *Sifrei*, which has recently been published on the basis of a number of manuscripts.[35]

In recent generations, and currently, various rabbis and scholars have published critical editions of halakhic *midrashim* on the basis of variant readings in printed editions and manuscripts, together with commentary and explications.[36]

B. The *Tosefta*

Commentaries devoted to the *Tosefta* began to appear mainly in the period of the *aḥaronim*,[37] and even of these, a goodly number have not survived.[38] The following two commentaries are considered to be classics in the field:

32. As to Rabad's Talmud commentaries and novellae, *see infra* pp. 1123–1124. As to his responsa, *see* Appendix C. As to his codificatory work, *see infra* pp. 1173–1174, 1223–1225. Rabad also wrote commentaries on the Mishnah, of which the commentaries on Tractates *Eduyyot* and *Kinnim* are extant; they are printed in regular editions of the Talmud. For Rabad's life and work, *see* I. Twersky, *Rabad of Posquières*, JPS, 1980.

33. Published by I.H. Weiss, Vienna, 1862; *see* his Introduction, pp. VII–VIII. Rabad also wrote a commentary on the *Sifrei* that is referred to in various other commentaries on the *Sifrei* but has not survived.

34. Rabbenu Hillel lived in the twelfth century; very little is known about his life. *See* S. Koliditzky, *Sifra im Perush Rabbenu Hillel* [*Sifra* with the Commentary of Rabbenu Hillel], 1948, Introduction; *id.*, *Sifrei im Perush Rabbenu Hillel*, 1961, Introduction.

35. *See supra* n. 34. For other commentaries on the halakhic *midrashim*, *see* M. Kasher, *Sarei ha-Elef*, 1959, pp. 4–8. A comprehensive commentary on the *Sifrei* on Numbers and Deuteronomy was written by Naftali Ẓevi Judah Berlin (Neẓiv), the head of the renowned *yeshivah* of Volozhyn. Another extensive commentary is that of Meir Leibush Malbim on the *Mekhilta*, the *Sifra*, and the *Sifrei* (Numbers and Deuteronomy). It reflects Malbim's unique style of interpretation (as to which *see supra* p. 308) and is printed together with his commentary on the Torah.

36. For details as to the halakhic *midrashim*, *see supra* pp. 1047–1049. A critical edition of the *Mekhilta de-R. Ishmael* has an English translation of the text: J.Z. Lauterbach, *Mekilta de-Rabbi Ishmael* (3 vols. including Introduction and notes), JPS, 1933–1935.

37. At least one of the *rishonim* wrote a commentary on part of the *Tosefta*. *See* S. Lieberman, Preface to *Ḥasdei David*, Part IV, Jerusalem, 1970, and *corrigenda* and *addenda* in *Tashlum Tosefta*, pp. 64–65 (*see infra* n. 43), where Lieberman refers to a commentary on *Tosefta* Tohorot by Ibn Sahula, a contemporary of Rashba (*see also* Lieberman, *Marx Jubilee*

1. *ḤASDEI DAVID* BY DAVID PARDO

David b. Jacob Pardo was a leading halakhic authority in the eighteenth century in Turkey and the Land of Israel.[39] He composed important commentaries on the Mishnah, the *Tosefta*, the *Sifrei*, and various Talmudic topics, as well as other works.[40] *Ḥasdei David* is the classic commentary on the *Tosefta*. As a commentator of our own time has put it:

> The rabbi [*i.e.*, Rabbi David Pardo] did not neglect anything, great or small, but discussed every matter extensively and in depth, simply and with good sense, in the context of [a comprehensive inquiry into] the entire field of Torah literature. Even with all of the other works [on the *Tosefta*] that have been written to the present day, one cannot properly study the *Tosefta* without studying what he had to say. Examine it and examine it again, for it contains everything.[41]

Ḥasdei David covers the entire *Tosefta*; the first part (on the Orders of *Zera'im*, *Mo'ed*, and *Nashim*) and the second part (on the Order of *Nezikin*) were published in the author's lifetime. The third part (on the Order of *Kodashim*) was published toward the end of the nineteenth century, and the fourth part (on the Order of *Tohorot*) was published in 1970, 1971, and 1977 in Jerusalem.[42]

2. *TOSEFTA KI-FESHUTAH* BY SAUL LIEBERMAN

Saul Lieberman (1898–1984), a leading Talmudic scholar, published an edition of the *Tosefta* that includes the text, according to variant readings in printed editions and manuscripts, together with *Masoret ha-Tosefta*, in which (in the style of the *Masoret ha-Shas* on the Talmud) he indicates the

---

Volume, p. 292ff., as quoted in *Tashlum Tosefta*). In his preface to *Ḥasdei David*, Lieberman corrected the statement he had made in his Introduction to *Tosefta* Zera'im, p. 14, that no commentary on the *Tosefta* by any of the *rishonim* is known.

38. *E.g.*, the commentaries of Abraham Yakhini in the seventeenth century and Isaiah Berlin in the eighteenth. *See* Lieberman, *supra* n. 37.

39. Ca. 1710 (Venice)–ca. 1792 (Jerusalem). He served as rabbi in various communities outside the Land of Israel; and when he settled in Jerusalem, he was chosen as the head of the *yeshivah* Ḥesed le-Avraham u-Vinyan Shelomo. *See* A.L. Frumkin, *Toledot Ḥakhmei Yerushalayim* [Biographies of the Scholars of Jerusalem], III, pp. 95–98; M. Benayahu, *Rabbi Ḥayyim Yosef David Azulai*, II, pp. 357–360.

40. *See* Frumkin and Benayahu, *supra* n. 39.

41. S. Lieberman, Preface to *Ḥasdei David*, Part IV.

42. Vol. 1 on Tractates *Kelim* and *Ahilot*; vol. 2 on Tractates *Nega'im*, *Parah*, and *Niddah*; vol. 3 on Tractates *Mikva'ot*, *Tohorot*, *Makhshirim*, *Zavim*, *Yadayim*, and *Tevul Yom*. It should be noted that the Vilna-Romm edition of the *Tosefta* includes an abridgement of the *Ḥasdei David* commentary that is not always faithful to the original. The original *Ḥasdei David* should therefore always be consulted, as Lieberman has pointed out. *See Tosefta ki-Feshutah*, I, Introduction, p. 16 n. 10.

other sources in which the paragraph referred to appears, and a brief explanatory commentary.[43] He published a larger, detailed commentary in the companion volumes, which are called *Tosefta ki-Feshutah* [The *Tosefta* According to Its Plain Meaning]. This work exhaustively considers all Talmudic and post-Talmudic literature relevant to each point discussed, and explains the *Tosefta* on the basis of meticulous textual study of the laws it sets forth. The commentary is thus extremely valuable, not only for an understanding of the particular part of the *Tosefta* under discussion but also for a general overview of the subject as dealt with throughout rabbinic literature. Lieberman did not succeed in finishing his commentary on the entire *Tosefta*,[44] and part of the work is being published posthumously.[45]

IV. COMMENTARIES ON THE BABYLONIAN TALMUD

A. The Geonic Period

The first commentaries in the geonic period were not comprehensive commentaries on the Talmud but were confined mainly to explaining difficult words and expressions. They were generally responses to inquiries from outside Babylonia:

> The *geonim* directed their commentaries mainly to those outside the *yeshivah*—more precisely, to people in other countries. The Babylonian Jews themselves had very little need for commentaries on the Talmud, for they still spoke the language of the Talmud. Hai Gaon, in his explanation of various Talmudic terms, states: "This is known in Babylonia even by women and children." Aramaic was spoken by them until the end of the geonic period. For the scholars and students of the ancient *yeshivot* [in Babylonia], the mode of life described in the Talmud was not something out of the distant past but a reflection of their own experience.

43. A critical edition of the *Tosefta*, with v.l. according to various mss., was published by M.S. Zuckermandel in 1881/1882 and has become accepted as the standard text. A second edition, including *Tashlum Tosefta* by S. Lieberman, was published in 1938.

44. The following have been published: *Tosefta Zera'im* (1955), *Mo'ed* (1962), *Nashim* (Tractates *Yevamot, Ketubbot, Nedarim*, and *Nazir*, 1967; Tractates *Sotah, Gittin*, and *Kiddushin*, 1973), *Nezikin* (Tractates *Bava Kamma, Bava Meẓi'a*, and *Bava Batra*, 1988), accompanied in each instance by *Tosefta ki-Feshutah*, comprising ten parts in all. A supplement with corrections and additions to *Tosefta ki-Feshutah*, Mo'ed, appeared in 1962. In 1938/1939, Lieberman published a commentary on the entire *Tosefta*, called *Tosefet Rishonim*, in which he compiled interpretations and explanations of *Tosefta* texts scattered through works of *rishonim*.

45. Another extensive contemporary commentary on the *Tosefta* is *Ḥazon Yeḥezkel* by Y. Abramsky (1886–1976), one of the foremost halakhic authorities of the twentieth century. This commentary covers, to the date of the present work, the Orders of *Zera'im, Mo'ed, Nashim, Nezikin*, and *Kodashim*.

> The Talmudic tradition lived on in the Babylonian *yeshivot* for hundreds of years after [the Talmud's] completion, even though a new and transformed world had already come into existence outside the walls of the academy. Thus, Babylonian scholars, generally speaking, had no need for a commentary on the Talmud. The Talmudic concepts were familiar to them; only occasionally did an unfamiliar word in the Talmud require explanation, or a forgotten concept require new definition. . . .
>
> We see the opposite in the Jewish diasporas distant from the Babylonian center. To them, the Talmud was a closed book. Its language was strange and required explanation; the Talmudic mode of discussion was also foreign and not understood. At that time, even distinguished scholars could stumble over run-of-the-mill Talmudic passages that, thanks to Rashi's commentary, are understood today by a beginning student.[46]

Indeed, scholars outside Babylonia turned to the Babylonian *geonim* with requests to explain particular words and legal concepts, as well as the content of Talmudic passages.

The geonic commentaries on the Talmud have reached us in a fragmented state; they are found in the thousands of responsa by the *geonim* to questions asked of them, in the order they were asked, and not according to the order of the tractates. Although they would sometimes explicate full Talmudic passages in minute detail, the explanations were not arranged according to the Talmudic passages themselves and were thus not readily accessible. In recent times, the geonic commentaries have been collected and arranged according to the order of the Talmudic tractates by Benjamin Menashe Lewin in *Oẓar ha-Geonim* [A Geonic Treasury], a thesaurus of the geonic responsa and commentaries. This work covers a substantial number of the Talmudic tractates but has not yet been completed for the entire Talmud.[47]

B. Rabbenu Hananel's Commentary

Over the course of time, Talmudic commentary evolved from translation of terms and clarification of legal concepts to comprehensive commentary on the substance of the Talmudic discussions.

46. Assaf, *Geonim*, p. 137.

47. Lewin published only twelve volumes, from Tractate *Berakhot* through *Bava Kamma* (and a part of *Bava Meẓi'a*), and since his death in 1944 this major project has not been continued except for Tractate *Sanhedrin*, by H. Z. Taubes, which appeared in 1967. *Oẓar ha-Geonim* includes a separate section of geonic responsa in the sequence of the Talmudic tractates (*see infra* pp. 1472–1473), as well as other halakhic material from the period; *see infra* n. 50. A. Kimmelman, "Luaḥ Ezer le-Ferushim mi-Tekufat ha-Geonim (me-Ereẓ Yisra'el, Bavel, ve-Kairouan)" [Citator to the Commentaries of the Geonic Period (in the Land of Israel, Babylonia, and Kairouan)], *Shenaton*, XI-XII (1984–1986), pp. 463–564, is quite helpful for locating geonic commentaries on the Bible, the Mishnah, and the Talmud.

The first commentary of the latter type was written at the end of the geonic period, not in Babylonia but in North Africa. It was composed in the first half of the eleventh century by Rabbenu Hananel b. Ḥushiel b. Elhanan. Ḥushiel was a halakhic authority in southern Italy, who moved to Kairouan in North Africa.[48] After his death, his position as head of the *yeshivah* there was filled by his son Rabbenu Hananel, together with his colleague Nissim b. Jacob, known as Nissim Gaon.[49]

Rabbenu Hananel made extensive use of the various commentaries of the Babylonian *geonim* and also referred frequently to the Jerusalem Talmud. His commentary is clear and straightforward; it does not explain the Talmudic discussion step by step but rather gives a summary of its content, focuses on its difficult parts, and omits what seemed clear. Rabbenu Hananel attempted especially to determine the correct text of the Talmud, and for this purpose he made use of early manuscripts. In addition to providing commentary, an important objective of Rabbenu Hananel was to state the governing law, which he frequently did at the end of his comments on the problem under discussion. It is probably for this reason that his commentary covers only the parts of the Talmud dealing with laws relevant to practical conduct—the Orders of *Mo'ed, Nashim,* and *Nezikin,* and a few other tractates from the remaining Orders that cover matters with practical relevance (such as Tractate *Berakhot* in the Order of *Zera'im* and Tractate *Ḥullin* in the Order of *Kodashim*).[50]

C. Rabbenu Gershom Me'or ha-Golah and His Students

Talmudic commentary reached its zenith not in Babylonia, where the Talmud was created and developed, nor in the centers attached to Babylonia by political, cultural, and commercial ties (such as the North African center), which received their instruction directly from the Babylonian *geonim,* but rather in Germany and France.

48. According to Rabad (*Sefer ha-Qabbalah,* trans. and ed. G. Cohen, JPS, 1967, pp. 63–64), Ḥushiel was one of the "four captives" who left southern Italy by sea and were captured by pirates. He was ransomed by the Jewish community of Kairouan. However, from a letter of Ḥushiel discovered in the Cairo *Genizah,* it appears that he did not come to Kairouan as a captive but of his own free will. *See* Margaliot, *Sefer Hilkhot ha-Nagid,* Jerusalem, 1962, pp. 6–7, and sources cited, *ad loc. See also id.* at 61–62.

49. As to Nissim Gaon, *see* S. Abramson, *Rav Nissim Gaon, Ḥamishah Sefarim* [R. Nissim Gaon, Five Books], Jerusalem, 1965, Introduction, pp. 17ff.

50. Rabbenu Hananel's commentary to some of the tractates of *Mo'ed* and *Nezikin* has been printed in the margin of the pages of the Talmud in ed. Vilna-Romm and other editions that followed it. In *Oẓar ha-Geonim,* his commentary to Tractate *Berakhot* and to the tractates from *Yevamot* to *Bava Kamma,* which B.M. Lewin compiled from books of *rishonim* and mss. fragments, appears as a separate section. As to citation of TJ by Rabbenu Hananel, *see infra* p. 1132.

At the end of the tenth and the beginning of the eleventh centuries C.E., a center of Jewish learning developed in Germany. Rabbenu Gershom Me'or ha-Golah ("The Light of the Exile"), the leading German halakhic authority,[51] had many students, through whom many of his Talmudic commentaries have reached us.[52] His outstanding students succeeded him and headed the *yeshivot* at Worms and Mainz; two such students were Jacob b. Yakar of Worms and Isaac b. Judah of Mainz.

D. Rashi's Commentary on the Talmud[53]

Jacob b. Yakar[54] and Isaac b. Judah raised a disciple who was to become one of the greatest authorities on the *Halakhah* and the foremost explicator of Judaism in general—Solomon b. Isaac (Solomon Yiẓḥaki), known as Rashi.[55]

Rashi's great accomplishments are his commentaries on the Bible and on the Babylonian Talmud. By virtue of his Talmudic commentary, the Babylonian Talmud has become a book studied by young and old, by people to whom it is an avocation as well as by scholars for whom such study is their main vocation. The wonderful artistry in Rashi's commentary on the Talmud is reflected in his ability to integrate his explanation into the Talmudic discussion itself; his comments so well fit the discussion that they seem to be part of it. His comments are brief and to the point, his language is precise and clear, and he guides the student through the most complex discussions with a steady hand and with remarkable ease. As a result, even a neophyte in the study of the Talmud is greatly helped by Rashi's commentary, which is also very helpful to accomplished scholars. This is what makes Rashi's commentary unique among all the Talmudic commentaries ever written.

Rashi's commentary has become an inseparable part of the Talmud, and this fact has given him a decisive influence on the responsa and the codificatory literature. Because all three of the major types of halakhic literature are based on the Talmud, his commentary, which made the Talmud

51. As to Rabbenu Gershom, *see further supra* pp. 783–786.

52. Compilations of commentaries by Rabbenu Gershom on only a few tractates are extant: *Ta'anit, Bava Batra,* and a few tractates in *Kodashim;* they are printed in the Vilna-Romm edition of the Talmud. However, most of his commentary has reached us by way of the Talmud commentary of Rashi, a disciple of his disciples.

53. For Rashi's biography and activities, *see* E.M. Lipschuetz, *R. Shelomo Yiẓḥaki* (in E.M. Lipschuetz, *Ketavim,* I, 1947, and republished as a separate volume by Mosad ha-Rav Kook, 1966). *See id.* at 19 n. 1 for additional source references.

54. After Jacob b. Yakar's death, Isaac ha-Levi ("Segan Leviyyah") headed the *yeshivah* at Worms, and Rashi stayed on as a student. Later, Rashi attended the *yeshivah* at Mainz, which was headed by Isaac b. Judah.

55. 1040 (Troyes, northern France)–1105. He is buried in Worms, southern Germany.

an open book for all, necessarily influenced the other types of halakhic literature as well.

The genesis of Rashi's commentary is noteworthy. Students would record their teachers' statements and comments in notebooks (*kunteres*; plural, *kuntresim*). Rashi recorded Jacob b. Yakar's comments on a number of Talmudic tractates in this manner. When Rashi moved to Mainz, he added the *kunteres* of Mainz to the one he brought with him from Worms. Various *kuntresim* based on Rabbenu Gershom's commentary circulated in the *yeshivot,* and every student would add his own notes of what he had heard from his teacher. Rashi edited, adapted, perfected, and organized these *kuntresim,* and so evolved his commentary on the Talmud.[56] As stated, Rashi's commentary includes many of his teachers' comments, which were based on Rabbenu Gershom's commentary; but those comments were fragmentary and disjointed, and Rashi's great skill succeeded in transforming them into a complete and coherent work suitable for use by everyone. The commentary on the Talmud by Rashi that we possess is generally the third version, which is the best. For some tractates, the second version, and sometimes even the first version, has survived. For some tractates, Rashi's commentary is incomplete.[57]

Rashi made clear in his commentary what he believed to be the accurate reading of the text, but he refrained from correcting the text itself. His students and their students after them inserted the text as determined by Rashi into the body of the Talmud itself, and therefore it is sometimes difficult to distinguish between the earlier text of the Talmud and the text as corrected by Rashi.[58]

Rashi's commentary has been accepted as the classic commentary on the Talmud. All previous commentaries have been relegated to a secondary position, and no one since Rashi has succeeded in composing as comprehensive and masterful a commentary on the entire Talmud. Beginning with the first printing of the Talmud, Rashi's commentary has always accompanied the Talmudic text on the inside margin of every page.[59]

56. On this account, the Tosafists referred to Rashi's commentary as "*kunteres*"; and when they cited it they usually wrote, "*Kunteres* commented. . . . "

57. Judah b. Nathan (Riban), Rashi's son-in-law, completed the commentary on Tractate *Makkot,* from 19b. Samuel b. Meir (Rashbam), Rashi's grandson, completed the commentary on Tractate *Bava Batra,* from 29a. Rashi's commentaries on Tractates *Nedarim, Nazir,* and *Me'ilah,* as well as on the tenth chapter of *Pesaḥim,* are first versions.

58. Rabbenu Tam objected strenuously to the insertion of Rashi's readings into the Talmudic text itself—a step from which Rashi himself refrained. *See* Rabbenu Tam's Introduction to his *Sefer ha-Yashar,* ed. S. Schlesinger, Jerusalem, 1959, p. 9, and *see* Urbach, *Tosafot,* p. 528.

59. The name Rashi has been popularly seen as an acronym for **Ra***bban* **Sh***el* **I***srael* ("the teacher of Israel"); and, indeed, Rashi's commentaries on the Torah and the Talmud

V. NOVELLAE ON THE BABYLONIAN TALMUD

A. The Ashkenazic Novellae; the Tosafists

1. IN GENERAL

With Rashi, Talmudic commentary reached its zenith.

The commentary was not only a teacher and guide. It also paved the way for a new and profound method of examination of the inner recesses of the Talmud—the analytical and critical approach of the Tosafists. From the days of the *amoraim* in the academies of Pumbedita, Sura, and Nehardea, there had been no centers for the study of the Torah comparable to the academies of the Rhine cities, Lotharingia and Champagne.[60]

It was in those academies that the Tosafists studied and produced their great works, beginning the literature of the novellae. The Tosafists resembled the *amoraim* not only in their diligence in studying and analyzing the Talmudic *Halakhah,* but even more so in their methodology and in the collective form of study they adopted. They carried forward the creativity of the Talmud from the point where it had come to a halt in the sixth century C.E. Perhaps this was the reason that the Tosafists earned a favored position akin to that of Rashi. From the earliest printed editions of the Talmud, their novellae have appeared on the outside margins of the Talmudic text—opposite Rashi's commentary on the inside margins. These three—the Talmud, Rashi, and the *Tosafot* (the "additions" of the Tosafists)—have become a single unit.[61] The Tosafists completed Rashi's effort to make the Talmud the heritage of the entire Jewish people. As Menahem b. Aaron b. Zeraḥ, a Spanish halakhic authority in the fourteenth century, put it:

> It is due to R. Solomon [Rashi] and his descendants [the Tosafists] that the Talmud has been and is being studied everywhere. . . . They are both the remote and the immediate cause.[62]

The Tosafists were active over a period of approximately two hundred years, in the twelfth and thirteenth centuries. The *Tosafot* were the collective creation of the halakhic authorities of Germany and France, and also, to a

---

are indispensable for all students—young and old, beginning and advanced. As to Rashi's responsa, *see infra* p. 1477 and Appendix C.

60. Urbach, *Tosafot,* p. 15.

61. Known as *GeFeT,* an acronym for *Gemara* (Talmud), *Perush* [which becomes *F*erush after "Ge" according to the principles of Hebrew vocalization] (commentary, *i.e.,* Rashi), and *Tosafot.*

62. *Ẓeidah la-Derekh,* Introduction. *See also* Urbach, *Tosafot,* pp. 16ff., 525–526.

limited degree, of England, Italy, and the Slavic countries. The first Tosafists were students of Rashi. They wrote down their comments and novellae as "additions" (*tosafot*) to "the commentary of the[ir] great master," because they viewed Rashi's commentary as the *ne plus ultra* of Talmudic commentary, to which their observations and novellae were merely an incidental supplement. However, in the course of time these "additions" expanded until they became annotations to the Talmud and thereafter were viewed as being more than merely glosses to Rashi's commentary.

2. HOW THE NOVELLAE OF THE TOSAFISTS WERE CREATED

The students and scholars of the academies attended the study hall with their teachers and discussed and debated the Talmud and its commentaries. The teachers, and especially the students, took notes on the discussions. These notes were called "the *tosafot* of student A written in the presence of teacher B," *e.g.*, "the *tosafot* of Rashbam written in the presence of Rashi." Students moved from one academy to another, bringing with them the novellae of their study hall, which became known as "the *tosafot* of the study hall at X or Y." Thus, many collections of *tosafot* appeared, each one bearing the name of its study hall.[63]

There is consequently a strong resemblance between the Tosafists' notes and the form in which the Talmud itself was written and put together. Both the Talmud and the *Tosafot* contain the discussion and debate in the study halls on halakhic questions and interpretations; the Talmud records the debates in Sura and Pumbedita, and the *Tosafot* the debates in the French and German academies. There are, to be sure, certain external differences. Thus, in the Talmud, the discussion is recorded in the form of a dialogue (*e.g.*, "Rava said to him," "Come and hear," etc.) whereas the *Tosafot* are in question-and-answer form (*e.g.*, "The question was asked by Rabbenu Tam," "Ri responded," "If you will say," "It can be said," etc.). However, this difference is essentially one of form, not substance.

The body of learning the Tosafists had to study and analyze was much more extensive than that which the *amoraim* had to master. The Tosafists

63. *E.g.*, *Tosafot ha-Ri* (*Tosafot* of Isaac the Elder), *Tosafot R. Judah of Paris*, *Tosafot Tukh* (*Tosafot* of Eliezer of Touques), *et al.* Occasionally, the teachers or other halakhic authorities commented that the students did not report the discussions correctly; and in one instance Rabbenu Tam rejected notes from the study hall of Riba (Isaac b. Asher ha-Levi, one of the first Tosafists in Germany): "That which Riba [is recorded as having] answered he did not answer, nor did he compose those *tosafot* that the copyists called by his name. Do not rely on them, because most are erroneous. I examined [them] and I have so discovered" (*Sefer ha-Yashar*, ed. Schlesinger, #315, p. 197). In the course of time, the compilations of notes were revised and reedited. Some of these compilations are extant, either printed on the pages of the Talmud itself or published separately; but a significant number have not survived. *See* Urbach, *Tosafot*, pp. 19–20.

had to consider not only what the *amoraim* needed to take account of but all the post-Talmudic halakhic literature as well.[64] Consequently, their deliberations were considerably more extensive. They compared different passages within the Babylonian Talmud; they contrasted the law in the Babylonian Talmud with the treatment of the same subjects in the Jerusalem Talmud; they discussed and examined the *baraitot*, the *Tosefta*, and the halakhic *midrashim*; and they also investigated textual variations and took a position with regard to them. In addition, they debated the statements of the *geonim* and *rishonim* who preceded them—primarily the statements of Rashi.

3. THE LEADING TOSAFISTS

The leading Tosafists include the following:

a. SAMUEL b. MEIR (RASHBAM)

Rashbam was Rashi's grandson; his mother was Rashi's daughter. He was born between 1080 and 1085 C.E. and died after ca. 1158. Not only was Rashbam one of the leading Tosafists in France, but he wrote commentaries on some Talmudic tractates.[65] He was also a leading Bible commentator, whose interpretations follow the plain meaning of the text.

b. JACOB b. MEIR (RABBENU TAM)

Rabbenu Tam[66] was Rashbam's brother. He was born ca. 1100 and died in 1171. He was the foremost halakhic authority in France in his generation and one of the great and powerful leaders of his time.[67]

c. ISAAC b. SAMUEL (RI)

Ri, also known as Isaac the Elder, lived in the twelfth century in Dampierre, France, and was a nephew and student of Rashbam and Rabbenu Tam. He was also called "*The* Tosafist," and his name is mentioned in almost all the passages of the printed version of the *Tosafot*.[68]

64. The Tosafists also had available to them edited compilations of halakhic literature from the Talmudic period, which the *amoraim* themselves never had in that form, such as TJ, various *midrashim*, "minor tractates," etc.

65. *See supra* n. 57. Rashbam also wrote a commentary on the tenth chapter of Tractate *Pesaḥim*.

66. As to the appellation "*tam*," *see* Genesis 25:27: "Jacob was an *ish tam* who stayed in camp [lit. dwelled in tents]." *Ish tam*, translated by the JPS *Tanakh* as "mild man," connotes qualities of integrity, completeness, and purity.

67. As to Rabbenu Tam's responsa, *see infra* p. 1478 and Appendix C.

68. Menahem b. Aaron b. Zeraḥ (*Ẓeidah la-Derekh*, Introduction) describes the method of study in Ri's study hall:

> Rabbenu Isaac [Ri] was the nephew of Rabbenu Tam, the famous Tosafist, and studied and taught in the *yeshivah*. My teachers from France have testified in the name of their

d. SAMSON b. ABRAHAM (RASH) OF SENS

Rash of Sens, France, was one of the leading Tosafists in the second half of the twelfth and the beginning of the thirteenth centuries. He was the most outstanding student and the spiritual heir of Ri. In addition to the many *tosafot* he composed, mention should be made, among his other halakhic works, of his commentary on two mishnaic Orders—*Zera'im* and *Tohorot*—for which (except for Tractate *Berakhot* in *Zera'im* and Tractate *Niddah* in *Tohorot*) there is no Babylonian Talmud. He settled in the Land of Israel in 1211 C.E. and is therefore also called "The Jerusalemite," or "Rabbi Samson of the Land of Israel."[69]

e. MEIR b. BARUCH (MAHARAM) OF ROTHENBURG

Maharam of Rothenburg was one of the last of the Tosafists and one of the leading molders of Jewish law, especially civil and public law (communal enactments and administration of the autonomous Jewish self-government).[70] He was born in Worms in approximately the third decade of the thirteenth century. Because of the persecution of the Jews of Germany, he encouraged their emigration and himself attempted to flee. However, he was caught, identified by an apostate, and imprisoned by order of Kaiser Rudolph. He died in prison in 1293. Maharam of Rothenburg was the leader of German Jewry and among its foremost halakhic authorities.[71]

> teachers that it was well known that sixty rabbis studied under him, each one of whom heard the *Halakhah* he taught. Furthermore, each one [of the sixty rabbis] studied a tractate his colleagues did not study, and they used to review [the tractates] orally. Rabbenu Isaac would not teach a *halakhah* unless all of the *gemara* was thoroughly known by them. . . . Any *halakhah* or tannaitic or amoraic statement that seemed wrong or was contradicted by another source, he would explain in his own way, as is clear to anyone who has seen their *tosafot*, responsa, and commentaries, and his critical glosses on the work of their grandfather, Rabbenu Solomon [Rashi].

Ri's study hall was thus considered the main creative source for the *Tosafot* where, as Solomon Luria (Maharshal) put it:

> They made the Talmud as one ball [*i.e.*, they harmonized it] . . . and turned it around and rolled it from place to place. Matters that to us seem incomprehensible [they explained by saying] that one subject is to be interpreted thus, and the other so. The Talmud was thereby harmonized and became coherent . . . and the correctness of its rulings was confirmed . . . [quoted by Urbach, *Tosafot*, p. 210].

69. As to Rash of Sens and his study of TJ, *see infra* p. 1132.

70. *See supra* pp. 679ff. and *passim*.

71. As to compilations of the responsa of Maharam of Rothenburg, *see infra* p. 1478 and Appendix C. Maharam's outstanding disciple, Asheri (Asher b. Jehiel, also known as Rosh), settled in Spain and brought the teachings of Maharam and other German and French halakhic authorities to that Jewish center. This development had a crucial effect on the study and determination of the *Halakhah*. *See infra* pp. 1251–1253.

4. DECISIONS AND RESPONSA IN THE *TOSAFOT*

The vast literature of the Tosafists consists for the most part of novellae but also includes a great deal of material in the nature of responsa and, particularly, codificatory literature. Scattered about in the compilations of the various Tosafists are responsa to inquiries and many decisions on legal points arrived at during their deliberations. These decisions were intended to be of more than merely theoretical interest; they were intended to govern practical conduct. However, the Tosafists did not compile their legal decisions in a separate code. They viewed the Talmud as the definitive and conclusive source for the determination of the law; and, in order to preserve the link between that source and their halakhic conclusions, they incorporated their legal decisions as an integral part of the discussion and debate that preceded their final legal conclusion.[72] They acted similarly with regard to their responsa, which also were intended to declare the governing law. E. E. Urbach has described this special characteristic of the Tosafists' work:

> The various types of geonic compositions and the works of the commentators developed very differently [from the *Tosafot*]. Prior to the Tosafists, the distinctions between the types of compositions were fixed and rigid. Commentary, responsa, and codes were separate categories, each having its own clearly identifiable characteristics. The Tosafists began where the Talmud ended, and their compositions became new "Talmuds." Like the Talmud, they recorded whatever occurred in the study hall: the debate during study, the *ma'asim* and legal decisions rendered orally by authoritative decisionmakers, the epistles, and the written legal decisions and *halakhot*. This external similarity [between the *Tosafot* and the Talmud] is the product of the Talmudic Sages' method of study, which was renewed in the study hall of the Tosafists.[73]

A subsequent work, *Piskei ha-Tosafot* [The Rulings of the *Tosafot*], abstracts the essence and the conclusion of each section of the *Tosafot*.[74] The identity of the author is disputed; some attribute it to Asheri, others to Asheri's son, Jacob b. Asher, the author of the *Turim*, and still others to an

72. As will be demonstrated below in the discussion of the codificatory literature, the problem of maintaining the connection between the codified law and the Talmudic sources was a central problem of codification. *See infra* pp. 1144–1148, discussing the approach of various codifiers to this problem.

73. Urbach, *Tosafot*, pp. 525–526.

74. Each separate section of *Tosafot* is called a *dibbur* (lit. "statement," "speech," or "talk"); the accepted method of citation to *Tosafot* in English is: *Tosafot*, tractate, folio, and side, s.v. (*sub verbo* = "under the word"). . . . In Hebrew, s.v. is replaced by *d.h.* = *dibbur ha-matḥil* = "statement beginning with . . . ."

unknown author.[75] The relevant section of the *Piskei ha-Tosafot* is printed at the end of each tractate in the large editions of the Talmud.[76]

B. The Sephardic Novellae/Commentaries

The following are a few of the major Sephardic authors of commentaries and novellae (including the halakhic authorities of Provence).

1. JOSEPH ibn MIGASH (RI MIGASH)

Ri Migash[77] was the outstanding disciple of Alfasi. He composed novellae on the Talmud, but only those on Tractates *Bava Batra* and *Shevu'ot* have survived. Some of what he wrote, however, has been preserved through quotation by later authors. Maimonides thought very highly of him:

> As God lives, that man's grasp of Talmud amazes everyone who studies his writings and perceives the depth of his analysis, so that I may say of him, "His methodology surpasses that of all his predecessors." I have also collected all the laws I found in his commentary. [78]

2. ABRAHAM b. DAVID (RABAD) OF POSQUIÈRES[79]

Rabad's novellae/commentaries on the Talmud[80] did not reach as wide an audience as his other halakhic writings, although his interpretations were frequently quoted by the major commentators on the Talmud who followed him, such as Rashba and Meiri. They called him "The Great Commentator" (*gedolei ha-meforshim*). Similarly, a great many of his comments were incorporated into the *Shittah Mekubbeẓet* of Beẓalel Ashkenazi, discussed below. Rabad's style is explicit and easy to study. Unlike Rashi, he did not write a full commentary on the complete text and content of a Talmudic discussion; instead, he discussed the halakhic issues in the course

75. *See* Urbach, *Tosafot,* pp. 566–567; *infra* p. 1285 n. 187.

76. As to the responsa of the Tosafists, *see infra* Appendix C.

77. 1077 (Seville, Spain)–1141.

78. Maimonides, *Commentary on the Mishnah,* Introduction (ed. Mosad ha-Rav Kook, Jerusalem, 1965, transl. J. Kafaḥ, p. 25b). Maimonides' codificatory methodology was also influenced by Ri Migash; *see infra* pp. 1183–1184. As to the responsa of Ri Migash, *see infra* pp. 1476–1477 and Appendix C.

79. For biographical notes on Rabad, *see supra* pp. 1110–1111 and n. 32.

80. Ḥasdai Crescas wrote: "And also the great rabbi Abraham b. David [Rabad] composed commentaries on the whole Talmud" (*Or ha-Shem,* Vienna, 1859, p. 2a). David of Estella noted that, in addition to his other halakhic works, "Rabbenu Abraham b. David of Posquières" also "wrote an explanatory commentary on most of the Talmud." *See* Twersky, *supra* n. 32 at 77.

of comparing the various halakhic sources. Thus, the method of his commentary is closer to that of the Tosafists. Only relatively recently have Rabad's novellae/commentaries on Tractates *Bava Kamma* and *Avodah Zarah* been printed on the basis of manuscripts.[81]

3. MEIR ABULAFIA (RAMAH)

Ramah[82] was the head of an important *yeshivah* in Toledo, Spain, and wrote a book of novellae on the Talmud, called *Peratei Peratin* [Details of Details]. The only part of this work extant is the part on Tractates *Bava Batra* and *Sanhedrin,* which is known as *Yad Ramah* [The Upraised Hand—a play on the acronym "Ramah"]. Ramah discussed every minute detail of each topic, whether directly relevant or only peripheral, arising in the course of the Talmudic discussion; and he generally included a summary of the main points at the end of the discussion. Ramah wrote in Talmudic Aramaic, which sometimes gives rise to difficulties in understanding his novellae.[83]

4. NAḤMANIDES (RAMBAN)

Naḥmanides[84] was born and lived for most of his life in Gerona, Spain. He wrote novellae, known as *Ḥiddushei ha-Ramban,* on almost all the tractates of the Talmud. By an amalgam of the methodology of the Tosafists and the "plain meaning" approach of earlier *rishonim,* he penetrated to the core of Talmudic problems. His novellae display a strong tendency to distill the halakhic conclusion from the Talmudic discussion.[85]

5. SOLOMON b. ABRAHAM ADRET (RASHBA)

Rashba[86] was the leader of Spanish Jewry in the second half of the thirteenth century. He was one of the outstanding disciples of Jonah

81. Rabad's commentary on *Bava Kamma* was published by S. Atlas in 1940 (facsimile ed., 1963). His commentary on *Avodah Zarah* was published by A. Sofer in 1961. *See* A.H. Freimann's critique of the Atlas edition, *Kiryat Sefer,* XX (1943–1944), pp. 25–28, and Freimann's critical comments (p. 27) regarding the title "*Ḥiddushei ha-Rabad*" [Novellae of Rabad], which Atlas gave the work, instead of "*Perush ha-Rabad*" [Commentary of Rabad], as it was called by the *rishonim.* For further details, *see* Twersky, *supra* n. 32 at 77–82; Atlas, *supra,* Introduction, pp. 13ff. *See also supra* p. 1111 n. 32.

82. Ca. 1170 (Burgos, Spain)–1244.

83. This is also true of the style of his responsa. *See infra* p. 1510 n. 172.

84. Ca. 1194 (Gerona, Spain)–ca. 1270 (Acre, Land of Israel). Several monographs have been written about Naḥmanides. *See, e.g.,* Y. Unna, *Rav Moshe ben Naḥman (Ha-Ramban), Ḥayyav u-Pe'ulato* [Naḥmanides—His Life and Work], Jerusalem, 1954 (2nd expanded ed.); C. Chavel, *Rabbenu Moshe ben Naḥman,* Jerusalem, 1967.

85. As to Naḥmanides' methodology, *see* S. Abramson, *Kelalei ha-Talmud be-Divrei ha-Ramban* [Talmudic Principles in the Works of Naḥmanides], Jerusalem, 1971, pp. 7–41. As to Naḥmanides as a commentator on Alfasi and as a codifier, *see infra* pp. 1174–1175, 1242–1243. As to his responsa, *see infra* p. 1478 and Appendix C.

86. 1235 (Barcelona, Spain)–1310.

Gerondi[87] and Naḥmanides. His novellae, which are extant on most of the tractates, are characterized by depth of analysis and understanding. He followed the methodology of his teacher, Naḥmanides, in amalgamating the methodology of the Tosafists and the "plain meaning" approach. His novellae are very extensive and contain many new halakhic principles, particularly in the area of *mishpat ivri.* Rashba, too, displayed a marked tendency to make definitive legal rulings.[88]

6. YOM TOV ISHBILI (RITBA)

Ritba[89] was the outstanding disciple of Rashba and wrote various types of halakhic literature, but his main work was his many novellae on most of the tractates of the Talmud. They are outstanding for clarity and detail, and they analyze in great depth all topics dealt with in the Talmudic discussion. Ritba's novellae also contain a great deal of material ranging over the areas of *mishpat ivri* as well as numerous legislative enactments adopted in his time. Portions of Ritba's novellae have been published at various times and, in the aggregate, cover most tractates of the Talmud; they recently have been collected and printed in several volumes. Novellae on some tractates had long been erroneously attributed to Ritba; the authentic Ritba novellae on those tractates have now been published from manuscript.[90]

7. NISSIM GERONDI (RAN)

Ran[91] was the leader of Spanish Jewry in the middle of the fourteenth century and, like Rashba, headed the *yeshivah* and was the principal religious authority in Barcelona. He composed novellae/commentaries on a

87. Jonah Gerondi is also known as "Rabbi Jonah the Pious." A contemporary of Naḥmanides, he died in 1263.

88. As to Rashba's codificatory methodology and his responsa, *see infra* pp. 1273–1277, 1478, and Appendix C. As to his activities in regard to communal enactments and Jewish public law, *see supra* pp. 679ff. and *passim.*

89. Ritba lived in Spain at the end of the thirteenth and the beginning of the fourteenth centuries.

90. Six volumes of Ritba's novellae have been published (Or ha-Torah, Tel-Aviv, 1958) on most of the tractates of the Orders of *Mo'ed, Nashim,* and *Nezikin,* as well as on Tractates *Ḥullin* and *Niddah.* In 1954, M. ha-Kohen Blau published Ritba's novellae on Tractate *Bava Batra* from mss. In 1962, E. Halpern published *Ḥiddushei ha-Ritba ha-Ḥadashim* [The New Novellae of Ritba] on Tractate *Bava Meẓi'a* from mss.; the text of these corresponds to the quotations from Ritba in *Shittah Mekubbeẓet* and differs from that of the previously printed novellae on that tractate. In 1967, the novellae of Ritba on Tractate *Shabbat* were printed from mss.; there, too, the text differs from the novellae on that tractate which had been attributed to him but which were actually written by Nissim Gerondi (Ran). *See* the introductions to the books cited. For other works of Ritba, *see infra* p. 1242 n. 24 and Appendix C. M. Blau has published *Kitvei ha-Ritba* [The Writings of Ritba], New York, 1957, which includes *Sefer ha-Zikkaron, Hilkhot Berakhot,* and responsa of Ritba.

91. Beginning of fourteenth century (Barcelona)—ca. 1380.

number of Talmudic tractates, some of which have only recently been published from manuscript. Particularly well known is his commentary on Tractate *Nedarim,* which is printed together with Rashi's commentary in the commonly used editions of the Talmud. It is the classic commentary on that tractate.[92]

8. MENAHEM MEIRI

Bet ha-Beḥirah [The Chosen House—usually connoting the Temple] by Menahem Meiri,[93] a commentary on most of the tractates of the Talmud, occupies a unique place in Talmudic commentary.[94] Meiri lived most of his life in Perpignan, France, and corresponded with Rashba and many halakhic authorities in France and Germany. Meiri's method was to assemble from both Talmuds, the *Tosefta,* the halakhic *midrashim,* and the then extant literature all the passages and laws relevant to the topic under discussion. His commentary is written in clear and lucid Hebrew that is unique among Talmudic commentaries.[95] The format of his commentary is as follows: Meiri first explains the *mishnah* and then the Talmud's discussion insofar as it relates directly to the laws set forth in the *mishnah.* Thereafter, the commentary goes on to explain and discuss with great clarity all the other matters dealt with in the Talmud's discussion, bringing to bear the views of many of the foremost prior authorities. Thus, Meiri's work is not merely a systematic commentary on the Talmud, but is a kind of encyclopedia of prior halakhic opinion; it is therefore one of the most popular and useful aids to understanding the Talmud. Meiri also wrote novellae on the Talmud, only a few of which are extant.

9. BEẒALEL ASHKENAZI

Novellae/commentaries were also written in Turkey and the eastern countries. At the close of the period of the *rishonim* in the sixteenth century, one of the leading halakhic scholars of Egypt and Jerusalem, Beẓalel Ashkenazi, compiled the main commentaries and novellae of the *rishonim* on the tractates of the Talmud. The title of the work is *Asefat Zekenim* [The Compendium of the Elders] or *Shittah Mekubbeẓet* [A Systematic Compila-

92. Rashi's commentary on Tractate *Nedarim* is his first version and therefore is sometimes difficult to understand. As to Ran as a commentator on Alfasi, and as to Ran's responsa, *see infra* pp. 1175–1176 and Appendix C.

93. 1249 (Provence)–1315.

94. Most of Meiri's works remained in ms. for approximately six hundred years, and only a few were printed. By now, nearly all have appeared in print on the basis of ms. Parma (Italy). *Bet ha-Beḥirah* covers thirty-seven tractates, mainly in the Orders of *Mo'ed, Nashim,* and *Nezikin.*

95. The only earlier work with a comparable Hebrew style was a codificatory work—Maimonides' *Mishneh Torah; see infra* pp. 1206–1210.

tion].[96] Ashkenazi was a disciple of David ibn Zimra (Radbaz),[97] the Chief Rabbi of Egypt; and when Radbaz settled in the Land of Israel, Ashkenazi replaced him until he too took up residence in Jerusalem somewhat later.

The *Shittah Mekubbeẓet* covers many tractates of the Talmud and quotes excerpts from the commentaries of Rabbenu Gershom, Rabbenu Hananel, Ri Migash, and many other *rishonim.* Frequently, it is the only source of our knowledge of the contents of the works it quotes. Many *rishonim* whose commentaries and novellae are extant are also included in the *Shittah Mekubbeẓet,* which is thus an invaluable source for comparison with the text of the volumes of commentaries and novellae themselves. The collection of the commentaries and novellae of many *rishonim* in a single work greatly facilitates the study and understanding of the Talmud.[98]

C. Novellae in the Period of the *Aḥaronim*

The writing of novellae flourished in the various centers of Jewish life, particularly in Europe, from the sixteenth century onward, *i.e.,* from the beginning of the period of the *aḥaronim.* However, the novellae of this later period are different from those of the *rishonim.* The *rishonim* concentrated mainly on the Talmud itself, whereas, to a large extent, the *aḥaronim* concerned themselves with the novellae of the *rishonim.* Although the *aḥaronim* indirectly explain the Talmud and do arrive at novel interpretations, their comments are directly addressed to the statements of Rashi, the Tosafists, and other *rishonim.*

The later period also saw a widespread change in the method of study and the writing of novellae. In the writings of even the most innovative of the *rishonim,* the central objective is the discovery of the plain meaning of the Talmud, and their comments focus on the central issue of the Talmudic discussion. However, the works of many of the *aḥaronim* (who had the benefit of the writings of the *rishonim*) are to a great extent devoted to abstract conceptual analysis characterized by *pilpul* (finespun dialectics) to the point that their discussions frequently wander far off the central subject of the Talmud's concern.[99]

96. *Shittah Mekubbeẓet* quotes the commentaries and novellae; but, in contrast to Meiri's *Bet ha-Beḥirah,* it does not explain them or integrate them as part of a connected discussion of the topic under review.

97. As to Radbaz, *see infra* pp. 1233, 1486, and Appendix C.

98. To date, *Shittah Mekubbeẓet* has been printed for Tractates *Bava Kamma, Bava Meẓi'a, Bava Batra, Ketubbot,* and a few tractates of *Mo'ed* and *Nashim.* Other parts of the work are still in ms.

99. For a more detailed discussion of this change in the methodology of study in Poland and Germany, and of the views of the halakhic authorities of those countries in the

The novellae literature of this period is wide-ranging and rich; it is distinguished by the acuity of its thought-processes and analysis. The following are two examples of this literature, written by two of the greatest of the *aḥaronim*, each one of which is an archetype for a distinct theoretical and literary approach.[100]

1. *ḤIDDUSHEI HALAKHOT* BY SAMUEL ELIEZER EDELS (MAHARSHA)

Maharsha[101] was one of the foremost halakhic authorities of Poland. His book *Ḥiddushei Halakhot* [Halakhic Novellae] covers a great number of tractates and is printed in nearly all editions of the Talmud. It explains with precision and great insight the statements of Rashi and the Tosafists, and on occasion directly addresses the text of the Talmud. Although the elucidation of the statements of the *rishonim* indirectly casts light on the Talmud itself, Maharsha's direct point of reference was usually the *rishonim*. He did not range far afield in his novellae but rather explained each Talmudic problem on the basis of the material contained in the Talmud's own discussion. This work became very widely accepted and is studied together with the text of the Talmud, Rashi, and the *Tosafot*.[102]

---

sixteenth and seventeenth centuries as to the proper method of studying the Talmudic literature, *see infra* pp. 1380, 1383, 1395, *et al.*

100. Glosses (*haggahot* or *he'arot*) to the Talmud and to the writings of the *rishonim* are a literary category unto themselves. They are not full-fledged commentaries or novellae but rather are in essence brief notes, source references, and critical comparisons between TB and TJ, between different sources in TB, and between different commentaries. To this category belong *Gilyon ha-Shas* [Marginal Notes to the Talmud] by Akiva Eger, the *Haggahot* [Glosses] of Z.H. Chajes, and the *Haggahot ve-Ḥiddushei ha-Rashash* [Glosses and Novellae of Samuel Strashun].

Of the glosses concentrating on critical comparisons and source references, mention should be made of *Me'ir Nativ* by Shabbetai Zussman and *Yefeh Einayim* by Aryeh Loeb Jellin of Bielsk. The latter displays enormous erudition and a penetrating critical sense in regard to the relationships among various sources in both Talmuds, the *Tosefta,* and the tannaitic *midrashim,* and particularly between the sources in TJ and those in TB. (For an evaluation of Jellin's work, *see* Ginzberg, *Perushim,* I, Introduction, p. 131).

These glosses are printed in the large editions of the Talmud, some on the actual page to which they refer (such as Eger's *Gilyon ha-Shas*), but most at the end of each tractate. A similar work is *Ẓiyyun Yehoshu'a* by Joshua Heshel b. Elijah Ze'ev of Volozhyn, which lists, with great erudition and acuity, parallel sources in TJ; it was first printed in Vilna, 1869, and a facsimile edition was published in Jerusalem, 1970.

101. 1555 (Cracow, Poland)–1631; for a biography of Maharsha, *see* R. Margaliot, *Toledot Adam, Korot Yemei Ḥayyei ha-Maharsha* [The Story of a Man: A Biography of Maharsha], Lemberg, 1911.

102. As to Maharsha's methodology of study and of determining the law, *see infra* pp. 1383–1384.

2. *PENEI YEHOSHU'A* BY JACOB JOSHUA FALK

Jacob Joshua Falk[103] served as rabbi and head of the *yeshivah* in many communities. His work *Penei Yehoshu'a* [The Face of Joshua—a play on Falk's name] treats various topics in unusual depth. Its focus, as a rule, is generally on statements of *rishonim*, but they are a vehicle for clarifying the Talmud itself. Unlike Maharsha, Falk was not content to confine himself to the Talmudic passage he was explaining; rather, he reasoned analogically from one issue to another and from one Talmudic passage to another, ranging throughout the entire Talmud. He contributed a prodigious number of novellae. *Penei Yehoshu'a* covers most tractates of the Talmud and has been accepted by students of the Talmud as one of the classics of the *aḥaronim*.

The two works described above are basic in the halakhic literature of the *aḥaronim*; they are examples of two different forms of the rich and vast literature of that period. That literature,[104] which still continues to be written, has been enriched by several literary forms in addition to these.[105]

103. 1680 (Cracow, Poland)–1756.

104. A partial listing of other works of novellae by outstanding *aḥaronim* includes the following:

The sixteenth and seventeenth centuries: Ḥokhmat Shelomo, by Solomon Luria (author of *Yam Shel Shelomo*); *Me'ir Einei Ḥakhamim*, by Meir b. Gedaliah of Lublin (Maharam of Lublin); *Meginei Shelomo*, by Joshua b. Joseph of Cracow (mainly devoted to a defense of Rashi against the criticisms of the Tosafists); *Ḥiddushei Halakhot Maharam Schiff*, by Meir Schiff.

The eighteenth century: Turei Even and *Gevurat Ari*, by Aryeh Loeb b. Asher (author of *Sha'agat Aryeh*); *Ẓiyyun le-Nefesh Ḥayyah* (abbreviated to its acronym *Ẓelaḥ*), by Ezekiel Landau (author of *Noda bi-Yehudah*); *Sha'ar Yosef* (on Tractate *Horayot*), by Ḥayyim Joseph David Azulai (Ḥida).

The nineteenth century: Derush ve-Ḥiddush, by Akiva Eger; *Ḥiddushei Ḥatam Sofer*, by Moses Sofer; *Arukh la-Ner*, by Jacob Ettlinger; *Ḥiddushei ha-Rim*, by Isaac Meir Alter of Gur.

The twentieth century: In the great *yeshivot* established in the twentieth century in the Jewish centers in Poland and Lithuania, the main emphasis was on learning through composing novellae, and a significant portion of the novellae literature of this period was a by-product of the system of studying and teaching prevalent in the *yeshivot*, particularly in Lithuania. Most works of novellae in the twentieth century take the form of discussions of Maimonides' *Mishneh Torah* or the *Shulḥan Arukh*, or are organized according to various Talmudic topics. The following are a few of the better known works: *Or Same'aḥ*, by Meir Simḥah ha-Kohen of Dvinsk; *Ḥiddushei Rabbenu Ḥayyim ha-Levi*, by Ḥayyim ha-Levi Soloveitchik; *Ẓofnat Pa'ne'aḥ*, by Joseph Rosen (known as "The Rogochover"), consisting of glosses/notes on other sources; *Sha'arei Yosher*, by Shimon Judah Shkop; *Levush Mordekhai*, by Moses Mordecai Epstein; *Even ha-Ezel*, by Isser Zalman Meltzer; *Ḥazon Ish*, by Abraham Isaiah Karelitz.

105. The Babylonian Talmud itself has been translated into various languages, of which the following are a few:

VI. COMMENTARIES AND NOVELLAE ON THE JERUSALEM TALMUD[106]

A. The Jerusalem Talmud—Its Study and Use as a Basis for Legal Decisions

Commentaries and novellae were at first written mainly on the Babylonian Talmud. It is true that the Jerusalem Talmud was often cited or quoted in novellae just as it was in the other types of halakhic literature; some authorities did this frequently and others rarely, depending on the period and on how well the particular author was acquainted with the Jerusalem Talmud.[107] However, the central starting point for commentary and novellae was the Babylonian Talmud, which for a long time was the focus of most such literature.

This situation was the result of a number of factors. It has already been

---

1. *Talmud Bavli im Targum Ivri u-Ferush Ḥadash* [Babylonian Talmud with Hebrew Translation and New Commentary], 1952–1960, published by Devir and Masada, Tel Aviv (Tractates *Bava Kamma, Bava Meẓi'a,* and *Bava Batra* translated into Hebrew, with explanatory commentary, notes, and v.l. by E.Z. Melamed, S. Abramson, *et al.*, edited by J.N. Epstein).
2. *Der Babylonische Talmud . . . übersetzt . . . von Lazarus Goldschmidt* [The Babylonian Talmud Translated into German], with v.l., explanatory commentary, and notes by Eliezer Goldschmidt, 1st ed. (9 vols.), 1897–1935; 2d ed. (12 vols.), 1929–1936.
3. *The Babylonian Talmud, Translated into English with Notes, Glossary and Indices under the Editorship of Rabbi Dr. I. Epstein* [individual tractates translated by various scholars], London, The Soncino Press, 1948–1952. The subject index, the index of Talmudic Sages, and the table of Biblical citations refer to the page numbers of the translation, not the regularly used editions of the Talmud, and are therefore of limited utility.

These translations can aid the student unskilled in the Talmud to overcome language difficulties; and they also provide brief explanatory notes for difficult passages, as well as variant readings from mss., which are especially valuable. It goes without saying, however, that these translations—as indeed translations of any work—must be used with caution in attempting to draw specific conclusions.

Adin Steinsaltz of Jerusalem has recently been publishing tractates of TB with vocalization and punctuation together with the accompanying texts of Rashi and the *Tosafot* with punctuation but no vocalization. The edition contains a running commentary on the text, which includes a translation into modern Hebrew. Various notes on biography, language, realia, and *Halakhah* are also added; and each volume concludes with useful indexes. Random House has recently begun publication of various tractates of TB in English by Steinsaltz in the same format as the Hebrew edition.

106. *See* Ginzberg, *Perushim,* I, Introduction, pp. 83–132. This and succeeding references to *Perushim* are to the Hebrew Introduction.

107. Several *rishonim* wrote commentaries on the Jerusalem Talmud that are not extant and are known only from references by later authors. *See* S. Lieberman, "Mashehu al Mefarshim Kadmonim la-Yerushalmi" [On Early Commentators on the Jerusalem Talmud], *Alexander Marx Jubilee Volume,* 1950, pp. 287–301.

noted that because of the harsh economic and political conditions at the time in the Land of Israel, the redaction of the Babylonian Talmud was superior, in both content and organization, to that of the Jerusalem Talmud.[108] The *geonim* made the Babylonian Talmud the controlling authority; they ruled that all conflicts between the Babylonian and Jerusalem Talmuds were to be resolved in favor of the Babylonian Talmud. Two reasons were given: (1) according to Hai Gaon, the devastation and persecutions in the Land of Israel halted instruction in the law, so that the laws in the Jerusalem Talmud were inadequately clarified;[109] and (2) according to Alfasi, the Babylonian *amoraim* finalized their Talmud and reached their conclusions after the *amoraim* of the Land of Israel, and the general rule of decision making that "the law is in accordance with the views of the later authorities" requires that the Babylonian Talmud prevail.[110]

Although in the Land of Israel and in nearby countries—Egypt and southern Italy—the Jerusalem Talmud was for some time the final authority, in the course of time the Babylonian Talmud supplanted it and became "The Talmud," while the Jerusalem Talmud was almost forgotten. With the ascension of the Abbasid dynasty (747 C.E.), Babylonia became the political center of the Arab-Moslem empire. Baghdad was the site of the caliphate, and roads to and from there were open and heavily traversed by caravans and travelers. Babylonia was "the center of the world," while the Land of Israel "was relegated to a corner of the Mediterranean Sea," with which communication became difficult and was almost severed.[111]

As a result of its physical accessibility, Babylonia became the spiritual center of Jewish life, and the queries of Jews in the diaspora were submitted to the Babylonian *geonim*. Their responsa were based on the Babylonian Talmud, which they regarded as the binding authority; the natural consequence was that the study of the Jerusalem Talmud declined. The Babylonian *geonim* engaged very little in the study of the Jerusalem Talmud.[112] The inhabitants of the Land of Israel followed the rulings of the Jerusalem Talmud so long as a Jewish community existed there. When that community was destroyed by the Crusaders at the end of the eleventh century, the "dominion" of the Jerusalem Talmud ended even in the Land of Israel. Those

108. *See supra* p. 1097.

109. *See* S. Assaf, *Teshuvot ha-Geonim* [Responsa of the *Geonim*], 1929, pp. 125–126.

110. Alfasi, *Sefer ha-Halakhot*, Eruvin (end). As to the paramount authority of TB, *see* additional references, *supra* p. 1098 n. 68.

111. Ginzberg, *Perushim*, pp. 90, 107; M. Margaliot, *Ha-Ḥillukim she-bein Anshei Mizraḥ u-Venei Ereẓ Yisra'el* [The Differences between the People of the East and the Residents of the Land of Israel], Jerusalem, 1938, Introduction, pp. 3–9. *See further infra* p. 1469 as to the representatives of the Babylonian academies in the various Jewish centers who forwarded questions to the Babylonian *geonim* and relayed their responsa.

112. Ginzberg, *Perushim*, pp. 100ff.; Abramson, *supra* n. 49 at 212 and nn., *ad loc.*

who later migrated from other countries to the Land of Israel maintained their previous adherence to the Babylonian Talmud.[113]

As has been noted, the Jerusalem Talmud was cited, to a certain extent, by some halakhic authorities, especially Nissim Gaon, Rabbenu Hananel, Alfasi, Maimonides, Naḥmanides, and other early Spanish authorities. On the other hand, the early *rishonim* of France and Germany did not study the Jerusalem Talmud; according to scholarly opinion, Rashi never even saw the complete Jerusalem Talmud.[114] It was only at the beginning of the twelfth century that the French and German halakhic authorities began to take account of the Jerusalem Talmud, and they continued to study it until the beginning of the fourteenth century. In this connection, particular mention should be made of Rash of Sens, whose commentary on Mishnah *Zera'im* made substantial use of the Order of *Zera'im* in the Jerusalem Talmud.[115]

As a result of the fate of the Jerusalem Talmud, no satisfactory comprehensive commentary on it was written, and the absence of such a commentary necessarily increased the already great difficulty of mastering that Talmud. For hundreds of years, the Jerusalem Talmud was caught in a vicious circle: it was not studied, so no commentary was written on it; there was no commentary written on it, so it was not studied. This circle was broken as a result of the great renaissance of the Jewish community in the Land of Israel in the sixteenth century, which marked the beginning of a comprehensive literature of commentaries and novellae on the Jerusalem Talmud.

B. Solomon Sirillo's Commentary

The earliest extant commentary on the Jerusalem Talmud is by Solomon Sirillo. Sirillo lived in the first half of the sixteenth century and, as a child,

113. Ginzberg, *Perushim*, p. 105. As to the destruction of the Jewish community in the Land of Israel by the Crusaders, the consequent effect on the spiritual status of the Land of Israel vis-à-vis the diaspora, and the effect of renewed immigration and resettlement upon the status of the Land of Israel as a Jewish spiritual center, *see* S. Klein, *Toledot ha-Yishuv ha-Yehudi be-Ereẓ Yisra'el me-Ḥatimat ha-Talmud ad Tenu'at Yishuv Ereẓ Yisra'el* [A History of Jewish Settlement in the Land of Israel from the Completion of the Talmud until the Movement for the Resettlement of the Land of Israel], Tel Aviv, 1928, pp. 126ff.

114. Ginzberg, *Perushim*, pp. 110–111. Italian authorities such as Nathan b. Jehiel, the author of the *Arukh*, did know TJ and made frequent use of it. They did not, however, write commentaries specifically upon TJ. As has been noted, there was a strong connection, dating from ancient times, between the Jews of southern Italy and the Land of Israel.

115. *See* Ginzberg, *Perushim*, pp. 107–114; Lieberman, *supra* n. 107 at 287–289; Lipschuetz, *supra* n. 53 at 98 n. 7; Urbach, *Tosafot*, pp. 223, 246. As to Rash of Sens and his immigration to the Land of Israel, *see supra* p. 1121.

was one of the Spanish exiles. From Spain, he left for Turkey and later moved to the Land of Israel. He was one of the leading halakhic authorities in both these last-mentioned Jewish centers.

Sirillo's commentary deals mainly with the Order of *Zera'im*. The focus on this Order is closely related to a significant turn of events connected with the writing of commentaries on the Jerusalem Talmud. In the first half of the sixteenth century, known as the "Safed Period," the Jewish population of the Land of Israel increased due to the arrival there of many Spanish exiles, including a number of important personages. The Jewish community there became well established, and its economy revived. As a result, the Land of Israel once again became a spiritual center for world Jewry.[116] The existence of a Jewish settlement in the Holy Land raised many questions concerning the laws directly relating to the Land of Israel, such as the laws of tithes, the sabbatical year, and the mixture of species (*kilayim*); and their solution required recourse to the Order of *Zera'im* in the Jerusalem Talmud, there being no Babylonian Talmud on that Order.[117]

The halakhic authorities therefore increasingly consulted the Jerusalem Talmud on *Zera'im*, and this in turn stimulated the need for a comprehensive commentary on that Order. It is instructive that the very reason that apparently caused the Talmud on *Zera'im* to be written only in the Land of Israel was the same reason that, some 1200 years later, led to the writing of a comprehensive commentary on that very Order of the Jerusalem Talmud.[118] Sirillo's commentary is concise and lucid, in the manner of the *rishonim*; and from his time on, commentaries on the Jerusalem Talmud became more numerous.[119]

116. As to the economic factors that led to the rise of Safed and its transformation into a center of the Jewish community, *see* Kena'ani, "Ha-Ḥayyim ha-Kalkaliyyim bi-Ẓefat u-Sevivotehah ba-Me'ah ha-Shesh Esreh va-Ḥaẓi ha-Me'ah ha-Sheva Esreh" [The Economic Life of Safed and its Environs in the Sixteenth and the First Half of the Seventeenth Centuries], *Zion* (Me'asef), VI (1934), Jerusalem, pp. 172ff.; S. Aviẓur, "Ẓefat Merkaz le-Ta'asiyat Arigei Ẓemer ba-Me'ah ha-Tet Vav" [Safed, A Center of the Wool Weaving Industry in the Fifteenth Century], *Sefer Ẓefat*, I, Jerusalem, 1962.

117. *See supra* p. 1094.

118. As a result of the Jewish people's current return to the Land of Israel and resettlement there, the Jerusalem Talmud has once again acquired practical relevance; and renewed interest in it has arisen. Similarly, in an earlier time, Rash of Sens, the Tosafist, who immigrated to the Land of Israel, wrote a comprehensive commentary on Mishnah *Zera'im* that relied largely on that Order in the Jerusalem Talmud. *See supra* p. 1121.

119. Some fifty years after Sirillo, another halakhic authority of the Land of Israel, Eleazar Azikri (sometimes Azkari) wrote a commentary on TJ, of which only the commentary on Tractate *Berakhot* is extant. Similarly, a commentary on the aggadic material in TJ, called *Yefeh Mar'eh* [Beautiful in Appearance] (a play on the author's name "Jaffe," which means "beautiful"), written by Samuel Jaffe Ashkenazi of the same period, is extant. *See* Ginzberg, *Perushim*, pp. 117–118; Lieberman, *supra* n. 107 at 301ff.

C. *Sedeh Yehoshu'a* by Joshua Benveniste

Joshua Benveniste, one of Constantinople's leading rabbis in the seventeenth century, composed the first major commentary covering most of the Jerusalem Talmud, entitled *Sedeh Yehoshu'a* [Joshua's Field]. Unlike Sirillo's commentary, Benveniste's is very expansive. It quotes variant readings and includes glosses based on manuscripts and on references to the Jerusalem Talmud in works of *rishonim*. Benveniste's remarks in his Introduction concerning the extent to which the Jerusalem Talmud was studied in his day are illuminating:

> Since I saw this pearl of a Talmud neglected, with no one bothering to harvest it so as to explain its words, reveal its mysteries, and disclose to us the secrets of the wisdom it contains, I arose and, relying on the Lord, studied the literature, and decided to interpret and explain the halakhic part [and not the aggadic part][120] of the Jerusalem Talmud.

The Sephardic scholars were the first to write commentaries on the Jerusalem Talmud; but subsequently the Ashkenazic scholars took over most of this work and were particularly responsible for expanding the study of the Jerusalem Talmud. The earliest and most important of these Ashkenazic commentators was Elijah of Fulda.

D. Elijah of Fulda's Commentary and Novellae

At the beginning of the eighteenth century, Elijah of Fulda, Germany,[121] composed a commentary on the Order of *Zera'im* and on Tractates *Shekalim, Bava Kamma, Bava Meẓi'a,* and *Bava Batra.* His commentary is concise; when he felt it necessary to discourse at length, he set out his further comments separately. Consequently, he divided his commentary into two sections—one similar to Rashi's on the Babylonian Talmud, and the other consisting of novellae like those of the Tosafists. In this manner, he established the model for two commentators on the Jerusalem Talmud in the succeeding generation.

Elijah of Fulda's commentary greatly popularized the study of the Jerusalem Talmud among Ashkenazic scholars, who in turn wrote additional commentaries and glosses on it. Below are described two of the most sig-

120. A commentary on the aggadic part of TJ had previously been written by Samuel Jaffe Ashkenazi; *see supra* n. 119.

121. Apparently, Elijah of Fulda never served as a rabbi, but, as he put it on the title page of his books, was "a resident of the city of Fulda." *See* Ginzberg, *Perushim,* p. 121 n. 29. *See also id.* as to the commentary's influence on the spread of the study of TJ.

nificant commentators of this group—David Fraenkel and Moses Margoliot.

E. David Fraenkel's Commentary and Novellae

David Fraenkel,[122] one of the foremost rabbis in eighteenth-century Germany, served as the Chief Rabbi of Greater Berlin. Like Elijah of Fulda, he divided his commentary on the Jerusalem Talmud into two sections: an explanatory commentary that he called *Korban ha-Edah* [The Communal Sacrifice], and a second and distinct section consisting of novellae, entitled *Sheyarei Korban* [The Leftovers of the Sacrifice]. Fraenkel's work—particularly the novellae—is more extensive than that of Elijah of Fulda, and includes the Orders of *Mo'ed* and *Nashim* and the Tractates *Sanhedrin, Makkot,* and part of *Shevu'ot.*[123]

F. Moses Margoliot's Commentary and Novellae

The greatest commentary on the Jerusalem Talmud, both quantitatively and qualitatively, is that of Moses Margoliot, who was born in Kedainiai, Lithuania, between 1710 and 1720 C.E. He served as rabbi in several Lithuanian communities and died in Brody, Galicia, in 1780. Margoliot was the first to write a commentary on the entire Jerusalem Talmud; and he too divided his commentary into two parts—*Penei Moshe* [The Face of Moses], an explanatory commentary, and *Mar'eh ha-Panim* [The Look of the Face], novellae. His commentary is superior to its predecessors both in erudition and in sharpness of analysis. Margoliot made use of various manuscripts in order to establish correct readings.[124]

122. 1707–1762.

123. *I.e.,* up to TJ Shevu'ot 5:4, at which point he died. *See* the printer's note at the end of Fraenkel's commentary to that tractate.

124. *See* Margoliot's own remarks in *Mar'eh ha-Panim,* Shevu'ot 7:6, s.v. Rabbi Ḥanina:

> I call heaven and earth as my witnesses that the commentary on this [Jerusalem] Talmud that I have written was the result of vast research, study, diligence, and labor night and day [lit. "In the evening she came and in the morning she returned," *cf.* Esther 2:14]. [I set myself] to research, study, and examine all parts of this Talmud, the entire *Tosefta,* and all sections of the Babylonian Talmud with the views and explanations of the *geonim,* as far as I could.
>
> Thanks be to God that I have had the merit to discover here many explanations and interpretations of the Babylonian Talmud and many manuscripts of the early *geonim* that were not to be found in our country. I have also found an ancient copy of the *Tosefta* on parchment more than a thousand years old, very carefully written, with meticulous attention to the text. I found many things in it that are missing in the printed versions.

It is interesting that Margoliot's name has been found on the list of students registered in the Department of Botany in the University of Frankfort-on-Oder. Apparently, he enrolled in order to acquire the botanical knowledge necessary for a full understanding of the laws in the Order of *Zera'im* in the Jerusalem Talmud,[125] which are applicable to the Land of Israel and which raise various botanical questions.

G. The Gaon of Vilna's Commentary

Another important and original commentary on the Order of *Zera'im* of the Jerusalem Talmud is that of Elijah b. Solomon Zalman, the Gaon of Vilna.[126] In his other works as well, he frequently cited the Jerusalem Talmud, and he was a major factor contributing to the increased study of that Talmud.[127]

As has been seen, a literature of commentary and novellae on the Jerusalem Talmud began to develop in the sixteenth century, at first written by Sephardic and later by Ashkenazic scholars. Nevertheless, our knowledge of the Jerusalem Talmud is still incomplete; it remains difficult to study and understand. Considerable portions are obscure, and the correct reading is frequently uncertain. The Jerusalem Talmud has not yet had the benefit

---

May God be praised that I have succeeded in composing the commentary and the *Mar'eh* [*i.e.*, the novellae] on these three Orders—*Nashim* and *Nezikin*, now brought to press, and *Zera'im*, which is now written in clear manuscript. May God grant me the grace He grants to the undeserving and allow me to complete the commentary on the Order of *Mo'ed*, so that this entire Talmud will then be illuminated as with the light at the front of the *menorah* [*cf.* Numbers 8:2], and also the unclear statements of Maimonides, of blessed memory, will become clear and shine brightly. [Margoliot compiled indexes to his discussions of the *rishonim* on each Order and organized them along the lines of Maimonides' *Mishneh Torah*.] And, thanks be to God, I have been able to explain fully and clearly every cryptic reference in this Talmud to the *Tosefta*, inasmuch as, in almost all instances, the word "*tani*" introduces a reference to the *Tosefta*, and only rarely to *Torat Kohanim*, the *Sifrei*, or the *Mekhilta*. Those references that I could not find after a long search in the *Tosefta*, *Sifra*, *Sifrei*, *Mekhilta*, and *Pesikta* (both *Rabbata* and *Ze'irata*) I designated simply as a *baraita* that they [the Sages of the Talmud] had, but that we do not.

125. *See* Ginzberg, *Perushim*, pp. 124–125. *See also* S. Lieberman, *Ha-Yerushalmi ki-Feshuto* [TJ according to Its Plain Meaning], 1935, Introduction (at the beginning).

126. 1720–1797.

127. There is no certainty that all the comments attributed to the Gaon of Vilna in his commentary on TJ *Zera'im* are indeed his. The commentary was not printed from his ms. but by his students, who took notes on what they had heard from him orally. The commentary exists in two versions (each by a different student) which occasionally contradict each other. The only work printed directly from the Gaon of Vilna's own ms. is his commentary on the *Shulḥan Arukh*, and there he also copiously cites TJ. For further discussion, *see* Ginzberg, *Perushim*, pp. 125–129.

of a clear and definitive commentary similar to the masterwork of Rashi on the Babylonian Talmud, which opened up that work to both the ordinary student and the serious scholar. Although, in recent generations, several halakhic authorities and scholars have written brief glosses and commentaries on the Jerusalem Talmud,[128] that Talmud, which, together with the Babylonian Talmud, constitutes the basis of the Oral Law, still awaits a complete and comprehensive commentary that will establish the correct text and will fully illuminate its contents.[129]

128. Books written on TJ in recent times include:

1. *No'am Yerushalayim,* by Joshua Isaac Slonimer, Vilna, 1863, two vols. (on the entire TJ).
2. *Sefer Nir* by Meir Marim, *av bet din* of Kobrin and environs, 1875–1932, two vols. (Orders *Zera'im* and *Mo'ed* and Tractates *Gittin, Kiddushin, Nazir, Yevamot,* and *Sotah*).
3. *Ahavat Ẓiyyon vi-Yerushalayim,* by Dov Ber Ratner, Vilna, 1901–1917; twelve vols. (Tractates *Zera'im* and *Mo'ed*).
4. *Seridei ha-Yerushalmi,* by Louis Ginzberg, New York, 1909.
5. *Netivot Yerushalayim,* by Israel Ḥayyim Daiches, 1900–1927 (Tractates *Bava Kamma, Bava Meẓi'a,* and *Bava Batra*).
6. *Yerushalmi le-Seder Zera'im,* with commentary of Solomon Sirillo and *Emunat Yosef;* new edition, Jerusalem, 1934 *et seq.,* eleven vols.
7. *Ha-Yerushalmi ki-Feshuto,* by Saul Lieberman, Jerusalem, 1935, vol. I (Tractates *Shabbat, Eruvin,* and *Pesaḥim*).
8. *Sha'arei Torat Ereẓ Yisra'el,* by Ze'ev Wolf Rabinowitz, Jerusalem, 1940.
9. *Perushim ve-Ḥiddushim ba-Yerushalmi,* by Louis Ginzberg, New York, 1941–1961, four vols. (Tractate *Berakhot,* chs. 1–5), with a comprehensive Introduction.
10. *Yerushalmi Massekhet Shekalim* with Commentaries of Rabbenu Meshullam and of a Disciple of Rabbenu Samuel b. Shneur, published by A. Sofer, New York, 1944.
11. *Hilkhot ha-Yerushalmi le-ha-Rambam,* by Saul Lieberman, New York, 1948.
12. *Talmud Yerushalmi, Order of Zera'im According to Readings of Elijah, the Gaon of Vilna,* by Abraham Jacob Neumark, Tel Aviv, 1956.
13. *Yerushalmi Shevi'it,* with Commentaries of Solomon Sirillo, Elijah of Fulda, *Sefer Nir,* the Gaon of Vilna and Ḥazon Ish, Givatayim, 1959.
14. *Ha-Yerushalmi ha-Meforash,* by Shlomo Goren, Jerusalem, 1961 (Tractate *Berakhot* chs. 1–5).

See also supra n. 100, regarding books of glosses to the Babylonian Talmud, many of which are devoted to a critical comparison of sources in both Talmuds (*e.g., Yefeh Einayim*).

129. As to the importance of study and research in TJ both with respect to halakhic content and literary form, and for an understanding of the historical, political, and social factors that influenced the development of various legal principles, *see supra* pp. 1095–1097 and nn. 63 and 64. The return of the Jewish people to the Land of Israel in modern times and the establishment of a Jewish sovereign state have increased the importance and the urgency of thorough study of the Jerusalem Talmud—the Talmud of the Land of Israel.

Chapter 32
THE CODIFICATORY LITERATURE: NATURE AND STRUCTURE; THE PROBLEM OF CODIFICATION

I. The Relationship of Codificatory Literature to Commentaries, Novellae, and the Responsa Literature
II. The Two Basic Types of Codes
III. Codification in Other Legal Systems
  A. The Term "Codification"
  B. Codification in Continental Europe
  C. Codification in Common-Law Countries
IV. The Nature and Problem of Codification in Jewish Law

I. THE RELATIONSHIP OF CODIFICATORY LITERATURE TO COMMENTARIES, NOVELLAE, AND THE RESPONSA LITERATURE

In addition to commentaries and novellae, another principal type of literary source of Jewish law in the post-Talmudic period is the codificatory literature. The distinctive feature of this literature is that it aims to set forth the law in a definitive and organized fashion, and its conclusions are arrived at by theoretical analysis of the relevant material contained in the various literary sources of the law.

All the major types of literary sources of Jewish law in the post-Talmudic era are interconnected, and each influences the others. Thus, both the commentator and the author of novellae study for their own purposes all the available halakhic literature, including the codificatory and responsa literature; and the author of a responsum or a code must study the commentaries and novellae and their conclusions. In this respect, each type of literary source sustains and enriches the others.

At the same time, there are important differences; each type has a special character and purpose of its own. The commentaries/novellae literature differs from responsa and codes in that its aim is to explain and clarify a particular halakhic subject and its purpose is essentially theoretical rather than practical. By contrast, the purpose of a responsum or a code is more than a theoretical analysis or explanation of the law; a responsum or code is intended to set forth the binding law governing practical conduct.

Although responsa and codes share the common objective of determining the law to be applied in practice, they differ in the methods by which they reach their conclusions and in the manner in which the conclusions are presented. A codificatory work states conclusions arrived at by theoretical analysis, but generally does not indicate the reasoning process. By contrast, to read a responsum is to be propelled into the vortex of an actual halakhic and legal confrontation, to hear the facts and the arguments of the parties, and to follow the halakhic authority through every stage of the analysis leading to the decision which resolves the problem.

II. THE TWO BASIC TYPES OF CODES

Codificatory literature consists mainly of two types—books of *halakhot* and books of *pesakim.* The difference between them reflects a fundamental difference in approach to the problem of codification in Jewish law. Books of *halakhot* state the final conclusion after some discussion, generally brief and to the point, that cites and explains the sources on which the conclusion is based. The outstanding example of this type of code is the *Sefer ha-Halakhot* [Book of the Laws] by Isaac Alfasi. By contrast, books of *pesakim* state the final halakhic conclusion without any discussion and without indicating the sources on which the conclusion is based. The outstanding example of a work of *pesakim* is Maimonides' *Mishneh Torah.* In the course of time, a third type of code developed, which blended the qualities of each of the other two.

In addition to and as a corollary of this difference in content between books of *halakhot* and books of *pesakim,* there is also a difference in literary form. Books of *halakhot,* which cite, briefly discuss, and explain the sources of the law they set forth, are naturally organized to correspond with the organization of whatever literary source contains the material on which the statement of the law is based. Alfasi's *Sefer ha-Halakhot* is therefore organized according to the order of the tractates of the Talmud, and other books of *halakhot* have various other methods of organization described below.

On the other hand, books of *pesakim* are organized topically, setting forth in one place under each topic all the relevant laws, which in their original sources may be scattered throughout various parts of tannaitic, Talmudic, and post-Talmudic literature. A code that sets forth only the halakhic conclusion, with no discussion or citation of source, is organized topically because that is the most convenient and useful arrangement. This was the method used in the fourteen books of Maimonides' *Mishneh Torah*.

Thus, books of *halakhot*, unlike books of *pesakim*, maintain, both in content and in literary form, a link to the sources of the *Halakhah*.

III. CODIFICATION IN OTHER LEGAL SYSTEMS

As indicated, the distinction between books of *halakhot* and books of *pesakim* reflects a fundamental difference in approach to the problem of codification in Jewish law. A full understanding of the problem requires a brief preliminary review of the nature and function of codification in other legal systems.[1]

A. The Term "Codification"

The term "codification," in its historical sense, means the reduction to writing of law previously extant only orally. In time, codification came to have a different meaning, similar to but not identical with legislation. Legislation involves the establishment of a particular normative rule by an authorized legislator or legislative body. It may involve one or more legal provisions, and its object is to amend an existing legal norm or to create a new one. In Jewish law, this type of legislation, termed *takkanah* or *gezerah*, has been enacted by various authorized legislative bodies.[2]

Codification, on the other hand, has a broader function. It involves at least a significant area of the law, if not the entire legal system. Codification stems from and is motivated by the need to address shortcomings resulting from various juridical, historical, and national factors. These factors include: proliferation of laws scattered in different literary sources, awkwardness and lack of uniformity in the literary style of the laws, inconsistency of legal norms within a legal system due to haphazard development of numerous *ad hoc* provisions over a long period of time, and inconsistency of

1. As to the problem of codification in the various legal systems, *see* C. Ilbert, *The Mechanics of Law Making*, New York, 1914, pp. 32–41, 150–180; M.E. Lang, *Codification in the British Empire and America*, Amsterdam, 1924; E. Freund, *Legislative Regulation*, New York, 1932, pp. 3–17; *Encyclopaedia Britannica*, 1966, VI, pp. 8–12, s.vv. Code, Code Napoleon; *Encyclopaedia of the Social Sciences*, 1949, III, pp. 606–613, s.v. Codification; *International Encyclopaedia of Social Sciences*, 1968, IX, pp. 214 *et seq.*, s.vv. Legal systems, Code law systems; pp. 229 *et seq.*, s.vv. Legislation, Interpretation, and Codification of statutes; Y. Pokrovsky, *Ha-Problemot ha-Yesodiyyot Shel ha-Mishpat ha-Ezraḥi* [The Fundamental Problems of Civil Law] (Hebrew trans., A. Litai), Jerusalem, 1922, pp. 28–41.

2. *See supra* pp. 477ff.

legal provisions as a result of the amalgamation of different legal systems following the political union of different states and nations. The legislator generally sees a particular legal problem requiring solution, whereas the codifier operates from the perspective of the legal system as a whole in order to meet systemic needs.

B. Codification in Continental Europe

The proponents of the major Continental codes, beginning with the middle of the eighteenth century, had high hopes and ambitious aspirations for codification, which have been only partly vindicated by the acid test of experience. The major codes of that period, such as the Prussian Code at the end of the eighteenth century and the Napoleonic Code in the early nineteenth century, aspired to compile all the normative provisions in a given area of law, organize them in a scientific and logical order, and express them in clear and concise language understandable to everyone. The declared goal of the codification movement in that period was not merely to make the code the single source of the law supplanting all previous legal rulings, but to make it a complete, clear, and easily understood work of the highest quality, so that, as Frederick the Great declared, "the whole army of lawyers will be utterly superfluous" because the code—as the French codifiers believed—will make the law "simple, democratic, and accessible to every citizen."[3]

Furthermore, the codes explicitly provided that they were not to be interpreted by means of any kind of "philosophical speculations."[4] The code was to be the sole source of law; there was to be none other, before or after it. It was to be comprehensive in every respect; adding to it or subtracting from it was forbidden and, indeed, would be unnecessary.

These inflated expectations were not realized. It became apparent that no code, however comprehensive, can contain the answers to all the legal questions that continue to arise, and that interpretation, whether by analogy or by other means, is inescapable. The vision of the law as being stated so simply that it could be accessible to everyone also proved to be a mirage. Notwithstanding all the effort expended on language and style, the codes were still intelligible only to jurists, and even they frequently disagreed about the meaning and application of particular provisions in a given case. It became clear that no code can be self-sufficient; every code needs to be supplemented, explained, clarified, and interpreted.

This realization led to a more correct and realistic appraisal of the ob-

3. *Encyclopaedia of the Social Sciences*, III, p. 612.
4. Pokrovsky, *supra* n. 1 at 29–30; *see Encyclopaedia of the Social Sciences*, *supra* n. 3.

jectives that codification could be expected to achieve. These objectives, on which there is now general agreement, are three:

1. A code should include fundamental provisions that establish principles and guidelines; it should not attempt to be comprehensive and all-inclusive. It is the judges and jurists who should apply and interpret the code's general guidelines in the light of the specific circumstances that may arise.
2. A code should be well organized, well written, and easy to study. It should, as far as possible, be clear and succinct, but it cannot meet the eighteenth-century aspiration of accessibility and intelligibility to everyone. Jurisprudence, like any other scientific discipline, has special terms and expressions; its language and style are not easily understood by laymen. Any oversimplification in style runs the risk of obscurity and imprecision, which are the bane of all legal draftsmen. The style must be professional-legal, but care should be taken to avoid, as far as possible, prolixity, ambiguity, and obscurity.
3. Finally, a code is the authoritative source for every law in any legal field covered by it. However, while its provisions supplant any other prior provisions to the contrary, a code is not intended to preclude future legal development. On the contrary, it is manifest from the outset that a code, standing alone, cannot cover all questions, and that only future interpretation, whether in the course of adjudication or of theoretical study and analysis, can make the code reasonably comprehensive and fully useful.

C. Codification in Common-Law Countries

The great movements toward codification originated in Continental Europe; and, to the present day, many of the systems of continental law, such as the French, the German, and the Swiss, have remained staunch advocates of codification. There are, however, important legal systems, such as the common law, that take a negative view of the basic concept of codification because they disagree with the advocates of codification on a fundamental issue that goes beyond the question of codification itself.

This issue—deeply rooted in ideology and history—is: What is the most appropriate way for a legal system to deal with the continuing development and creativity of the law? Continental legal systems support the principle that amendments and improvements whereby the law is continuously developed are exclusively the province of the legislature, and that the best way for the legislature to articulate the law is by drafting a code that the legislative imprimatur makes authoritative.

The common law, however, views adjudication of actual problems arising in daily life as the principal method of carrying on the process of creating, shaping, and developing the law. The common-law approach prefers new legal principles to emerge from the crucible of practical life rather than out of the abstract thought processes of a legislature prospectively drafting a statute. The common law, therefore, confers binding force on legal principles derived from judicial precedents; the courts are significant participants in the creation and development of the law.[5] It is instructive that in the second half of the eighteenth century and the beginning of the nineteenth century an outstanding English jurist and scholar, Jeremy Bentham, ardently championed the cause of codification but, despite some posthumous influence on the movement for codification in the British colonies, such as occurred in India, he failed to effect any significant advance toward that goal in England itself.

The common-law system has not been immune to the proliferation and complication of statute law enacted over a period of centuries. One method of coping with this problem has been to compile the most recent texts of the various statutes and to organize them according to subject matter. These compilations are sometimes called "codes," but they are not codifications in the generally accepted sense of the term as used in the present discussion. The text in such compilations is only presumptive evidence of the actual text of any given statute, and the statutory text prevails when inconsistent with the text of the compilation.

Another approach to a solution is statutory revision, or consolidation, which also arranges the statutes systematically by subjects and issues. Revision, unlike compilation, is generally considered to be new and binding legislation; it must be accepted by authorized governmental agencies as conclusive proof of the statutory text, and it occasionally changes the original text of the law.[6]

A considerable number of scholars believe that revision constitutes codification; others, particularly in England, reserve the term "codification" exclusively for a binding legislative enactment, systematically arranged and classified, encompassing all the legal material, both common-law and statutory, on a particular subject. To date, there are very few codifications in that sense in England. It should also be noted that compilations and revisions both involve only statutory enactments.

5. *See supra* pp. 979–980.

6. *See* the Israeli Law and Administration Ordinance, 1948, sec. 16 (as amended in 1972), for the difference in the Israeli legal system between a "new version" and a "consolidated version." "New version" is closer to "revision," while "consolidated version" is closer to "compilation." According to Section 16, in both categories the most recently enacted text, whether "new" or "consolidated," states the binding law. *See* Gali v. State of Israel, 40(iv) *P.D.* 169 (1986).

In the United States, in the beginning of the nineteenth century, there was some movement toward codification; and in several states, codes were enacted covering civil and criminal procedure, as well as various areas of the civil law. In fact, later in the nineteenth century, David Dudley Field, the great advocate of codification, prepared a civil code for New York State, but after a stormy debate his code was rejected by the legal community of New York. Even in the United States, where there has been more codification of parts of the law than in England, the bulk of the law consists of both common law and statutory enactments, whereas in continental Europe the law is almost entirely codified.[7]

IV. THE NATURE AND PROBLEM OF CODIFICATION IN JEWISH LAW

The foregoing discussion of codification and the various approaches to it in other legal systems is helpful in understanding various aspects of the codificatory literature of Jewish law. These aspects will be noted in the course of the ensuing discussion of the various halakhic codes. One matter, however, which is central to consideration of the codificatory literature of Jewish law, must be dealt with at the outset.

As has been seen, it is a basic tenet of the theory of codification (even in its present less ambitious form) that not only is the code the exclusive authorized source for the law it contains, but any inconsistent prior law is thereby abrogated.

That principle is not tenable within the Jewish legal system; no one has ever even suggested it. The very nature, as well as the binding force, of Jewish law derives from its continuity—the chain of tradition from generation to generation. Every rule or norm added to the corpus of the law by means of any of the halakhic legal sources[8] is effective because it draws its

7. In the United States, the vast tangle of judicial precedents (in which there are conflicts not only between the courts of different states, but even between federal appellate courts) has been "codified" after a fashion in the American Law Institute's "Restatements of the Law," which have been published in the areas of Conflict of Laws, Property, Trusts, Contracts, Torts, Agency, Foreign Relations, Judgments, Restitution, etc. However, the Restatements are not binding, although they can be very persuasive authority. *See Restatement of the Law, Conflict of Laws,* 1934, p. VII *et seq.; Restatement in the Courts,* Permanent Edition (1945), pp. 1–23; *International Encyclopaedia of the Social Sciences,* 1968, IX, p. 212 *et seq.* It is significant that virtually all the Restatements have been restated in a second series, that new Restatements have been undertaken to encompass newly emerging legal areas, and that a third series of some Restatements is being prepared.

8. *See supra* pp. 228ff. and Part Two of the present work.

sustenance from the Written Law and the Oral Law, including the legal rules added throughout the generations.

This quality of Jewish law is axiomatic and beyond dispute. Not even Maimonides, who compiled the greatest and most nearly perfect halakhic code of all, sought to establish his work as the source of halakhic authority, superseding all prior *Halakhah.* This is true notwithstanding his clearly stated ambitious purpose in writing his code:

> In brief, a person will not need to have recourse to any other work to ascertain any of the laws of Israel. This work is intended as a compendium of the entire Oral Law, including the enactments, customs, and decrees instituted from the days of Moses, our teacher, until the redaction of the Talmud, as expounded for us by the *geonim* in all the works composed by them since the completion of the Talmud.
>
> Hence, I have entitled this work *Mishneh Torah* [Recapitulation of Torah], for the reason that a person who first reads the Torah and then this work will know from it all of the Oral Law, and there will be no need to read any other book [written] between them.[9]

Nor did Maimonides entertain even the slightest idea of introducing any change in the law through his work. In fact, he began his Introduction, which contains the far-reaching statement just quoted, with a description of the chain of tradition from the Revelation at Sinai, including a detailed list of the names of those who transmitted the tradition. He then concluded:

> Everything in the Babylonian Talmud is binding on all Israel. Every town and country must follow all the customs, give effect to the decrees, and carry out the enactments of the Talmudic Sages, because the entire Jewish people accepted everything contained in the Talmud. The Sages who adopted the enactments and decrees, instituted the practices, rendered the decisions, and derived the laws, constituted all or most of the Sages of Israel. It is they who received the tradition of the fundamentals of the entire Torah in unbroken succession going back to Moses, our teacher.

The Torah revealed at Sinai—the Oral as well as the Written Law—is both the supreme value of Jewish law and the source of halakhic authority; and everything in the Torah is "binding on all Israel."

The clear implication of this emphatic statement was explicitly stated in Maimonides' response to a letter of inquiry from Phinehas b. Meshullam, the *dayyan* (judge) of Alexandria:[10]

9. *MT,* Introduction (ed. Constantinople), Mosad ha-Rav Kook, 1963, p. 14; *see infra* pp. 1185–1186.

10. *Koveẓ ha-Rambam,* I, #140, p. 25c.

> I have never said (Heaven forbid!): "Do not occupy yourselves with the Talmud or the *Halakhot* [Book of Laws] of Rabbi Isaac [Alfasi]—or anyone else." God is my witness that this last year-and-a-half I have not taught my work [the *Mishneh Torah*]. Only three people have studied some of the books. Most of the students wished to study the *Halakhot* of the Master [Alfasi], and I taught them all the *Halakhot* several times. Two also requested to learn Talmud, and I taught them the tractates that they requested. Have I instructed or even contemplated that on account of my work all the books written before my time should be burned?

Thus, Maimonides acknowledged that the halakhic literature prior to his own work remained valuable for academic study and research into the sources of the law. He also must have appreciated its importance for ongoing legal creativity and the solution of new problems. The foremost requirements for creative solutions to such problems are profound study of the Talmud, and analogical reasoning from the vast reservoir of laws and discussions in Talmudic and post-Talmudic literature.

Maimonides intended no more than that his work would be the sole resource to which recourse would be necessary in order to find the correct statement of the law. He was convinced that his code included the totality of Jewish law up to his time and that there could not be any conflict between his work and the law stated as binding in the works of prior halakhic authorities.[11]

In view of the link between Jewish law and its sources, and in view of the authority of the codifier (in the modern sense of the word) to change the law in the process of codification, it is clear that codification and even revision are incompatible with the essential nature of the Jewish legal system. Only a compilation of the laws is acceptable. Innovation, creativity, and modification within the Jewish legal system are effectuated only by means of the legal sources of the system and are not within the prerogative of the author of a halakhic "codificatory" work.[12]

On the other hand, the halakhic system is able to recognize a "codificatory" work as an authoritative compilation of the law and to have recourse to it as the sole resource for making legal decisions. Indeed, that was Maimonides' purpose. In this respect, the *Mishneh Torah* shares the quality of a code in the currently accepted sense of the term, since it was intended

11. *See further infra* pp. 1185–1187.

12. *See* in detail *supra* pp. 228ff. and Part Two of this work. Obviously, even the author of a book of *halakhot* or *pesakim* is occasionally likely in the course of his work to formulate or develop a particular legal principle, especially as a result of the use of interpretation or legal reasoning. In such a case, however, the innovation and creativity are the result of the codifier's use of interpretation or legal reasoning as a legal source, and not of the act of codification as such.

to encompass the whole of the Jewish legal system and to be not merely presumptive evidence but a source from which anyone deciding a legal question will know "all of the Oral Law, and there will be no need to read any other book."

The great problem that has faced all the codifiers of Jewish law throughout the ages has been whether a compilation like that of Maimonides—theoretically compatible with the halakhic system though it may be—is desirable and good for the system. Does not such a code that purports to include the totality of the law, and that sets forth only conclusions without prior discussion, tend to sever the law from the sources that give it life and nourishment? Does not the very nature of Jewish law, with its principle that "the words of both are the words of the living God," require continual study and discussion of the range of opinions on every issue, and does it not reject—indeed, as a matter of principle—setting forth the law on the basis of only one view? Jewish law has developed historically by solving concrete, practical problems and not by establishing binding rules and principles *a priori.*[13] Therefore, is it not entirely conceivable that there is no place for codification in Jewish law, just as, generally speaking, there is no place for it in the common law, which developed in much the same way?

These considerations point to a conclusion that the Jewish legal system could—and possibly even should—reject both the codification and the compilation of its laws. However, certain countervailing factors made codification, in the sense of a comprehensive compilation of the laws, desirable and even necessary. Some motivating factors were similar to those in other legal systems favoring codification, but others were uniquely grounded in Jewish history and in the condition of Jewish law itself. These motivating factors operated in three areas: (a) historical circumstances—both external and internal—of the Jewish people (such as the difficult political situation and the schismatic sects); (b) academic and educational circumstances (such as the difficulty involved in studying the halakhic material and attaining familiarity with it); and (c) circumstances inherent in Jewish law itself (such as lack of uniformity).

These clusters of conflicting pressures and considerations for and against codification operated during the various processes and stages through which Jewish codificatory literature passed,[14] and the main task of the codifiers of Jewish law has always been to strike a proper balance

13. *See supra* pp. 950–957, 1072–1073; *infra* pp. 1456–1457.

14. These factors are discussed in detail below in connection with the various works in their respective periods. *See further* M. Elon, "Meni'im ve-Ekronot be-Kodifikaziyah Shel ha-Halakhah" [Motive Forces and Principles in the Codification of the *Halakhah*], *Hagut ve-Halakhah,* 1968, pp. 75–119 (*Gevilin,* 1967, pp. 71–85).

among them. Some of the factors involved have already been discussed in connection with the composition of the first code of the Oral Law, namely, the Mishnah of R. Judah Ha-Nasi. On the one hand, the desire to restore uniformity to the law,[15] the fear that the academic level and the number of students were declining due to new tribulations, the spread of the "kingdom of wickedness" in the world,[16] and the aim of facilitating the knowledge and study of the *Halakhah*[17]—all played a part in persuading R. Judah Ha-Nasi to undertake the redaction of the Mishnah. On the other hand, the need to maintain the continuity of the tradition and to preserve the connection between the halakhic system and its sources led him to incorporate variant opinions in his Mishnah and to identify the Sages who maintained them, even where he held that the law was otherwise.[18]

R. Judah Ha-Nasi's solution was appropriate and necessary for his own time but did not seem adequate for subsequent codifications. Starting with the geonic period, there began a series of attempts to find other answers to the question of how Jewish law should be codified. These attempts produced three main types of codificatory literature: (a) books of *halakhot,* (b) books of *pesakim,* and (c) a combination of the two. Within each type, different literary forms developed in various periods. A substantial portion of the following chapters is devoted to these types and forms, and to the halakhic, didactic, and historical factors that gave rise to them.

15. *See supra* pp. 1061–1070.

16. Maimonides, *supra* n. 9 at 6; *see supra* p. 1069.

17. *See* Maimonides, *supra* n. 16: R. Judah Ha-Nasi "composed a work [*i.e.,* the Mishnah] to be in everyone's hand so that they can study it quickly and it will not be forgotten."

18. For a fuller discussion, *see supra* pp. 1070–1071.

Chapter 33

THE CODIFICATORY LITERATURE FROM THE GEONIC PERIOD UNTIL MAIMONIDES' *MISHNEH TORAH*

I. Codificatory Works in the Geonic Period
  - A. *Sefer ha-She'iltot* by Aḥa of Shabḥa
  - B. *Halakhot Pesukot* by Yehudai Gaon
  - C. *Halakhot Gedolot*
  - D. Motivating Factors for and against Codification in the Geonic Period
  - E. Halakhic Monographs
    1. Saadiah Gaon
    2. Samuel b. Ḥophni Gaon
    3. Hai Gaon
    4. The Objectives of Halakhic Monographs

II. *Sefer ha-Halakhot* by Isaac Alfasi (Rif)
  - A. The Nature and Content of *Sefer ha-Halakhot*
  - B. Commentaries on *Sefer ha-Halakhot*
    1. Zeraḥiah ha-Levi Gerondi (Rezah)
    2. Abraham b. David (Rabad) of Posquières
    3. Naḥmanides (Ramban)
    4. Jonathan of Lunel
    5. Nissim Gerondi (Ran)
    6. Joseph Ḥabiba
    7. Joshua Boaz b. Simon Baruch
    8. Other Commentators

III. Codificatory Works from Alfasi to Maimonides
  - A. Spain
    1. Isaac ibn Ghayyat (Riẓag)
    2. Judah al-Bargeloni
  - B. France and Germany
    1. The School of Rashi
    2. Eliezer b. Nathan (Raban)

I. CODIFICATORY WORKS IN THE GEONIC PERIOD

A. *Sefer ha-She'iltot* by Aḥa of Shabḥa

Commencing with the eighth century C.E., the considerable halakhic literature of the geonic era that is extant reveals ever-increasing activity in regard to codification of the *Halakhah.* The codificatory literature of this period took several forms, but the feature common to them all is that they are books of *halakhot, i.e.,* their declared aim is to present the halakhic conclusion and final ruling after a concise discussion of the underlying Talmudic and post-Talmudic sources.

The first such book of known authorship written after the completion of the Talmud[1] is *Sefer ha-She'iltot* by Aḥa from the town of Shabḥa near Basra in Babylonia, who lived in the first half of the eighth century C.E. Aḥa was not officially designated as *gaon.* As Sherira Gaon relates,[2] Aḥa was a candidate for the office of *gaon* in the academy of Pumbedita, but Exilarch Solomon b. Ḥasdai appointed Natronoi Kahana, who was a student of Aḥa, whereupon Aḥa settled in the Land of Israel, where he resided until he died.

Scholars have extensively considered the nature and purpose of *Sefer ha-She'iltot.*[3] The most likely hypothesis is that it is essentially a collection of sermons. It is in the same style and form as the sermons that the leading Sages, as early as in the Talmudic era, would deliver on sabbaths and various other occasions. However, "it is more halakhic than aggadic; its codificatory motive is quite prominent and it very soon came to be used and relied upon to provide the answers to practical legal questions."[4]

Sefer ha-She'iltot is unique in its literary form. It is not arranged either by subject or in the order of the Talmudic tractates, but rather, like mid-

1. The authors of books such as the "minor tractates" and the various *midrashim* written between the completion of the Talmud and *Sefer ha-She'iltot* are anonymous; *see* Assaf, *Geonim,* p. 154. *See also* Tractate *Semaḥot,* ed. D. Zlotnick, Introduction (rejecting the proofs advanced for dating that tractate to a later period); A. Goldberg's review of Zlotnick, *Kiryat Sefer,* XLII (1967), pp. 460ff.

2. *Iggeret Rav Sherira Gaon,* ed. B. M. Lewin, p. 103. *See* Rabad (Abraham ibn Daud), *Sefer ha-Qabbalah* [Book of Tradition], trans. and ed. G. Cohen, JPS, 1967, pp. 47–48.

3. *See* the bibliography in Assaf, *Geonim; Sefer ha-She'iltot,* ed. S. Mirsky, 1960, I, Introduction, pp. lff. Our citations *(e.g., she'ilta* 33, discussed *infra)* follow the numbers in Mirsky's edition.

4. Assaf, *Geonim,* p. 155.

rashic literature, follows the sequence of the Torah. Each *she'ilta* (singular of *she'iltot*—the origin of the term is explained below) discusses a particular halakhic subject that is conjoined to the Biblical passage directly relevant or otherwise appropriate to it. Interestingly, in the case of some of the *she'iltot*, the passage to which the *she'ilta* is linked does not contain the halakhic source on the particular subject, but merely refers to the subject in the course of a narrative. For example, the laws of robbery and theft in the *She'iltot* are not linked to the verses that are their halakhic source,[5] but to the passage relating the story of Noah and the Flood, where it is said: "The earth is filled with *ḥamas* [lawlessness, violence, or oppression, connoting lack of respect for property] because of them; I am about to destroy them with the earth."[6] Thus, *she'ilta* 4, to the Biblical portion of Noah, begins:

> It is forbidden for Jews to rob or steal from one another; indeed the punishment for these transgressions is more severe than for [violations of] all [other] prohibitions. Thus we find in the case of the generation of the Flood that their doom was sealed only on account of robbery. As R. Eleazar said: "Come and see how severe is the effect of lawlessness (*ḥamas*), for the generation of the Flood was guilty of every transgression, but their doom was sealed only on account of *ḥamas*, as it is said, 'For the earth is filled with lawlessness because of them; I am about to destroy them with the earth.'"

After some aggadic reflections, the *she'ilta* goes on to discuss the substance of the laws of robbery and theft. Similarly, an extensive discussion of the law of betrothal and marriage, particularly betrothal through an agent, is presented in *she'iltot* 16 and 17 in connection with Genesis 24, which tells of the marriage of Isaac and the appointment of Abraham's servant, Eliezer, as agent to betroth a wife for Isaac. Likewise, the laws of bailees, for which the source is Exodus 22:6ff., are discussed in *she'ilta* 20 on Genesis 29:15ff., which tells of the entrustment of Laban's flocks to Jacob. The laws of suretyship are presented in *she'ilta* 33 in connection with the story of Judah's undertaking to Jacob to be surety for Benjamin's safety, in which Judah said: "I myself will be surety for him; you may hold me responsible."[7] The beginning of this *she'ilta* has an ethical-aggadic flavor:

> The House of Israel are duty bound to have compassion one for another. Whoever needs sustenance should be sustained, and whoever needs a loan

5. Leviticus 19:11: "You shall not steal; you shall not deal deceitfully or falsely with one another."

6. Genesis 6:13.

7. Genesis 43:9. TB Bava Batra 173b rejects the possibility of deriving the laws of suretyship from this verse, and that Talmudic passage is actually quoted in *she'ilta* 33. The textual version of the passage quoted in the *she'ilta* resolves a difficulty with the passage that troubled Maharsha. *See Masoret ha-Shas, ad loc.*

should be granted it. If one grants a loan guaranteed by a surety, he should claim in the first instance not against the surety but against the debtor; only if the debtor does not repay should he proceed against the surety.

The structure of the *she'iltot* is also unique. A complete *she'ilta* consists of four parts. The first is a kind of general introduction to the central halakhic subject to be discussed. This part reviews the ethical-religious value involved, together with pertinent halakhic material. The second part sets forth a pertinent halakhic problem opening (in Aramaic) with "But you must learn." The third part is the discourse, opening with "Blessed be the Name of the Holy One, blessed be He, who has bestowed upon us Torah and commandments through Moses, our teacher, in order to teach His people, the House of Israel." In this part, the subject is discussed at length in full detail, heavily spiced with halakhic and aggadic sources. The fourth part gives the answer to the specific halakhic problem initially posed, and opens: "And as to the query we posed to you" (a convention of humility—the accurate introductory formula would be "as to the question that you asked me").[8] It is by reason of the Aramaic formula introducing the fourth part—*u-le-inyan she'ilta di-sha'ilna*—that the book is called *She'iltot.* As it has reached us, most *she'iltot* are lacking various parts, mainly the "discourse."[9]

From this brief description of *Sefer ha-She'iltot,* its characteristic feature is clear: *Halakhah* and *Aggadah* are employed together in the style of the ancient discourses, with a view to determining halakhic conclusions. A comparison with the usual forms of codificatory literature raises the question as to whether this book should really be classified in that category. However, there are two reasons why *Sefer ha-She'iltot* must be considered before discussing the books of *halakhot* produced in the geonic period. First, *Sefer ha-She'iltot* brings together in one place a substantial number of problems and laws in various halakhic areas, and one of its purposes is to set forth correctly the controlling law and make clear the reason for the legal conclusion. Second, *Sefer ha-She'iltot* served as an important and highly authoritative source for a series of classic books of *halakhot* written subsequently, as indicated by the following statement of Abraham ibn Daud in his *Sefer ha-Kabbalah*:[10]

After R. Samuel bar Mari there was a great scholar [by the name of] R. Aḥa of Shabḥa, who composed his *She'eiltot* [*She'iltot*] on all the commandments

8. *See* Rashi, Shabbat 30b, s.v. Di-she'ilna kadameikhon; Mirsky, *supra* n. 3 at 20, and *she'ilta* 1, p. 19.

9. *Sefer ha-She'iltot* contains 171 *she'iltot;* for an example of a *she'ilta* complete in all its four parts, *see she'ilta* 1.

10. Rabad, *supra* n. 2 at 47.

specified in the Torah. This book, which has survived to this day, was examined and scrutinized by all who lived after him; we have heard that to this day not a single error has been detected in it.[11]

A tradition regarding the composition of *Sefer ha-She'iltot* reported by Menahem Meiri has evoked considerable wonder and speculation among scholars.[12] In *Bet ha-Beḥirah,*[13] Meiri wrote:

> We have a clear tradition about R. Aḥa, of blessed memory, that he had a son who was not at all inclined to study. He therefore composed for him *Sefer ha-She'iltot,* so that on every sabbath, as the weekly Torah portion would be read, there would be explained to him through the book well-known laws from the Talmud.

However, without entering into the specific details of this tradition, it should be pointed out that its basic concept—the objective of composing a concise halakhic work understandable by young and old, scholar and layman—appears often in one form or another in the works of quite a number of codifiers.[14] This objective is no reason for wonderment: it is implicit in the very concept of a code summarizing Jewish law—or the law of any legal system—as previously discussed in connection with the eighteenth-century proponents of codification in various legal systems.[15]

B. *Halakhot Pesukot* by Yehudai Gaon

Halakhot Pesukot [Settled Laws], written shortly after *Sefer ha-She'iltot,* and attributed to Yehudai Gaon, is the first classic example of a book of *halakhot.*[16]

11. *See further* Mirsky, *supra* n. 3 at 12–16.

12. *See, e.g.,* Ginzberg, *Geonica,* I, p. 89; Mirsky, *supra* n. 3 at 17–18.

13. Meiri, *Bet ha-Beḥirah,* Avot, Jerusalem, 1944, Introduction, pp. 64–65 (ed. B.Z. Prag, Jerusalem, 1964, p. 52).

14. *See infra* pp. 1185, 1265–1266, 1271, 1321–1322, 1372.

15. *See supra* p. 1141. It is true that Meiri went on to say that he viewed the tradition he reported as evidence of a different, even opposite, purpose, *i.e.,* to compose books for the use of certain individuals only, "not that they should be intended for general use by all the people, for they had no need of it." However, the tradition does not prove Meiri's conclusion unless it is taken to mean that the book was in fact written only for the use of the son of Aḥa of Shabḥa.

16. The book was not written by Yehudai Gaon himself (who was blind) but by his disciples, on the basis of his teachings and legal decisions. *See* Assaf, *Geonim,* p. 167. For a long time, the book was known only from quotations in geonic literature and in the literature of the *rishonim* and the Karaites. In 1911, David Sassoon found in San'a, Yemen, a manuscript of the Aramaic original; but not until 1950 was it published in full by his son Solomon Sassoon (Mekiẓei Nirdamim, Jerusalem, 1950). As to the book *Halakhot Pesukot* and the ms., *see* Sassoon's Introduction to his 1950 publication; Assaf, *Geonim,* p. 168;

Yehudai Gaon was one of the great personages of the geonic period. He was associated with the academy of Pumbedita; but when the *gaon* of the academy of Sura died and there was no scholar of Yehudai's stature there, Exilarch Solomon b. Ḥasdai appointed him head of the academy at Sura.[17] Yehudai was the first *gaon* to establish communication with Jewish communities in North Africa (Tunisia, Algeria, and Morocco); he also held discussions on various halakhic matters with the halakhic authorities of the Land of Israel, whom he considered bound by the authority of the Babylonian scholars in regard to determining the law. He is also the first *gaon* from whom many responsa—more than one hundred—have survived. These are characterized by extreme brevity, an indication of his great authority.[18]

Halakhot Pesukot decisively influenced succeeding generations and opened a new era in codificatory literature. The book encompasses all parts of the *Halakhah* then applicable and is arranged by subject, *e.g.*, sabbath, festivals, Passover, interest and usury, loans, *ketubbot*, betrothal, divorce, etc. It does not include laws then totally inapplicable or laws applicable only within the Land of Israel and hence not followed in practice in Babylonia, such as the commandments directly relating to the Land of Israel (*e.g.*, the various tithes and the sabbatical year) and the laws of sacrificial offerings and ritual purity. Thus, Yehudai Gaon set an example for all subsequent codificatory literature, which, with limited exceptions, was also confined to codifying only the law having practical relevance at the time the books were written.

From the standpoint of both style and organization, *Halakhot Pesukot* is a book of *halakhot*. The final halakhic conclusion is generally preceded by a concise précis of the Talmudic sources upon which the conclusion is based. The subjects are for the most part arranged in the order of the tractates of the Talmud, in consequence of which all the material on a particular subject is not always brought together. Written originally in Aramaic, the book was translated into Hebrew; according to most scholars, the translation was done in the Land of Israel.[19]

Abramson, *Ha-Enẓiklopedyah ha-Ivrit* [The Hebrew Encyclopedia], XIV, p. 532, s.v. Halakhot pesukot.

17. This was at the end of the sixties and the beginning of the seventies of the eighth century. In *Ha-Enẓiklopedyah ha-Ivrit*, X, p. 135, s.v. Gaon, it is stated that Yehudai Gaon was the head of the academy of Sura in the years 757–761 C.E.; Assaf, *Geonim*, p. 165, gives 760–763 C.E. as the period Yehudai Gaon held this position.

18. Assaf, *Geonim*, pp. 166ff.

19. In Hebrew, the book is called *Hilkhot Re'u* on account of its opening words, which deal with the laws of *eruvin: "Re'u ki"*—"Mark that [the Lord has given you the sabbath]"; Exodus 16:29.

Halakhot Pesukot substantially facilitated halakhic research. This advantage, together with the recognition of the great authority of the author, led to its rapid and widespread circulation throughout the diaspora. Many copies were made, and various abridged versions of it were composed, such as *Halakhot Ketu'ot* ("Cut" *Halakhot*), *Halakhot Keẓuvot* ("Cut", "Fixed," or "Set" *Halakhot*), *Halakhot Ketannot* (Abridged *Halakhot*), and others.[20]

C. *Halakhot Gedolot*

Two generations later, in the ninth century C.E., a book of *halakhot* was written that was the largest, in size and scope, of the geonic era, namely, *Halakhot Gedolot.* According to most halakhic authorities,[21] its author was Simeon Kayyara, whose surname means "wax vendor" (from *keira* = wax). He lived in Basra, Babylonia.

Halakhot Gedolot, before stating the governing law, briefly presents the sources.[22] Its organization follows the order of the tractates of the Talmud. Its arrangement is in general similar to that of *Halakhot Pesukot,* except that it subsumes more of the material culled from a variety of sources under specific subject headings, sometimes even establishing nomenclature for new legal topics. It also includes some laws relating to commandments that no longer had practical relevance when the book was written, such as various laws relating to sacrificial offerings. Important sources for *Halakhot Gedolot* include, in addition to the Talmud, *Halakhot Pesukot, Sefer ha-She'iltot,* and geonic responsa.[23]

Halakhot Gedolot is also noteworthy in that it is the first Hebrew book with a preface. Moreover, the preface itself is unusual in that it says nothing about the nature and purpose of the book. The preface has two parts: (a) praise of the Torah and its students, based on various Scriptural verses and aggadic sayings; and (b) a list of the 613 commandments divided into 365 negative and 248 affirmative commandments. *Halakhot Gedolot* is the first

20. *See further infra* nn. 24 and 29.

21. Sherira Gaon, Hai Gaon, and the halakhic authorities of Spain and Provence. Some of the authorities of Northern France and Germany attributed the work to Yehudai Gaon. *See* Assaf, *Geonim,* pp. 168–169; *Ha-Enẓiklopedyah ha-Ivrit,* XIV, p. 530, s.v. Halakhot gedolot.

22. *Halakhot Gedolot* is extant in two versions: (1) the Babylonian, first printed in Venice in 1548 (which is the earlier and preserves the original text of the book), and (2) the Spanish (Aspamia), published by R.A. Hildesheimer, Berlin, 1888 (which contains many later additions). *See* A. Epstein, "Al Sefer Halakhot Gedolot" [On the Book *Halakhot Gedolot*], *Ha-Goren,* III, 1902, p. 46; *id., Kadmoniyyot ha-Yehudim* [Early History of the Jews], II, p. 378.

23. As to the relationship between *Halakhot Pesukot* and *Halakhot Gedolot, see further* Halevy, *Dorot,* III, pp. 200–211; Weiss, *Dor Dor ve-Doreshav,* IV, pp. 29–35, 315–316; Ch. Tchernowitz, *Toledot ha-Posekim* [History of the *Posekim*], 1946, I, pp. 70–84.

book to list and enumerate the commandments. Many later authorities also undertook such enumeration but differed with the enumeration in *Halakhot Gedolot.*

D. Motivating Factors for and against Codification in the Geonic Period

The codificatory activity in the first half of the geonic era, the chief literary products of which have been briefly reviewed,[24] was accompanied by all the tensions between the conflicting tendencies previously discussed that have characteristically been at work with regard to the codification of Jewish law.

On the one hand, the times called for a short and concise summary of the law. To find any law, it was necessary to research comprehensively the vast corpus of material in the Talmud, augmented in the period between Yehudai Gaon's book and Simeon Kayyara's work by halakhic material contained in enactments, responsa, and similar sources.[25] As stated in *Seder Olam Zuta*:[26]

> R. Yehudai Gaon, of blessed memory, . . . was as great a sage as those of former times, of blessed memory. It was he who gave fixed form to his wisdom and demonstrated it in *Halakhot Gedolot, Halakhot Ketu'ot,* and *Halakhot Keẓuvot,* which could be studied and relied upon by people unable to master the Orders and tractates [of the Talmud].

An internal historical factor of great importance—the emergence of Karaism in Babylonia in the eighth century C.E.—also spurred the codification of the *Halakhah.* The founder of Karaism, Anan b. David, was of the family of the exilarchs. When, in the latter part of the eighth century C.E., the exilarch died and Anan, having been found unfit to replace him, was passed over in favor of his younger brother, Anan placed himself at the head of the remnants of the religious sects that then existed among Babylonian-Persian Jewry, merged them, and founded the Karaite sect. The Karaites

24. For additional codificatory works, *see Halakhot Keẓuvot,* ed. M. Margaliot, Jerusalem, 1942, and Introduction, pp. 170–171; *Ha-Enziklopedyah ha-Ivrit,* XIV, p. 534, s.v. Halakhot keẓuvot. *Halakhot Keẓuvot* is unique in that it generally states short and concise halakhic rulings without citing sources from the Talmud (Margaliot, *supra,* Introduction at 20ff.) Another such work is *Sefer Metivot,* ed. B.M. Lewin, Jerusalem, 1934; *see* Assaf, *Geonim,* pp. 203ff., and the ensuing discussion by Assaf concerning additional halakhic works by the *geonim. See also infra* p. 1203 n. 63.

25. *See supra* pp. 643ff. and *infra* pp. 1468–1473.

26. Neubauer, *Seder ha-Ḥakhamim,* I, p. 178.

denied the authority of the Oral Law; Anan reportedly stated: "Forsake the words of [the] Mishnah and Talmud and I will make for you a Talmud of my own."[27] The *geonim,* commencing with Yehudai Gaon, took the offensive against Karaism in a battle that lasted some two centuries. In these polemics, the *geonim* and other halakhic authorities produced a rich and vast legal and philosophical literature; and it is a reasonable assumption that, particularly after the ideological battle against the Karaites heated up, one of the methods of consolidating the position of traditional Judaism—based as it is upon the rules of the Oral Law—was to compose books that clearly and concisely summarized the rules of the Oral Law.[28]

On the other hand, this trend toward codification aroused anew the apprehension that study and research in the wide expanse of Talmudic literature itself would be neglected, and that such neglect would lead to the severance of the law from its sources. These conflicting pressures are instructively reflected in a query addressed in the middle of the ninth century to Paltoi b. Abbaye, Gaon of Pumbedita from 842 to 858 C.E., and in his response. Paltoi Gaon was asked:

> [W]hich is preferable and commendable—to engage in the study of the *halakhot* [*i.e.,* the Talmud] or to engage in the study of *halakhot keti'ot*[29] [*i.e.,* codes]? We would not be asking such a thing except that most people tend to study *halakhot keti'ot,* saying, "Of what use are the laborious argumentations of the Talmud to us?"

The Gaon replied:

> They are not acting properly. It is forbidden to act as they do, for they are diminishing Torah, whereas Scripture states [Isaiah 42:21]: "That he may magnify and glorify [His] Torah." What is more, they cause the study of the Torah, God forbid, to become forgotten; *halakhot keti'ot* were composed to be reviewed by one who has studied the entire Talmud and continues to apply

27. *Seder Rav Amram* [R. Amram's Order of Prayers, commonly called his *Siddur*], Warsaw, 1865, p. 38.

28. *See* Assaf, *Geonim,* pp. 117ff., 167; B.M. Lewin "Mi-Seridei ha-Genizah" [Some *Genizah* Fragments], *Tarbiẓ,* II, pp. 383ff., especially pp. 386–393. *See also* Tchernowitz, *supra* n. 23 at I, 64–69. On Karaism generally, *see* H.H. Ben-Sasson, *Perakim Be-Toledot ha-Yehudim bi-Mei ha-Beinayim* [Studies in Jewish History in the Middle Ages], pp. 156–171.

29. *Keti'ot* means "fixed" in the sense of "finally determined" or "settled." *See Oẓar ha-Geonim,* Ketubbot, p. 89, n. 7: "Thus said R. Yehudai Gaon . . . who has settled (*kitta*) the *Halakhah*. . . . " *See also* J. Schor, Introduction to *Sefer ha-Ittim* [Book of Seasons] of Judah al-Bargeloni, p. XXI n. 12, for an explanation of the term *halakhot ketu'ot* (*ketu'ot* is a variant form of *keti'ot)* and a discussion of the composition of books of *halakhot* in the Talmudic and post-Talmudic periods.

himself to it; if such a person is in doubt regarding some point or cannot fully understand it, he may then consult the code books.[30]

From the query, it is evident that most people were in favor of codification, because, as they put it, "Of what use are the laborious argumentations of the Talmud to us?" It was easier to reach a conclusion by consulting a code than by undertaking the arduous study of the many twists and turns of the argument in the passages of the Talmud. Paltoi Gaon condemned the popular trend that favored codification: even if codes were easier and more convenient for learning the law, that very fact increased the danger that there would be less study of Torah, that the Torah would be forgotten, and that the law would be severed from its sources.

Paltoi therefore limited the use of the codes: they are not a substitute for the Talmudic sources. Rather, they may properly be used only to supplement the study of the sources themselves. Only when some doubt still remains after due research should a code be consulted to help clarify and resolve a problem. Thus, in Paltoi Gaon's opinion, a code is not a primary source but a reference work, like a commentary, to be consulted in case of some problem in understanding a particular matter in the Talmudic sources.

E. Halakhic Monographs

The almost completely negative attitude toward codification reflected by Paltoi Gaon may well explain why during the entire geonic era hardly any additional works in the style of *Halakhot Pesukot* and *Halakhot Gedolot* were composed. For about a century, until Saadiah Gaon, no codificatory work was written.[31] Halakhic creativity in this era largely took the form of responsa, which were becoming more numerous. Then, beginning with the first half of the tenth century C.E., a new literary form began to appear—summaries of the law that were different from the previous code books. The new form was the monograph, an exhaustive summary of the law on a single subject. These monographs for the most part dealt with subjects within *mishpat ivri, i.e.,* civil, criminal, and public law, and responded to the needs of Jewish communities and their courts, which judged according to Jewish law. They were, in the main, written by three of the leading Babylonian *geonim,* Saadiah Gaon, Samuel b. Ḥophni Gaon, and Hai Gaon.

30. *Ḥemdah Genuzah* [Hidden Treasure] #110; Assaf, *Teshuvot ha-Geonim* [Responsa of the *Geonim*], 1929, #158, p. 81; *Ha-Eshkol,* ed. Auerbach, II, Laws of the Torah Scroll, p. 50.

31. The one exception was *Seder Rav Amram Gaon,* which does not deal with matters of *mishpat ivri.* This *siddur* (order of prayers) was sent to Isaac b. Simeon of Spain at his request. *See* the critical edition by E.D. Goldschmidt, Jerusalem, 1972, and *id.,* Introduction.

1. SAADIAH GAON

Saadiah Gaon was born in Egypt in 882 C.E. He immigrated to the Land of Israel; but as a result of various halakhic controversies there—especially his famous dispute with Aaron b. Meir, the head of the *yeshivah* in the Land of Israel, regarding the reckoning of the calendar[32]—he lost confidence in the halakhic authorities of the Land of Israel and emigrated to Babylonia. After a few years, in 928, he was appointed Gaon of the *yeshivah* at Sura, which he continued to head, except for one interruption, until his death in 942. Saadiah was a prolific writer in a wide variety of fields, including *Halakhah*, Biblical commentary, philosophy, and Hebrew philology.

Besides Saadiah's broad-ranging literary activity, he was one of the great spiritual leaders of the geonic period. He was the key figure in maintaining the spiritual hegemony of the Babylonian halakhic authorities throughout the diaspora, and he fought fiercely against the Karaites and their sympathizers. Saadiah's halakhic works include commentaries and introductions to the Talmud and to specific halakhic subjects; his *Siddur* (Prayer Book, lit. Order [of Prayers]), in which he standardized the text of the prayers and benedictions, is especially noteworthy. However, his major halakhic works were his monographs on various subjects, *e.g.*, *Sefer ha-Yerushot* [Book of Inheritances], *Sefer ha-Mattanot* [Book of Gifts], *Sefer ha-Pikkadon* [Book of Bailments], *Sefer Shevu'ot* [Book of Oaths], and monographs on ritual slaughter and *terefah* (animals unfit to eat because of physical defects), interest and usury, and ritual purity and impurity. Of all these books, only one has survived intact—*Sefer ha-Yerushot*; the others are known from *Genizah* fragments or quotations in the works of subsequent authorities. All Saadiah's works were written in Arabic—he was the first *gaon* who wrote halakhic books in that language—and this fact seems to have been one of the main reasons they were little used and were eventually lost after Arabic ceased to be spoken among Jews.[33]

These works of Saadiah, like those of Samuel b. Ḥophni Gaon and Hai Gaon who followed him, were clear, thorough, and logically organized, with each subject preceded by an introduction and a summary of the general principles. Thus, for example, *Sefer ha-Yerushot* begins:[34]

32. For the nature of this dispute, *see* M.D. Cassuto, "Al Mah Neḥleku Rav Saadiah Gaon u-Ven-Meir?" [What Was the Dispute between Rabbi Saadiah Gaon and Ben-Meir?], *Sefer Rav Saadiah Gaon* [Rabbi Saadiah Gaon Volume], Jerusalem, 1943, pp. 333ff.

33. Assaf, *Geonim*, pp. 185–188. Apparently, it is uncertain whether Saadiah Gaon wrote *Sefer Shevu'ot; see* S. Abramson, *Inyanot be-Sifrut ha-Geonim* [Studies in Geonic Literature], pp. 62–64.

34. *Sifrei Rabbenu Saadiah Gaon b. Yosef ha-Faiyumi* [The Collected Works of Rabbenu Saadiah Gaon b. Joseph of Faiyum], published by Joseph Naphtali Derenbourg, IX. This

> Ownership of property may be transferred by one person to another by means of [any one of] three methods: inheritance, sale, or gift. Each of these three [methods] has basic principles [lit. "roots"] and refinements [lit. "branches"]. . . . [The discussion of] inheritances is divided into four parts. . . . The second section of the part on inheritance by children deals with the division of the estate among grandchildren, and this section has four subsections [lit. "gates"] which you need to know.

Thus, Saadiah sets out the subject in minutest detail.[35] This systematic and exhaustive arrangement and classification was later of great help to Maimonides in his monumental code, the *Mishneh Torah.*[36]

According to Müller[37] and Assaf,[38] *Sefer ha-Yerushot* manifests an additional codificatory characteristic that later became one of the principles in Maimonides' approach to codification. Assaf stated:

> The halakhic books of Saadiah Gaon exhibit two different methodologies. In his *Sefer ha-Yerushot* and in his *Siddur,* he neither cited any source nor documented his opinions; he couched his legal propositions as statements of settled law. He neither referred to even one passage from the Talmud nor mentioned the name of a single Sage of the Mishnah or Talmud. Thus, he paved the way and provided a model for Maimonides.
>
> On the other hand, in *Sefer ha-Shetarot* [Book of Legal Instruments] and in *Sefer ha-Pikkadon* and several other works, he followed an entirely different methodology. While he was just as meticulously systematic, defined his terms appropriately, and set forth every legal rule in his own words, he also cited the Talmudic source upon which he relied. In this methodology, he was followed by the *geonim* who succeeded him, R. Samuel b. Ḥophni and R. Hai.
>
> This change marked a turning point in his methodology; it is reasonable to assume that he used this new format in his later works because his earlier method of omitting citations of the Mishnaic and Talmudic sources may have aroused opposition like that later directed at Maimonides on account of his *Mishneh Torah.*

---

part contains *Sefer ha-Yerushot* in the Arabic original, together with a translation into Hebrew by H.S. Horwitz, with an introduction and notes by J. Müller. The passage quoted is from *Sefer ha-Yerushot,* pp. 9, 20–21.

35. *See Sefer ha-Yerushot,* Subject Index and Introduction, pp. XI–XV.

36. *See infra* p. 1196.

37. Müller, *supra* n. 34, Introduction to *Sefer ha-Yerushot,* p. X:

We also note that he did not cite any law or rule in the name of the one who stated it; that he set forth the rules as if they were the laws of the Torah, in the manner of a legislator, not referring to the Mishnah or the Talmud or the *tannaim* or the *amoraim;* and that he did not mention a single verse of the section of the Torah on inheritance. In this, he set the example for Maimonides, who followed him.

38. Assaf, *Geonim,* p. 189.

It appears, however, that this assumption regarding Saadiah's methodology in *Sefer ha-Yerushot* is incorrect, as Abramson has demonstrated:[39]

> The printed *Sefer ha-Yerushot* is merely an abridgement of Saadiah's book on the subject of inheritance. The abridgement omitted the documentation from Scripture and Talmud and left only the rules derived from them.

Sefer ha-Yerushot as Saadiah wrote it included documentation from Scripture and the Talmud.[40] Saadiah thus followed in this book the same methodology as in his other halakhic works—he did cite the sources from which he derived his conclusions.[41]

2. SAMUEL b. ḤOPHNI GAON

Samuel b. Ḥophni, the Gaon of the *yeshivah* of Sura from 977 to 1013, also composed a number of detailed monographs summarizing various areas of the law. These monographs set a record in halakhic literature for quantity. Like Saadiah, Samuel b. Ḥophni wrote not only in the area of *Halakhah* but also in many other fields, including Biblical commentary, philology, and philosophy. Also like Saadiah, he wrote in Arabic, and his books suffered the same fate as the works of Saadiah: of the dozens of his halakhic works, not one has been printed in its entirety; and of most of them, all that has survived is their name. Of the rest, there remain only scattered fragments that were discovered in the *Genizah.*

The overwhelming majority of Samuel b. Ḥophni's halakhic works cover subjects within the purview of *mishpat ivri, e.g., Sefer be-Dinei ha-Kinyanim* [Book of the Laws of Acquisition], *Sefer ha-Mattanah* [Book of Gifts], *Sefer ha-Tena'im* [Book of Contracts], *Sefer ha-Mashkon* [Book of Pledges], *Sefer be-Mikaḥ u-Mimkar* [Book of Purchase and Sale], *Sefer ha-Shutafut* [Book of Partnership], *Sefer be-Hilkhot Gezelah* [Book on the Laws of Robbery], *Sefer be-Hilkhot Shekhenim* [Book on the Law of Neighbors],

39. S. Abramson, "Ha-Genizah she-be-Tokh ha-Genizah" [The *Genizah* within the *Genizah*], *Proceedings of the Rabbinical Assembly of America,* XV (1951), pp. 227–228.

40. *See id.*, regarding the existence of such ms. fragments of Saadiah's *Sefer ha-Yerushot* and pointing out that the Introduction to Saadiah's *Sefer ha-Shetarot* indicates that, contrary to the opinion of Assaf, *Sefer ha-Shetarot* was composed before *Sefer ha-Yerushot. See* H. Hirschfeld, "Arabic Portion of Cairo *Genizah* at Cambridge," *JQR* [Old Series], XVI (1904), p. 299.

41. As to matter in Saadiah's books within the province of *mishpat ivri, see* further A. Karlin, "Ha-Halakhah ve-ha-Mishpat be-Torato Shel Rabbenu Saadiah Gaon Zal" [*Halakhah* and Law in the Teachings of Rabbenu Saadiah Gaon, of Blessed Memory], *Sefer Rav Saadiah Gaon: Koveẓ Torani-Madda'i* [Rabbi Saadiah Gaon: A Religious and Scientific Anthology], Mosad ha-Rav Kook, Jerusalem, 1943, pp. 428ff. On Saadiah Gaon, *see further* S. Bialoblotzky, "Rav Saadiah Gaon," reprinted in Bialoblotzky, *Em la-Masoret: Meḥkarim u-Ma'amarim,* Ramat Gan, 1971, pp. 127–206.

Sefer ha-Arvut ve-ha-Kabbelanut [Book of Ordinary and Special Contractual Suretyship], *Sefer ha-Shevu'ot* [Book of Oaths], *Sefer al ha-Katnut ve ha-Bagrut* [Book on Minority and Adulthood], *Sefer be-Dinei Ishut* [Book of Family Law], *Sefer ha-Yerushot* [Book of Inheritance], *Sefer be-Hilkhot Ẓava'ot* [Book of the Laws of Wills], and a long list of other monographs treating all the areas of civil law, evidence, and procedure, as well as some of the criminal law. He is even reported to have written *Sefer be-Dinei ha-Neharot, ha-Te'alot ve-ha-Borot* [Book of the Laws of Rivers, Canals, and Cisterns].[42]

Judging from the fragments which have survived, these books were remarkably systematic, organized topically according to a consistent classification, and written in an easy, straightforward style. Fragments of *Sefer ha-Arvut ve-ha-Kabbelanut,* published from manuscript, are an interesting illustration of Samuel b. Ḥophni's methodology.[43] The book opens with a discussion somewhat similar to the introductory statements in *Sefer ha-She'iltot,* involving the ethics, as well as the law, of suretyship.

> Said the author: Blessed be God, the God of Israel, the faithful Surety, who has pledged to His servants, to whom He has given His commandments, a great reward and eternal bliss, recompense for the commandments they perform, and reward for their good deeds; and this [pledge] He has the power to fulfill, praised be He to all eternity. . . . It is beyond possibility that He should cease to be Almighty. Nothing can prevent Him from fulfilling what He has decreed, and nothing can hinder Him from carrying out His will. Hence His suretyship will not fail in any respect or from any aspect. Everyone has faith in it and every human heart relies upon it.
>
> These qualities distinguish the guaranty by God, may He be blessed, to His servants for their recompense and reward, from the suretyship of human beings to guarantee money or the like, because sometimes they [human sureties] are unable to perform the guaranties they have undertaken, or their performance may be hindered or delayed. Hence, the Sage [King Solomon] decried the suretyship which some people undertake, and cautioned against undertaking it after their manner, saying: "Do not be one of those who give their hand [who stand surety for debts] lest [your bed be taken from under you when] you have no money to pay."[44] He went on to rebuke one who undertakes suretyship for a stranger, saying, "Harm awaits him who stands surety for a stranger [or, "for another"]; he who spurns pledging shall be

42. Assaf, *Geonim,* pp. 194–197; Abramson, *supra* n. 39 at 229–231.

43. These fragments, which contain the Introduction and chs. 1–4 and part of ch. 5, were published by Assaf in *Sinai,* XVII, pp. 135–155. Chs. 29, 30, and 31 were subsequently published by A. Greenbaum in *Kiryat Sefer,* XLVI, pp. 154–169, with source references and notes.

44. Proverbs 22:26–27. Suretyship in the Biblical era was created by a handshake. *See supra* pp. 1026–1027.

secure."[45] Therefore, the early Sages said, "A person should always keep away from three things: from taking to wife an orphan who is a minor [because she may disaffirm the marriage], from accepting bailments, and from standing surety."[46]

If a person does undertake to be a surety, it is his duty to perform his undertaking [if necessary], but he should [first] do everything he can to extricate himself from it, as the Sage [King Solomon] has said, "My son, if you have stood surety for your fellow, given your hand for a stranger [or, "for another"], you have been trapped by the words of your mouth. . . . Do this, then, . . . [my son, to extricate yourself, for you have come into the power of your fellow: Go grovel—and badger your fellow; give your eyes no sleep, your pupils no slumber. Save yourself like a deer out of the hand (of a hunter), like a bird out of the hand of a fowler]."[47]

This [*i.e.*, the undertaking of suretyship] is binding only if he [the surety] has certain characteristics, if he has become a surety in a particular manner, and if the subject of the guaranty, as well as the obligee, meets particular requirements. These four parts comprise thirty-one chapters of the laws of suretyship and indemnity agreements. We elucidate and explain the laws and support them by proofs from the Talmud. May the God of Israel grant us aid in all matters that promote good and welfare.

Following this introduction is a description of the contents of the thirty-one chapters which comprehensively and brilliantly cover all the legal problems of the law of suretyship. The following list of a few of the chapters is representative:

The first chapter of this our book deals with the definition and nature of suretyship; the second chapter, with the form of words by which a person becomes a surety; the third chapter, with the form of words by which a person becomes an *arev kabbelan*;[48] the fourth chapter, with the substantive difference between an ordinary surety and an *arev kabbelan*; the fifth chapter, with the legal position of the surety bound by the suretyship obligation.

Next follows a detailed discussion of the various subjects relevant to each chapter, and a brief treatment of the Talmudic and post-Talmudic

45. Proverbs 11:15.

46. TB Yevamot 109a; the current printed version varies slightly but not materially from the text as quoted by Samuel b. Ḥophni.

47. Proverbs 6:1–5. Samuel b. Ḥophni quoted only verses 1–3, and those only partially. The rest of the verses 1–5 have been supplied in our text in brackets.

48. Under Jewish law, there are two kinds of surety—an ordinary surety, whose liability is secondary to that of the principal debtor, and an *arev kabbelan*, whom the obligee may sue directly, without the necessity of first proceeding against the principal debtor. *See* TB Bava Batra 173b-174a; the codes cited in *Ein Mishpat*, *ad loc.*; and *supra* p. 1096 n. 63.

sources for the author's conclusions. The few fragments that have been found and published indicate the contents and organization of the work. It is indeed a pity that the greater part of such a valuable intellectual achievement has been lost.

3. HAI GAON

Hai Gaon, the last, and one of the greatest and most famous of the *geonim,*[49] continued the pattern of composing halakhic monographs on particular subjects. Hai,[50] son of Sherira, Gaon of Pumbedita, and son-in-law of Samuel b. Ḥophni Gaon, was born in 939 C.E. In 986 C.E., he was appointed president of the High Court of the *yeshivah* at Pumbedita; and a few years later, while his father (who lived to the age of one hundred) was still alive, he was appointed Gaon of the *yeshivah* of Pumbedita, which he headed for forty years. He died at the age of ninety-nine, in 1038.

His passing marked the close of the geonic period, and with it, the spiritual hegemony of Babylonia over the other Jewish centers. This hegemony had actually begun to wane a century earlier, because of external political reasons and the rise of large Jewish centers in Africa and Europe.[51] However, on the strength of the personalities of Sherira Gaon and his son Hai Gaon, Babylonia continued to maintain some degree of general authority over all Jewry. With the death of Hai Gaon, in the words of Samuel ha-Nagid, "the Jews of Babylonia, North Africa, and Spain have become equal."[52]

Like Saadiah and Samuel b. Ḥophni, Hai Gaon, too, was highly productive in various fields, including Biblical exegesis, linguistics, and philosophy. However, his preeminence was primarily in *Halakhah,* and it was said of him that "he spread Torah abroad throughout Jewry more than all of the other *geonim,* and those who sought the Torah from east and west walked by his light. . . . Of the *geonim* before him, there was none like him; and he

49. "Gaon," as used by Alfasi and most *rishonim,* designates Hai Gaon. *Cf.* the designation of R. Judah Ha-Nasi simply as "Rabbi" in Talmudic sources.

50. According to Assaf, *Geonim,* p. 198, "Hai" is the Babylonian form of the name "Ḥiyya." *See also* S. Morag, "Hai-Ḥayyim (le-Mahut Shemo Shel ha-Rav Hai Gaon)" [Hai-Ḥayyim (On the Nature of the Name of Hai Gaon)], *Tarbiẓ,* XXI (1962), p. 188, to the effect that the name comes from Ḥayyim. *See also id.* at 190, concerning the two forms of Hebrew spelling of the name.

51. *See supra* p. 43.

52. Elegy by Samuel ha-Nagid on the death of Hai Gaon; *see Kol Shirei R. Shemu'el ha-Nagid* [The Collected Poems of Samuel ha-Nagid], ed. H. Brody, Warsaw, 1911, p. 12 and n. 41. In *Diwan Shemu'el ha-Nagid,* ed. D. Sassoon, p. 13, the reading is not *nishvu venei Vavel* ("the Jews of Babylonia . . . have become equal") but *nishvu penei tevel* ("the face of the world has become equal," *i.e.,* the world has become stale and flat). The correct reading seems to be *benei Vavel; see also Diwan Shemu'el ha-Nagid, Ben Tehillim,* ed. D. Yarden, Jerusalem, 1966, p. 235.

was the last of the *geonim.*"[53] He responded to queries addressed to him from within Babylonia and from other areas of the diaspora. His responsa constitute more than a third of all the extant responsa of the *geonim* issued over a period of approximately four hundred years.[54]

The overwhelming majority of Hai Gaon's monographs are on subjects within *mishpat ivri.* He wrote *Sefer ha-Dayyanim* [Book of Judges], *Sefer Shevu'ot* [Book of Oaths], *Sefer ha-Mikaḥ ve-ha-Mimkar* [Book of Purchase and Sale], *Sefer Mishpat ha-Tena'im* [Book of the Law of Contracts], *Sefer Mishpetei Halva'ot* [Book of the Laws of Loans], *Sefer be-Dinei Maẓranut* [Book of the Law of Adjoining Property Owners], and others.[55] Following the example of Saadiah and Samuel b. Ḥophni, Hai Gaon composed these works in Arabic (although he wrote responsa in both Hebrew and Aramaic);[56] but some of them have survived, as a result of their translation into Hebrew at an early period. Thus, *Sefer Shevu'ot,* translated by an unknown translator and entitled *Mishpetei Shevu'ot* [Laws of Oaths],[57] and *Sefer ha-Mikaḥ ve-ha-Mimkar* [Book of Purchase and Sale], which is his greatest work and one of the classics of the codificatory literature, have survived intact. The latter work was translated by Isaac b. Reuben al-Bargeloni[58] in 1078, *i.e.,* forty years after the author's death.[59] This work, consisting of sixty chapters (called "gates"), comprehensively treats all the legal problems involved in the broad subject of acquisitions and obligations. Each "gate" deals with a specific subject, which is defined and clarified on the basis of Talmudic and post-Talmudic sources. Thus, for example, the first gate treats the definition

53. Rabad, *supra* n. 2 at 58–59.

54. Assaf, *Geonim,* p. 200.

55. *Id.* at 201–202.

56. *See infra* pp. 1472, 1510.

57. Printed in Venice, 1602; Hamburg, 1782; reprinted relatively recently in Jerusalem (undated), with source references and subject index. As to the various translations of the book, *see* Abramson, *supra* n. 33 at 133, and *id.* "Min ha-Makor ha-Aravi Shel Sefer ha-Mikaḥ ve-ha-Mimkar le-Rav Hai Gaon" [From the Arabic Original of Rabbi Hai Gaon's Book of Purchase and Sale], *Jubilee Volume for J.N. Epstein,* Jerusalem, 1950, pp. 296, 298.

58. Al-Bargeloni was a liturgical poet and author of halakhic works, who served as judge in the community of Dania in the district of Valencia, Spain. His remarks at the beginning of the book are of interest:

> This is a work entitled *Sefer ha-Mikaḥ ve-ha-Mimkar,* written by Rabbenu Hai Gaon b. Rabbenu Sherira Gaon . . . may they rest in Paradise. He wrote it in Arabic for those who used that language, because they did not understand the language of our Sages very well. Therefore, I, Isaac b. Reuben al-Bargeloni, have studied the book carefully to the best of my poor ability, and have restored it to the Hebrew language for our brethren in the Land of Edom [*i.e.,* Christian Spain] who do not understand Arabic.

59. The Hebrew translation was printed in Venice in 1602 and in Vienna in 1800. At the end of *Sefer ha-Mikaḥ ve-ha-Mimkar,* the translation of three short books is also included—*Sefer ha-Mashkon* [Book of Pledges], *Mishpetei Tena'im* [Law of Contracts], and *Mishpetei Halva'ot* [Law of Loans]; but these are not by Hai Gaon; *see* Abramson, *supra* n. 39 at 230.

of sale (in the narrow sense of transfer of ownership in exchange for money) and the kind of transaction properly included in that concept. The second gate discusses what can and cannot be sold. The third gate discusses the legal capacity—particularly mental capacity—required to be a party to a sale. The book's lucidity and the precision of its legal definitions have made it one of the basic works in this broad legal field, and many *rishonim* quoted from it and relied upon it. It has even been the subject of a number of commentaries.[60]

4. THE OBJECTIVES OF HALAKHIC MONOGRAPHS

The *geonim* had various objectives in composing their legal monographs. One of the most important was to make available to judges treatises that were thorough and comprehensive, yet succinct and convenient for reference in connection with the various legal matters brought before them. Meiri has written:

> We are told by Rabbenu Saadiah, of blessed memory, in his *Sefer ha-Pikkadon*, that he wrote it after a judge had been appointed in his town, which was a commercial center where the merchants were in the habit of entrusting money to each other. They were constantly involved in contentious disputes regarding their deposits. The judge was sometimes perplexed and requested him [Saadiah] to give a general overview of the law of bailments.[61]

This literature may also have been designed to facilitate systematic reference and study and thus help students of the Talmud organize and summarize their learning.[62]

60. Another work of Hai Gaon that is of great importance to *mishpat ivri* is his *Sefer ha-Shetarot* [Book of Legal Instruments], published by S. Assaf, Supplement to *Tarbiẓ*, I, Book III; *see infra* p. 1536. *See also Sinai*, II, pp. 461ff., for essays on the subject of Jewish law in the works and responsa of Hai Gaon; A. Karlin, "Dinei Mekhirah Lefi Tokhnit Sefer ha-Mikaḥ ve-ha-Mimkar Shel Rav Hai Gaon" [Laws of Sale according to *Sefer ha-Mikaḥ ve-ha-Mimkar* of Rabbi Hai Gaon], *Divrei Mishpat*, IV (1956).

61. Meiri, *supra* n. 13. *See also* S. D. Goitein, *Sidrei Ḥinnukh bi-Mei ha-Geonim u-Vet ha-Rambam* [Educational Systems from the Geonic Period to Maimonides], Jerusalem, 1962, pp. 18–19.

62. *See* Goitein, *supra* n. 61 at 154–155:

> Only a small part of the many halakhic monographs of the Babylonian *geonim* whose names appear in the *Genizah* lists have reached us. For the most part, only fragments have been preserved; but from the scant material that is available, one can tell that these were systematic lectures, meticulously arranged in paragraphs and subparagraphs in a pedagogically reiterative style. There are grounds to conclude that these were lectures to students, and that the lectures were compiled into textbooks. Just as every half-year the *geonim* designated for the scholars and students a different tractate of the Talmud, first for individual study and then for group discussion, so their practice was apparently to lecture to the rabbinical students each school "term" on a different

The pattern of books of *halakhot* along the lines of *Halakhot Pesukot* and *Halakhot Gedolot* was abandoned in the latter part of the geonic era, probably, among other reasons, because of the apprehension, expressed by Paltoi Gaon in the mid-ninth century, that codificatory works tend to cause the Torah to become forgotten, inasmuch as they sever the law from its sources. Although the books cited the Talmudic sources on which their statements of the law were based, these citations were generally so terse that the sources were swallowed up in the conclusions and rulings. Each monograph, on the other hand, dealt with a single legal subject, not the entire halakhic system; it was well organized and analytically structured, and it clearly explained both the reasons for its conclusions and the sources on which the conclusions were based.

II. *SEFER HA-HALAKHOT* BY ISAAC ALFASI (RIF)

A. The Nature and Content of *Sefer ha-Halakhot*

As the geonic period came to an end, the need arose once again for a code that covered the entire halakhic system yet was succinct and definitive. Several factors were at work. The increased volume of responsa[63] and legislative enactments[64] in various fields of the law necessarily involved the continuing expansion and development of the law. Moreover, for a considerable time, such activity had been going on not only in Babylonia, but also in North Africa and Europe. The fact that the number of Jewish centers had increased also led inevitably to marked differences in laws and customs.

While such differences had existed in the geonic period, and even ear-

---

> halakhic topic, *e.g.*, laws of purchase and sale, laws of oaths, laws of prayer, and the like. These lectures are the books on those subjects that we read today.
>
> This is the best explanation for the remarkable fact that these spiritual leaders, whose word was law for the entire Jewish diaspora, did not write a single work covering the entire *Halakhah.* Moreover, the fact that the three named *geonim* wrote for the most part on the same topics is also explained on the basis that their halakhic works were essentially lectures to students, or, rather, study material dictated to the students, who then learned them by heart.

Goitein's remarks do explain the objective, or at least one of the objectives, of these monographs. However, his explanation does not sufficiently account for the absence of a comprehensive work covering the entire *Halakhah;* the composition of a legal monograph for the purpose stated does not preclude a comprehensive work. It is submitted that the main reason why none of the *geonim* wrote a comprehensive work was the fear expressed by Paltoi Gaon; *see supra* pp. 1157–1158

63. *See infra* pp. 1468–1473.

64. *See supra* pp. 643ff.

lier—between the Land of Israel and Babylonia, and between different *yeshivot* and localities within each of these centers—the differences became much more prominent as the centers in the diaspora increased in number and spread over a broader area.[65]

These factors, and others discussed below,[66] led to the composition of one of the greatest and most important works in the halakhic system—a work that left its mark on the study and determination of the *Halakhah* in every subsequent generation. This work is *Sefer ha-Halakhot* [Book of the Laws] by Isaac b. Jacob ha-Kohen Alfasi, known in Hebrew by his acronym, "Rif" [***R***abbi ***I***saac of ***F***ez].

Alfasi was born in 1013 in the town of Qal'at Ḥammad in North Africa,[67] which is why he is sometimes called ha-Kala'i (the Qala'ean). He studied in Kairouan and in the *yeshivot* of Nissim b. Jacob (Nissim Gaon) and Rabbenu Hananel b. Ḥushiel, and eventually settled in Fez, North Africa (hence his appellation Alfasi), where he taught Torah to many students. At the age of seventy-five, he was forced to flee Fez after being denounced to the government; he moved to Spain, where, after a few months, he settled in Lucena, which was then a spiritual center of Spanish Jewry. After a short time, upon the death of Isaac b. Judah ibn Ghayyat, Alfasi headed the famous *yeshivah* in Lucena, where he attracted many students, including Joseph ibn Migash (Ri Migash) and Judah Halevi. Alfasi died in 1103, having designated Ri Migash to succeed him.

Alfasi was regarded in his generation as the leading Talmudic authority in Spain, and he left a legacy of hundreds of responsa to queries addressed to him from all the communities of Spain and North Africa. His major work, however, is *Sefer ha-Halakhot,*[68] which generally follows the pattern of organization of *Halakhot Gedolot* of Simeon Kayyara, although with some significant differences. Like *Halakhot Gedolot,* Alfasi's work is arranged in the order of the tractates of the Talmud, and presents the Talmudic sources before stating a conclusion as to the governing law. The sources, moreover, are not merely cited but are summarized and discussed.

65. *See supra* pp. 676–677, 936.

66. Namely, the authoritative resolution of halakhic questions that had been disputed, and the need for "an abridged Talmud" *(Talmud katan)* to make the contents of the Talmud more accessible and easier to learn. *See infra* p. 1171.

67. As to Alfasi's birthplace, *see* I.M. Toledano, *Ner ha-Ma'arav, Toledot Yisra'el be-Marokko* [The Light of the West: A History of the Jews of Morocco], Jerusalem, 1911; A.V. Aptowitzer, *Mavo le-Raviah,* p. 373; B.Z. Benedikt, "He'arot le-Toledot ha-Rif" [Notes on the Life of Alfasi], *Kiryat Sefer,* XXVII, pp. 119–120; H.Z. Hirschberg, *Toledot ha-Yehudim be-Afrikah ha-Ẓefonit* [History of the Jews of North Africa], I, p. 79.

68. The full title of Alfasi's code is *Sefer Halakhot Rabbati; see* S. Friedman's Introduction to *Sefer Halakhot Rabbati le-Rabbenu Yiẓhak Alfasi,* ms. New York, Jerusalem, 1974, pp. 52ff. As to Alfasi's responsa, *see infra* pp. 1476–1477 and Appendix C.

Alfasi's work is confined strictly to that portion of the *Halakhah* that retained practical relevance after the destruction of the Temple. (It will be recalled that Simeon Kayyara sometimes included laws, such as the laws of sacrificial offerings, that had no practical application in post-Temple times.) The work does not, therefore, encompass the entire Talmud, but only three of the six Orders, *i.e., Mo'ed, Nashim,* and *Nezikin,* together with Tractate *Berakhot* (which covers the laws of blessings and prayers) in the Order of *Zera'im,* and Tractate *Ḥullin* (which deals with dietary laws and ritual slaughter) in the Order of *Kodashim.* The laws that are scattered through the Orders of *Kodashim* and *Tohorot* and still have practical relevance, *e.g.,* the laws of the ritual defilement of priests, and the laws relating to Torah Scrolls, *mezuzah,* phylacteries, and fringes (*ẓiẓit*), were codified by Alfasi in a separate work entitled *Halakhot Ketannot.*

Even with respect to material contained in the three Orders he covered, Alfasi meticulously followed the principle of treating only laws having practical relevance. Thus, for example, he omitted Chapters 5 through 8 of Tractate *Pesaḥim,* because they discuss the paschal lamb, no longer sacrificed since the destruction of the Temple. He treated only the last chapter of Tractate *Yoma,* which deals with the five privations prescribed for the Day of Atonement and with the rules of repentance; he did not treat the other chapters that deal with the Temple ritual on that day.[69]

As has been noted, Alfasi concisely discussed the relevant Talmudic sources before stating his final conclusion. His discussion is far more extensive than in the books of *halakhot* of the *geonim.* Alfasi succinctly set out the main points of the Talmudic discussion and quoted the relevant statements on which he based his conclusions. Thus, Alfasi's work includes the general structure of the Talmudic discussion, so that studying *Sefer ha-Halakhot* provides the student with a recapitulation of the main points of the pertinent Talmudic sources.

69. Similarly, Alfasi did not deal with laws which applied only in a specific historical context. For example, M Rosh ha-Shanah 3:1 states:

> If the court itself and all Israel had seen the new moon and the witnesses had been examined, yet night fell before they could proclaim, "It is hallowed!" then it is an intercalated month [a thirty-day month, as that day had not been proclaimed the first of the new month before nightfall]. If the court alone saw it, two [of the judges] should stand and bear witness before them [the other judges] and then they may say, "It is hallowed! It is hallowed!" If it was seen by three who themselves constitute a court, two of them should stand up and seat two of their colleagues [not previously sitting on that court] beside the [remaining] single [judge of the original court] and bear witness before them [the three judges now sitting] and then they may say, "It is hallowed! It is hallowed!"; for no single person may be deemed trustworthy by himself [to declare the advent of the new moon].

This *mishnah* is omitted by Alfasi, because by his time it had no practical relevance; the calendar was calculated and known in advance, and the months were no longer established one at a time by judicial proclamation.

Occasionally, when significant for a definitive legal ruling, Alfasi discussed the meaning of the Talmudic passage and cited various views, in most instances indicating his own supporting or opposing arguments. In this respect, he undertook an important additional function, namely, to resolve many halakhic problems that had previously been disputed. In the face of the vast halakhic material contained in the two Talmuds and the rest of Talmudic literature, as well as the extensive halakhic literature from the geonic era, Alfasi, in his *Sefer ha-Halakhot,* had to decide between conflicting opinions. This task had heavily engaged the halakhic authorities in earlier periods. Rules for such decision making can be found throughout the Talmud[70] and were augmented by the *savoraim* and *geonim*; indeed, treatises were written on the subject.[71] Alfasi applied these rules in determining the law. Not infrequently, he disagreed with the law established by the *geonim* and with Simeon Kayyara's conclusions in *Halakhot Gedolot.*[72]

Alfasi frequently cited or quoted the Jerusalem Talmud, "the Talmud of the westerners" as he called it; but when the law in the Babylonian Talmud conflicts with that of the Jerusalem Talmud—even only implicitly—he followed the Babylonian Talmud. He explicitly established this as a rule of decision making, relying on the principle, settled as early as the geonic period, that ever since the time of Abbaye and Rava, "the law is in accordance with the views of the later authorities (*hilkheta ke-vatra'ei*)":[73]

> Since our [Babylonian] Talmud adopts the more lenient view, it does not matter to us that in the Talmud of the westerners [the Jerusalem Talmud] the act is forbidden; for we rely upon our Talmud because it is later [*i.e.,* was redacted after the Jerusalem Talmud], and they [the Sages of the Babylonian Talmud] were more versed than we are in the westerners' Talmud. If they had not felt certain that this statement of the westerners should not be followed, they would not have ruled it permissible for the thing to be done.[74]

Sefer ha-Halakhot also includes a certain amount of Talmudic *Aggadah.* The Talmud contains, in addition to its halakhic material, a great quantity and variety of aggadic matter, including ethical and philosophical reflections and concepts, sometimes interwoven with legal discussion. Alfasi undertook the arduous and difficult task of distinguishing between *Aggadah* that has only speculative or anecdotal significance and *Aggadah* that serves

70. *See supra* p. 1089.
71. *See* Assaf, *Geonim,* pp. 223ff.
72. *See* Tchernowitz, *supra* n. 23 at 141ff.
73. *See supra* pp. 267–271.
74. Alfasi to Eruvin (end), at the conclusion of #697.

as a basis for halakhic rules governing practical conduct. His keen discernment and deep insight enabled him to succeed in this undertaking.

For example, the Talmud states:[75]

> If a person prays for divine favor for his fellow when he himself is in need of the same thing, his need will be responded to first. . . . If a person complains to Heaven against his fellow [instead of taking the case to a human tribunal], he himself will be punished first.

Of these two aggadic *dicta,* Alfasi included only the second, because a rule governing practical conduct may be derived from it, *i.e.*, that a dispute with one's fellow should be brought to a court; but Alfasi did not include the first because it does not involve a binding rule of conduct.

The broad inclusion by Alfasi of the main points of the Talmudic discussion—both the halakhic and the aggadic portions—earned for *Sefer ha-Halakhot* the additional title "The Abridged Talmud" (*Talmud Katan*); and the author himself apparently intended his work to be just that, in order to make it easier for people to engage in Talmudic study.[76]

Alfasi's *Sefer ha-Halakhot* was the crowning masterpiece of this genre of codificatory literature; and, thanks to its scope and contents as well as to the personality and authority of its author, it became the authoritative code of the halakhic system. Maimonides' Introduction to his *Commentary on the Mishnah,* after discussing the codificatory literature of the *geonim,* went on to say:

> The *Halakhot* by the great master Rabbenu Isaac, of blessed memory, succeeded in replacing all of them [*i.e.*, the other codes], since it includes all the decisions and laws that are needed in this era, *i.e.*, the era of exile. In this work, he cleared up all the errors that had crept into the rulings of his predecessors. I have found difficulty in only a few rulings, certainly not amounting to even ten.[77]

The halakhic authorities of France and Provence were also appreciative of the magnitude of Alfasi's achievement. Isaac the Elder, one of the

75. TB Bava Kamma 92a (the first *dictum*), and *id.* 93a (the second *dictum*); Alfasi to Bava Kamma, ch. 8, #167. *See also infra* p. 1192 n. 34.

76. The name "Abridged Talmud" (*Talmud Katan)* for Alfasi's work is to be found as early as in *Sefer ha-Qabbalah, supra* n. 2 at 84. *See also* B.Z. Benedikt, "Le-Toledotav Shel Merkaz ha-Torah be-Provenẓ" [On the History of the Center for the Study of Torah in Provence], *Tarbiẓ,* XXII, p. 105; *id.*, *supra* n. 67 at 120 and nn.; *see also* Tchernowitz, *supra* n. 23 at 146–147.

77. Maimonides, *Commentary on the Mishnah,* ed. Kafaḥ (Hebrew only), Introduction, p. 25. In one of his responsa, Maimonides wrote that in his *Mishneh Torah* he differed from Alfasi in approximately thirty instances; *see Resp. Maimonides,* ed. Blau, #251 (p. 459).

great Tosafists, said of him: "A human being could never compose a work like this without the help of divine inspiration."[78] Rabad, the keen critic of Maimonides and of many other great halakhic authorities, wrote of Alfasi: "I would rely on Alfasi, of blessed memory, even if he were to say that right is left."[79]

Alfasi's work supplanted many books of *halakhot* written in his own time and even later;[80] and an entire literature of commentary was composed around it, partly to explain and supplement it, and partly to query or defend it.[81] The tremendous influence exerted by Alfasi's work in the Jewish legal system is evidenced by the fact that after some five centuries and the appearance of many other codificatory works such as Maimonides' *Mishneh Torah,* Asheri's *Piskei ha-Rosh,* and Jacob b. Asher's *Sefer ha-Turim,* Alfasi continued to be one of the most influential authorities to be reckoned with in Jewish legal decision making. This status of Alfasi was authoritatively established by the rule of decision making declared by Joseph Caro in the sixteenth century as the basis of his works *Bet Yosef* and the *Shulḥan Arukh*:[82]

> Since I concluded that the three pillars of instruction upon which the House of Israel rests are Alfasi, Maimonides, and Asheri, of blessed memory, I resolved that when two of them agree on any point I will determine the law in accordance with their view, except for those few instances when all or most [of the other] halakhic authorities disagree with that view and a contrary practice has therefore become widespread.

In this way, many of Alfasi's rulings found their way into the authoritative *Corpus Juris* of the *Halakhah,*[83] where they remain to this day.[84]

78. Quoted by Menahem b. Zeraḥ in *Ẓeidah la-Derekh,* Introduction.

79. *Katuv Sham, Hassagot ha-Rabad al Ba'al ha-Ma'or le-Massekhet Rosh ha-Shanah ve-Sukkah be-Ẓeruf Mavo* [*Katuv Sham,* Rabad's Critique of the *Ma'or* on Tractates *Rosh ha-Shanah* and *Sukkah,* with an Introduction], ed. I.D. Bergman, Jerusalem, 1957, p. 3 (critique of the *Ma'or* on Sukkah 14a); *see also Temim De'im,* Lvov, 1812, #238 (p. 34c, s.v. Hineh), quoted *infra* p. 1174. Regarding the expression "right is left," *see supra* pp. 247ff. *See also* Rabad, *Commentary on Bava Kamma,* ed. S. Atlas, pp. 138–139.

80. *See infra* pp. 1177–1179.

81. *See infra* pp. 1173–1176.

82. Preface to *Bet Yosef* on *Tur* OḤ; *see infra* pp. 1317–1319.

83. If one takes into account Maimonides' strong reliance on Alfasi (*see supra* p. 1171 and n. 77) and the fact that *Piskei ha-Rosh,* Asheri's code, incorporates a considerable part of Alfasi's *Sefer ha-Halakhot* (*see infra* p. 1251), it becomes clear that Alfasi's influence, including that exerted through the other two "pillars of instruction," is exceedingly great.

84. Ed. Sabbioneta, 1554–1555, contains an index of the laws found in Alfasi, arranged in the order of Maimonides' *Mishneh Torah;* this index permits the location of the laws in Alfasi without reference to the sequence of the Talmudic tractates. The index was reprinted in the Vilna edition of TB (and subsequent facsimiles) at the end of the Talmud.

B. Commentaries on *Sefer ha-Halakhot*

An extensive literature developed around *Sefer ha-Halakhot*. Some was critical, some defended it against the critics, and some explained and supplemented it. Thereafter, such works in the nature of commentaries or glosses (called in Hebrew *nos'ei kelim*, lit. "armor bearers")[85] were written on the main Jewish codes.[86] Those on Alfasi are by some of the greatest halakhic authorities. A few of the important commentators on Alfasi are next discussed.

1. ZERAḤIAH HA-LEVI GERONDI (REZAH)

Rezah lived in the twelfth century in the town of Lunel in Provence, and was one of the outstanding halakhic authorities of his day. At the age of nineteen, he wrote *Sefer ha-Ma'or* [Book of the Luminary], consisting of critical glosses and supplementations to Alfasi's *Sefer ha-Halakhot*. *Sefer ha-Ma'or* is in two parts: *Ha-Ma'or ha-Gadol* [The Great Luminary] on the Orders of *Nashim* and *Nezikin*, and *Ha-Ma'or ha-Katan* [The Lesser Luminary] on the Order of *Mo'ed*.[87]

Rezah apologized profusely for questioning Alfasi's work "for there has not been written as fine a work on the Talmud since it was finally redacted." Yet he felt bound to seek out the truth; "as the Philosopher [Aristotle], refuting his master, said, 'Truth and Plato are at odds and both are beloved, but Truth is the more beloved.'" Consequently, he explained, his criticisms only added honor and glory to Alfasi's work.[88]

2. ABRAHAM b. DAVID (RABAD) OF POSQUIÈRES

Rabad,[89] a contemporary of Rezah, wrote critical glosses (*hassagot*) on Alfasi, albeit very apologetically:

85. The term is a metaphorical adaptation of the military term signifying one who carries his superior's weapons. *See* I Samuel 14:13: "And Jonathan clambered up . . . , his armor bearer behind him," and *id.*, vv. 1, 7, 12, *et al.* The author of a commentary on the work of a great authority is conceived of as "assisting" that authority in the battle on behalf of Torah, thus figuratively "bearing the arms" of a warrior greater than himself.

86. *See, e.g., infra* pp. 1231–1235, 1302–1304, 1424–1432.

87. *See* Rezah's Introduction to *Sefer ha-Ma'or* on Alfasi; it is printed in the large editions of the Talmud, preceding Alfasi to Berakhot.

88. For further details, *see* Rezah's Introduction. For the same reason, Rezah also said (*id.*):

> In the name of the Everlasting, I adjure every copyist of this book of mine to copy also this Introduction . . . and not toss it away as copyists in these lands are wont to do. It is evidence to clear me before all readers of any guilt for [writing] this book of mine . . . and to judge me favorably.

89. For further information about Rabad, *see supra* pp. 1123–1124 and *infra* pp. 1223–1225.

> Truly, I ought to have closed my eyes and sealed my lips and followed him unswervingly to the right and to the left; but this is a task for the sake of Heaven. . . . So I did not refrain from critically reviewing [his work] as far as I was able, whether [that review] refuted or was supportive . . . ; for the Almighty desired, for the sake of His righteousness, to magnify and glorify His Torah.[90]

Rabad sharply attacked Rezah for his criticisms of Alfasi, and frequently defended Alfasi against them, sometimes criticizing Rezah with extreme asperity.[91]

3. NAḤMANIDES (RAMBAN)

Naḥmanides[92] viewed Alfasi as the leading authority for determining the law, and wrote two books defending Alfasi against both Rezah and Rabad:

a. *Milḥamot ha-Shem* [The Wars of the Lord] took issue with Rezah's critiques:

> I was moved by intense zeal for our great master, R. Isaac Alfasi, of blessed memory, for I have seen among those who dispute him that their challenge is so broad that they did not concede to him the merit of having made even a single correct statement, worthwhile comment, or sound ruling.[93]

Naḥmanides went on to state that although it is not always possible to demonstrate the correctness of a halakhic opinion with the compelling force of a mathematical proof, nevertheless the proper approach is to accept the reasoning that conforms most closely to the plain meaning of the laws and the Talmudic passages.[94]

90. *Temim De'im, supra* n. 79.

91. *See Katuv Sham, supra* n. 79, *passim.* Every critique by Rabad begins with the words *katuv sham* ("It is written there"). *See also infra* pp. 1223–1225 as to the style of Rabad's critical glosses to Maimonides' *Mishneh Torah.*

92. As to Naḥmanides, *see supra* p. 1124.

93. Naḥmanides, *Milḥamot ha-Shem,* Introduction, printed in large editions of TB preceding Alfasi to Berakhot. For a critical edition, *see* C. Chavel, *Kitvei Ramban* [Collected Works of Naḥmanides], Jerusalem, 1963, I, p. 410. As to the two parts of *Milḥamot ha-Shem* and the difference between them, *see* Chavel at n. 1.

94. *See* Naḥmanides' interesting remarks in *Milḥamot ha-Shem, supra* n. 93, Introduction:

> And you, dear reader, do not feel that I view all my rejoinders to Rabbi Zeraḥiah, of blessed memory, as so overwhelmingly persuasive that you will glory in being able to engender a doubt on any of them in the minds of the students, or that you will strain your argument through the eye of a needle to escape the force of my arguments. I hold no such view. Any student of Talmud knows that where the commentators differ, no view can be absolutely demonstrated to be correct and, generally speaking, no

b. *Sefer ha-Zekhut* [The Book of Merit] answers Rabad's critiques on Alfasi. Naḥmanides was very temperate in his expressions about Rabad and accorded him great respect.[95]

Rezah, Rabad, and Naḥmanides essentially were critics or defenders of Alfasi and only incidentally his explicators. The main purpose of the commentators next discussed was to explain Alfasi and, incidentally, also to supplement him.

4. JONATHAN OF LUNEL

Jonathan of Lunel, who lived in the second half of the twelfth and the beginning of the thirteenth centuries, was a disciple of Rabad and the foremost halakhic authority of Lunel in his generation. He wrote a commentary on Alfasi's *Sefer ha-Halakhot,* of which only the part on Tractate *Eruvin* is included in the printed editions of the Talmud; but his commentaries on additional tractates have recently been published separately.[96] He carried on a correspondence with Maimonides, who held him in the highest regard. Toward the end of his life (1210), he was one of the "three hundred rabbis of England and France" who settled in the Land of Israel, where he lived until his death.[97]

5. NISSIM GERONDI (RAN)

Ran, a judge and head of the *yeshivah* in Barcelona, was one of the leading Spanish halakhic authorities of the fourteenth century.[98] He wrote

---

counterargument is completely unanswerable. For, in this field, there can be no proof to a certainty as in mathematics or astronomy. However, we do our best and are satisfied if, on balance of the arguments, we can reject one of the opinions . . . and accept the view that most closely accords with the plain meaning of the laws as well as with good sense. That is the goal of our endeavor, and it is the aim of every pious scholar who engages in the study of Talmud.

95. Of the *Sefer ha-Zekhut,* only the part on Tractates *Yevamot, Ketubbot,* and *Gittin* have appeared in print in large editions of TB, *in loco.*

96. Commentary of Jonathan of Lunel on Alfasi on the following tractates: *Berakhot* (New York, 1957, ed. M. Blau); *Sukkah* (in *Ginzei Rishonim,* Jerusalem, 1962, ed. A. Liss); *Rosh ha-Shanah* and *Yoma* (in *Ginzei Rishonim,* Jerusalem, 1963, ed. M. Hirschler); *Ta'anit* (in *Ginzei Rishonim,* Jerusalem, 1963, ed. A. Liss); *Bava Kamma* (Jerusalem–New York, 1969, ed. S. Friedman, with a detailed introduction by Friedman); *Sanhedrin* (ed. J. Kuperberg, in *Sanhedrei Gedolah* [The Great Sanhedrin], II, Jerusalem, 1969); *Ḥullin* (in *Avodat ha-Levi'im,* annotated by S. Bamberger and S. Stern, Frankfurt, 1871; facsimile ed., New York, 1957).

97. *See* Friedman's Introduction, *supra* n. 96 at 24, and sources cited, *id.* at n. 207.

98. *See also supra* pp. 1125–1126.

a commentary on Alfasi covering fourteen tractates, but it is possible that a few of these have been erroneously attributed to him. Today, Ran's is the most widely accepted commentary on Alfasi.

6. JOSEPH ḤABIBA

Joseph Ḥabiba, a disciple of Ran, lived in Spain at the beginning of the fifteenth century. His work *Nimmukei Yosef* [The Argumentations of Joseph—a play on the author's name] is a commentary on the entire *Sefer ha-Halakhot* of Alfasi; but the printed editions of the Talmud contain his commentary only on the seven tractates on which there is no commentary by Ran. The bulk of Ḥabiba's published commentary is on *Nezikin*; his commentary on additional tractates has only recently been published. In terms of acceptance, *Nimmukei Yosef* ranks a close second to Ran's commentary on Alfasi.

7. JOSHUA BOAZ b. SIMON BARUCH

Joshua Boaz was among the Jews exiled from Spain. He immigrated to Italy, where he lived during the first half of the sixteenth century. His book *Shiltei Gibborim* contains supplementation to Alfasi as well as critiques and divergent views of leading authorities, including Isaiah of Trani (Riaz; known also as Isaiah the Latter), who lived in Italy at the end of the thirteenth century.[99]

8. OTHER COMMENTATORS

There were many other commentators on Alfasi's work, and an extensive halakhic literature developed around his *Sefer ha-Halakhot,* which to this day remains the first of the "three pillars" of the edifice of Jewish law.[100]

99. Joshua Boaz was also the author of *Masoret ha-Shas* and *Ein Mishpat-Ner Miẓvah,* which are printed on the page in standard editions of TB and contain parallel citations to Talmudic and codificatory literature. *See* Boaz's Introduction, printed in large editions of TB preceding Alfasi on Tractate *Berakhot,* where he discussed his books above cited, as well as others he wrote, but not his *Shiltei Gibborim. See also* R.N.N. Rabinowitz, *Ma'amar al Hadpasat ha-Talmud* [Essay on the Printing of the Talmud], ed. A.M. Haberman, 1952, pp. 48ff. and p. 51 n. 6.

100. *See* B.Z. Benedikt, "Tchernowitz, Chaim, *Toledot ha-Posekim,*" *Kiryat Sefer,* XXV, pp. 164–176; Friedman *supra* n. 96, Introduction. *See also infra* pp. 1243–1244 (on Meshullam b. Moses of Beziers, author of *Sefer ha-Hashlamah,* to the effect that his book was intended to supplement, explain, and take issue with Alfasi); *infra* p. 1269 n. 142 (as to the commentary on Alfasi by the author of *Sefer ha-Ittur,* entitled *Me'ah She'arim).*

III. CODIFICATORY WORKS FROM ALFASI TO MAIMONIDES

During Alfasi's time, and in the immediately succeeding generations, several other important books of *halakhot* were written. The following are the leading authors and their works:

A. Spain

1. ISAAC ibn GHAYYAT (RIẒAG)

Riẓag lived in the eleventh century in Spain and was the halakhic authority of that Jewish center until the arrival of Alfasi. He is also known for his liturgical and poetic compositions. His book *Halakhot Kelulot* [Comprehensive *Halakhot*] apparently contained most or all of the laws applicable after the destruction of the Temple, but only a part, printed under the title *Sha'arei Simḥah* [Gates of Joy] and treating mainly the laws of the sabbath and the festivals, has survived and been published.[101]

The laws in this work are topically arranged. The discussion of each subject commences with the basis and origin of each law and continues with the rulings of the *geonim* and the *rishonim*. Spanish halakhic authorities in the succeeding generations, such as Naḥmanides, Rashba, and Asheri, frequently cited Riẓag's works. *Halakhot Kelulot* is an important source for works written in the post-Talmudic period up to Riẓag's time that are no longer extant.[102]

2. JUDAH al-BARGELONI

Judah al-Bargeloni, who lived in twelfth-century Barcelona, wrote an extensive halakhic work which, according to Menahem Meiri,[103] was a "comprehensive codification of most Talmudic subjects. 'Its measure is longer than the earth and broader than the sea [Job 11:9].'" His work apparently included all the laws applicable after the destruction of the Temple.

The work consists of three treatises: (a) *Sefer ha-Ittim* [Book of the Seasons] on the laws of the sabbath, the festivals, and benedictions; one part, mainly dealing with the laws of the sabbath, is extant;[104] (b) *Yiḥus*

101. The title page reads: "*Sefer Sha'arei Simḥah,* Part I, by Rabbenu Isaac b. R. Judah ibn Ghayyat, also called *Me'ah She'arim,* accompanied by a commentary, *Yiẓḥak Yeranen,* by R. Isaac Dov ha-Levi Bamberger, Fürth, 1861." Part II appeared in 1862; *see* Bamberger's Introduction.

102. Another halakhic work of Alfasi's time that has not survived is *Kuppat ha-Rokhelim* by Isaac b. Baruch Albalia, a leading Spanish authority. *See* Meiri, *Bet ha-Beḥirah,* Avot, ed. Jerusalem, 1944, Introduction, p. 68.

103. Meiri, *supra* n. 102 at 67.

104. Published by J. Schor, Berlin, 1902.

She'er [Consanguinous Relationships] on family law, which is not extant; and (c) *Sefer ha-Din* [The Book of Law] on civil law, of which only fragments have survived, including a portion of *Sefer ha-Shetarot* [Book of Legal Instruments].[105]

The work is topically arranged and very detailed.[106] The author usually quotes Alfasi's *Sefer ha-Halakhot,* adds his own conclusions, and also introduces opinions and clarifications of the law by the *geonim* and his predecessors among Spanish halakhic authorities. His work thus constitutes a mine of information on the post-Talmudic halakhic literature up to his time.[107]

B. France and Germany

1. THE SCHOOL OF RASHI

In France and Germany, too, a considerable number of codificatory works were composed during this period. Several emanated from the school of Rashi, *e.g., Sefer ha-Orah,*[108] *Sefer ha-Pardes,*[109] and *Siddur*

105. *Sefer ha-Shetarot* contains seventy-three forms of documents; *see infra* pp. 1536–1537. Additional excerpts from *Sefer ha-Din* were published by S. Assaf, *Madda'ei ha-Yahadut,* II, pp. 16ff. The extant parts of al-Bargeloni's book constitute mere fragments in relation to its original size and scope.

106. Large parts of the three sections of the book were apparently lost because their length made them difficult to copy. Various authors composed abridgments or put together selections from it. The copyist of *Sefer ha-Shetarot* explicitly stated that he copied only the laws relating to legal instruments and did not copy the documents themselves. *Sefer ha-Ittim,* particularly, appeared in many abridged editions. According to some scholars, *Sefer ha-Eshkol,* by Abraham b. Isaac, *Av Bet Din* of Narbonne (generally known as Rabad II), is an abridgment of *Sefer ha-Ittim. Sefer ha-Eshkol* treats the festivals and other matters of religious law. *See Sefer ha-Eshkol,* ed. S. Albeck, Introduction, pp. 31ff.

107. The collections of geonic responsa entitled *Sha'arei Teshuvah* and *Lik* are selections from the works of Judah al-Bargeloni. *See* J. Mueller, *Mafte'aḥ li-Teshuvot ha-Geonim* [Index to Responsa of the *Geonim*], pp. 19–23; S. Albeck, *Tiferet Yisra'el* [Jubilee Volume in Honour of Israel Levy], pp. 119ff.; *Sefer ha-Eshkol,* ed. Albeck, Introduction, p. 42; *Sha'arei Teshuvah,* ed. Z.W. Leiter, 1946, Introduction. The book *Hilkhata Gavrata* [Strong (*i.e.,* well-supported) *Halakhot*], by Samuel ha-Nagid (Spain, first half of the eleventh century), was among his important sources. *See Sefer Hilkhot ha-Nagid,* published by M. Margaliot, Jerusalem, 1962, pp. 43ff.

108. The title page of a modern edition reads: "*Sefer ha-Orah, Kolel Piskei Dinim ve-Halakhot, Meyuḥas le-Rabbenu Shelomo b. R. Yiẓḥak, Zal, ha-Noda be-Shem Rashi* [Book of Illumination, Including Legal Rulings and *Halakhot,* Attributed to Rabbenu Solomon b. R. Isaac, of Blessed Memory, Known as Rashi], Part I, Published with an Introduction by Solomon Buber, Lvov, 1905."

109. The title page of a modern edition reads: "*Sefer ha-Pardes le-Rashi, Zal, Kolel Teshuvot u-Fiskei Dinim mi-Geonim Kadmonim u-le-Rabbenu Shelomo b. Yiẓḥak, ha-Noda be-Shem Rashi* [Book of the Orchard by Rashi, of Blessed Memory, Including Responsa and Rulings of the Early *Geonim* and Rabbenu Solomon b. R. Isaac, of Blessed Memory, Known as Rashi], Published with an Introduction by H.J. Ehrenreich, Budapest, 1924."

Rashi,[110] as well as *Maḥzor Vitry* by Simḥah b. Samuel of Vitry, a disciple of Rashi.[111] These books deal mostly with the laws of benedictions, the sabbath, and the festivals; dietary laws; and, in part, the laws of marriage and divorce, and sexual prohibitions.

2. ELIEZER b. NATHAN (RABAN)

An important codificatory work of this period is *Even ha-Ezer* by Raban, who lived in the twelfth century in Mainz and was one of the first Tosafists in Germany. His book is also called *Ẓofenat Pa'ne'ah* [Revealer of Secrets]. One part of the book contains responsa,[112] and another part halakhic rulings. The rulings are arranged in the order of the Talmudic tractates, and cover *Berakhot*, *Ḥullin*, *Avodah Zarah*, and *Niddah*, as well as the Orders of *Mo'ed*, *Nezikin*, and *Nashim*. Raban interwove commentary on the Talmud with halakhic rulings. The book includes quotations from Rabbenu Hananel's commentary on the Talmud and from the writings of the *geonim*. Subsequent generations esteemed Raban highly as one of the great early codifiers and made much use of his book.[113]

Throughout the entire period covered by this chapter, Alfasi's *Sefer ha-Halakhot* remained the essential and authoritative codificatory work, which was widely accepted as such in the various Jewish centers.[114] A new and "revolutionary" stage was introduced into halakhic codification when Maimonides wrote his great work, the *Mishneh Torah*, discussed in the next chapter.

110. The title page of a modern edition reads: "*Siddur Rashi, Kolel Piskei Dinim ve-Halakhot* [The Prayer Book of Rashi, Including Rulings and *Halakhot*], Published with an Introduction by Solomon Buber and Jacob Freimann, Berlin, 1912."

111. The title page of a modern edition reads: "*Maḥzor Vitry le-Rabbenu Simḥah, Eḥad mi-Talmidei Rashi, Zal* [The Vitry Prayer Book for the Annual Prayer Cycle, by Rabbenu Simḥah, a Disciple of Rashi, of Blessed Memory], Published with an Introduction by S. Horowitz and supplements by A. Berliner, S.A. Wertheimer, and H. Brody, Berlin, 1889–1897."

112. *See infra* Appendix C.

113. As to Raban and his book, *see* S. Albeck, *Mavo le-Even ha-Ezer me'et ha-Raban* [Introduction to *Even ha-Ezer* by Raban], Warsaw, 1905; Urbach, *Tosafot*, pp. 148ff. Codificatory works of a specialized nature were also written in Provence, *e.g.*, *Sefer ha-Eshkol* of Rabad II (*see supra* n. 106), and *Sefer ha-Ittur* of Isaac b. Abba Mari of Marseilles, an elder contemporary of Maimonides. Because of the unusual form of its organization, *Sefer ha-Ittur* is discussed in detail *infra* pp. 1267–1269.

114. *Sefer ha-Halakhot* achieved acceptance in North Africa and Spain during Alfasi's lifetime and in France (where Rashbam wrote supplements to it) approximately two generations later. In Germany, the first to mention Alfasi was Raban, whose grandson Raviah (Eliezer b. Joel ha-Levi of Bonn, *see infra* pp. 1238–1239) quoted Alfasi frequently. From that time on, Alfasi's work was also accepted in Germany as authoritative. For further details, *see* Aptowitzer, *Mavo le-Raviah* [Introduction to Raviah], p. 92 and pp. 372ff.

Chapter 34

THE CODIFICATORY LITERATURE: MAIMONIDES' *MISHNEH TORAH*

I. Strengthening of the Tendency toward Codification at the Beginning of the Rabbinic Period

II. Maimonides and his Codificatory Work
   - A. Goals
   - B. Compiling and Reworking the Halakhic Material
   - C. Topical Arrangement and Classification
   - D. Categorical Statement of Legal Rules with No Reference to Sources or Contrary Opinions
   - E. Style and Draftsmanship of the *Mishneh Torah*
   - F. Factual-Casuistic Formulation
   - G. A Legal Code for the People

III. Critical Reaction to Maimonides' Codificatory Methodology
   - A. Correspondence with *Dayyan* (Judge) Phinehas b. Meshullam of Alexandria
   - B. Correspondence with Joseph ibn Aknin; Rendering Decisions on the Basis of the *Mishneh Torah*
   - C. Rabad's Critical Glosses
   - D. Asheri's Reaction
   - E. Interim Summary of the Stages of Codification of Jewish Law

IV. Commentaries on the *Mishneh Torah*
   - A. *Migdal Oz* by Shem Tov ibn Gaon
   - B. *Maggid Mishneh* by Vidal of Tolosa
   - C. *Kesef Mishneh* by Joseph Caro
   - D. *Yekar Tiferet* by David ibn Zimra (Radbaz)
   - E. *Leḥem Mishneh* by Abraham di Boton
   - F. *Mishneh la-Melekh* by Judah Rosanes
   - G. *Haggahot Maimuniyyot* by Meir ha-Kohen of Rothenburg

V. The Ultimate Achievement of the *Mishneh Torah*

I. STRENGTHENING OF THE TENDENCY TOWARD CODIFICATION AT THE BEGINNING OF THE RABBINIC PERIOD

The turn toward codification of the *Halakhah,* manifested in Alfasi's *Sefer ha-Halakhot,*[1] continued to gather momentum until it brought about a significant change in the methodology of codification. The supreme expression of this change was achieved in the monumental and most original halakhic code ever written, namely, the *Mishneh Torah* of Maimonides. Steps in this new direction appear to have commenced as early as the beginning of the twelfth century, immediately following the death of Alfasi. A responsum of Joseph ibn Migash (Ri Migash), the foremost student of Alfasi, who became Alfasi's successor as the head of the *yeshivah* at Lucena and was the leading halakhic scholar of his time in Spain, well evidences the change. Ri Migash was asked:[2]

> What is our Master's opinion about a man who has never learned *Halakhah* [*i.e.,* the Talmud] with a teacher and does not know the way of the *Halakhah* or what it means or how to read it, but has read widely in the responsa of the *geonim,* of blessed memory, and in the codes? Is a person who has no understanding of the basis for the law and no knowledge of its Talmudic source permitted to instruct [*i.e.,* make authoritative legal pronouncements]? Is it proper to rely on him in any matter? Would our Master clarify for us the law on this issue and provide a sufficient explanation?

The query itself is far-reaching. It asks not only whether a code possesses intrinsic authority and is not (as Paltoi Gaon thought) merely a reference to be consulted in case of doubt as to a legal issue. The question goes further. It asks whether a judge who does not have an adequate knowledge of the Talmud and does not even understand the basis of the applicable law or its source in the Talmud is permitted to make legal rulings on the strength of responsa and books of *halakhot,* and whether it is proper to rely on decisions of such a judge.[3] Ri Migash responded:

1. *See supra* pp. 1167–1172.
2. *Resp. Ri Migash* #114.
3. The questioners also pointed out that the geonic responsa may have been "corrupted by reason of their copyists" and are therefore not always reliable, that one cannot always identify their authors, and that sometimes the decision in a responsum was later retracted. The responsum of Ri Migash did not address these matters. *See also infra* n. 4, p. 1227 n. 135, and p. 1512.

You should know that this man is more fit to be allowed to judge than many others who have set themselves up to judge nowadays, most of whom do not have even one of these two qualifications, namely, understanding of the *Halakhah* [Talmud] or a grounding in the rulings of the *geonim*. It is rather those who presume to make authoritative legal pronouncements on the basis of their study of the *Halakhah* and on the basis of the strength of their Talmudic knowledge who ought to be restrained from doing so, for nowadays no one is qualified [on that basis] to do so. No one in our time has attained such expertise in the Talmud as to be thereby qualified to make legal rulings on the strength of Talmudic analysis without taking account of what the *geonim*, of blessed memory, have held.

But one who makes rulings on the basis of the geonic responsa and finds support in them for his rulings is more suitable and praiseworthy, even though he does not understand the Talmud, than one who thinks that he knows his way through the Talmud and relies upon himself. For one who makes a ruling, even though flawed in reasoning, in reliance on what the *geonim* have said does not really err; he at least acts on the basis of a decision of a distinguished and expert court. However, one who makes a ruling on the basis of his independent analysis of a legal rule [in the Talmud] may misunderstand the rule or be misguided in his reasoning, and may be wrong in concluding that the legal rule requires the result he reaches, when in fact it does not.

No one in our time has attained such distinction in Talmud as to be qualified on that account to make authoritative pronouncements on the law. I have already seen the responsa of some persons who believed that the rightness of their decisions was as clear as day, but were wrong; their decisions were based on inapposite sources, and the sources upon which they based their conclusions did not support them. There was a fine distinction—so subtle that it escaped them—between the case they were dealing with and the legal rule [in the Talmud] that purportedly controlled their decision. They seized on a legal rule that they took at face value without sensing its finer points, and they applied that rule to their case without being aware of the subtle distinction.

[Things have reached] such a state that I say that someone who does not rely on himself but [instead] bases his decisions on the geonic responsa and rulings, which are authoritative and well-settled, and which set forth clearly and succinctly the reasoning [supporting their conclusion], is more praiseworthy than one who presumes to base his rulings directly on the Talmud.[4]

4. From the standpoint of both law and historical fact, another aspect of this responsum is particularly interesting. Ri Migash was also asked whether it is permitted to rely on a judge "if he is not God-fearing and evidence has been given against him with regard to many wicked acts." (The query also emphasized that the judge in question was not consistent in his decisions.) Ri Migash responded:

This explicit statement by Ri Migash indicates the palpable change in attitude on the part of some halakhic authorities as to the course and proper place of codification in Jewish law.[5] Books of *halakhot* were not, as Paltoi Gaon had thought in the mid-ninth century, merely reference works to help solve problems that were difficult to resolve solely on the basis of the Talmudic sources. According to Ri Migash, a book of *halakhot* carries weight in its own right, and it is not necessary to study the Talmudic sources. Indeed, the change cuts deeper still: Recourse to books of *halakhot* is superior to the research and analysis of the Talmud itself as a means of ascertaining the law; in the search for a clear legal rule in the dense foliage of the Talmud, there is a risk that something will be misunderstood and an improper distinction will be made. If, however, the basis of the judge's decision is the clear and easily grasped formulation of the codifier, the judge can at least be certain that he has based his decision on the law as declared by a learned halakhic authority; and this is true even though it is possible that the ruling in the book of *halakhot* differs from the conclusion fairly to be drawn from the Talmudic discussion itself.

Why was it necessary to go so far? Because, according to Ri Migash, "no one in our time has attained such distinction in Talmud as to be qualified on that account to make authoritative pronouncements on the law." Therefore, deciding cases and declaring the law require that there be a book setting out the content of the law in clear, concise, and easily readable form.

The author of this forthright and far-reaching statement that a code is

---

> And as to your mentioning his not being God-fearing, if he holds judicial office, one ought to investigate the matter, for it is not fitting to put an unsuitable judge in office. That is tantamount to [the idolatrous act of] "planting an *asherah* [a tree or grove involved in idol worship] in Israel" [TB Sanhedrin 7b]. However, if he does not hold a judicial office but hears only those cases in which the parties select him, we ought not to interfere.

See supra pp. 19–33 regarding arbitration and lay tribunals.

5. For the approach of Rabbi Jacob, a Spanish halakhic authority of that period, that diverged from that of Ri Migash, *see* two letters discovered in the Cairo *Genizah* and published by S.D. Goitein, in *Sidrei Ḥinnukh bi-Mei ha-Geonim u-Vet ha-Rambam* [Educational Systems from the Geonic Period to Maimonides], Jerusalem, 1962. *See also* I. Ta-Shema, "Yeẓirato ha-Sifrutit Shel Rabbenu Yosef ha-Levi ibn Migash" [The Literary Works of R. Joseph ha-Levi ibn Migash], *Kiryat Sefer,* XLVI (1971), pp. 547–550 and n. 13. For additional discussion of this responsum of Ri Migash, *see* I.H. Weiss, *Bet Talmud,* I (1881), pp. 119–120; L. Blau, "Das Gesetzbuch des Maimonides Historisch Betrachtet" [A Historical View of Maimonides' Code], in *Moses Ben Maimon,* 1914, II, pp. 343–345. For the circumstances accounting for the difficulty of extracting the law from the Talmud, *see* the Introduction to *Sefer ha-Mafte'aḥ le-Man'ulei ha-Talmud* [Book of the Key to the Locks of the Talmud] of Nissim Gaon in S. Abramson, *Rav Nissim Gaon, Ḥamishah Sefarim* [Rabbi Nissim Gaon, Five Books], 1965, p. 3.

a better basis for making legal decisions than the Talmud itself was an eminent halakhic authority of whom Maimonides wrote, "That man's grasp of Talmud amazes everyone who studies his writings and perceives the depth of his analysis, so that I may say of him, 'His methodology surpasses that of all his predecessors.'"[6]

It is a fair assumption that Ri Migash's responsum encouraged Maimonides to undertake the important and difficult task of composing a code of Jewish law in such a form and on such a scale that it would suffice, even standing alone, as a basis for making legal rulings and deciding cases. Maimonides performed the task with prodigious genius and much artfulness by pioneering a new form of codificatory literature: a book of *pesakim*—authoritative, concise statements of legal rules.

II. MAIMONIDES AND HIS CODIFICATORY WORK

A. Goals

It is hardly surprising that a man such as Maimonides, whose work superbly reflects systematic organization, would make clear, both to himself and to his readers, his motives and objectives in writing his masterpiece. He did so in detail in the Introduction to his *Sefer ha-Mizvot* [Book of the Commandments],[7] in the Introduction to his *Mishneh Torah,* and in several responsa and epistles that he wrote to those who sought his guidance or took issue with him. Maimonides set forth as the background and motivation for his work the familiar reasons that led in all periods to the writing of compendious but concise codes, namely, the vastness of the halakhic material, the difficulty of understanding the sources and of finding one's way in them, and the social and historical milieu:[8]

> At the present time, when dire calamities keep following one another and the needs of the moment brush aside all things, our wise men have lost their wisdom, and the understanding of our astute people is hidden. Hence, the commentaries, the codes of law, and the responsa that were written by the *geonim,* who strove to make them easily intelligible, have presented difficulties in our days, so that only a few are capable of understanding them properly. Needless to say, this applies to the Talmud itself (the Babylonian as well

6. Maimonides, *Commentary on the Mishnah,* Introduction (Hebrew trans. Kafaḥ, without the Arabic original), p. 25.

7. *Sefer ha-Mizvot* was written as a preparatory work for the *Mishneh Torah; see* Maimonides, *Sefer ha-Mizvot,* ed. Rambam la-Am, Mosad ha-Rav Kook, 1958, Introduction, pp. 3 and 5.

8. *MT,* Introduction, following the text of ed. Constantinople, Mosad ha-Rav Kook, 1964, p. 13. Our citations to *MT,* Introduction, are to this edition.

> as the Jerusalem), the *Sifra,* the *Sifrei,* and the *Tosefta*—works that require wide knowledge, a learned mind, and ample time before one can discern from them the correct practice as to what is prohibited or permitted, and the other laws of the Torah.
>
> Therefore, I, Moses ben Maimon, the Sephardi, bestirred myself and, relying upon the Creator, blessed be He, have made a thorough study of all these books, and have determined to compose a work containing the results derived from all these books concerning what is prohibited or permitted, unclean or clean, as well as the other laws of the Torah.[9]

One of the goals Maimonides hoped his code would achieve was to make "all the laws—the rules of each and every commandment, and of all the enactments promulgated by the Sages and prophets—clear and manifest to young and old."[10] This aspiration, of course, is similar to that of all codifiers of any legal system.[11]

The background and purpose of the *Mishneh Torah* described to this point were not particularly novel; similar motives and aims had led to the composition of books of *halakhot* in earlier periods. The great innovation of Maimonides involved an additional revolutionary objective for the *Mishneh Torah*—a completely new approach as well as a novel form for setting forth the authoritative distillation of the *Halakhah.* Maimonides, as usual, expressed this grand and bold objective clearly and without equivocation:[12]

> In brief, a person will not need to have recourse to any other work to ascertain any of the laws of Israel. This work is intended as a compendium of the entire Oral Law, including the enactments, customs, and decrees instituted from the days of Moses, our teacher, until the redaction of the Talmud, as expounded for us by the *geonim* in all the works composed by them since the completion of the Talmud.
>
> Hence, I have entitled this work *Mishneh Torah* [Recapitulation of Torah], for the reason that a person who first reads the Torah and then this work will know from it all of the Oral Law, and there will be no need to read any other book [written] between them.

9. *See also* Epistle of Maimonides to Jonathan ha-Kohen of Lunel, Provence *(Resp. Maimonides,* ed. A.H. Freimann, 1934, Introduction, p. LXI): "My intention in this work was none other than to clear the way and remove the stumbling blocks in the path of students, to keep them from becoming discouraged by the extensive [Talmudic] debates and thereby falling into error in determining the law." On the correspondence between Maimonides and the scholars of Provence, *see* S.M. Stern, "Ḥalifat ha-Mikhtavim Bein ha-Rambam ve-Ḥakhmei Provinẓa" [The Correspondence between Maimonides and the Scholars of Provence], *Zion,* XVI, pp. 18–29.

10. *MT,* Introduction, p. 14.

11. *See supra* p. 1185.

12. *MT,* Introduction, p. 14.

As previously stated,[13] Maimonides did not mean by this statement that his code was to be the authoritative legal source of Jewish law. The very introduction to the *Mishneh Torah,* in which the statement just quoted was made, opens with a description of the "chain of the tradition." It specifies the names of all those who were links in the chain, commencing with the Revelation at Sinai—the seminal event and the source of authority for the Jewish legal system. Indeed, it makes clear that everything set forth in the Written Law and in the Oral Law as handed down in the Talmud "is binding on all Israel."[14] Consequently, all the prior halakhic literature would remain as material for study and analysis, and as a source for legal pronouncements on new problems arising in the future;[15] but finding and ascertaining the *Halakhah* as crystallized up to Maimonides' time was to be done exclusively by means of his code, for he was fully confident that his code included the entire Oral Law and that there could be no inconsistency between it and the binding halakhic literature up to that time.

The Introductions to his various works and his responsa indicate that Maimonides set for himself four basic objectives in the preparation and composition of the *Mishneh Torah,* similar to the guidelines used even today for any type of code in every legal system. Maimonides' objectives were:

1. To compile the entire corpus of Jewish law from the Torah up to his own day and to rework this material scientifically and systematically.
2. To select and arrange the material topically.
3. To set forth the law categorically and prescriptively, without associating it with particular Sages, without mentioning conflicting opinions, and without source references.
4. To achieve a polished literary style that clearly and succinctly expresses the content of the concepts expounded.

Fulfilling these objectives in codifying the law of any legal system calls for superior skills; fulfilling them in codifying the *Halakhah* calls for genius of the highest order. Let us see how Maimonides set about achieving each of these objectives.

B. Compiling and Reworking the Halakhic Material

Maimonides regarded the compilation and reworking of the entire corpus of Jewish law as the primary task of his code. He stated in his Introduction to *Sefer ha-Mizvot*:

13. *Supra* pp. 1145–1146.

14. *MT,* Introduction, p. 11. For a full quotation *see supra* p. 1145.

15. *See* Maimonides' response to Phinehas b. Meshullam, quoted *supra* p. 1146; *supra* n. 9.

> I deemed it advisable to compile a compendium that will include all the laws and precepts of the Torah, with nothing missing from it . . . , so that this compendium would include all the laws of the Torah of Moses, our teacher, whether or not they have practical relevance in this time of exile.
>
> And I will include in it everything of the Torah that has been established and recorded, omitting no relevant question that might arise, or at least I will mention the principle by means of which that question can easily be resolved without reflecting too deeply. Such is my goal in this work: to be brief yet comprehensive, so that the reader might encompass all that is found in the Mishnah, the Talmud, the *Sifra,* the *Sifrei,* the *Tosefta,* and all enactments of the *geonim,* of blessed memory, who came afterwards, as well as all that they have explained and commented upon concerning what is prohibited or permissible, ritually impure or pure, and invalid or valid, [and who is] guilty or not guilty, liable or not liable to pay, and required or not required to take an oath. In short, there should be no need for any book written since the Torah other than this one from which to ascertain anything required anywhere in the entire Torah, including both Biblical and rabbinic laws.[16]

In this enormous labor of compilation, Maimonides was aided by the commentaries and books he had previously written. In his youth, he had written a commentary on the Orders of *Nashim, Nezikin,* and *Mo'ed* as well as on Tractate *Ḥullin* of the Babylonian Talmud;[17] and on the Jerusalem Talmud, he had written *Hilkhot ha-Yerushalmi* [Laws of the Jerusalem Talmud].[18] (These books have been largely lost.) When he was twenty-three years old,[19] he began his classic commentary on the Mishnah, based, as he himself attested,[20] on the halakhic *midrashim,* the *Tosefta,* the Talmud, and the geonic literature. In addition, he wrote the *Sefer ha-Miẓvot* as a preparatory exercise for the *Mishneh Torah.*[21] Only after all these preparations did

16. *Sefer ha-Miẓvot,* Introduction, p. 1b. The Introduction to the *Mishneh Torah* states (p. 14):

> This work is intended as a compendium of the entire Oral Law, including the enactments, customs, and decrees instituted from the days of Moses, our teacher, until the redaction of the Talmud, as expounded for us by the *geonim* in all the works composed by them since the completion of the Talmud.

17. *Commentary on the Mishnah,* Introduction, p. 25. *See also Ḥiddushei ha-Rambam la-Talmud* [Maimonides' Novellae on the Talmud], containing passages attributed to Maimonides' commentary on the Talmud, published by Zachs, Jerusalem, 1963.

18. Maimonides, *Commentary on the Mishnah,* M Tamid 5:1. *See also* S. Lieberman, *Hilkhot ha-Yerushalmi le-Rabbenu Moshe b. Maimon* ["Laws of the Jerusalem Talmud" by Maimonides], New York, 1948, Preface and Introduction.

19. *See* Maimonides' statement upon completing his *Commentary on the Mishnah,* at the end of Tractate *Ukẓin.*

20. At the beginning of his Introduction to the *Commentary on the Mishnah,* p. 1.

21. *Sefer ha-Miẓvot,* Introduction, pp. 3 and 5.

he begin at the age of approximately forty-one to compose the *Mishneh Torah,* on which he worked for about ten years.[22] It should also be pointed out that throughout this period, fortune did not smile on him. He was exiled from city to city and from country to country—from Cordoba in Spain to Fez in North Africa, then to the Land of Israel, and finally to Cairo, Egypt.

In reworking the halakhic material that he assembled, Maimonides examined, on the basis of "old texts," the nature and accuracy of various legal rules his predecessors had established; and he also pointed out errors in the texts that had been responsible for erroneous halakhic conclusions. For example, the *Mishneh Torah* states:[23]

> If one lends money to another in the presence of witnesses and tells him, "Pay me only in the presence of witnesses," the borrower must pay him in the presence of witnesses. . . . If the borrower says, "I did what you told me and paid you in the presence of So-and-so and So-and-so, who have gone overseas or died," he is believed. If, however, he [the lender] has told him

22. The *Mishneh Torah* mentions three different dates in connection with its composition:

1. *1176* C.E. Maimonides stated in *Hilkhot Shemittah ve-Yovel* 10:4: "According to this reckoning, the current year, which is the 1107th since the destruction [of the Temple], which coincides with the 1487th of the Seleucid era [*minyan shetarot*] and with the 4936th year since Creation, is a sabbatical year and the 21st year in the jubilee cycle." Thus, Maimonides wrote *Hilkhot Shemittah ve-Yovel* in 1176 (4936 A.M.).
2. *1177* C.E. In *MT,* Introduction, p. 13, Maimonides wrote: " . . . up to this time, which is the 1108th year since the destruction of the Temple, which coincides with the year 4936 from the creation of the world" (= 1176); *but see,* in the note to line 147, that the correct reading is 4937 (= 1177).
3. *1178* C.E. *Hilkhot Kiddush ha-Ḥodesh* 11:16 states: "We therefore made it a principle that we always make the start for this reckoning from the beginning of Thursday night, the day after which will be the third day of the month of Nisan of the current year, which is the seventeenth year of the 260th cycle, coinciding with the 4938th year from Creation [= 1178], the 1489th year of the Seleucid era, and the 1109th year since the destruction of the Second Temple."

The date 1177 C.E. mentioned in the Introduction was thus apparently not the year Maimonides started work on the *Mishneh Torah;* for in the previous year, 1176, he was already at work on *Hilkhot Shemittah ve-Yovel.* He must have written the Introduction after some sections of the work had been completed. The only thing that is certain is the length of time he took to write it, namely, ten years, as he himself attested. *See Koveẓ ha-Rambam,* I, 1860, #49.

From the two dates given in *Hilkhot Shemittah ve-Yovel* and *Hilkhot Kiddush ha-Ḥodesh,* it follows that Maimonides did not write the various parts of the *Mishneh Torah* in the sequence in which they appear in the work as we now have it; for in our version, *Shemittah ve-Yovel* comes after *Kiddush ha-Ḥodesh,* and in *Shemittah ve-Yovel* he wrote that the year was the 4936th since Creation, whereas in *Kiddush ha-Ḥodesh* he wrote that the year was the 4938th. *See* I.H. Weiss, "Toledot ha-Rav Rabbenu Moshe b. Maimon" [A Biography of Maimonides], *Bet Talmud,* I (1881), pp. 225–226.

23. *MT,* Malveh ve-Loveh 15:1–2.

> [the borrower], "Pay me only in the presence of So-and-so and So-and-so," and the borrower says, "I paid you in the presence of others who have died or have gone overseas," he is not believed.

The next paragraph continues:

> There are Talmudic texts in which it is written: "If one tells another, 'Pay me only in the presence of witnesses,' and he [the borrower] says, 'I paid you in the presence of So-and-so and So-and-so, who have gone overseas,' he is not believed." This is a scribal error that has misled those who have rendered decisions in accordance with those texts.[24] I have examined the old texts and found therein: "he is believed." In Egypt, I obtained a fragment of an old text of the Talmud written on parchment of the type upon which they used to write some five hundred years ago, and I found two versions of this *halakhah* written on two specimens of parchment, both of which state: "If he says, 'I paid in the presence of So-and-so and So-and-so, who have gone overseas,' he is believed."
>
> Because of this scribal error, whch has occurred in some texts, some *geonim* have taught that if he [the lender] tells him [the borrower], "Pay me only in the presence of So-and-so and So-and-so," and he pays in the presence of others, he is not believed, even if he produces the witnesses in whose presence payment was made. This, too, is a serious error. The correct rule is that if witnesses come and testify that the borrower has paid the lender in their presence, the borrower is released, and there is no room here for any doubt. . . . My conclusion is also supported by the [context of the] *Gemara*.

In deciding that there was a scribal error, Maimonides brought common sense to bear on the subject, stating:[25]

> Furthermore, what I have said [that the borrower is believed when he says he paid in the presence of witnesses who have gone overseas or have died] finds support in reason. For what could the borrower do? The lender said to him, "Pay me only in the presence of witnesses," and he did repay him in the presence of witnesses. Is he supposed to imprison the witnesses for the rest of their lives to prevent them from leaving? And, if they died, what should he do? Should he keep paying time and again forever until he is able to produce witnesses?[26]

In order to achieve the maximum utility for his code, Maimonides made use of non-Talmudic sources whenever necessary for the understand-

24. Namely, Alfasi; *see* Alfasi, Shevu'ot, ch. 6, #1156. *See also* Ran, *ad loc.*, on the methodologies and texts of Alfasi and Maimonides.

25. *MT,* Malveh ve-Loveh 15:2.

26. For additional examples, *see MT,* Yom Tov 2:12 (*see also Migdal Oz, ad loc.*); Ishut 11:13 (*see also Maggid Mishneh* to par. 12); *Sefer ha-Mizvot,* Negative Commandment #199 (pp. 265–266).

ing of Talmudic laws. The laws of *kiddush ha-ḥodesh* (sanctification of the New Moon) are an example. These laws deal with establishing the date of Rosh Ḥodesh (the New Moon), the annual calendar, and related subjects, which led Maimonides to discuss at length the method of calculating the seasons. He learned mathematical astronomy, as he himself attested, from the books of Greek scholars, because Talmudic literature was lacking in material on this subject:[27]

> As regards the logic for all these calculations—why we add a particular number or deduct it, how all these rules were discovered and proved—all this is part of the science of astronomy and mathematics, about which many books have been written by Greek scholars; and these books are available to the scholars of our time. But the books that had been written by the Sages of Israel, of the tribe of Issachar, who lived in the time of the Prophets, have not come down to us.
>
> Since all these rules have been established by sound and clear proofs, irrefutable and free from any flaw, we need not be concerned about the identity of their authors, whether they were Hebrew prophets or gentiles.[28] For when we deal with rules and propositions that have been demonstrated by sound reasoning and verified by flawless proofs, we may rely upon the author who has discovered them or the person who has transmitted them [and] upon the quality of the proofs and reasoning that support them.

Maimonides went on to explain why he introduced these mathematical calculations into his work:[29]

> We have now expounded all the methods of calculation required for the determination of the visibility of the new moon and for the examination of the witnesses [to its appearance], so that discerning students might be able to learn everything about the subject. Thus, they will not be deficient in this one

27. *MT,* Kiddush ha-Ḥodesh 17:24.

28. *See also* Maimonides, *Shemonah Perakim,* Introduction, in *Ha-Hakdamot le-Ferush ha-Mishnah* [The Introductions to the Commentary on the Mishnah], ed. Rambam la-Am, Mosad ha-Rav Kook, 1961, p. 155:

> Know that the ideas presented in these chapters and in the following commentary are not of my own invention, nor did I originate the explanations they contain. Rather, I have gleaned them from the words of the Sages in the *midrashim,* in the Talmud, and in other works by them, as well as from the words of the philosophers, ancient and recent, and also from the works of many authors, as one should accept the truth from whatever source it comes.

See also MT, Kiddush ha-Ḥodesh 11:2–3, and *The Guide for the Perplexed,* II, ch. 8. To similar effect, *see* the responsum of Maimonides to the scholars of the community of Marseilles (Southern France) in *Kovez̧ ha-Rambam,* II (Epistles), pp. 24ff. This responsum is also noteworthy for Maimonides' astringent rejection of the claims of astrology and similar "sciences" to predict the future.

29. *MT,* Kiddush ha-Ḥodesh 19:16.

> of the many pathways of the Torah, and will have no need to roam and ramble in other books in search of such information. "Search and read in the scroll of the Lord: not one of these shall be absent."[30]

Thus, Maimonides' reason for including this material was that he desired to meet the need to concentrate in one place, to the fullest possible extent, all the material—even that generated by non-Jewish scientists—affecting each law, so that the reader would not be required to consult other works in order to obtain needed information.

As noted in the Introduction to *Sefer ha-Mizvot,* Maimonides included in his work the entire *corpus juris* of the Jewish legal system, "whether or not they have practical relevance in this time of exile."[31] In this respect, he broke with the pattern followed by the overwhelming majority of the prior books of *halakhot* (commencing with the *Halakhot Pesukot* of Yehudai Gaon), which did not include laws that no longer had practical relevance. He went even further; his code also includes principles relating to Jewish thought, theology, and ethics, and to the mental and physical aspects of human conduct. He believed that these subjects also deserved to be covered in a book of *pesakim,* and he set them forth in numbered paragraphs, in the classic code style, in *Sefer ha-Madda* [The Book of Knowledge], the first book of the *Mishneh Torah.* This integration of philosophy, faith, and ethics with the law characterizes even the purely halakhic sections of Maimonides' code. Sometimes, he prefaced a legal topic with a relevant historical-ethical introduction, and in other instances, he concluded a legal topic with pertinent ethical comments and philosophical reflections.

For example, the laws of *Hanukkah* are introduced by the following three paragraphs:

> In the time of the Second Temple, when the Greeks ruled over Israel, they issued evil decrees against them, proscribing their religion and forbidding them to study the Torah or to fulfill the commandments. They laid hands on their property and on their daughters, and they entered the Temple, made breaches in it, and defiled that which was ritually pure. The Jewish people were in dire straits and suffered great persecution, until the God of our fathers took pity on them and saved and delivered them from the hands of the Greeks. For the Hasmonean family of High Priests won a victory in which they slew the Greeks and saved the Jews from their hands. They set up a king from among the priests and restored Israel's kingdom for a period of more than two hundred years, until the destruction of the Second Temple.
>
> The day on which the Jews were victorious over their enemies and de-

30. Isaiah 34:16.
31. *Sefer ha-Mizvot,* Introduction, p. 1.

stroyed them was the twenty-fifth day of the month of Kislev. When they reentered the Temple, they found within its precincts only one cruse of ritually pure oil—enough to burn for only a single day. Yet, with it they kept burning the required number of lights for eight days, until they could press olives and produce ritually pure oil.

Consequently, the Sages of that generation enacted that the eight days beginning with the 25th of Kislev should be days of rejoicing on which the Hallel [psalms of praise] is to be recited and that on each one of the eight nights lights should be lit in the evening at the entrances of the houses to manifest and publicly demonstrate the miracle. These days are known as *Hanukkah.* Funeral eulogies and fasting are forbidden on them, just as on *Purim;* and kindling lights on those days is a commandment based on the authority of the Scribes, analogous to the commandment to read the *Megillah* [the Scroll of Esther, on *Purim*].[32]

This historical introduction, based in the main on Talmudic sources,[33] is not essential to the halakhic rules—the laws of kindling the *Hanukkah* lights and the like—which Maimonides thereafter set forth. Nevertheless, he saw fit to preface his treatment of the laws of *Hanukkah* with the historical-religious background of the festival, in order to convey a deeper understanding of its laws.[34] Maimonides concluded the laws of *Hanukkah* as follows:[35]

The commandment to kindle the *Hanukkah* lights is exceedingly precious, and one should be particularly careful to fulfill it in order to publicize the

32. *MT,* Megillah ve-Hanukkah 3:1–3.

33. *See Maggid Mishneh, ad loc.*, and the commentary to *Mishneh Torah,* Zemanim, vol. V, in ed. Rambam la-Am, Mosad ha-Rav Kook, 1957, pp. 656–657.

34. It is interesting to compare the treatment of *Hanukkah* in the *Mishneh Torah* with that in Alfasi's *Sefer ha-Halakhot* and in the codificatory literature after Maimonides. Alfasi, (*Hilkhot Hanukkah,* ch. 2 of Tractate Shabbat), quotes from TB only the *baraita* "What is *Hanukkah*? . . . When the Hasmoneans prevailed over them and defeated them, they searched and found only one cruse of oil." He does so because the *baraita* ends with "they proclaimed those eight days as holidays for psalms of praise and thanksgiving [*i.e.*, reciting *Hallel* and *Al ha-Nissim*]." This is the source for the law that *Hanukkah* lights should be kindled and a benediction recited on each of the eight days. Alfasi limited himself to quoting just this "historical" item, in line with his usual approach of quoting only so much of the *Aggadah* as is of practical importance in supporting the validity of halakhic norms (*see supra* p. 1169).

Sh. Ar. OḤ ch. 670ff. includes no historical information. It begins directly with the laws ("On the 25th of Kislev, the eight days of *Hanukkah* [commence]. . . . ") in accordance with Caro's general approach, which omits introductions, reasons for the laws, and the like (*see infra* p. 1327). *Sefer ha-Turim* gives a brief summary of the history. (For the general method of the *Turim, see infra* pp. 1295–1302, 1327, and Appendix B.) *Kiẓẓur Shulḥan Arukh* ch. 139 incorporates Maimonides' text, as does *Mishnah Berurah,* Sh. Ar. OḤ, *loc. cit.* For further comparisons of the respective styles of the *Mishneh Torah,* the *Turim,* and the *Shulḥan Arukh, see infra* pp. 1327–1340 and Appendix B.

35. *MT,* Megillah ve-Hanukkah 4:12–14.

miracle and to offer additional praise and thanksgiving to God for the wonders He wrought for us. Even if one has no food to eat except what he receives from charity, he should pawn or sell his garment to buy oil and lamps, and kindle the lights.

If one has no more than a single *perutah* and needs wine for the sanctification *(kiddush)* of the sabbath and oil to kindle the *Hanukkah* light, he should give priority to the purchase of oil for the *Hanukkah* light over the purchase of wine for the sabbath *kiddush.* Since both commandments are based on the authority of the Scribes, it is best to give priority to the *Hanukkah* light, since it serves as a commemoration of the miracle of *Hanukkah.*

If such a poor man must choose between sabbath candles [which there is a positive duty to light in order to brighten the home on the sabbath and foster domestic harmony] and a *Hanukkah* lamp, or between sabbath candles and wine for the sabbath *kiddush,* the sabbath candles have priority, for the sake of domestic harmony, since even the Divine Name may be erased [in the oath of purgation, Numbers 5:12–31] in the interest of harmony between husband and wife. Great indeed is peace; for the purpose for which the whole of the Torah was given is to bring peace to the world, as it is written, "Her ways are pleasant ways, and all her paths, peaceful."[36]

Maimonides thus incorporated and stressed the religious-ethical grounding[37] of the legal rules he expounded,[38] and concluded with a reference to the value of peace between husband and wife, all humankind, and all God's creatures.[39]

The arduous labor involved in finding and "unveiling" every law in

36. Proverbs 3:17.

37. *See Tur* and Sh. Ar. OḤ ch. 678, which set forth the rules regarding which commandment is given priority, but do not mention the ethical grounding of the rules. For additional historical introductions by Maimonides, *see MT,* Avodat Kokhavim ve-Ḥukkoteihem ch. 1; Tefillah 1:3ff.; Ishut 1:1. For chapters concluding with general ethical concepts, *see* Issurei Bi'ah 22:21; Sheḥitah 14:16; Roẓe'aḥ u-Shemirat ha-Nefesh 13:14; Me'ilah 8:8; Tum'at Ẓara'at 16:10.

38. Maimonides' practice of giving reasons for laws has engendered extensive discussion among the halakhic authorities. *See* Maimonides' own statement in one of his responsa: "[I]t is my intention in all of this work [*Mishneh Torah*] to provide a rational basis for the laws and to make them more understandable to most people." (*Resp. Maimonides,* ed. Blau, #252, p. 461.) *See also* J. Levinger, *Darkhei ha-Maḥashavah ha-Hilkhatit Shel ha-Rambam* [Methodology of Maimonides' Halakhic Thought], 1965, pp. 92ff.; B.Z. Benedikt, "Le-Darko Shel ha-Rambam be-Ta'amo Shel Din" [On Maimonides' Methodology in Regard to Rationales for Legal Rules], *Kovez Torah she-be-al Peh* [Collected Essays on the Oral Law], Mosad ha-Rav Kook, 1964, pp. 87ff.; E.S. Rosenthal, *Perakim,* Year Book of Schocken Institute, I, pp. 183ff.

39. Just as Maimonides included material from outside the Talmud as well as his own supplementary comments, he also omitted many matters contained in the Talmud with reference to demons, the evil eye, baleful stars, bad dreams, and infliction of harm through magic. Alfasi and the later codifiers do include the Talmudic passages on these subjects. *See* Levinger, *supra* n. 38 at 106 and nn. 53, 54, and at 118ff.

the vast Talmudic literature—where sometimes a law is mentioned only incidentally in the course of a debate dealing essentially with an entirely different subject—was described by Maimonides himself, in a letter to *Dayyan* (Judge) Phinehas of Alexandria, recounting an incident from Maimonides' own life. As discussed below, Maimonides did not indicate in his code the sources in the Talmudic literature from which the laws he set forth were derived. Maimonides wrote to Phinehas:

> A certain *dayyan,* a pious man, came to me with a section of the work [*Mishneh Torah*] in his hand, containing the laws of homicide from *Sefer Nezikin* [The Book of Damages], and he showed me a certain law. He said, "Read this"; so I read it. I said, "What is the problem here?" He said, "What is the source for what is stated here?" I said, "In the [appropriate] place, either in [Chapter] *Ellu Hen ha-Golim* [Tractate *Makkot,* ch. 2] or in [Tractate] *Sanhedrin* among the laws of homicide." He said, "I have already gone over all of that, but I could not find [the source]—not [even] in the Jerusalem Talmud or the *Tosefta.*"
>
> I was taken aback for a while; and then I said, "I remember that in a certain place in [Tractate] *Gittin* this point is explained." I took out *Gittin,* and searched, but I could not find [the source]. I was totally confounded and said, "Where indeed is the source for this statement? Leave it for a while until I remember where!" After he left, I remembered. I sent a messenger and brought him back, and I showed him the matter clearly explained in Tractate *Yevamot,* in a passage entirely incidental to the main topic of the discussion. He could hardly believe what had happened, and went off.[40]

The difficulty and the burden of responsibility involved in finding, assembling, and reworking the entire *corpus juris* of the *Halakhah* was acknowledged and appreciated even by those halakhic authorities who strongly took issue with the other basic guidelines followed by Maimonides in writing the *Mishneh Torah.* Rabad of Posquières, the severe critic of Maimonides, observed in one of his critical glosses:

> Abraham [Rabad] says: All he writes here has no basis in *Gemara* or *Tosefta,* nor is it indicated by reason . . . and, for the life of me, if he had not achieved such a prodigious accomplishment in gathering together the statements of the *Gemara,* the Jerusalem Talmud, and the *Tosefta,* I would have convened a public council [against him], including the elders and halakhic authorities of the people; for he has changed the vocabulary and the rhetoric [of the *Hala-*

40. *Kovez ha-Rambam,* II (Epistles), p. 26a/b. Because of this incident, Maimonides regretted that he did not indicate the Talmudic source for his statement of the law where the source is elsewhere than in the main treatment of the subject in the Talmud. He even intended to write a separate book citing such sources. *See id.* (continuation), and also Maimonides' statements quoted *infra* pp. 1197, 1216–1221.

khah], has altered the meaning of laws handed down by tradition, and has turned them into something else.[41]

The merit of Maimonides' great accomplishment in finding, assembling, and reworking the corpus of Jewish law seems to have stood him in good stead.

C. Topical Arrangement and Classification

The task of topical arrangement and classification was without a doubt one of the most complex and formidable challenges in Maimonides' undertaking. The Introduction to *Sefer ha-Miẓvot* describes the task as follows:[42]

> As I directed my attention toward this goal, I began thinking about how the organization of this work and the arrangement of its parts should be accomplished. [I wondered:] Should I organize it according to the organization of the Mishnah and in the same sequence, or should I organize it in some other way, arranging the subjects in the order that logic dictates, since this is the proper and easier way for learning? Then it became clear to me that it would be best to organize this work into groups of *halakhot* rather than according to the tractates of the Mishnah, *e.g.*, "The Laws of the Tabernacle" *(Sukkah)*, "The Laws of the Palm Branch" (*Lulav*), "The Laws of the *Mezuzah*," "The Laws of the Fringes" (*Ẓiẓit*); and that I should divide every such general section of *halakhot* into chapters and paragraphs, in the format of the Mishnah, so that, for example, "The Laws of the Phylacteries" (*Tefillin*) would consist of chapters one, two, three, and four, with each chapter being divided into paragraphs, so as to facilitate memorization by those who wish to learn any part of it by heart.
>
> With this kind of organization, it would clearly not be appropriate to organize the laws relating to any particular topic under two general sections—affirmative and negative commandments—but all necessary divisions would be made within the chapters of each general section.
>
> At times, one general section would contain a number of commandments, either because they all relate to a single general topic or because many commandments involve a single objective. For example, in dealing with idolatry, I would entitle this section, "The Laws of Idolatry," and then I would proceed to discuss under this general topic a number of commandments: [the prohibitions against] enticing an individual Israelite [to idol worship, Deuteronomy 13:7ff.], leading a community astray [Deuteronomy 13:13ff.], causing [one's offspring] to pass [through the fire] in the worship of Moloch [Leviticus

41. Rabad, *Hassagot*, Kilayim 6:2.

42. Our translation follows the Hebrew of J. Kafaḥ, ed. Rambam la-Am, *supra* n. 7 at 2–3. *See MT*, Introduction, p. 14: "This work is organized according to subject, not according to the numerical order of the *miẓvot*."

> 18:21], prophesying in the name of an idol [Deuteronomy 13:2ff.], worshipping idols, and other similar commandments relating to idolatry. Similarly, in the general section entitled "The Laws of Things Forbidden to Be Brought on the Altar," I would mention [the commandments against offering] leaven or honey, blemished offerings, the hire of a harlot or the price of a dog, and similar commandments, since they all concern a single general subject, namely, things forbidden to be brought on the altar.

The organization of the Mishnah did indeed serve in some measure as a starting point for Maimonides, but it was not adequate to provide him much help in sorting the material and arranging it topically because, as we have seen, the organization of the Mishnah is not completely topical. Tractate *Kiddushin* (on marriage), for instance, includes a great deal of material on the laws of acquisition, and Tractate *Gittin* (on divorce) includes many laws in various areas, including agency and creditors' rights.[43] This lack of consistent organization grew even more marked in the Talmud: although the Talmud was redacted to follow the sequence of the Mishnah, the material it discusses is often not even relevant to the *mishnah* to which it is appended.

The form of post-Talmudic literature was cast in the same mold. Occasionally, the halakhic material followed the sequence of the Torah, as in the case of *Sefer ha-She'iltot*. Other works, such as *Halakhot Pesukot, Halakhot Gedolot,* and Alfasi's *Sefer ha-Halakhot,* were arranged in the order of the Talmudic tractates. While it is true that in some of these books of *halakhot* the material began to be arranged topically (*e.g.*, laws in a single area such as evidence, or interest and usury, being treated together),[44] and Maimonides was undoubtedly influenced by this development, the earlier efforts were only a modest first step: not all the material relating to the topic was covered, and only a relatively small number of topics were so treated. Some *geonim,* as we have seen, wrote monographs on various topics, like *Sefer ha-Yerushot* [Book of Inheritances] by Saadiah Gaon, *Sefer ha-Arvut ve-ha-Kabbelanut* [Book of Ordinary and Special Contractual Suretyship] by Samuel b. Ḥophni Gaon, *Sefer ha-Mikaḥ ve-ha-Mimkar* [Book of Purchase and Sale] by Hai Gaon, and others; and it is a fair assumption that the concentration of material on a particular subject in each of the monographs greatly assisted Maimonides in his efforts to classify the law and organize it topically.

However, these monographs encompassed only a few subjects, and there was as yet no comprehensive work encompassing all the areas of Jewish law, fully classified and topically arranged. With all the assistance

43. *See supra* pp. 1055–1056.
44. *See supra* p. 1154.

that Maimonides could derive from the works of his predecessors, he was, as a practical matter, compelled to plow deeply through all the available halakhic material, break it down into individual rules, and insert each rule in its proper place under the appropriate general heading. Maimonides pointed out in his letter to Phinehas of Alexandria[45] how tedious this task was:

> Only a great scholar like yourself can understand the toil involved in this work. Most students will imagine that it [simply] follows the order of the Talmud, merely omitting the questions and answers. I can certify that many chapters in it contain *halakhot* distilled from ten or more places in the Babylonian and Jerusalem Talmuds and in *baraitot* [*i.e.*, *Tosefta* and halakhic *midrashim*]. I have not followed the order of the Talmud or the Mishnah, but under each topic I have gathered all of the relevant laws regardless of their source, so that the laws relating to that subject should not remain scattered and dispersed throughout the sources. This was my ultimate aim in this work; for no one in the whole world can remember everything in the three main sources of laws—the Babylonian and Jerusalem Talmuds and the *baraitot*.[46]

Maimonides composed the *Mishneh Torah* in conformity with these principles. The Hebrew name *Mishneh Torah* has the same meaning as the Greek "Deuteronomy" ("Recapitulation of the Law"): just as the Biblical Moses recapitulated the Torah in the Book of Deuteronomy, so Moses Maimonides recapitulated the *Halakhah* in his day. The "work" (*ḥibbur*, lit. "composition"), as Maimonides called it,[47] contains fourteen books. This number is expressed in Hebrew by the two letters (*yod* and *dalet*) forming the word *yad* (hand). The work is therefore also called *Ha-Yad ha-Ḥazakah* ("The Mighty Hand")—an allusion to the verse "For all the great might [lit. "the mighty hand"] and awesome power that Moses displayed before all Israel."[48]

Each book of the *Mishneh Torah* is divided into sections, each of which is entitled *Hilkhot* ("Laws of") followed by the name of the legal topic covered;[49] the entire work contains eighty-three sections. Each section in turn is divided into chapters, of which there are a total of one thousand; and

45. *Kovez̩ ha-Rambam*, I, #140 (p. 26), s.v. Ve-zeh she-amarta.

46. *See also MT*, Avodat Kokhavim ve-Ḥukkoteihem 2:6, and the introductory captions to *Hilkhot Bekhorot* and *Hilkhot Evel*. *See also* Levinger, *supra* n. 38 at 13 and n. 2.

47. *See supra* pp. 1185, 1194, *et al.*

48. Deuteronomy 34:12. There was some reluctance to call the work of a human being *Mishneh* (="Deutero") *Torah* (="nomy"). *Devarim* is the usual Hebrew name for the Book of Deuteronomy, which is also called *Mishneh Torah*.

49. *See infra* for examples of the sections of the books dealing with civil and criminal law.

each chapter is divided into paragraphs, of which there are nearly fifteen thousand in all.[50] Each paragraph is called a *halakhah* (law).

The titles and subjects of the first ten books are:[51]

I. *Sefer ha-Madda* [The Book of Knowledge], consisting of five sections, treats the principles of the Jewish faith. The sections include *Yesodei ha-Torah* [Fundamentals of the Torah], *De'ot* [Ethical Principles], and *Teshuvah* [Repentance].

II. *Sefer Ahavah* [The Book of Love (of God)] deals mainly with laws of prayers and benedictions.

III. *Sefer Zemanim* [The Book of Seasons] treats the laws of sabbath and festivals.

IV. *Sefer Nashim* [The Book of Women], which deals with family law, is more fully summarized below.

V. *Sefer Kedushah* [The Book of Holiness] treats sexual prohibitions (*arayot*), ritual slaughter (*sheḥitah*), and dietary laws (*kashrut*).

VI. *Sefer Hafla'ah* [The Book of Asseveration] includes the laws of oaths, vows and Nazirites, and votive gifts to the Temple.

VII. *Sefer Zera'im* [The Book of Seeds] deals with the precepts directly relating to the Land of Israel, such as laws relating to mixed species (*kilayim*), tithes, gifts to the poor from produce (and other alms), sabbatical and jubilee years, and the like.

VIII. *Sefer Avodah* [The Book of Temple Service] covers the laws of Temple service.

IX. *Sefer Korbanot* [The Book of Sacrifices] includes the laws of various types of sacrificial offerings.

X. *Sefer Tohorah* [The Book of Purity] deals with the laws of ritual purity and impurity.

50. 14,909 *halakhot* precisely. H.S. Neuhausen, in *Torah Or le-ha-Rambam* [Scriptural Index for Maimonides], Baltimore, 1942, Introduction, p. VII, and p. 104, took great pains to determine the precise number. His book is an index of scriptural verses in the *Mishneh Torah* and contains a short subject index, various appendixes listing books on Maimonides' terminology, etc.

51. In Hebrew, a law of the *Mishneh Torah* is cited: Rambam [**R.** **M**oses **b.** **M**aimon], *Hilkhot Ishut* [Ch.] 10, [*halakhah*] 9. *Hilkhot Ishut* [Laws of Personal Status] is in *Sefer Nashim* [The Book of Women], the fourth book, but the book is not cited. Nor is it usual in Hebrew to cite the work by either of its names—*Mishneh Torah* or *Yad ha-Ḥazakah*. "Rambam" in the Hebrew citation suffices to identify the work cited, because throughout halakhic literature, wherever the name "Rambam" is cited without qualification, the reference is to the *Mishneh Torah*, which is his *magnum opus*.

In English, the common forms of citation are: (Maimonides,) *MT*, Ishut 10:9 (used in the present work) or (Maimonides,) *Yad*, Ishut 10:9. It is clear from certain statements of Maimonides that he did not write his code in the sequence of the books and sections as they now appear; *see supra* n. 22.

The last four books, *Sefer Nezikin* [The Book of Damages], *Sefer Kinyan* [The Book of Acquisitions], *Sefer Mishpatim* [The Book of Civil Laws], and *Sefer Shofetim* [The Book of Judges], together with *Sefer Nashim* (Book IV, above), include the substance of *mishpat ivri.*[52] The following is a short survey of the contents of these five books.

Book IV, *Sefer Nashim,* contains five sections:

1. *Hilkhot Ishut* [Laws of Personal Status], twenty-five chapters.
2. *Hilkhot Gerushin* [Laws of Divorce], thirteen chapters.
3. *Hilkhot Yibbum va-Ḥaliẓah* [Laws of Levirate Marriage and Release Therefrom], eight chapters.
4. *Hilkhot Na'arah Betulah* [Laws of a Virgin Maiden], three chapters.
5. *Hilkhot Sotah* [Laws of the Suspected Wife], four chapters.

Book IV contains the whole of family law, which is for the most part civil law but also includes some provisions of the criminal law such as the laws of seduction and rape. The title, *Sefer Nashim,* is based on the title of the mishnaic *Seder Nashim* (Order of Women).

Book XI, *Sefer Nezikin,* contains five sections:

1. *Hilkhot Nizkei Mamon* [Laws of Damages Caused by Property], fourteen chapters.
2. *Hilkhot Genevah* [Laws of Theft], nine chapters.
3. *Hilkhot Gezelah va-Avedah* [Laws of Robbery and Lost Property], eighteen chapters.
4. *Hilkhot Ḥovel u-Mazzik* [Laws of Wounding and Damaging], eight chapters.
5. *Hilkhot Roẓe'aḥ u-Shemirat ha-Nefesh* [Laws of Homicide and Preservation of Life], thirteen chapters.

Book XI contains the laws relating to property damage and personal injury, both civil and criminal. This book is named after the mishnaic *Seder Nezikin* (Order of Damages). However, while all the law we have classified as *mishpat ivri* (except for family law) is dealt with in this one mishnaic Order, Maimonides parceled out this material among four books of the *Mishneh Torah*: *Nezikin* [Damages], *Kinyan* [Acquisitions], *Mishpatim* [Civil Laws], and *Shofetim* [Judges]. He confined *Sefer Nezikin* to those matters connected in the main with torts and crimes against persons or property.

52. This statement is not without exception. Certain subjects that we have classified as part of *mishpat ivri* (*see supra* p. 105) are treated in other books of the *Mishneh Torah, e.g.,* the laws of sexual prohibitions in *Sefer Kedushah,* and some parts of the laws of oaths. Conversely, these five books include subjects that are not part of *mishpat ivri, e.g.,* the laws of mourning, contained in *Sefer Shofetim* (*see infra* p. 1202). This lack of congruence in both directions stems from the commonality of the nature and sources of all branches of the *Halakhah; see supra* pp. 111–122.

Book XII, *Sefer Kinyan,* also contains five sections:

1. *Hilkhot Mekhirah* [Laws of Sales], thirty chapters.
2. *Hilkhot Zekhiyyah u-Mattanah* [Laws of Entitlement and Gifts], twelve chapters.
3. *Hilkhot Shekhenim* [Laws of Neighbors], fourteen chapters.
4. *Hilkhot Sheluḥin ve-Shutafin* [Laws of Agency and Partnership], ten chapters.
5. *Hilkhot Avadim* [Laws of Slaves], nine chapters.

Book XII treats the laws included in the concept *kinyan* in its two main senses, namely, modes of acquisition, and rights in property already acquired.[53]

Hilkhot Mekhirah includes part of the laws of contracts as well as rules of interpretation and some of the laws of legal competency.[54] *Hilkhot Zekhiyyah u-Mattanah* includes the laws of wills, *i.e.,* the laws as to gifts made by a person in sound health, and the will of a *shekhiv me-ra* (a person facing imminent death).[55] *Hilkhot Shekhenim* discusses reciprocal rights of neighbors, the laws of *maẓranut* (adjoining property), and matters involving municipal law (affecting town residents as such). The laws of slavery are also a part of *Sefer Kinyan,* since the master had property rights in his slave. The laws of slavery became obsolete very early; but, as noted, Maimonides included in his work even laws that no longer had practical application.

Book XIII, *Sefer Mishpatim,* is also divided into five sections:

1. *Hilkhot Sekhirut* [Laws of Leasing and Hiring], thirteen chapters.
2. *Hilkhot She'elah u-Fikkadon* [Laws of Borrowing and Bailment], eight chapters.
3. *Hilkhot Malveh ve-Loveh* [Laws of Creditor and Debtor], twenty-seven chapters.
4. *Hilkhot To'en ve-Nit'an* [Laws of Plaintiff and Defendant], sixteen chapters.
5. *Hilkhot Naḥalot* [Laws of Inheritance], eleven chapters.

In Book XIII, Maimonides included several legal areas, but it is difficult to find their common thread. The first two sections deal with the hire of persons and things, *i.e.,* the right to the services or property of another. The

53. These two senses of the term *kinyan* are very common in Jewish law. Thus, when the term *kinyan* appears in a halakhic text, careful study is required in order to assign to it the meaning that correctly fits the context. *See* Gulak, *Yesodei,* I, p. 88.

54. Other laws relating to legal competency are found in *MT,* Ishut, ch. 2.

55. In Jewish law, the will of a person in sound health is essentially an *inter vivos* disposition; only "the gift of a person facing imminent death (*mattenat shekhiv me-ra*) is regarded by the Sages as a legacy" (TB Bava Batra 149a). *See infra* pp. 1681–1682, 1877–1878.

laws in these sections are based on the laws of the four categories of bailees in Jewish law: the unpaid bailee, the paid bailee, the bailee who pays for the use of the bailed property, and the borrower. These two sections also include labor laws and the laws of trusteeship.

The third section, *Hilkhot Malveh ve-Loveh,* includes a substantial portion of the laws of obligations as well as the laws of suretyship, liens and pledges, mortgages, interest and usury, and execution of judgments.

The fourth section, *Hilkhot To'en ve-Nit'an,* treats civil procedure and some of the laws of evidence. In this section, Maimonides included the laws of *ḥazakah* (proof of ownership of land by three years' adverse possession), because in Jewish law that topic is part of the law of procedure; this kind of *ḥazakah* is a substitute for direct proof (such as a deed or witnesses) that the property was legally acquired, and not a matter of substantive law (such as where possession effects transfer of ownership).[56]

The fifth section, *Hilkhot Naḥalot,* belongs to another area of law, namely, intestate succession. As noted, the laws of entitlement by will were included in *Hilkhot Zekhiyyah u-Mattanah* in *Sefer Kinyan,* whereas *Hilkhot Naḥalot* in *Sefer Mishpatim* deals with the right to inherit because of relationship by blood or marriage. *Hilkhot Naḥalot* also includes the laws of guardianship, which is closely related to estate administration, and thus to inheritance.

Book XIV, *Sefer Shofetim,* has five sections:

1. *Hilkhot ha-Sanhedrin ve-ha-Onshin ha-Mesurin Lahen* [Laws of the Sanhedrin and Its Penal Jurisdiction], twenty-six chapters.
2. *Hilkhot Edut* [Laws of Evidence], twenty-two chapters.
3. *Hilkhot Mamrim* [Laws of Rebels], seven chapters.
4. *Hilkhot Evel* [Laws of Mourning], fourteen chapters.
5. *Hilkhot Melakhim u-Milḥamoteihem* [Laws of Kings and Their Wars], twelve chapters.

Book XIV, the last of the "legal" books as well as the last book of the *Mishneh Torah,* deals for the most part with Jewish public law (sections 1, 3, and 5). The first section discusses the composition and jurisdiction of the courts in the judicial hierarchy. It also includes various laws of civil and criminal procedure, substantive penal laws, and the execution of judgments in criminal cases.

The second section, *Hilkhot Edut,* deals with laws of judicial proof by means of testimony; it includes everything that affects the competency of

56. *See* Z. Warhaftig, *Ha-Ḥazakah ba-Mishpat ha-Ivri* [*Ḥazakah* in Jewish Law], Jerusalem, 1964; M. Elon, EJ, VII, pp. 1516–1522, s.v. Ḥazakah (reprinted in *Principles,* pp. 590–596).

witnesses, as well as laws relating to the penalties for false testimony, and the like.

The third section, *Hilkhot Mamrim,* deals with the binding authority of the superior courts over lower courts and with the law regarding the rebellious elder (*zaken mamre*)—a judge who refuses to follow a decision of the High Court. It includes provisions relating to the legislative process, *i.e.,* the adoption of *takkanot* and *gezerot,* and also contains the laws pertaining to the rebellious son and the honor due to parents.

The fourth section, *Hilkhot Evel,* deals with the laws of mourning, and is an anomaly in *Sefer Shofetim;* Maimonides himself acknowledged the anomaly, and explained it as the result solely of formalistic reasons.[57]

The last section, *Hilkhot Melakhim,* deals with the complex of laws affecting the king (who was the executive authority and, to a limited extent, also had authority to legislate),[58] the laws of war, and other matters of public and international law.

As noted, the five books described above cover the type of material included in almost every legal system. Maimonides usually began with a general description of the legal area about to be treated and then continued with a detailed treatment of the laws relating to that area. From time to time, he defined, either before or after the laws, various legal concepts in the section under discussion. The topical arrangement and interconnections of the laws are constructed with consummate artistry.

Occasionally, however, something seems to be strangely out of place, and things placed next to each other seem to lack any meaningful connection, *e.g.,* the laws of mourning in *Sefer Shofetim* [Book of Judges], the laws of inheritance in *Sefer Mishpatim* [Book of Civil Laws] rather than in *Sefer Kinyan* [Book of Acquisitions], the juxtaposition of the laws governing honor due to parents with the laws relating to the rebellious elder, and the like.

There are various reasons for these apparent anomalies. Maimonides' arrangement of his work was influenced by the sequence of the precepts (*mizvot*) in the Torah, by the arrangement of the Mishnah and the Talmud, by linkages on a basis other than content, and by other such considerations.[59] In any discussion of the arrangement and systemization of the Jewish legal system, it must be borne in mind that the classifications generally accepted in other legal systems (*e.g.,* civil and criminal law, substantive and procedural law, and the like) do not completely correspond to the classifi-

57. *See* the listing of the precepts relating to mourning in the section of the Introduction to *Mishneh Torah* describing the organization of the books and chapters, and in the introductory caption to *Hilkhot Evel.*

58. *See supra* pp. 55–57, 486–487.

59. *See supra* pp. 1053–1056.

cations in Jewish law; and such divergences between different legal systems are not unusual.[60] Moreover, the connection between, and the reciprocal influence of, the religious and the legal strands of the *Halakhah* have affected not only the substance of legal norms, but also their categorization and placement within the legal system.[61] For example, this connection explains why Maimonides placed immediately after the laws of homicide the laws relating to the duty to erect a parapet around a flat roof. The common basis for these two sets of the laws, as expressed in the heading of that section, is the preservation of life, *i.e.*, the sanctity of human life and the prohibition against treating it lightly.

It was probably thanks to this great work of Maimonides in putting together a sophisticated and systematic code that his successors—Jacob b. Asher, who wrote the *Sefer ha-Turim* about 150 years later, and Joseph Caro, the author of the *Shulḥan Arukh*, about four hundred years later—were able to classify into clear and well-defined categories the halakhic material that accumulated since Maimonides, making only minor changes in his system of classification. If not for the great achievement of Maimonides, it would be impossible today to find a path through the vast accumulation of halakhic material.

D. Categorical Statement of Legal Rules with No Reference to Sources or Contrary Opinions

Maimonides attained his first two objectives through his extraordinary ability to assemble, rework, and classify material. His third objective was attained in consequence of two characteristics to be expected in someone of his stature—a capacity for boldness, and a readiness to pioneer beyond the conventional. As has been seen,[62] the codification of Jewish law involves a fundamental problem: Can the Jewish legal system, which is, by its very nature, a continuous chain of tradition harking back to the Torah, tolerate a code containing only a definitive and categorical statement of each law, with no citation of differing opinions and without source references?

The codificatory literature reviewed to this point has shown that until the time of Maimonides no work had been written that briefly set forth the laws without stating the names of those by whom the laws were transmitted or the Talmudic sources of the laws.[63] In Maimonides' view, this tended to

60. *See supra* pp. 75–76.

61. *See supra* pp. 111–122.

62. *See supra* p. 1144–1148.

63. The one possible exception is *Halakhot Keẓuvot Meyuḥas le-Rav Yehudai Gaon* ["Fixed *Halakhot*" Attributed to Yehudai Gaon], in which halakhic rules are given without reference to the Talmudic sources; *see id.*, ed. M. Margaliot, Jerusalem, 1942, and Introduc-

make it more difficult to arrive at a legal conclusion and made the existing codes difficult to understand and of limited utility. He therefore created a new genre of codificatory literature—a systematic halakhic work presenting legal rules categorically in prescriptive form, with no reference to sources or contrary opinions. Maimonides explained his method and motives:

> I decided to put together the results obtained from all those [previous] works, as to what is forbidden or permitted, [ritually] pure or impure, together with the other laws of the Torah, all in plain and concise language. Thus, the entire Oral Law, systematically arranged, will become familiar to all, without citing arguments and counterarguments—one person saying one thing and another something else. Rather, [the law will be stated] clearly, pointedly, and accurately, in accordance with the conclusions drawn from all these compilations and commentaries that have appeared since the time of Moses to the present, so that all the laws, whether [Biblical] precepts or enactments adopted by the Sages and Prophets, will be accessible to old and young alike.[64]

In his Introduction to *Sefer ha-Mizvot,*[65] Maimonides added:

> In this compendium, I will try, as is my custom, to avoid mentioning differences of opinion and rejected teachings; and I will include in it only the established law, so that this compendium will include all the laws of the Torah of Moses, our teacher, whether they have practical relevance in the time of the exile or not. It also appears to me to be advisable to omit citation of the bearers of the Tradition as support and proof [for the various laws]; thus, I will not say with each and every law, "These are the words of this Rabbi," or "This Rabbi says thus-and-so.". . . All this [I will do] for the sake of brevity.[66]

---

tion, p. 20. Other abridgments of books of *halakhot* also did not contain references to sources; *see supra* p. 1155. As to *Sefer ha-Yerushot* of Saadiah Gaon, *see supra* p. 1160–1161 for the views of Müller and Assaf and the proofs to the contrary by Abramson.

64. *MT,* Introduction, pp. 13–14.

65. *Sefer ha-Mizvot,* p. 1.

66. Maimonides' Introduction to *Sefer ha-Mizvot* continues:

> Instead, I will mention in a general way at the beginning of this compendium all the Sages of the Mishnah and the Talmud, of blessed memory, and I will say that all the laws of the Torah—namely, the Oral Law—have been received and handed down from person to person [going back] to Ezra, [and thence] to Moses, our teacher. Together with the leader of every generation that received the Tradition, I will also mention the outstanding persons in his generation who were associated with him in the imparting of the Oral Teaching.

Maimonides, in fact, did this in his Introduction to the *Mishneh Torah* and thereby gave assurance that the source of the authority of the Jewish law is the Torah given at Sinai and the chain of tradition, and that his work, notwithstanding its categorical and monolithic

Maimonides' code was faithful to this approach, nearly always stating the law categorically, prescriptively, and without reference to contrary opinions. The only exceptions are the more than 120 *halakhot* which Maimonides himself added on his own[67] (indicated by such expressions as: "It appears to me," "I say," "It seems likely to me") and about fifty *halakhot* where he determined the law himself on the basis of his review of the opinions of the *geonim* and *rishonim* who preceded him.[68] Only in these instances does the *Mishneh Torah* give any indication as to the sources of the law and the method by which it was determined.[69]

This was the most revolutionary aspect of Maimonides' code, and it aroused the strongest opposition. Rabad, who was among Maimonides' severest critics, rendered the following assessment.[70]

---

style, does not pretend to be the source of legal authority but rather is a compendium containing all the halakhic laws as crystallized up to his time. *See also supra* p. 1145.

67. *See* Levinger, *supra* n. 38 at 210–219. *See also Koveẓ ha-Rambam*, I, #140 (p. 26), s.v. Ve-zeh she-amarta.

68. Levinger, *supra* n. 38 at 220–225.

69. Maimonides' omission of source references has led many halakhic authorities and scholars to search for the sources upon which his statements of the law were based. This search is particularly difficult because Maimonides had available to him Talmudic sources since lost, the contents of which are unknown. The discovery of some such Talmudic sources has brought to light the sources of several laws in Maimonides' code. *See, e.g.*, M. Kasher, *Ha-Rambam ve-ha-Mekhilta de-Rabbi Shim'on b. Yoḥai* [Maimonides and the *Mekhilta* of R. Simeon b. Yoḥai], New York, 1943, for some interesting examples.

Maimonides sometimes cited as the source for a law a different Scriptural verse than is cited in the Talmud. *See MT*, Melakhim 1:2: "The appointment of a king precedes the war against Amalek, as it is written, 'I am the one the Lord sent to anoint you king. . . . Now go, attack Amalek'" [I Samuel 15:1–3]. TB Sanhedrin 20b cites a different verse, involving a strained interpretation. *See Kesef Mishneh* and Radbaz, *ad loc.*, noting the difference and stating that it requires further consideration, but not pursuing the matter further. *But see Leḥem Mishneh, ad loc.*:

> This [citation by the Talmud in Tractate *Sanhedrin* 20b] is mere homiletics (*derashah*), but what our Master [Maimonides] cites is more straightforward. Perhaps he found it in some text, for, although it is not mentioned in our *Gemara*, our Master's method is known: When it comes to the matter of Scriptural proofs, if the substance of the law is not affected by the choice between possible supporting verses from Scripture, he was not wedded to our *Gemara*. He cited the supporting verse that seems most straightforward wherever he had found it so used—the Jerusalem Talmud, or *Sifrei*, or some other source. . . . This is why our Master cited this supporting verse [from I Samuel] and omitted the one cited in the Talmud, even though that was from the Pentateuch [and therefore of greater authority than the verse from the Prophets cited by Maimonides], because that [verse from the Pentateuch] was not quite so straightforward.

See further MT, Roẓe'aḥ u-Shemirat ha-Nefesh 10:8; *Haggahot Maimuniyyot, ad loc.*; *Yad Malakhi*, II, Kelalei ha-Rambam [Principles of Maimonides], #4.

70. Rabad, *Hassagot* to Maimonides' Introduction to the *Mishneh Torah*. Rabad's critical glosses start with the Hebrew letters *alef alef*, the first letters of the words, *Amar Avraham*, "Abraham [Rabad] says."

> Abraham [Rabad] says: He [Maimonides] sought to improve but he did not improve, for he has forsaken the method of all authors who preceded him; they adduced proof and cited the authority for their statements. . . . This is simply overweening pride in him.

It is true that the omission of the sources gave rise to difficulties; Maimonides himself was aware of these problems and considered how to overcome them.[71] However, generations later, it turned out that in his essential innovation in the codification of the halakhic system—stating the law prescriptively and categorically without naming sources—he not only "sought to improve" but in fact did improve, since he paved the way, in substantial measure, for the codificatory form that achieved general acceptance about four centuries later when Joseph Caro wrote the *Shulḥan Arukh.*[72]

E. Style and Draftsmanship of the *Mishneh Torah*

Maimonides' fourth basic objective for his code involved style and draftsmanship. The question of the style and language of legal provisions, particularly of a code encompassing a complete legal system, is a matter of the highest importance; and Maimonides gave it explicit and careful consideration:[73]

> I also found it advisable not to compose it [the *Mishneh Torah*] in the style of Scripture, since that sacred tongue is too limited for us now to express the laws in all their complexity. I also will not compose it in the language of the Talmud [Aramaic], because only a few of our people now understand it [Aramaic], and even those who are expert in the Talmud find many of its words strange and difficult. Instead, I will compose it in the style of the Mishnah, so that it will be easily understood by most people.

The style of the *Mishneh Torah* reveals that the statement just quoted reflects the modesty of a great man. Although the Mishnah did serve as a basis for the style of the *Mishneh Torah,* the stylistic structure of the *Mishneh Torah* was an innovation in Jewish legal literature. It is characterized by two features: (1) lucid and pleasant Hebrew legal style; and (2) clear and precise legal draftsmanship, easy to read and to understand. The creation of this Hebrew legal style is one of the prime achievements of the codificatory work of Maimonides; indeed, it has not been equaled to this day. Thus, an examination of the *Shulḥan Arukh* immediately reveals the substantial difference between its style and that of the *Mishneh Torah.* The *Shulḥan Arukh*

71. *See infra* pp. 1220–1221.
72. *See infra* pp. 1312–1313.
73. *Sefer ha-Mizvot,* Introduction, p. 1.

consists of several linguistic layers. One is in the style of Maimonides, which appears in those *halakhot* taken from Maimonides' code that Caro incorporated with no change in language.[74] Another is in Caro's own style which appears in the *halakhot* he himself added, and a third is in the style of prior codes, such as the *Turim,* whose language Caro also adopted.

In evaluating Maimonides' style, one must constantly bear in mind that the various sources from which he drew were written in different languages and dialects. He used both the Babylonian Talmud, written in Babylonian [= Eastern] Aramaic, and the Jerusalem Talmud, written in Syro–Land-of-Israel [= Western] Aramaic. In certain respects, these two dialects can be as different as two completely unrelated languages. Maimonides also used the early halakhic *midrashim,* written in the Hebrew idiosyncratic to them, and the Mishnah and the *baraitot,* written in a Hebrew style of their own. Indeed, even mishnaic Hebrew is not uniform; one of the distinguishing features of the various historical layers making up the Mishnah is the difference in the style of various tractates, chapters within the same tractate, and, occasionally, individual paragraphs within the same chapter. In addition to all this, there is the Babylonian Aramaic of the geonic period, which already had become somewhat different from the Aramaic of the Talmud, so that the *geonim* sometimes felt the need to explain the language of the Talmud.[75] Lastly, there was the language of the post-geonic halakhic literature up to Maimonides' own time.

Out of this mélange, Maimonides created a consistent, uniform style that gave no indication of its genesis from many different languages and dialects. The same type of transformation was also wrought by Maimonides' legal draftsmanship. With consummate artistry, Maimonides succeeded in reworking and polishing every single paragraph, drafting it in a legal style usually so perspicuously clear that it set forth precisely the meaning he intended to convey and left no room for ambiguity.

It was the good fortune of the Hebrew language that in writing the

74. *See also* the end of Joshua Falk's Introduction to *Sefer Bet Yisra'el u-Me'irat Einayim* (referred to by its acronym *Sema*). This Introduction was reprinted in the El ha-Mekorot edition of the *Shulḥan Arukh,* 1956, beginning of ḤM, I; also in the Pe'er ha-Torah edition, 1967, beginning of ḤM, III: "Even as to the laws that the *Turim* had written, Maharik [Joseph Caro], for the most part, set them down not in the language of the *Turim,* but in that of Maimonides; but he arranged them in the order of the chapters of the *Turim.*" Caro also made slight changes in style even when copying *in extenso* from Maimonides. *Compare, e.g., MT,* Malveh ve-Loveh 25:1–2 *with* Sh. Ar. ḤM 129:1–2. For further details, *see* Appendix B, example 3.

75. In addition, Saadiah Gaon, Samuel b. Ḥophni Gaon, and Hai Gaon had written a substantial number of monographs in Arabic (*see supra* pp. 1159, 1161–1162, 1164–1165), and Maimonides had to translate into Hebrew whatever he introduced into his code from these monographs.

Mishneh Torah, Maimonides departed from his previous practice in regard to the language in which the work was written. All his other books had been written in Arabic. Even the most successful translations are obviously translations, and the translators of Maimonides' books into Hebrew were not always successful. The Hebrew of the *Mishneh Torah,* however, is Maimonides' own; it is a precious treasure, a Hebrew legal style of wonderful beauty and precision. Very much to the point is the reply he sent to a letter from "the dear and honored elder, the student, Mar Joseph . . . , who earnestly endeavors to study Torah and assiduously occupies himself with our *Commentary on the Mishnah* but who does not understand the code we composed, namely, the *Mishneh Torah,* because it is in Hebrew."[76] Mar Joseph therefore requested Maimonides to translate it into Arabic. Maimonides replied:

> It would also be well for you to learn this lesson from this work in the sacred tongue in which we composed it, for it is easy to understand and well suited for self-instruction; once you master one section, you will be able to understand the whole work. I do not want, under any circumstances, to publish it in Arabic, because it would then lose all its beauty. I now would like to render the *Commentary on the Mishnah* and the *Sefer ha-Miẓvot* into the Holy Tongue; how much less would I be likely to turn this code into Arabic! Do not in any way ask this of me.

The following examples reflect Maimonides' creativity in Hebrew style and legal draftsmanship:[77]

The Talmudic-Aramaic principle *kol de-alim gaver*[78] (whoever is the stronger [of the claimants to property] prevails), which in certain limited circumstances remits the parties to self-help, he rendered *kol ha-mitgabber yittol* (whoever prevails by self-help will retain the property);[79] *shuda de-dayyanei*[80] (judicial discretion) he rendered *harei ha-davar masur la-dayyanim* (the matter is entrusted to the judges).[81] For the Aramaic word *te'una* (a

76. *Koveẓ ha-Rambam,* II (Epistles), p. 15.

77. Maimonides' style in the *Mishneh Torah* has been the subject of many articles and studies. One worthy of particular mention is W. Bacher, "Zum Sprachlichen Charakter des Mischna Tora" [On the Linguistic Character of the *Mishneh Torah*], in *Moses Ben Maimon,* Leipzig, 1914, II, pp. 280–305. *See also* Bacher's article on the subject, published as an appendix to *Erkhei Midrash,* translated into Hebrew by A.S. Rabinovitz, Tel Aviv, 1923. For additional bibliography, *see* J.J. Dienstag, "Le-Yaḥas Maran el Mishpat ha-Rambam" [On the Attitude of Rabbi (Kook) to Maimonides' Teaching], *Sinai,* LIX, pp. 59–60 and n. 29; Levinger, *supra* n. 38 at 14ff.

78. TB Bava Batra 34b and other sources indicated there.

79. *MT,* To'en ve-Nit'an 10:6.

80. TB Kiddushin 74a and other sources indicated there.

81. *MT,* Zekhiyyah u-Mattanah 5:6.

load)[82] he coined a Hebrew equivalent *te'on,* as in "a load of fruit that was lying in the public domain."[83] In the interest of uniform style, he used the term *arvanut* for suretyship (in lieu of *arvut)* to make it correspond to the form of *kabbelanut* (contractorship).[84]

Sometimes, Maimonides gave currency to a legal term he adopted from much earlier halakhic literature. For example, Leviticus states:[85] "You shall have an honest balance, honest weights, an honest *ephah,* and an honest *hin.*" The *Sifra*[86] expounds the verse as follows:

> "Honest balance" means "adjust [*ẓaddek,* from the same root as *ẓedek*—justice, honesty] the balance properly." "Honest weights" means "adjust the weights properly." "Honest *ephah*" means "adjust the *ephot* properly." "Honest *hin*" means "adjust the *hin* properly."

Adopting this felicitous Hebrew term (*ẓaddek* = adjust), Maimonides wrote:[87] "It is a positive commandment to adjust (*leẓaddek*) balances, weights, and measures accurately and to calibrate them carefully at the time of their manufacture, for Scripture says, 'You shall have an honest balance, etc.'" Further,[88] "it is the duty of the court to appoint officers in every province and in every district to visit the shops, adjust balances and measures, and fix prices."

Sometimes, in order to achieve greater clarity and eliminate any possibility of ambiguity, Maimonides phrased a law somewhat differently than the source from which he took it, as in the following examples:

The first *mishnah* of Tractate *Kiddushin* reads: "A wife is acquired by three methods: by money, by document, and by sexual intercourse." The meaning is that any one of these methods is sufficient, not that all three are required to effect a marriage,[89] but the language of the *mishnah* is ambiguous, and allows the interpretation that all three methods are required. In stating this rule, Maimonides introduced a slight change: "A wife is acquired by any one of the following three methods: by money, or by docu-

82. TB Bava Meẓi'a 32a ("It means that they and their load (*te'unayhu*) are lying on the ground"), and the passage following. *See also* TB Sotah 34a ("There is a tradition that the weight [*te'una*] that a man can raise upon his shoulder is a third of the weight he can carry [when others help to set it on his shoulder]").

83. *MT,* Mekhirah 4:5.

84. *MT,* Malveh ve-Loveh 25:5 ("All of them are covered by the term *arvanut*"). The term *kabbelanut* does not, in fact, appear in Maimonides, but does appear in the Talmudic discussion, TB Bava Batra 174a.

85. Leviticus 19:36.

86. *Sifra,* Kedoshim, ch. 8.

87. *MT,* Genevah 8:1.

88. *Id.* 8:20.

89. *See* TJ Kiddushin 1:1, 1a (1:1, 58b).

ment, or by sexual intercourse."[90] Thus, the meaning is clarified and the ambiguity eliminated.

Deuteronomy 19:15 states: "A case (*davar)* can be valid only on the testimony of two witnesses." The Talmudic principle in the law of evidence is, "a case (*davar*) but not *ḥaẓi davar."*[91] Under this principle, both witnesses must testify to the same facts, and it is not sufficient if each testifies to a different part of the facts. The Hebrew word *ḥaẓi* is ambiguous, since it may mean either "a half" or "a part." By changing the word *ḥaẓi* to *mikẓat,*[92] which always means "a part," Maimonides set forth clearly and correctly the precise meaning of this principle.

A *mishnah* states:[93]

> If two persons [appearing before the court] lay hold of a cloak and one says, "I found it," and the other says, "I found it," [or] one says, "All of it is mine," and the other says, "All of it is mine," one shall swear that not less than half of it belongs to him, and the other shall swear that not less than half of it belongs to him, and they shall divide [the value of] it [equally between them].

The way this *mishnah* is expressed gave rise to much discussion in the Talmud. The repetition of "I found it" and "all of it is mine" is redundant and convoluted, resembling more the verbatim report of the claims of the parties than a statement of a legal principle. Also, the constant repetition of words, *e.g.,* "one says . . . and the other says . . . , one shall swear . . . and the other shall swear . . . ," disturbs the flow of the thought. Maimonides phrased the rule this way:[94]

> If two persons were holding onto an object . . . one says, "All of it is mine" and the other says, "All of it is mine"—each of them shall take an oath over a sacred object that not less than half belongs to him, and they divide [the value of] it [equally between them].

The rule is the same as in the Mishnah, but worded differently. Maimonides omitted the allegation "I found it," which is not legally germane, thus reducing to once the need for stating what each litigant claims. He also substituted "object" for "cloak," thus stating the rule more generally and comprehensively. The result is a clearer and simpler legal style.

90. *MT,* Ishut 1:2.
91. TB Bava Kamma 70b; Bava Batra 56b *et al.*
92. *MT,* Edut 4:7.
93. M Bava Meẓi'a 1:1.
94. *MT,* To'en ve-Nit'an 9:7.

F. Factual-Casuistic Formulation

Although Maimonides is notable for his innovations in the methodology of halakhic codification, he made no substantial change in one important aspect of codificatory style. Our previous discussion of the Mishnaic style[95] noted that R. Judah Ha-Nasi formulated most legal rules in a casuistic style; rules were couched in the form of the concrete factual instances to which they applied, rather than as normative generalizations or abstract statements of a general norm not fleshed out by concrete examples. Only a small portion of the Mishnah is written in a combined casuistic-normative style in which the normative part sums up the principle inferable from the casuistic part; and a purely normative style is even more rare. This essentially casuistic style is also typical of the entire post-Mishnaic halakhic literature.

Maimonides, too, continued in the same pattern and included in the *Mishneh Torah* all of the factual instances previously included in the halakhic literature. He was not content merely to extract the legal principle implicit in the concrete instances contained in the Talmudic literature, but he also included, albeit in his own wording and style, the concrete instances themselves. The only difference from prior literature is that Maimonides made greater use of the combined casuistic-normative style.

For example, the legal rule discussed above concerning two persons claiming the same object is stated in the Talmud with respect to a variety of concrete cases involving a cloak, an animal, etc. In each instance, the rule in the *mishnah* is that when each claimant says, "All of it is mine," each is entitled to half of the value, and each must take the required oath. However, the oath is not to the entire claim ("All of it is mine"), because one of the claimants would then be swearing falsely. Consequently, each claimant swears that he owns not less than the half that the law awards him; under this form of oath there is a possibility that neither of the oaths is false because both claimants may in fact have an equal right to the object.

Maimonides briefly sets forth the concrete details contained in the Talmud,[96] the form of the oath, and what each claimant is entitled to; but he concludes with a generalization all his own: "Hence we learn that everyone who takes an oath in order to be awarded property, whether the oath be a

95. *See supra* pp. 1072–1078.

96. *MT,* To'en ve-Nit'an 9:7–8, which also includes the case from the Mishnah where one claims that "all of it is mine" and the other that "half of it is mine": the first swears that not less than three-quarters of it belongs to him, the second swears that not less than one-quarter of it belongs to him, and the value is apportioned three-quarters and one-quarter, respectively. Maimonides added another concrete example ("Two people who are sitting beside a heap of grain in an alley or a courtyard belonging to both"), the source of which is not clear.

light or severe one, does not swear to what he claims, but to what he is awarded, even though he claims more."

In the foregoing example, Maimonides stated the casuistic element before the normative. In other instances, he stated the normative element first. For example:[97]

> It is forbidden to buy anything that can [reasonably] be presumed to have been stolen, either in whole or in part. Hence, one may not buy wool or milk or kids from a shepherd [since the shepherd may have stolen them]. However, one may buy milk and cheese from a shepherd in the desert [since there the owner of the flock forgoes his rights to the milk and cheese], but not in an inhabited area. One may buy four sheep or four fleeces of wool from a shepherd of a small flock, or five from a [shepherd of a] large flock, for we do not presume that these would be stolen [since these are substantial quantities and their theft would be noticed by the sheepowner]. This is the general rule: Anything sold by a shepherd, [the loss of] which the sheepowner would have noticed, may be bought from the shepherd, but what the owner would not have noticed may not be bought [from the shepherd].

The various examples of this law, together with the general rule stated at the end, are taken from the Talmud,[98] but the principle stated by Mai-

97. *MT,* Genevah 6:1–2.

98. M Bava Kamma 10:9; TB Bava Kamma 118b. For further instances of Maimonides' inclusion of all the examples set forth in the Talmud, *see infra* pp. 1327–1340 (the examples from the *Mishneh Torah)* and nn., *ad loc.* Other instances where Maimonides included the concrete examples contained in the Talmudic sources even when he also stated a general principle, either preexisting or original with him, include the following:

1. *MT,* Melakhim 5:7
   Regarding the prohibition against returning to Egypt (Deuteronomy 17:16), Maimonides concluded, "and Alexandria is included in the prohibition." He specifically mentioned Alexandria because of what is said about Alexandria in TB Sukkah 51b in regard to this very prohibition (*see Kesef Mishneh, ad loc.*), although the statement at the beginning of that *halakhah* clearly includes Alexandria, since Alexandria is located within the boundaries of Egypt as Maimonides defined them.
2. *MT,* Sanhedrin 24:1
   This *halakhah* states: "A judge should decide civil cases *(dinei mamonot)* in accordance with what his mind is inclined to believe and his heart is convinced is the truth, even if there is no clear proof; it goes without saying that when he knows to a certainty what is the fact, he is to decide accordingly." This is a general principle Maimonides formulated on the basis of examples relating to various cases dealt with in the Talmud. Subsequently, Maimonides referred to these specific examples:
   i. When the judge is inclined to believe that the defendant will perjure himself (the case of Rava and his wife, the daughter of R. Ḥisda, TB Ketubbot 85a). In such a case, the defendant's obligation to take an oath to support his defense will be shifted to the plaintiff, who, upon taking an oath to support his claim, will obtain a judgment.

monides at the outset—"It is forbidden to buy anything that can [reasonably] be presumed to have been stolen"—was original with him, although it follows from the Talmudic examples. Even though he started with the normative principle, he followed with all the illustrative concrete examples contained in the Talmud.

Why did Maimonides' innovations not include changing the casuistic style? There were apparently three reasons: First, he could not assume the very heavy responsibility of formulating the law solely in terms of general principles and still feel secure that the principles, without further elaboration, would embrace all the factual situations already dealt with in the halakhic literature. Maimonides did not wish to be a source of the law but rather its authoritative expositor and summarizer; thus, only by including

---

ii. When the judge is inclined to believe that a promissory note or bill of indebtedness has been paid (the case of R. Papa and Abba Mari, TB Ketubbot 85a). Here, Maimonides described various factual circumstances that could arise in accordance with the different interpretations of the Talmudic passage.

iii. When the judge is inclined to believe a person who claims to have entrusted personal property to someone who died leaving no instructions with regard to the property. In such a case, the claimant may prove his claim by describing features that clearly identify the property (TB Ketubbot 85b).

After stating these examples, Maimonides concluded: "The rule is the same for all similar cases, for it is a matter for the judge to decide as he perceives the truth in the case. That being so, why did the Torah require two witnesses? So that when two witnesses appear before the judge, he is to decide in accordance with their testimony, even if he does not know whether they testified truthfully or falsely."

3. *MT,* To'en ve-Nit'an 12:15
This *halakhah* states: "If one takes possession of an unguarded area outside the fence of a field and sows it and has the benefit of it . . . , this is not considered to be adverse possession. . . . The same rule applies to anyone who sows a space left unguarded and readily accessible to man and beast."

The source for the first part is TB Bava Batra 36a; the general principle "The same rule applies . . . " is Maimonides' own addition.

4. *MT,* Nezirut 5:10,13,16
These *halakhot* discuss three prohibitions imposed on a Nazirite. Concerning the first, the drinking of wine, the Mishnah (M Makkot 3:7–8) states: "A Nazirite who drinks wine the entire day commits only one transgression. But if he is told, 'Do not drink,' 'Do not drink,' he commits a transgression each time [he disregards the warning]." The same rule is repeated in regard to the other two prohibitions: against cutting the hair and against becoming ritually impure. Chapter 5 of *MT,* Nezirut repeats all three cases: in *halakhah* 10, the drinking of wine; in *halakhah* 13, the cutting of hair; and in *halakhah* 16, becoming ritually impure. The reason for the repetition is that the same casuistic specification occurs in the Mishnah.

all the concrete cases mentioned in the literature up to his time could he feel confident that he had in fact included all the existing law.

Second, by the casuistic presentation, Maimonides retained a strong link between his code and the Talmud. One of the inevitable results of his new codificatory style was the severance of his code, at least so far as external form is concerned, from all prior halakhic literature. In order to avoid the undesirable results that might arise from this discontinuity in form, and in order to preserve the substantive link between the content of his work and that of the Talmud, he retained the casuistic details of the law as set forth in the Talmud. Thus, as a result of Maimonides' utilization of the concrete cases found in Talmudic literature, one who studies the *Mishneh Torah* enters the milieu of the entire Talmudic literature.

Third, but by no means least important, the casuistic style is essential to the continued development of Jewish law. Keeping the determination of the law closely tied to concrete factual situations gives the law flexibility. New problems can more easily be solved by drawing analogies from one case to another or by distinguishing among different cases, in accordance with the inner logic of the law and the felt needs of the time and place as weighed by the particular halakhic authority making the decision. This basic characteristic of the halakhic system has influenced the casuistic form of all the codes in that system, including Maimonides' *Mishneh Torah.*[99]

G. A Legal Code for the People

Maimonides achieved the four basic objectives he set for himself. He created a new *genre* of codificatory literature: a code that (1) includes all the laws of the halakhic system, (2) classifies and topically arranges the law, (3) couches the law in original, clear, and easy Hebrew, and, most importantly, (4) states the law categorically, without reference to source or to contrary views. In a letter to his outstanding disciple, Joseph b. Judah ibn Aknin, Maimonides expressed his view of his achievement:

> [I am letting you] know that I have not composed this work in order to aggrandize myself among the Jews, or to attain any glory. The One-Whose-Name-Is-To-Be-Blessed knows that at first I labored on it only for my private use, to gain some respite from probing, debating, and searching out whatever I may need. Now that I have become old, thanks be to God and may He be praised that I am alive, a zeal for the Lord of Hosts has taken hold of me, seeing that the people were without a legal code that would contain only the

99. *See supra* pp. 1072–1078, concerning the style of the Mishnah, and pp. 1142–1143, concerning the similar background and development of the common law and its approach to codification.

correct determinations, free from differences of opinion and from errors. So I have acted solely for the honor of Him-Whose-Name-Is-To-Be-Blessed.[100]

Truly, Maimonides did prepare for the people a "legal code"—the best crafted and most comprehensive book of *pesakim* in the history of Jewish law.[101]

III. CRITICAL REACTION TO MAIMONIDES' CODIFICATORY METHODOLOGY

As might have been expected, the boldly innovative form of Maimonides' code aroused fierce debate and sharp critical reaction, some of which was directed at Maimonides during his lifetime. His replies bespeak his deep conviction of the correctness of his approach and of the vital need of the Jewish legal system for his work. However, most of the criticism arose after Maimonides' death and generated profound and penetrating debates about the nature and methodology of Jewish legal codification.[102]

100. *Koveẓ ha-Rambam,* II (Epistles), p. 30. *See also* the version in *Iggerot ha-Rambam* [Epistles of Maimonides], ed. D.Z. Baneth, Jerusalem, 1946, Epistle 6, p. 50:

> [I am letting you] know that I have not composed this work in order thereby to become great among the Jews, or to become famous in the world, that I should be offended by opposition to my purpose in writing it. Not so; God is my witness that from the outset I wrote it for myself, in order to be relieved of the [necessity to] probe and search [anew each time] for the [*halakhot* that are] needed, and for [my] old age and for the sake of the Lord, Who is to be blessed. For, by God, a zeal has taken hold of me for the Lord God of Israel when I see [before me] a people without a comprehensive book that sets out matters truly and is accurate and precise in [the] views [it expresses]. Therefore, I have acted purely for the sake of Heaven.

101. Maimonides continued to correct and perfect his work, sometimes even retracting or changing various statements of the law. This can be seen from his responsa, as well as from an examination of manuscript passages of the *Mishneh Torah* available to us in Maimonides' own handwriting. These changes, the widespread popularity swiftly attained by his works, and the errors made by copyists brought about variant readings and inconsistencies. One who studies Maimonides must bear this in mind and be alert to the possibility of different versions of the text.

As to variant readings in Maimonides, *see, e.g.,* Lieberman, *supra* n. 18, Introduction, pp. 1ff.; S. Atlas, *Keta'im mi-Sefer Yad ha-Ḥazakah la-Rambam* [Excerpts from Maimonides' *MT*], London, 1940, Introduction, pp. 6–8; *Mishneh Torah,* ed. Rome, 1480, facsimile ed., Jerusalem, 1956, Introduction by J.L. Maimon, pp. 9ff. *See also* M. Elon, "He-Arev, ha-Ḥayyav ha-Ikkari ve-Ekron Ḥofesh ha-Hatna'ah be-Dinei Arvut ba-Mishpat ha-Ivri" [The Surety, the Principal Debtor, and the Principle of Freedom of Contract in the Jewish Law of Suretyship], *Proceedings of the Fourth International Congress of Jewish Studies,* 1967, I, pp. 203ff., for an example of a radical difference between the law in *MT,* Malveh ve-Loveh 25:4, as set forth in the text of the *Mishneh Torah* in extant printed editions and as set forth in the text of ed. Rome, 1480.

102. Many halakhic authorities and scholars have addressed themselves to the critical reactions to the *Mishneh Torah. See,* among the more recent studies, I. Twersky, "Al Hassagot

A. Correspondence with *Dayyan* (Judge) Phinehas b. Meshullam of Alexandria

Mention has already been made of the correspondence between Maimonides and Phinehas b. Meshullam, who served as a *dayyan* (judge) in Alexandria. Phinehas wrote to Maimonides:[103]

> The contents of your work are enlightening only to someone who has studied the Talmud and knows the identity of the Sages who participated in the discussions in the Talmud and the *Gemara,* but it is not [satisfactory] to occupy oneself solely with them [the contents of *Mishneh Torah*], for that would cause the names of the *tannaim* and *amoraim* to become forgotten.
>
> Certainly, those who study [the *Mishneh Torah* without being versed in the Talmud] do not understand what they are studying; they err in regard to what your work says and do not fathom the depth of your meaning or plumb the source from which your text is derived. It is concerning such [students] that the *tanna* has said:[104] "Sages, be cautious with your words [lest you incur the penalty of exile and be banished to a place of evil waters that the disciples who come after you may drink], and [then] they will die, and the Heavenly Name will be profaned.". . . It is befitting your glory to tell the world not to abandon the study of the *Gemara.*

Replying to these comments, which tended to deny the *Mishneh Torah* its essential purpose as a code, namely, to permit the law to be declared without requiring consultation of any other source, Maimonides did not mince words:[105]

> On this whole matter, you should be reproved and told that I well understand what is in your mind, although you merely hinted at it. [Phinehas did not accuse Maimonides openly, but said only that the book could well lead to forgetting the names of the *tannaim* and *amoraim* and to cutting off the *Halakhah* from its sources.] Let me tell you first, that I have never said (Heaven forbid!): "Do not occupy yourselves with the Talmud or the *Halakhot* [Book of Laws] of Rabbi Isaac [Alfasi]—or anyone else."
>
> God is my witness that this last year-and-a-half I have not taught my work. Only three people have studied some of the books. Most of the students wished to study the *Halakhot* of the Master [Alfasi], and I taught them all the

---

ha-Ra'avad le-Mishneh Torah" [On Rabad's Critical Glosses to the *Mishneh Torah*], *Harry Wolfson Jubilee Volume* (Hebrew Section), 1965, pp. 169–186; *id.*, *Rabad of Posquières*, JPS, 1980, pp. 128ff.; *id.*, "The Beginnings of *Mishneh Torah* Criticism," *Biblical and Other Studies*, ed. A. Altmann, pp. 161–182. In these works (and in the notes thereof), there is also a comprehensive bibliography.

103. *Kovez ha-Rambam*, I, #140 (pp. 25–26).

104. M Avot 1:11.

105. *Kovez ha-Rambam*, I, #140 (p. 25).

> *Halakhot* several times. Two also requested to learn Talmud, and I taught them the tractates that they requested. Have I instructed or even contemplated that on account of my work all the books written before my time should be burned? I explicitly stated in the Introduction to my work that I wrote it only to relieve the frustration of those who are unable to plumb the depths of the Talmud and learn from it how to tell what is forbidden and what is permitted; and I have gone into this at great length.[106]
>
> As to what you say about the names of the Sages, I did mention the names of most of the Sages—*tannaim* and *amoraim*—at the very beginning of the work [in the Introduction]. Is it really true that whoever has set forth the law and has made pure fine flour [*i.e.*, stated the law elegantly and accurately] has caused the name of Heaven to be profaned, as you seem to think? *Geonim* and great masters before me have written books and made legal pronouncements in Hebrew and Arabic on particular subjects. But in codifying the entire Talmud and all the laws of the Torah, I have had no predecessor since our sainted master [R. Judah Ha-Nasi] and his colleagues. Because this [work] is comprehensive, is the Heavenly Name on that account profaned? How astonishing! And as to the students who, you say, do not understand [it], no author of any book has it in his power to follow it around and deny to everyone except certain selected individuals permission to read it.

Maimonides went on to explain his view of the essential difference between the literary form of a book of *pesakim* and a commentary *(perush)*, *i.e.*, a reference work or handbook that explains and gives reasons:[107]

> You should know, my good friend, that whoever writes a book . . . follows one of two methods, either that of a *ḥibbur* [book of *pesakim*, lit. "composition"] or that of a *perush* [commentary]. The method of a *ḥibbur* is to state only the correct legal principles, omitting both the problems and their solutions, as well as any kind of proof, as our sainted master [R. Judah Ha-Nasi] did in the Mishnah. But the method of *perush* is to set forth, in addition to the correct legal principles, the inconsistencies and problems with respect to each issue; to respond to the difficulties; and to prove that one view is true and another false, or that one view is preferable to another. This is the style

106. In regard to this statement of Maimonides to Phinehas b. Meshullam, S.D. Luzzatto wrote in a letter to a certain scholar (Z.H. Chajes?) (*Kerem Ḥemed*, IV [1839], p. 290):

> Yet, with all respect to Maimonides, of blessed memory, what he says here is not the same as what he said in his Introduction. . . . In fact, for the sake of peace, the Master, of blessed memory, changed the tenor of his words in this letter from what he wrote in his Introduction.

Luzzatto's remark is incorrect; *see supra* pp. 1145–1146. *See also* Ziemlich, "Plan und Anlage des Mischne Tora" [Plan and Design of the *Mishneh Torah*], in *Moses Ben Maimon*, I, pp. 254–256. *See also* the subsequent portion of Luzzatto's letter quoted *infra* n. 141, and Z.H. Chajes' statement there referred to.

107. *Kovez̩ ha-Rambam*, I, #140 (p. 25).

> of the Talmud—the Talmud is the *perush* on the Mishnah. I did not produce a *perush* but a *ḥibbur,* after the manner of the Mishnah.

As to the omission of the names of the Sages, Maimonides also found support in the way the Mishnah was written:[108]

> You should know that if I have caused the names of the Sages to be forgotten by stating the correct legal rules without the names of their authors, I have followed in the footsteps of our sainted master [R. Judah Ha-Nasi], who was my predecessor in this as well. Everything that he stated without attribution of authorship had been declared by other Sages, and those other Sages in turn did not make their statements on their own authority but received them from others, who in turn received them from still others back to Moses, our teacher.
>
> Just as the *tannaim* and *amoraim* were not meticulous about recording the names of all the Sages from the days of Moses, our teacher, until their own day (which would be a virtually endless task), we also should not be concerned whether or not their names were mentioned. What is the practical benefit of it? It is explicitly stated in a number of instances:[109]
>
> > Rabbi [Judah Ha-Nasi] thought that Rabbi A was correct in a particular matter, and he included Rabbi A's opinion [in the Mishnah] without attribution of source; and [he thought] that Rabbi B was correct in another matter and included Rabbi B's opinion without attribution of source.
>
> This makes clear that what Rabbi [Judah Ha-Nasi] thought was a correct statement of the law, which was to be followed in practice, he stated without naming the source. In many instances it is stated:[110] "This anonymous opinion is that of one individual," but Rabbenu [R. Judah Ha-Nasi] does not give the name of anyone. On those points as to which the opinion of the Sages was divided and Rabbi [Judah Ha-Nasi] did not favor either of the contending views, he stated both opinions, each in the name of its author: "Rabbi A says thus and so, and Rabbi B says thus and so"—and he named the Sages from whom he heard [those opinions] or who lived close to his time; but [he did] not [give] the names of their teachers and their teachers' teachers, for at that time there were many adherents of each of the contending views.
>
> The Sages, of blessed memory, have indeed told us why he explicitly mentioned the names he did in [regard to] some laws:[111]
>
> > Why are the names of Shammai and Hillel recorded in cases where their views were rejected [and the proponent of the rejected view later reversed himself]? To teach future generations [that a person should not stubbornly persist in his views]. And why are individual opinions re-

108. *Id.* at 25–26.
109. *See supra* p. 1060.
110. *See supra* p. 1072 and n. 147.
111. M Eduyyot 1:4–6.

> corded along with the opinion of the majority [when the majority view is law]? So that a court that favors the individual's opinion may use that opinion to support its decision. Why [else] is an individual's opinion recorded with that of the majority when the individual's opinion is rejected? So that if someone will say, "I hold such a tradition," [another may reply, "True, but it is the tradition of Rabbi A (a minority opinion)"].
>
> This clearly means that the proper course is to state only the law as settled, but since at that time some acted in one manner and followed the opinion of one [Sage], and others acted differently, following the opinion of another [Sage], it was necessary to record [names]. Since I have written [my work] in the style of the Mishnah, and the Talmud has already settled every law either specifically or generally by means of the general principles of decision making, and there is no longer divergence in the law as applied in practice, why should I mention the name of one whom the law does not follow, or mention the name of a particular individual noted in the Talmud, *e.g.*, Abbaye or Rava, when the law is the view not merely of that individual, but of the many who received the tradition from the many?

In principle, Maimonides was certainly correct. R. Judah Ha-Nasi also omitted the names of some of the transmitters of the tradition, stated the law as he thought correct without mentioning the particular Sages who held that view, and used other similar methods. But this parallel does not resolve the problem completely. The Mishnah of R. Judah Ha-Nasi, despite its manner of transmitting and declaring the law, is replete with the names of *tannaim* and records differences of opinion as to the law. The body of the *Mishneh Torah,* however, does not mention even one name of a transmitter of a law, and the entire book states the law monolithically and without attribution of source. Possibly in order to explain this difference, Maimonides added a new and interesting rationale, rooted in the Jewish historical reality of his time:[112]

> The reason why I chose [not to indicate the Sages' names] was to deny an opportunity to the sectarians [*i.e.*, the Karaites, whose influence in Maimonides' time was considerable] to gain ascendancy, for they argue, "You rely upon the statements of individuals." That, however, is not true; it is thousands and tens of thousands [who received the tradition] from thousands and tens of thousands. This is why I said at the beginning of my work, "So-and-so and his court received [the tradition] from So-and-so and his court" [Maimonides listed the links in the chain of tradition in the Introduction to the *Mishneh Torah*]: to make known that the tradition is that of the many from the many and not of individual from individual.
>
> Hence my wish and aim that each and every law shall be found [in it]

112. *Kovez ha-Rambam,* I, #140 (p. 26).

> without attribution of source, *i.e.*, as the one and only rule. It should not be stated in the name of a particular individual, for that [*i.e.*, stating the law in the name of particular individuals] will lead to much damage from these sectarians who reject the entire Oral Law because they see it as the product of various individuals and imagine that the Oral Law was not transmitted, but rather made up by particular individuals.

In Maimonides' day, when there was bitter conflict with the Karaite sect, whose main attack was against the validity and authority of the Oral Law, it was desirable and even necessary that a book of *pesakim* should reflect Jewish law's monolithic nature and transcendence of individual contributions—and that the *Halakhah* be seen not as something handed down by individuals but as grounded in the "thousands and tens of thousands" who received it "from thousands and tens of thousands."[113]

Later in his letter, Maimonides conceded the justice of one criticism; the *Mishneh Torah* classified the entire halakhic system topically, as a result of which there were sometimes assembled in one chapter "halakhic rules from ten or more places in the Babylonian and Jerusalem Talmuds and the *baraitot*." Consequently, it was often difficult to ascertain the source for a given law, whether for the purpose of academic-theoretical study or adjudicating an actual case.[114] Even Maimonides himself, as has been noted, experienced that difficulty when asked by a judge for the source of a certain law in *Hilkhot Roẓe'aḥ u-Shemirat ha-Nefesh*, which Maimonides finally found in Tractate *Yevamot*, where it is mentioned only incidentally in another connection. The solution, however, Maimonides went on to say, is not to change the form of the book of *pesakim* itself, but to write a separate source book to supplement it:

> This is why I regret that I did not write, as a companion piece to this work, the kind of composition I have been discussing. I do intend, God willing, to do it, even though it will be very onerous to give a source reference for every relevant law located elsewhere in the Talmud than in the main body of law on the topic. What do I mean? Take, for example, the laws of the sabbath set forth in my work. Nothing explicitly discussed in Tractates *Shabbat* or *Eruvin* [both dealing essentially with the laws of the sabbath] needs a source refer-

113. Disputes with sects of heretics and Karaites as a factor inducing codification existed as early as in the geonic era in connection with the need for books of *halakhot* (*see supra* pp. 1156–1157), but Maimonides pointed to this factor as also influencing the literary form appropriate to a codificatory work. *See also supra* p. 810 as to Maimonides' *takkanot* against the Karaites.

114. *E.g.*, to find answers to new problems for which the existing law provided no solution. *See supra* pp. 1146, 1186.

> ence. But for the sabbath laws taken from Tractates *Avodah Zarah* or *Pesaḥim* or *Zevaḥim* or *Keritot,* I would indicate the source: "This law in chapter so-and-so of my work comes from chapter so-and-so of such-and-such tractate." This would be a separate book, for it cannot be incorporated in the [codificatory] work, which, as I told you, is not in the style of a commentary.[115]

This detailed explanation once again clearly summarizes Maimonides' objective in writing the *Mishneh Torah*—that the work was to have a unique status in determining and declaring the law as crystallized in his day, and that it was to be the sole source for ascertaining the law for purposes of conduct and adjudication. A categorical statement of the law, without attribution of source or reference to contrary opinion, was designed to enable his work to attain that status. Maimonides contended that setting forth the laws in this manner, far from impairing the continuity of the Jewish law and the preservation of its sources, would, on the contrary, present the law as something handed down by all the Jewish Sages, as opposed to the view of the Karaites, who denied that the halakhic system represented the heritage of the entire Jewish people and claimed that it represented merely the opinions of certain individuals.

However, Maimonides had no intention whatever of making any change with respect to study and analysis in the halakhic system, and it never entered his mind that the study and analysis of the rich Talmudic literature then extant should be abandoned. Moreover, the study of Talmudic literature in all its periods and subperiods is sometimes necessary for the purpose of determining the law notwithstanding the existence of the most comprehensive code, as, for example, when a new problem arises for which the existing law provides no solution. The novelty of Maimonides' work is related only to the methodology of codification, not to study (or "commentary"), whether such study is purely theoretical or for the purpose of determining the law in particular cases.[116]

115. *Kovez ha-Rambam,* I, #140 (p. 26). Here, Maimonides pointed the way to the codificatory form that was later to be adopted, first by Rashba and then by Joseph Caro, *i.e.,* a set of two separate books, one a book of *halakhot* and the other a book of *pesakim; see infra* pp. 1273–1277, 1312–1313.

116. *See supra* p. 1146; Blau, *supra* n. 5 at 342ff.; Ziemlich, *supra* n. 106 at 258–259. The observation of Tchernowitz, *Toledot ha-Posekim,* I, pp. 235–236, that Maimonides did not intend the *Mishneh Torah* to be used to determine the law for purposes of practical application but intended it to be "only in the nature of a textbook or an encyclopedia of the Talmud, and nothing more," is untenable and indeed astonishing. *See also* S.Z. Havlin, "Mishneh Torah le-Rambam—Sof Ge'onut" [Maimonides' *Mishneh Torah*—The End of the Geonate], *Ha-Ma'ayan* (Isaac Breuer Institute), V (1965), pp. 41ff.

B. Correspondence with Joseph ibn Aknin; Rendering Decisions on the Basis of the *Mishneh Torah*

Maimonides' clear statement of his objectives was not enough to prevent fierce controversy in his own time and in subsequent generations. He foresaw the severe criticism his work would be subjected to and forthrightly addressed that probability in a letter to his outstanding disciple, Joseph b. Judah ibn Aknin:[117]

> I well knew when I was writing it [the *Mishneh Torah*] that without doubt it will fall into the hands of an envious evildoer who will disparage what is most praiseworthy in it and will see himself as having no need of it or as entitled to denigrate it; and into the hands of an ignoramus and simpleton who will not appreciate its value and will think it worthless; and into the hands of a starry-eyed and confused neophyte who will find some passages difficult because he will not know their source or will not have the intelligence to understand the precise nuances of what I have written; and into the hands of a pious, thick-headed, and dyed-in-the-wool conservative who will attack my exposition of the foundations of faith embodied in it. [All] these will be the majority. [However], without doubt it will also come into the hands of the remnant whom the Lord calls upon, men of justice and fairness and good sense, who will recognize the worth of what I have done—of whom you are the first. If in my generation I had no one but you, it would be enough for me.

Since Maimonides held these views as to the bases of the anticipated criticism of his book, he concluded his letter with the high optimism of every great artist confident that his creation represents authentic and inevitable truth:[118]

> However, all I have described to you about those who will not give it the acceptance it merits—that will not last longer than my lifetime. But in the future, when envy and egocentric ambitions will subside, all Jewry will use it exclusively and, without doubt, will not turn to any other [book of *Halakhah*], except for those who, throughout their lives, devote themselves to study and research, even if it may have no practical application.

Maimonides' ambitious and optimistic wish was in substantial measure fulfilled; he himself attested that in his own lifetime legal rulings in the

117. Baneth, *supra* n. 100 at 51; for a different version, *see Kovez ha-Rambam*, II (Epistles), p. 30. Baneth, in his Introduction, asserts that the name of the disciple was Joseph b. Judah ibn Simeon, that Joseph b. Judah ibn Aknin was not a disciple but a colleague of Maimonides, and that because both were named Joseph b. Judah they became confused with each other, with the result that ibn Aknin has erroneously been identified in nearly all the scientific literature as the disciple.

118. Baneth, *supra* n. 100 at 52.

majority of *yeshivot* in Babylonia were based on his code,[119] that his code had "been accepted in the island of Sicily, as it was accepted in the East, in the West, and in Yemen,"[120] and that letters reached him even "from the halakhic authorities of France and others in their name saying that they are impressed by the work and request [to receive] the rest of it; and [the work] has already spread to the most far-flung areas of human habitation."[121] This acceptance continued after Maimonides died. In many countries and communities, Maimonides' work was accepted as the definitive code, and enactments were even adopted by which "they agreed among themselves and legislated that in regard to all their laws and legal matters, they will conduct themselves in accordance with all that is written in the books of Maimonides, of blessed memory, whether permissive or prohibitory, [and] whether relating to monetary matters or to marriage, *ketubbah*, or divorce."[122]

However, the main controversy around Maimonides' work did not turn on the points raised in his letter to Joseph ibn Aknin. Many halakhic authorities, although they understood, appreciated, and were impressed by the greatness of Maimonides' work, were strongly opposed to a code intended to be the sole source for determining the law and reaching decisions, in which the law is stated categorically and monolithically without referring to the sources or to contrary opinion. This opposition gathered strength and made increasing headway.

C. Rabad's Critical Glosses

Maimonides' severest critic arose in his own lifetime: Abraham b. David (Rabad) of Provence. Rabad, known as one of the greatest halakhic author-

119. *Resp. Maimonides,* ed. Freimann, #69, p. 69: "Our work has already reached the later authorities in Babylonia, and we have heard that the majority of the *yeshivot* use it as a basis for making legal decisions."

120. *Kovez ha-Rambam,* II (Epistles), pp. 24–25 (epistle to the rabbis of Marseilles).

121. Baneth, *supra* n. 100 at 52 (Maimonides' epistle to Joseph b. Judah ibn Aknin); *see also* Maimonides, "Ma'amar Teḥiyyat ha-Metim" [Essay on the Resurrection of the Dead], *Kovez ha-Rambam,* II (Epistles), p. 8: "Our work has become well known throughout the world and has spread to the outermost parts." *See also* Blau, *supra* n. 5 at 343; I.Z. Kahane, "Ha-Pulmus mi-Saviv Kevi'at ha-Hakhra'ah ke-ha-Rambam" [The Controversy Concerning Determination of the Law in Accordance with the Views of Maimonides], *Sinai,* XXXVI (1956), p. 392. Kahane's article was published in installments in *Sinai,* XXXVI, XXXVII, and XXXVIII.

122. *Resp. Ran* #62. The quotation is from the question put to Ran. Such enactments were adopted in even earlier periods. *See* the enactment of the community of Tudela of 1305, quoted in Baer, *Spain,* pp. 220–221; *Resp. Rashba,* I, #253. *See also supra* p. 711 for many other sources regarding countries and communities that agreed to accept Maimonides' views as the basis for legal decision making; A.H. Freimann, "Die Ascheriden" [The Descendants of Asheri], *JJLG,* XIII (1920), pp. 174–175, 194, 221; Kahane, *supra* n. 121.

ities,[123] was the head of a *yeshivah* in Posquières. He appreciated some of the extraordinary merits of the *Mishneh Torah*[124] and expressed agreement with many of the laws in it.[125] His severe strictures on the *Mishneh Torah* were certainly not intended *ad hominem* or as an expression of personal pique or anger.[126] Nor was he jealous of the fame of Maimonides' *Mishneh Torah,* which was never achieved by the comprehensive book of *halakhot* written (according to some scholars) by Rabad but no longer extant.[127] Rabad's strong disagreement was with Maimonides' method of declaring the law without citing the sources and without setting out the range of opinions on each legal issue—information which is vital to the very essence of Jewish law and to the methodology of halakhic decision making.

Rabad took aim at this feature of Maimonides' code from the very start, in the first of his critical glosses *(hassagot)* to Maimonides' Introduction to the *Mishneh Torah.* Against that very "revolutionary" passage of Maimonides—"Hence, I have entitled this work *Mishneh Torah,* for the reason that a person who first reads the Torah and then this work will know from it all of the Oral Law, and there will be no need to read any other book [written] between them"—Rabad leveled the following charge:

> Abraham [Rabad] says: He sought to improve, but he did not improve, for he has forsaken the method of all authors who preceded him; they adduced proof and cited the authority for their statements. This [traditional method] was of great value, for often a judge is inclined to declare something prohibited or permitted on the basis of a particular source, but if he knew that an authority greater than himself took a different view, he would change his

123. *See, e.g.,* Rashba, *Torat ha-Bayit,* Introduction to *Bet ha-Nashim* (end); *Resp. Radbaz,* Li-Leshonot ha-Rambam [On Maimonides' Statements of Law], #267 (1630); *see also* Twersky, *supra* n. 102, *Harry Wolfson Jubilee Volume* at 169 for additional sources.

124. *See supra* pp. 1194–1195; for detailed discussion, *see* Twersky, *supra* n. 102, *Harry Wolfson Jubilee Volume* at 176ff.; *id., Rabad of Posquières* at 131ff.

125. *See* the list of references in R. Margaliot, "Ha-Rambam ve-ha-Ra'avad" [Maimonides and Rabad], *Sinai,* XXXVI, pp. 387–390; *see also* Twersky, *supra* n. 124.

126. Some recent scholars hold the contrary view. *See, e.g.,* Graetz, *History of the Jews,* JPS, Philadelphia, 1894, III, p. 490; *id., Divrei Yemei Yisrael* [History of the Jews], Hebrew trans. S.P. Rabinowitz, IV, pp. 402–403 and Rabinowitz's n. 2 there. For details, *see* Twersky, *supra* n. 102, *Harry Wolfson Jubilee Volume* at 170. Even some *rishonim* asserted that sometimes Rabad unjustifiably attempted to attribute errors to Maimonides. *See further* Twersky, *loc. cit.;* Margaliot, *supra* n. 125; and H. Michael, *Or ha-Ḥayyim,* pp. 542–543, all of which deal with this issue in detail.

127. Such a view was expressed by Joseph Sambari; *see* Neubauer, *Seder ha-Ḥakhamim,* I, p. 124. *See also* S. Abramson, "Sifrei Halakhot Shel ha-Ra'avad" [Rabad's Books of *Halakhot*], *Tarbiẓ,* XXXVI, pp. 158–179, thoroughly discussing the view that Rabad wrote a comprehensive book of *halakhot,* and proving that this view is without basis. Rabad's extant works include books of *halakhot* on limited subjects, such as *Ba'alei ha-Nefesh,* which treats the laws of menstrual purity *(taharat mishpaḥah)* and sexual relations (ed. J. Kafaḥ, Jerusalem, 1965).

> mind. Now, I do not know why I should retract my tradition and my proof on account of the work of this author [Maimonides]. If the one who takes issue with me is greater than I, well and good; but if I am greater than he, why should I yield my opinion in favor of his? Furthermore, on some matters the *geonim* were divided, and this author chose one opinion [over the others] and put it in his book. Why should I be governed by his choice if it seems wrong to me, and I do not know whether the holder of the opposing view is entitled to deference? This is simply overweening pride in him.

In Rabad's opinion, the *Mishneh Torah*'s statement of only a single unattributed view deprives the judge of the means to make up his own mind and impairs his power of decision. The judge may be aware of an opinion opposed to the one stated in the *Mishneh Torah*, but he cannot know which opinion should prevail, because he does not know the weight of the nameless authority whose view is set forth in the *Mishneh Torah*. The judge may sometimes be unaware of a difference of opinion among the *geonim*, which, had he known of it, he would have, in the exercise of his independent judgment, resolved one way; but Maimonides' method of stating the law has preempted this opportunity and has decided the case for him the other way. The effect is to deny to the judge the power of independent judgment essential to his basic function, which is to decide the case before him.[128]

Rabad was not content merely to express general opposition in principle to Maimonides' methodology. He was justified in his fear that a work so excellent and comprehensive and so easy to study and understand would gradually supplant the study of all the rest of halakhic literature. Therefore, in spite of his advanced age,[129] he reviewed the entire *Mishneh Torah* and wrote critical glosses to many of the laws it contains. These glosses were terse, and often sharp. Their object was to draw attention to incongruities and inconsistencies between the law as set forth by Maimonides and the law in the Talmudic sources, and to instances where Maimonides reached legal conclusions on the basis of halakhic methods and analyses that were not generally accepted. In this way, Rabad hoped to impel the readers of Maimonides' code to check the correctness of Maimonides' statements against the Talmudic sources and the geonic literature.[130]

128. In Rabad's view, a book of *halakhot* should be modeled on the Mishnah in that it should state different opinions. Rabad's position was directly contrary to the view expressed by Maimonides in his letter to Phinehas b. Meshullam (*see supra* pp. 1216–1220), in which he said that in their day such a model was not appropriate for a book of *pesakim*.

129. Rabad was older than Maimonides; *see Resp. Tashbeẓ*, I, #72: "We found in a responsum of Rabad that he said about Rabbi Moses [Maimonides], 'He is young and we are old'" (quoted in Michael, *supra* n. 126 at 542).

130. Among the well-known halakhic authorities who were contemporaries of Maimonides and who also wrote critical glosses on the *Mishneh Torah* was Moses ha-Kohen of Lunel (Remakh). His glosses were known to various authors, and were used particularly by

D. Asheri's Reaction

Criticism of Maimonides' codificatory methodology continued after the time of Rabad and his contemporaries. Some of it even came from halakhic authorities who esteemed Maimonides' work highly and made considerable use of it in their own writings.[131]

The severest reaction—and the one having the greatest consequence—came about a century later from one of the great halakhic codifiers and commentators, Asheri (Asher b. Jehiel, also known as Rosh), the outstanding disciple of Meir of Rothenburg (Maharam). After the death of Maharam, Asheri became the leader of Ashkenazic Jewry and later settled in Spain, where he became one of the foremost halakhic authorities and leaders in that Jewish center as well.[132]

Asheri expressed his opposition to the *Mishneh Torah* in a case referred to him for review after it had been decided by another judge.[133] A judge named Mazli'aḥ had rendered a decision on a certain issue on the basis of the *Mishneh Torah*. Asheri ruled that the decision was erroneous. By a close study of the Talmudic source for Maimonides' statement, Asheri established that Mazli'aḥ had misunderstood Maimonides' meaning. Mazli'aḥ's failure to consult the Talmudic source moved Asheri to conclude his responsum with the following highly significant comment:

> Anyone who decides cases on the basis of the law set forth by Maimonides, of blessed memory, errs if he is not sufficiently expert in *Gemara* to be aware of Maimonides' sources. Such a judge renders decisions permitting what is forbidden and forbidding what is permitted. For he [Maimonides] did not follow the lead of other authors who adduced proofs for their opinions and provided source references to the *Gemara* that enable him [the reader] to grasp the underlying principle and arrive at the truth of the matter. Instead, he [Maimonides] wrote his book like one delivering a prophetic message from the Almighty,[134] providing neither reason nor proof. Thus, anyone read-

---

Joseph Caro in his commentary on the *Mishneh Torah*, entitled *Kesef Mishneh (see infra* p. 1233). Remakh's glosses on the Books of *Madda, Ahavah,* and *Zemanim* were published with notes and explanations by S. Atlas, *HUCA*, 1956 and 1963 (facsimile ed., Jerusalem, 1969); and his glosses on the Books of *Madda, Ahavah, Zemanim, Nashim, Kedushah,* and *Shofetim* with notes by D.M. Schmiedl were published by J. Cohen, Jerusalem, 1970.

131. *See, e.g., Sefer Miẓvot Gadol* by Moses of Coucy; *see also infra* p. 1262 n. 112 and accompanying text.

132. For further details concerning Asheri, *see infra* pp. 1251–1252.

133. *Resp. Asheri* 31:9.

134. *See* Rema's similar observation regarding the *Shulḥan Arukh, infra* p. 1362. The observation there is with reference to Caro's method of decision making; here, it is with reference to stating the law without giving reasons or adducing proofs.

ing it [the *Mishneh Torah*] imagines that he understands it, but he really does not. For if he is not expert in *Gemara*, he cannot really and truly understand the subject, and he will err in the decisions he renders and the legal pronouncements he makes. Let no one, therefore, rely upon his reading of his [Maimonides'] book to give judgment or make legal pronouncements unless he [also] finds support in the *Gemara* [for the law as stated by Maimonides].

Asheri added:

I have heard an outstanding individual in Barcelona, who is an expert in three [Talmudic] Orders [*Mo'ed, Nashim,* and *Nezikin*], say: "I am amazed at people who have not learned *Gemara* but who read the books of Maimonides, of blessed memory, and on that basis adjudicate cases and give legal instruction, thinking that they understand what they have read. For I know from my experience that in [regard to] the three Orders that I have studied, I understand what I read in his books; but in his books on the laws of *Kodashim* and *Zera'im* I do not understand a thing, and I am convinced that for those people this is the case with regard to all his books."

Asheri thus categorically rejected Maimonides' main objective. According to Asheri, the function of a halakhic code is not, as Maimonides thought, to be the sole work that needs to be consulted in determining the law and in rendering decisions; relying solely on such a book for these purposes is likely to lead to misunderstanding of what has been written in categorical and monolithic form.[135] According to Asheri, the aim of a codificatory work is not to be a self-sufficient source; it is rather to be used in connection with the Talmudic sources of the laws it seeks to summarize. Only by keeping close to the sources of a legal rule can one arrive at the true meaning of the rule stated in the code.[136]

135. *See also Resp. Asheri* 43:12 regarding decision making on the basis of the book *Sefer Mizvot Katan* (*see infra* pp. 1263–1265):

> Woe unto those who undertake to render decisions on the basis of books and compendia of great scholars without themselves knowing either Mishnah or *Gemara*! For sometimes the scribe may erroneously write "liability" when he means "exemption" or write "prohibited" when he means "permitted," or because of their deficient knowledge they fail to understand fully what the authors have written and so they fall into error.

Asheri here added another argument: that the scribe or copyist may have made a mistake. The same concern had previously been expressed by those who asked Ri Migash about decision making on the basis of the books of the *geonim*, but Ri Migash did not address the point in his reply; *see supra* p. 1181 n. 3.

136. In several places, Asheri added that not only ought one not render decisions on the basis of a code because it may mislead the reader, but an opinion stated without attribution of source or supporting Talmudic citations is entitled to less weight than an opinion based on proofs adduced from the Talmud. *See, e.g., Resp. Asheri* 94:5:

> It seems to me that since Rabbenu Isaac Alfasi, the Tosafist Rabbenu Isaac the Elder, and Rabad, of blessed memory, all cited clear and well-known authority for their

Asheri's view of the limited function and authority of a codificatory work corresponds to his view of the process of legal decision making. He held that a judge is bound only by "the Talmud as compiled by R. Ashi and Ravina." When the judge has clear and convincing arguments for his own view, he is free to differ with rulings made by post-Talmudic halakhic authorities (including the *geonim*) that are not explicitly rooted in the Talmud itself.[137] Therefore, he needs to have before him all opinions on a subject in order to be able to decide which one to accept. Apart from the concern about possible mistakes in the code and the difficulties of truly understanding the law solely from its text, Maimonides' central idea that the *Mishneh Torah* should serve as the exclusive and binding code runs counter to the very nature of Jewish law, in which multiplicity of opinions is a positive and vital feature. Jewish law does not recognize any decision made after the completion of the Talmud as final and beyond challenge.[138] No book of

---

> conclusions, their opinions are entitled to more weight than the opinion of Rabbi Moses [Maimonides], who wrote like a prophet and cited no authority. Furthermore, they were more distinguished than he in wisdom and number—not that I am capable of weighing their respective merits, but that is the tradition that we have heard and accepted.

This responsum was cited by Maharshal in his Introduction to *Yam Shel Shelomo*, Bava Kamma, in connection with the account of the differences of opinion between the Spanish halakhic authorities, on the one hand, and the French and German authorities, on the other. *See infra* p. 1386 n. 58. Likewise in *Resp. Asheri* 100:2, at the end of the first responsum, Asheri wrote:

> I have carefully deduced this from the *Gemara* and the *Tosefta*, and we are not prepared to accept as law given to Moses at Sinai (*halakhah le-Moshe mi-Sinai*) what the author [Maimonides] has written. Had he also written down his proofs and explained his views, we would have had to accept them if his arguments were sound.

137. *Piskei ha-Rosh*, Sanhedrin, ch. 4, #6; *cf. Resp. Asheri* 55:9. The subject is extensively discussed *supra* pp. 269–271, 984–986. Rabad's critique of Maimonides' Introduction to the *Mishneh Torah* (*supra* pp. 1224–1225) made the point that a judge should be in a position to decide which of the various opinions to follow. Asheri went even further than Rabad. According to Rabad, as quoted in *Piskei ha-Rosh, supra:* "We are not now free to rule contrary to a *gaon* on the basis of our own reasoning which is opposed to his view of the law, unless there is [in the *gaon*'s reasoning] an egregious problem—and that kind of situation does not occur"; hence, according to Rabad, one who rules contrary to a *gaon* has committed the equivalent of an error on a law of the Mishnah. Asheri rejected the view of Rabad and held that a judge's authority to decide for himself extends to all post-Talmudic law, including that of the geonic era; *see also supra* p. 668 n. 10.

138. Interestingly, Maimonides agreed that no post-Talmudic ruling is final. *See* his Introduction to the *Mishneh Torah* regarding the binding force of all that is stated in TB, which all Jewry is obliged to follow, "because the entire Jewish people accepted everything contained in the Talmud." Such a statement, as he pointed out earlier in his Introduction, cannot be made about post-Talmudic times:

> After the redaction of the Talmud by R. Ashi's court and the completion of that task in the lifetime of his son, the Jews became dispersed throughout the world. The people migrated to the ends of the earth and to far-off isles. Violence was widespread, and

pesakim, however masterly, can be the sole source for legal decisions; that prerogative is reserved for the Talmud alone.

E. Interim Summary of the Stages of Codification of Jewish Law

Thus far, three stages in the development of the attitude of post-Talmudic halakhic authorities regarding the form and substance of codification have been identified. In the ninth century, Paltoi Gaon was firmly opposed to giving books of *halakhot* an independent status and insisted that they were to be used only as reference works in cases where it was difficult to find in

---

> armed bands made the roads unsafe. . . . After the completion of the Talmud, when a court in any country issued decrees, adopted enactments, or instituted customs for the Jews of its own country or of a number of countries, its rulings did not gain acceptance by the entire Jewish people, because of the distances between the [Jewish] settlements and the difficulties of communication.
>
> Since the court of any particular country is composed of individuals [whose authority has not been universally accepted], and since the High Court of seventy-one [members] ceased to exist many years before the redaction of the Talmud, the residents of one country cannot be compelled to conduct themselves according to the custom and practice of another country, nor is a court in one country under any obligation to issue a decree that has been issued by a court of another country. So, too, if one of the *geonim* taught that a certain approach should be taken and it is clear to a subsequent court that this approach was not in accordance with the approach in the Talmud, the earlier authority is not [necessarily] followed, but the view—whether of the earlier or the later authority—that seems more reasonable is adopted.

See also Resp. Maimonides, ed. Blau, #310 (II, p. 576):

> I would make it a general rule that any pronouncement of one of the *geonim*, of blessed memory, who is an accepted legal authority, for which we cannot find clear proof should not be rejected or declared to be mistaken, but we should say that he may have had some proof. However, it would not be proper for us to rely upon that pronouncement or to act upon it until its rationale becomes clear to us. This is a principle that our Sages, of blessed memory, have also clarified for us in their statement [TB Bava Batra 130b, quoted *supra* p. 982], "Do not tear it up, but do not deduce the law from it."

See also id., I, pp. 226–267 and nn.; *supra* p. 645 n. 6.

Maimonides' statement is quoted here at length, because it indicates clearly that his opinion on the issue of freedom to decide between different post-Talmudic views is similar to that of Asheri. Furthermore, like Asheri (*see supra* n. 137), Maimonides held that one should not rely upon the view of a halakhic authority, even a *gaon*, if there is no clear proof for that view. However, Maimonides did not draw the same conclusion as Asheri, namely, that he himself was not authorized to write a book of *pesakim* for the halakhic system stating the law monolithically and without attribution of source. Maimonides believed that because he arrived at his conclusions by analyzing and weighing the entire breadth of Talmudic literature, and because he explicitly pointed out whenever a given law in his book is not based upon Talmudic sources (*see supra* p. 1205), his statements and conclusions had the same force as if supported by "clear proof." *See also supra* pp. 981–986.

the Talmudic literature the solution to some particular problem. The primary source for finding and determining the law must, he said, be the Talmud itself.

Some three centuries later, Joseph ibn Migash reached precisely the opposite conclusion as to the books of *halakhot;* he thought that they should be the main source for determining the law and that they were preferable to the complicated discussions of the Talmud for that purpose because it is in researching the Talmud that error is most likely to occur. As has been noted, this attitude of Ibn Migash attained its high point in Maimonides' book of *pesakim,* which he called *Mishneh Torah* [Recapitulation of Torah], because anyone desirous of ascertaining the law needed no books other than the (Written) Torah and its "Recapitulation."

In the third stage, Rabad, in Maimonides' own lifetime, and Rabad's successors thereafter—particularly Asheri, a century later—reverted to the position advocated by Paltoi Gaon: the law must be determined primarily from the study of the Talmudic sources; the purpose of a book of *halakhot* is merely to assist in finding the law in Talmudic literature itself. This view became increasingly accepted by the halakhic authorities after Asheri—particularly in Spain,[139] France, and Germany.[140]

The halakhic authorities began to search out new and different codificatory methods that would be consistent with the purpose of halakhic codification, namely, to help find and determine the law. In these efforts, they sought to preserve an essential characteristic of Jewish law—awareness by the judge of the multiplicity of opinions vital to the correct decision in the particular case before him.[141] However, even though Maimonides' codifi-

139. *Resp. Ribash* #44. A contemporary and colleague of Ribash, the philosopher Ḥasdai Crescas, was also opposed to Maimonides' codificatory approach, and expressed his opposition in terms reminiscent of Rabad: "Since he [Maimonides] omitted the names of the *geonim* and the differences of opinion among them, and also did not refer to the sources where the subject at hand could be found, we are not saved from the doubt and confusion that beset us when we find in some other great author's books conclusions and opinions contrary to his." (Introduction to *Or ha-Shem,* ed. Vienna, 1859, p. 2).

140. *See* Kahane, *supra* n. 121, *Sinai,* XXXVIII at 243–246; ET, IX, p. 336.

141. This essential feature of halakhic decision making was expressed, in the course of a severe critique of Maimonides, in S.D. Luzzatto's letter to S.J. Rapoport (*Kerem Ḥemed,* III (1838), pp. 66–67):

> Now Maimonides with all his philosophizing did us no good, because formerly the words of the Sages were like prods whereby to direct the animal [*i.e.,* the multitude] as the Sages thought was good and beneficial according to the time and place. But Maimonides formulated them as if written in stone; he set forth *halakhot* categorically and sought to remove all doubts, consign all differences of opinion to oblivion, and subject all of Jewry and all of its halakhic authorities in every generation to the conclusion favored by the Talmudic Sages or by himself. In the Mishnah, however, minority opinions are also mentioned, so that later generations may know both opinions and, after investigation, decide which to follow, as they see fit and as the times require.

catory objective was not accepted, the *Mishneh Torah* profoundly influenced the codification of Jewish law. Maimonides was the "second pillar" upon whom Joseph Caro based his legal pronouncements in *Bet Yosef* and the *Shulḥan Arukh*,[142] and many of the basic approaches of Maimonides' codificatory methodology were adopted in the subsequent halakhic codes, particularly the *Shulḥan Arukh*.[143]

IV. COMMENTARIES ON THE *MISHNEH TORAH*

The appearance of a comprehensive code naturally stimulates the composition of a literature of commentaries[144] that seek to probe the code's comprehensiveness, accuracy, and other qualities. The high esteem in which Maimonides' *Mishneh Torah* was held, on the one hand, and the sharp controversy it engendered, on the other, sparked the creation of an extensive and voluminous literature of commentary on this work. These commentaries had various objectives: some to criticize Maimonides, others to defend him against the critics, or to explain or supplement his treatment of particular subjects. The central function of most of the commentaries, particularly the earlier ones, was to trace the Talmudic sources from which Maimonides distilled his *halakhot*. No other halakhic work has had the distinction of

---

> If Rabad had not opposed Maimonides and stood in the breach, the Mishnah and the Talmud might have been lost and forgotten. We, our children, and our grandchildren would have been enslaved to Maimonides and Aristotle, and denied the ability to go back to the sources and acquire a sound knowledge of the subject. I say "and Aristotle," for there are several topics in the *Mishneh Torah* that are derived not from the Sages but from Aristotle and his Arabic commentators, such as in *Hilkhot Yesodei ha-Torah* and *Hilkhot De'ot*.

See further another letter of Luzzatto (*Kerem Ḥemed*, IV, pp. 287–293) to a certain scholar (Z.H. Chajes?) elaborating, explaining, and correcting what he said in the first letter. *See also supra* n. 106, regarding Luzzatto's letters on this subject.

There is a thorough critique of the foregoing comments of Luzzatto in Z.H. Chajes, "Tiferet le-Moshe" [The Glory of Moses], reprinted in *Kol Kitvei Maharaẓ Chajes* [The Collected Works of Z.H. Chajes], 1958, I, pp. 395ff. Luzzatto's remarks are quoted on p. 403. *See also id.* at 435ff. for the essay "Darkhei Moshe" [The Ways of Moses], which deals with Maimonides' halakhic and philosophic methodology. That essay has been reprinted in *Koveẓ Rabbenu Moshe b. Maimon* [Maimonides Anthology], ed. J.L. Fishman (Maimon), with notes by the editor, Jerusalem, 1935, II, pp. 1ff. *See also* Freimann, *supra* n. 122 at 185–190.

142. *See supra* p. 1172 and *infra* pp. 1317–1319.

143. *See infra* pp. 1273–1275, 1285–1287, 1312–1313, *et al.*

144. For explanation of the Hebrew term for such commentaries (*nos'ei kelim*, lit. "armor bearers"), *see supra* p. 1173 n. 85. *See also supra* pp. 1173–1176 for the commentaries on Alfasi's *Sefer ha-Halakhot* and *infra* for commentaries on many other books of *halakhot*.

being the subject of so many commentaries;[145] indeed, commentaries on the *Mishneh Torah* are still being written. Some of the commentaries are usually printed on the pages of the *Mishneh Torah*. They include:[146]

A. *Migdal Oz* by Shem Tov ibn Gaon

Shem Tov ibn Gaon, Rashba's disciple, was a Spanish halakhic authority and kabbalist of the mid-fourteenth century. He was the first to supply source references for Maimonides' text, and he also included references to Maimonides' responsa. His main objective was to defend Maimonides and counter Rabad's criticisms. He also corrected scribal errors in the text.[147]

B. *Maggid Mishneh* by Vidal of Tolosa

Vidal of Tolosa, a colleague of Nissim Gerondi (Ran), was a leading Spanish halakhic authority in the fourteenth century. His goals in *Maggid Mishneh*[148]

145. In *Kuntres Ozar Mefarshei Mishneh Torah* [Bibliography of Commentaries on the *Mishneh Torah*], by Judah Rubinstein (printed at the end of the fifth vol. of the *Mishneh Torah*, ed. Shulsinger Bros., New York, 1947), 341 books are listed and briefly described. Regarding the exact number of the books on the list, *see* Rubinstein's Introduction.

Rubinstein's list is not fully exhaustive. Makhon Moshe (the institute for research into the work of Maimonides), organized by the Agudat Halikhot Am Yisrael, has been publishing an edition of the *Mishneh Torah* based on Yemenite manuscripts edited by J. Kafaḥ. Thirteen volumes appeared (1984–1992), covering the Books of *Madda, Ahavah, Zemanim, Nashim, Kedushah, Hafla'ah, Zera'im, and Avodah*. Kafaḥ, in addition to writing his own commentary, summarized parts of approximately three hundred other commentaries, and his list shows that Rubinstein's list is not complete. Also, Rubinstein did not include unpublished manuscripts, *e.g.*, the commentary by Saadiah b. David Adani (al-Adani), a Yemenite scholar of the fifteenth century, on the Books of *Ahavah, Zemanim,* and *Tohorah,* of which the original manuscript is in the Bodleian Library at Oxford, and a photostat is in the possession of Y.S. Nahum. *See* Nahum, *Zohar le-Ḥasifat Ginzei Teiman* [Light on the Discovery of the Archives of Yemen], Tel Aviv, 1986, p. 67. *See also* the remarks by S. Assaf on this commentary, *Kiryat Sefer,* XXII (1945), pp. 240–244. There are also extant fragments of the commentary by Zechariah ha-Rofe (a Yemenite scholar of the sixteenth century); *see* Nahum, *supra,* as well as other Yemenite manuscripts of commentaries on *Hilkhot Sheḥitah. See also The Yemenite Manuscripts in the Ben-Zvi Institute,* ed. Dr. I. Tuvi, Ben-Zvi Institute, Jerusalem, 1982, pp. 46–53.

146. In a sense, Rabad, the great critic of Maimonides, may also be considered a commentator on Maimonides: as noted above, Rabad sometimes explained Maimonides' text and indicated the source of particular laws. Rabad's glosses also appear in the usual editions of the *Mishneh Torah* on the pages to which they are relevant.

147. *Migdal Oz* also traces the changes Maimonides made in the various editions of his work; *see supra* n. 101.

148. It is accepted practice in halakhic literature to link the title of a commentary with the title of the book it expounds; hence, the title *Maggid Mishneh,* indicating that the work is a commentary on the *Mishneh Torah.* There is the same linkage with the titles of the other commentaries mentioned *infra.* The title is frequently also derived from a Scriptural phrase, *e.g.*, *Maggid Mishneh* from Zechariah 9:12, *Kesef Mishneh* from Genesis 43:12; *Leḥem Mishneh* from Exodus 16:22; *Mishneh la-Melekh* from Esther 10:3.

were to explain Maimonides' text, to indicate the halakhic sources, to suggest reasons why Maimonides preferred the views he adopted over those he rejected, and to defend Maimonides against his critics, especially Rabad. Unlike the author of *Migdal Oz,* Vidal did not always agree with Maimonides, but at times was inclined to accept the opinion of Rabad or of other critics. *Maggid Mishneh* is extant on six of the fourteen books of the *Mishneh Torah.*[149]

C. *Kesef Mishneh* by Joseph Caro

Joseph Caro, the author of the *Shulḥan Arukh,* wrote a comprehensive commentary on the *Mishneh Torah,* entitled *Kesef Mishneh.*[150] His aims were largely similar to those of the *Maggid Mishneh,* which he often cited and discussed. His commentary also covers books of the *Mishneh Torah* for which *Maggid Mishneh* is lacking.[151]

D. *Yekar Tiferet* by David ibn Zimra (Radbaz)

Radbaz, the foremost halakhic authority of the sixteenth century in Egypt (until he immigrated to the Land of Israel), provided a commentary on the portion of the text of Maimonides for which there was no *Maggid Mishneh.* He defended Maimonides against criticism but did not particularly concern himself about supplying source references. Parts of his commentary have been printed in several recent editions of works by Maimonides, as well as separately.[152]

E. *Leḥem Mishneh* by Abraham di Boton

Abraham di Boton, a leading halakhic authority in Salonika in the sixteenth century, was a disciple of Samuel de Medina (Maharashdam). His book *Leḥem Mishneh*[153] attempts to ascertain Maimonides' sources and reconciles inconsistencies between the *Mishneh Torah* and the Talmudic

149. The six books are: *Zemanim, Nashim, Kedushah, Nezikin, Kinyan,* and *Mishpatim.* Even in these, *Maggid Mishneh* on certain sections is not extant, *e.g., Hilkhot Kiddush ha-Ḥodesh* in *Zemanim, Hilkhot Na'arah Betulah* and *Hilkhot Sotah* in *Nashim,* and *Hilkhot Sheluḥin ve-Shutafin* in *Kinyan.* As to various aspects of *Maggid Mishneh,* such as the order in which it was written, *see* I.S. Spiegel, "Sefer Maggid Mishneh she-al Mishneh Torah le-Rambam" [The Book *Maggid Mishneh* on Maimonides' *Mishneh Torah*], *Kiryat Sefer,* XLVI, pp. 554–579.

150. *See supra* n. 148.

151. For further information on *Kesef Mishneh, see infra* p. 1320.

152. *See Yekar Tiferet,* ed. S.B. Werner, 1945, and Werner's Introduction.

153. *See supra* n. 148.

sources. When he was in the midst of his commentary to *Hilkhot Tefillah* [Laws of Prayer], Caro's *Kesef Mishneh* reached him, and he found in it explanations and novellae similar to those he had also written. He therefore decided that for the rest of his commentary, "I will write down only those points of mine that are novel,"[154] *i.e.*, only comments adding to what was said by Caro.

F. *Mishneh la-Melekh* by Judah Rosanes

Judah Rosanes lived in the second half of the seventeenth and the early part of the eighteenth centuries. He was the Rabbi of Constantinople and was regarded as the leading Turkish halakhic authority of his generation. His book *Mishneh la-Melekh*[155] is different from the other commentaries. If, for purposes of comparison, we distinguish between commentaries and novellae,[156] the books above referred to would be classified as commentaries, whereas *Mishneh la-Melekh* would be novellae. Judah Rosanes actually wrote his novellae without reference to Maimonides, as a work on various Talmudic subjects, but his disciple, Jacob Kuli, who printed his books, arranged them to correspond to the organization of the *Mishneh Torah.*[157]

G. *Haggahot Maimuniyyot* by Meir ha-Kohen of Rothenburg

Haggahot Maimuniyyot [Maimonidean Glosses] by Meir ha-Kohen of Rothenburg is different in kind and purpose from all the other commentaries previously mentioned, which is why it is discussed last although it was

154. *Leḥem Mishneh* to *MT*, Tefillah 11:15:

> Today, 5th Adar 5335 [A.M. = 1575 C.E.], I received the commentary of the great Rabbi Joseph Caro, of blessed memory, to [the code of] the Master [Maimonides], of blessed memory, and I saw that it had many things that I had gone into and questioned in the *halakhot* concerning which I have written up to this point; so from now on, I will write down only those points of mine that are novel.

The date is corrected to 8th Adar 5338 by D. Tamar, "Le-Verur Shenat Petiratam Shel Gedolei Ḥakhmei Ereẓ Yisra'el ve-Turkiyah" [On the Clarification of the Date of Death of Leading Scholars of the Land of Israel and of Turkey], *Sinai,* LXX, p. 231. Tamar points out that a printer mistook the Hebrew letter *ḥet* (numerical value 8) for the similar-looking letter *he* (numerical value 5) and that 5th Adar 5335 (= 1575) should be 8th Adar 5338 (= 1578). The correct date is given in *Leḥem Mishneh,* ed. Venice, 1609. Caro died on 13th Nisan 5335 (1575), approximately five weeks *after* 5th Adar 5335, yet in the corrupted text of *Leḥem Mishneh* he is mentioned as being "of blessed memory," an honorific expression reserved for those who have died.

155. *See supra* n. 148.

156. *See supra* p. 1105.

157. *See* Introduction of Jacob Kuli to *Mishneh la-Melekh,* s.v. Melekh menaḥem. The Introduction is printed in the usual editions of the *Mishneh Torah* at the beginning of *Sefer ha-Madda.*

composed before some of the others. The author lived at the end of the thirteenth and the beginning of the fourteenth centuries and was a disciple of Maharam of Rothenburg. The purpose of *Haggahot Maimuniyyot* was not to criticize or defend Maimonides, or to find his sources, but to supplement the *Mishneh Torah* with the responsa and decisions of the German and French halakhic authorities wherever appropriate.[158]

Only a few of the hundreds of commentaries that are part of the extensive literature on Maimonides' *Mishneh Torah* have been discussed here.[159] In addition to the commentaries directly on the *Mishneh Torah,* there are discussions of laws as set forth by Maimonides interspersed throughout the general literature of commentaries, novellae, and responsa.

V. THE ULTIMATE ACHIEVEMENT OF THE *MISHNEH TORAH*

In no other instance in all halakhic literature is there such a stark discrepancy between an author's purpose and the actual results of his work as that which occurred in the case of Maimonides' *Mishneh Torah* and its commentaries. Maimonides' essential purpose in composing the *Mishneh Torah* was to restore to the *Halakhah* its uniform and categorical character, "without citing arguments and counterarguments—one person saying one thing and another something else. Rather, [the law will be stated] clearly, pointedly, and accurately."[160] Yet, precisely because of its categorical style, hundreds of books were written on Maimonides' code raising "arguments and counterarguments—one person saying one thing and another something else," so that not only did the law fail to achieve clarity and uniformity, but further problems and debates were directly generated by Maimonides' statements of the law and the opposition they engendered. Nevertheless, while Maimonides did not achieve the aim that he set for himself, his code has enriched every area of halakhic literature to this very day.

158. Another part of *Haggahot Maimuniyyot* is called *Teshuvot Maimuniyyot* [Maimonidean Responsa]. These appear at the end of each Book of the *Mishneh Torah.* This part consists mainly of the responsa of the German and French halakhic authorities relevant to each subject. To some extent, these are also set forth in the *Haggahot.* For further discussion, *see* Urbach, *Tosafot,* pp. 434–436. Similar instances in which books of *halakhot* composed in one center were supplemented by decisions of halakhic authorities of other centers occurred also in later times; *see, e.g., infra* pp. 1359–1363.

159. *See supra* n. 145.

160. Maimonides, *MT,* ed. Rambam la-Am, Introduction, p. 15.

Chapter 35

THE CODIFICATORY LITERATURE: FROM MAIMONIDES UNTIL THE *SHULḤAN ARUKH*; THE *SEFER HA-TURIM*

I. Codificatory Literature until the *Sefer ha-Turim*
  A. Books Following the Order of the Talmud, and/or Organized in Whole or in Part According to Topic
    1. *Sefer Avi ha-Ezri* and *Sefer Avi'asaf* by Eliezer b. Joel ha-Levi (Raviah)
    2. *Sefer ha-Roke'aḥ* by Eleazar b. Judah
    3. *Sefer ha-Terumah* by Baruch b. Isaac
    4. *Sefer ha-Manhig* by Abraham b. Nathan ha-Yarḥi
    5. *Or Zaru'a* by Isaac b. Moses (Riaz)
    6. Codificatory Works by Naḥmanides
    7. *Sefer ha-Hashlamah* by Meshullam b. Moses of Beziers
    8. *Sefer ha-Terumot* by Samuel Sardi
    9. *Sefer Shibbolei ha-Leket* by Zedekiah b. Abraham ha-Rofe
    10. *Sefer ha-Tanya*
    11. *Sefer ha-Neyar*
    12. *Sha'arei Dura* by Isaac b. Meir of Düren
    13. *Sefer ha-Mordekhai* by Mordecai b. Hillel ha-Kohen
    14. *Piskei ha-Rosh* by Asheri, and Its Commentaries
      a. *Piskei ha-Rosh*
      b. Commentaries on *Piskei ha-Rosh*
        (1) *Haggahot Asheri* by Israel of Krems
        (2) *Peri Megadim et al.* by Yom Tov Lipmann Heller
        (3) *Korban Netanel* by Nethanel Weil
    15. *Sefer ha-Tashbeẓ* by Samson b. Ẓadok and *Sefer ha-Parnas* by Moses Parnas of Rothenburg
    16. *Sefer Eẓ Ḥayyim* by Jacob b. Judah Ḥazzan
    17. *Sefer Orḥot Ḥayyim* by Aaron b. Jacob ha-Kohen
    18. *Sefer Kol Bo*
  B. Books Organized on the Basis of an Enumeration of the Biblical Commandments
    1. *Sefer Yere'im* by Eliezer b. Samuel (Re'em)
    2. *Sefer Miẓvot Gadol* (*Semag*) by Moses of Coucy
    3. *Sefer Miẓvot Katan* (*Semak*) by Isaac of Corbeil
    4. *Sefer ha-Ḥinnukh*
  C. Books Organized According to Idiosyncratic Criteria
    1. *Sefer ha-Ittur* by Isaac of Marseilles
    2. *Sefer Meisharim* and *Toledot Adam ve-Ḥavvah* by Rabbenu Jeroham b. Meshullam

D. The Codificatory Methodology of Solomon b. Abraham Adret (Rashba)
1. *Torat ha-Bayit ha-Arokh, Torah ha-Bayit ha-Kaẓer,* and Other Codificatory Works by Rashba
2. *Bedek ha-Bayit* and *Mishmeret ha-Bayit*
II. *Sefer ha-Turim* by Jacob b. Asher
A. Jacob b. Asher's Codificatory Methodology
B. The Structure and Organization of *Sefer ha-Turim*
III. Commentaries on *Sefer ha-Turim*
A. *Bet Yosef* by Joseph Caro and *Darkhei Moshe* by Moses Isserles (Rema)
B. *Bet Yisra'el* by Joshua Falk
C. *Bayit Ḥadash* (*Baḥ*) by Joel Sirkes
D. Compilations of Responsa Arranged According to the Organization of *Sefer ha-Turim*
IV. Codificatory Literature from *Sefer ha-Turim* to the *Shulḥan Arukh*

I. CODIFICATORY LITERATURE UNTIL THE *SEFER HA-TURIM*

Between Maimonides' *Mishneh Torah* at the end of the twelfth century and Jacob b. Asher's *Sefer ha-Turim* (also known simply as the *Turim*) toward the middle of the fourteenth century, a substantial number of codificatory works were composed. During this period, there was a strong current of opposition to the methodology of the *Mishneh Torah* on the ground that the presentation of only one view of the law without reference to sources or variant opinions would sever the *Halakhah* from its sources and was inconsistent with the very nature of Jewish law and its decision-making process; a judge had to be aware of all the various views as to the law so that he could discharge the nondelegable responsibility of deciding which view is to prevail in the particular case before him.

Even though the works written during this period differ from one another in their literary form and arrangement, most of them are alike in one respect: they are books of *halakhot, i.e.,* they state the controlling legal conclusion in each instance, but only after a brief discussion of the Talmudic sources and the various opinions.

There were two main reasons why such books of *halakhot* were necessary: (1) increased halakhic creativity, and (2) proliferation of conflicting opinions. These have always been primary factors motivating codification. There was a need for a suitable work that would facilitate research and summarize the law for the decisionmaker. This period was blessed with creativity in all branches of the law through the activities of the Tosafists in

Germany and France, the scholars of Provence, and Naḥmanides and his disciples in Spain. In addition, the polemic surrounding Maimonides' methodology provided further stimulus to discover different literary forms for books of *halakhot*.

Some of the books continued to be organized in the conventional manner, *i.e.*, either in the order of the Talmudic tractates (with some attempt to accommodate the need for topical arrangement), or solely on the basis of subject matter. Others took on new literary forms: some were arranged in the order of the commandments (*mizvot*) in the Torah and others in the form of a book of *halakhot* and a book of *pesakim* as companion works. Still others were arranged according to idiosyncratic guidelines, such as the order of a particular mnemonic or the order of events in the human life-cycle.

A considerable number of these books deal mainly with matters beyond the scope of *mishpat ivri*, but they deserve brief mention for their codificatory methodology. Some of the books are known only from secondary sources that quote or refer to them, some have remained in manuscript for centuries and have been printed only recently, and some are of unknown or uncertain authorship.[1]

The variety of patterns and designs of the codificatory works in this period may well correlate with the extent to which one or another codificatory approach gained ascendancy during the course of the development of codification in the halakhic system. The following is a brief review of some of these codificatory works, classified according to their methodology.

A. Books Following the Order of the Talmud, and/or Organized in Whole or in Part According to Topic

1. *SEFER AVI HA-EZRI* AND *SEFER AVI'ASAF* BY ELIEZER b. JOEL HA-LEVI (RAVIAH)

Sefer Avi ha-Ezri and *Sefer Avi'asaf*[2] were written by Raviah, one of the important Tosafists, who was active in Germany in the second half of the twelfth and the beginning of the thirteenth centuries. *Sefer Avi ha-Ezri* follows the order of the Talmudic tractates and also includes novellae and responsa.[3] However, it aims to summarize and settle the law after clarifying and discussing the sources. It deals for the most part with topics found in Tractate *Berakhot*, the Order of *Mo'ed*, Tractate *Ḥullin*, and the laws of *pros-*

1. For examples in each category, *see infra*.
2. *Avi* (lit. "father of") is the acronym of Eliezer b. Joel.
3. Following the methodology of the Tosafists, *see supra* p. 1122.

bul. Sefer Avi'asaf is devoted in the main to topics in the Orders of *Nashim* and *Nezikin.*

Sefer Avi ha-Ezri has been published from manuscripts only in the latter part of the twentieth century, and then only in part.[4] An additional volume of Raviah's works was published in 1964, containing, in the main, topics in the Order of *Nashim,* and also an appendix on the laws of the *ketubbah.*[5]

Raviah is most frequently quoted in the works of the leading German codifiers, who were his disciples, or students of his disciples; and he had a strong and decisive influence on subsequent codificatory literature. He himself frequently quoted Rabbenu Hananel and Alfasi as well as leading German and French halakhic authorities, thus contributing to the integration of the rulings of the Ashkenazic and the early Sephardic authorities, a fusion that halakhic authorities also achieved during subsequent periods.[6]

2. *SEFER HA-ROKE'AḤ* BY ELEAZAR b. JUDAH

Eleazar b. Judah, of the Kalonymus family (known as *Ba'al ha-Roke'aḥ*), was a halakhic authority in Germany and a contemporary of Raviah. *Sefer ha-Roke'aḥ* is arranged mainly by topic. It discusses the sources of each law and then succinctly states the legal rule. It deals mainly with the laws of blessings and prayers, festivals, and other "religious" law (*issur*). The book begins with the laws of piety and repentance, and it details methods of repentance commensurate with the nature of the sin—an approach developed by the *Ḥasidim* of Germany in the twelfth and thirteenth centuries.[7]

3. *SEFER HA-TERUMAH*[8] BY BARUCH b. ISAAC

Baruch b. Isaac of Worms was an outstanding disciple of the Tosafist Isaac b. Samuel of Dampierre (Isaac the Elder, known as Ri). In 1237, he

4. *Sefer Raviah,* ed. Avigdor Aptowitzer, published by Mekiẓei Nirdamim together with a one-volume introduction, *Mavo la-Raviah.* A second edition of *Sefer Raviah* in three volumes was published by the Harry Fischel Institute for Talmudic Research in 1964, supplemented by a fourth volume (ed. E. Priesman and S.Y. Cohen). *See infra* n. 5.

5. *See supra* n. 4. *Sefer Avi'asaf* was known to Ḥida (Ḥayyim Joseph David Azulai [1724–1806]). Priesman and Cohen believe that the material in their additional volume is *Sefer Avi'asaf. See* their Introduction to Volume IV, pp. 14ff., which also gives their view as to the difference between *Avi ha-Ezri* and *Avi'asaf.*

6. *See infra* p. 1251 n. 65, p. 1353, *et al.* For Raviah's biography, works, and halakhic methodology, *see* Aptowitzer, *Mavo la-Raviah, supra* n. 4; Urbach, *Tosafot,* pp. 315–321.

7. As to Eleazar b. Judah and his works, *see* Urbach, *Tosafot,* pp. 321–341. *See also id.* at 325, on the similarity between the beginning of *Sefer ha-Roke'aḥ* and the beginning of Maimonides' *Mishneh Torah.* For the significance of the name *Sefer ha-Roke'aḥ, see id.* at 327.

8. *Sefer ha-Terumah* was so named by the author "because its doctrines are taken from the most select [doctrines] (*mi-terumot*) of men of insight, the holy ones of the Lord, Who

moved to the Land of Israel and on his way passed through the island of Crete, where he promulgated legislative enactments for the community.[9]

Sefer ha-Terumah is arranged mainly by topic. To a certain extent, it also follows the order of the Talmud (as, for example, in regard to the laws of the sabbath). The book discusses ritual law, festivals, family law, prayers, and relations with non-Jews; there is also a chapter devoted to the laws of the Land of Israel.[10] At the beginning of the book, there is an overview of the contents,[11] briefly describing the substance of each paragraph in every topic. Before the final conclusion as to each legal rule, there is a comprehensive discussion of the Talmudic sources, which includes the various relevant opinions.[12]

4. *SEFER HA-MANHIG* BY ABRAHAM b. NATHAN HA-YARḤI

Abraham b. Nathan ha-Yarḥi[13] was active in France, Germany, Spain, and other countries at the end of the twelfth and the beginning of the thirteenth centuries. He, too, was a disciple of Isaac b. Samuel, and composed his work (as he says) "so that the Jewish people might know how to conduct themselves on the sabbaths, the New Moons, and the festivals, including their intermediate days . . . , and I called this book *Manhig Olam* [A Guide for Everyone], because in it I set forth all the orders of prayers and I

---

dwells on high." *See* the comments at the end of the book, which are actually in the nature of a brief introduction. For another example of a similar use of the term *terumot, cf.* TB Gittin 67a: "My doctrines are the most select of the best (*terumot mi-terumot*) doctrines of R. Akiva."

9. *See supra* p. 811. *Sefer ha-Terumah* treats as a distinct subject the "Laws of the Land of Israel" (found in the printed edition between the Laws of Phylacteries and the Laws of the Sabbath). The Introduction to this subject reads as follows:

> For Zion's sake I will not remain silent, and for Jerusalem's sake I will not be still, until its righteousness shall shine forth brightly [*cf.* Isaiah 62:1] and the Teacher of Righteousness shall come to us with the holy men of surpassing brilliance who have passed away but will awaken and arise and enlighten us as to the path we are to follow. Truly is the Land of Israel beloved, and happy is the man who dwells there. For even those who left it, Jehoiachin and those exiled with him, took with them stones and soil of the Land of Israel and built a synagogue . . . in Babylonia [TB Megillah 29a] to fulfill the Scriptural verse, "Your servants take delight in its stones, and cherish its dust" [Psalms 102:15]. . . . He who dwells there and observes the commandments directly relating to it will surely merit to be in the company of the Holy One, blessed be He.

10. *See supra* n. 9.

11. *See Sefer ha-Terumah,* Introduction.

12. For further details, *see* Urbach, *Tosafot,* pp. 286–299.

13. Born in Lunel, southern France. His name, ha-Yarḥi, is the Hebrew equivalent of Lunel, since the Hebrew *yare'aḥ* and Latin *luna* both mean "moon"; and ha-Yarḥi and Lunel both mean "lunar" or "of the moon." Lunel was a center of Torah study, inhabited by many great scholars. *See infra* n. 33. *See also* EJ, XI, pp. 565–566, s.v. Lunel, and bibliography cited.

also thoroughly discuss customs, so that everyone may know everything about his customs—their reasons, their basis, and their history."[14] The book is topically arranged and includes, in connection with each law, a review of the Talmudic sources and the opinions of the *geonim* and the Spanish and French authorities.

5. *OR ZARU'A*[15] BY ISAAC b. MOSES (RIAZ)

Riaz[16] was active in Vienna at the end of the twelfth and the first half of the thirteenth centuries. He was a disciple of Raviah and incorporated in his book a great many of his teacher's rulings. *Or Zaru'a* is topically arranged, in the order in which the topics appear in the Talmud. Riaz's discussion, preceding each definitive statement of the law, is comprehensive and exhaustive. In addition to the Talmudic sources, he quotes, among others, the *geonim,* Rabbenu Hananel, Alfasi, Maimonides, Rashi, and the Tosafists. The book is an important—and sometimes the sole—source for the works of earlier halakhic authorities and has had great influence on later codificatory literature.[17]

In its extant form, *Or Zaru'a* consists of four parts. The first discusses the laws of blessings and prayers; topics in the Order of *Zera'im;* ritual laws, including laws of ritual purity; marriage, including levirate marriage and *ḥaliẓah;* and divorce and the *agunah.* The beginning of this part discusses the law of charity, based on the verse "[they shall] keep the way of the Lord by doing what is just [in the Hebrew, *ẓedakah,* which means "charity" as well as "justice"] and right."[18] The second part deals, *inter alia,* with the laws of festivals.[19] The third and fourth parts include rulings on subjects covered in Tractates *Bava Kamma, Bava Meẓi'a, Bava Batra, Sanhedrin,* and *Avodah Zarah.*[20] The book also contains novellae and responsa.[21]

14. *Sefer ha-Manhig,* Introduction.

15. In the Preface, the author explained that he chose this title for his work "because of a special affection for the Scriptural verse, 'A light is sown [*or zaru'a*] for the righteous, and joy for the upright in heart' [Psalms 97:11], of which the final letters of the Hebrew words spell 'R. Akiva.'" At the beginning of the book the author, like R. Akiva, expounded interpretively on each letter of the alphabet.

16. Isaiah b. Elijah of Trani (the "Latter Isaiah," *see infra* p. 1258 n. 98) is also known by the acronym Riaz; care must, therefore, be taken to determine which of these two authorities a reference to "Riaz" identifies.

17. *Or Zaru'a* is frequently quoted from the abridgment by the author's son; *see infra* n. 21.

18. Genesis 18:19.

19. These two parts were first published in Zhitomir, 1862.

20. The third and fourth parts were published in Jerusalem, 1888–1890. The rulings relating to Tractate *Shevu'ot* were published by A.H. Freimann in *Tiferet Yisra'el,* a *Festschrift* in honor of Israel Lewy, 1911, pp. 10–32.

21. Riaz's son, Ḥayyim Or Zaru'a, who wrote *Resp. Maharaḥ Or Zaru'a,* composed an abridged version of his father's work, entitled *Simanei Or Zaru'a* [Highlights of *Or Zaru'a*],

6. CODIFICATORY WORKS BY NAḤMANIDES

Naḥmanides (Ramban) lived in Spain in the first half of the thirteenth century. In his codificatory works, he employed three different styles. First, in his books on the laws of *Nedarim* (Vows), *Bekhorot* (Firstlings), and *Ḥallah* (Dough-Offering), he followed Alfasi's method in the *Sefer ha-Halakhot*,[22] explaining his purpose as follows:

> I will begin with the laws of *Nedarim* and *Bekhorot*; I have written them so as to complete the *Sefer ha-Halakhot* of the great master [Alfasi], from which these laws have been omitted. However, because they apply at all times and in all places, he did treat some of them as they appear in different parts of the Talmud. And I, the least of the students of his disciples, have followed in the straight path of his footsteps.[23]

Like Alfasi, Naḥmanides in these works also followed the sequence of the Mishnah and the discussions in the Talmudic tractates—*Nedarim*,[24] *Bekhorot*, and *Ḥallah*.[25] Naḥmanides briefly discussed the Talmudic sources, and also—like Alfasi—referred to the *geonim* and Rabbenu Hananel, after which he stated the legal rule.

Naḥmanides employed a second and completely different codificatory style in *Hilkhot Niddah* [The Laws of the Menstruant Woman]. This work is a short monograph, covering a single limited subject in the style *par excellence* of a book of *pesakim*. The material is arranged in chapters, and the chapters are divided into sections; the law is stated categorically without attribution of authority and only rarely is a contrary view mentioned as *ve-*

---

and it was from that version that Israel of Krems, author of *Haggahot Asheri* [Glosses to Asheri], quoted *Or Zaru'a*; the end of each such quotation states: "from *Or Zaru'a*." As to this and Riaz generally, *see* Urbach, *Tosafot*, pp. 359–370. For the particular history of the ms. of *Or Zaru'a*, *see* M. Samet, *Kiryat Sefer*, XLIII, p. 435.

22. *See supra* pp. 1167–1172.

23. Naḥmanides, Introduction to *Hilkhot Bekhorot ve-Ḥallah*. The book appeared with a commentary called *Hilkhot Yom Tov* by Yom Tov b. Israel Jacob Algazi (Maharit Algazi) of Jerusalem who served as *Rishon le-Ziyyon* (chief Sephardic rabbi of the Holy Land) in the second half of the eighteenth century. It is printed in the Vilna edition of the Talmud, and Naḥmanides' Introduction appears at the end of the book. It was also published as a separate volume, Vilna, 1903.

24. Naḥmanides' *Hilkhot Nedarim* is printed in the Vilna edition of the Talmud together with Alfasi's *Sefer ha-Halakhot* to Tractate *Nedarim*. Naḥmanides, however, was more discursive and detailed than Alfasi. The commentary on Naḥmanides (also printed in the Vilna edition) is by Ritba (Spain, fourteenth century).

25. *See supra* n. 23. Naḥmanides supplemented M Ḥallah, for which there is no corresponding tractate in the Babylonian Talmud, with various pertinent sources scattered throughout other tractates of the Babylonian Talmud.

yesh she-horah ("but someone [else] has ruled"). The style is clear and simple. Naḥmanides wrote this book at the request of "some God-fearing colleagues."[26]

A third codificatory work by Naḥmanides—in yet another style—is *Torat ha-Adam.*[27] This work, in the style of a geonic monograph,[28] discusses the laws relating to the sick and their treatment, the relaxation of religious restrictions when life is endangered, the legal status and responsibility of the physician, and the laws of *viddui* (the confessional prayer before death) and of burial and mourning; it concludes with a discussion of reward and punishment, entitled *Sha'ar ha-Gemul* (The Gate of Recompense). The book is divided into sections ("gates") and topics, and is engagingly written in a clear and easy style. On each topic, *Torat ha-Adam* brings to bear all the discussion in the Talmudic sources and the wide range of opinion of the *geonim* and the *rishonim* up to Naḥmanides' time, and then sets forth a definitive statement of the law.

Torat ha-Adam, in the legal areas covered by it, served as a foundation for the most important later codes, especially the *Turim* and the *Shulḥan Arukh.* It also created a new subject heading in the codification of the *Halakhah,* namely, the laws of physicians and medical treatment.[29]

7. *SEFER HA-HASHLAMAH* BY MESHULLAM b. MOSES OF BEZIERS

Meshullam b. Moses was a halakhic authority in Provence, at the end of the twelfth and the first half of the thirteenth centuries. *Sefer ha-Hashlamah* was designed to supplement Alfasi's *Sefer ha-Halakhot.*[30] Like Al-

26. *See* Introduction to *Hilkhot Niddah.* The book has been printed several times, most recently together with Rabad's *Ba'alei ha-Nefesh* (Jerusalem, 1956). *See* Naḥmanides' Introduction to the effect that he believed his own book to be unnecessary, since *Ba'alei ha-Nefesh* had already appeared, but he yielded to his friends and produced a work written in plain, simple, and easily understandable language.

27. *Torat ha-Adam* has been reprinted many times, most recently by C. Chavel, *Kol Kitvei ha-Ramban* [Naḥmanides' Collected Works], 1964, II, pp. 9–311, with Introduction and notes. The name *Torat ha-Adam* is an allusion to II Samuel 7:19; *see* Chavel, *supra* at 9 n. 1 and 10 n. 4.

28. *See supra* pp. 1158–1167.

29. *See Tur* YD ch. 335 (Laws of Visiting the Sick, Medicine, the Terminally Ill, and Persons *in Extremis*). This section begins: "The following is a synopsis of the contents of *Torat ha-Adam,* which the great rabbi Ramban wrote, together with a few other opinions I will insert." *See also* Sh. Ar. YD ch. 336, entitled "Laws of the Physician," which also deals with a physician's legal responsibility. Maimonides' *Mishneh Torah* does not devote a separate section to the law of physicians; the fourth chapter of *Hilkhot De'ot* discusses hygiene and health generally. *See* M. Elon, "Ha-Halakhah ve-ha-Refu'ah ha-Ḥadishah" [*Halakhah* and Modern Medicine], *Molad,* XXI (231), 1971, pp. 228ff.

30. As to Alfasi's *Sefer ha-Halakhot, see supra* pp. 1167–1172.

fasi, Meshullam followed the order of the Talmudic tractates, but he discussed only those topics for which he felt Alfasi required supplementation. Meshullam's brief Introduction succinctly sets out his objective:[31]

> I saw that our Master, Rabbi Isaac Alfasi, of blessed memory, was very terse in his *Sefer ha-Halakhot,* so I proposed to supplement his discussion, sometimes supporting his conclusions (although they require no support, especially from one as unworthy as I) and sometimes to raise a query. I called this book *Sefer ha-Hashlamah* after my name[32] and after its purpose, which is to supplement the *Sefer ha-Halakhot* of Alfasi. I hereby notify the reader that on many matters I follow the opinions of the author of the *Sefer ha-Ma'or.*[33]. . . However, I have no intention of committing myself either to Alfasi or to Maimonides, who made a thorough study of the Torah of Moses, our teacher. Rather, to the best of my own meager ability, I will attempt to separate the food from the waste and extract the wheat from the chaff.

Thus Meshullam made clear his independence in declaring the law, notwithstanding the views of earlier codifiers. His opinions and rulings were quoted by subsequent halakhic authorities, particularly by his fellow countryman, Menahem Meiri.[34] *Sefer ha-Hashlamah* began to be printed only in the nineteenth century; and to date, a substantial part has been published on the Orders of *Mo'ed* and *Nezikin,* and the Tractates *Yevamot* and *Ḥullin.*[35]

8. *SEFER HA-TERUMOT* BY SAMUEL SARDI

Samuel Sardi[36] was a Spanish halakhic authority in the first half of the thirteenth century. He lived in Barcelona, engaged in commerce, and

31. The Introduction appears at the beginning of *Sefer ha-Hashlamah* to the Order of *Nezikin,* part I, Tractates *Bava Kamma* and *Bava Meẓi'a,* published by J. Lubetzky, 1885.

32. *Hashlamah* is derived from the same root as Meshullam.

33. Zeraḥiah ha-Levi, who composed *Sefer ha-Ma'or* as a critical gloss to Alfasi; *see supra* p. 1173. Meshullam continued: " . . . I follow the way of the *Ma'or,* although not as one who plagiarizes his words, since I received them thus from my father, of blessed memory, because when both [*i.e.,* Meshullam's father and Zeraḥiah ha-Levi] were alive, they sometimes disagreed in the Tower of Lunel from where Torah spread [*see supra* n. 13], and they sometimes agreed."

34. As to Meiri, *see supra* p. 1126.

35. The part on Tractates *Bava Kamma* and *Bava Meẓi'a* was published in 1885 (*see supra* n. 31); on *Bava Batra, Sanhedrin,* and *Shevu'ot,* by J. Lubetzky, Warsaw, in 1908; on *Berakhot,* by M.M. Shaḥor, Berlin, in 1893. *Sefer ha-Ma'or* and *Sefer ha-Hashlamah* on *Berakhot, Pesaḥim, Shabbat, Eruvin, Mo'ed Katan,* and *Ḥullin* were published by M. Blau, New York (4 vols.), 1964–1967; *Sefer ha-Hashlamah* is included in *Ginzei Rishonim* on *Sukkah, Berakhot, Rosh ha-Shanah, Yoma,* and *Ta'anit,* published by M. Hershler, Jerusalem, 1962–1967; *Sefer ha-Hashlamah* on *Yevamot* was published by A. Ḥafuta, Tel Aviv, in 1965. For more detailed information on Meshullam b. Moses, *see* the Introductions of Lubetzky to *Sefer ha-Hashlamah* on *Bava Kamma* and *Bava Meẓi'a,* and H. Brodie to *Sefer ha-Hashlamah* on *Berakhot,* Berlin, 1893.

36. So called after Sardinia, his place of birth.

amassed substantial wealth. He was a student and colleague of Naḥmanides, with whom he discussed halakhic issues both in person and by correspondence. *Sefer ha-Terumot*[37] exhaustively discusses an important part of Jewish civil law—the law of loans, and related matters.[38] A prime factor motivating the writing of the book was the author's personal knowledge of daily commercial life, which made evident the need for a succinct book of laws on commercial transactions for easy reference by those engaged in business, and perhaps even for use by judges, as we learn from his Introduction:

> I wrote it . . . so that all laws relating to loans by written instrument or oral agreement, or relating to the rights and obligations of lenders and borrowers, can be found in one place. Sometimes they [the debtors] defraud their creditors by chicanery, deceit, falsehood, wantonness, and trickery. Some default on account of lack of means because of the troubled times. Some have their assets conveyed or encumbered to others. Some borrow on usury and include the interest in the face amount of the loan. And by all these means they take the property and invade and consume the assets of others, sometimes legally and sometimes not, as it is written: "The wicked man borrows and does not repay."[39] I decided, therefore, to bring them to judgment for all these things and instruct them as to the path they should follow.[40]

Sefer ha-Terumot is an excellent example of a book of *halakhot.* It is arranged according to topics and issues rather than the sequence of the Talmudic tractates. To some extent, it can be considered the first code devoted solely to Jewish civil law.[41] It is divided into seventy "gates" (*she'arim*), each dealing with a particular subject, and subdivided into chapters, which the author calls *inyanim* (subjects) or *ḥalakim* (sections), that are further subdivided into paragraphs, called *peratim* (details). This pattern of division is reminiscent of the division of Maimonides' *Mishneh Torah* into sections,

37. Samuel Sardi entitled his book *Sefer ha-Terumot* for the same reason that Baruch b. Isaac chose the name *Sefer ha-Terumah* for his work (*see supra* n. 8). *See* Sardi's Introduction: "Now I will teach and separate a tithe of my tithes (*terumah mi-terumati*), following the custom of R. Simeon, who used to say to his disciples, 'My sons, learn my doctrines, for my doctrines are the most select of the best (*terumah mi-terumot*) doctrines of Rabbi Akiva [TB Gittin 67a]. . . . Therefore, I gave it the title *Sefer ha-Terumot.*"

38. These laws contain a considerable portion of the Jewish law of obligations; *see* M. Elon, EJ, XII, pp. 1310–1316, s.v. Obligations, law of (reprinted in *Principles,* pp. 241–246).

39. Psalms 37:21.

40. In the time of Samuel Sardi, debtors commonly made fraudulent conveyances of their assets to avoid paying their debts. There were also cases of default because of inability to repay. *See* Elon, *Ḥerut,* pp. 118ff.

41. *Sefer ha-Terumot* is more of a code, in the sense of a definitive statement of the law, than the monographs of the *geonim,* which also in the main treat civil law. *See supra* pp. 1158–1167.

chapters, and paragraphs. It may indeed be assumed that Samuel Sardi, who frequently quoted Maimonides in his work, was influenced by Maimonides' method of arranging his material.[42]

In content, however, *Sefer ha-Terumot* is clearly a book of *halakhot* and not a book of *pesakim*. On every point it starts with a discussion of the Talmudic source and the various opinions of the post-Talmudic halakhic authorities; only after that discussion does it proceed to a definitive conclusory statement of the law. Samuel Sardi (like his contemporary, Naḥmanides) extensively referred to the works of the earlier halakhic authorities of Spain, France, and Germany, and also included responsa that he received from Naḥmanides. The text is preceded by a brief table of contents of the "gates" and chapters, in order to enhance the usefulness of the work and to facilitate finding particular laws: "I have indicated the place of each law at the beginning of my work so that the laws and their explication will be readily accessible to the reader."[43] The influence of *Sefer ha-Terumot* continues to the present day, by virtue of the *Sefer ha-Turim* of Jacob b. Asher, who often quoted *Sefer ha-Terumot* in *Tur Ḥoshen Mishpat*.[44]

A comprehensive commentary on *Sefer ha-Terumot*, entitled *Giddulei Terumah*, was written by Azariah b. Ephraim Figo, of Italy, in the first half of the seventeenth century. This commentary explicates the text of *Sefer ha-Terumot*, sets out the sources, and expresses Figo's own opinion on points as to which Samuel Sardi and other authorities disagreed.[45]

42. The sequence of the subject matter in *Sefer ha-Terumot* also largely parallels the sequence of Maimonides' *Hilkhot Malveh ve-Loveh*. It is interesting, however, that *Sefer ha-Terumot* does not treat the laws of interest and usury, which were codified by Maimonides in chs. 4–10 of *Hilkhot Malveh ve-Loveh*. Similarly, both the *Turim* and the *Shulḥan Arukh* put those laws in *Yoreh De'ah* and not in *Ḥoshen Mishpat*. *See also infra* p. 1289 and n. 206.

43. *Sefer ha-Terumot*, Introduction.

44. On Samuel Sardi, *see* the Introduction to his book. *See also* S. Assaf, *Sifran Shel Rishonim*, 1935, pp. 53–55. A large number of Naḥmanides' responsa quoted by Assaf were addressed to Sardi. Sardi's book transmits selected readings of texts of *rishonim* and occasionally discusses their correctness. *See, e.g.*, gate 35, ch. 1, par. 28 (end): "Some have cited Maimonides as having written in his book, *'mi-mi she-erẓeh teḥillah'* ('from whomever I so desire first'), but I examined his book and found that he had in fact written, *'mi-mi she-erẓeh goveh'* ('from whomever I will desire to claim'); and this is the text of our *mishnah*." *See further* M. Elon, "Ḥofesh ha-Hatna'ah be-Dinei Arvut" [Freedom of Contract in the Law of Suretyship], *Proceedings of the Fourth International Congress of Jewish Studies*, 1967, I, pp. 197ff. (at pp. 203ff.).

45. *Giddulei Terumah* was first printed together with *Sefer ha-Terumot* (Venice, 1643); this edition was republished in facsimile in Jerusalem, 1961. *See* the author's Introduction at the beginning of the book, describing how he moved from general studies to the study of *Halakhah*, and his method in composing his book.

9. *SEFER SHIBBOLEI HA-LEKET* BY ZEDEKIAH b. ABRAHAM HA-ROFE

Zedekiah b. Abraham ha-Rofe, of the Anavim family, was an Italian halakhic authority of the thirteenth century.[46] The first part of *Sefer Shibbolei ha-Leket*[47] is divided into twelve sections (*arugot,* rows), each of which is subdivided into chapters (*shibbolim,* lit. "ears [of corn]"). This part contains 372 chapters,[48] and discusses the laws of prayer, the sabbath, blessings, festivals, mourning, circumcision, *ẓiẓit* (fringes), and other subjects.[49]

The second part of the work contains 157 chapters,[50] and discusses ritual law, personal status, marriage and the *ketubbah,* divorce and *ḥaliẓah,*

46. In ch. 263 of his book (ed. Buber, p. 252), which deals with the four fast days, Zedekiah b. Abraham ha-Rofe referred to the edict for the burning of the Talmud, which took place in his lifetime:

> Since we deal here with the laws of fasting and the matter of the burning of the Torah, we have written this in memory of what happened in our own day, when, because of our many sins, the Torah of our God was burned in 5004 A.M [= 1244 C.E.] on the Friday of the weekly Torah portion Ve-Zot Ḥukkat ha-Torah. Some twenty-four wagonloads full of books of Talmud, laws, and *aggadot* were burned in France, as we have heard. We also heard from rabbis who were present that they asked a *she'elat ḥalom* [*i.e.,* a question by way of a dream] to determine whether it had been so decreed by the Creator, and they were answered, "Ve-da gezerat oraita" ["And this is the decree of the Torah"; these words are identical with Onkelos' Aramaic translation of Numbers 19:2, the second verse of that week's Torah portion, except for the letter *vav* ("and") in the word *ve-da*]. The meaning [of the inserted *vav*] is that the sixth day [*i.e.,* Friday, the sixth day of the week, indicated by the letter *vav,* which also signifies the number six] of the [week when the Torah] portion Zot Ḥukkat ha-Torah [is read in the synagogue service] is the date called for by the edict. From that day onward, some have taken it upon themselves to fast every year on the Friday of the [week when] Zot Ḥukkat ha-Torah [is the Torah] portion [read during the synagogue service].

See also infra p. 1263.

47. The first part was first published under the name *Shibbolei ha-Leket ha-Shalem,* by Solomon Buber, Vilna, 1887 (facsimile ed., Jerusalem, 1962), with an introduction but without notes. (*See* Introduction, p. 32, as to Buber's inability to provide annotations.) The second part of the book was published by M.Z. Ḥasida, with notes and source references, in the journal *Ha-Segullah,* 1934–1937 (facsimile ed., Jerusalem, 1969). Another edition of the first part, also called *Shibbolei ha-Leket ha-Shalem,* with v.l. of additional mss., commentary, notes, and introduction, was undertaken by S.K. Mirsky, New York, 1966; but only the first two sections, on prayer and the sabbath, have appeared.

48. "And their mnemonic is 'the seven [Hebrew *sheva,* the Hebrew letters of which have the numerical value of 372] healthy ears,'" an allusion to Genesis 41:24: "And the thin ears swallowed the seven healthy ears." *See* the author's Introduction (end), after his table of contents.

49. These last laws are not arranged in *arugot* and *shibbolim* but in *halakhot* (laws) and *dinim* (rules). *See further* Buber, *supra* n. 47, Introduction, p. 2.

50. In ed. Ḥasida (*supra* n. 47), *but see* Buber, *supra* n. 47 at 2–3 and n. 8, for a different total number that he saw in ms.

and many aspects of civil law. The Talmudic sources and the opinions of the *geonim,* as well as German, French, and Italian halakhic authorities, are discussed in detail.

10. *SEFER HA-TANYA*

Sefer ha-Tanya[51] was written about the same time as *Sefer Shibbolei ha-Leket,* by an Italian author whose identity has not been established. *Sefer ha-Tanya* is based in large measure upon *Sefer Shibbolei ha-Leket*[52] but also includes laws from other sources.[53] The book is arranged according to subject matter and discusses, *inter alia,* the laws of blessings, prayer, the sabbath, and festivals.

11. *SEFER HA-NEYAR*

Sefer ha-Neyar[54] was written by a thirteenth-century French author whose identity is unknown.[55] The book contains forty-four chapters, and is in the main arranged by topic. It treats, *inter alia,* the laws of the sabbath and the festivals, mourning, *orlah* (produce of the first three years of a tree's growth), *kilayim* (mixed species), *ḥallah, sheḥitah* (ritual slaughter), *terefot* (prohibited foods), blessings, and personal status (*e.g.,* prohibited sexual unions, the laws of marriage and the *ketubbah,* divorce, and levirate marriage and *ḥaliẓah*). It also discusses the law of wills and inheritance. The Talmudic sources and the opinions of *geonim* and of Spanish and French halakhic authorities on each point are briefly discussed, followed by a summary statement of the law on the point involved.

12. *SHA'AREI DURA* BY ISAAC b. MEIR OF DÜREN

Sha'arei Dura (also known as *Sefer Issur ve-Hetter*)[56] was written by Isaac b. Meir of Düren, a thirteenth-century German halakhic author-

51. Many editions have been printed, most recently under the name *Sefer Tanya Rabbati* with commentary by Simon b. Saul ha-Levi Horowitz (facsimile ed., Jerusalem, 1963).

52. Ḥida, *Shem ha-Gedolim,* Books, Letter *shin,* par. 27 ("*Sefer Tanya* was derived from *Shibbolei ha-Leket*").

53. *See Shibbolei ha-Leket ha-Shalem,* ed. Mirsky, Introduction, pp. 40–49. As to *Sefer ha-Tanya,* its relationship to *Shibbolei ha-Leket,* and its authorship and date, *see id.;* Horowitz, *supra* n. 51, Introduction; Buber, *supra* n. 47, Introduction at 28–31.

54. Part I, consisting of twenty-five chapters, was first published from mss. by G. Appel, New York, 1961, with introduction and notes. For the source and meaning of the title, *see* the Introduction, pp. 19–22.

55. *See id.* at 22–38.

56. Reprinted many times, most recently under the name *Sefer Sha'arei Dura ha-Shalem ha-Nikra Issur ve-Hetter,* in two volumes (vol. I, to ch. 37, by I.N. Freilich), undated (1932?), with introduction and notes, together with glosses and comments by Israel Isserlein (extracted from his book, *She'arim be-Dinei Issur ve-Hetter*) and other commentators, includ-

ity.[57] The book deals solely with dietary laws. It contains ninety-six chapters on the laws of ritual slaughter, the salting of meat, prohibited foods, and similar matters. In form, it is a book of *pesakim*. Its style is extremely spare; it does not discuss Talmudic sources, and it states the opinions of the *rishonim* with the utmost brevity. The work was accepted as authoritative in its field and was very quickly the subject of annotations and commentaries.[58]

13. *SEFER HA-MORDEKHAI* BY MORDECAI b. HILLEL HA-KOHEN

Mordecai b. Hillel ha-Kohen was a German halakhic authority in the second half of the thirteenth century. An outstanding disciple of Maharam of Rothenburg, he was martyred in 1298, apparently in the Rindfleisch massacres. His work *Sefer ha-Mordekhai* (also called "the *Mordekhai*") follows the sequence of Alfasi's *Sefer ha-Halakhot.* His objective was to supplement Alfasi's work with the opinions of the halakhic authorities of Germany and France as expressed in their responsa, novellae, and rulings. To the present day, the *Mordekhai* has been an important source for the teachings of the French and German authorities during the period beginning with the teachers of Rashi and ending with Maharam of Rothenburg. Certain halakhic works are known to us only because they are quoted in the *Mordekhai.*[59] The *Mordekhai* also liberally quotes the *geonim,* Rabbenu Nissim, Rabbenu Hananel, and many Spanish and Provençal authorities.

The *Mordekhai* is a compendium of all types of Talmudic and post-Talmudic halakhic literature from every center of Talmudic learning. However, the sources quoted in the extant version of the *Mordekhai* cannot be uncritically accepted as authentic, because the work has survived in a truncated and corrupt form; various copyists and compositors have supplemented it, changed its text, and deleted parts of it. From very early on, there were two different editions: a longer one, known as the "large Austrian

---

ing the sixteenth-century scholars Nathan Nata b. Samson Spira and Solomon Luria (Maharshal).

57. Scholars disagree as to whether Isaac b. Meir lived in the thirteenth century (as a contemporary of Maharam of Rothenburg or as his disciple) or in the fourteenth century (as a disciple of Asheri). We have taken the first view. *See* Freilich, *supra* n. 56, Introduction; I.S. Elfenbein, "Minhagim Shel Kol ha-Shanah me-Ashkenaz le-Rabbenu Yiẓḥak mi-Dura" [Customs for the Entire Year from Ashkenaz by R. Isaac of Düren], *Ḥorev,* X (1948), pp. 129ff.; I. Ta-Shema, "Al Sefer Issur ve-Hetter Shel R. Yeruḥam ve-al R. Yiẓḥak mi-Dura" [On *Sefer Issur ve-Hetter* of R. Jeroham and on R. Isaac of Düren], *Sinai,* LXIV (1969), pp. 256–257.

58. *See supra* n. 56.

59. *E.g., Sefer ha-Dinim* of R. Judah ha-Kohen and *Sefer ha-Ḥokhmah* of Baruch b. Samuel.

Mordekhai," and a shorter one, known as the "Rhenish edition."[60] Many halakhic scholars have noted errors in the text of the *Mordekhai.*[61]

Although, as previously indicated, the *Mordekhai* follows the sequence of Alfasi's *Sefer ha-Halakhot,* the connection is only superficial. Alfasi is quoted no differently than other leading authorities, without discussion or explanation. Moreover, the *Mordekhai* does not resemble a typical book of *halakhot.* While it cites all the Talmudic sources (Babylonian, Jerusalem, and *baraitot*) as well as all the post-Talmudic sources, and it identifies them with great precision, it does not discuss the merits of conflicting opinions in an effort to arrive at a definitive statement of the law. The opinions are quoted *verbatim* (or paraphrased when, in the author's view, they are too extensive to be quoted), and set off against each other; occasionally, the author states that a specific opinion is "the heart of the matter" or "such is the custom."

Thus, the *Mordekhai* is essentially a compendium of halakhic sources, commencing with the Talmud, that presents the various opinions in a convenient form for the consideration of the reader. In later periods, the author of the *Mordekhai* was considered an outstanding halakhic authority. Joseph Caro included the *Mordekhai* among the five authorities on whom he relied when he could not reach a clear decision on the basis of the opinions of the "three pillars of instruction" (Alfasi, Maimonides, and Asheri).[62] Moses Isserles (Rema) quoted the *Mordekhai* in almost every one of his glosses to the *Shulḥan Arukh.* Indeed, the *Mordekhai* has had a marked influence on subsequent codification and decision making.[63]

60. The *Mordekhai* now printed in all large editions of the Babylonian Talmud after Alfasi's *Sefer ha-Halakhot* is the shorter version.

61. *See, e.g., Resp. Rema* 100:5:

> For you are acquainted with *Sefer ha-Mordekhai* and its language; in many instances the language is unclear because it was pieced together from many books, and thus it has in it many glosses and cryptic statements of laws divorced from their original context.

See also Bayit Ḥadash to *Tur* OḤ ch. 692, s.v. Kol ḥet yemei Hanukkah; Urbach, *Tosafot,* pp. 436–438. For a comprehensive study of the life and works of Mordecai b. Hillel ha-Kohen, *see* the article of A.S. Cohen, which appeared in installments, translated from the German, in *Sinai,* IX to XVI. For v.l. of the *Mordekhai, see* S. Rosenthal, "Shinnuyei Nusḥa'ot be-Sefer ha-Mordekhai" [Textual Variances in *Sefer ha-Mordekhai*], *Shanah be-Shanah* (Heichal Shelomo Annual), 1968, pp. 234ff.

62. *See infra* pp. 1317–1319.

63. Various helpful indexes of *Sefer ha-Mordekhai* have been compiled to facilitate its use. The edition of 1554/1555 included an alphabetical index arranged according to the order of the sections in the *Mishneh Torah* and entitled "An Abridged Version of All the Laws in the *Mordekhai.*" According to its colophon, it was compiled by Joshua Boaz b. Simon Baruch, the author of *Shiltei ha-Gibborim* on Alfasi. It was printed as a separate volume in Cremona in 1557 under the name *Kiẓẓur ha-Mordekhai* [The Abridged *Mordekhai*]. In 1559, an index by Joseph Ottolenghi, an Italian scholar, was printed in Riva di Trento according

14. *PISKEI HA-ROSH* BY ASHERI, AND ITS COMMENTARIES

a. *PISKEI HA-ROSH*

Piskei ha-Rosh (also known as *Hilkhot ha-Rosh* and *Sefer Asheri*) was written by Asheri (Asher b. Jehiel, also known as Rosh), a German and Spanish halakhic authority of the second half of the thirteenth and the beginning of the fourteenth centuries. *Piskei ha-Rosh* is one of the classic books of *halakhot*. It follows the pattern of Alfasi's *Sefer ha-Halakhot* in a number of respects: its external structure, *i.e.*, the sequence of the Talmudic tractates; its internal arrangement, *i.e.*, a synopsis of the Talmudic discussion as a prelude to a definitive statement of the law; and its language, *i.e.*, it almost always quotes Alfasi in full. Indeed, the work may very well have been intended as a complementary work to *Sefer ha-Halakhot*.[64]

There is a greater quantity and variety of halakhic material in Asheri's work than in Alfasi's; two centuries had passed since Alfasi, and much additional material had accumulated in the various areas of the law. Asheri also included in his work the doctrines and approaches of the French and German halakhic authorities, and passed judgment on the issues on which they differed from the Spanish authorities.[65]

Asheri was born in Germany and was the outstanding disciple of Maharam of Rothenburg, even serving as the leader of German Jewry after the latter's death. Later, he fled Germany; and when he reached Spain, he was

---

to the sequence of the tractates and chapters of the Talmud. The two indexes appear in the Vilna edition of the Talmud (and facsimiles); the alphabetical index is printed at the end of the Talmud, following the index to Alfasi.

64. Many scholars have noted the extremely close relationship between *Piskei ha-Rosh* and Alfasi's *Sefer ha-Halakhot*. *See, e.g.*, the statement of Asheri's son Jacob, the author of the *Turim*, in his Introduction to *Tur* ḤM: "*Piskei ha-Rosh*, by my father, of blessed memory, . . . are based on the foundation laid by the great Rabbi Isaac Alfasi, of blessed memory" (more fully quoted *infra* p. 1284); and the statement of Asheri's disciple, Rabbenu Jeroham, in his Introduction to *Sefer Meisharim*: "Also the rulings he [*i.e.*, Asheri] wrote based on the books of Rabbi Alfasi." *See also* Maharshal's Introduction to *Yam Shel Shelomo*, Bava Kamma, and the introduction of *Sema* to Sh. Ar. ḤM. As to Asheri's attitude to Alfasi, *see Resp. Asheri* 84:3 (p. 78b), citing Maharam of Rothenburg: "For our teacher Meir [Maharam], of blessed memory, would take all Rabbi Alfasi's words as stating the essence of the law and wrote several times in his responsa that Rabbi Alfasi never made an unnecessary statement."

65. Citation of the opinions of the halakhic authorities of these two centers, and discussion and treatment of them together in a single work, had been done to some extent before Asheri by Isaac of Marseilles (*see infra* p. 1269), Raviah (*see supra* p. 1239), Naḥmanides (*see supra* pp. 1242–1243), and Moses of Coucy (*see infra* pp. 1261–1262), as well as by Rashba and Mordecai b. Hillel ha-Kohen, in Asheri's own time. However, Asheri surpassed his predecessors and contemporaries in these respects, and in the determination of which view should be followed when there is a conflict of opinion. On the nature of the differences of opinion between these two centers and their different approaches to decision making, *see infra* pp. 1279, 1386, *et passim*.

acknowledged as one of the leading authorities of that diaspora. Since Asheri served in a position of leadership in both of these centers, he was uniquely situated to put the teachings of the leading halakhic authorities of both countries "under one roof," and to discuss and pass judgment upon their views. Moreover, Asheri provided extensive explanations, more comprehensive than Alfasi's, of the passages he incorporated in his work from the Talmud. If Asheri felt that some halakhic conclusion could be derived from parts of the Talmud that Alfasi omitted, he would include them. His method of dealing with and explaining the Talmudic passages lends his book of *halakhot* something of the character of a commentary on the Talmud.[66]

Asheri's methodology is a natural consequence of his basic position, discussed above,[67] that only a law contained in the Talmud itself is absolutely binding; if a judge relies on proofs acceptable to his contemporaries, he is free to reject any post-Talmudic (even geonic) opinion. As previously noted,[68] Asheri opposed books of *pesakim* that contained no attribution of authority, no indication of sources, and no references to conflicting views as to the law. He was of the opinion that the law can be ascertained only by studying the relevant passages of the Talmud itself, and not by depending solely on a book of *pesakim*. Asheri's book of *halakhot* was the practical embodiment of this basic position. Each conclusion is preceded by a synopsis of the relevant Talmudic discussion and of the differences of opinion to which the issue had given rise, and even the arrangement of the book follows the order of the tractates in the Talmud.[69]

66. According to A.H. Freimann, "Ascher Ben Yechiel, Sein Leben und Wirken" [Asher b. Jehiel, His Life and Works], *JJLG*, XII (1918), p. 302, Asheri's primary objective in writing this work was to provide the definitive commentary on the Talmud. However, it appears that Freimann was not precisely correct. Asheri's primary objective was to compose a book of *halakhot* according to his own codificatory approach, in light of the considerations discussed in our text; however, because of his particular method of treating Talmudic passages, his work also took on, to some extent, the qualities of a commentary. Freimann's reliance on *Yad Malakhi*, II, Principles of Rashi, Tosafot, and Asheri, #32, is not well founded. The statement there that "Asheri's way is to explain and Alfasi's way is to state without explanation" merely means that Alfasi quotes the original words of the Talmud without adding any explanation of his own, whereas Asheri explains his own views in addition to quoting the language of the Talmud. This is also the meaning of the sources quoted in *Yad Malakhi*, *supra* (*Bayit Ḥadash* to *Tur* OḤ 356:2 is a mistaken reference). *Bayit Ḥadash* to *Tur* YD 142:16 (*Yad Malakhi*'s reference to 142:6 is an error), s.v. U-mah shekatav ha-Ramah (end), is particularly clear on this point: "Although Alfasi also quotes the Mishnah without explanation, it is clearly Asheri's way to explain his rulings more fully."

67. *See supra* pp. 269–270, 984–986, 1226–1229.

68. *Supra* pp. 1226–1229

69. Asheri, like Alfasi, treated only those laws still applicable after the destruction of the Temple, and therefore did not write on the Orders of *Zera'im* (except for Tractate *Bera-*

Piskei ha-Rosh excels in still other respects. The extensive material it discusses before stating Asheri's legal conclusion is presented simply, clearly, and succinctly. The distinctive feature of Asheri's work is his independence of judgment. He states the law in accordance with the view to which his reasoning leads, even if the opposing view was espoused by an outstanding post-Talmudic authority, such as a *gaon,* Alfasi, Rabad, or even his own teacher, Maharam of Rothenburg.

Asheri's work was soon acknowledged as binding by many halakhic authorities; in many communities, its conclusions were frequently given greater weight than those of Maimonides' *Mishneh Torah.*[70] The influence of *Piskei ha-Rosh* on codificatory literature is still felt strongly today. Asheri's son Jacob disseminated his father's rulings and opinions throughout Jewry in his *Sefer ha-Turim;* and Joseph Caro, two centuries later, made Asheri the "third pillar" of Caro's own "house," *i.e.,* his commentary on *Sefer ha-Turim,* entitled *Bet Yosef* [House of Joseph]:

> Since I concluded that the three pillars of instruction upon which the House of Israel rests are Alfasi, Maimonides, and Asheri . . . , I resolved that when two of them agree on any point I will determine the law in accordance with their view.[71]

b. COMMENTARIES ON *PISKEI HA-ROSH*

An extensive literature of commentaries on *Piskei ha-Rosh* has developed, of which three are here noted:

(1) *Haggahot Asheri* by Israel of Krems

Israel of Krems, Austria, the author of *Haggahot Asheri* [Glosses on Asheri], was a fourteenth-century Ashkenazic halakhic authority. He was the great-grandfather of Israel Isserlein, the author of *Terumat ha-Deshen.*

---

khot), *Kodashim* (except for Tractate *Ḥullin*), or *Tohorot* (except for Tractate *Niddah*). *Piskei ha-Rosh,* Menaḥot includes *Halakhot Ketannot* [Abridged *Halakhot*], which deals with laws such as those pertaining to the Torah Scroll, ritual impurity, *ḥallah,* and *orlah,* which are covered in those Orders, yet are currently applicable.

70. *See Yad Malakhi, supra* n. 66, #36. However, various communities in Spain, Egypt, and North Africa continued to follow the rulings of Maimonides. *See supra* p. 1223 and n. 122; A. Hirschmann, *Rabbi Yiẓhak bar Sheshet* (*ha-Ribash*), pp. 38–40, 172. *See also Resp. Zikhron Yehudah* #54.

71. *Bet Yosef* to *Tur* OḤ, Introduction. *See also supra* pp. 1172, 1231. On the abridged version of *Piskei ha-Rosh* by Asheri's son Jacob, *see infra* p. 1285. For a comprehensive treatment of Asheri's life and works, *see* Freimann, *supra* n. 66 at 237ff.; *id.,* "Die Ascheriden" [The Descendants of Asheri], *JJLG,* XIII (1919), pp. 200ff.; Baer, *Spain,* pp. 316ff. (Hebrew ed., p. 185); Urbach, *Tosafot,* pp. 459–468.

The glosses in *Haggahot Asheri* set out various laws and rulings that supplement *Piskei ha-Rosh.* A substantial part of his material was taken from the Tosafist Isaac b. Samuel (Ri)[72] and from *Or Zaru'a.*[73] *Haggahot Asheri* is printed in regular editions of the Talmud as marginal notes to *Piskei ha-Rosh.*

(2) *Peri Megadim et al.* by Yom Tov Lipmann Heller

Yom Tov Lipmann Heller was a halakhic authority of Bavaria and Poland at the end of the sixteenth and the first half of the seventeenth centuries. He pioneered a distinctive method of Mishnaic commentary in his *Tosafot Yom Tov,* which has been previously discussed;[74] and he was a participant in the great debate as to the best approach to halakhic codification.[75] He was of the opinion that the proper form for a code is a book of *halakhot,* and he regarded *Piskei ha-Rosh* as a worthy exemplification of such a book in both form and content. Even *Piskei ha-Rosh,* however, he maintained, required commentary and supplementation. Textual errors had to be corrected; and sometimes, in Heller's opinion, Asheri was substantively wrong in his statement of the law.[76]

Consequently, Heller wrote a comprehensive commentary on *Piskei ha-Rosh,* divided into four parts: (1) *Peri Megadim,* printed in most editions of the Talmud, covering Tractate *Berakhot, Halakhot Ketannot* [Abridged *Halakhot*] (a compilation by Asheri), and several tractates in the Orders of *Kodashim* and *Tohorot;* (2) *Nofet Ẓufim,* not yet published, on the Order of *Mo'ed;* (3) *Ashishot,* not yet published, on the Order of *Nashim;* and (4) *Pilpula Ḥarifta,* printed in most editions of the Talmud, on the Order of *Neẓikin. Peri Megadim* and *Nofet Ẓufim* each consists of two books: *Ma'adanei Melekh,* which elucidates, explains, and corrects Asheri; and *Leḥem Ḥamudot,* which quotes various halakhic authorities and arrives at definitive statements of the law.

72. Cited in *Haggahot Asheri* by a Hebrew acronym for "Commentary of Ri Taken from the Book of Rulings of Hezekiah of Magdeburg." Hezekiah was a contemporary of Maharam of Rothenburg.

73. *See supra* n. 21.

74. *See supra* pp. 1108–1109.

75. *See infra* pp. 1403–1407.

76. *See* his Introduction to his *Sefer Ma'adanei Melekh ve-Leḥem Ḥamudot* on *Piskei ha-Rosh* (printed preceding *Piskei ha-Rosh,* Berakhot); and his Introduction to *Pilpula Ḥarifta* (printed preceding *Piskei ha-Rosh,* Bava Kamma). *See also* the further discussion, *infra* p. 1407. In some printed editions, the two parts are called *Ma'adanei Yom Tov* and *Divrei Ḥamudot; see* N.N. Rabinowitz, *Al Hadpasat ha-Talmud* [On the Printing of the Talmud], pp. 112, 130; title page of Vilna ed. of the Talmud; Friedberg, *Eked Sefarim,* s.v. Ma'adanei melekh ve-leḥem ḥamudot; Ḥida, *Shem ha-Gedolim,* Books, Letter *mem,* par. 165 ("*Ma'adanei Melekh Leḥem Ḥamudot* . . . but printed ed. B has *Ma'adanei Yom Tov ve-Divrei Ḥamudot,* because of an incident that occurred").

(3) *Korban Netanel* by Nethanel Weil

Nethanel Weil was a German halakhic authority in the first half of the eighteenth century. *Korban Netanel* was written on the Orders of *Mo'ed* and *Nashim*. It explains Asheri's comments, clarifies Asheri's text, and cites Asheri's sources in the Talmud and *midrashim*.[77] It is printed in the regular editions of the Talmud with *Piskei ha-Rosh*.

15. *SEFER HA-TASHBEẒ* BY SAMSON b. ẒADOK AND *SEFER HA-PARNAS* BY MOSES PARNAS OF ROTHENBURG

Samson b. Ẓadok and Moses Parnas, thirteenth-century German halakhic authorities, were disciples of Maharam of Rothenburg, and most of their works are devoted to recording the doctrines and practices of their teacher. Samson b. Ẓadok even recorded the practices followed by Maharam during Maharam's imprisonment. *Sefer ha-Tashbeẓ* and *Sefer ha-Parnas* were considered sufficiently authoritative to be included as part of the recognized codificatory literature by later authorities, who cite and rely on them. *Sefer ha-Tashbeẓ* consists of 590 chapters, and *Sefer ha-Parnas*, 428. Each law is stated concisely and without elaboration. The main topics include the laws of sabbath and festivals; benedictions; prayer; mourning; and—to a certain extent—marriage and the *ketubbah*, divorce, *ḥaliẓah*, levirate marriage, and various civil law topics.[78]

16. *SEFER EẒ ḤAYYIM*[79] BY JACOB b. JUDAH ḤAZZAN

Jacob b. Judah Ḥazzan,[80] of London, England, sometimes called Jacob of London, was a halakhic authority at the end of the thirteenth century. The Introduction to *Sefer Eẓ Ḥayyim*[81] reviews the chain of tradition of the Oral Law until the redaction of the Talmud and then refers to several codificatory works composed by the *geonim*, Alfasi, Maimonides, and others up to the time of Moses of Coucy,[82] of whom the author wrote:

77. *See* the author's brief, lyrical Introduction, printed preceding *Piskei ha-Rosh*, Shabbat.

78. *Sefer ha-Tashbeẓ* was printed in 1556 in Cremona, and has since been reprinted several times (most recently in Jerusalem, starting in 1951). Rabbenu Pereẓ of France added notes that are printed in the various editions of *Sefer ha-Tashbeẓ*. *Sefer ha-Parnas* was first published by M.S. Horowitz, Vilna, 1891, with notes by Horowitz and David Luria.

79. *Sefer Eẓ Ḥayyim* was first published in three volumes (1962–1967) by I. Brodie with a Preface (in vol. I), Introduction (in vol. III), and notes.

80. As to the meaning of this title and the function of a *ḥazzan*, *see Sefer Eẓ Ḥayyim*, *supra* n. 79, Introduction, vol. III, at x.

81. This Introduction is patterned after Maimonides' Introduction to the *Mishneh Torah*, which was a model generally for *Sefer Eẓ Ḥayyim*.

82. As to Moses of Coucy, *see infra* pp. 1261–1263.

> [He] brought many Jews back to the right path with the sermons that he preached, and he composed a work on the entire Torah based on the work of our great master, Maimonides. He supplied proofs for most of his statements, and he quoted the decisions of the later *geonim* in his book *Sefer ha-Darshan.*[83] Because of these proofs and geonic citations, his work was disseminated throughout most of the diaspora.

However, Moses of Coucy did not provide an exhaustive treatment of the *Halakhah*; "he omitted a number of laws mentioned by Maimonides, Isaac b. Samuel (Ri), Rabbenu Tam, Alfasi, the *Tosefta,*[84] *Halakhot Gedolot,* and Amram Gaon."[85] Jacob b. Judah therefore wrote his work to supply these omissions, and also to add the opinions of English halakhic authorities.[86]

Sefer Eẓ Ḥayyim is arranged by topic, based mainly but not inflexibly on the order of the *Mishneh Torah.*[87] It does not generally review the relevant Talmudic discussions, but simply states the law in general terms, followed sometimes by an extremely brief summary of the various opinions of *geonim* and *rishonim.* The work is thus essentially a book of *pesakim.*

Sefer Eẓ Ḥayyim is divided into two parts. The first, called *Sefer ha-Torah,* contains sixty chapters. It includes instructions in the laws of prayer, benedictions, festivals, ritual law, a considerable part of the laws directly relating to the Land of Israel (such as *orlah, ḥallah,* and *kilayim*), and the whole field of family law—marriage, the *ketubbah* and its conditions (*tena'ei ketubbah*), and levirate marriage and *ḥaliẓah.* The second part, called *Sefer ha-Mishpat,* contains forty-nine chapters that cover the entire civil and criminal law and then, at the end, the laws relating to kings, the Land of Israel, charity, and the Messiah. Jacob of London appears to be the first person to apply the term *mishpat* to the civil and criminal law of the halakhic system.[88]

83. *I.e., Sefer Miẓvot Gadol. See infra* p. 1261 n. 108.

84. The insertion of *Tosefta* here is puzzling. It may be an error and perhaps should read *Tosafot* rather than *Tosefta,* in which case the reference would be to the rulings of the Tosafists. Later in the Introduction the phrase appears again: "Alfasi, the *Darshan,* the *Tosefta,* and *Halakhot Gedolot.*" Further study seems necessary; it is strange that the editor was not troubled by this difficulty.

85. *Sefer Eẓ Ḥayyim,* Author's Introduction.

86. *Id.,* Editor's Preface, vol. I, and Editor's Introduction, vol. III.

87. *Id.,* Author's Introduction (end): "And note that I have arranged it at times following Maimonides' chapters and at times following a different arrangement." *See also Sefer Eẓ Ḥayyim,* III, p. 159, to the effect that he removed the laws of slaves from where Maimonides dealt with them (at the end of *Sefer Kinyan* [The Book of Acquisitions] before *Sefer Mishpatim* [The Book of Civil Laws]) and inserted them after *Hilkhot Melakhim* [Laws of Kings], "because they are no longer presently applicable." *See* Introduction, III, p. XII.

88. Family law, including the financial relationships between spouses, is included in *Sefer ha-Torah* and not in *Sefer ha-Mishpat. See further supra* pp. 105–108 and p. 107 n. 70.

17. *SEFER ORḤOT ḤAYYIM*[89] BY AARON b. JACOB HA-KOHEN

Aaron b. Jacob ha-Kohen of Lunel was a halakhic authority in southern France at the beginning of the fourteenth century. He was exiled from France in the Expulsion of 1306.[90] This event motivated the composition of his work, because, for lack of a fixed domicile, "when I need to know a law in order to guide conduct, or when I am asked to render true judgment [between litigants], this priest (*kohen*) is at a loss for an answer—I cannot answer 'yes' when that should be the answer, or 'no' if that is appropriate."[91] Since he could not always obtain the required books because of his wanderings, he wrote, "I collected their statements as I needed them, little by little, until I succeeded in compiling their holy words in this book to bring along with me in my wanderings. I called the book *Orḥot Ḥayyim* [The Ways of Life], for they that go in the 'ways of life' will achieve an abundance of happiness."[92]

The book is arranged by topic. The first part[93] discusses the laws of benedictions and prayer according to the sequence of a person's day, from waking in the morning until bedtime at night, and then discusses the laws relating to the sabbath and festivals. This part contains sixty-one chapters, each subdivided into paragraphs. The order of topics in this part resembles the order in *Tur Oraḥ Ḥayyim,* which is discussed later in this chapter. The second part, in the extant edition, consists of seventy-three chapters, each subdivided into paragraphs. It is also arranged by topic, but the theory of its organization is not clear. It begins with the laws of circumcision, the redemption of the first-born, and the honor due to parents. It then goes on to the laws of marriage, the *ketubbah,* prohibited sexual unions, menstruant women, divorce, levirate marriage and *ḥaliẓah, mezuzah,* enclosure of parapets, and some of the laws directly relating to the Land of Israel. Next, it deals with the laws of idolatry, forbidden wine (*yein nesekh*), forbidden foods and other ritual practices, charity, restoring lost and stolen property, evidence, pledges, the sabbatical year, overcharging, oaths and vows, judges, gossip, castration, and arrogance. It then returns to such topics as weights and measures, modes of acquisition, notice, *asmakhta,* and other

89. Part I was printed in Florence, 1750, and was reset and published by J.D. Shtitzberg and Son, Jerusalem, 1956. Part II was first published in two volumes by Moses b. Eliakim Schlesinger, Berlin, 1902, with detailed notes and an introduction; and there have since been several reprintings and facsimile editions.

90. *See* the Introduction to *Sefer Orḥot Ḥayyim,* printed at the beginning of Part I, commencing "I am the man who has known wandering . . . , and with those exiled by the Expulsion have I wandered from my home to a land of great darkness," and continuing at length.

91. *Id.*

92. *Id.*

93. Or, as the author put it in his Introduction, "the first Order (*Seder*)."

areas of civil law. One of the last topics is the laws of mourning, and the very last chapter discusses the reason "why the patriarchs wished to be buried in the Land of Israel."[94]

18. *SEFER KOL BO*

The authorship of *Sefer Kol Bo* is uncertain, but the book was written sometime at the end of the thirteenth or the beginning of the fourteenth century.[95] It is related in structure and pattern to *Sefer Orḥot Ḥayyim;* some scholars believe it to be an abridgment of *Sefer Orḥot Ḥayyim* composed by an unknown author; others are of the opinion that it is the first edition of *Sefer Orḥot Ḥayyim,* from the pen of Aaron b. Jacob ha-Kohen himself, who later expanded that book to its present form.[96]

Sefer Kol Bo contains 148 chapters, and includes the laws of benedictions and prayer, festivals, personal status, divorce and levirate marriage, civil and ritual matters, mourning, the first-born, and the Land of Israel. Here, too, the topics are arranged in an order that is difficult to understand. The last part of the book includes the *takkanot* of Rabbenu Gershom and of Rabbenu Tam, as well as the *Takkanot* of "Shum" (the enactments of Speyer, Worms, and Mainz),[97] in addition to selected responsa and halakhic rulings of various authorities.[98]

94. On Aaron ha-Kohen of Lunel and *Sefer Orḥot Ḥayyim, see* Ḥida, *Shem ha-Gedolim,* Persons, Letter *aleph,* par. 130; H. Michael, *Or ha-Ḥayyim,* pp. 143–144; and, for a detailed treatment, M. Schlesinger's Introduction, *supra* n. 89.

95. Various editions of *Sefer Kol Bo* have been published.

96. For a detailed discussion of the various opinions, *see* Schlesinger's Introduction to *Orḥot Ḥayyim, supra* n. 89 at XXIV–XXVII. Zunz, who believed that *Kol Bo* is an abridgment of *Orḥot Ḥayyim,* identified the author as Shemariah b. Simḥah but offered no persuasive proof; *see id.*

97. *See supra* pp. 783–789.

98. In addition to books of *halakhot* covering all the laws on one or more given subjects, others were composed that contain rulings on specific issues. *See, e.g., Sefer ha-Makhri'a* of Isaiah b. Mali of Trani, the Elder (known as Rid), a thirteenth-century Italian halakhic authority who wrote *Tosafot Rid,* one of the foremost commentaries on the Talmud. *Sefer ha-Makhri'a* contains ninety-two rulings on various issues in the laws of benedictions, prayer, festivals, personal status, and civil law. Isaiah the Elder's *Piskei ha-Rid* was published by Makhon ha-Talmud ha-Yisra'eli ha-Shalem, Jerusalem, 1971, together with *Piskei ha-Ri'az* by Isaiah b. Elijah of Trani (Isaiah the Elder's grandson, known as the Latter Isaiah), on the tractates of the Order of *Mo'ed* and the laws of *ẓiẓit* (ritual fringes), phylacteries, etc.

A similar type of book sets out customs and usages relating to various halakhic matters, but the coverage of the subjects is not exhaustive, *e.g., Magen Avot* by Menahem Meiri. That volume contains a thorough discussion of twenty-four different customs practiced in Meiri's home town, Perpignan, in Southern France, relating to benedictions, prayers, and dietary laws. The book was first published by I. ha-Levi Last in 1909, with an introduction and notes, and has been reprinted several times. Meiri wrote the book in defense of the customs instituted by previous generations—the ancestors (*avot,* lit. "fathers")—in Perpignan, and as a reaction to the criticism of Spanish halakhic scholars who had come there and questioned the validity of the local customs. For further details, *see* Meiri's Introduction.

B. Books Organized on the Basis of an Enumeration of the Biblical Commandments

One of the most common forms of organization of books of *halakhot* in the period under discussion was based on an enumeration of the Biblical commandments. As we have seen, Maimonides wrote *Sefer ha-Mizvot* [The Book of the Commandments], in which he listed each of the 613 commandments of the Torah. However, Maimonides' book was a preparatory exercise for his *magnum opus*, the *Mishneh Torah*, to ensure that he would not inadvertently omit any commandment relating to the subjects he treated.[99] This was the reason he briefly described each of the 248 affirmative and 365 negative commandments, sometimes indicating the Scriptural source, particularly when the Torah sets forth the commandments explicitly. Maimonides thus regarded his *Sefer ha-Mizvot* not as a codificatory work in its own right but merely as a preparation for his code, the *Mishneh Torah*. However, a substantial number of authors adopted this literary model for their own books of *halakhot*, on the assumption that this method of codification would facilitate a knowledge of the Biblical commandments and the laws connected with each of them; some of these works are classic examples of the genre.[100]

1. *SEFER YERE'IM* BY ELIEZER b. SAMUEL (RE'EM)

Re'em lived in the twelfth century in Metz, France, and was the outstanding disciple of Rabbenu Tam and the teacher of Raviah.[101] Re'em stated in the brief Introduction to *Sefer Yere'im* [The Book of the God-Fearing][102] that he came to write it as a result of

> seeing that those poor in Torah[103] wear themselves out in rounds of casuistic grappling with fine points of Talmudic discussion[104] and pay no attention to the source of the commandments that the Lord has commanded. How then shall they carry out His laws and rules?

99. *Sefer ha-Mizvot*, ed. Kafaḥ, Introduction, p. 3.

100. *See infra* for the rationales advanced by the authors for the composition of the various books organized on the basis of an enumeration of the Biblical commandments. That the assumption referred to in the text was frequently correct is attested by the great popularity of three of these books, namely *Semag*, *Semak*, and *Sefer ha-Ḥinnukh*, as to all of which *see infra*. pp. 1261–1267.

101. *See supra* pp. 1238–1239.

102. *See Sefer Yere'im* with *To'afot Re'em*, a commentary by Abraham Abba Schiff, Vilna, 1892, and republished in facsimile.

103. The printed version reads "*inyanei Torah*" ("matters of Torah"); J.N. Epstein emended it to "*aniyyei Torah*" ("those poor in Torah"), following TB Sanhedrin 24a; *see* Urbach, *Tosafot*, p. 137 n. 46.

104. *See To'afot Re'em, supra* n. 102 at n. 7.

He therefore called his book *Sefer Yere'im* "because from it they will learn to fear the Lord." The book is thus intended to be a book of *halakhot* summarizing all the laws relating to each commandment, with a view to providing the information necessary to carry out the "laws and rules." Re'em divided the book into seven "pillars" (*ammudim*), each pillar into "hooks" (*vavim*),[105] and each "hook" into paragraphs. The book contains only 464 paragraphs, because some paragraphs cover more than one commandment. Each paragraph quotes the Scriptural verse that is the source of the commandment, briefly discusses the relevant Talmudic passages, cites the explanations of Rashi, Rashbam, Rabbenu Tam, and others (including occasionally the *geonim*), and concludes with a summary statement of the law.

Each of the seven pillars represents a category of commandments. The first pillar treats the commandments relating to forbidden sexual unions, such as incest and forbidden marriages (paragraphs 1–45); the second and third pillars include all the commandments relating to forbidden foods and things from which one is not permitted to benefit. The fourth pillar discusses "prohibitions against taking money from one's fellow or holding back payment when the Torah requires payment to be made." It treats the laws of interest, theft, robbery, withholding wages, bribery, trespass, pledges and other security interests, the gratuity given to a Hebrew slave, and the financial relationship between spouses. It also includes the laws relating to *terumah* and tithes, the share of the poor in the harvest (*leket, shikhḥah,* and *pe'ah*), and charity (paragraphs 136–173). The fifth pillar treats "those prohibitions against wrongs to God and human beings that do not involve stealing or financial benefit," namely, part of the criminal law, such as murder, kidnapping, perversion of justice, and dishonesty in weights and measures, as well as such prohibitions as "You shall not act toward him [*i.e.,* your debtor] as a creditor" (Exodus 22:24) and the prohibition against oppression of an orphan or widow (paragraphs 174–278). The sixth and seventh pillars discuss prohibitions against acts that offend the Lord but cause no harm to human beings; they include the laws of blasphemy, false oaths, desecration of the sabbath and festivals, sacrificial offerings, sanctity, and ritual purity.[106]

Notwithstanding the author's aim to arrange the commandments so as to make it easy to find the law,[107] the classification and arrangement of the

105. After Exodus 26:32, describing the Tabernacle: "pillars of acacia wood . . . hooks of gold. . . ."

106. *See* the list of all the laws in the table of contents of *Sefer Yere'im.*

107. *See* the author's Introduction: "All the laws that share a certain similarity I will discuss together under one heading . . . , and I will be brief so that the reader may run through it, and those who seek the Lord will find [the law] correctly."

various commandments in each of the seven pillars make it very difficult to locate desired material in the book.

2. *SEFER MIẒVOT GADOL (SEMAG)* BY MOSES OF COUCY

Moses b. Jacob of Coucy, France, was a Tosafist who lived in the first half of the thirteenth century. His book *Sefer Miẓvot Gadol* is generally known as *Semag,* the Hebrew acronym for the title. The Introduction explains the author's motivation for his work. He traveled widely and preached in Jewish communities in various countries to encourage the observance of the commandments and the study of Torah;[108] and his experience as an itinerant preacher alerted him to the need for a book of *halakhot* organized on the basis of an enumeration of the Biblical commandments:[109]

> It happened when Heaven called and I traveled through countries to preach to the Jewish diasporas, I decided to arrange the commandments in my mind, each one as it is stated—the fundamentals, without all the details—so that I should not err in my sermons. In several places, they asked me to write a book containing the essence of each commandment according to the sources, placing all the affirmative commandments in one part and all the negative commandments in the second. Therefore, I, Moses b. Jacob, have set about composing two books; and I have learned from everyone I could, to the best of my ability, how to set forth proofs concisely, not exactly in the language of the Talmud; in many places I have changed the language and made it clearer and more concise, so that the reader may run through it. I have also divided the material into short sections to permit a pause for reflection after each one.

The first part of the book discusses the 365 negative commandments, and the second discusses the 248 affirmative commandments.[110] For each commandment, the Biblical source verse is cited, together with the rabbinical exegesis, the relevant Talmudic sources, and comments and rulings by the *geonim,* Alfasi, Rashi, Maimonides, previous Tosafists, and other halakhic authorities; and finally, the author's conclusions are set forth. In the course of the presentation, the author interweaves aggadic and ethical material.

Moses of Coucy emphasized in his Introduction that he disagreed with

108. He was also known as Rabbi Moses the Preacher, and therefore the book is also called *Sefer ha-Darshan* [The Book of the Preacher]. *See supra* pp. 1255–1256 for Jacob of London's statement about him in the Introduction to *Sefer Eẓ Ḥayyim. See also* I.D. Gilat, "Shetei Bakkashot le-R. Moshe mi-Kuẓi" [Two Requests of R. Moses of Coucy], *Tarbiẓ,* XXVIII (1959), pp. 54–58.

109. *See Semag,* Introduction.

110. In both *Sefer ha-Miẓvot* and the listing of the commandments at the beginning of the *Mishneh Torah,* Maimonides first listed the affirmative and then the negative commandments.

Maimonides' method of categorical statement of the law without attribution of authority or citation of sources. However, he had great admiration for Maimonides' work; he quoted from it copiously—occasionally quoting it *verbatim* without giving credit to the source. He frequently accepted Maimonides' legal conclusions, and, in general, even arranged the commandments not according to their order in the Torah but in the order in which they appear in the *Mishneh Torah.* In one respect, however, Moses of Coucy did change the order of the commandments from that in the *Mishneh Torah.* The laws that Maimonides dealt with in the last four books of the *Mishneh Torah—Sefer Nezikin, Sefer Kinyan, Sefer Mishpatim,* and *Sefer Shofetim*—are put before those which, in the *Mishneh Torah,* are dealt with earlier, in *Sefer Hafla'ah, Sefer Zera'im, Sefer Avodah, Sefer Korbanot,* and *Sefer Tohorah.*[111]

Following the general order of the *Mishneh Torah*—rather than the sequence in which the commandments are scattered throughout the Torah—facilitates finding the law, since the rules are subsumed within the framework of a topical classification. At the beginning of each part of the work, there is also a table of contents called *remazim* ("hints"), listing the commandments discussed in that part. This table of contents also helps to make *Sefer Miẓvot Gadol* a convenient book for study.

Notwithstanding Moses of Coucy's admiration for Maimonides and his following of Maimonides' general pattern in the organization of *Semag,* he generally held with the leading French and German authorities such as Rashi, Rabbenu Tam, and Ri when they disagreed with Maimonides either as to the law or the enumeration of the commandments.[112]

111. The order of the commandments in *Semag* is as follows: First, the commandments that relate primarily to *Sefer ha-Madda* [The Book of Knowledge] and *Sefer Zemanim* [The Book of Seasons] of Maimonides; next, the commandments dealt with in *Sefer Nashim* [The Book of Women], including the laws of forbidden sexual unions; then dietary prohibitions and the rules regarding the preparation of kosher food (in the positive commandments section); then civil law, in a section that includes, by and large, the laws contained in Maimonides' *Sefer Nezikin* [The Book of Damages], *Sefer Kinyan* [The Book of Acquisitions], *Sefer Mishpatim* [The Book of Civil Laws], and *Sefer Shofetim* [The Book of Judges]; then matters concerning oaths and vows, such as by a nazirite. Only after all the foregoing are laws relating to the Temple set forth, apparently relegated to this position because they no longer had any practical application. At the end of the positive commandments, the book deviates from Maimonides' order and discusses five commandments that are not Biblical but rabbinic.

112. *See Semag,* Introduction:

> And that great man arose, our master, Moses b. Maimon, who was from Cordoba and moved to the land of the Ishmaelites [*i.e.,* Egypt] and composed a work on the entire Torah, a fine and valuable work, and he enlightened Israel.
>
> He wondrously mastered all branches of learning; no one like him has been known in recent generations, and many have been strengthened in Torah by his books, which have become popular in both Christian and Moslem countries. However, this great scholar cited no proofs in his books, and therefore anyone who uses

Semag had a genesis that was unique. Moses of Coucy was one of the four rabbis summoned in 1240 to a religious disputation with the apostate Nicholas Donin, to answer Donin's charges against the Talmud. On March 3, 1240, Pope Gregory IX ordered all copies of the Talmud confiscated; in 1242,[113] the copies were ordered burned, and Talmudic study was prohibited. Apparently, the need that then arose for a comprehensive halakhic work summarizing the main Talmudic and post-Talmudic sources contributed in large measure to the rapid popularity and widespread distribution of *Semag.*[114] Its influence on subsequent codification of the *Halakhah* is manifested by the fact that Joseph Caro accepted it as one of the five authorities on which he drew when he could not determine the law from his "three pillars of instruction."[115]

3. *SEFER MIẒVOT KATAN (SEMAK)* BY ISAAC OF CORBEIL

Isaac b. Joseph lived in the thirteenth century in Corbeil, France. His book *Sefer Miẓvot Katan,* known as *Semak,* the acronym of its title, and also called *Sefer Ammudei Golah* and *Sefer Miẓvot Kaẓar,* was written shortly after Moses of Coucy's *Semag.* Like *Semag,* it is arranged according to the order of the Biblical commandments. It draws heavily on Moses of Coucy's work, as indicated by Isaac of Corbeil himself:

> Also, any person who does not understand it should study the book of the commandments that Rabbi Moses of Coucy wrote. If he still does not understand, he should ask someone more learned than himself.[116]

> his books as the basis for issuing rulings and looks to them for a prooftext will find that he has a riddle without an answer if he has forgotten or has never known the source. Furthermore, many of the greatest pillars and personages of the Torah disagree with his interpretations and rulings, such as Rabbenu Solomon b. Isaac [Rashi], Rabbenu Jacob b. Meir [Rabbenu Tam], and Rabbenu Isaac b. Samuel [Ri], whom all the recent halakhic authorities regard as most venerable. They disagree with him even on the enumeration of the commandments.

See also Resp. Rema #67 for the view of Maharshal that *Semag* disagreed with Maimonides only when Maimonides held contrary to the Tosafists, and Rema's conclusion that, in the matter there under discussion, *Semag* disagreed with Maimonides. *See also supra* pp. 1226.

113. As to the date of the edict that the Talmud be burned, *see* Urbach, *Tosafot,* pp. 375–376. *See also supra* p. 1247 n. 46.

114. Many mss. of *Semag* have survived. The leading halakhic authorities of the fifteenth and sixteenth centuries accepted it as an authoritative work and composed glosses and commentaries on it. Joshua Boaz, in his reference work *Ein Mishpat* on TB, included references to *Semag* along with references to the *Mishneh Torah* and *Sefer ha-Turim.*

115. *See infra* pp. 1317–1319.

116. Letter of Isaac of Corbeil, quoted at the beginning of his book. P. Buchholz, "Historischer Überblick über die Mannigfachen Codificationen des Halachastoffes, von ihren Ersten Anfängen bis zu ihrem Letzten Abschlusse" [A Historical Overview of the Manifold

In simple language, without discussion, the book very briefly sets out the Talmudic law and a few rabbinic opinions. It follows the example of Moses of Coucy by spicing the text with aggadic and ethical material.

Semak is divided into seven parts, corresponding to the days of the week,[117] for the reason explained by the author as follows:[118]

> I have written the commandments to which we are presently subject in seven pillars,[119] corresponding to the seven days of the week, and I ask every man to read one pillar every day, so that it may be well with him.

The method by which the laws are classified and organized makes it very difficult to find any particular law, or even to locate the treatment of a general subject area. The division of the material into seven sections is based not on any criterion relating to subject matter but on totally different considerations. For example, the laws of marriage are set forth in the fourth section along with other totally unrelated laws because, as the author put it,[120] "As our Rabbis taught: A virgin should be wed on Wednesday [*i.e.*, the fourth day of the week]."[121] The fifth section contains the dietary laws and the laws of adjudication and judicial procedure—the latter because, according to Ezra's enactment,[122] "courts shall sit on Thursdays."[123] Similarly, Friday's section includes monetary (*i.e.*, civil) law, because "the sixth commandment [of the Decalogue] is 'You shall not murder,' and most murders are motivated by money,[124] as it is written, 'Let us set an ambush to shed

---

Codifications of the Corpus of the *Halakhah,* from Their First Beginnings to Their Final Conclusion], *MGWJ,* XIII (1864), p. 247 n. 5, contains a bizarre error. Buchholz claimed that Isaac of Corbeil's letter stated that he wrote his book because even the rabbis had an inadequate knowledge of the *Halakhah* ("dass selbst die Rabbinen nicht genau die uns obliegenden Gesetze kennen"). He reached this conclusion on the basis of Isaac's statement that "because, through [our] sins, the Torah is being forgotten and I am apprehensive that *rabbis* (*rabbanim*) do not have a thorough knowledge of the explanation of the commandments to which we are subject, I have written about these commandments." However, Buchholz was led into error by a copyist's or a printer's mistake. The correct reading is "that *many* (*rabbim*) do not have a thorough knowledge." The editions of Liady (1795), Kapust (1810), and Satu-mare (1935) all have the reading "*rabbim,*" which is clearly correct.

117. The division of *Sefer Yere'im* by Eliezer of Metz into seven "pillars" (*see supra* pp. 1259–1261) apparently influenced the author of *Semak.*

118. Letter of Isaac of Corbeil, *supra* n. 116.

119. Hence the book's name, *Ammudei Golah Hem Shiv'ah Ammudei Olam* [The Pillars of the Diaspora That Are the Seven Pillars of the World]. *See also* the author's statement at the end of his letter, discussed *supra* n. 116.

120. *See* the table of contents at the beginning of the book.

121. M Ketubbot 1:1.

122. TB Bava Kamma 82a.

123. *See* the table of contents at the beginning of the book.

124. *See id.*

blood, let us lie in wait for the innocent,'[125] and very closely thereafter it is written, 'we shall fill our homes with loot.'"[126] That is to say, civil law was treated in the sixth section because the sixth of the Ten Commandments is "You shall not murder," and generally it is disputes over money matters that lead to killing, as is taught by the proximity between the two verses quoted from the Book of Proverbs. Clearly, these "criteria" have no intrinsic significance and are merely pegs to ensure that every law is included somewhere in the seven parts of the work.

Semak is not a typical book of *halakhot.* The author intended it for popular usage by those not well versed in the *Halakhah;* therefore he warned that "no rulings should be based on it," except by persons who are able to clarify the issue from the Talmud itself. Thus, the author saw it as a kind of popular text from which any Jew could come to know the commandments and how to perform them. However, as it ultimately turned out, the book's simple language and easy presentation caused it to be accounted by later halakhic authorities as a book of *pesakim,* and some of the leading authorities composed glosses to it and relied on its rulings.[127]

4. *SEFER HA-ḤINNUKH*

The author of *Sefer ha-Ḥinnukh* (whose identity is not clear and has been much debated by scholars)[128] lived in the thirteenth century in Spain. As a basis for his definitive statements of the law, he selected the rulings of Alfasi, Maimonides, and Naḥmanides:

> Most of the book has been culled from the works of those pillars of the world whose fame for excellence and wisdom is known to all, namely, Rabbi Isaac Alfasi and Rabbi Moses b. Maimon [Maimonides], may they be remembered for good (who are accorded primacy in glory and greatness in the present work) and, to complete the threefold cord in wisdom, understanding, and knowledge, Rabbi Moses b. Naḥman [Naḥmanides], of blessed memory.[129]

The book also cites opinions of Rashi, Rabad, the Tosafists, and other *rishonim.*[130] The author pointed out that his work was meant for young

125. Proverbs 1:11.

126. Proverbs 1:13.

127. *Semak* also achieved widespread distribution. *See* Urbach, *Tosafot,* pp. 447–453.

128. *See, e.g., Sefer ha-Ḥinnukh,* ed. Chavel, 5th ed., 1962, Introduction, pp. 5ff., and Appendix, pp. 797ff.; S.H. Kook, *Iyyunim u-Meḥkarim,* II, pp. 316–320. For the effect of the identity of an author on the weight to be accorded his book in subsequent decisions, *see Sedei Ḥemed,* Rules of Decision, ch. 15, par. 36 (vol. VI, p. 108b) and *infra* n. 133.

129. *See* the author's letter at the beginning of the book. His language is reminiscent of Joseph Caro's reference to the "three pillars" (*infra* p. 1317), but Caro's third pillar was Asheri, whereas for *Sefer ha-Ḥinnukh,* whose author was a contemporary of Asheri, it was Naḥmanides.

130. *See* Chavel, *supra* n. 128, Introduction at 12–16 and nn., *ad loc.*

people, so that they may know the *Halakhah* and study it[131]—a sentiment we have seen expressed also with regard to other codificatory works.[132] However, the work must have also been intended to provide a brief summary of the laws for people of all ages and to assist in learning and determining the law—which, of course, are the objectives of every codifier.[133]

Sefer ha-Ḥinnukh lists the commandments according to the sequence of the weekly Torah readings. For each Torah reading, it first lists the affirmative and then the negative commandments. The treatment is brief, the language simple and readily understandable, and the Hebrew style clear and lucid. The discussion of each commandment is divided into four sections: (1) the basis of the commandment—its source in the Torah and its explanation in the Talmud; (2) the roots of the commandment—its reasons and rationale, in which the author engagingly expounds the conceptual and philosophical underpinnings of the commandment; (3) the laws relating to the commandment—a brief statement of the main rules connected with the commandment; and (4) the applicability of the commandment—to whom, when, and where the commandment applies.

The felicitous style and convenient form of *Sefer ha-Ḥinnukh* have made it a very popular work; it has been regularly published in many editions, both in manuscript and printed form, and it has been the subject of

131. The author stated in his letter, *supra* n. 129:

> Perhaps because of it [the book], the youths will become more conscious of them [the commandments], pay attention to them on sabbaths and festivals, and turn from foolish behavior in the city streets to the brightness of the Light of Life (*Or ha-Ḥayyim*). Youngsters will ask each other, "How many commandments does this sabbath have?" and the world will thus become full of knowledge and benevolent purpose because the correct explanation of each will be readily available, and they will be able to find easily what they seek by consulting the signs [*i.e.*, table of contents]. The holy seed will be blessed of God, they and their children and all they possess, in all their habitations. I too will be included with them in the blessing.

This may well be the reason that the book was named *Sefer ha-Ḥinnukh* [The Book of Education], after the verse, "Train (*ḥanokh*) a lad in the way he ought to go; he will not swerve from it even in old age" (Proverbs 22:6). In his text, the author frequently turns to the reader in terms such as: "And now, my son" (Commandment #420) and "Please remember, my son" (#606). *See also* Chavel, *supra* n. 128, Introduction at 7.

132. *See supra* pp. 1153, 1185 and *infra* pp. 1270, 1321–1322, 1372. This approach to codification exists also in other legal systems; *see supra* p. 1141.

133. *See, e.g.,* Commandment #329 for a detailed discussion of commercial law; *see also* Chavel, *supra* n. 128, Introduction at 7. The book was accepted as an authoritative work on a par with other *rishonim,* and many halakhic authorities composed glosses and commentaries on it; *see infra* n. 134. However, it is possible that the attribution of the book to Aaron ha-Levi, a famous contemporary of Rashba, contributed to its recognition as an authoritative work; *see supra* n. 128.

many glosses and commentaries.[134] However, it is not really a book of *halakhot* in the pure sense; in a book of *halakhot*, the author states the law as he derives it on the basis of his own analysis of the halakhic sources, whereas *Sefer ha-Ḥinnukh*, as pointed out in the statement quoted above, relies primarily on prior authorities for its legal conclusions.

C. Books Organized According to Idiosyncratic Criteria

1. *SEFER HA-ITTUR* BY ISAAC OF MARSEILLES

Isaac b. Abba Mari of Marseilles lived in the twelfth century in southern France. He was an older contemporary of Maimonides, and it is very doubtful that he ever saw the *Mishneh Torah*.

Sefer ha-Ittur, also known as *Ittur Soferim*,[135] is arranged in a unique way described in its Introduction. The book contains the "six things that halakhic scholars and their disciples should be familiar with," as specified in the Talmud:[136] writing, ritual slaughter, circumcision, phylacteries, marriage benedictions (*i.e.*, nonmonetary laws of marriage), and *ẓiẓit* (fringes). Following Rabbenu Tam's explanation, the author takes "writing" to mean the laws of written legal instruments (*shetarot*),[137] and he devotes a section (which he calls a *sha'ar*, "gate") to the subject of legal documents in civil law.

This "gate" is subdivided into two parts. The first is a kind of introduction which consists of ten chapters and discusses the laws of written instruments generally. The first chapter discusses the dating of legal instruments; the second, direct modes of acquisition; the third, indirect acquisition (*kin-*

134. *E.g.*, the glosses of Judah Rosanes, the author of *Mishneh la-Melekh*, and those of Isaiah Berlin-Pick, among others. For details as to these glosses, as well as for mss. and printed editions, *see* Chavel, *supra* n. 128, Introduction at 18–22, and pp. 741ff. The best known of the commentaries on *Sefer ha-Ḥinnukh* is *Minḥat Ḥinnukh*, a pilpulistic work by Joseph Babad, 1st ed., Lvov (Lemberg), 1869, with many editions since.

135. This name appears in the title the author gave to his Introduction to Part I and in his Introduction to the section entitled "The Ten Commandments." *See also* the end of the book (p. 77c/d) and Ḥida, *Shem ha-Gedolim*, Books, Letter *ayin*, par. 32. *Sefer ha-Ittur* has been infrequently printed, and the text is replete with errors. The edition now generally used is that of Meir Jonah, who reprinted the book in its entirety, including the "Ten Commandments" section, and added glosses, source references, and citations to halakhic authorities who refer to and discuss *Sefer ha-Ittur*. The glosses contain some commentary and present a great deal of information very succinctly. The book was printed serially: Vilna, 1874; Warsaw, 1883, 1885.

136. *See* TB Ḥullin 9a.

137. *See* the author's Introduction to *Sefer ha-Ittur*: "'Writing' was interpreted by Rabbenu Tam as meaning 'written legal instruments'; in accordance with this, I have put in order the various written legal instruments and the respective laws relating to them."

yan agav), etc. The second part of the "gate" treats specific types of instruments, discussing each type and its relevant laws under a special mnemonic heading:

> I have provided letter signs for them so that the reader will quickly find [lit. "run through"] the subjects: *TSKP BGZA HKhMH* [*TiShKoPh Be-GeZA ḤoKhMaH,* a Hebrew mnemonic meaning "Look into the Source (or Trunk) of Wisdom"], and through them you will find all the [laws of] written legal instruments: T = *Tena'ei Mamon* (monetary conditions) . . . [and] *Temurah* (barter and exchanges); S = *Shover* (voucher or receipt), *Shittuf* (partnership), *Sekhirut* (leasing and renting), and *Shuma* (court appraisals and judicial sales); K = *Kiyyum* (validation of documents) . . . , *Kabbalat Edim* (acceptance of testimony), and *Kabbelanut* (a type of suretyship). . . . [138]

The subjects continue in the same vein to the end of the entire mnemonic.

The author, although purporting to be addressing only "halakhic scholars and their disciples," nevertheless felt it necessary to find a criterion for organizing and explicating his material that would enable the reader to "quickly find the subjects." According to the organization adopted, the financial aspects of marriage are treated in the section on "writing," under letter signs corresponding to the names of the various written instruments, *e.g.*, conditions of the *ketubbah* (*tena'ei ketubbah*), or the various forms of *ketubbah,* while the ceremonial and ritual aspects of marriage are discussed under the topic "marriage benedictions." Such fragmentation of subject matter occurs even within the section on "writing" itself: In "S," under the heading "*Sekhirut,*" the validity of leases is discussed, but the liability of the lessee for damage to the leased property is discussed in "P," under *Pikkadon* (deposit, pledge), together with the liability of other types of bailees. A law that fits under two subject headings is generally dealt with under each heading, or reference is made under one heading to the other.[139] In addition to the six main headings mentioned above, there is another section, called "The Ten Commandments,"[140] which discusses the festivals.

138. Author's Introduction to *Sefer ha-Ittur.*

139. *See, e.g.,* the discussion concerning who is required to search for *ḥamez̤* (leaven) in a house as to which a lease takes effect on the fourteenth of Nisan (the eve of Passover). This matter is considered under letter "S," in connection with the laws of leasing (*sekhirut*) (ed. Meir Jonah, p. 50b, #54) and in the laws of *ḥamez̤ u-maz̤z̤ah* (leaven and matzoh) in the "Ten Commandments" section (p. 121b, #143). As to this section, *see infra* n. 140 and accompanying text.

140. The title does not refer to the Decalogue but to "those ten commandments that are clarified and explained in it [the book], namely, *Sukkah, Lulav, Hallel, Shofar, Bi'ur Ḥamez̤, Maz̤z̤ah* and *Maror, Yom ha-Kippurim, Megillah, Hanukkah,* and Festivals." Author's Introduction to "The Ten Commandments."

Sefer ha-Ittur uses as its sources the Babylonian and Jerusalem Talmuds, the *Tosefta*, geonic responsa (it is the only extant source for certain responsa),[141] Rabbenu Hananel, Alfasi,[142] Rashi, Rashbam, Rabbenu Tam, and other *rishonim*. It merges the traditions of Babylonia with those of the Land of Israel, and frequently cites laws derived from the Jerusalem Talmud. Similarly, it integrates, apparently for the first time, the teachings of Spanish authorities with the responsa and rulings of the authorities of northern France.

Sefer ha-Ittur is a classic book of *halakhot*; it cites the sources, discusses them briefly, and arrives at conclusions that are frequently independent and original. It is quoted by many of the leading *rishonim* and also by *Sefer ha-Turim* and *Bet Yosef*; and the authorities subsequent to Caro also quote it extensively. Notwithstanding the author's avowed aim in organizing and classifying his subject matter, the unique arrangement of the rules of civil law, as well as the difficult Hebrew style and the many errors that have crept into the text, make the work difficult to use, whether for study or practical guidance.[143]

2. *SEFER MEISHARIM* AND *TOLEDOT ADAM VE-ḤAVVAH* BY RABBENU JEROHAM b. MESHULLAM

Rabbenu Jeroham lived in Provence in the fourteenth century. In 1306, when the Jews were expelled from France, he moved to Spain, where he became a disciple of Asheri.

His books *Sefer Meisharim* [The Book of Equity] and *Toledot Adam ve-Ḥavvah* [The Chronicle of Adam and Eve] together constitute a book of *halakhot* encompassing all the laws applicable after the destruction of the Temple. Rabbenu Jeroham first wrote *Sefer Meisharim*, the great bulk of which is devoted to civil law, including the civil aspects of family law (such as support and maintenance and the *ketubbah*) as well as the laws of interest

141. *See* S. Assaf, "Mafte'aḥ li-She'elot u-Teshuvot ha-Geonim ha-Muva'ot be-Sefer ha-Ittur" [An Index of the Geonic Responsa Cited in *Sefer ha-Ittur*], *Ha-Ẓofeh le-Ḥokhmat Yisra'el*, VI (1922).

142. *Sefer ha-Ittur* regularly sets forth Alfasi's opinions, expressed in Alfasi's own style, but generally condensed. The author also wrote a brief commentary on Alfasi, called *Me'ah She'arim*, which is printed in the Vilna edition of TB with Alfasi on tractates in the Orders of *Nashim* and *Nezikin*.

143. Occasionally, the book treats subjects in alphabetical order, which makes for greater ease of use. *See, e.g.*, the laws of ritual slaughter in Book II, Gate 2, regarding the various blemishes that cause an animal to be unfit for slaughter (ed. Meir Jonah, pp. 29d *et seq.*). *See also* Tchernowitz, *Toledot ha-Posekim*, II, p. 162. For the various commentaries on *Sefer ha-Ittur* and the errors in the text, *see* Ḥida, *Shem ha-Gedolim*, Books, Letter *ayin*, par. 32, and *supra* n. 135. Although Meir Jonah in his glosses suggests various emendations, there are still a great many passages requiring critical examination and correction.

and usury.[144] Thereafter, he wrote *Toledot Adam ve-Ḥavvah,*[145] in which the material is arranged according to an original and interesting principle that is hinted at in the title.[146] This book contains all the "religious" laws, including that part of family law not involving the financial relationship between spouses; thus, it includes the laws of betrothal, marriage, and divorce. The contents are treated in the chronological order of occurrence in a person's life, from birth to death. The first part, called *Adam,* deals with such things as birth, circumcision, the study of Torah, benedictions, festivals, and the like. The second part, called *Ḥavvah* (Eve), continues with all those laws pertaining to a person's conduct starting with marriage, such as the laws of marriage and divorce, levirate marriage, and forbidden sexual unions; it concludes with the laws of burial, mourning, and similar matters.

Rabbenu Jeroham gave careful consideration to the arrangement and classification of the material in these works. He discussed at length the importance of arrangement and classification as a means of facilitating the finding of legal rules, and he noted the great difficulty involved in finding the laws on any particular subject, scattered as they are throughout the vast Talmudic literature.[147] He reviewed the previous books of *halakhot,* evaluated their strengths and weaknesses, and criticized various aspects of their codificatory methods. He explained the purpose of his work and the methodology that he arrived at as a result of his study of earlier codificatory works:

> Therefore, in order to make things easier for students and others, I decided to arrange each subject separately with all the laws pertaining to it, and to indicate each place in the Talmud where it can be found, so that the student can examine it there if he so desires. . . . If there is a difference of opinion among the codifiers, I will mention it to the extent I can, and in most instances I will give the names of the codifiers involved . . . , but for the sake of brevity I will not recite any of their proofs or arguments and counterargu-

144. Similarly, in Maimonides' *Mishneh Torah* the laws of interest and usury appear in *Hilkhot Malveh ve-Loveh* [Laws of Creditor and Debtor]; *see supra* p. 1201. In *Sefer ha-Turim* and the *Shulḥan Arukh,* however, they are in YD and not ḤM. *See infra* p. 1289 and n. 206.

145. *See* the beginning of the Introduction to *Toledot Adam ve-Ḥavvah:* " . . . that I wrote in my previous book, which I called *Sefer Meisharim,* where I revealed my motives for writing it."

146. *See* the Introduction to *Toledot Adam ve-Ḥavvah:* "I will explain at the very outset, so that the reader may quickly find what he seeks. Know, dear reader, that I have divided it into two parts: part one, 'Adam,' and the other, 'Eve' [Ḥavvah]. The part entitled 'Adam' covers from birth to marriage, and the part entitled 'Eve' covers from marriage to death. Therefore, I called the book *Toledot Adam ve-Ḥavvah.*"

147. Introduction to *Sefer Meisharim; see also* the Introduction to *Toledot Adam ve-Ḥavvah.*

> ments . . . , except that if I find a disagreement among the codifiers where my humble opinion favors one particular view that I can support with proof, I will say that the view I favor is the more persuasive, even though I may not give my proofs for it, just as I have not recited their proofs.

Indeed, Rabbenu Jeroham adopted a very detailed and well-designed arrangement of his subject matter. Each main subject is discussed in a separate subdivision, which is called a *nativ* ("path"). *Sefer Meisharim* contains thirty-two such "paths";[148] *Adam*, twenty-one; and *Ḥavvah*, seven. Each "path" is divided into sections, each of which is further divided into paragraphs. Occasionally, a subject is treated in two different places—once in detail and once by way of cross-reference to the detailed treatment. Rabbenu Jeroham explained:

> If one is looking for a particular law that could properly be treated in either of two "paths" and examines only one "path," he might not find it because it will be treated in the other "path," which he did not examine. Therefore, I have written about it in both of them so that he will find it in whichever he examines.[149]

In addition, Rabbenu Jeroham's Introduction explains how his books are organized and shows how to find the points of law for which one is looking. There is also a detailed index for each "path," and every "path" and section has its own concise table of contents.

The Introduction to *Sefer Meisharim* summarizes the nature of the organization of the book, its helpfulness in finding the law, and the reason for the book's title:

> [I chose this method of organization] because it is straightforward [*yashar*, the root word of *meisharim*]. It enables any person to find every law he seeks, whether he is a great scholar, a beginner, or an intermediate student; whether he wants to accept the law as written in my book or to see its source in the Talmud; whether he wishes to examine all the places in the Talmud where it is mentioned, or to review the differences of opinion among the codifiers, or to see one of the fine points of the Tosafists or any of the other codifiers or commentators with regard to a particular law. Therefore, I called it *Sefer Meisharim* . . . according to the verse . . . "It was You who established equity (*meisharim*), You who worked righteous judgment in Jacob."[150]

148. Rabbenu Jeroham's books are therefore sometimes called *Netivot* [Paths].

149. Introduction to *Sefer Meisharim;* also in the Introduction to *Toledot Adam ve-Ḥavvah.*

150. Psalms 99:4.

Rabbenu Jeroham's organization does facilitate finding the material in *Sefer Meisharim,* and conveniently arranges the topical treatment of the subject matter. For example, all the legal material in Maimonides' *Hilkhot Mekhirah* [Laws of Sales] is divided into more clearly and specifically defined units: Path 9 treats the laws of commercial negotiations, overcharging, and mistake; Path 10 treats the acquisition of personalty; Path 11 treats the acquisition of real property, and so on.[151] However, the organization of *Toledot Adam ve-Ḥavvah* according to the order of events in a person's life is awkward and makes the laws difficult to find. Furthermore, one occasionally finds different and unrelated subjects in the same "path" or section.

As useful and practical books of *halakhot,* both *Sefer Meisharim* and *Toledot Adam ve-Ḥavvah* were displaced by *Sefer ha-Turim,* written by Rabbenu Jeroham's contemporary Jacob b. Asher, which is discussed later in this chapter. Moreover, Joseph Caro, some two centuries later, criticized what he viewed as Rabbenu Jeroham's failure to fully achieve one of his main objectives, namely, to provide adequate source references for each law.[152] However, Rabbenu Jeroham's opinions were accepted by both Caro and Moses Isserles (Rema) as one of the important sources for determining the law;[153] and, as a consequence, his opinions exerted influence on later authorities.[154] Various glosses and commentaries were composed on both books, but most have not survived. *Netivot Mishpat* by Ḥayyim Algazi is extant but covers only part of *Sefer Meisharim.*[155]

151. *See* the Introduction to *Sefer Meisharim.* These and succeeding "paths" also contain subject matter which in Maimonides' *Mishneh Torah* is included in other sections. On the other hand, all of the law of torts—damages caused by property (such as by an ox), damage caused by a person (such as assault and battery, theft, robbery, defamation), and damage caused by neighbors—is included in one "path" (#31), whereas in the *Mishneh Torah* the same subject matter is divided into four or five separate sections. Rabbenu Jeroham apparently believed that including all these laws in a single "path" would make it easier to find whatever law one was looking for. Similarly, the laws of interest and usury—including those relating to *iska* (*i.e.,* casting a transaction in the form of a partnership to overcome the prohibition against interest)—are all in one "path" (#8), whereas Maimonides divided them between *Hilkhot Malveh ve-Loveh* [Laws of Creditor and Debtor] and *Hilkhot Sheluḥin ve-Shutafin* [Laws of Agency and Partnership].

152. *See* Caro's Introduction to his *Bet Yosef* to *Tur* OḤ.

153. *See id.* Rabbenu Jeroham is also frequently cited by Rema in his glosses to the *Shulḥan Arukh.*

154. *See Yad Malakhi,* II, Kelalei She'ar ha'Meḥabrim ve-ha-Meforeshim [Principles of the Other Authors and Commentators], #19 ("Rabbenu Jeroham should be relied upon more so than Ribash") and sources cited there; Ḥida, *Shem ha-Gedolim,* Persons, Letter *yod,* par. 382.

155. *Netivot Mishpat* is a very detailed commentary on *Sefer Meisharim,* from Path 1 to Path 27 and, to a minor extent, on Path 31. As to glosses and commentaries on Rabbenu Jeroham's work, *see* Ḥida, *supra* nn. 143, 154. For biography and bibliography of Rabbenu Jeroham, *see* Freimann, *supra* n. 66 at 283–285.

D. The Codificatory Methodology of Solomon b. Abraham Adret (Rashba)

1. *TORAT HA-BAYIT HA-AROKH, TORAT HA-BAYIT HA-KAẒER,* AND OTHER CODIFICATORY WORKS BY RASHBA

It would be remiss to conclude this survey of codification from Maimonides to the *Turim* without consideration of the codificatory methodology of Rashba. Rashba was an outstanding halakhic authority and the recognized leader of Spanish Jewry in the second half of the thirteenth and the beginning of the fourteenth centuries. The form of Rashba's codes was different from that of all other books of *halakhot* and was the precursor of what was destined to become, some two centuries later, the accepted methodology of halakhic codification. Rashba's code, *Torat ha-Bayit* [The Law of the House], is, in fact, two books: *Torat ha-Bayit ha-Arokh* [The Long *Torat ha-Bayit*] and *Torat ha-Bayit ha-Kaẓer* [The Short *Torat ha-Bayit*]. *Torat ha-Bayit ha-Arokh* discusses in detail the relevant Talmudic and post-Talmudic sources, whereas *Torat ha-Bayit ha-Kaẓer* states, without citation of source or attribution of authority, the bare legal conclusion that follows from the discussion in *Torat ha-Bayit ha-Arokh.*

The two volumes treat a part of what is generally classified as "religious" law that includes ritual slaughter, animals unfit for food (*terefot*), salting of meat, and forbidden mixtures. *Torat ha-Bayit* is divided into seven "houses," each of which is further subdivided into "gates." Rashba prefaced his work with a table of contents that contains a concise précis of the subjects treated in each "house" and "gate." He called the table of contents *Mevo ha-She'arim* [The Entranceway to the Gates]. He explained the objective of his elaborate organization:

> I have divided this work into seven houses and I will divide each house into gates, in order to make the reader's task easier so that he should feel at home in the Law of the House. . . . Therefore, I called this work *Torat ha-Bayit.*[156]

In his Introduction to *Torat ha-Bayit,* Rashba described his motives for undertaking this work, and further explained his objectives and his methodology. He pointed out that "there are people who desire to apply themselves diligently to their studies and seek [knowledge] from God's book"; there are also many people who, because of the demands made on their time by the need to earn a livelihood, "will not be able to achieve [knowledge] in the little time [available] . . . from the books of the *Gemara* and the *rishonim.*"

156. Rashba, *Torat ha-Bayit,* Introduction.

As a result:

> Some of them are eager that a gate be opened for them [to know] how to fulfill their obligations, that a table should be set[157] before them on matters of religious law (*issur ve-hetter*), and that they should be informed along which way the light of those laws shines in order to fulfill their obligations in two ways, namely, that which is desired and that which is required—study and practical application. [They desire] that there should be written, in brief as well as at length, the way in which the commandments should be performed.

Rashba undertook to compose such a work along both lines—the long and the short:

> And so I have entered into this task, . . . and I will, with the help of God, set forth the explanations that show how each point was developed, so that the interested reader will discover the spring from which the waters flow—and his waters will be pure—whether from the *Gemara* or from the *rishonim.* Afterward, I will write brief statements of the *Halakhah* in matters as to which we are possessed of a tradition [alternative reading: "as though the matters were transmitted to us by tradition"]. Thus, the reader will fulfill his obligation to study by diligently applying himself to the examination and study of the law, and will fulfill his obligation to perform [the commandments] on the basis of the short statements [of the law]. I have waited for the Lord and hoped for Him so that my work should be a firm house and restore the souls of the soulful who sit before the Lord.

Rashba's work was meant for all, both for students who desired to apply themselves to their studies and for those whose only desire was to know how to observe the laws and who were satisfied with a summary statement of the legal rules. He therefore composed two books; one book in the style of the Talmud, *i.e.,* discussion building on the *Gemara* and the *rishonim,* and the other in the style of "brief statements of the *Halakhah*" for practical application. Rashba's methodology marked a new and original method of halakhic codification. One part of his opus, *Torat ha-Bayit ha-Arokh,* discusses every halakhic subject fully and systematically, reviewing the Talmudic sources, as well as the relevant opinions of the *geonim* and the *rishonim.* On the basis of these discussions, Rashba drew his conclusions. This part of the work, therefore, is a typical book of *halakhot.* The second part, *Torat ha-Bayit ha-Kaẓer,* presents without attribution of source or citation of authority the conclusions that emerge from the discussions in the first part

157. It is interesting that Rashba used the same figure of speech, "setting a table," that Caro used for his book of *pesakim,* the *Shulḥan Arukh; see infra* p. 1322 and n. 36.

and is thus, viewed standing alone, a typical book of *pesakim*; it states the law categorically without discussion or reference, "as though the matters were transmitted to us by tradition."[158]

By means of this "dual method," Rashba solved the fundamental problem of the codification of the *Halakhah* to which we have repeatedly referred: on the one hand, the need for a book of categorical directives for practical purposes, without citation of sources or reference to differences of opinion, and, on the other, the danger that such a formulation may sever the law from its sources, may lead to errors in the interpretation of the categorically stated law, and may impede the judge's consideration of divergent opinions when ruling on an actual case. Rashba solved the problem by the device, original with him, of composing two separate companion volumes: (1) a book of *halakhot* containing a discussion of the law and, (2) a book of *pesakim* stating the legal rules emerging from the discussion in the book of *halakhot*. Both of Rashba's books are also outstanding for their logical arrangement of the laws and for their clear and concise style, which facilitate both reference and study. Rashba's codificatory methodology enables students and judges to use either or both of the two volumes as necessary or appropriate in light of their abilities and the circumstances.[159]

In addition to *Torat ha-Bayit,* Rashba wrote other codificatory works.[160]

158. A similar form of expression—"like one delivering a prophetic message from the Almighty, providing neither reason nor proof"—was used by Asheri (*see supra* p. 1226) in his strictures against the method of Maimonides. Rashba used that very method for his *Torat ha-Bayit ha-Kaẓer.*

159. For more on his methodology in this work, *see Resp. Rashba,* I, #494. For an interesting parallel in the codification of Moslem law, *see* I. Meron, "Nekudot Magga Bein ha-Mishpat ha-Ivri le-Vein ha-Mishpat ha-Muslemi" [Points of Contact between Jewish and Moslem Law], *Shenaton,* II (1975), pp. 343ff. (at 356–359).

In various places and at various times, *Torat ha-Bayit* has been printed as two separate books. In 1882, both books were printed together in Jozepaf (reprinted New York, 1952; Jerusalem, 1963), with the text of *Torat ha-Bayit ha-Kaẓer* printed in the margins, corresponding to the discussion on the respective pages in *Torat ha-Bayit ha-Arokh.* This manner of presentation emphasizes the basic difference in the codificatory form of the two parts of *Torat ha-Bayit* on the one hand, and the complementary relationship between them in meeting codificatory needs, on the other. In the course of time, halakhic authorities adopted as a principle of decision making that "when there is an inconsistency between *Torat ha-Bayit ha-Arokh* and *Torat ha-Bayit ha-Kaẓer,* we follow *Torat ha-Bayit ha-Kaẓer,* because that purports to state the law" (*Peri Megadim* to Sh. Ar. YD, Introduction, Rules for Decision Making in Matters of *Issur ve-Hetter,* par. 9). *See also Sedei Ḥemed,* VI, Rules of the *Posekim,* par. 10:3.

160. Rashba's other books are:

1. *Sefer Avodat ha-Kodesh,* which discusses the laws of festivals. It is divided into two "houses" (*battim*): (a) *Bet Netivot* [The House of Paths], covering the laws of *eruvin* and ritual baths, and (b) *Bet Mo'ed* [The House of Festivals]. Each "house" is divided into "gates." Only the summary rulings in this work have appeared in print, and even these have suffered abridgment and deletions by

2. *BEDEK HA-BAYIT* AND *MISHMERET HA-BAYIT*

When Rashba's *Torat ha-Bayit* appeared, one of his contemporaries, Aaron ha-Levi, composed critical glosses on it, and in his Introduction he explained the importance of his critique:

> Sages from early generations have been in the habit of writing codes, each in the form he chose. And . . . they would criticize them [*i.e.*, one another's works], as they saw fit, so that the truth of the matters should emerge, because no partiality to persons may be shown in regard to matters of the living God, may He be exalted. And now a work by one of the sages of this generation has come into my hands that contains things with which I do not agree, and I have seen fit to point them out and express my own opinion so that the matters shall be clarified and those who perceive will have the benefit [of additional enlightenment] and the wise man will make up his mind for himself.

Aaron ha-Levi's criticism is thus not directed at Rashba's "dual method," which is the one best suited for preserving both the continuity and uniformity of the *Halakhah*, but rather at the substance of certain of Rashba's conclusions. It was for this reason that Aaron ha-Levi named his book *Bedek ha-Bayit* [Repair of the House]:

> The work that has come into my hands is called *Torat ha-Bayit* [The Law of the House]; I have therefore called my critique *Bedek ha-Bayit* [Repair of the House], because it is my intention, with God's help, to find and set right everything in it that requires correction.[161]

Rashba replied to the criticisms contained in *Bedek ha-Bayit* in a book he called *Mishmeret ha-Bayit* [Defense of the House], which was published

---

the printers. One must therefore ascertain whether one has the full, or only an abridged version.

2. *Sha'ar ha-Mayim*, on the laws of *mikveh* (ritual baths). This book is divided into eleven "gates," each of which comprehensively discusses the Talmudic and post-Talmudic literature on a particular point, in a fashion similar to that of *Torat ha-Bayit ha-Arokh*. A parallel book, *Bet ha-Mayim*, states in concise form the legal conclusions following from *Sha'ar ha-Mayim*, in the manner of *Torat ha-Bayit ha-Kaẓer*. Both *Sha'ar ha-Mayim* and *Bet ha-Mayim* have been published together from mss. (along with both volumes of *Torat ha-Bayit*) by M. Hershler, Jerusalem, 1963, with an introduction and explanatory commentary called *Shulei ha-Aderet*. As to the previous printed edition and the name of the book, *see* Hershler's Introduction.
3. *Piskei Ḥallah*, which treats the laws of the separation of the dough-tithe. It contains four "gates," and was published by I.D. Bergman, with an explanatory commentary called *Kedushat Leḥem*, Jerusalem, 1970.

161. *Bedek ha-Bayit*, Introduction.

anonymously.[162] Rashba's objective was to reply to all of Aaron ha-Levi's criticisms and thus protect the house he had built: "And I come to protect the house . . . ; therefore, I have called this book *Mishmeret ha-Bayit*."[163] The Introduction to *Mishmeret ha-Bayit* discusses at length various methods of writing critiques and critical glosses and vigorously attacks Aaron ha-Levi; and the book itself contains sharp rebuttals of the criticisms in *Bedek ha-Bayit.*

In regular editions of *Torat ha-Bayit ha-Arokh,* the text of that work is printed in the center of the page, with *Bedek ha-Bayit* on the inside margin and *Mishmeret ha-Bayit* on the outside margin.[164] This "triptych" is highly esteemed and respected.

Rashba's methodological innovation in codificatory literature did not, in his own time, achieve the full approbation it deserved. Although *Torat ha-Bayit* was regarded as a basic halakhic text on the subjects it treated and, as such, was widely recognized as having achieved an important position in codificatory literature,[165] nevertheless, its essential codificatory innovation, *i.e.,* two complementary volumes, inspired no emulation for a long period. One of the reasons may be that Rashba did not apply this method—or perhaps was unable to apply it—to more than a small segment of the *Halakhah.* However, the beginning Rashba made was followed up some two centuries later in the codificatory works of Joseph Caro, which brought about the final crystallization of the methodology of halakhic codification.

II. *SEFER HA-TURIM* BY JACOB b. ASHER[166]

A. Jacob b. Asher's Codificatory Methodology

As shown by the discussion up to this point, from the time of Maimonides' *Mishneh Torah,* codifiers of the *Halakhah* wrestled strenuously with the problem of methodology. Maimonides' bold attempt to introduce into the halakhic system a self-contained and consolidated code reawakened and even intensified the fear that a definitive restatement of the law could lead to the severance of the law from its sources and could restrict the range of

162. The Introduction to *Mishmeret ha-Bayit* does not state the identity of its author, but other sources do. *See, e.g.,* Ḥida, *Shem ha-Gedolim,* Persons, Letter *shin,* par. 19; Michael, *supra* n. 94 at 579, s.v. Rabbenu Shelomo b. R. Avraham b. Adret.

163. *Mishmeret ha-Bayit,* Introduction.

164. In a recent edition, *Torat ha-Bayit ha-Kaẓer* also appears in the margin; *see supra* n. 159.

165. There is reason to believe that *Torat ha-Bayit* was the basis for *Tur* YD. *See* Freimann, "Die Ascheriden," *supra* n. 71 at 185 and n. 1. *See also infra* pp. 1289–1290.

166. For a biography and bibliography of Jacob b. Asher, *see* Freimann, "Die Ascheriden," *supra* n. 71 at 160–211.

judicial options by omitting reference to divergent opinions. Maimonides' experiment had no emulators. Instead, various attempts were made to draft codes in the style of books of *halakhot,* whether following the order of the Talmudic tractates or the Biblical commandments, or organized topically or according to the days of the week or even the events in a person's life-cycle. Rashba's experiment of two complementary volumes—a book of *halakhot* side by side with a book of *pesakim,* a form that had the potential for resolving the problem of codificatory methodology—remained an isolated effort and had no immediate effect on halakhic codificatory literature.

While all these various forms of codification preserved the link with the sources and made available the full range of halakhic opinions, the great majority of them did not fulfill the essential codificatory objectives: easy style, simple language, logical organization that made it easy to find the law, a clear and unequivocal statement of the law, and comprehensive coverage of the entire *corpus juris* currently applicable. The existing state of affairs gave rise to an urgent and vital need to develop a suitable method for the codification of Jewish law; and, in the first half of the fourteenth century, a work exemplifying such a method was both successful and well received. This work is the *Sefer ha-Turim* [The Book of the Rows] (also called the *Turim* or the *Arba'ah Turim* [The Four Rows]).[167] It was written by Jacob b. Asher, who is also called, after the name of his work, "Jacob Ba'al ha-Turim" (Jacob, the Author of the *Turim*), or simply "Ba'al ha-Turim" (The Author of the *Turim*). Jacob was the third son of Asheri, who, as has been noted, was sharply opposed to the methodology of the *Mishneh Torah* and had composed his own book of *halakhot,* namely, *Piskei ha-Rosh.*

Jacob b. Asher was born in Germany ca. 1270 C.E. and, together with his father, fled from there to Spain in 1303. He served as a judge (*dayyan*) in the rabbinical court of Toledo and died there ca. 1343.[168] By the time of Jacob b. Asher, various additional factors intensified the urgency of the need for a code of Jewish law. During the twelfth and thirteenth centuries, the Tosafists had created a vast and highly significant halakhic literature. Although that literature consisted mainly of novellae to the Talmud, anyone faced with the need to ascertain the governing law in any particular case was obviously required to consider the opinion of those eminent halakhic

167. Certain aspects of the codificatory methodology of the *Turim*—setting forth the Talmudic principle, together with the various opinions of named *rishonim* with regard to specific applications—can be found, to some degree, in various contemporaneous and immediately prior works such as *Sha'arei Dura, see supra* pp. 1248–1249, and *Eẓ Ḥayyim, see supra* pp. 1255–1256. However, in the *Turim* the method is far more crystallized and encompasses the entire *corpus juris* of Jewish law that was then applicable.

168. As to the date of Jacob b. Asher's death, *see* Freimann, "Die Ascheriden," *supra* n. 71 at 164 and n. 4.

authorities. Furthermore, it was characteristic of the Tosafists that interspersed throughout their discursive novellae were a vast number of halakhic rulings.[169] Thus, authoritative legal rulings became even more widely scattered and more difficult to find.

Still another factor adding to the urgency of the need for a comprehensive code was the proliferation of books of *halakhot,* which, as in the earlier periods, resulted in conflict of opinion on a great many legal issues, so that it had become increasingly difficult for judges to find their way in the material and determine what view to follow.

The burgeoning halakhic literature in the two great Jewish centers—Germany and France on the one hand, and Spain on the other—also contributed to the multiplicity of opinions. The Tosafists in Germany and France included some of the leading authors of responsa, such as Rabbenu Tam and Maharam of Rothenburg, whose thousands of responsa constituted authoritative rulings entitled to deference by Jewish courts. In Spain, among the greatest achievements in the development of Jewish law were the commentaries, novellae, and responsa of such authorities as Meir ha-Levi Abulafia (Ramah), Naḥmanides, Rashba, and others. As the codificatory works and responsa proliferated, so did the conflicts of opinion.

As we have already seen, some of the leading halakhic authorities of this period did begin to try to reconcile the divergent rulings of these two centers or, where this was not possible, to decide on a principled basis which rulings should be followed.[170] Thus, Moses of Coucy, in *Sefer Miẓvot Gadol,* followed the leading Tosafists when they disagreed with Maimonides.[171] Asheri went even further. He incorporated into his *Piskei ha-Rosh* an almost complete summary of the discussions of the Tosafists and much of the doctrine of his own teacher, Maharam of Rothenburg, together with the rulings and interpretations of the *geonim* and the early Spanish authorities, particularly Alfasi; and he declared the law in accordance with the opinion he believed correct. However, much work remained to be done. A great many opinions were barely mentioned by Asheri—particularly opinions of his contemporaries or immediate predecessors;[172] and Asheri's code did not include many new rulings made in the decisions and responsa of Asheri

169. *See supra* p. 1122.

170. Raviah, *supra* p. 1239, and Isaac of Marseilles, *supra* p. 1269, had to some degree amalgamated the doctrines of Spanish, French, and German halakhic authorities. On the divergences of view between the various centers, *see* Joshua Falk's Introduction to *Bet Yisra'el* and *Sefer Me'irat Einayim* (*Sema*), which is printed at the beginning of Sh. Ar. ḤM (reprinted in Sh. Ar. ḤM, ed. El ha-Mekorot, 1956, beginning of Part I, and in ed. Pe'er ha-Torah, 1960, beginning of Part III).

171. *See supra* p. 1262.

172. *E.g.*, Maimonides, Isaac of Marseilles, Naḥmanides, Ramah, Moses of Coucy, Isaac of Corbeil, Samuel Sardi, and Rashba. *See* Falk, *supra* n. 170.

himself. Even the arrangement of *Piskei ha-Rosh,* which follows the order of the tractates of the Talmud, and its statement of the law in conjunction with discussion of the relevant Talmudic passages, made it difficult for a student or judge to find what he was looking for.[173] All these factors intensified the need for a code that would meet the yet unfulfilled requirements.

In his introductions to the various parts of the *Turim,* Jacob b. Asher explained the factors that motivated him to compose this code. The Introduction to one of the four *turim, Yoreh De'ah* (which is similar to the Introduction to another of the *turim, Oraḥ Ḥayyim*), states:

> Since we are already a long time in exile, legal analysis has deteriorated, opinions have proliferated, and conflicts of authority abound. There is no longer any clear and undisputed law, so that many wander about to seek the word of the Lord but cannot find it.[174] Therefore, my ideas and thoughts stirred me to consider the statements . . . and understand the books and the words of their authors . . . and I determined to compose a work on the subject of religious law and all the other matters needed at this time.[175]

Although Jacob b. Asher described the halakhic and historical background of his work in his introductions to the parts dealing with ritual law and the laws of benedictions, prayer, and festivals, his description was much more thorough in the parts of his work covering the field of *mishpat ivri,*

173. Jacob b. Asher, perhaps out of respect for his father, did not mention this factor as a reason for writing his book, but it is stated in Falk's Introduction to *Sema, supra* n. 170. Falk, pointing out that Asheri followed the sequence of the Talmud and discussed the meaning of the Talmudic passages, stated:

> [Not everybody] can be an expert in the entire Talmud . . . and can locate where the various legal rules may be found. In order to correct that state of affairs, his son arose . . . and saw that Asheri's words were pleasing . . . to enlighten [his readers], but that for the reason above stated, they needed a better form if this generation was to benefit from them. . . . He [Jacob b. Asher] wrote in it [*Sefer ha-Turim*] all the laws in the order of the *halakhot* [*i.e.,* logically arranged by subject] . . . in the fashion of Maimonides . . . in clear and concise language. He began each chapter with a quotation from the source [of the law] in the *Gemara,* and followed with a brief explanation so that the reader might easily understand it. He also included references to the conflicting opinions with regard to the law in question.

174. After Amos 8:12 ("Men shall wander from sea to sea and from north to east to seek the word of the Lord, but they shall not find it"). *Cf. Tosefta* Eduyyot 1:1; *and see supra* p. 1067.

175. The Introduction continues:

> Then, I reflected: "Behold, is it not experience that tells and years which give wisdom? You are young and have neither knowledge nor skill. . . . Therefore, give up your ideas lest you be embarrassed in your latter days by what you did in your youth!" But I answered and said, "I will arise and do it no matter what, because the work is for [the sake of] Heaven. I will seek help from Him and He will be my eyes; He will open my ears to hear and my mouth to speak clearly, and He will bring my ideas to fruition, and I will rejoice with all my heart."

particularly the area of civil law. Thus, his Introduction to *Tur Ḥoshen Mishpat* (which deals with civil law) states:

> Blessed be the Lord, God of Israel, who has chosen us from among all peoples and given us the true Torah and just and perfect laws. . . . He commanded us in the matter of [civil] law: "If a case is too baffling for you to decide . . . ,"[176] [which means] that if one person disagrees with others, they must go to the judge at the time and he will declare the law to them, so that the Torah will not become like two Torahs, one saying one thing and the other saying the opposite, but rather one Torah and one law for all of us. . . .
>
> The Sanhedrin sat, and from it went forth Torah and law for all Israel; for it is by the merit of doing justice according to the law of the Torah that the Divine Presence rests on Israel. In addition [to the Sanhedrin], there were two courts of twenty-three members each in the Temple—one at the entrance to the [Temple] courtyard and the other at the entrance to the Temple Mount; and there were 481 other courts in Jerusalem, in addition to innumerable courts in all the other towns.[177]
>
> I, Jacob, son of Rabbi Asher, of blessed memory, saw that because of our manifold sins, the Temple was destroyed and all these [courts] disappeared . . . and there is no just judge and no longer anyone to assure that necessary corrections are made. . . . Every man does as he deems fit. . . . Therefore, the law has become distorted. There are those who seek the law on a matter but receive no illumination because their intelligence is inadequate [*i.e.*, they have difficulty in finding and understanding the law]. There are others on whom the light of the law does shine, but who deliberately darken it because they fear that the weight of the law is against them. These say, "I will select the law in the matter from one of the writers on the *Halakhah*, which I will pronounce [as the correct position] and it will be good for me. 'My rod' (*makli*) will tell me the law."[178] Therefore, I bestirred myself and decided to compose a book on the civil law.

Jacob b. Asher thus indicated how the lack of a binding code of Jewish law was a much more acute problem in the "legal" parts of the *Halakhah*,

176. Deuteronomy 17:8. For discussion of the significance of this verse in halakhic jurisprudence, *see supra* pp. 266–267.

177. *See* TB Sanhedrin 88b, and *cf. Tosefta* Ḥagigah 2:9 and S. Lieberman, *Tosefta ki-Feshutah*, pp. 1297ff. *See also supra* p. 1063. Identification of the source for the author's enumeration of 481 courts in Jerusalem requires further study.

178. The allusion is to Hosea 4:12, "My people . . . consults its stick,/Its rod (*maklo*) directs it," and a play on words is intended: *makel* means "rod," and *mekel* means "one who is lenient in his ruling." The same phraseology appeared earlier in *Resp. Rashba*, I, #253 ("And he who relies upon one who rules leniently (*ha-mekel*) in matters of Torah commits a transgression and is one of those of whom it is said . . . , 'His rod directs him'"). Similar statements appear in *Resp. Asheri* 108:11 ("Know that the French in our land have relaxed their practice in regard to usury, and their rod directs them") and *Resp. Zikhron Yehudah* #49 ("He wanted to accept [the law] from those who permit and not from those who forbid, for his rod directs him").

i.e., in laws concerning monetary matters, than in the laws of prayer, festivals, and ritual matters. As was pointed out at the end of the passage just quoted, the difference is that divergent opinions in the wide field of civil law allow a defendant who fears that he will lose his case ("they fear that the weight of the law is against them") to assert that he follows a particular view, according to which he would not be liable; and as Jacob b. Asher put it, he will say, "I will select the law in the matter from one of the writers on the *Halakhah*, which I will pronounce [as the correct position] and it will be good for me."[179]

The technical name for such a plea is *kim li*, "It is established for me [that the law is in accordance with a particular authority, who favors my position]." According to many halakhic authorities, this plea first appeared in Jewish civil law in the thirteenth century. The plea is grounded on the basic principle that the burden of proof is on the claimant. The original meaning of this principle in the Talmud was that the claimant must prove the facts that entitle him to recover from the defendant. The *kim li* plea as it developed added a new dimension to the principle: if there are conflicting opinions as to the law, one in favor of the plaintiff and the other in favor of the defendant, the latter can argue that in his view, the opinion that favors him is correct, and thus nothing can be taken from his possession unless it is affirmatively proved that the view favoring his position is incorrect. That such a plea could be tendered and that it could result in judgment for the defendant was possible only because of the multiplicity of opinions and the lack of authoritative resolution of the conflicts between them. Also, needless to say, the plea tends to undermine the foundation of a rational and orderly process of adjudication.[180]

179. Jacob b. Asher seems to mean that the litigant rather than the judge presumes to select the rule to be followed. Maharshal (*Yam Shel Shelomo*, Bava Kamma, Introduction) later explicitly stated this as a reason why there was a need for a code that definitively states the law: "Because of this [*i.e.*, the absence of an authoritative code of this character], a litigant can disagree and say, '*Kim li*.'" (For an explanation of this plea, *see infra* and n. 180.) That Jacob b. Asher meant that it is the litigant rather than the judge who so states is implied by the clause "because they fear that the weight of the law is against them," which can only refer to litigants. Consequently, he did not adduce this reason in his Introductions to *Tur* OḤ or *Tur* YD, which deal with "religious" law, because a plea of *kim li* is applicable only in civil litigation.

Freimann, "Die Ascheriden," *supra* n. 71 at 175, interprets this language of Jacob b. Asher as referring to a judge who wants to make things easier for himself by not making a decision on his own but relying instead on the writings of one of his predecessors. This interpretation, for the reasons stated, is erroneous.

180. The *kim li* plea is one of the most important and complicated subjects in Jewish law. It is closely connected with the proliferation of local rulings after the geonic period and with the consequent large increase in the number of divergent opinions and approaches with regard to every law. *See supra* pp. 666–667, 936. As to the connection between the plea

Jacob b. Asher thus set himself two goals, which ultimately merge into one. The first was to restore definitiveness to Jewish law, and to express the law clearly and unequivocally. The second was to find a suitable method of codification, which, in the light of the sharp controversy as to the relative merits of books of *halakhot* and books of *pesakim,* would enable the law to be clearly, definitively, and categorically stated, without attribution of authority or citation of source, yet, at the same time, would maintain the continuity of the law, preserve the link with its sources, and keep alive the knowledge of the wide spectrum of opinions within it.

---

of *kim li* and the problem of codification, *see* Maharshal, *Yam Shel Shelomo,* Bava Kamma, Introduction, quoted *supra* n. 179. *See also infra* p. 1386 and n. 59.

As pointed out, later halakhic authorities attributed the efficacy of the plea of *kim li* to the authorities of the thirteenth century. *See Resp. Maharam of Rothenburg,* ed. Cremona, #159 (quoted in *Mordekhai,* Ketubbot, ch. 4, #154), ed. Berlin, #25 (p. 154), *et al.; Resp. Asheri* 1:8, 67:2, 84:3, 85:11; *Resp. Maharik* #149 (end), #182; *Resp. Radakh,* II, #10; *Resp. Maharibal,* I, #75 (73); *Resp. Torat Emet* #207; *Resp. Maharshdam,* ḤM, #29, #61, #154; *Resp. Maharshakh,* II, #81; *Keneset ha-Gedolah,* ḤM ch. 25, *Haggahot Bet Yosef,* pars. 6–19; Shabbetai Kohen, *Tokfo Kohen,* ##93, 94, 95.

In the course of time, many limitations were attached to the availability of such a plea in order to mitigate the negative impact of the plea on orderly judicial proceedings. *See, e.g., Resp. Radbaz,* II, #825; IV, #1187 (#116); *Resp. Maharif* (Jacob Faragi) #61; *Halakhot Ketannot,* I, #182: "For if so [*i.e.,* if you allow the *kim li* plea], you have completely abrogated the *Ḥoshen Mishpat.*" *Urim ve-Thummim,* abridgment of *Tokfo Kohen* (ḤM, following ch. 25) #124 (end), states:

> In the whole area covered by *Ḥoshen Mishpat,* not one law in a thousand is decisively settled . . . so it is really a matter of might making right. Because of our many sins, we have forgotten the Torah to the extent that in all *Ḥoshen Mishpat* there is not even one law that is undisputed either generally or in some particular by one or more authorities, *rishonim* or *aḥaronim.* That being so, the codifiers and authors have labored in vain to adduce various proofs [for their views] and futilely exerted themselves in fine-spun analysis of the Torah, because the defendant will always plead *kim li* and so our Torah will—Heaven forbid!—be in complete disorder.
>
> Therefore, great consideration is required, particularly with regard to a law in the *Shulḥan Arukh* as to which the author [Joseph Caro] and Rema made no reference to a contrary opinion. [In such a case], a tradition has been handed down to me—and I have seen expert judges act accordingly, and so I, too, have done when sitting as a judge—not to accept a plea of *kim li* based on a contrary opinion. Since both *Bet Yosef* and Rema put all reference to it [the contrary opinion] behind the door [*i.e.,* omitted all reference to that opinion], it need not be taken into account; and the authorities of this generation have agreed to abide by and carry out everything that is concisely set forth in the *Shulḥan Arukh* and the glosses of Rema. . . . Therefore, Heaven forbid that anyone should plead *kim li* against the ruling of the author [Caro] and Rema.

Questions such as when the plea of *kim li* was first entertained, the extent of its availability, and the restrictions placed upon it in the various Jewish diasporas, as well as the connection between it and the problem of Jewish juridical autonomy, still await exhaustive basic research.

In his introductions, Jacob b. Asher tells how he set about to achieve these two goals. One passage states:

> I decided to write a book of laws after the fashion of *Piskei ha-Rosh,* by my father, of blessed memory, which are based on the foundation laid by the great Rabbi Isaac Alfasi, of blessed memory, who minutely examined and sifted the Talmud and revealed all its mysteries. In the few places where his opinion does not agree with that of other authors such as Maimonides, I present their opinions and that of my father Asheri, together with his [Asheri's] ruling, so that the reader may quickly find [lit. "run through it"] and act in accordance with what is to be found there, not deviating from it to the right or to the left.[181]

Another passage adds:[182]

> I do not intend to include protracted proofs, but to set down[183] the law as it has been authoritatively declared; when there are differing opinions, I will set them forth and then state my father's conclusion.

Jacob b. Asher thus took the rulings of Alfasi as his basis for determining the law; and when Maimonides or others—who include an array of important German, French, and Spanish authorities—disagreed with Alfasi, the *Turim* discusses the varying opinions and generally follows the decision of the author's father.[184] This is not just an expression of filial piety, but an expression of the principle of *hilkheta ke-vatra'ei, i.e.,* that the law is in accordance with the views of the later authorities.[185] As far as Jacob b. Asher was concerned, his father was the latest authority, whose decision was therefore definitive and binding. The adoption of the principle of *hilkheta ke-vatra'ei* with regard to Asheri was particularly appropriate in that he, as the leader of Ashkenazic Jewry and, later, one of the leading authorities in Spain, had considered a substantial portion of the opinions of the halakhic

181. Continuation of Introduction to *Tur* ḤM; an allusion to Deuteronomy 17:11 regarding rulings of the Sanhedrin ("You must not deviate from the verdict that they announce to you either to the right or to the left").

182. Introductions to *Tur* YD and OḤ.

183. Introduction to *Tur* OḤ reads: *lehavi,* "to bring."

184. There are exceptional cases in which he explicitly disagreed with his father; *see infra* n. 192.

185. For detailed discussion of this principle, *see supra* pp. 267–271, 983–986. *See also Resp. Elijah Mizraḥi* #66 (ed. Jerusalem, p. 223b):

> R. Asher's [Asheri's] rulings are most important in all matters because he came last and saw all the rulings of the *geonim,* sifted them well, and then ruled as he did. This most certainly applies when the [author of the] *Turim,* who was the most recent authority, agrees with him. Thus, it is fitting to follow such rulings.

authorities in both centers and, in the event of conflict, had decided between them.[186]

In a sense, therefore, acceptance of Asheri's rulings resolved conflicts between the halakhic authorities of these two great Jewish centers. The authoritativeness that Jacob b. Asher ascribed to his father's rulings had led him, before embarking on the *Turim*, to compose a digest of Asheri's decisions, entitled *Sefer ha-Remazim* [The Book of Hints] or *Simanei Asheri* [Highlights of Asheri].[187]

The foregoing quotations from the *Turim* also shed light on the fulfillment of Jacob b. Asher's second goal relating to the literary form of halakhic codification. He chose a middle course between a book of *halakhot* and a book of *pesakim*. However, he did so not by way of complementary volumes, as Rashba had done in his *Torat ha-Bayit*; rather, he combined the two literary forms in a single work. This work first states the law briefly, in a form only slightly changed from the original Talmudic formulation, and generally without indicating the sources in the Talmud or the names of the Talmudic Sages involved.[188] In this respect *Sefer ha-Turim* is a book of *pesakim*.

However, immediately after stating the law in this manner, the work sets out briefly the essence of all the various relevant opinions of prior authorities, identifies the author of each opinion—whether one of the *geonim* or one of the leading *rishonim* of the Jewish centers of Germany, France, or Spain—and then indicates with which of the authorities the author agrees.

186. As has been seen, *supra* p. 1279 and n. 172, Asheri did not cite the opinions of all the previous halakhic authorities; and this was true particularly in regard to his contemporaries and immediate predecessors. Even when the *Turim* does cite opinions not referred to by Asheri, its ruling still follows Asheri's view.

187. *See* Ḥida, *Shem ha-Gedolim*, Persons, Letter *yod*, par. 208; this digest is printed in all large editions of the Talmud under the name *Kiẓẓur Piskei ha-Rosh* [The Abridged Rulings of Asheri]. As to Jacob b. Asher's objective in preparing the digest, *see Resp. Rabbenu Beẓalel Ashkenazi* #22, quoted in *Yad Malakhi*, II, Kelalei ha-Ribah u-Moharika [Principles of the *Turim* and Caro], #21; Freimann, "Die Ascheriden," *supra* n. 71 at 176. Jacob b. Asher also wrote an abridgment of his father's responsa, which has not survived. *See Resp. Rabbenu Beẓalel Ashkenazi, loc. cit. supra;* Michael, *supra* n. 94 at 262, 488; Freimann, *supra* at 208. Ḥida, *Shem ha-Gedolim*, Books, Letter *pe*, par. 120, cites the opinion of Jacob Emden that Jacob b. Asher also wrote *Piskei ha-Tosafot* [The Rulings of the *Tosafot*], which is also printed in the large editions of the Talmud. However, the attribution is doubtful. Ḥida also cites an opinion that Asheri was the author, but it seems that the author was some unknown scholar. *See* Urbach, *Tosafot*, pp. 566–567 and n. 1.

188. It is only in his preface to each of the *Turim* or to particular groups of laws relating to a single subject that Jacob b. Asher quoted Talmudic statements in the names of their authors. A significant proportion of such statements are aggadic and constitute a kind of philosophic foreword to the halakhic subject under discussion. This will be more fully discussed *infra* pp. 1295–1299.

Frequently, however, this indication is not explicit but only implicit.[189] Possibly, in this way, Jacob b. Asher desired to carry on the literary form that cites the whole range of halakhic opinion,[190] notwithstanding his clearly expressed intention to make definitive rulings.[191] As stated, he generally ruled in accordance with his father's view;[192] and, in so doing, he also sometimes quoted or summarized Asheri's responsa.

Thus, in this middle way, Jacob b. Asher found the desirable solution to the problem of codifying Jewish law: on the one hand, a categorical and prescriptive statement of the basic legal principle, without attribution of authority or citation of source, and, on the other hand, a presentation of the various opinions of the post-Talmudic authorities on the ramifications of the principle, and his conclusion as to how the law should be definitively declared.

Careful study of the *Turim* reveals that essentially it is modeled on the codificatory method employed by R. Judah Ha-Nasi in the Mishnah. As has been seen, Maimonides' response to the criticism of the *Mishneh Torah* by Phinehas b. Meshullam, the *dayyan* of Alexandria, contended in part that the *Mishneh Torah* had in fact followed the method of R. Judah Ha-Nasi in that the Mishnah had also not given the chain of tradition for every law:

189. In the majority of cases, the *Turim* does not state in terms that any particular opinion is the law. Rather, after referring to a specific opinion, the author would state: "From the formulation of my . . . father [Asheri], of blessed memory, this appears to be so," or simply, "And my father Asheri ruled," or "And that seems correct (*ve-hakhi mistabra*)." This lack of explicitness led to the perception that there was a need for various rules to determine precisely what the *Turim* was deciding. *See, e.g., Yad Malakhi,* II, *supra* n. 187, ##5–10, 13, 23, 27, 30.

190. Like that employed by R. Judah Ha-Nasi in the Mishnah; *see infra.*

191. *See* the Introductions to OḤ, YD, and ḤM, quoted *supra* pp. 1281–1284. ("So that the reader may quickly find and act in accordance with what is to be found there, not deviating from it to the right or to the left"). The plain meaning is that the reader shall "not deviate from" the law as definitively determined in the *Turim.*

See also the Introduction to *Sema* (printed at beginning of Sh. Ar. ḤM):

> The book of the *Turim* and its legal rulings followed those of Rosh [Asheri] without deviation to the right or the left . . . even when various great scholars and halakhic authorities disagree with him. Therefore, there still exists a measure of confusion as to whose view the law follows, since not everyone is able to decide for himself; and this shortcoming was dwelt on at length by Rabbi Joseph Caro, who wrote his own work for that reason.

This language implies that Jacob b. Asher's intended meaning was that there should be no deviation from his father's decisions either "to the right or the left." *See infra* n. 192.

192. *See supra* pp. 1284–1285. *See also Yad Malakhi, supra* n. 187, #30 ("The methodology of the *Turim* is to cite the views of the [other] authorities first and then to state Asheri's decision, in order to indicate that the latter is to be followed"). *See also id.,* # 23 ("The author of the *Turim* never disagrees with his father unless he explicitly says so") and #27.

"Rabbi [Judah Ha-Nasi] . . . named the Sages from whom he heard [the opinions recorded in the Mishnah] or who lived close to his time; but [he did] not [give] the names of their teachers and their teachers' teachers."[193] However, Maimonides' comparison between the *Mishneh Torah* and R. Judah's Mishnah is flawed: Maimonides never referred to *any* Sages by name,[194] whereas the Mishnah does refer by name to the Sages who reported a tradition, even if it does not mention earlier bearers of the tradition.

The comparison with the Mishnah is apt, however, as regards the *Turim*. R. Judah Ha-Nasi omitted reference to the source and the names of prior Sages in the chain of tradition of every law, but set forth, in addition to the essential legal rule or principle, the relevant conflicting opinions and the names of the *tannaim* who held these opinions. Similarly, Jacob b. Asher did not trace the origin and development of every law back to the Talmudic sources and Sages, but contented himself with stating the law and adding the conflicting opinions of the post-Talmudic authorities (whom he identified) concerning the various ramifications of the law. In addition, Jacob b. Asher also followed R. Judah Ha-Nasi in sometimes expressly stating which view, in his opinion, was correct and sometimes indicating his preference only indirectly.

Nevertheless, care must be taken not to overstate the similarity between the Mishnah and the *Turim*, since in both style and structure the *Turim* is more variegated and complex than the Mishnah. Still, the basic approach of the *Turim* to the methodology of halakhic codification is comparable to that of the Mishnah; and it is interesting that after approximately 1100 years the methodology of halakhic codification had come full circle.

B. The Structure and Organization of *Sefer ha-Turim*

One of Jacob b. Asher's principal aims in writing his code was to make it easy to use "so that the reader may run through it"[195] and "so that every point may be easily found."[196] For this reason, he did not follow the se-

193. *Kovez ha-Rambam*, I, #140 (p. 25). *See supra* p. 1218.

194. As pointed out *supra* (p. 1219), this is why Maimonides made the additional argument that in his time, because of the Karaites, it was imperative to present the *Halakhah* without reference to individual authorities, as a tradition received by "the many from the many."

195. Introduction to *Tur* ḤM, quoted *supra* p. 1284.

196. Introductions to *Tur* ḤM and YD, toward the end. The quoted language was used in the context of the composition of a table of contents (*simanim*) to provide a capsule summary of the contents of each of the *Turim*: "I also decided to write *simanim* to describe each subject in very few words at the beginning of the book, giving the number [of the

quence of the tractates in the Talmud, as his father had done;[197] nor did he adopt an arbitrary pattern of organization. Instead, he organized his work according to subject matter.[198]

The book is divided into four "rows" (*turim*; singular, *tur*).[199] Each *tur* is divided into sections, called *halakhot,* which in turn are subdivided into chapters, called *simanim*; and in extant editions, the chapters are further divided into paragraphs (*se'ifim*). The division of the material into sections, and the names of the various sections in early printed editions, are not the same as in later editions; therefore, close study is necessary in order to ascertain with certainty the original form of the work. In early editions, the chapters are not divided into paragraphs. The following discussion relates to the organization and structure of the *Turim* in the editions currently used.[200]

---

chapter], so that every point may be easily found." However, this statement also more generally expresses the author's overall objective in regard to the structure and organization of his work.

197. *See* the Introduction to *Sema, supra* n. 173, to the effect that on this point Jacob b. Asher did not follow his father's pattern of organization because the organization of a code according to the sequence of the tractates of the Talmud makes it difficult to find the law.

198. Consequently, his first step in writing his own work was to prepare a digest of his father's rulings and responsa so that he could include his father's determinations in his own work under the appropriate subject headings. *See supra* p. 1285.

199. The name is an allusion to the four rows of precious stones on the High Priest's breastplate (Exodus 28:15–30). The name *Arba'ah Turim* [Four Rows] appears only in the Introduction to the last *tur,* ḤM; in the Introduction to the others, the author refers to his work as "the book (*sefer*)."

200. In the Soncino edition of ca. 1490 and the Fano edition of 1516, the division into sections, etc., is not the same as in later editions. This is especially striking in ḤM, which in those editions is divided into only two sections: *Hilkhot Edut* [Laws of Evidence] and *Hilkhot Halva'ot* [Laws of Loans]. On the other hand, even these early editions contain at the beginning of each *tur* a list of the chapters in that *tur,* together with a brief description of the content of each chapter, in the nature of chapter headings, although perhaps somewhat fuller than chapter headings normally are. It was to these descriptions (*simanim*) that Jacob b. Asher referred in his Introduction, *supra* n. 196. Joseph Caro expanded these descriptions, as he noted at the end of *Bet Yosef* to *Tur* OḤ, Introduction:

> Since the table of contents of *Sefer ha-Turim* is very skimpy, and sometimes anyone looking for a particular law cannot tell whether it is in one chapter or another or even in the book at all, I determined to prepare another table of contents listing in detail all the laws contained in each chapter, and then I made a list of all the new laws that I present in my commentary entitled *Bet Yosef,* so that everyone will be able to find easily the law he seeks.

These tables of contents to *Bet Yosef* are printed at the end of each of the *Turim; see infra* p. 1319 n. 28. The Cremona edition of 1558 contains a more detailed description of the sections in ḤM, but both the names and contents of the sections are quite different from the present editions. The Riva di Trento edition of 1560 is very similar to the Cremona edition of 1558. The Sabbioneta edition of 1559, which already has the *Bet Yosef* commen-

The names of the four *turim* and the general contents of each are as follows:

1. *Tur Oraḥ Ḥayyim* [The Path of Life] contains all the laws governing a person's daily life, such as the laws relating to conduct on arising in the morning and the laws of benedictions, fringes (*ẓiẓit*), phylacteries, prayer, sabbath, and festivals. As Jacob b. Asher put it: "I called it *Oraḥ Ḥayyim* because from it issues life."[201]
2. *Tur Yoreh De'ah* [It Will Teach Knowledge] discusses matters of *issur* ("religious" law), such as the laws of ritual slaughter, animals unfit for food (*terefot*), other forbidden foods, idolatry, menstruant women and the ritual bath, vows and oaths,[202] circumcision and the redemption of the first-born, visiting the sick, and burial and mourning.[203]

   Tur Yoreh De'ah includes a number of laws that, although classified as *issur,* are properly subsumed under *mishpat ivri* as the term is used in the present work.[204] For example, chapters 159–177 of *Tur Yoreh De'ah* treat the laws of interest and usury; chapters 240–241 deal with the respect and honor due to parents, and include laws regarding filial financial obligations;[205] and there are other examples.[206] On the name and

---

tary next to the text of the *Turim,* is very similar to the editions currently in use in regard to the names and contents of the sections, although there are still some differences. (It should be pointed out that Jacob b. Asher's Introductions to the various *turim* contain quite detailed lists of the subjects treated in each *tur.*) Comprehensive research is needed to clarify the matter of these differences between the various editions. The division of the chapters into paragraphs first appears in the Sabbioneta edition, which has paragraph indications in the margin rather than the body of the text. The division into paragraphs in contemporary editions is not meticulous—occasionally a new paragraph is started in the middle of a subject or even of a line.

201. Introduction to *Tur* ḤM. *See also* Introduction to *Tur* OḤ: "I called this book *Oraḥ Ḥayyim* because it will remove the deadly pitfalls from [the path of] those who walk in its ways." *Tur* OḤ contains 693 chapters.

202. In some instances, these laws involve matters that are clearly within *mishpat ivri, e.g.,* the use of oaths and vows to establish obligations (*see supra* pp. 119–120). Ch. 334 treats bans and excommunication, which were used as sanctions in matters of *mishpat ivri* and were particularly instrumental in the maintenance of communal organization and the enforcement of communal enactments (as were also the laws treated in the last part of ch. 228). *See supra* pp. 678ff.

203. *Tur* YD contains 403 chapters.

204. *See supra* p. 105.

205. *E.g.,* the obligation to support parents. Laws relating to support of children are in *Tur* EH ch. 71.

206. *E.g.,* the laws exempting a halakhic scholar (*talmid ḥakham*) from taxes are in YD ch. 243. The main treatment of tax laws is in ḤM ch. 163. As to exemption from taxation, *see* M. Elon, EJ, XV, pp. 840ff., s.v. Taxation, at p. 854 (reprinted in *Principles,* pp. 662ff., at p. 675). *See* Appendix A to the instant work for cross-reference tables of comparable provisions of the *Mishneh Torah* and the *Shulḥan Arukh.*

content of this *tur,* Jacob b. Asher wrote:[207] "It deals with that which is prohibited,[208] to teach the Children of Israel what is permitted and what is forbidden. I called it *Yoreh De'ah* because it will teach knowledge and will make tradition understandable."[209]

3. *Tur Even ha-Ezer* [The Stone of the Helper] treats family law. It is divided into the following sections: (a) Procreation (chapters 1–25), which, *inter alia,* deals with marriages forbidden because of consanguinity or other reasons, and includes (chapter 17) the laws of the *agunah* (because her remarriage is forbidden) and the various methods by which an *agunah* may become eligible to remarry;[210] (b) marriage (chapters 26–65), which deals mainly with the methods of effecting betrothal and marriage;[211] (c) the *ketubbah* (chapters 66–118), which discusses the financial relations between the spouses arising out of that document;[212] (d)

It should be noted that in the *Mishneh Torah,* the laws of interest and usury are in *Sefer Mishpatim* [The Book of Civil Laws], *Hilkhot Malveh ve-Loveh* [Laws of Creditor and Debtor], chs. 4–10, and in *Sefer Kinyan* [The Book of Acquisitions], *Hilkhot Sheluḥin ve-Shutafin* [Laws of Agency and Partnership], chs. 6–8; and the laws of respect due to parents are in *Sefer Shofetim* [The Book of Judges], *Hilkhot Mamrim* [Laws of Rebels], chs. 5–7. However, Maimonides, too, sometimes treated matters of *mishpat ivri* elsewhere than in the "legal" books of his *Mishneh Torah, e.g.:* (1) the laws of *prosbul,* which Maimonides treated in *Sefer Zera'im* [The Book of Seeds], *Hilkhot Shemittah ve-Yovel* [Laws of the Sabbatical and Jubilee Years], ch. 9; and (2) some of the laws of forbidden marriages, which Maimonides treated in *Sefer Kedushah* [The Book of Holiness], *Hilkhot Issurei Bi'ah* [Laws of Forbidden Sexual Unions], chs. 1–3, 12, 14–16. In the *Turim,* these laws are in the "legal" sections: laws of *prosbul* in ḤM ch. 67, and forbidden marriages in the first chapters of EH. *See* Appendix A.

207. Introduction to *Tur* ḤM.

208. The Hebrew is *ha-holekh kidmat assur,* a play on *kidmat Asshur* ("east of Asshur") in Genesis 2:14: "The name of the third river is Tigris, the one that flows east of Asshur."

209. *Cf.* Isaiah 28:9 ("To whom would he give instruction [*yoreh de'ah*]?/To whom expound a message [*yavin shemu'ah*]?"). *Cf. also* the Introduction to *Tur* YD ("I called this book *Yoreh De'ah* because it will give a person knowledge to rule on all matters [relating to laws] that apply in our time").

210. The laws relating to the abandoned wife (*agunah*) in themselves constitute a sizable part of codificatory and responsa literature because they are so extensive—particularly the laws that relate to finding ways to "release" the *agunah* so as to permit her to remarry (*see supra* pp. 522–530, 846–879). A major project, *Oẓar ha-Posekim* (*see infra* p. 1442), which proposes to collect a large part of the halakhic material that has accumulated since the appearance of the *Shulḥan Arukh* and organize it in the same sequence, has produced six large volumes (III–VIII) devoted to chapter 17 of Sh. Ar. EH alone.

211. The other subjects covered include financial obligations (other than those based on the *ketubbah*) arising out of betrothal and marriage, such as: ch. 3 (the return of the betrothal money and wedding gifts of the spouses); ch. 51 (acquisitions which can be effected merely by oral statements); and ch. 55 (laws with regard to the rights of a betrothed woman to support, burial, and inheritance).

212. This section also discusses widow's rights and the support of daughters. *See also supra* n. 211.

divorce (chapters 119–154); (e) disaffirmance (chapter 155), which discusses the laws concerning a fatherless bride below the age of legal capacity (given in marriage by her mother or brothers), who may "disaffirm the marriage" when she reaches maturity, and in that event does not require a divorce; (f) levirate marriage (chapters 156–168) and *ḥalizah* (chapters 169–176); (g) rape and seduction (chapter 177); and (h) wives suspected of infidelity (*sotah*) (chapter 178).

The laws in *Tur Even ha-Ezer* are conveniently and logically organized, following the normal chronological sequence: first, laws relating to betrothal and marriage and how each status is effected; second, the relationship between the spouses resulting from the marriage status; third, the laws of divorce; and finally, after dealing with the normal course of events, unusual matters such as disaffirmance, and levirate marriage and *ḥalizah*. *Sefer Nashim* [The Book of Women] in Maimonides' *Mishneh Torah*, as has been seen, organized the laws in the same order; but in *Tur Even ha-Ezer*, the laws of Maimonides' *Hilkhot Ishut* [Laws of Personal Status] are divided into two separate sections: *Hilkhot Kiddushin*, which deals with how betrothal and marriage are effected, and *Hilkhot Ketubbot*, which discusses the personal and financial obligations arising out of marriage.

Jacob b. Asher explained the name *Even ha-Ezer* that he gave to the *tur* dealing with family law as follows: "The third *tur* is *Even ha-Ezer* because there I made for man a fitting helper [*ezer ke-negdo*][213] . . . and I called it *Even ha-Ezer* because it is both useful and helpful."[214]

4. *Tur Ḥoshen Mishpat* [The Breastplate of Decision]. Jacob b. Asher wrote: "I called it *Ḥoshen Mishpat*, and I have placed in it the *Urim* and *Thummim* [the oracle the High Priest wore on his breast], because it is needed by every inquirer to enlighten his eyes and to open his lips, [to speak]

213. *Cf.* Genesis 2:18 ("The Lord God said, 'It is not good for man to be alone; I will make a fitting helper for him [*ezer ke-negdo*]'") and 2:20.

214. Introduction to *Tur* ḤM. The word *even* ("stone") in the title may be an allusion to the precious stones that formed the four rows (*turim*) of the High Priest's breastplate, *see supra* n. 199. On the basis of the penchant for word play in the *Turim*, it appears that the word "*ezer*" ("help," or "helper") is used in two senses: first, this *tur* treats the various laws governing how a man effects betrothal and marriage to his "fitting helper" (*ezer ke-negdo*); and second, it contains the laws for the benefit of the "helper" (*ezer*), *i.e.*, her rights against her husband (*ke-negdo*). *See also* Introduction to *Tur* EH (end) for a poetic play on the word *ezer*, expressing the prayer that God will be "a helper" to the author and ending with the verse (I Samuel 7:12), "Samuel took a stone and set it up between Mizpah and Shen and named it Eben-ezer [stone of help]: 'For up to now,' he said, 'the Lord has helped us.'" (The quotation is not exact in the *Turim*, in which "he said" is replaced by "saying.") It is not clear whether the quotation is meant to indicate another reason for the name of this *tur*; it may be that the verse is the basis for the juxtaposition of "*Even*" and "*ha-Ezer*."

straight and true."[215] This *tur* contains the great bulk of the civil law and certain parts of the criminal law.

Tur Ḥoshen Mishpat has an interesting pattern of organization, which differs from that of the *Mishneh Torah.* Jacob b. Asher's civil code begins with the laws of judges (chapters 1–27), which deal with the composition of courts, the appointment of judges, jurisdiction, and part of the laws of procedure. Next are the laws of evidence (chapters 28–38) and other matters relating to proof of claims. Following thereafter are various areas of civil law (monetary matters) such as loans,[216] partnership, acquisition, sales, inheritance, and bailments (chapters 39–347). The code concludes with the laws of theft (chapters 348–358), robbery (chapters 359–377), torts and informers (chapters 378–388), damage caused by property (chapters 389–419), and assault and battery (chapters 420–426).

As will be recalled, Maimonides had chosen an almost diametrically opposite pattern of organization for his *Mishneh Torah*: The first of his books dealing with the subject matter of *mishpat ivri*—after Book IV, *Sefer Nashim*—is Book XI, *Sefer Nezikin* [The Book of Damages], which contains the laws relating to damage caused by property and the laws of theft, robbery, lost property, assault and battery, and homicide and the preservation of life. Books XII and XIII, *Sefer Kinyan* [The Book of Acquisitions] and *Sefer Mishpatim* [The Book of Civil Laws], discuss many substantive areas of civil law, such as the law of sales, acquisitions and gifts, leasing and hiring, creditor and debtor, and inheritance. The last Book (XIV), *Sefer Shofetim* [The Book of Judges], contains the laws of the Sanhedrin, which include the composition and jurisdiction of the various courts, and portions of the law of evidence.

Thus, *Tur Ḥoshen Mishpat* reversed Maimonides' order, beginning where Maimonides ended—with the rules governing courts and evidence—and ending where Maimonides began—with the "pathological" part of the law, namely, theft, damages, and assault and battery. As has been pointed out, Maimonides was influenced by the order of the tractates in the Talmud, in which the Order of *Nezikin* begins with Tractate *Bava Kamma,*

215. *Cf. also* Exodus 28:30 ("Inside the breastplate of decision you shall place the *Urim* and *Thummim,* so that they are over Aaron's heart when he comes before the Lord. Thus Aaron shall carry the instrument of decision for the Israelites over his heart before the Lord at all times"). The Introduction to *Tur* ḤM goes on to say: "The fourth *tur* is *Ḥoshen Mishpat;* there I inscribed law and judgment." Though the style of the last clause is Biblical, there is no verse with that language in Scripture, and the clause was not intended to echo any particular verse.

216. The Laws of Loans also include that part of the law of evidence in connection with loans that is not contained in the general treatment of the laws of evidence.

dealing with the laws of damages, robbery, theft, and assault and battery; only at the end of the Order of *Nezikin* come the tractates—*Sanhedrin, Shevu'ot,* and *Makkot*—that treat the composition of courts and the law of evidence. *Tur Ḥoshen Mishpat* departed from the conventional organization of halakhic codes and followed the inner logic of the subject matter "so that every point may be easily found."[217]

In regard to classification in Jewish law, it is instructive to examine the analytical categorization of the material in the various sections of *Tur Ḥoshen Mishpat* and to note the criteria according to which the sections were organized.[218] Except for family law, which Maimonides included in *Sefer Nashim* and Jacob b. Asher included in *Tur Even ha-Ezer,* Maimonides included the halakhic material encompassed by *mishpat ivri* in four books: *Nezikin, Kinyan, Mishpatim,* and *Shofetim.* That material was divided by Maimonides into nineteen sections, not including *Hilkhot Evel* (Laws of Mourning), which cannot be considered part of *mishpat ivri.* In contrast, *Tur Ḥoshen Mishpat* is divided into fifty-eight sections—more than three times as many as the *Mishneh Torah.*

The reason for this difference is that the classification in the *Turim* is much more refined. For example, separate sections are devoted to loans (chapters 39–66), legal instruments executed in non-Jewish courts (chap-

217. Introductions to *Tur* YD and ḤM, toward the end, and *see supra* pp. 1287–1288. It should be pointed out that in the *Turim,* as well as in the *Mishneh Torah,* the laws of *To'en ve-Nit'an* (Plaintiff and Defendant) are set out after the laws of loans, fiduciaries, and pledges. The laws of *To'en ve-Nit'an* include laws governing pleading and evidence, which are regarded as procedural. Nevertheless, they are codified in the substantive part of Jewish law, unlike other aspects of the laws of evidence and judicial procedure, which are codified either immediately after the beginning (as in the *Turim*) or close to the end (as in the *Mishneh Torah*). The reason is that in Jewish law the distinction between substance and procedure does not have the same significance as in other systems. *See* Elon, *Ḥakikah,* pp. 79–84.

The arrangement of the sections in *Tur* ḤM may have been influenced by the order of the tractates of the Talmud as the *geonim* arranged them and as described by Meiri, *Bet ha-Beḥirah,* Berakhot, Introduction (ed. Dykman, 1960, p. 33): "The arrangement of the three Orders as we have become accustomed to study them has been substantially changed. . . . The arrangement of the Order of *Nezikin* [as revised by the *geonim*] was as follows: *Sanhedrin, Makkot, Shevu'ot, Avodah Zarah, Horayot, Avot, Eduyyot, Bava Kamma, Bava Meẓi'a,* and *Bava Batra*—in all, ten tractates." *See also id.* at 32, indicating that the reference is to the arrangement in the geonic period. Meiri explained why the *geonim* changed the order fixed by R. Judah Ha-Nasi: "Indeed, it is only fitting that the tractates of the Order of *Nezikin* should begin with *Sanhedrin,* because at the beginning of every claim and the start of every litigation, he [the party involved] must seek out judges to hear his claim, and it is therefore appropriate first to explain the subject of judges and the way they must act in every type of case, whether civil or criminal" (*id.* at 35).

218. The discussion in the text relates to the organization of the *Turim* in current editions. *See supra* p. 1288 and n. 200. Even if it was not Jacob b. Asher who fixed this internal organization, it is still of quite an early date and it is therefore worthwhile to examine this work—one of the most important codes of Jewish law—for the light it sheds on the development of the classification of Jewish law.

ter 68), holographic promissory notes (chapter 69), creditor and debtor (chapter 70), fiduciaries (chapter 71), pledges (chapters 72–74), creditors' rights generally (chapters 97–106), creditors' rights against orphans (chapters 107–110), creditors' rights against encumbered property (chapters 111–116), mortgages (chapters 117–119), satisfaction and release of obligations (chapter 120), and suretyship (chapters 129–132). Thus, twelve separate sections are devoted to material that Maimonides included in a single section of *Sefer Mishpatim,* namely, *Hilkhot Malveh ve-Loveh* [Laws of Creditor and Debtor].[219] To a certain degree, this minute classification is useful and justified, as, *e.g.,* (a) the treatment of the law of mortgages and of creditors' rights against orphans and encumbered property separately from the treatment of the laws relating to the loan transaction itself; and (b) the treatment of the laws of suretyship separately from the law relating to loans generally. However, it is difficult to justify separate sections for loans, holographic promissory notes, and creditor and debtor, or separate sections for mortgages and for creditors' rights against encumbered property.

The following example also illustrates problematic aspects of Jacob b. Asher's classification. The material included by Maimonides in *Hilkhot Sekhirut* [Laws of Leasing and Hiring] in *Sefer Mishpatim* is presented in *Tur Ḥoshen Mishpat* under the following separate headings: paid bailee (chapters 303–306), hirer (lessee) (chapters 307–319), sharecropper (chapters 320–330), and employer and employee (chapters 331–339). A good case can be made for separate treatment of the laws governing the relationship of employer and employee, but the laws of leasing or hiring property could certainly have been treated together with sharecropping.

Even if the analytical division of the material in the *Turim* into sections is sometimes too fine,[220] this division, generally speaking, was a forward step in the classification of Jewish law. Thus, the material contained in Maimonides' *Hilkhot Shekhenim* [Laws of Neighbors] in *Sefer Kinyan* is divided in the *Turim* into the following sections: damage done by neighbors (chapters 153–156), concurrent ownership of land (chapters 157–beginning of 175), and rights of adjoining landowners (most of chapter 175). Similarly, Maimonides' *Hilkhot To'en ve-Nit'an* [Laws of Plaintiff and Defendant] in

219. As previously stated (*supra* n. 206), the laws of interest and usury are included in the *Mishneh Torah* in *Hilkhot Malveh ve-Loveh* [Laws of Creditor and Debtor] chs. 4–10. In the *Turim,* they constitute a separate section of YD (chs. 159–177).

220. Another prime example of overrefined classification in the *Turim* is the devotion of a separate section to each of the following subjects: acquisition of real property, acquisition by *sudar,* acquisition of slaves, acquisition of animals, acquisition of chattels, etc. (*Tur* ḤM, from ch. 190 on). The *Mishneh Torah* includes all this material in *Hilkhot Mekhirah* [Laws of Sales]. In the *Shulḥan Arukh,* Joseph Caro reconsolidated some of these laws that the *Turim* treated separately; *see infra* pp. 1324–1325.

Sefer Mishpatim is divided in the *Turim* into the following sections: plaintiff and defendant (chapters 75–86), oaths in court (chapters 87–96), possession of movable property (chapters 133–139), and possession of real property (chapters 140–152). This increased refinement in classification undoubtedly stemmed from the fact that the law had substantially increased in bulk, largely as a result of new court judgments and the proliferating responsa literature, both of which created a need for more refined classification.

Our examination of the various books of *halakhot*,[221] and of Maimonides' *Mishneh Torah*,[222] has disclosed that codifiers occasionally interweave aggadic with halakhic material, particularly at the beginning or end of a section, where the author would insert philosophical and ethical comments relevant to the legal material discussed in that section. Jacob b. Asher also followed this practice in the *Turim* and even expanded on it by writing long prefaces to the various *turim* or to specific sections, which he spiced with aggadic material and ethical concepts. In these prefaces, he included quotations from the Talmud and the Midrash, together with the names of the Sages quoted. The beginning of chapter 1 of *Tur Ḥoshen Mishpat* is an especially interesting example in that it discusses the place of law in Judaism. The greater part of it is therefore quoted here:

> Rabban Simeon b. Gamaliel said: "The world exists because of three things—justice, truth, and peace."[223] Rabbenu Jonah, of blessed memory, explained:[224]
>
>> This does not mean that the world was *created* for the sake of these three things, inasmuch as the beginning of the chapter[225] states: "The world rests on [*i.e.*, came into being for the sake of] three things," and those are not the same three things mentioned here. Rather, at the beginning, it [the Mishnah] states that the world was *created* for the sake of three things, namely, Torah, the Temple service, and deeds of loving kindness.[226] . . . This statement [of Rabban Simeon b. Gamaliel] is that the

221. *See supra* pp. 1150–1153, 1161–1164, and *passim*.

222. *See supra* pp. 1191–1193.

223. M Avot 1:18. Our printed editions have: "The world stands" (*ha-olam omed*), but Jacob b. Asher and apparently Rabbenu Jonah Gerondi, who is quoted by the *Turim* later in the passage, and by Joseph Caro in *Bet Yosef*, had "The world exists" (*ha-olam kayyam*), as do other texts; *see* v.l. in the Mishnah, *ad loc.*, and *see* H. Albeck, *Commentary on M Nezikin*, Hosafot ve-Hashlamot, p. 494.

224. Commentary of Rabbenu Jonah on M Avot 1:2.

225. M Avot 1:2. Rabbenu Jonah's commentary reads: ". . . for below it states . . . ," since his statement was a comment on M Avot 1:2 and not 1:18. The *Turim* modified the quoted language because the discussion there started with reference to 1:18.

226. Rabbenu Jonah's commentary continues: "Torah, as it is written [Proverbs 8:22], 'The Lord created me at the beginning of His course.' Torah said, 'I was created before any other creature, and it was for my sake that all other creatures were created.' Similarly, with

> world *exists* [*i.e.*, after it has been created, it continues to exist] on the strength of these things: justice, by which law is applied to disputes in human affairs, because were it not for justice, might would make right;[227] truth, as the Sages said, "Falsehood has no legs"[228] [*i.e.*, cannot survive], but truth is the foundation and strong support of all things; and peace, as they said,[229] "Pray for the welfare of the government, since but for the fear of it men would swallow each other up alive."[230]

This was also the intent of our Sages when they said,[231] "Everyone who gives a judgment that is completely and truly correct [lit. "a true judgment to its very truth"][232] is deemed a partner of the Holy One, blessed be He, in the act

---

regard to the Temple service, for the Holy One, blessed be He, chose Israel from all the nations and the Temple from all the places so that they [Israel] should serve Him there; and because of this the world was created. Similarly, regarding deeds of lovingkindness, which . . . lead to the favor of God, may He be blessed."

227. *See* TB Gittin 60b *et al.*

228. *Cf.* TB Shabbat 104a: "Falsehood stands on one leg."

229. M Avot 3:2.

230. In current printed editions of Rabbenu Jonah's commentary, the text is somewhat different from the quotation in the *Turim*.

231. TB Shabbat 10a.

232. For the double mention of "truth" (*emet*) in the formula "a true judgment to its very truth," *see* the various explanations offered in *Bet Yosef, Bayit Ḥadash, Perishah,* and *Derishah, ad loc.* The explanation offered in *Derishah,* quoted *supra* p. 159, is especially interesting:

> What is meant by "a judgment that is completely and truly correct" [*din emet la-amito,* lit. "a true judgment to its very truth"] is that one should judge in accordance with the particular place and time, so that the judgment is in full conformity with the truth, rather than always inflexibly apply the law precisely as it is set forth in the Torah. For sometimes a judge's decision must go *lifnim mi-shurat ha-din* [*i.e.*, not hew to the strict line of the law] and reflect what is called for by the particular time and circumstances. When the judge does not do this, then even if his judgment is correct, it is not "a true judgment to its very truth." This is the meaning of the statement of the Sages: "Jerusalem was destroyed because they based their judgments on the law of the Torah and did not go *lifnim mi-shurat ha-din.*" As to this, it was written, "You shall not deviate to the right or to the left from what they instruct you" [*cf.* Deuteronomy 17:11], which the Sages interpret to mean that you may not deviate even if they tell you that right is left.

See also supra pp. 155–158, 243–261, and the Commentary of Elijah, Gaon of Vilna, on Proverbs 6:4, quoted in part *supra* p. 180:

> Scholars need only know the law of the Torah, so that their doctrine not be contrary to that law; but they do not need to be experts in worldly matters. . . . [However], judges must also be experts in worldly matters so that they do not rule erroneously; for if they are not expert in such matters, then even if they are expert in Torah law, the result will not be "a completely and truly correct" judgment; *i.e.*, even if the judge renders a true judgment, it will not be so in the fullest sense of truth, because the judge has been misled into a false view of the case. Therefore the judge must be an expert in both fields. And so it is written, "For bribery blinds the eyes of the wise," namely, wise in matters of Torah, and "bribery blinds the eyes of the astute," namely, astute with regard to worldly affairs.

of creation," for He created the world that it may exist. The wicked who steal and do violence destroy it with their deeds, as happened in the generation of the Flood, whose fate was sealed only because of robbery,[233] as it is written: "For the earth is filled with lawlessness," after which it is written, "I am about to destroy them with the earth."[234] It follows, therefore, that the judge who thwarts the machinations [lit. "breaks the arms"] of the wicked, and takes the prey from them and returns it to its owners, enables the world to exist and fulfills the will of the Creator, blessed be His name, who created it so that it may exist. It is as though he had become a partner to the Holy One, blessed be He, in the act of creation.

Indeed, God singled out Abraham, our father, and called him "he who loves Me" because Abraham followed the path of justice and guided his children to follow it, as it is written,[235] "For I have singled him out, that he may instruct his children and his posterity to keep the way of the Lord by doing what is just and right." And Moses, our teacher, peace be upon him, the greatest of all the prophets, also heeded the advice of Jethro regarding justice, namely, to appoint judges to warn Israel and instruct them concerning justice; and God agreed to it.[236] And Joshua, after he made a covenant with the people of Israel to serve God, concluded by addressing himself to the matter of justice, as it is written: "On that day at Shechem, Joshua made a covenant for the people and laid down for them law and judgment (*ḥok u-mishpat*)."[237] For justice is an important and fundamental principle in the service of God.

After Joshua, each of the judges judged his generation and brought it back from its evil way to the service of God, to follow the path which Abraham, our father, trod, to do righteousness and justice; and that is why they were saved from their enemies. [This period lasted] until Samuel, a faithful prophet of God, arose. He judged Israel all the days of his life, and every year made the circuit of Bethel, Mizpah, and Gilgal, and judged Israel in all those places.[238] The Sages said that the route he took one year he did not take the following year;[239] and that was in order to turn the heart of the whole people back to the service of God and follow in the path that Abraham, our father, peace be upon him, had taken. Samuel anointed David king over Israel and he, too, followed the ways of God more than anyone who had preceded him,

233. TB Sanhedrin 108a.

234. Genesis 6:13.

235. Genesis 18:19.

236. *Cf.* Exodus 18:23–24. *See also* the Commentary by the author of the *Turim* (unabridged version) on Exodus 18:19: "R. Abraham [ibn Ezra] explained . . . he [Jethro] told him [Moses] to ask permission from God, because he said to him, '[If you do this]—and God so commands you—you will be able to bear up' [Exodus 18:23]. Thus, he most certainly must have asked God."

237. Joshua 24:25. The 1985 JPS *Tanakh* has " . . . and he made a fixed rule for them." The more literal translation in our text is closer to Jacob b. Asher's point.

238. *Cf.* I Samuel 7:15–16.

239. *Cf.* TB Shabbat 56a. *See also* *Ḥiddushei Haggahot* to *Tur* ḤM, Introduction, Letter *dalet* (ed. Koenigsberg, Letter *he*).

as it is written, "And David did justice and righteousness."[240] The Sages explained the verse "And Joab rebuilt [lit. "revived"] the rest of the city"[241] as meaning that, because of the justice and righteousness that David did, Joab was able to revive the rest of the city.[242] David was succeeded by his son after him, beloved of the Lord, who loved to follow the practices of his father;[243] and he asked God for an understanding and sensitive heart to judge his people and to discern between good and evil. His request was favorably received by the Lord and He gave him a wise and understanding heart, such as had not existed before him or was to exist after him; and all Israel were in awe of him, because they saw that the wisdom of God was in his heart to do justice.[244]

And also Jehoshaphat, who walked in his father's ways and whose heart was elevated in the Lord's ways,[245] was very vigorous in the matter of justice, and appointed judges in every town. He told the judges, "Consider what you are doing, for you judge not on behalf of man, but on behalf of the Lord. He is with you when you pass judgment."[246] This is also true of Josiah, of whom Scripture says,[247] "There was no previous king like him who turned back to the Lord with all his heart"—on which the Sages commented that he restored [at his own personal expense] the proceeds of all the judgments he had rendered before he became eighteen years of age.[248] Scripture also praises the Messiah, may he come speedily in our days, in the matter of justice, as it is written,[249] "Thus he shall judge the poor with equity and decide with justice for the lowly of the land."

As the reward is great, so too is the punishment for denying or perverting justice, as we have been taught,[250] "The sword comes upon the world because of delaying and perverting justice." Similarly, David said,[251] "I have done what is just and right; do not abandon me to those who would wrong me"—from which it follows that he who withholds justice will be so abandoned. Jerusalem was destroyed and Israel was exiled only because they forsook justice,[252] as it is written,[253] "The faithful city that was filled with justice,

240. II Samuel 8:15, where the text is: "David executed true justice [lit. "did justice and righteousness"] among all his people."

241. I Chronicles 11:8.

242. *Cf.* TB Sanhedrin 49a.

243. *Cf.* I Kings 3:3.

244. *Cf.* I Kings 3:9,10,12,28.

245. *Cf.* II Chronicles 17:6.

246. II Chronicles 19:6.

247. II Kings 23:25.

248. TB Shabbat 56b, where the text reads: "Every judgment he had given between the ages of eight and eighteen he restored."

249. Isaiah 11:4.

250. M Avot 5:8.

251. Psalms 119:121.

252. *Cf.* TB Shabbat 139a.

253. Isaiah 1:21.

where righteousness dwelt—but now murderers," and[254] "They do not judge the case of the orphan, and the widow's cause never reaches them"—after which it is written,[255] "Ah, I will get satisfaction from My foes; I will wreak vengeance on My enemies."

Similarly, Jerusalem will be redeemed through justice, as it is written:[256] "Zion shall be saved by justice, her repentant ones by righteousness"; and,[257] "Devote yourselves to justice, aid the wronged, uphold the rights of the orphan, defend the cause of the widow"; after which it is written,[258] "Be your sins like crimson, they can turn snow-white." [Administering justice] also brings the Redemption nearer, as it is written,[259] "Observe what is right and do what is just; for soon My salvation shall come and My deliverance be revealed." The Holy One, blessed be He, desires justice more than all the sacrificial offerings, as it is written,[260] "To do what is just and right (*mishpat u-ẓedakah*) is more desired by the Lord than sacrifice." Scripture does not say "more than a sin offering or a burnt offering," but "more than sacrifice" [*i.e.*, more than all sacrifices].

Moses, our teacher, also warned us . . . :[261] "You shall not be partial in judgment. . . . Fear no man, for judgment is God's." He also formulated this as a positive commandment: "Judge your neighbor fairly"[262] and "Govern the people with due justice."[263]

He also commanded to appoint judges in every place, as it is written,[264] "You shall appoint judges and officials in all your settlements." "Judges" are the duly constituted adjudicators, and "officials" are those with the rod and the lash who stand before the judges to carry out their sentence.[265]

After this instructive preface[266] on the importance of justice, Jacob b. Asher proceeded to discuss the jurisdiction, composition, and competence of the

254. Isaiah 1:23.
255. Isaiah 1:24.
256. Isaiah 1:27.
257. Isaiah 1:17.
258. Isaiah 1:18.
259. Isaiah 56:1.
260. Proverbs 21:3, where the reading is "To do what is right and just (*ẓedakah u-mishpat*). . . . "
261. Deuteronomy 1:17.
262. Leviticus 19:15.
263. Deuteronomy 1:16.
264. Deuteronomy 16:18.
265. *See Sifrei,* Deuteronomy, sec. 15 (end); Rashi to Deuteronomy 16:18. *Cf.* TB Sanhedrin 7b, where "the rod and the lash" refers to R. Huna, who was a judge.
266. For similar prefaces containing philosophical and ethical material relevant to the subject of a particular *tur, see* the Preface to ch. 1 in OḤ and that to ch. 1 in EH. As stated, such prefaces can occasionally be found within a *tur* at the outset of the discussion of a particular subject. *See, e.g.,* the Preface to the Laws of the Sabbath, OḤ ch. 242; the Preface to the Laws of *Sukkah,* OḤ ch. 625, *et al. See also Bayit Ḥadash* (*Baḥ*) to EH ch. 1 and OḤ chs. 242 and 625 for the rationale for these prefaces in the *Turim.*

various courts, and similar subjects. He included in the *Turim* only those laws that were still applicable after the destruction of the Temple,[267] and thus reverted to the policy first adopted at the very beginning of Jewish codificatory literature in the *Halakhot Pesukot* of Yehudai Gaon[268] and followed by the great majority of codifiers. Maimonides' *Mishneh Torah* was unique in treating the entire corpus of the *Halakhah.*[269]

The difference between the scope of the *Turim* and that of the *Mishneh Torah* is well exemplified by the relative proportion of each work devoted to the subjects included in *mishpat ivri.* In the *Mishneh Torah,* the law comprising *mishpat ivri* takes up less than one-third of the work,[270] whereas in the *Turim,* approximately one-half (*Even ha-Ezer* and *Ḥoshen Mishpat*) is devoted to that area of the law.[271] It is also worthy of note that *Ḥoshen*

267. At times, laws that apply exclusively in the Land of Israel were included if relevant to the general subject and to laws that apply also outside the Land of Israel. *See, e.g., Tur* ḤM 376:1: "If a person encroaches on his neighbor's property and forcibly appropriates even as little as a fingerbreadth of his neighbor's land as his own, he is a robber; and if he stealthily encroaches and appropriates, he is a thief. If the encroachment takes place in the Land of Israel, the trespasser also transgresses the prohibition 'You shall not move your neighbor's landmarks'" (Deuteronomy 19:14).

On the other hand, some specific laws that do not apply outside the Land of Israel were not included even if the general subject to which they relate has practical relevance outside of the Land of Israel. *See, e.g., Tur* ḤM 231:26–30, where various laws of profiteering are discussed, but the prohibition that applies in the Land of Israel against trafficking in commodities needed for survival and the prohibition against exporting such commodities from the Land of Israel, although relevant to the general subject of profiteering, were not mentioned because they apply exclusively in the Land of Israel; *see* TB Bava Batra 90b-91a. The *Mishneh Torah,* of course, includes both these laws (*Hilkhot Mekhirah* 14:4,8); and, interestingly, so does Joseph Caro's *Shulḥan Arukh* (ḤM 231:23,26). *See also Sema, ad loc.,* subpar. 42, 44. Caro lived in the Land of Israel in Safed, in his time a developed commercial center that exported goods. *See supra* p. 1133 and n. 116.

268. *See supra* pp. 1153–1155.

269. Jacob Ḥazzan's *Eẓ Ḥayyim* also included laws that were no longer applicable, but not to the same extent (even in regard to the number of subjects) as the *Mishneh Torah. See supra* pp. 1255–1256.

270. Five books (*Nashim, Nezikin, Kinyan, Mishpatim,* and *Shofetim*) out of fourteen. The proportion in the Mishnah is similar—two Orders (*Nashim* and *Nezikin*) out of six. A more precise assessment can be made by examining the *Mishneh Torah,* Rome edition of 1480 (facsimile ed., Jerusalem, 1955). That edition, in which no commentaries—not even Rabad's glosses—are printed, contains 673 pages (not including the Introduction or the list of the commandments). Of those 673 pages, *Sefer Nashim, Sefer Nezikin, Sefer Kinyan, Sefer Mishpatim,* and *Sefer Shofetim* (excluding the laws of mourning) occupy 217 pages—less than one-third.

271. *Tur* OḤ has 697 chapters; YD, 403; EH, 178; and ḤM 426. However, in the *Turim,* too, as in the *Mishneh Torah,* it is not the number of chapters that is important but their scope and length. Thus, in the 1540 Soncino edition of the *Turim* (printed without *Bet Yosef*) the division is as follows: OḤ—89 folios, YD—78, EH—49, ḤM—120. In the Augsburg edition of the same year (also without *Bet Yosef*), OḤ has 77 folios, YD 64, EH 43, and ḤM 106.

Mishpat is the largest and most comprehensive of the four *Turim*[272]—another indication of the extent to which Jewish civil law was applied in practice in the daily life of the diaspora in that period.

The methodology of the *Turim* in regard to both form and content was highly successful. It is true that Maimonides' *Mishneh Torah* is, in some respects, a superior work; it excels the *Turim* in consolidation of the laws into complete and homogeneous units and particularly in clarity and beauty of style and diction. However, the *Turim* succeeded in concentrating in a convenient and well-organized form the entire *corpus juris* of Jewish law (so far as it still had practical applicability) as it had then developed, and in classifying and organizing the law into clear and well-defined subject areas, so that both students and judges could easily find whatever was necessary for their study or rulings.

Most significantly, the *Turim* successfully achieved a middle course between a book of *pesakim* and a book of *halakhot*. On the one hand, it does not suffer from the awkwardness inherent in a full presentation of Talmudic discussion and the identification of all the Sages involved; it states the basic legal principles unequivocally, categorically, and without reference to source or authority. On the other hand, it presents the various opinions of the leading *rishonim* on particular ramifications and indicates, either explicitly or indirectly, which of the conflicting views is deemed correct. Thus, the work has the advantages of both a book of *pesakim* and a book of *halakhot*: it is convenient to use and definitively states the law, yet preserves the continuity of Jewish law and its link to the chain of tradition, and brings to the attention of the decisionmaker the whole range of relevant opinions.

Jacob b. Asher realized his aspiration to create a work such "that the reader may quickly find and act in accordance with what is to be found there, not deviating from it to the right or to the left." The *Turim* was very soon accepted in a large part of the Jewish world. Although a part of the eastern Jewish communities continued to accept Maimonides' *Mishneh Torah* as the authoritative code,[273] the great Jewish centers in the west—particularly in Germany, Italy, and Poland—followed the rulings of the

272. *See supra* n. 271.

273. *See supra* p. 1233 and n. 122. In some eastern Jewish communities, *Sefer ha-Turim* was accepted as the definitive statement of the law; *see, e.g., Resp. Tashbez,* III, #257 and #327 as to *"gelilot Sefarad"* ("the Spanish provinces") that followed the rulings of the *Turim.* The *Turim* was similarly authoritative in North Africa and even Egypt, as well as other Jewish centers in the East. *See also* Elijah Mizraḥi, *Resp. Mayim Amukkim* #1: "Nevertheless, we have determined the law according to the author of the *Turim,* of blessed memory, because he is the most recent authority, and, from the time of Abbaye and Rava, we follow the later authority." *See further* Freimann, "Die Ascheriden," *supra* n. 71 at 191ff.

Turim.[274] It is an indication of the popularity of the *Turim* that it was the second Hebrew book to appear in print,[275] whereas many other codificatory works remained in manuscript for centuries. Furthermore, the contents and even the topical arrangement of the *Turim* served, two centuries later, as the basis for the most widely accepted halakhic code, the *Shulḥan Arukh* of Joseph Caro.

III. COMMENTARIES ON *SEFER HA-TURIM*

The widespread popularity of the *Turim* and its recognition by the halakhic authorities resulted, as in the case of many other codificatory works, in a rich literature of commentaries. The commentaries on the *Turim* traced its sources, took issue with it, explicated it, reconciled perceived inconsistencies in it, and supplemented its rulings.

A number of the leading Sephardic[276] and Ashkenazic[277] halakhic authorities of the fifteenth century wrote commentaries and glosses to the *Turim*, but the classic commentaries extant were written for the most part

274. *See* Michael, *supra* n. 94 at 489, s.v. Rabbenu Ya'akov b. R. ha-Rosh. Jacob Landau wrote in *Sefer ha-Agur* (*see infra* p. 1305): "This is a general rule for readers: When I do not give a source for a quotation, it is from the *Turim.*" Mahari Minẓ (Judah Minẓ, Italy, fifteenth century) reported an interesting fact: "Some rabbis refuse even to read *Tur* OḤ on the ground that laymen [*ba'alei battim*] study it" (*Resp. Mahari Minẓ u-Maharam mi-Padua,* Section Resp. Mahari Minẓ, #15, 6th par., s.v. U-ve-inyan ha-de'ot). However, it was said of Maharil (Jacob b. Moses Moellin) that "he would take the *Turim* with him to the synagogue and study it whenever the cantor prolonged his renditions, as well as during the *kedushah* and *kaddish* prayers" (*Sefer ha-Maharil,* Warsaw, 1874, Hilkhot Tefillah, p. 61b).

275. In 1475. The first Hebrew book to be printed was Rashi's commentary on the Pentateuch, on Adar 10, 1475—the same year that the *Turim* was printed. *See* A. Freimann, *Thesaurus Typographiae Hebraicae,* A1, plates 1–3, for examples of *editio princeps* of Rashi; A2, plates 1–6, for examples of *Tur* OḤ, EH, and ḤM of 1475; A4, plates 1–2, for *Tur* OḤ printed Sivan 14, 1476; A5, plates 1–2, for *Tur* YD printed Av 15, 1477. All these editions were printed in Italy.

276. Joseph Caro's Introduction to *Bet Yosef* on *Tur* OḤ mentions a commentary on the *Turim* by Isaac Aboab (the latter), a Spanish authority during the period of the Expulsion from Spain, who was a disciple of Isaac Canpanton and the teacher of Abraham Zacuto and Jacob Berab. This Introduction also mentions "the beginnings of a treatise" on *Tur* OḤ and YD by Jacob b. Solomon ibn Ḥabib. (Ibn Ḥabib was also a Spanish authority at the time of the Expulsion and compiled the well-known *Ein Ya'akov,* a collection of all the aggadic passages in the Talmud, with commentaries of the *rishonim,* as well as one of his own.) Moses b. Isaac Alashkar, known as Maharam Alashkar, a halakhic authority in Spain and Egypt at the end of the fifteenth and beginning of the sixteenth centuries, composed a commentary on the *Turim* called *Geon Ya'akov; see* Ḥida, *Shem ha-Gedolim,* Persons, Letter *mem,* par. 102; Michael, *supra* n. 94 at 489ff. *See also id.*, s.v. Rabbenu Ya'akov b. R. ha-Rosh, for a listing of many other glosses and commentaries.

277. Such as the glosses of Elijah of Prague, a fifteenth-century Ashkenazic authority. *See* Isaac Tirnau, *Sefer Minhagim,* Minhag of *Purim,* Glosses, subpar. 2.

by leading Ashkenazic authorities in the sixteenth and early seventeenth centuries. A partial listing includes the following:

A. *Bet Yosef* by Joseph Caro and *Darkhei Moshe* by Moses Isserles (Rema)

Since both these commentaries are closely connected with the codificatory methodology of their authors and with the *Shulḥan Arukh*, they will be discussed in the next chapter, which deals with Caro's and Rema's codificatory works.

B. *Bet Yisra'el* by Joshua Falk

Joshua b. Alexander ha-Kohen Falk, a student of Solomon Luria (Maharshal) and Rema, was a halakhic authority in Poland in the second half of the sixteenth and beginning of the seventeenth centuries. His work *Bet Yisra'el*[278] is divided into three parts: *Perishah*, *Derishah*, and *Haggahot*. *Perishah* is a commentary that explains the text of the four *Turim* and traces the sources of their laws. The second part, *Derishah*, discusses at length the various opinions of the *rishonim* and other prior authorities. This pattern, however, was not always adhered to; occasionally, *Perishah* is more discursive than *Derishah*. The third part, *Haggahot*, consists of glosses to Rema's *Darkhei Moshe* and contains rulings and decisions, mainly from the responsa literature, rendered after the composition of the *Turim* and of *Bet Yosef*.[279]

C. *Bayit Ḥadash (Baḥ)* by Joel Sirkes

Joel Sirkes was a halakhic authority in Poland at the end of the sixteenth and in the first half of the seventeenth centuries. *Bayit Ḥadash*, generally known by its acronym *Baḥ*, is a classic commentary on the *Turim*. It explains and comments on the text, indicates sources, discusses the various opinions cited in the text and in *Bet Yosef* and *Darkhei Moshe*, and states the

278. Falk called his work *Bet Yisra'el* [House of Israel] because it is "valuable and helpful to the whole House of Israel" and it memorializes the name of his father-in-law, Israel b. Joseph, who financed the *yeshivah* that Falk headed. *See* Falk's Introduction (end) to *Bet Yisra'el* and to *Sefer Me'irat Einayim* (*Sema*), printed at the beginning of Sh. Ar. ḤM.

279. Originally, the third part was also written on the *Turim*, but later Joshua Falk wrote it as glosses to Rema's *Darkhei Moshe* instead; *see* Falk's Introduction. As to the fourth part (*i.e.*, *Sema*, which he wrote on Sh. Ar. ḤM), and for a detailed discussion of Falk's codificatory methodology and his objectives in writing on the *Turim* and on the *Shulḥan Arukh*, *see infra* pp. 1408–1414.

author's view of the law on disputed points.[280] *Bayit Ḥadash* exhibits the same well-developed critical sense in its textual analysis of the *Turim* that appears in Sirkes's writings on the Talmud and other halakhic works.[281]

The works of both Joshua Falk and Joel Sirkes were deeply influenced by their approach to codifying the *Halakhah*, which is further discussed below.[282]

D. Compilations of Responsa Arranged According to the Organization of *Sefer ha-Turim*

In the course of time, books were composed mainly for the purpose of supplementing the *Turim* and *Bet Yosef* with halakhic material that these works had omitted and adding material that had later accumulated. The first two works of this type were written about a century after *Bet Yosef*: *Panim Ḥadashot*, by Isaac Jesurun, and *Keneset ha-Gedolah*, by Ḥayyim Benveniste. Later, as it became necessary from time to time to review and update the substantial amount of halakhic material accumulated since the *Turim* and *Bet Yosef* and to arrange it according to the pattern of organization of these two works, additional compilations and supplementations appeared. Since they are directly based on both the *Turim* and *Bet Yosef*, they will be covered after our discussion of *Bet Yosef*.[283]

IV. CODIFICATORY LITERATURE FROM *SEFER HA-TURIM* TO THE *SHULḤAN ARUKH*

Sefer ha-Turim achieved widespread popularity and was recognized as the main code of Jewish law, notwithstanding the many codificatory works that appeared contemporaneously with it or afterward, during the fourteenth and fifteenth centuries. Most of the other works treated subjects such as the laws of prayer and benedictions, festivals, and ritual slaughter and other

280. *See further infra* pp. 1415–1417 as to *Bayit Ḥadash* and Joel Sirkes' codificatory methodology.

281. Another commentary on the *Turim*, called *Va-Yiggash Yehudah*, was written in the sixteenth century by Judah Liba b. Meir Ḥanlish, an Ashkenazic authority in Posen. In the course of time, a digest of this commentary was composed, called *Ḥiddushei ha-Gaon Maharlaḥ* or *Ḥiddushei Haggahot*. This digest is printed in all recent editions of the *Turim*. *See* Ḥida, *Shem ha-Gedolim*, Books, Letter *vav*, pars. 3–4; Michael, *supra* n. 94 at 489ff.; Tchernowitz, *Toledot ha-Posekim*, II, pp. 299–300.

282. *See infra* pp. 1408–1417.

283. *See infra* pp. 1432–1443.

dietary laws. The following is a brief survey of some of the better-known works.

In Spain during the fourteenth century, several books of *halakhot* in various areas of the law of festivals were written by Yom Tov b. Abraham Ishbili (Ritba).[284] *Sefer Abudarham,* by David b. Joseph Abudarham, treats the laws of prayer and benedictions;[285] and *Sefer Ohel Mo'ed,* by Samuel b. Meshullam Yerudani, treats the laws of benedictions, prayer, festivals, and other ritual matters.[286]

In the same period in Germany, many books were written on customs and practices; to a certain degree, these may be properly classified as codificatory literature. They include: in the fourteenth century, *Sefer Minhagim de-vei Maharam b. Baruch me-Rothenburg*[287] and *Sefer ha-Minhagim* by Abraham Klausner;[288] in the fifteenth century, *Sefer ha-Minhagim*[289] by Yiẓḥak Isaac Tirna, a Hungarian authority who had been a student of Abraham Klausner, and *Sefer ha-Maharil* by Jacob b. Moses Moellin.[290] The books of customs addressed themselves mainly to the laws of prayer, benedictions, festivals, and ritual law. In the fields of law covered by *Tur Oraḥ Ḥayyim* and *Tur Yoreh De'ah,* two additional books were written in the fifteenth century: *Sefer Issur ve-Hetter ha-Arokh* by a German halakhic authority[291] and *Sefer ha-Agur* by Jacob Landau, an authority in Germany and Italy.[292] Such books

284. Of these works by Ritba, only the one dealing with the laws of benedictions has survived; it was printed at the end of *Resp. Ḥayyim va-Ḥesed* by Ḥayyim Isaac Musafia and more recently by M. Blau in *Sefer Kitvei ha-Ritba* [Collected Works of Ritba], New York, 1956, pp. 52–129, with the commentary *Me'ein ha-Berakhot. See* Blau's Introduction at 3–5 as to other halakhic works of Ritba (on the laws of the Day of Atonement, Rosh ha-Shanah, etc.) which have not survived.

285. Reprinted many times; of late, *Sefer Abudarham ha-Shalem,* ed. S. Kroyzer, 1959, with Introduction.

286. The book was published in two parts, Jerusalem, 1886–1904, with commentary and glosses by Ḥayyim Abraham Gagin and his son Moses Ḥai Gagin. The book is divided into "gates" (*she'arim*), which are subdivided into "paths" (*netivim*).

287. First published by I. Elfenbein, New York, 1938, with Introduction and notes.

288. Reprinted many times; *e.g.,* ed. I.H. Ehrenreich, 1929, with Introduction and notes.

289. Frequently reprinted. Apparently, this is the first halakhic work to emerge from Hungary.

290. Frequently reprinted.

291. Last published in Vilna, 1891, by A. Braun, who wrote a commentary on it, called *Zer Zahav.* The author's name is Jonah; he was a disciple of Israel Isserlein, but the book was mistakenly attributed to Jonah Gerondi (*see* title page), who was a thirteenth-century Spanish authority.

292. *Sefer ha-Agur* has been reprinted many times and has most recently appeared as *Sefer ha-Agur ha-Shalem,* with Introduction and notes by M. Hershler, Jerusalem, 1960. Jacob Landau stated in his Introduction that he wrote the book for his disciple Ezra b. David Obadiah ha-Rofe, who, because of the press of his medical practice, was unable to study the

of *halakhot* and customs played a large role in shaping the life-style of Ashkenazic Jewry, and many of the laws and rulings they contain are included by Rema in his glosses to the *Shulḥan Arukh.*

A few of the books of *halakhot* of this period also treat family and civil law. In Germany, Alexander Suslin ha-Kohen, who was martyred in the pogroms at the time of the Black Death, wrote *Sefer ha-Agudah,* containing rulings and novellae on all the tractates of the Talmud, arranged in the order of the tractates. Subsequent Ashkenazic authorities, including Jacob Weil, Maharil, and Rema, frequently relied on Suslin.[293] In Spain, too, several codificatory works were written, some of which have only recently been printed.

From the standpoint of the history of halakhic codification, the most significant work of the period between the *Turim* and the *Shulḥan Arukh* is *Sefer Ḥukkot ha-Dayyanim* [The Book of the Laws of the Judges] by Abraham b. Solomon ibn Tazarti in fourteenth-century Spain.[294] Unlike the other halakhic works of the period, it deals solely with family and civil law. Its style is similar to that of the *Turim* in that it first states basic legal principles without reference to authority or source, generally not citing or quoting the relevant discussion in the Talmud. Thereafter, it indicates the various relevant opinions, but more briefly than the *Turim.*

A further interesting similarity between *Sefer Ḥukkot ha-Dayyanim* and the *Turim* is in their organization. *Sefer Ḥukkot ha-Dayyanim,* like *Tur Ḥoshen Mishpat,* begins its treatment of civil law with the rules pertaining to judges—qualifications, composition of the courts, procedure, and the prohibition against bribery. Then follow the laws relating to witnesses, such as competency, grounds for disqualification, plotting witnesses (*edim zomemim*), and examination of witnesses. Next come the laws of witnesses to documents, admissions, officers of the court, scribes of the court, and pleading. However, the similarity is mostly in the general organization; there are differences in the sequence in which particular topics are discussed. For

---

Halakhah in the Talmudic sources. The book quotes entire passages from the *Turim; see* author's Introduction and *supra* n. 274.

293. *See* Ḥida, *Shem ha-Gedolim,* Books, Letter *aleph,* par. 16; Michael, *supra* n. 94 at 224. *Sefer ha-Agudah* has been reprinted frequently, most recently by A.J. Szyck, New York, 1959; *see* the Introduction to that edition. The part relating to Tractates *Shabbat, Megillah, Ta'anit, Yoma,* and *Beẓah* was published by E. Brissel, Jerusalem, 1966, with comparative readings from ms. Oxford and glosses and commentary.

294. The book was first published in Jerusalem in 1970–1971: *Sefer Ḥukkot ha-Dayyanim,* by Rabbenu Abraham b. Solomon ibn Tazarti, a disciple of Rashba, with a commentary, *Shimru Mishpat,* by Abraham Ashkenazi, Introduction by Isaac Nissim, and notes by Isaac Ashkenazi entitled *Konan la-Mishpat. See id.,* Introduction at 16–20, as to the identification of Abraham b. Solomon ibn Tazarti as the author.

example, *Tur Ḥoshen Mishpat* begins with the question of the power of the courts to adjudicate civil and capital cases after the destruction of the Temple (chapters 1–2), whereas *Sefer Ḥukkot ha-Dayyanim* discusses that subject after the laws relating to witnesses (chapter 76). The *Turim* discusses the laws of compromise and settlement in chapter 12; *Sefer Ḥukkot ha-Dayyanim*, in chapter 75. Many further examples could be given.

Sefer Ḥukkot ha-Dayyanim has only recently been published,[295] with a detailed commentary by Abraham Ashkenazi, a nineteenth-century halakhic authority in Jerusalem and Sephardic Chief Rabbi of the Holy Land from 1869 to 1880. The commentary traces the book's underlying sources, particularly Rashba. Abraham Ashkenazi's son Isaac added notes and supplements to the commentary.[296]

Another work that is in part specifically devoted to civil law is *Ẓeror ha-Ḥayyim* and *Ẓeror ha-Kesef* by Ḥayyim b. Samuel, a disciple of Rashba. This book of *halakhot* is in the main topically arranged. Before summarizing the law, it briefly reviews the Talmudic sources and the opinions of prior *rishonim*. *Ẓeror ha-Ḥayyim* treats the laws of prayer, benedictions, and festivals;[297] *Ẓeror ha-Kesef* treats civil law "and it is divided into *derakhim* (paths) and *she'arim* (gates)."[298]

Another book of *halakhot* written in this period is *Sefer Zevadin de-Urḥa—Ẓeidah la-Derekh* by Menahem b. Aaron ibn Zeraḥ, a fourteenth-century Spanish halakhic authority. His father had been expelled from France in 1306 and had settled in Italy, where Menahem was born. Menahem was forced to leave Italy after his whole family was killed in pogroms; he moved to Spain, where he became a disciple of Judah the son of Asheri. There, too, he suffered great tribulations. The Introduction to his book gives an account of his life was well as a detailed history of the *Halakhah* and

295. Vol. I of *Sefer Ḥukkot ha-Dayyanim*, containing one hundred chapters, appeared in 1970, and vol. II, containing chs. 101–241, in 1971. The beginning of each volume contains an index of names of persons. Vol. II also includes (at the end) a cross-reference table between chapters in *Sefer Ḥukkot ha-Dayyanim* and the *Shulḥan Arukh* that is helpful for studying the differences between the two books in organization and contents and for locating parallel passages. *See supra* n. 217 to the effect that variations in organization existed as early as in geonic times; the *geonim* put Tractate *Sanhedrin* at the beginning of the Order of *Nezikin*, rather than where R. Judah Ha-Nasi placed it and where we have it today.

296. The parallels between *Sefer Ḥukkot ha-Dayyanim* and *Tur* ḤM are very striking and have not yet been thoroughly studied; *see supra* n. 295. Another interesting point is worthy of note: chs. 20 and 21 begin: "If two witnesses testify against Manasseh, one saying . . . and the other saying. . . . " The use of "Manasseh" as a fictitious name for a party to a case is unusual in rabbinic literature; such fictitious names are conventionally the names of the sons of the patriarch Jacob: namely, Reuben, Simeon, Levi, Judah, etc.

297. This part was published by S. Ḥagi, Jerusalem, 1966, with Introduction and notes.

298. *See* Ḥida, *Shem ha-Gedolim*, Books, Letter *ẓadi*, pars. 32, 37; *id.*, Persons, Letter *ḥet*, par. 20. This part is as yet unpublished (*see* Editor's Introduction to *Ẓeror ha-Ḥayyim*).

halakhic literature, particularly in the post-Talmudic period. This Introduction is thus an important historical source for biographical material on halakhic authorities of Germany, France, and Spain. It points out that the book was composed in honor of Don Samuel Abrabanel, who helped the author in time of trouble, and who, because of the many other pressures that preoccupied him, did not have the time to study the Talmud. Therefore, ibn Zeraḥ wrote the book for Abrabanel and for "others at the court of our lord, the king . . . and particularly for travelers and officials and those privy to the king."

Ẓeidah la-Derekh concisely sets forth most of the *Halakhah* in an easy and clear style. Generally, it does not discuss the Talmudic sources, but presents the basic rules and the various relevant opinions without identifying the authorities who held them. The book is distinctive in that it is replete with philosophical rationales not only for "religious" law, but also for family law, divorce, and similar legal areas.[299]

The book is divided into five sections (*ma'amarim*, lit. "articles" or "essays"): the first treats the laws of benedictions, prayer, etc.; the second—"religious" law, such as dietary laws; the third—personal status, marriage, the financial relationship between spouses, divorce, levirate marriage, *ḥaliẓah*, etc.; the fourth—sabbath and festivals; the fifth—fasts, mourning, the Messiah, etc. Each section is divided into *kelalim* (rules), and each *kelal* into *perakim* (chapters).[300]

For approximately two centuries, Jacob b. Asher's *Sefer ha-Turim* remained the primary and most widely accepted code of Jewish law. Its methodology suited the codificatory needs of the time and maintained the link with the sources of the law by means of copious citations of differing opinions. Furthermore, it encompassed the totality of the law applicable at the time. It therefore met the needs of judges, students, and the community at large.[301] In the sixteenth century, at the end of the period covered by this chapter, various halakhic and historical factors combined to bring about the composition of a new code of Jewish law by Joseph Caro and Moses Isserles, which is discussed in the next chapter.

299. *See, e.g.*, the philosophical explanation of the subject of divorce, essay 3, rule 3, ch. 1.

300. *See* Ḥida, *Shem ha-Gedolim*, Persons, Letter *mem*, par. 49; *id.*, Books, Letter *ẓadi*, par. 4.

301. *See* Mahari Minẓ's observation, *supra* n. 274. For a comparison of the literary characteristics of the *Turim*, the *Mishneh Torah*, and the *Shulḥan Arukh*, *see further infra* pp. 1327–1341 and Appendix B.

Chapter 36

THE CODIFICATORY LITERATURE: THE WORKS OF JOSEPH CARO AND MOSES ISSERLES

I. Joseph Caro and His Codificatory Achievement
  A. Historical and Halakhic Circumstances
  B. A Two-Part Code: A Book of *Halakhot* and a Book of *Pesakim*
  C. *Bet Yosef*
    1. Compendious Presentation of All the Halakhic Material
    2. Methodology of Determining the Law
  D. The *Shulḥan Arukh*
    1. Codificatory Approach
    2. Structure and Arrangement
    3. Language and Style as Compared to the *Turim* and the *Mishneh Torah*
  E. The Crystallization of the Methodology for Codifying Jewish Law
II. Moses Isserles (Rema) and His Contribution to the Codificatory Literature
  A. The Polish Jewish Community
  B. Jacob Pollack and Shalom Shakhna, and Their Attitude toward Codification
  C. Moses Isserles (Rema)
  D. *Darkhei Moshe:* Its Purpose and Methodology
  E. *Torat Ḥattat* and Its Methodology
  F. Glosses to the *Shulḥan Arukh:* The *Mappah*—Its Objectives and Methodology
  G. The *Shulḥan Arukh* as the Authoritative Code of Jewish Law

I. JOSEPH CARO AND HIS CODIFICATORY ACHIEVEMENT

A. Historical and Halakhic Circumstances

The era between Jacob b. Asher, author of the *Turim,* and Joseph Caro was notable in Jewish history, as in world history, for many significant, and even crucial, events.[1] Some Jewish centers in the diaspora suffered decline or

1. Important events in world history during this period included the fall of the Eastern Roman Empire (1453), the discovery of America (1492), the Reformation of Martin Luther

destruction, and others arose to take their place and carry on their traditions. The center in Germany, already battered by a long series of calamitous persecutions for many years, was shaken to its very foundations by the outbreak of the Black Death in the middle of the fourteenth century (1348–1350) and by the ensuing pogroms against the Jewish communities as a result of the accusation that the Jews had poisoned the wells. In Spain, the persecutions and oppressive laws against the Jews intensified in the second half of the fourteenth century, reached a high point in the mass forced conversions to Christianity in 1391, and continued into the fifteenth century, culminating in the total destruction of the Spanish Jewish community by the Expulsion of 1492.

Entire Jewish populations, together with their rabbis and leaders, were forced to migrate and reestablish themselves in new centers. The Jewish center in Poland was built from the ruins of the Jewish communities of Germany; and the Jews of Spain found refuge in a number of Jewish centers, primarily in North Africa, the Middle East (Turkey, the Land of Israel, and Egypt), and Italy. As a result, the Jewish communities of Salonika, Adrianople, Constantinople, and Cairo, among many others, were transformed into major centers of Jewish learning; and the High Court of Safed became renowned as a leading halakhic tribunal throughout world Jewry. Many of the leading halakhic authorities became exiled wanderers. Joseph Caro, the son of Ephraim Caro, was one of them.

Joseph Caro was born in Spain in 1488. At the age of four, he, together with his parents, was exiled in the Expulsion of 1492. The family wandered through several way stations—Constantinople, Adrianople, Nikopol in northern Bulgaria, Salonika, and Egypt—until it reached Safed, in the Land of Israel. In Safed, Caro was appointed to the *bet din* presided over by Jacob Berab, who reintroduced the ancient practice of rabbinical ordination. Caro was one of the first whom Berab ordained. When Berab died, Caro, together with Moses b. Joseph Trani (Mabit), headed the *Bet Din* of Safed, which served as a leading tribunal for world Jewry.[2]

(1483–1546), and, of no less moment than these, the invention, in the fifteenth century, of movable type for printing.

2. *See* J. Katz, "Maḥaloket ha-Semikhah bein Rabbi Ya'akov Beirav ve-ha-Ralbaḥ" [The Dispute over Ordination between Rabbi Jacob Berab and Ralbaḥ (Rabbi Levi b. Ḥabib)], *Zion*, XVI, pp. 28–45; M. Benayahu, "Ḥiddushah Shel ha-Semikhah bi-Ẓefat" [The Reinstitution of Ordination in Safed], *Sefer Yovel Likhevod Yiẓḥak Baer* [Jubilee Volume in Honor of Yitzhak Baer], 1961, pp. 248ff.; D. Tamar, *Meḥkarim be-Toledot ha-Yehudim be-Ereẓ Yisra'el u-ve-Italyah* [Studies in the History of the Jews in the Land of Israel and in Italy], Jerusalem, 1970. As to the period in general, *see* H.H. Ben Sasson, "Toledot Yisra'el bi-Mei ha-Beinayim" [A History of the Jews in the Middle Ages], and bibliography cited, in *Toledot Am Yisra'el* [A History of the Jewish People], II. As to the economic background of Safed's

These migrations and wanderings of entire Jewish communities produced a number of social and halakhic effects. Jews began to long for the Final Redemption and for a restored and renewed supreme halakhic authority that would once again consolidate the Jewish people scattered throughout the diaspora. The attempt by Jacob Berab to renew the ancient institution of ordination was one manifestation of this yearning.[3] The expulsions and wanderings that uprooted entire communities and replanted them in new locations created a whole complex of halakhic problems arising out of the conflict between the laws and customs[4] of the older inhabitants and those of the newcomers. It was this conflict that gave rise to a vast and remarkably creative output of responsa, legislative enactments, and codificatory works.[5] As this halakhic creativity grew in scope, it became increasingly difficult to navigate through the vast literature. Differences of opinion intensified, and conflicting decisions multiplied.

In his *Bet Yosef*,[6] Caro described the condition of Jewish law in his day:

> As time has passed, we have been poured from vessel to vessel. We have become scattered, and terrible trials and tribulations, one after the other, have come upon us, to the extent that, as a result of our sins, the verse "And the wisdom of its wise shall fail [and the prudence of its prudent shall vanish]"[7] has become applicable to us. The Torah and its students have become helpless. For the Torah has become not [only] two Torahs; rather, it has been fragmented into innumerable Torahs because of the multitude of books written to explicate its laws and rules. Although all those writers, peace be upon them, meant to enlighten our darkness, the "light" we have enjoyed from them has brought great doubt and confusion because each author has composed his own work in which he either has repeated what previous writers had already written or has stated the law contrary to his predecessors without

---

growth, *see* S. Avitzur, "Ẓefat Merkaz le-Ta'asiyat Arigei Ẓemer be-Me'ah ha-Ḥamesh Esreh" [Safed, The Center of the Woolen Cloth Industry in the Fifteenth Century], *Sefer Ẓefat*, I, 1962, pp. 41ff.

3. *See* sources cited *supra* n. 2.

4. Joseph Caro accorded custom considerable force. Thus, he held that a prohibitory custom must be followed even where his own opinion was that the conduct in question was in fact permissible. Indeed, if a custom, whether prohibitory or permissive, is widespread, it is to be followed, since its acceptance indicates that most, if not all, the halakhic authorities disagree with the contrary result reached by Caro's decision-making methodology. (*See Bet Yosef* to *Tur* OḤ, Introduction, quoted *infra*, and *cf. Resp. Avkat Rokhel* #32.) The prodigious increase in the number of customs gave rise to a new form of legal literature, namely, compilations of the various customs having the force of law.

5. The multiplicity of local customs and legislation resulted in the development of conflict of laws as a distinct branch of the law. *See supra* pp. 78–79, 677, 936.

6. *Bet Yosef* to *Tur* OḤ, Introduction.

7. Isaiah 29:14.

> mentioning the conflict. You will sometimes find that several codifiers have stated a rule categorically as though it is universally accepted, but when you investigate, you discover that leading halakhic authorities have rejected it. Innumerable instances of this kind will be apparent to anyone who examines the books of the codifiers and then traces their sources to the Talmud and the ancient authorities. And, if one attempts to trace the source of every law from the Talmud through all the commentaries and codes, he will find this task to be exceedingly difficult and will surely become exhausted in the search for the source of the law in the Talmud.[8]

The wounds of exile and dispersion had left their scars on Jewish law; the one Torah had become not two but innumerable Torahs, and "the Jews of that generation needed a book such as this that collects all the laws and reveals their sources so that a correct conclusion can be reached as to what the *Halakhah* prescribes."[9] There were many great halakhic authorities in that generation, but of them all, Joseph Caro alone undertook this momentous task so vitally needed by both his own and later generations.[10]

B. A Two-Part Code: A Book of *Halakhot* and a Book of *Pesakim*

How did Joseph Caro propose to accomplish this task, and what was the method chosen by him to solve the problems involved in the codification of Jewish law?

Caro's statements and works reveal that his codificatory method was to create a single work consisting of two parts or books that, although separate and distinct in form and content, would, taken together, achieve a single overall objective. This approach to codification was not entirely original. A similar approach had already been suggested in the letter to Phinehas of Alexandria in which Maimonides stated that he was thinking of writing a separate book that would contain the sources for some of his rulings in the *Mishneh Torah*.[11] However, this statement was no more than a bare

8. These remarks of Caro in his Introduction were intended to describe not only the tribulations of exile generally that were suffered by the Jewish people, but also the particular tribulations of the expulsions that had occurred just before his time, as well as of those in his own lifetime. These tribulations produced an unusual and inordinate increase in halakhic disputes—differing views as to the details of legal rules—leading, as he put it, to "innumerable Torahs." *See also* Ḥida's remark, quoted in the next sentence of the text.

9. Ḥida, *Shem ha-Gedolim*, Books, Letter *bet*, #59.

10. *See further id.*: "In that generation, there were three rabbis worthy of the task: Joseph Taitaẓak, our teacher [Caro], and Maharibal [Joseph ibn Lev]. Any one of them could have accomplished the work, but Heaven decreed that the law should be given by our holy teacher [Caro] because of his extreme humility."

11. *See supra* pp. 1220–1221.

suggestion. Moreover, Maimonides did not intend to write a book that would contain all the disparate opinions on every point. He contemplated including only the sources for the opinions that he had adopted, and only for the laws for which the source was not readily ascertainable in the Talmud; and he never carried out even this more limited project.

Rashba's two-part work, *Torat ha-Bayit ha-Arokh* and *Torat ha-Bayit ha-Kaẓer,* was a much larger step in the direction of Caro's approach; it consisted of a book of *pesakim* stating the law in succinct, categorical style, complemented by a book of *halakhot* describing the development of each legal rule or principle and presenting all the relevant opinions.[12] However, Rashba's work covered only some of the laws relating to matters of *issur* and festivals. Moreover, it did not in its time noticeably influence the methodology of codificatory literature; each of the many codes written during the next two and one-half centuries followed its own distinct pattern of style and content. Caro succeeded in transforming Rashba's methodology into the accepted approach to halakhic codification by his adoption of that methodology for the creation of his own great code: a single work made up of two parts—*Bet Yosef* and the *Shulḥan Arukh.*

C. *Bet Yosef*

1. COMPENDIOUS PRESENTATION OF ALL THE HALAKHIC MATERIAL

Bet Yosef [The House of Joseph] was Joseph Caro's first, and, in point of scope and content, his major work. He composed it as an extension of the *Turim* and followed the organization of that work. Following the passage in his Introduction, quoted above, he clearly and explicitly described the two objectives of his work. The first was:

> To compose a work that includes all the laws currently applicable, together with an explanation of their roots and origins in the Talmud, as well as an exposition of the different opinions of all the authorities, omitting none.[13]

The first objective of *Bet Yosef* was thus to collect all the halakhic material up to Caro's own time concerning "the laws currently applicable," *i.e.*, the laws applicable after the destruction of the Temple, to indicate the Tal-

12. *See supra* pp. 1273–1275.

13. *Bet Yosef* to *Tur* OḤ, Introduction. The quoted passage begins: "Therefore, I, the poorest of the thousands, Joseph, the son of Ephraim the son of Joseph Caro, have been zealous for the Lord of Hosts, have girded my loins to clear the way, and have decided to compose. . . . "

mudic sources, and to present all the different opinions bearing on each law. Caro also described how he intended to carry out that objective:

> I decided not to write the book as an independent work, so that I would not have to repeat what my predecessors wrote; I therefore decided to attach it to one of the famous codes,[14] . . . the book of the . . . *Turim* of Rabbenu Jacob b. Asher, because it [the *Turim*] includes most of the opinions of the authorities.

Attaching his work to the *Turim* thus spared Caro the burden of repeating the opinions of the halakhic authorities already collated in that work; he needed merely to indicate the Talmudic sources of the laws stated in the *Turim,* explain and sometimes criticize the various opinions presented there, and occasionally correct errors that had found their way into the text. Caro continued:

> This is the purpose of the work [*Bet Yosef*] and its methodology: to explain each law that the author of the *Turim* wrote [and to indicate its source], be it a *mishnah,* a *baraita,* a *Tosefta,* a statement in the Babylonian or Jerusalem Talmud, or a passage of the *Sifra, Sifrei,* or *Mekhilta.* [It is also intended to indicate] whether the law is unanimously agreed upon or whether there are conflicting views respecting it among the *tannaim* or *amoraim,* and, if so, why the author [of the *Turim*] adopted the view of the particular authority he followed.
>
> When the author [of the *Turim*] sets forth conflicting opinions among halakhic authorities with respect to a law, the reasons for each opinion will be explained and its root and source in the Talmud will be stated. When the author [of the *Turim*] omits the opinion of an authority,[15] . . . the view of that authority will be presented and explained. When the statements of an authority, whether or not quoted in the *Turim,* are difficult to understand, they will be explained—particularly the statements of Maimonides, because in many instances his rulings are cryptic and enigmatic; these will be explained in our book according to the interpretations of *Maggid Mishneh* and Ran.[16] . . . And when the author of the *Turim* [queries or] poses an objection to the opinion of an authority, the objection or query will be answered. If there is a

14. Caro stated that he had originally intended to attach his work to Maimonides' *Mishneh Torah,* "since he is the most famous halakhic authority in the world, but I gave up the idea because he gives only one opinion and I would have had to set out at length the opinions and the rationales of all the other authorities."

15. In this regard, Caro stated: "As you will find, he [the author of the *Turim*] frequently omits the opinion of Alfasi or Maimonides or other authorities." It should be borne in mind that Alfasi and Maimonides were two of the three "pillars of instruction" on which *Bet Yosef* was based, as discussed *infra.*

16. Ran is mentioned here, together with *Maggid Mishneh,* as an author of a commentary on the *Mishneh Torah.* As far as is known, Ran never wrote such a commentary; Caro's statement requires investigation.

new law mentioned by a codifier or commentator that the *Turim* does not present, it will be presented and explained.[17]

Caro then set out a detailed listing of more than thirty halakhic works by leading prior authorities[18]—commentaries, novellae, responsa, and codes[19]—whose statements and opinions are presented and discussed in *Bet Yosef:*

It thus follows that whoever has this book will have arranged before him: the statements of the Talmud with the commentaries of Rashi, *Tosafot,* and Ran; the rulings of Alfasi, Asheri, the *Mordekhai,* [the *Mishneh Torah* of] Maimonides and . . . [its] commentators,[20] *Maggid Mishneh,* Rabbenu Jeroham, *Sefer ha-Terumah, Shibbolei ha-Leket, Roke'aḥ, Sha'arei Dura, Sefer ha-Tashbeẓ,*[21] *Sefer ha-Ittur, Nimmukei Yosef, Semag, Semak, Orḥot Ḥayyim, Torat ha-Bayit, Haggahot Asheri, Sefer ha-Manhig, ha-Agur, Sefer Ba'alei ha-Nefesh* by Rabad; and the responsa of Asheri, Rashba,[22] Isaac b. Sheshet, Simeon b. Ẓemaḥ [Duran],

17. Further in his Introduction, Caro referred to the commentaries on parts of the *Turim* by Isaac Aboab and Jacob ibn Ḥabib, and stated that he did not always agree with their comments. Caro also undertook to correct the copyists' errors that had crept into the text of the *Turim:* "Since the *Four Turim* is full of copyists' mistakes in a number of places, I will point out the mistakes and write down the proper readings according to carefully edited and correct copies that I have reviewed."

18. Each of these works has been described *supra* in the sections treating the commentaries, novellae, and codificatory literature, or is discussed *infra* in connection with the responsa literature. For the treatment of each individual book and author, *see* the references in the indexes to this work.

19. Caro did not include among the books he listed as sources for *Bet Yosef* either Naḥmanides' or Rashba's novellae to the Talmud, as well as other novellae, perhaps because they are essentially not books of normative law. Subsequently, Caro did mention Naḥmanides' and Rashba's novellae in his discussion of how to demonstrate the correctness of particular rulings on the basis of proofs from the Talmud and its commentaries; *see infra.* However, he listed Rashi's commentary and the *Tosafot* among his sources (in addition to mentioning them along with the novellae of Naḥmanides and Rashba in his discussion regarding the demonstration of the correctness of particular rulings). Caro's listing of Ran as one of his sources and as one of the five authorities for determining the law apparently refers to Ran's commentary on Alfasi. (*Nimmukei Yosef,* another commentary on Alfasi, is also listed as one of the sources.) Naḥmanides is also named as one of the five authorities; there is a question whether this designation is on the basis of Naḥmanides' books of *halakhot.* All of this requires further study and clarification.

20. The reference is to *Haggahot Maimuniyyot; see supra* pp. 1234–1235.

21. The reference is to *Sefer ha-Tashbeẓ* by Samson b. Ẓadok, a disciple of Maharam of Rothenburg, and not to *Resp. Tashbeẓ,* the book by Simeon b. Ẓemaḥ Duran, whom Caro subsequently mentioned.

22. Caro took great care to identify correctly the authors of the books he quoted. *See* his subsequent remarks concerning the responsa of Rashba that were attributed to Naḥmanides: "Some responsa of Rashba, written with a pen of iron and lead in print [*i.e.,* printed], have come into my possession, at the beginning of which it is written that they are the responsa of Naḥmanides. Although I know that they are responsa of Rashba, when I quote from them, I write, 'It is written in the *Responsa Attributed to Naḥmanides,'* since the printed

Mahari Colon, and *Terumat ha-Deshen*. All their statements will be fully explained; and in, a few instances, passages from the *Zohar* [will be quoted].[23]

2. METHODOLOGY OF DETERMINING THE LAW

After this thorough description of his first objective in writing *Bet Yosef*, Joseph Caro went on to discuss his second objective: to determine the law by selecting which of the many conflicting opinions of the halakhic authorities to follow. He described his methodology for accomplishing this objective as follows:

> I decided that after presenting all the opinions I will state the legal conclusion, deciding which opinion to accept, for that is the ultimate purpose—that we should have one Torah and one law. But I realized that if we try to determine which authority is correct on the basis of Talmudic arguments and proofs, [we will find that] the *Tosafot* and the novellae of Naḥmanides, Rashba, and Ran are replete with arguments and proofs for each of their opinions, and who will be so presumptuous as to undertake to add to them? And who can be so audacious as to pass judgment on such giants [lit. "as to put his head between the mountains—the mountains of God"], to decide between them by appraising arguments and proofs, to contradict their conclusions, or to decide, when they withheld decision? For, because of our many sins, our minds are too weak even to understand them fully, let alone to presume to be wiser than they. Moreover, in any event, even if we were capable of taking this path, we could not keep going on it, because it would be an exceedingly long journey.

---

books are available to everyone, and whoever wishes to examine the actual responsum will be able to identify it."

23. The reference to the *Zohar*, a major kabbalistic work, in a purely halakhic work such as *Bet Yosef* must be viewed in light of the circumstances of Jewish life in the sixteenth century. At that time, some of the greatest kabbalists flourished in Safed, the major city of the Galilee; they were led by Isaac Luria (known by his acronym as "Ari" ha-Kadosh—the Holy "Lion"), his colleagues, and his disciples; and a kabbalistic work, known as *Maggid Meisharim*, has even been attributed to Caro himself. However, the carefully restrained way in which Caro stated that he would quote "in a few instances . . . from the *Zohar*" indicates the limited influence that mysticism and *Kabbalah* had on Caro's halakhic work. In any case, Caro was explicit that statements in the *Zohar* are not to be given any weight "when they conflict with the Talmud or its commentators" (*Bet Yosef* to *Tur* OḤ ch. 25, s.v. Vi-yevarekh asher kiddeshanu be-miẓvotav ve-ẓivanu le-hani'aḥ tefillin; *cf. id.* ch. 31 (near the end) and *id.* ch. 141, s.v. U-mi-tokh leshon ha-Rosh). *See also Sedei Ḥemed*, VI, Rules for Decision Making #2, subpars. 9, 12, 13 (p. 60b *et seq.*); Ch. Tchernowitz, *Toledot ha-Posekim*, II, pp. 223–224; I. Tishbi, *Mishnat ha-Zohar*, I, pp. 41–42; R.J.Z. Werblowski, *Joseph Karo, Lawyer and Mystic*, London, 1962, and the review of Werblowski's book by D. Tamar, *Kiryat Sefer*, XL (1965), pp. 65–71.

Logically, when there are differences of opinion among the halakhic authorities, it would seem that the law should be determined by adducing arguments and proofs from the Talmudic sources and appraising the merits of each opinion. However, although this would, in principle, be the correct methodology, Caro contended that as a practical matter it was almost impossible to employ. He gave two reasons: (1) all the *rishonim* based their opinions on arguments and proofs, and "who can be so audacious as to put his head between the mountains . . . of God, . . . [and] decide between them by appraising arguments and proofs?"; and (2) such a course would involve "an exceedingly long journey" too onerous to ever complete. The lengthy analysis that would be required to show that one opinion is more persuasive than another would take so much time and would be so exhausting that it would allow no reasonable hope of ever reaching the desired objective of presenting a final and unequivocal determination of all the rules of Jewish law.[24]

In view of these considerations, Caro chose a different and original method to determine the binding legal rules:

> Since I concluded that the three pillars of instruction upon which the House of Israel rests are Alfasi, Maimonides, and Asheri, of blessed memory, I resolved that when two of them agree on any point I will determine the law in accordance with their view, except for those few instances when all or most [of the other] halakhic authorities disagree with that view and a contrary practice has therefore become widespread.[25]
>
> When one of the three above-mentioned pillars[26] expresses no opinion on a particular matter and the other two do not agree, we will turn to Naḥmanides, Rashba, Ran, the *Mordekhai,* and *Semag* . . . and declare the law in accordance with the view of the majority of these authorities. When none of the three above-mentioned pillars expresses an opinion, we will declare the

24. *See also* Caro's remarks, *Bet Yosef* to *Tur* OḤ, Introduction (in the beginning, following the quotation *supra* pp. 1311–1312), for a thorough explanation of the difficulties involved in clarifying and finally ascertaining the law on the basis of the Talmudic and post-Talmudic sources.

25. As to this reservation, *see* Caro's further remarks quoted here and *see infra* p. 1355.

26. In *Resp. Avkat Rokhel* #201, Caro called them "the three pillars of the world." The heading of that responsum reads: "The above question was answered by Maharashdam," and the responsum concludes, "Until here [is what] I [the publisher of the responsum] have found." The responsum bears no signature. However, it is clear that Caro was its author since it contains the sentence, "And in my work *Bet Yosef* I wrote. . . . " The purpose of the heading is simply to call attention to the fact that Maharashdam wrote a responsum on a similar question (*Resp. Maharashdam,* ḤM, #1). There is also other evidence proving that Caro wrote the responsum; for further discussion, *see* H. Dimitrovsky, "Vikku'aḥ she-Avar bein Maran Rabbi Yosef Caro ve-ha-Mabit" [A Dispute between Our Master, Rabbi Joseph Caro, and Mabit], *Sefer Ẓefat,* I, pp. 82–83 and nn., *ad loc.*

> law according to the well-known halakhic authorities who have expressed their opinion on the particular matter.
>
> This method is the most feasible way (lit. "the royal road"); it is correct, easy to apply, and the most efficient solution to the problem. And if, despite our ruling that certain things are permissible, the practice in some countries has been to prohibit those things, those countries should continue to follow their custom, since they have already accepted the opinion of the halakhic authority holding those things prohibited, and they are therefore not permitted to act in accordance with the permissive ruling, as is stated in chapter *Makom she-Nahagu.*[27]

The criterion for determining the law on a question disputed by the halakhic authorities was thus not an evaluation of the arguments on the merits of the question, but rather a technical and mathematical formula based on the number of proponents of a particular opinion among a preselected group of halakhic authorities.

Caro understood and emphasized that his method was not ideal but was chosen only because of its utility, as "the most feasible . . . and . . . efficient solution." It was entirely possible that the final ruling based on his mathematical reckoning would sometimes be inconsistent with the conclusion that would perhaps more accurately conform to the Talmudic sources. Furthermore, this mechanical approach could sometimes lead to internal inconsistencies in the law as finally determined. For example, although rulings of Maimonides on two different issues may be logically interconnected, if Maimonides and Alfasi agreed on the result on one issue and Asheri disagreed, the law on that issue would be determined according to the result reached by Maimonides and Alfasi; yet if Alfasi and Asheri agreed against Maimonides on the other issue, the law would not follow Maimonides' view, although this result would be inconsistent with the theory of his ruling on the first issue.

Nevertheless, with all its drawbacks, this methodology for decision making was better than relying on an appraisal of the merits of each question, both because of the substantive difficulty involved in making a choice from among the different opinions, and because the laborious efforts required to reach a conclusion as to every single issue would have been a never-ending process. In effect, Caro established preselected "judicial benches." The first "bench" was composed of Alfasi, Maimonides, and Asheri; the second consisted of one or two of them together with Naḥmanides, Rashba, Ran, and the authors of the *Mordekhai* and *Semag.* Any question the first bench was not able to decide was referred to the second; and, in

27. TB Pesaḥim 50b–51a; for detailed discussion, *see supra* p. 900 n. 14 and pp. 933–934.

accordance with accepted judicial procedure, the decision of the majority was accepted as law. This was a good method in view of the personal attributes and stature of those who constituted the "benches." It was efficient because the "benches" were permanent and always in session; and the opinions of the "judges" could be found in the books they had written. The decisionmaker had only to review their opinions and apply the formula for selecting the opinion that would control.

It was the vast increase in halakhic material and the multitude of differences of opinion among the halakhic authorities that led Caro to adopt this methodology. It was the only way by which he could undertake the enormous and difficult task of composing a book of *halakhot* that would include a final categorical definitive statement of law on every subject in the halakhic system.[28]

D. The *Shulḥan Arukh*

1. CODIFICATORY APPROACH

Joseph Caro's main objectives in writing his *Bet Yosef* were to collect into a single work the different opinions concerning the rules of the *Halakhah,* and, by means of the methodology he had formulated, to determine which opinion should be accepted as law. Caro, however, saw this work as only one part of his solution to the problem of codifying Jewish law. He knew that while a book of *halakhot* (containing a complete discussion of the sources of the law and the views of all the authorities as well as a final normative decision) was essential, it was not itself sufficient to satisfy the needs of halakhic codification. He appreciated Maimonides' fundamental premise that the essential characteristics of a convenient and efficient code are clarity and brevity—the code must present each law clearly, categorically, and definitively. Therefore, after composing his *Bet Yosef,* and as a

28. In order to make it easier to find a particular law in *Bet Yosef,* Caro provided a table of contents that had two purposes: (1) to give a more detailed listing of the subjects dealt with in the *Turim* than is contained in the table of contents of the *Turim* itself (*see supra* p. 1288 n. 200), and (2) to list the new laws contained in *Bet Yosef. See Bet Yosef* to *Tur* OḤ, Introduction (near the end):

> Since the table of contents of *Sefer ha-Turim* is very skimpy, and sometimes anyone looking for a particular law cannot tell whether it is in one chapter or another or even in the book at all, I determined to prepare another table of contents listing in detail all the laws contained in each chapter, and then I made a list of all the new laws that I present in my commentary entitled *Bet Yosef,* so that everyone will be able to find easily the law he seeks.

The table of contents for each of the four parts of the *Turim* is printed at the end of the part to which it applies.

complement to it, Caro provided Jewish law with a classic book of *pesakim*—the *Shulḥan Arukh.*

Caro made his position very clear as to the need for a book of *pesakim.* It will be remembered[29] that Rabad had criticized Maimonides severely for having, in his *Mishneh Torah,* "forsaken the method of all authors who preceded him" in that Maimonides omitted the sources on which his decisions were based and presented only the view with which he agreed. Caro responded to Rabad's strictures as follows:[30]

> But I say that the master's [Maimonides'] reason was that if he had wanted to follow the method of the authors who preceded him, what purpose would there have been in writing anything beyond what had already been written by Alfasi, whose rulings he generally followed? Therefore, he intended to introduce a new method: to state the law clearly and briefly in the style of the Mishnah, so that every intelligent person thereafter can rely on Maimonides' statement of the law. And should some great scholar not be prepared to accept that choice without first weighing the matter himself—who prevents him from studying the Talmudic literature and the other halakhic works? It follows that the method Maimonides adopted is of benefit to everyone except the scholar who stands head and shoulders above the rest of his generation—and even for such a person it is of value, because if he must make a quick decision, he can rely on Maimonides' opinion; and even if he is not pressed for time, it is no small matter for him to know Maimonides' opinion.

Far from contradicting Caro's methodology in *Bet Yosef,* his statement quoted above supplies the additional element essential to achieve his overall approach to codification of Jewish law. He believed that a halakhic code must have two components: one that cites all the sources and differing opinions, and another that presents a single statement of the law—final, categorical, and monolithic. Caro described clearly his theory of the "double" code in his Introduction to the *Shulḥan Arukh.*[31] He began by describing his *Bet Yosef:*

> The major work that I wrote on the . . . *Turim,* which I called *Bet Yosef,* includes all the laws to be found in all the [books of the] codifiers, new and old, together with their sources in the Babylonian and Jerusalem Talmuds, the *Tosefta, Sifra, Sifrei, Mekhilta,* commentaries, codes, and responsa, new and old, with each law fully and appropriately explained in its proper place.

29. *See supra* p. 1224.

30. *Kesef Mishneh* to Maimonides' Introduction to the *Mishneh Torah.*

31. The Introduction can be found in early printed editions and in some more recent printed and facsimile editions, such as the El ha-Mekorot edition of the *Shulḥan Arukh,* Jerusalem, 1954, and the Pe'er ha-Torah edition, Jerusalem, 1960 (in Sh. Ar. ḤM, vol. II).

He continued:

> I realized that it would be beneficial to gather the lilies and the sapphires [*i.e.*, the halakhic conclusions] of its [*Bet Yosef*'s] discussion, [and present them] briefly, clearly, and comprehensively, in an elegant and pleasant style, so that God's perfect Torah[32] may be fluent on the tongue of every Jew. Thus, when a scholar will be asked a matter of *Halakhah*, he will not need to hesitate.[33] . . . The law to be applied in practice on any question that he will be asked will be clear to him because he will be fully familiar with this book [the *Shulḥan Arukh*], which is so excellently constructed. It is divided into thirty parts, so that if one studies one part each day, he will have reviewed its contents every month.[34] Of such a person it will be said, "Happy is he who comes here with his knowledge readily in hand."[35]
>
> Furthermore, the younger students will study it constantly and commit it to memory. Practical *Halakhah* will thus become "childhood learning" absorbed in their earliest years; and when they grow old, it will not depart from them. The intelligent students will shine like the heavens because they will be spared the pain of great toil and will enjoy studying this book; it is entirely

32. *See* Psalms 19:8.

33. *See Sifrei*, Deuteronomy, Va-etḥanan, sec. 34 (ed. Finkelstein, p. 60), to Deuteronomy 6:7; TB Kiddushin 30a and *Tosafot*, *ad loc.*, s.v. Al tegamgem ve-tomar lo. Caro continued: "But he will 'say to Wisdom, "You are my sister"' [Proverbs 7:4]; just as it is clear to him that his sister is forbidden to him [*see* TB Sanhedrin 7b], so too it [*i.e.*, a matter of *Halakhah*] will be as clear."

34. The notion of reviewing one's studies each month is found in the Talmud; *see* TB Berakhot 38b ("R. Ḥiyya b. Abba would review his learning every thirty days"); TB Pesaḥim 68b ("R. Sheshet would review his learning every thirty days"). There were places where this practice was applied to the *Shulḥan Arukh*; *see Shem-ha-Gedolim*, Books, Letter *zayin*, #23. *See also* Sh. Ar. ḤM 43:29 (at the end) where the phrase "[one should study] up to this point on the twenty-first day" appears—a vestige of the division of the *Shulḥan Arukh* into thirty parts. *See also Sema*, *ad loc.*, subpar. 53. This phrase is missing from early editions; *see, e.g.*, ed. Venice 1565, 1567 (Gryphio), 1574. However, it is found in ed. Venice 1567 (Cavalli) and 1594, and ed. Cracow, 1594.

The division into thirty parts is made in ed. Venice 1567 (Cavalli) at the top of each page and at the end of each chapter; since that edition is not readily available, the divisions are set forth here: Day 1—OḤ 1–88 (at the end of ch. 88 appears, "[one should study] up to this point on the first day"; similar statements are found at the end of each of the divisions); Day 2—OḤ 89–169; Day 3—OḤ 170–259; Day 4—OḤ 260–317; Day 5—OḤ 318–372; Day 6—OḤ 373–467; Day 7—OḤ 468–544; Day 8—OḤ 545–684; Day 9—OḤ 685–697, YD 1–61; Day 10—YD 62–124; Day 11—YD 125–182; Day 12—YD 183–220; Day 13—YD 221–259; Day 14—YD 260–297; Day 15—YD 298–342; Day 16—YD 343–403, EH 1–12; Day 17—EH 13–66; Day 18—EH 67–118; Day 19—EH 119–153; Day 20—EH 154–173; Day 21—EH 174–178, ḤM 1–43; Day 22—ḤM 44–74; Day 23—ḤM 75–102; Day 24—ḤM 103–141; Day 25—ḤM 142–175; Day 26—ḤM 176–224; Day 27—ḤM 225–263; Day 28—ḤM 264–311; Day 29—ḤM 312–388; Day 30—ḤM 389–427. As noted *supra*, there were books of *halakhot* that were divided into seven parts for a weekly study cycle. *See supra* p. 1264, concerning *Semak*.

35. TB Mo'ed Katan 28a, where this was said in regard to a Sage who reviewed his learning in thirty days.

> pleasurable, containing clear and definitive statements of the applicable law, without discursive debate or argument.
>
> I called this book *Shulḥan Arukh* [The Set Table][36] because the reader will find set out in it all kinds of delicacies meticulously arranged, preserved, systematized, and clarified. I trust that, by divine grace, the earth will be filled with the knowledge of God by virtue of this book—the small and the great, the student and the accomplished scholar.

This, then, was Caro's approach to codifying the *Halakhah. Bet Yosef* included the disparate opinions on all the laws and their sources; but, "so that God's perfect Torah may be fluent on the tongue of every Jew," Caro composed another book "containing clear and definitive statements of the applicable law, without discursive debate or argument." This latter work would be written "briefly, clearly, and comprehensively, in an elegant and pleasant style," so that when a judge or scholar is asked a question, "he will not need to hesitate, . . . [and] the law to be applied in practice on any question that he will be asked will be clear to him." Like all codifiers—in Jewish law[37] as well as in other legal systems[38]—Caro was convinced that not only would his code serve Talmudic scholars and experts, but also "the younger students will study it constantly and commit it to memory," so that "practical *Halakhah* will thus become 'childhood learning.'" Caro's two-part work—a book of *halakhot* and a book of *pesakim*—indeed constitutes the halakhic code *par excellence,* fully appropriate to the nature, and responsive to the needs, of the *Halakhah.*[39]

36. The term *shulḥan arukh* as referring to an arrangement of rules and laws appears in *Mekhilta,* Mishpatim, ch. 1 (ed. Lauterbach, III, p. 1; ed. Horowitz-Rabin, p. 246): "R. Akiva says: . . . 'Set them [*i.e.,* the laws] out before them like a set table [*ke-shulḥan arukh*].'" *See also* Rashi on Exodus 21:1, s.v. Asher tasim lifneihem. *Cf. Sifrei,* Numbers, Pinḥas, sec. 136 (ed. Horowitz-Rabin, p. 182): "R. Akiva says: 'The verse discloses that the Almighty showed all the hidden chambers of the Land of Israel to Moses like a set table.'" In this passage, R. Akiva used the metaphor to indicate how easy it was to see what was set out, and to distinguish each item from the others. Rashba also used the term in connection with his book *Torat ha-Bayit; see* his Introduction to the book and *supra* pp. 1273–1275 (noting the similarity between the codificatory methodologies of Caro and Rashba).

See also Proverbs 9:1–2: "Wisdom has built her house, she has hewn her seven pillars. She has prepared the feast, mixed the wine, and also *set the table*" (emphasis supplied). Jacob ibn Ḥabib wrote in the Introduction to his *Ein Ya'akov:* "It was for this reason that Alfasi, and Asheri after him, realized that it was good in the sight of God to be beneficent to Israel and to arrange before them a set table [*shulḥan arukh*] in one special book [which would contain] all the parts of the aforesaid laws." Ibn Ḥabib died in Salonika about 1516, some fifty years before the completion of the *Shulḥan Arukh.*

37. *See supra* pp. 1153, 1185, 1265–1266, 1270.

38. *See supra* p. 1141.

39. It should be noted that, in the opinion of many scholars, Caro deviated in the *Shulḥan Arukh* from the policy he followed in *Bet Yosef,* which was to declare the law in accordance with the majority view among Alfasi, Maimonides, and Asheri; instead, he

2. STRUCTURE AND ARRANGEMENT

The *Shulḥan Arukh* is divided into four parts, in the same manner as the *Turim;* and the parts are called by the same names: *Oraḥ Ḥayyim, Yoreh De'ah, Even ha-Ezer,* and *Ḥoshen Mishpat.* This design follows from the fact that the laws in the *Shulḥan Arukh* are distillations of the conclusions reached in *Bet Yosef,* which, as will be remembered, was structured around and follows the arrangement of the *Turim.*[40] Like the *Turim,* each of the four parts of the *Shulḥan Arukh* is divided into sections (*halakhot*) subdivided into chapters (*simanim*) and further subdivided into paragraphs[41] (*se'ifim*).[42]

---

tended to favor Maimonides. *See* Yom Tov Lipmann Heller, *Divrei Ḥamudot* to *Piskei ha-Rosh,* Ḥullin 8:185; Solomon (b. Isaac) le-Vet ha-Levi, *Resp. Maharash le-Vet ha-Levi* (Salonika, 1652), OḤ #9 (near the beginning of the responsum); Ḥayyim Benveniste, *Keneset ha-Gedolah,* OḤ #462, glosses to *Bet Yosef,* subpar. 5. *See also* I.Z. Kahane, "Ha-Pulmus mi-Saviv Kevi'at ha-Hakhra'ah ke-ha-Rambam" [The Controversy Concerning Determination of the Law in Accordance with the Views of Maimonides], *Sinai,* XXXVII (1956), pp. 226–227.

There are some laws included in *Bet Yosef* that are omitted in the *Shulḥan Arukh.* As to these laws, *see* Ḥida, *Resp. Ḥayyim Sha'al* #48, p. 3a: "We sometimes find correct laws presented in *Bet Yosef* that are omitted from the *Shulḥan Arukh,* as is known to all who are familiar with the subject. With respect to this, the later rabbis used to say that he [Caro] regarded these laws as either obvious or very rarely applicable." *See also* M. Drori, "Shegagah ba-Mishpat ha-Ivri: Ta'ut be-Din ve-Ta'ut be-Uvda" [Mistake in Jewish Law: Mistake of Law and Mistake of Fact], *Shenaton,* I (1974), pp. 72ff. at 87–88.

40. Occasionally, Caro referred in the *Shulḥan Arukh* to a ruling contained in the *Turim; see, e.g.,* Sh. Ar. ḤM 129:5: "Just as the surety . . . only with regard to the lien of a *ketubbah,* as is explained in *Tur* EH." Similarly in Sh. Ar. ḤM 427:9: "Some of them are explained in *Tur* YD ch. 116." With regard to Sh. Ar. ḤM ch. 427, *see further infra.* p. 1326.

41. The division of the *Shulḥan Arukh* into sections, chapters, and paragraphs appeared in the very first edition (Venice, 1565) and in all subsequent editions—those published in Caro's lifetime as well as after his death. The division was undoubtedly made by Caro himself. There are slight variations between the earlier and later editions, *e.g.,* in ed. Venice 1565, 1567, 1574, and some later editions, chs. 39–96 are called *Hilkhot Halva'ot* [Laws of Loans], whereas in later and current editions, chs. 39–74 are called *Hilkhot Halva'ah* [Laws of Lending] and chs. 75–96 are called *Hilkhot To'en ve-Nit'an* [Laws of Plaintiff and Defendant]. However, on the whole, the division in current editions is very similar to that of the early editions; *see further* the table in Appendix A of the present work. In subsequent discussions in the present work, the references to the *Shulḥan Arukh* are to current editions. *See supra* p. 1288 and n. 200 concerning the differences between various editions of the *Turim.*

42. Since the division of the *Shulḥan Arukh* and the subjects of each of the four parts are generally identical with those of the *Turim,* care must be taken in citing the two books. If the reference is to *Ḥoshen Mishpat* in the *Turim,* the citation is "*Tur* ḤM," followed by the chapter number. If the reference is to *Ḥoshen Mishpat* in the *Shulḥan Arukh,* the citation is "Sh. Ar. ḤM," followed by the chapter and paragraph numbers. To a certain extent, it has become common practice that a reference to *Ḥoshen Mishpat* without specification refers to the *Shulḥan Arukh.* References to the *Shulḥan Arukh* always include both the chapter number and the paragraph number, *e.g.,* Sh. Ar. ḤM 201:1, but it is not customary to cite the paragraph as well as the chapter number in the *Turim.*

Although the *Shulḥan Arukh,* like the *Turim,* is arranged topically, the analytical breakdown of the various subjects, *i.e.,* in the sections within each part, is somewhat different from that of the *Turim.*[43] We have already discussed the excessive subdivision of subject matter in the *Turim* (in the form in which that work has come down to us), as contrasted to Maimonides' inclusion of various subjects under one heading in his *Mishneh Torah.* In the *Shulḥan Arukh,* Caro, to a considerable extent, regrouped various subjects under a single heading. For example, in *Tur Ḥoshen Mishpat* the material contained in chapters 39–74 consists of seven sections, each of which has its own heading.[44] The seven sections, however, are really subdivisions of one central subject in the law of loans, and it is more appropriate to subsume them under one heading than to split them up under seven headings. In the *Shulḥan Arukh* they all appear under the heading "Laws of Lending."[45]

Another example pertains to the modes of acquisition. In the *Turim,* the material in chapters 190–226 is divided into twelve separate sections (such as "Acquisition of Real Property," "Acquisition by *Sudar,*" "Acquisition of Animals," etc.), whereas in the *Shulḥan Arukh* all these laws are treated under the single heading, "Laws of Purchase and Sale."[46]

Caro also gave a title to every chapter.[47] This served a twofold purpose:

It should be noted that Maimonides' *Mishneh Torah* is cited differently from the *Turim* and the *Shulḥan Arukh.* The *Mishneh Torah* is cited by the title of the section, the chapter, and the paragraph, *e.g., MT,* Sekhirut 1:5.

43. The reference in the text is to the division into sections as it appears in current editions of the *Turim; see also supra* p. 1288 and n. 200. In the two parts containing the laws on the subjects of *mishpat ivri,* the main differences between the two works are in *Ḥoshen Mishpat;* in *Even ha-Ezer* the differences are minor.

44. *See supra* pp. 1293–1294.

45. In early editions, chs. 75–96 are also included under the heading *Hilkhot Halva'ot* [Laws of Loans], but they were later given the separate heading of *Hilkhot To'en ve-Nit'an* [Laws of Plaintiff and Defendant]. *See supra* n. 41.

46. In the *Mishneh Torah, Hilkhot Mekhirah* [Laws of Sales] includes all of the subjects dealt with in the *Turim* in chs. 190 *et seq.* and in Sh. Ar. ḤM *Hilkhot Mekhirah* chs. 189–240. (Ch. 189 in the *Turim* is part of Laws of Agency.) In current editions of the *Turim,* this material is divided into many sections (*see supra* p. 1294 n. 220). In the *Shulḥan Arukh,* it is divided into two sections: chs. 189–226 are entitled *Hilkhot Mikaḥ u-Mimkar* [Laws of Purchase and Sale] and chs. 227–240 are entitled *Hilkhot Ona'ah u-Mikaḥ Ta'ut* [Laws of Overreaching and Mistake]. However, the latter heading does not accurately describe all the laws in the section—*e.g.,* ch. 235 par. 28 (dealing with acquisition on the sabbath) and the laws starting at ch. 237.

47. Various books of *halakhot* contain a listing of chapters and a short summary of the contents of each chapter at the beginning of the book (*see supra* pp. 1239–1240, 1271, 1273, *et al.*) Similarly, early editions of the *Turim* contain such tables of contents at the beginning of each part (*see supra* p. 1288 n. 200). However, it appears that Caro inserted titles and descriptive headings at the beginning of each chapter of the *Shulḥan Arukh* in addition to

(1) to permit a quick overview of the contents of each chapter[48] (the lack of such chapter titles is very much felt in the *Mishneh Torah,* where a substantial number of chapters on subsidiary topics are subsumed under a single general subject heading); and (2) to permit a number of subsidiary topics to be dealt with in the same section, since the title of each chapter clearly indicates the particular subject treated in it.

Although occasionally one also finds the reverse situation, where several subjects treated in the *Turim* under one heading are subdivided in the *Shulḥan Arukh*—sometimes for obvious reasons[49] and sometimes for no clear reason[50]—the general tendency in the *Shulḥan Arukh* is to subsume numerous subsidiary topics under a single general heading. The difference is reflected in the number of sections in the *Turim* as compared to the *Shulḥan Arukh.* For example, *Tur Ḥoshen Mishpat,* as we have it, contains fifty-eight sections, while the same material in *Shulḥan Arukh Ḥoshen Mishpat* occupies forty-one sections.[51] The organization of the *Shulḥan Arukh* thus represents a middle path between (1) the overbroad subject headings of Maimonides' *Mishneh Torah* (in which the four books, *Nezikin, Kinyan, Mishpatim,* and *Shofetim,* whose material is parallel to that of *Ḥoshen Mishpat,* consist of only nineteen sections) and (2) the excessively narrow and fragmented subject headings of the *Turim.*

---

the tables of contents that appear at the end of each part, thus making it easier to find one's way through the material. The fact that the headings appear in the first edition, Venice 1565, suggests that it was Caro himself who did this. Joshua Falk in his Introduction to his *Bet Yisra'el* and *Sema* stated: "The author [Joseph Caro] also wrote at the head of each chapter a specific caption stating what the chapter discusses" (end of Introduction, printed at beginning of Sh. Ar. ḤM).

48. In order to make it easier to find the law, Caro also prepared a detailed table of contents of the *Turim* and of the laws appearing for the first time in *Bet Yosef; see supra* n. 28.

49. *E.g., Hilkhot Shomer Sakhar* [Laws of the Paid Bailee] in *Tur* ḤM (ed. Sabbioneta, 1559, chs. 303–306; in earlier editions, the heading and chapter numbers are different) are divided in the *Shulḥan Arukh* into *Hilkhot Shomer Sakhar* (chs. 303–305) and *Hilkhot Umanim* [The Laws of Craftsmen] (ch. 306), which are in fact two separate categories of laws.

50. *E.g., Hilkhot Shutafin be-Karka* [Laws of Concurrent Ownership of Real Estate], which appears in *Tur* ḤM (ch. 157 to the beginning of ch. 175), is divided in the *Shulḥan Arukh* into *Hilkhot Shutafin be-Karka* (chs. 157–170) and *Hilkhot Ḥalukat Shutafut* [Laws of Severance of Concurrent Ownership] (chs. 171–175:2). It would seem that both subjects could readily be included in one section entitled "Laws of Concurrent Ownership of Real Estate," as in the *Turim; see also* Appendix A *infra.*

51. *See* Appendix A. Our comparison does not take into account the last chapter (ch. 427) of Sh. Ar. ḤM, since its subject is not treated at all in the *Turim.* In the *Shulḥan Arukh,* its heading is "The Positive Commandment to Remove Any Obstacle that Presents a Danger to Life and to Build a Parapet on One's Roof." This formulation is based on Maimonides, *MT,* Roẓe'aḥ u-Shemirat ha-Nefesh, ch. 11. *See infra.* p. 1326.

The *Shulḥan Arukh* also sometimes differs from the *Turim* in the classification of its material. Occasionally, Caro moved certain laws from one part to an entirely different part, when he felt that logic required the change.[52] There are also instances when he included a whole area of the law that was not dealt with at all in the *Turim*. This was not because it was a new area that first developed after the *Turim* was written, but simply because he felt it appropriate to include it in the *Shulḥan Arukh*. An example is the last chapter of *Shulḥan Arukh Ḥoshen Mishpat*, chapter 427, for which there is no corresponding section in *Tur Ḥoshen Mishpat*. Chapter 427 is based on Maimonides' *Mishneh Torah, Hilkhot Roẓe'aḥ u-Shemirat ha-Nefesh* [Laws of Homicide and Preservation of Life],[53] and includes such rules as the obligation to build a parapet on a roof and to remove any obstacle that presents a danger to life. The *Turim* omitted these rules because in the *Mishneh Torah* they are part of the Laws of Murder, which the *Turim* does not cover.[54] However, although the *Shulḥan Arukh* also does not deal with the laws of homicide, Caro included in *Shulḥan Arukh Ḥoshen Mishpat* those laws not directly pertaining to homicide that were included in the *Mishneh Torah* with the laws of homicide because of a common ethical thread, namely, the protection of human life. Conversely, Caro some-

52. *See, e.g., Tur* ḤM 182:1–3, which discusses the prohibitions against forming a partnership with a non-Jew and trading in nonkosher meat, both of which Sh. Ar. ḤM ch. 182 omits. Caro treated those laws in a more appropriate place, namely, in Sh. Ar. OḤ and YD, respectively. *See Sema,* Sh. Ar. ḤM ch. 182, subpar. 1. The titles of some sections in the *Shulḥan Arukh* are shorter or longer than those of the same sections in the *Turim*, as the subject matter requires; *see* Appendix A, and *compare* the titles of the sections in the *Shulḥan Arukh with* the titles in the *Turim* as they appear in the various editions.

53. *MT,* Roẓe'aḥ u-Shemirat ha-Nefesh, ch. 11. *See also Sema,* Sh. Ar. ḤM ch. 427, subpar. 1.

54. As stated, both the *Turim* (*see supra* p. 1300) and the *Shulḥan Arukh* (*see supra* p. 1313 as to *Bet Yosef*) set forth only those laws currently applicable (as contrasted to Maimonides, who included all the laws in the halakhic system) and do not deal with the laws of capital punishment or other criminal penalties contained in the Torah, which are applicable only when there is a formally constituted Sanhedrin. Although criminal penalties—and even the death sentence—were administered in various Jewish centers in the diaspora (*see supra* pp. 10–11, 47), they were not based on the penal law in the Torah, but on the general authority to punish pursuant to the principle formulated by R. Eliezer b. Jacob that "the court may impose flogging and punishment not prescribed in the Torah" (TB Sanhedrin 46a; *see supra* pp. 515–519). Criminal sanctions on the basis of this general authority are mentioned in both *Tur* and Sh. Ar. ḤM, ch. 2, and are discussed in detail mainly in the responsa literature and in various books of *halakhot*. *See also supra* pp. 10–11, 47, 688–698; E.E. Urbach, "Mi-Darkhei ha-Kodifikaẓyah—Al Sefer ha-Turim le-Rav Ya'akov b. Rav Asher" [On Codificatory Methodology—the *Turim* of Rabbi Jacob b. Rabbi Asher], *Jubilee Volume,* American Academy of Jewish Studies, XLVI-XLVII (1979–1980), p. 1, concerning codification in *Tur* and Sh. Ar. ḤM, ch. 425, dealing with currently applicable criminal law.

times omitted laws that do appear in the *Turim*, when he thought they had no practical significance.[55]

3. LANGUAGE AND STYLE AS COMPARED TO THE *TURIM* AND THE *MISHNEH TORAH*

As has been stressed, Joseph Caro intended his *Shulḥan Arukh* to be a book of "clear and definitive statements of the applicable law, without discursive debate or argument"; and indeed a comparison of the *Shulḥan Arukh* with previous books of *pesakim* will reveal that the *Shulḥan Arukh* is more categorical and concise than all the others. Not only did Caro omit reference to the sources of the laws, the proofs that led him to his conclusions, and the names of the authors of the laws[56] (following the example of Maimonides in all of these respects), but he also omitted any additional comments not strictly necessary to the bare statement of the law. As has been seen, Maimonides frequently incorporated rationales or explanations into his statements of the law and sometimes even added a relevant philosophical or ethical preamble or epilogue to his exposition of the law. Such comments can also be found in the *Turim*. However, Caro, in his desire for the utmost conciseness, omitted all such comments; his statement of the laws themselves was also as terse as possible. The following four examples, comparing the draftsmanship of the *Mishneh Torah*, the *Turim*, and the *Shulḥan Arukh*, highlight this feature of the *Shulḥan Arukh*.[57]

EXAMPLE 1

Mishneh Torah[58]	*Turim*[59]	*Shulḥan Arukh*[60]
If one says to a woman, "Behold, you are betrothed to me " . . . on condition that I	If he says to her, "Be betrothed to me ". . . on condition that I am a student"—this	[If one says to a woman], "Behold you are betrothed to me with this

55. *E.g.*, *Tur* ḤM ch. 274 mentions the various laws contained in the enactments attributed to Joshua (*see supra* pp. 551–553), but Caro omitted them. *See* Rema to Sh. Ar. ḤM ch. 274 on this subject, *and see supra* p. 553 n. 34.

56. Except for a few instances where the name of a Sage is cited. *See, e.g.*, Sh. Ar. YD 251:11: "Rabbi [R. Judah Ha-Nasi], who was sorrowful . . . "; ḤM 386:1: "The law accords with R. Meir's view that we adjudicate liability for indirect damage (*dina de-garmi*)." Similarly, in OḤ 165:2: "And . . . [Asheri] was accustomed . . . "; ḤM 99:2: "Thus he wrote in the name of . . . [Asheri]."

57. The examples are given in the order in which they appear in Maimonides' *Mishneh Torah*. *See* Appendix B for three further examples.

58. *MT*, Ishut 8:4–5. The Talmudic source is TB Kiddushin 49b. The question discussed is, What constitutes fulfillment of various conditions to which a betrothal has been made subject?

59. *Tur* EH ch. 38.

60. Sh. Ar. EH 38:20, 27–32.

am a student"—this does not mean [that he must be as committed to his studies] as Ben Azzai or Ben Zoma, but [the condition is fulfilled] as long as he is capable of answering a question on the subject of his studies or even on the simple laws pertaining to a festival that are taught in public just before the festival so that all the people may be conversant with them.

". . . on condition that I am a sage"—this does not mean [that he must be as erudite] as R. Akiva and his colleagues, but [the condition is fulfilled] as long as he can answer a question involving a "matter of wisdom" on any subject.

". . . on condition that I am strong"—this does not mean [that he must be as strong] as Abner son of Ner or Joab; but [the condition is fulfilled] as long as his friends fear him for his strength.

". . . on condition that I am rich"—this does not mean [that he must be as rich] as R. Eleazar b. Harsom or R. Eleazar b. Azariah; but [the condition is fulfilled] as long as his fellow townspeople respect him for his wealth.

does not mean [that he must be as committed to his studies] as Ben Azzai, but [the condition is fulfilled] as long as he is capable of answering a question on the subject of his studies or even on the laws pertaining to a festival that are simple laws taught in public.

". . . on condition that I am a sage"—this does not mean [that he must be as erudite] as R. Akiva and his colleagues, but [the condition is fulfilled] as long as he can answer a question involving a "matter of wisdom"—*i.e.,* a matter where the answer can be reached by logical analysis—on any subject.

". . . on condition that I am strong"—this does not mean [that he must be as strong] as Abner or Joab; but [the condition is fulfilled] as long as his fellow townspeople fear him for his strength.

". . . on condition that I am rich"—this does not mean [that he must be as rich] as R. Eleazar b. Harsom, but [the condition is fulfilled] as long as his fellow townspeople respect him for his wealth.

". . . on condition that I am righteous"—even if he is totally wicked, it is a case of doubtful [and

". . . on condition that I am a student"—[the condition is fulfilled] as long as he is capable of answering a question on the subject of his studies or even on the simple laws pertaining to a festival that are taught in public just before the festival so that all the people may be conversant with them.

". . . on condition that I am a sage"—[the condition is fulfilled] as long as he can answer a question involving a "matter of wisdom"—*i.e.,* a matter where the answer can be reached by logical analysis—on any subject.

". . . on condition that I am strong"—[the condition is fulfilled] as long as his friends fear him for his strength.

". . . on condition that I am rich"—[the condition is fulfilled] as long as his fellow townspeople respect him for his wealth.

". . . on condition that I am righteous"—even if[61] he is totally wicked, she is betrothed because of doubt [as to whether the condition is fulfilled], for he may have had thoughts of repentance.

". . . on condition that I am wicked"—even if he

61. Eds. Venice 1565 and 1574 have "even if" (as in our translation), whereas current editions read "and even if."

". . . on condition that I am righteous"—even if he is totally wicked, she is betrothed because of doubt [as to whether the condition is fulfilled], for he may have had thoughts of repentance.
". . . on condition that I am wicked"—even if he is completely righteous, she is betrothed because of doubt [as to whether the condition is fulfilled], for he may have had thoughts of idolatry; idolatry is a great sin and as soon as one even thinks of committing it he becomes one of the wicked, as it is written, ". . . lest your heart be led astray,"[62] and it is also written, ". . . I will hold the House of Israel to account for their thoughts [because they have all been estranged from me through their fetishes]."[63]

thus presumably valid] betrothal, for he may have had thoughts of repentance.
". . . on condition that I am wicked"—even if he is completely righteous, it is a case of doubtful [and thus presumably valid] betrothal, for he may have had thoughts of idolatry.

is completely righteous, she is betrothed because of doubt [as to whether the condition is fulfilled], for he may have had thoughts of idolatry.

In this example, Maimonides included all the details contained in the Talmud. The *Turim* followed Maimonides in a slightly abbreviated form, particularly at the end, where it omitted the discussion of idolatry included by Maimonides so as to provide a rationale for the law.[64] Caro further abridged his statement of the law by making it more categorical: he omitted all references to the examples—comparisons to Ben Azzai, Ben Zoma, etc.—and stated only the requirements for fulfillment of each condition.

62. Deuteronomy 11:16.

63. Ezekiel 14:5. Regarding no other transgression is a person considered to be wicked for merely contemplating its commission. *See* TB Kiddushin 39b, 40a, stating on the basis of Ezekiel 14:5 that the Almighty considers the contemplation of idolatry as the equivalent of committing it.

64. Maimonides' comments about idolatry, which supplement the discussion in TB, parallel those of Alfasi, *Sefer ha-Halakhot,* Kiddushin, *ad loc.* Maimonides also quotes the verse " . . . lest your heart be led astray" (Deuteronomy 11:16), which is not in Alfasi.

EXAMPLE 2

Mishneh Torah[65]

Everything attached to land is like land, and is acquired either by money, or by deed, or by an act of dominion (*ḥazakah*). If it does not need the land, *e.g.*, grapes ready to be harvested, it is like movable property for the purpose of acquisition, and [the law of] *ona'ah* (overreaching) applies to it.[66]

Turim[67]

Everything attached to land has the same law as land, and is acquired by money, and by deed, and by an act of dominion. . . . Maimonides wrote that this rule applies only if the article needs the land, but that if it does not need the land, *e.g.*, grapes that are ready to be harvested, it has the same law as movable property in regard to acquisition and [the law of] *ona'ah* (overreaching). But it seems to me that such articles are to be considered as attached to the land, since in regard to oaths, the Rabbis considered them[68] as attached [to the land, and therefore not the proper subject of a judicial oath concerning disputed property rights in them], even though they are ready to be harvested.

Shulḥan Arukh[69]

Everything attached to land that needs the land is like land and is acquired by money, or by deed, or by an act of dominion. . . . But if it does not need the land, *e.g.*, grapes ready to be harvested, it is like movable property for the purpose of acquisition, and [the law of] *ona'ah* (overreaching) applies to it.

In this example, Maimonides stated the law briefly. The *Turim* cited and rejected Maimonides' reservation regarding articles that do not need the land. Caro ruled to the same effect as Maimonides and skillfully inte-

65. *MT,* Mekhirah 1:17.

66. *See* M Shevu'ot 6:5–6 and TB Shevu'ot 42b; Bava Batra 87a; *and cf. MT,* Mekhirah 3:17–18 and To'en ve-Nit'an 5:4. Modes of acquisition of movable property are different from modes of acquisition of land; movable property is not acquired by payment of money, by deed, or by an act of dominion (such as fencing, opening a gateway, or locking the premises). In addition, the laws of overreaching apply to movable property, but not to real property.

67. *Tur* ḤM ch. 193.

68. Current editions read "*ḥashvinan lehu,*" but ed. Cremona 1558 and ed. Sabbioneta 1559 read "*ḥashvi lehu,*" which is grammatically more correct.

69. Sh. Ar. ḤM 193:1.

grated Maimonides' reservation ("that needs the land") as part of his affirmative statement of the controlling legal principle.[70] Although of no legal consequence, the differences in style between Maimonides and the *Turim* (Caro copied Maimonides' language *verbatim*) are of interest: Maimonides says, "is like land," the *Turim* says "has the same law as land"; Maimonides—"either by money, or by deed, or by an act of dominion," the *Turim*—"by money, and by deed, and by an act of dominion";[71] Maimonides—"it is like movable property for the purpose of acquisition, and [the law of] *ona'ah* applies to it," the *Turim*—"it has the same law as movable property in regard to acquisition and [the law of] *ona'ah.*" Although the Hebrew style of the statement of the governing principle in the *Turim* is somewhat more terse, Maimonides and Caro are clearer.[72]

EXAMPLE 3

Mishneh Torah[73]	*Turim*[75*]	*Shulḥan Arukh*[76*]
The three years that we have mentioned[74*] must be from day to day	[To show sufficient] possession of bathhouses, dovecotes, olive	The three years that they mentioned must be from day to day; even if

70. Nevertheless, in order to make the entire law perfectly clear, Caro then specifically stated that if it does not need the land, it is like movable property. His addition of the qualifying language "that needs the land" serves to make the first clause symmetrical with the last clause by limiting the first clause to things that are attached to the land and need the land. The view of the *Turim,* which is contrary to Maimonides, is stated in a gloss by Rema to Sh. Ar., *ad loc.*

71. The *Shulḥan Arukh* here reads "by money, or by deed" and not, like Maimonides, "either by money, or by deed." *Cf. MT,* Ishut 1:2, dealing with betrothal: "by money, or by document, or by sexual intercourse"; *see also supra* pp. 1209–1210.

72. Particularly making clear that each one of the three stated modes of acquisition is a fully effective alternative.

73. *MT,* To'en ve-Nit'an 12:1. It will facilitate understanding of this example if M Bava Batra 3:1, which is the main source of this law, is quoted:

> [The period of] possession [needed to prove ownership] of: houses; pits, ditches, and caves [used as receptacles for water]; dovecotes; bathhouses; olive presses; irrigated fields [fields that are irrigated by hand and produce crops several times a year]; slaves [whose legal incidents are analogized to the law of real property]; and anything that is continually productive [*i.e.,* not just once a year]—is three years from day to day [*i.e.,* possession by the occupier for three complete years is sufficient to constitute proof that the property belongs to him]. In the case of a field not under irrigation [a field that uses only rainwater and therefore produces crops only once a year], [the period of] possession is three years, which need not be from day to day [*i.e.,* although the field must be occupied for three years, it need not be worked for the entire year since it produces crops only once a year]. R. Ishmael says: "[The period of possession need be only] three months during the first year and three months during the last year and twelve months in the middle year, totaling eighteen months." R. Akiva says: "One month during the first year and one month during the last year and twelve months during the middle year, totaling fourteen months." R. Ishmael says: "This refers only

* Footnotes 74, 75, and 76 appear on the next page.

[*i.e.,* three complete years]; even if one day is missing, he has not had sufficient possession and may be removed from it [*i.e.,* the property]. This applies to real property that is continually productive, such as houses; courtyards; pits, ditches, and caves [used as receptacles for water]; shops; lodging houses; bathhouses; dovecotes; olive presses; irrigated fields that are continuously watered, sown, and planted; vegetable gardens; and orchards. Also, ambulatory slaves, as we have explained.[77] However, fields not

presses, pits, ditches, caves, and slaves, he must bring proof that he used them and took what they produced for three years. [The period of] possession of a field, whether an irrigated field that continually produces crops, or a nonirrigated field, or a field of trees that does not continually produce crops, is three years from day to day, *i.e.,* the field must be in his control for three years during which he appropriates all the profits. Maimonides wrote that fields of grain [which are not irrigated] and fields of trees do not

one day is missing, he has not had sufficient possession and may be removed from it. This applies to real property that is (continually)[78] productive, such as houses; courtyards; pits, ditches, and caves; shops;[79] lodging houses; bathhouses; dovecotes; olive presses; irrigated fields that are continuously watered, sown, and planted;[80] vegetable gardens; and orchards. Also, ambulatory slaves. However, fields not under irrigation, which are watered only by rain, and fields of trees do not require three complete

---

to a field of grain; but in the case of an orchard, as soon as he has gathered in his crop [of grapes], harvested his olives, and gathered in his summer harvest [*i.e.,* figs], this period is [deemed the equivalent of] three years."

TB Bava Batra 36b notes additional sources for this law; *see further* nn. *infra.* For detailed discussion of the law relating to possession of real property as proof of ownership and the law's Talmudic source, *see supra* pp. 1007–1014 and *infra* n. 74.

74. *See MT,* To'en ve-Nit'an 11:1 *et seq.* In Jewish law, the rule of possession (*ḥazakah*) for three years as proof of ownership is as follows: If A has been in undisturbed possession of real property for three years and B claims and even proves that he is the legal owner of that property, A's contention that he lawfully acquired the property from B is accepted, because the fact that A had been in possession of the property for three years without any protest by B serves as proof that the field came into A's possession legally, *i.e.,* by purchase or gift or the like. This is true even if A has no other proof, such as a deed of sale or gift. Possession for three years in Jewish law thus serves as proof of ownership, *i.e.,* that the occupier of the property obtained it lawfully. However, the three years' possession does not itself directly operate to transfer the legal ownership to the possessor. *See* M. Elon, EJ, VII, pp. 1516–1522, s.v. Ḥazakah (reprinted in *Principles,* pp. 590–596). For the term *ḥazakah* in the sense of a mode of acquisition, and for other meanings, *see supra* pp. 79–80.

75. *Tur* ḤM ch. 141.

76. Sh. Ar. ḤM 141:1.

77. *See MT,* To'en ve-Nit'an 10:4.

78. Eds. Venice 1565, 1567, and 1574 do not have the word "continually."

79. Eds. Venice 1565, 1567, and 1574 have the Hebrew word for "shops" written *plene* (with an extra *vav*).

80. Eds. Venice 1565, 1567, and 1574 have the word "taken" (*notelim*) instead of "planted" (*not'im*)—clearly an error, since "taken" is meaningless in the context. Caro's source was Maimonides, where the word is *ve-not'in.*

under irrigation, which are watered only by rain, and fields of trees do not require three complete years, but once he has consumed [*i.e.*, taken the profits from] three crops of one kind, it is deemed the equivalent of three years. For example, if it was a field of dates and he harvested three crops, or grapes and he harvested three crops, or olives and he harvested three crops—it is deemed the equivalent of three years, and he has had sufficient possession [to excuse the absence of a deed to establish ownership].

require three complete years, but once he has consumed three crops of one kind, it is [deemed the equivalent of] three years; Raḥ [Rabbenu Hananel] and Ramah [Meir ha-Levi Abulafia] also wrote to the same effect. But my master and father, the Rosh [Asheri], of blessed memory,[81] favored the first opinion, and so did Rabbenu Jonah.

years, but once he has consumed three crops of one kind, it is deemed the equivalent of three years. For example, if it was a field of dates and he harvested three crops, or grapes and he harvested three crops, or olives and he harvested three crops—it is deemed the equivalent of three years, and he has had sufficient possession.

An examination of the three texts reveals several characteristics of each. Maimonides modeled his style on the Mishnah[82] but was clearer and more expansive. The Mishnah reads: "[The period of] possession [needed to prove ownership] . . . is three years from day to day." The *Mishneh Torah* reads: "The three years that we have mentioned must be from day to day; even if one day is missing, he has not had sufficient possession and may be removed from it." Maimonides also explained what the Hebrew term *sedeh bet ha-shelaḥin* (an irrigated field) means; and at the end of the paragraph he stated the three examples mentioned in the Mishnah and the *baraita* and elaborated on them.[83] Maimonides not only made stylistic changes, but also

81. Ed. Cremona 1558 reads: "My master, my father, may the memory of the righteous be for a blessing. . . ."

82. M Bava Batra 3:1; *see supra* n. 73. The Mishnah uses the word *tadir* for "continually" in the phrase "and anything that is continually productive." Maimonides uses the word *tamid*, which also means "continually." The *Turim* uses *tadir*. It is unclear what influenced Maimonides to change the Mishnaic term.

83. Here, too, Maimonides' style is interesting. The Mishnah reads: "As soon as he has gathered in (*kanas*) his crop [of grapes], harvested (*masak*) his olives, and gathered in (*kanas*) his summer harvest [*i.e.*, figs], this period is [deemed the equivalent of] three years." A *baraita* quoted in TB Bava Batra 36b reads: "But the Sages say: Until he harvests (*yidgor*) three crops (*gederot*) [of dates], harvests (*yivẓor*) three crops (*beẓirot*) [of grapes], or harvests (*yimsok*) three crops (*mesikot*) [of olives]," substituting dates for figs. Maimonides used the three examples of the *baraita*—dates, grapes, and olives—in the same order as the *baraita*, but elaborated on them, not only using the terms for "harvest," each of which is specifically appropriate for each particular fruit, but specifically mentioning the fruit to

added to the examples in the Mishnah others from the Talmud;[84] in this, he was faithful to his codificatory method of mentioning every concrete example stated in Talmudic literature, even when the specific case is included in a generalization that is stated in the Talmud and by Maimonides himself.[85]

The *Turim* differs from Maimonides in two respects. On one hand, it is briefer: it does not cite the specific examples of dates, grapes, and olives, but merely states, "once he has consumed three crops of one kind." It does not explain what a *sedeh bet ha-shelaḥin* is. Slaves are included together with the other items—as they are in the Mishnah—and not mentioned separately, as in the *Mishneh Torah*.[86] Finally, it states only the examples listed in the Mishnah and omits all the additional examples Maimonides took from various Talmudic sources and skillfully incorporated in a comprehensive list. On the other hand, the *Turim* refers to a difference of opinion among the *rishonim* regarding the requisite duration of possession of fields of grain and fields of trees. Rabbenu Hananel, Maimonides, and Meir Abulafia held that the consumption of three crops of one kind in such fields was sufficient, even if it occurred in less than three years, while Rabbenu Jonah and Asheri required a full three years in all cases, and the *Turim* endorses their view.

Caro reverted to Maimonides' style (including the additional examples) except for a few instances where he tightened the language;[87] and,

---

which the term is applicable, and thus leaving no doubt as to the meaning of each particular term.

84. Maimonides added the following to the examples in M Bava Batra 3:1: (a) *"courtyards"* (following M Bava Batra 3:5 as explicated in the Talmud—"The law of [three years'] possession applies to the following: . . . If one put cattle . . . in a courtyard"; *see* Rashbam, Bava Batra 57a); (b) *"shops"* (following TB Bava Batra 29b—"the shops of Meḥoza"); (c) *"lodging houses"* (perhaps by analogy from shops); and (d) *"vegetable gardens"* (perhaps on the basis of TB Bava Batra 68a—"What are irrigated fields? Vegetable gardens").

85. *See supra* pp. 1211–1214. As to the law of three years' possession, both the Mishnah and Maimonides (albeit with some slight variation, *see supra* n. 82) state the general principle ("anything that is continually productive"), which actually encompasses all the examples. However, both the general principle and the specific examples are set forth.

86. In the *Turim*, as in Maimonides, the laws relating to ambulatory slaves, as to whom the period of possession is three years, had previously been set forth (*see Tur* ḤM ch. 135), but the *Turim* did not follow the lead of Maimonides, who mentioned slaves separately and pointed out that he had treated the subject earlier: "Also, ambulatory slaves, as we have explained."

87. Such as omitting "as we have explained," after "also, ambulatory slaves" (Sh. Ar. ḤM 135:2 had also previously stated the law as applied to slaves). The *Shulḥan Arukh* reads: "The three years that they mentioned" (eds. Venice 1565, 1567, and 1574 also read this way), instead of Maimonides' reading: "The three years that we have mentioned." The *Shulḥan Arukh* as well as Maimonides had previously discussed the period of three years. *See* Sh. Ar. ḤM 140:7.

like Maimonides, he stated the law categorically—to the same effect as Maimonides—without mentioning the views of any of the other authorities, whether supportive of or opposed to Maimonides.[88]

EXAMPLE 4

One of the requirements for proof of ownership on the basis of three years' possession is that the possession must be continuous. Lesser noncontinuous periods may not be added or "tacked on" to each other to make up the three years. The reason is that when the occupation is not continuous, the original owner can claim that he did not protest against it because the occupier conducted himself not like an owner but like a thief, moving in and out, and the owner therefore saw no need to protest.[89] In connection with this requirement of continuous possession, the Talmud[90] discusses the question of two partners, one of whom occupies the property for one year and the other for the next, and so on alternately for six years. The Talmud's conclusion is stated differently in each of the three codes:

Mishneh Torah[91]

If two partners were in possession of a field for six years—the first one having taken the profits during the first, third, and fifth [years], and the other having taken the profits during the second, fourth, and sixth [years]—neither of them has sufficient possession [lit. "the possession is not sufficient for one of them"], because the [original] owner of

Turim[92]

If two persons were in possession of one field—one having taken the profits[93] during the first, third, and fifth years, and the other having taken the profits[94] during the second, fourth, and sixth years—and they claim ownership, they have not had sufficient possession, for the complainant may say, "I did not see the need to protest because they did

Shulḥan Arukh[95]

If two partners were in possession of a field for six years—the first one having taken the profits for [years] 1, 3, 5, and the other having taken the profits for [years] 2, 4, 6—the possession is not sufficient for either one of them. If they had made this arrangement in a written agreement, their possession is sufficient once three years have

88. In his gloss to the *Shulḥan Arukh,* Rema cited the opinions of Rabbenu Jonah, Asheri, and the *Turim* that three complete years are required for all property, and added: "and this view, in my opinion, should be followed" notwithstanding the contrary views of Maimonides and Caro.

89. *See supra* n. 74.

90. TB Bava Batra 29b.

91. *MT,* To'en ve-Nit'an 12:5.

92. *Tur* ḤM ch. 144.

93. Ed. Cremona 1558 and other early editions read: "one having taken the profits from it."

94. Ed. Cremona 1558 reads: "having taken the profits from it."

95. Sh. Ar. ḤM 144:1.

the property may say, "Since I neither saw nor heard that one person occupied it year after year, I did not protest." Therefore, if these partners had drawn up a written agreement between themselves to the effect that each would occupy the property in alternate years, their possession is sufficient once three years have passed, because there is public knowledge of a written agreement; and since he [the original owner] did not protest, he has lost his right. The same applies to a slave who worked for each of two persons, in alternate years; if they had a written agreement between themselves, they have had sufficient possession.

not occupy [the property] in the appropriate manner, one person alone for three years." Therefore, if they had made this arrangement in a written agreement, the complainant cannot make this argument, because it [the written agreement] is [a matter of] public knowledge and there is here sufficient possession[96] after the first three years.

passed. . . . The same applies to a slave who worked for them under the same conditions.

Here too, the results of a close examination of these three texts are significant. Maimonides set forth the two rules in a manner consistent with the explicitness of the Talmudic passage.[97] However, he deviated from the Talmud's formulation in that he began with the rule in regard to possession of a field, whereas the Talmud dealt with possession of a female slave; and he dealt with possession of slaves (and then in terms of a male and not a female) only at the very end, almost as if by way of afterthought.[98] Apparently, Maimonides chose land as his principal illustration for practical reasons: in his time, land was of more practical importance than slaves; from

96. Ed. Cremona 1558 and current editions read: "and it is sufficient possession."

97. TB Bava Batra 29b.

98. Moreover, in the case of the slave, Maimonides confined his reference to the second rule, namely, that if the partners have a written agreement to divide the slave's services between them, their possession is sufficient. The Talmud discusses the case of a female slave in the context of the first rule, namely, that if there is no written agreement, their possession is not sufficient; only thereafter does the Talmud mention the rule that if there is a written agreement, their possession is sufficient.

the Talmudic example of a female slave, he derived by analogy the law as to a field. However, in order not to omit entirely the specific fact situation discussed in the Talmud, he added, "The same applies to a slave. . . ."[99]

The *Turim* follows Maimonides in one respect only; otherwise its style is very different. It too states the law as to possession by partners in terms of a field, but completely omits reference to slaves, apparently because slavery was not important when the *Turim* was written.[100] The *Turim* is briefer than Maimonides. At the beginning, it omits "for six years" because that is self-evident from the context; in place of Maimonides' "the [original] owner of the property" it substitutes "the complainant";[101] it shortens Maimonides' "if these partners had drawn up a written agreement between themselves to the effect that each would occupy the property in alternate years" to "if they had made this arrangement in a written agreement."

The *Turim* sometimes changed the style even when the purpose was not brevity. Thus, in place of Maimonides' "Since I neither saw nor heard that one person occupied it year after year, I did not protest," the *Turim* has "I did not see the need to protest because they did not occupy [the property] in the appropriate manner, one person alone for three years." Similarly, Maimonides has, "since he did not protest, he has lost his right," while the *Turim* reads, "the complainant cannot make this argument."

The *Shulḥan Arukh* is quite different from the other two and presents an excellent example of Caro's much more terse and incisive style. To achieve this effect, he borrowed from the style of each of the other two codes as suited his purpose. At the beginning, he followed Maimonides, with two interesting variations. Instead of the full ordinal numbers "first, third, and fifth, . . . second, fourth, and sixth," the *Shulḥan Arukh* states them in an abbreviated form indicated by "1, 3, 5, . . . 2, 4, 6"; and instead of "the possession is not sufficient for one of them," Caro wrote, "the possession is not sufficient for either one of them." Caro's addition of the word "either" is both a stylistically and substantively significant clarification.[102]

99. This is another excellent example of the extent to which Maimonides took pains to mention all the examples given in the Talmud, even though substantively they add nothing.

100. Slavery did exist to a limited degree in this period; *see* S. Assaf, *Be-Oholei Ya'akov, Avadim u-Seḥar Avadim Eẓel ha-Yehudim bi-Mei ha-Beinayim* [In the Tents of Jacob—Slavery and the Slave Trade among Jews in the Middle Ages], pp. 223–256. However, it was only a marginal occurrence. *See also supra* p. 1256 n. 87.

101. *Cf.* the passage in TB Bava Batra 29b: "A *complaint* was lodged against him (emphasis supplied).

102. Literally, this passage in Maimonides could be interpreted to mean that *one* of them does not have sufficient possession, but the other one does, or both of them collectively

Caro followed Maimonides' "their possession is sufficient once three years have passed," but as to the clause concerning the written agreement, Caro adopted the formulation of the *Turim* ("if they had made this arrangement in a written agreement") since it is much more concise than Maimonides.[103] Caro's statement of the law is shorter than that in both the *Turim* and the *Mishneh Torah*—he omitted the two rationales they offer, one for the rule that possession by partners in alternate years is insufficient to prove ownership and the other for the rule that the existence of a written agreement changes this result.

The last sentence of the excerpt from the *Shulḥan Arukh* is also interesting. On the one hand, Caro followed Maimonides in adding the example of the slave (presumably for the same reason, *i.e.*, to enumerate every specific example given in the Talmud),[104] but on the other hand, his reference to it is much briefer and more precise: instead of "The same applies to a slave who worked for each of two persons, in alternate years; if they had a written agreement between themselves, they have had sufficient possession," he wrote, "The same applies to a slave who worked for them under the same conditions." Caro's version is not only shorter but more precise, in that it applies to a slave both rules previously stated with regard to a field, namely, (1) that alternating periods of possession by partners may not be "tacked" (*i.e.*, combined) and (2) that the rule is to the contrary if the arrangement for alternating possession is made in a written agreement.

An analysis of the parallel passages in the foregoing examples (to which many more could be added)[105] reveals several general features of the respective styles of the *Mishneh Torah*, the *Turim*, and the *Shulḥan Arukh*. Although Maimonides in his *Mishneh Torah* made no reference to the sources of the laws or to views contrary to those he codified, he stated the full particulars of each law and incorporated into his text the law's rationale as well as relevant philosophic considerations. The *Turim* states the substance of the law more briefly than Maimonides; but it too sometimes includes the law's rationale and sometimes discusses relevant philosophic considerations. It consistently refers to all differences of opinion among the *rishonim* on each law; such references are an essential feature of its codificatory method.

---

do. *Cf. supra* p. 1330, regarding the substitution of "or" for "and" in the *Mishneh Torah* and, subsequently, in the *Shulḥan Arukh*. Generally, Maimonides was very careful in this respect.

103. Caro also omitted the word "therefore" which is in the *Turim*, because he did not include the rationale to which the *Turim* refers. *See* the further discussion *infra*.

104. As in the previous example, with regard to the enumeration of types of property in connection with three years' possession; *see supra*. pp. 1333–1334.

105. *See* three additional examples in Appendix B.

The method of the *Shulḥan Arukh* is distinct from that of the other codes. The *Shulḥan Arukh* states the substance of the law briefly, sometimes adopting the formulation of the *Turim* for this purpose. However, when clarity is particularly needed, the *Shulḥan Arukh* frequently prefers Maimonides' text; and in these instances, the *Shulḥan Arukh* is more expansive than the *Turim.*[106] The *Shulḥan Arukh* presents only the normative rule; in contrast to Maimonides and the *Turim,* it includes neither rationales for the law nor any philosophic considerations. Laws are generally stated without attribution of source[107] and with no reference to contrary opinions.[108]

These differences between the three codes stem from the different approaches of their authors to codification. Maimonides intended his *Mishneh Torah* to encompass the entire halakhic system, such that "there will be no need to read any other book."[109] He therefore felt constrained to provide the full details of each law, together with its rationale and philosophical background. Although the *Turim* did not aspire to such exclusivity, it too was intended to be a code from which one could learn every law, as well as its rationale, the general aggadic concepts relevant to it, and any contrary opinions.[110] Joseph Caro, however, in writing the *Shulḥan Arukh,* could omit not only contrary opinions, but also rationales, because he had given them all—at length and in detail—in his *Bet Yosef,*[111] which was the preparation for the *Shulḥan Arukh* and an integral part of his code of Jewish law. In this respect, too, Caro's codificatory methodology—a book of *pe-*

106. *See, e.g., supra* examples 2 and 3, and example 1 in Appendix B. On rare occasions, the *Shulḥan Arukh* is lengthier (in the Hebrew) than both Maimonides and the *Turim*—a phenomenon that has not been satisfactorily explained; *see* Appendix B, example 1.

107. In a few instances, Caro mentioned names of Sages and halakhic authorities in the *Shulḥan Arukh; see supra* n. 56 and *infra* n. 108.

108. Occasionally, however, the *Shulḥan Arukh* does cite two, or even three, opinions on a point of law. *See, e.g.,* Sh. Ar. OḤ 166:1, where the *Shulḥan Arukh* cites two opinions ("There are those who say . . . , and there are those who say . . . ") and decides in favor of one ("it is preferable to take care"); Sh. Ar. ḤM 129:4, where three opinions are given, two in the form of "there are those who say" and the third in the name of Maimonides. Sh. Ar. ḤM 131:4 sets forth a law and concludes: "The matter requires consideration" (and *see* Rema, *ad loc.*). As a result, various principles were developed for determining the law when the *Shulḥan Arukh* presents more than one opinion and does not explicitly decide between them. *See Yad Malakhi,* II, Kelalei ha-Shulḥan Arukh u-Rema [Principles of the *Shulḥan Arukh* and Rema], ##9–17.

109. Maimonides, *MT,* Introduction; *see supra* p. 1145, *et al.*

110. *See, e.g.,* the introductions to various sections of the *Turim* and to specific subjects within the sections. *See supra* pp. 1295–1299 and n. 266.

111. Where the *Turim* includes an aggadic passage, *Bet Yosef* also contains various relevant philosophical passages; *see Bet Yosef* to the introductions of the *Turim,* and *supra* n. 110.

sakim alongside a book of *halakhot*—proved itself to be the correct and efficient one for the halakhic system.

Nevertheless, it should be reiterated that Maimonides' *Mishneh Torah* remains the preeminent code in terms of structure and style. No author of a book of *halakhot* or *pesakim*—not even the *Shulḥan Arukh*—has succeeded in producing a work so uniformly excellent in clarity of design, beauty of style, and unity of structure as the *Mishneh Torah*. The *Mishneh Torah* is a unified, tightly constructed work, written in consistently beautiful and clear Hebrew. The *Shulḥan Arukh*, on the other hand, contains a variety of styles with a confusing mixture of Hebrew and Aramaic; the work as a whole lacks the uniformity and harmony that distinguish every part of the *Mishneh Torah*.

The halakhic material in the *Shulḥan Arukh* is composed of several strata; parts of it include laws from the *Mishneh Torah*, but those parts sometimes also contain laws that are inconsistent with Maimonides' rulings and therefore stylistically different as well. The *Shulḥan Arukh* also includes many laws that originated in the course of the four centuries after the *Mishneh Torah*; these laws were taken from a great many books of *halakhot*, responsa, commentaries, and novellae, all of which had distinct styles and structures. While Maimonides welded all his sources into one uniform style and an integrated structure, Caro generally stated each law in the style of its source, whether Hebrew, Aramaic,[112] or a mixture of both.[113] No attempt was made in the *Shulḥan Arukh* to rework the material taken from the various sources and fuse them into a unified and harmonious structure. Caro's main effort was to declare the law briefly and comprehensively, with nothing extraneous.[114] His success in that effort was one of the main reasons

112. Occasionally, Caro stated a law in the original Aramaic formulation of the Talmud even when Maimonides had translated it into Hebrew. A good example is *MT*, Malveh ve-Loveh 27:15, where Maimonides described a case taken from the Talmud (TB Bava Batra 166b), translating it from its original Aramaic into Hebrew. *Tur* ḤM ch. 42 and Sh. Ar. ḤM 42:15 present the law in its original Aramaic. This law is also an example of a combined casuistic-normative style in all three works, but with a difference in the order of presentation. Maimonides first stated the concrete case (in line with his practice of not deleting any specific examples given in the Talmud) and then the generalization, whereas the *Turim* and the *Shulḥan Arukh* state the general principle first and then the example. For further discussion of the law here referred to, *see supra* p. 434.

113. As stated, Caro frequently adopted Maimonides' formulation, even at the cost of brevity, if necessary for clarity. There are also instances where Caro seemingly copied Maimonides' formulation, yet inserted various stylistic changes for no apparent reason. *See, e.g.*, Appendix B, examples 2 and 3. The matter requires further study.

114. Occasionally, a law is stated twice—once in each of two parts of the *Shulḥan Arukh*. *See, e.g.*, Sh. Ar. YD 267:16 and Sh. Ar. ḤM 369:11. In this duplication, Caro followed *Tur* (YD 267:32–33 and ḤM 369:13) and *MT* (Gezelah va-Avedah 5:16 and Avadim 1:8). The source for the law is TB Bava Meẓi'a 73b; *see* Elon, *Ḥerut*, p. 75 n. 35 and p. 85 n. 73. This duplication in the *Shulḥan Arukh* and the other codes also requires further study.

why the *Shulḥan Arukh* became the authoritative code of the halakhic system.[115]

E. The Crystallization of the Methodology for Codifying Jewish Law

Joseph Caro's methodology for codifying the *Halakhah* was the culmination of the efforts of a number of predecessors. Had it not been for Maimonides' bold and revolutionary innovation in the twelfth century—a monolithic book of *pesakim* containing a categorical statement of legal rules with no reference to sources or contrary opinions—or for the originality of Rashba's thirteenth-century undertaking (*Torat ha-Bayit ha-Arokh* and *Torat ha-Bayit ha-Kaẓer*—a book of *pesakim* as a companion to a book of *halakhot*), or for Jacob b. Asher's venture in the fourteenth century combining both these genres into one *magnum opus* in the *Turim,* it is unlikely that Joseph Caro's twofold work, *Bet Yosef* and *Shulḥan Arukh,* would have been accepted or even written.

The need for a code of Jewish law was recognized equally by Maimonides, Rashba, Jacob b. Asher, and Joseph Caro, and the background giving rise to the need was the same for each of them: the difficulty of finding one's way through the halakhic sources, the diffuseness of the laws, and the proliferation of conflicting views as to specific provisions. These authors all had a common aspiration: to create a code in which the law on any matter would be clearly and definitively stated and could be easily and efficiently found. However, they differed in the methods they chose to achieve this goal[116]—except that Caro essentially followed Rashba's system.[117]

Their commonality in the perception of the problem and the desire to solve it, and their difference in regard to the solution that each one offered, become strikingly clear from a comparison of Caro's statement of purpose in composing *Bet Yosef* and the *Shulḥan Arukh* with Maimonides' explanation of why he wrote the *Mishneh Torah.* Both Maimonides and Caro re-

115. As to the acceptance of the *Shulḥan Arukh, see* the discussion later in this chapter and in chapter 37.

116. One basic aspect of the methodology of codification—a topical arrangement of the material—was common to all four codifiers. As will be recalled, the question of the manner of arranging the material in a code—whether to follow the order of the Talmudic tractates or of the Biblical commandments or to use a topical arrangement or some other system—was for a long time an important question on which the halakhic authorities disagreed. Maimonides created a sophisticated structure for a code arranged topically; and Rashba, the *Turim,* and the *Shulḥan Arukh* all used the same basic structure, although they disagreed with Maimonides and with one another with respect to various other aspects of codification.

117. *See supra* pp. 1277, 1313.

marked on the difficulty of locating any particular law in the vast halakhic literature as well as on the multiplicity of conflicting views—problems that led them, as they both put it, to be "zealous for the Lord of Hosts"[118] and (as Maimonides wrote) "to compile a compendium that will include all the laws and precepts of the Torah, with nothing missing from it"[119] or (as Caro wrote) "to compose a work that includes all the laws currently applicable."[120]

However, as to the method to be used, Maimonides set himself the task of "put[ting] together the results obtained from all those [previous] works . . . , all in plain and concise language. Thus, the entire Oral Law, systematically arranged, will become familiar to all, without citing arguments and counterarguments—one person saying one thing and another something else. Rather, [the law will be stated] clearly, pointedly, and accurately"[121] with the result that "a person will not need to have recourse to any other work to ascertain any of the laws of Israel. This work is intended as a compendium of the entire Oral Law . . . [such] that a person who first reads the Torah and then this work will know from it all of the Oral Law, and there will be no need to read any other book [written] between them."[122]

In contrast to Maimonides, Joseph Caro had learned from the many attempts prior to his own that conciseness and brevity in themselves were not adequate to meet the particular needs of Jewish law. Although such a presentation is a necessary and significant part of the halakhic system and "is of benefit to everyone,"[123] its benefit could come about only after the sources of the law, together with the variant opinions and final halakhic conclusions, had been treated in another separate and larger work such as *Bet Yosef.* Only after the composition of such a larger work is there a need for a complementary work such as the *Shulḥan Arukh* to state the law categorically and definitively.[124]

Maimonides viewed his *Mishneh Torah* as his *magnum opus,* for which all his other and in his view lesser halakhic works were merely preparation and prologue. Caro, however, considered *Bet Yosef* to be his major achieve-

118. *See supra* p. 1214 and p. 1313 n. 13.

119. *See supra* p. 1187.

120. *See supra* p. 1313.

121. *See supra* p. 1204.

122. *See supra* p. 1145.

123. *See supra* p. 1320.

124. Tchernowitz's statement (*Toledot ha-Posekim,* III, p. 29) that "He [Caro] dashed off the latter work [the *Shulḥan Arukh*] almost without thought" is without support; it contradicts Caro's stated aim and is inconsistent with the categorical style of the *Shulḥan Arukh.*

ment; he devoted twenty years to writing it and twelve additional years to reviewing and correcting it. Even after it was published and had spread to all Jewish communities, he reexamined it and wrote corrections and addenda, which were at first printed in a separate volume, *Bedek ha-Bayit,*[125] and then incorporated into subsequent printings of *Bet Yosef.* Caro referred to *Bet Yosef* as his "great work,"[126] while the *Shulḥan Arukh* constituted a collection of "the flowers"[127] of that great and stately tree. This was the final pattern that Joseph Caro fashioned for the codification of Jewish law: a code made up of two complementary components, each different in form and content, together providing a brief, convenient, useful, clear, and definitive statement of the law, yet at the same time preserving the continuity of the law and the connection between the law and its sources.

We may note here one of the most remarkable and portentous coincidences of Jewish history. The first code of Jewish law after the Torah was the Mishnah of R. Judah Ha-Nasi, who lived in Bet She'arim and Sepphoris in the Lower Galilee. More than 1350 years later, in 1563, the most recent major code of Jewish law was completed by Joseph Caro in Biriyyah and Safed, in the Upper Galilee.[128] The mysterious ways of history had brought

125. *See* Caro, *Bedek ha-Bayit,* Introduction (printed before, and sometimes after, his Introduction to *Bet Yosef* to *Tur* OḤ):

> Thus says the young Joseph, the son of Ephraim the son of Joseph Caro, of blessed memory: As God has helped me until now to compose the book *Bet Yosef* and have it printed, and it has spread throughout the whole of Jewry, God has further enabled me to review it; and I have made additions and supplements to it and corrected it . . . particularly since the printers left out many things. It was my intention that these additions would be inserted in a second printing, but this did not occur, because they hurriedly made a second printing before they received my manuscript. I therefore decided to publish the above-mentioned additions in a separate booklet, so that it will be available to all. When *Bet Yosef* is printed [again], everything will be inserted in its proper place, and in any event all will benefit. God will have thus enabled me to do a service for the public.

126. In his Introduction to the *Shulḥan Arukh:* "The great work I wrote on the four *Turim,* which I called *Bet Yosef.*"

127. *Shulḥan Arukh,* Introduction.

128. In the first editions (Venice 1565, 1567 [printed twice], 1574 [printed twice], and others), the following colophons appear at the end of each of the parts:

> *At the end of Sh. Ar. OḤ:* "Completed and consummated Monday, Elul 2nd, in the year 'God considered it to be good' [the numerical value of the letters of the Hebrew for "considered" (*ḥashavah*) is (5)315 A.M. = 1555 C.E.], in the village of Biriyyah in the Upper Galilee, may it be speedily rebuilt."
>
> *At the end of Sh. Ar. YD:* "Completed and consummated Tuesday evening, the second day of the month of Tammuz, 5316, in Safed, may it be speedily rebuilt." (5316 A.M. = 1556 C.E.; in ed. Venice 1567, printed by Gryphio, the date is 5317, but this is most probably a typographical error since EH, which is later, was completed in Shevat 5317 and Shevat precedes Tammuz in the Hebrew calendar.)

the Torah back to its original lodging place; and from its rightful home in the Land of Israel, it once again spread throughout world Jewry. The four parts of the *Shulḥan Arukh* were printed for the first time in Venice in 1565 and quickly circulated to Jewish communities in both the east and the west. Even in Caro's own lifetime—he died in 1575 at the age of eighty-seven—the *Shulḥan Arukh* was reprinted a number of times.[129] This fact alone confirms how much Caro's own and succeeding generations needed his code.[130]

At the end of Sh. Ar. EH: "This important book was completed on Tuesday, Shevat 19, 5317 A.M., in Safed, may it be speedily rebuilt, in the Upper Galilee, may it be rebuilt speedily in our days, Amen." (5317 A.M. = 1557 C.E.) Ed. Venice 1574 has: "This important book was completed this day, Iyyar 1st, [5]334 [=1574 C.E.] here in Venice"—but this refers to the completion of the printing, and the printer's colophon was substituted for Caro's. Ed. Venice 1567, printed by Gryphio, has no colophon.

At the end of Sh. Ar. ḤM: "'With what shall I approach the Lord, do homage to God on high' [Micah 6:6]? For great has been His steadfast love for me [*cf.* Psalms 117:2], and He has granted me the privilege to complete this valuable work. May He, in His mercy and great kindness, take pity on me to renew my youth like an eagle and grant me to sire male children who will occupy themselves with the study of Torah and become halakhic scholars among the Jews. May reverence for the Lord be their treasure [*cf.* Isaiah 33:6] and may the Torah not be absent from my mouth nor from the mouth of my children nor from the mouth of my children's children—said the Lord—from now on, for all times [*cf.* Isaiah 59:21], Amen. This valuable book was completed Thursday evening, 16th Adar I, in the year 'I speak always of your precepts' [lit. 'Your precepts are my talk' (Psalms 119:99)]." The numerical value of the letters of the Hebrew for "talk" (*siḥah*) is (5)323 A.M. = 1563 C.E. or, possibly, on the basis of an alternate reading (*si'aḥ*), (5)318 A.M. = 1558 C.E.; both dates are possible, since the first printing was Venice, 1565. Since the composition of the four parts was continuous, 1558 C.E. might seem the more likely date, inasmuch as the first three parts were completed in 1555, 1556, and 1557, respectively. Nevertheless, we have chosen the year 1563, which is also the date indicated by *Shem ha-Gedolim,* Books, Letter *tet,* #12: "And know that in the *Shulḥan Arukh* printed in the master's [Caro's] lifetime without being proofread, it is written at its conclusion that it was completed on Thursday evening, 17th Adar I, (5)323." Ed. Venice 1567 (Gryphio) reads: "Sunday evening, Nisan 28, (5)327," but the reference is to the year of printing; *see* the title page: "Printed in the House of Juan Gryphio in the Month of Nisan, 5327 A.M., here in Venice the Capital."

129. *See supra* n. 128 and various places throughout this chapter for the editions that appeared in Caro's lifetime. *See also* R. Margaliot, "Defusei ha-Shulḥan Arukh ha-Rishonim" [The First Printed Editions of the *Shulḥan Arukh*], *Koveẓ Rabbi Yosef Caro* [The Rabbi Joseph Caro Anthology], ed. I. Raphael, Jerusalem, 1969, pp. 89ff.; N. Ben Menahem, "Ha-Defusim ha-Rishonim Shel ha-Shulḥan Arukh" [The First Printed Editions of the *Shulḥan Arukh*], *id.* at 101ff.

130. *See supra* p. 1312 for the quotation to this effect from *Shem ha-Gedolim. See also Shem ha-Gedolim,* Persons, Letter *yod,* #165.

II. MOSES ISSERLES (REMA) AND HIS CONTRIBUTION TO THE CODIFICATORY LITERATURE

A. The Polish Jewish Community

One of the Jewish centers to which Joseph Caro's code found its way was Poland, which had just begun a renaissance of Jewish life and scholarship. Jews are known to have lived in Poland since the end of the tenth century C.E.; and commencing at the end of the eleventh century, waves of Jewish immigrants fled to Poland in the wake of the Crusades. The Rindfleisch Massacres at the end of the thirteenth century, the pogroms that accompanied the spread of the Black Death in the middle of the fourteenth century, and the persecutions of 1391 in Christian Spain also substantially increased the flow of Jews to Poland. Masses of Jews fled from their persecutors in the German states, Central Europe, and Spain, and settled in Poland, Russia, and Lithuania. As early as 1264, the Jews were granted a Charter of Privileges by Boleslav the Pious, the Duke of Kalisz, which became effective throughout Poland when the Polish states were later unified. The Charter, which was the legal basis for the status of the Jews of Poland, was reissued by Cazimir the Great in 1334 and by subsequent kings. It served as the basic legal document for the Jews, and regulated Jewish rights with regard to dwelling, commerce, the judicial system, and similar matters.[131]

B. Jacob Pollack and Shalom Shakhna, and Their Attitude toward Codification

In Poland, as early as the thirteenth century, there is evidence of the emergence of Jewish cultural life; and Jewish culture became increasingly vigorous from the middle of the fourteenth century, when Torah scholars arrived in Poland from Spain, Portugal, and Germany. At the end of the fifteenth century, the immigration to Poland by Jacob Pollack, one of the greatest halakhic authorities of the age, marked the start of a new period in the study of the *Halakhah* and in Jewish cultural life generally in that country.

Jacob Pollack, a student of Jacob Margolioth in Regensburg, served as rabbi in Prague. In or about 1491, he moved to Cracow, Poland. There he established a prominent *yeshivah* where he developed the system of *pilpul* (finespun dialectics) and *ḥillukim* (extremely subtle distinctions) for the

131. *See* M. Balaban, "Korot ha-Yehudim bi-Mei ha-Beinayim" [Jewish History in the Middle Ages], in *Bet Yisra'el be-Folin* [The Jews in Poland], I, *passim*, and particularly pp. 1–8.

study of the Talmud. This method of study, with its acute and probing conceptual analysis, attracted a large number of students. Cracow became a major center for the study of Torah in Jacob Pollack's day, and his *yeshivah* produced important halakhic authorities for the Jewish communities of Poland and other countries. He headed the Cracow *yeshivah* for some thirty years, and became "the great luminary" and "leader of his generation" whose "renown has spread from one end of the world to the other." Hundreds who studied at his *yeshivah* spread the study of Talmud throughout Poland.[132]

Jacob Pollack's outstanding disciple was Shalom Shakhna, who became the rabbi of Lublin and the head of its *yeshivah*. Shalom Shakhna was described as "the light of the Exile, the breath of our nostrils, the anointed of God, the rabbi of rabbis, the genius of geniuses, the prince of Israel."[133] Scores of students studied at the *yeshivah* that he headed until 1559, and they disseminated their master's teachings throughout Poland and many other countries. Jacob Pollack and Shalom Shakhna mark the beginning of the golden age of Polish Jewry, which they equipped to assume its central role in world Jewry. Thousands of students flocked to the great *yeshivot* of Cracow, Lublin, Lemberg, Brest-Litovsk (Brisk), and other towns, and later returned to their homes throughout Europe with the knowledge they had gained from their teachers.

The great momentum in the spiritual development of Polish Jewry was accompanied by the growth of its economic and commercial life and the strengthening of its autonomous communal institutions. During the sixteenth and seventeenth centuries, Polish and Lithuanian Jewry organized broad-based autonomous countrywide bodies with authority in the fields of administration, law, and education. In Poland, the Council of the Four Lands was the supreme governing body, with authority over all the Jewish communities and associations of communities in that country. In Lithuania, similar authority was exercised by the Council of Lithuania, which split from the Council of the Four Lands in 1623. For a period of some two centuries, the general government accorded official recognition to the representative bodies of Polish and Lithuanian Jewry.[134]

Jacob Pollack and Shalom Shakhna, the two "founding fathers" of the Jewish spiritual center in Poland, left no halakhic literature except a few

132. *See* H.H. Ben Sasson, EJ, XIII, pp. 709ff., s.v. Poland; A. Siev, *Ha-Rema*, Jerusalem, 1957, pp. 9–13.

133. *See* the statement of his son Israel, quoted in *Resp. Rema* #25 (at the beginning of the responsum).

134. Balaban, *supra* n. 131 at 26; *Pinkas ha-Medinah*, ed. S. Dubnow, Introduction; Ben Sasson, *supra* n. 132.

isolated legal rulings.[135] The reasons for this strange dearth are highly pertinent to the problem of codification of Jewish law and to Moses Isserles' codificatory methodology. These reasons were stated by Shalom Shakhna's son Israel as follows:[136]

> And so I received a ruling to be applied in practice from my master, my teacher, my father, the *gaon*, the leader and the light of all the Exile, Rabbi Shalom, who is known as Shakhna *zakeẓ lehah hakham*,[137] who educated many students from one end of the world to the other, from whose mouth we live and whose waters we drink. In truth, many times I, together with many other students, asked him to write a book of his rulings, but—because of his great piety and humility, being the most humble of men on earth—he responded: "I know that in the future they will rule only according to what I write because [of the principle that] 'the law is in accordance with the views of the later authorities,' and I do not want everyone to rely on me." He was referring to those cases where there is a difference of opinion among halakhic authorities and he decided between them or differed with them. Since "a judge must be guided only by what his own eyes see," let each one do as the time requires, according to the dictates of his own heart. . . .
>
> It was for the same reason that his teacher, the great Rabbi Jacob Pollack, also did not write a book, nor did they keep a copy in their *yeshivah* of any of the responsa that they sent to far-off places. Even keeping such a copy seemed to them to be a mark of arrogance.[138]

135. *See, e.g., Bayit Ḥadash* to *Tur* OḤ ch. 214 for "a copy of a manuscript" of Jacob Pollack; a written responsum of Shalom Shakhna was published by J.L. Fishman (Maimon) in *Sinai*, IV, pp. 218–220.

136. *Resp. Rema* #25 (near the beginning of the second half of the responsum; ed. A. Siev, p. 156b); the responsum was written by Shalom Shakhna's son Israel; *see* the beginning of the responsum. For the issue dealt with by the responsum and the identity of the person to whom the responsum was addressed, *see Resp. Rema*, ed. A. Siev, Introduction, pp. 30–32, and pp. 147ff. in nn.

137. In Hebrew, an acronym for: "May the memory of this holy and pious man [stand] for life in the world to come; behold I am an atonement for his resting place." *See* TB Sukkah 20a and Rashi, *ad loc.*, s.v. Hareini kapparat; Sh. Ar. YD 240:9 and 242:28.

138. This attitude of Shalom Shakhna was also described by Ḥayyim b. Beẓalel, the brother of Maharal of Prague and a student of Shalom Shakhna, in his Introduction to his book *Vikku'aḥ Mayim Ḥayyim*, a volume of critical glosses to Rema's *Torat Ḥattat*. The Introduction does not appear in the various editions of *Vikku'aḥ Mayim Ḥayyim* that have been printed together with *Torat Ḥattat*, but it was printed in the first edition of the book, which was published as a separate volume, Amsterdam, 1712. Tchernowitz quotes it in its entirety in *Toledot ha-Posekim*, III, pp. 93–100. The second paragraph of the Introduction states:

> When we [Ḥayyim b. Beẓalel and Rema] studied together in the *yeshivah* of that outstanding luminary, our teacher, Rabbi [Shalom] Shakhna, of blessed memory, and heard his lectures on *Sha'arei Dura* [*see supra* pp. 1248–1249], we, his students, entreated him many times to compile all the laws of *issur* and *hetter* in an appropriate order, but he responded that our request was in vain, doubtless for the reason I have written.

Jacob Pollack and Shalom Shakhna thus rejected the basic notion of halakhic codification. Their reason—which has been noted several times in regard to earlier periods—was that a judge should decide each case on the basis of his own examination of the halakhic sources and his own analysis of the relevant opinions. Shalom Shakhna's son Israel alluded to another reason, possibly original with him, for opposing codification in principle: that the very act of reducing a decision to writing limits the freedom of judicial decision making, at least temporarily.[139] This is so because the principle that "the law is in accordance with the views of the later authorities"[140] will constrain a judge to follow the decision of the most recent halakhic authority and will deter him from making sufficient use of other rules of decision making, such as the principle that "a judge must be guided only by what his own eyes see" and the principle that the judge should act "as the time requires, according to the dictates of his own heart."[141]

Thus, in order not to limit this judicial freedom, Jacob Pollack and Shalom Shakhna not only reached the drastic conclusion that codificatory works should not be written, but they did not even make copies of their own responsa for collection in a book, since responsa also contain halakhic decisions that would constrict a judge. As the rest of this, and also the next chapter explain, this attitude of the great "founding fathers" of the Polish halakhic center had a significant influence on many of the halakhic authorities of Poland, who were their students or students of their students. Although not all of them accepted this position to the fullest extent, it influenced the views of many of them on the codification of Jewish law.

The reason given by Ḥayyim b. Beẓalel was that each person should arrive at his own decision based on his own analysis of the sources as to each issue; *see id.* Par. 2 of the table of contents at the beginning of the Introduction states: "He brings proof that one should not find another's ruling tempting [to rely on] and should certainly not look to and rely on 'the set table' of the *aḥaronim.*" *See also infra* pp. 1375–1379. As to the omission of the Introduction to *Vikku'aḥ Mayim Ḥayyim* after the first edition, *see infra* p. 1376 n. 26.

139. Although it had previously been maintained that one should not accept as final a ruling contained in a codificatory work, since a judge, upon examining the various opinions, may conclude to the contrary (*see, e.g.,* Rabad's critique of Maimonides, quoted *supra* pp. 1224–1225, and Asheri's statement on the same subject, quoted *supra* p. 1226–1227), this view had apparently never before been broadened to suggest that the very act of reducing a decision to writing would impel later judges to follow that decision on the strength of the rule that the law is in accordance with the views of the later authorities.

140. For detailed discussion of this principle of decision making, *see supra* pp. 267–271.

141. The judge must also consider the extent to which a legal rule has become established as a result of custom. *See infra* pp. 1354–1355.

C. Moses Isserles (Rema)

Moses Isserles[142] (Rema), one of Shalom Shakhna's outstanding disciples, had an entirely different approach to codification. Rema was born ca. 1530 in Cracow, where his father, Israel, was one of the dignitaries of the community. Rema studied in Shalom Shakhna's *yeshivah* until he was about nineteen years of age; and at the age of twenty, he was appointed Rabbi of Cracow. Despite his youth, he was accepted as one of the leading halakhic authorities of the time.[143] He served as Rabbi of Cracow for some twenty-two years and taught many disciples who served in Jewish communities throughout Europe. He composed books in all areas of Judaic studies (*Halakhah, Aggadah, Kabbalah,* philosophy, and Biblical commentary) and even astronomy. He assumed his leadership role at the very time when Caro's *Bet Yosef* and *Shulḥan Arukh* appeared, and Rema and Caro did in fact correspond with each other. Rema's illustrious career was cut short by his untimely death in 1572, at the age of approximately forty-two.

Not only did Rema refuse to accept the extreme position of his teachers that no copies of responsa should be made (he himself, in numerous instances, was careful to preserve copies of his own responsa),[144] but he believed that codificatory literature was vital to the halakhic system, as witness his own three codificatory works—*Darkhei Moshe, Torat Ḥattat,* and his glosses to Caro's *Shulḥan Arukh* known as the *Mappah.*

142. Siev (*Ha-Rema,* pp. 17ff., and *Resp. Rema,* Introduction, p. 10) explains the name Isserles as being a contraction of Isserl-Lazers, his father's full given name. However, this derivation is doubtful. A more likely derivation is that the name is the possessive form of Isserl, the Yiddish form of Israel (Isserl's = Isserles), which was the first name of his father. Edels, the family name of Maharsha, can be explained in the same way. It is derived from the name of Maharsha's mother-in-law, Edel, who provided financial support for him and his many disciples.

143. Rema married Golda, his teacher's daughter. She died in an epidemic in Cracow in 1551 or 1552, and shortly afterward he married the sister of Joseph Katz, the author of *Resp. She'erit Yosef; see* Siev, *supra* n. 142.

144. *See Resp. Rema* #40, addressed to his disciple, Hirsch Alzishar:

> Know, my dear friend, that I have copies of all your questions since we parted, as well as my answers to them, attached to my [other] responsa of which you know. Therefore, when I write to you, everything is available to me. You should also adopt this practice so that all relevant matters will be together, each matter in its proper place [lit. "a word fitly spoken"; *see* Proverbs 25:11. The JPS *Tanakh* translates the expression as "a phrase well turned"]. In this way, we will not need to constantly repeat the earlier material, but we can briefly address the matter under consideration.

See also Resp. Rema #81, at the end:

> And, my friend, after you have read my letter, send it back to me, because it is my custom to have copies made of everything connected with any law, so that they will be available in my old age, which I hope to reach, with God's help.

D. *Darkhei Moshe:* Its Purpose and Methodology

Like Caro, Rema, in the introductions to his books and in his responsa, described his codificatory methodology in detail. His methodology developed in stages. Apparently, in the first stage, he believed that a code had only two objectives: (1) to collect the different opinions on a specific halakhic subject, and (2) to present those opinions lucidly and briefly. In his Introduction to *Darkhei Moshe,*[145] he described his motives in writing a book that would meet these two objectives. At first, when he had to render a decision, he would compare "the statements of the Talmud, the *geonim,* Alfasi,[146] *Tosafot,* Naḥmanides, and the [other] earlier authorities, as well as the later authorities, namely, the *Mordekhai,* Asheri,[147] and the *Turim;* for they penetrated [the *Halakhah*] to its very core and are considered foremost among all the authors, and their decisions have also spread through the entire diaspora."[148] However, Rema became aware that the conclusions he reached on the basis of those sources were not always correct:

> But sometimes when I rendered a decision clearly based on those sources, others came . . . and showed from responsa of halakhic authorities . . . such as those of Asheri, Rashba, Maharik [Joseph Colon], Ribash, and Maharai [Israel Isserlein], who are the great authorities that enlighten all . . . and also the statements of Maharyu [Jacob Weil], Maharil [Jacob Moellin], and Maharif [Jacob Pollack], who are the masters . . . , that my decisions, made on the basis of the earlier authorities, were incorrect, and I and my colleagues were considered ignoramuses.[149]

Correct decision making thus required an investigation of the views of all these authorities; but such an investigation, and particularly the effort of searching out and finding all the views, involved such extensive and difficult labor that there was always uncertainty as to whether all the relevant and divergent views had actually been taken into account in making the

145. Introduction to *Darkhei Moshe ha-Arokh* (on which *see infra* p. 1356 and n. 176) to *Tur* OḤ (Fürth, 1760) and to *Tur* YD (Sulzbach, 1692; printed by Johanan Kremnitzer, the author of *Oraḥ Mishor,* on whom *see infra* p. 1360 n. 186). The two books have recently been reissued in facsimile editions. The Introduction to *Darkhei Moshe* is also printed in the editions of the *Turim* published by El ha-Mekorot, Jerusalem; our page references are to this edition.

146. The authors and works referred to here have either been discussed *supra* in our treatment of commentaries, novellae, and codificatory works or are discussed *infra* in our treatment of the responsa literature. As to each book and its author, *see* the various indexes at the end of this work.

147. The name given by Rema is *ha-Asheri, i.e.,* Asher b. Jehiel.

148. Introduction, *supra* n. 145 at 1a, end of col. 1 and beginning of col. 2. The phrase "and are considered foremost among all the authors" presumably refers not only to the last-mentioned authorities but also to those listed earlier.

149. *Id.,* continuation of the same passage.

decision.[150] Rema therefore came to the conclusion—as had others before him and as Caro did contemporaneously with him—that there was need for a work that would collect the various opinions on every subject and present them lucidly and briefly:

> I therefore decided to abridge it [the material] and briefly summarize the responsa, which is the right method [lit. "in which path the light resides"], so that there will be systematic knowledge of the responsa and their assertions as to the Mishnah and the Talmud. . . . [I also decided] to gather together all the novellae of the *posekim,* so that they should all be simultaneously at hand, and to commit them to writing so as to have a record of them.[151]

Like Caro, Rema realized that such a large and comprehensive work would be most useful if appended to an existing book that had already accomplished a part of the enormous task. The book he chose was the *Turim:*

> Its material is well arranged, and it is easy [for anyone] . . . old or young . . . to find in it what one seeks. . . . I have collected all the novellae and the responsa of the *posekim* and arranged them in the order of the *Turim.* . . . My desire was to present only practical conclusions and not lengthy argumentation, and occasionally I abandoned lengthy statements due to weariness; thus, in every instance, I extracted the basic principle and the essence and omitted the rest.[152]

This was the primary objective that Rema originally had for his book *Darkhei Moshe.* However, during the course of writing it, he substantially modified both its purpose and its form when Caro's *Bet Yosef* reached Poland and came to his attention. He realized that Caro, whom he respected and honored as "the light of Israel, the head of the Exile" and whom he addressed as "our teacher and master, a prince of God in our midst,"[153] had

150. *Id.:* "I could find no way to avoid examining all their statements, which were exceedingly lengthy. The task is great and time is short and I, the laborer, am sluggish [*cf.* M Avot 2:15]. I also suffered from eyestrain."

151. Introduction, *supra* n. 145 at 1a, toward the middle of col. 2.

152. *Id.* at 1a, middle of col. 2. Rema did not intend to present in his book all the opinions on every subject but rather, "according to my limited intelligence, I chose the better rather than the poorer opinions." *Id.* Later, in his criticism of Caro's methodology, he returned to the question of not presenting all the opinions; *see infra.*

153. *See Resp. Rema* #48 for his comments regarding Caro: "The great *gaon,* our teacher and master Joseph Caro, may God preserve him, whose waters we drink from his vessel. . . . Our teacher and master, a prince of God in our midst . . . Heaven forfend that we should disobey the words of his Torah Eminence; disagreement with him is like disagreement with the Divine Presence." *See also* the quotation, *infra* n. 154, from Rema's Introduction.

already written a work that, in its compilation and consolidation of the halakhic material, had achieved the objective Rema had set for his *Darkhei Moshe*. Rema's great esteem for Caro led him to acknowledge that Caro's *Bet Yosef* was superior to his own *Darkhei Moshe* both in quality and comprehensiveness.[154] Rema was in "a state of confusion for many days,"[155] but after he re-examined "the contents of *Bet Yosef* to its end"[156] and analyzed its methodology and the halakhic material it contained—particularly its method for determining the law—he perceived that there were three "reasons," as he put it, for him to continue to write *Darkhei Moshe*, and that because of those "reasons" he should expand his original objectives.

The first reason was the need for a work that would "present the material without lengthy discussion."[157] According to Rema, his book was superior with respect to the manner in which the different opinions were presented: *Darkhei Moshe* is much more concise than *Bet Yosef;* it is similar in this respect to Maimonides and the *Turim*. The *Turim* thus served Rema not only as the work to which he appended his *Darkhei Moshe*, but also as a model for the style[158] and brevity[159] of his presentation of the various opinions. Rema was fully aware of the danger that brevity can result in

154. Rema described his dilemma (Introduction, *supra* n. 145 at 1a, 2nd half of col. 2):

> "And when the turn [Hebrew: *tor*] of Esther . . . arrived . . . " [Esther 2:15; Rema here alludes to the time that he began to write his commentary to *Tur* YD, which deals with matters of "*issur ve-hetter*," which sounds similar to "Esther"], when I heard that the light of Israel, the head of the Exile, the lion had come out of his lair . . . and composed the book *Bet Yosef*, whose excellence and worth and wonderful contents will be recognized by all who see it, I was afraid that I had worked in vain and labored for naught and robbed my eyes of sleep for no purpose . . . because my words are as nothing compared to those of that sage. . . . And if in one place I said something [contrary to his opinion], he has rebutted it in another place, because his knowledge is all-encompassing. . . . He has overlooked nothing.

155. *Id.* at 1a, end of col. 2.

156. *Id.* at 1b, beginning of col. 1.

157. *Id.* at 1b, 1st half of col. 1. He continued:

> Such things [*i.e.*, lengthy discussions] are wearisome for students such as I who wish to study the Torah "on one foot," in a short time, . . . for lengthy discussion is one of the obstacles to effective study. Although I am aware of the statement in chapter 3 of [Tractate] *Sotah* [TB Sotah 22a] to the effect that the *tannaim* [*i.e.*, those who transmit mishnaic texts] destroy the world and are worse than ignoramuses, because by abbreviating the texts without explanation they can purify a creeping insect [which is clearly impure], nevertheless, I have followed the path of Maimonides and the *Turim*, who taught their students in a concise manner; and I have been brief, as is desired by this generation.

158. This is also evident from Rema's explanation quoted *supra* p. 1351 that he appended his book to the *Turim* because "its material is well arranged, and it is easy [for anyone] . . . old or young . . . to find in it what one seeks," which indicates that Rema also took the *Turim* as a model for presenting, formulating, and arranging the material. *See also infra* pp. 1358–1359 for his comments in his Introduction to *Torat Ḥattat*.

159. The extent of Rema's work in shortening and reworking the sources is indicated

misinterpretation and erroneous legal rulings. Nevertheless, he chose the way of brevity because lengthy discussion is an obstacle to study and analysis. By opting for conciseness "I will make it impossible for the poorer student to say, 'My studies overwhelm me and my mind is not adequate to understand the long discussions that are so wearying, much less draw conclusions on the basis of them.'"[160] To forestall misunderstanding that might result from the brevity of his presentation, Rema took the following precaution:

> In order to prevent error I added one thing. For Heaven is my witness that I have taken great pains in every instance to give the name of the author of each statement—I have left none out, and I have added none. Thus, for any person for whom my brevity is not satisfactory, I have in every case cited the source for my statement, and the matter can be found in the books available to him. If he does not believe, let him investigate and see with his own eyes.

The second reason for continuing with *Darkhei Moshe* was:[161]

> I have added much to his [Caro's] material [in *Bet Yosef*], and I have "burst forth to the south and the west" with opinions by *rishonim* and *aḥaronim*. . . . I have included many responsa of *geonim* and responsa of recent authorities such as those of Maharai [Israel Isserlein] and [material from] *Issur ve-Hetter*,[162] . . . which the author of *Bet Yosef* never saw.

Bet Yosef did not include a significant part of the literature of novellae, responsa, and codes, particularly of the Ashkenazic authorities listed by Rema at the beginning of his Introduction:[163]

---

by his remarks (Introduction, *supra* n. 145 at 1b, beginning of col. 2) concerning his use of the formula *"ad kan leshono"* [lit. "up to here is his language"]:

> Because it was my intention to shorten and to separate the wheat from the chaff, as far as I could, I sometimes presented the substance without using the precise words [of the source] and I sometimes omitted the details and included only the general principles, because that was my main intention. Nevertheless, after presenting a source in that manner, I have written *"ad kan leshono,"* even though I made changes, . . . because the word *lashon* [usually translated as "language"] has three definitions: It can refer to the tongue, as is known; it can refer to language, as it is written, " . . . a nation whose language you do not understand" [Deuteronomy 28:49]; and it can also refer to the intention of the speaker, because the tongue is the quill of the heart and articulates its ideas. Therefore, I have written *"ad kan leshono."*

In other words, Rema reworked the content of each source and extracted its central idea ("presented the substance without using the precise words"); he nevertheless concluded his presentation of the view of each authority with "up to here is his *lashon*," in the sense of "up to here is his idea."

160. Introduction, *supra* n. 145 at 1b, 1st half of col. 1.

161. *Id.*

162. The reference may be to *Sefer Issur ve-Hetter ha-Arokh. See supra* p. 1305. *Sha'arei Dura,* also known as *Sefer Issur ve-Hetter* (*see supra* pp. 1248–1249), is specifically mentioned *infra.*

163. Introduction, *supra* n. 145 at 1a, 1st half of col. 1.

For he did not include *Or Zaru'a*,[164] *Ha-Agudah, Sha'arei Dura, Issur ve-Hetter*,[165] Mahari Brin,[166] Maharil, Maharyu, Maharam Pado,[167] *Seder Gittin va-Ḥaliẓah*,[168] Benjamin Ze'ev, and other collected novellae too numerous to list.

That *Bet Yosef* did not include all the various opinions found in the halakhic sources is a serious deficiency in a work aiming to be a compendium of the halakhic literature, particularly when the omission is likely to affect halakhic decisions. This is apparent from Rema's explanation of his third reason for continuing with *Darkhei Moshe*:[169]

The third [reason], which is the main one, is the purpose our work seeks to achieve. It is well known that the author of *Bet Yosef* is disposed to follow the great halakhic authorities; and in all cases he states the law "according to two or three witnesses" [*cf.* Deuteronomy 17:6], who are the beloved masters—Alfasi, Maimonides, and Asheri—whenever two of them agree. He pays no attention to other rabbis who are giants of Torah; he follows only the great ones, deciding in accordance with any two of them, even though they are from an earlier period and are not recent authorities.

He ignores the principle established by the earliest of the *rishonim*, Alfasi, who held, at the end of the last chapter of [Tractate] *Eruvin*[170]—and many have agreed with him—that the law should always be determined in accordance with the views of the later authorities, and that the earlier authorities should not be followed, even if the difference of opinion is between a teacher and one of his students. The *aḥaronim*, as led by Maharik and Maharai, have always adhered to this principle. . . . He [Caro] is in conflict with all the customs followed in these lands, most of which are based, simply and straightforwardly, on this principle and are questioned by no one. Therefore, I, too, do not desire to dispute them. . . . Similarly, it is normal practice to follow the views of the *Mordekhai*, Asheri, and his son Riba [Jacob b. Asher, author of the *Turim*], and I have taken this path.

Rema's third reason, which he viewed as the most important, is thus related to the method for determining the binding legal rule that Caro

164. The observations in n. 146 *supra* apply to the authors and works referred to here.

165. *See supra* n. 162.

166. The reference is to Israel b. Ḥayyim Bruna.

167. The reference is to Meir Katzenellenbogen, known as Maharam of Padua.

168. The reference is to a book of this name by Jacob Margolioth; *see* Sh. Ar. EH ch. 154, *Seder ha-Get* (beginning): "Statement of the proofreader: Everything that is written in this *seder* without attribution is from the *seder* of Jacob Margolioth, of blessed memory." Similarly, EH ch. 169 (after par. 56 of Sh. Ar.) in *Seder Ḥaliẓah Keẓarah*: "Statement of the proofreader: Here too, wherever the glosses do not give the source, it can be assumed to be from the various *sedarim*, particularly that of Jacob Margolioth."

169. Introduction, *supra* n. 145 at 1b, 2nd half of col. 1.

170. *See supra* p. 1170.

adopted in *Bet Yosef.* Rema totally rejected Caro's method of determining the law on the basis of the views of Alfasi, Maimonides, and Asheri, because this method was inconsistent with the principle that Alfasi himself accepted and followed, namely, "the law is in accordance with the views of the later authorities." The acceptance of Caro's method would have resulted in overturning all the laws accepted and followed by Polish Jewry, "most of which are based, simply and straightforwardly, on this principle"; since Caro's legal conclusions were "in conflict with all the customs followed in these lands," they were unacceptable.[171]

As previously noted, the principle that "the law is in accordance with the views of the later authorities" was the basis for the refusal of Jacob Pollack and Shalom Shakhna to preserve a written record of their decisions. Although Rema did not apply this principle to reject the very idea of codificatory literature as his teachers did, he applied it rigorously in determining the law. He also demonstrated that there were instances where Caro himself was not consistent in applying his own method, "and since in those instances he [Caro] concedes [that his method of relying on the majority opinion of Alfasi, Maimonides, and Asheri does not yield the correct conclusion], there may also be other instances where his methodology should not be followed."[172] Not only did Rema reject Caro's method of determining the law, but he even took care—and warned others to take care—not to regard his own rulings as conclusive, even though his own rulings were based on the principle that the law accords with the views of the later authorities. He described his own methodology as follows:[173]

> I have written as to every matter that "this is the law as it is applied in practice"—and for good reason. I have identified the author of every statement, except where the statement is my own, in which case I have written, "It appears to me," to identify it as mine. Thus, if I have erred, the error will be attributed to me, and my mistake will not be attributed to others. . . . I was apprehensive . . . that if I were to write [the laws] categorically and absolutely, and without attribution of source, people in the future might rely on me. . . . Therefore, I decided to identify my own opinions as mine; and henceforth, whoever wishes may disagree with me, and whoever wishes to rely on me, let him do so. . . . In any case, a judge must be guided only by what his own eyes see.[174]

171. *See also* Introduction, *supra* n. 145 at 1a, beginning of col. 1 (Caro's rulings should not be followed "whenever the customs of Ashkenazic Jews, the residents of this diaspora who are the progeny of French Jewry, are to the contrary").

172. *Id.* at 1b, 2nd half of col. 1.

173. *Id.*

174. *Id.* Beginning with the words "I was apprehensive," the quotation is in the second half of col. 2, near the end of the Introduction. In addition to the three reasons given in

Rema thus placed the burden on the judge to examine all the different opinions in every case and determine which one to accept as the law in the circumstances of the case before him. In this, he followed Jacob Pollack and Shalom Shakhna, who insisted that each judge must reach his decision "as the time requires, according to the dictates of his own heart," by applying the fundamental principle of decision making that "a judge must be guided only by what his own eyes see."[175]

In short, the three "reasons"—the three major aims—that Rema advanced for his *Darkhei Moshe* were: (1) to state concisely, rather than at length like *Bet Yosef,* the different halakhic opinions; (2) to present the views omitted from *Bet Yosef* because Caro either did not value them or was not aware of them; and (3) to foster his teachers' principles of decision making, namely, that the law is in accordance with the views of the later authorities, and that each judge should make his own determination of the law by the exercise of his own judgment in the case before him.

The *Darkhei Moshe* currently printed in the regular editions of the *Turim* is the *Darkhei Moshe ha-Kaẓar* [The Abridged *Darkhei Moshe*] and is a condensation of the full work. In the full work, *Darkhei Moshe ha-Arokh,* Rema quoted *Bet Yosef* as well as many other opinions omitted in the short version.[176]

---

our text, Rema also stated that at times he "explained statements of *rishonim* differently than the way they were understood by the author of *Bet Yosef*" (*id.* at 1a, 1st half of col. 1); and he noted that at times "I have seen many things in his books that are not in their correct order and are obscure and out of place" (*id.* at 1b, 1st half of col. 1).

Rema then compared *Darkhei Moshe* to *Bet Yosef:*

> In the final analysis, I apply to us [*i.e.,* Caro and himself], although we are not equal, the verse "And Moses took with him the bones of Joseph, who had exacted an oath from the children of Israel" [Exodus 13:19; "Moses" = Moses Isserles; "Joseph" = Joseph Caro]. That is to say that I have taken the essence and the bones [of what he says], and left the remainder. Every wise man will see and decide whether my purpose was the discovery of the truth or whether I meant just to criticize and cavil.

(*Id.* at 1b, end of col. 1).

175. *See supra* p. 1347.

176. Siev (*Ha-Rema,* p. 62) states that Rema hinted in his Introduction to *Darkhei Moshe* (p. 1b, 1st half of col. 2: "What I did in the later edition") that he himself wrote *Darkhei Moshe ha-Kaẓar* as well as *Darkhei Moshe ha-Arokh.* However, it appears that Siev is in error; the "later edition" referred to is the long version of *Darkhei Moshe* that incorporates the revisions made after *Bet Yosef* reached Rema, as stated *supra.* This is clear from Rema's subsequent statement that in his book he first presents the views of *Bet Yosef* and then other opinions, novellae, etc., none of which appear in *Darkhei Moshe ha-Kaẓar* as we have it. There is no apparent source for Siev's opinion, or for the opinion of Tchernowitz (*Toledot ha-Posekim,* II, p. 230), that Rema himself wrote both books. It is possible that Rema wrote only one version—the full one—and that copyists and commentators later deleted the quotations from *Bet Yosef* and other sources and thus created *Darkhei Moshe ha-Kaẓar. See* I. Nissim, "Haggahot ha-Rema al ha-Shulḥan Arukh" [Rema's Glosses to the *Shulḥan Arukh*],

E. *Torat Ḥattat* and Its Methodology

The second important codificatory work written by Rema, *Torat Ḥattat,* also reflects the three objectives that motivated the writing of *Darkhei Moshe.*[177] *Torat Ḥattat* contains a significant portion of the "religious" laws (*issur ve-hetter*), such as the laws relating to *terefot* (animals unfit as food), *ta'arovet* (the admixtures of forbidden and permitted foods), the salting of meat, and the separation of meat and milk; it was composed as a sequel to *Sha'arei Dura.*[178]

Rema's Introduction to *Torat Ḥattat*[179] discusses the need to consider the opinions of the later halakhic authorities, in view of the principle that the law accords with the later authorities:

> [I have decided] to record the accepted law in every case on the basis of the later authorities (*aḥaronim*) of blessed memory, whom we follow. . . . I intend solely to examine the practices of the *aḥaronim* in order to learn and to instruct as to the proper conduct; for these purposes, the opinions of the *aḥaronim* have the greatest weight. [I will] also [record] what I have observed of the conduct of my teachers.

Rema's Introduction again emphasizes the freedom of decision that must be accorded to every judge to determine the law to be applied to the facts of the case before him:

> And behold! I do not say to others, "Accept [my view]!" because they have the prerogative and not I. . . . [My intention is] to inform the readers, so that they should know to take care. In every matter, I have given the reasons [for my rulings] and indicated the sources from which I drew them. Whoever wishes to rely on me, let him do so; whoever wishes to disagree—who can object? It makes no difference how much or how little [one may disagree], as long as he directs his heart to Heaven and is deliberate in judgment.

Sinai, Jubilee Volume, 1958, p. 31 n. 6. The matter still requires clarification. *See also supra* n. 145.

177. In all probability, Rema wrote *Torat Ḥattat* in 1568, and it was first printed in 1569; *see* Siev, *Ha-Rema,* p. 47.

178. As to *Sha'arei Dura, see supra* pp. 1248–1249.

179. Rema explained his choice of the name *Torat Ḥattat* as follows:

I decided to call this small treatise *Torat Ḥattat* [The Law of the Sin Offering] on the basis of the verse [Leviticus 10:16] "And Moses inquired about the goat of sin offering." I am afraid lest I have erred by making some ruling contrary to the law, for "there is not one good man on earth who does what is best and does not err" [Ecclesiastes 7:20], and a fearful and a fainthearted man like me [is apprehensive] lest he has made an error, heaven forfend, and his work be defective. I have, therefore, first offered a sin offering, which comes to atone for a sin of commission, in connection with this work, which is intended as a guide to proper conduct.

Rema reiterated that he based his decisions on those *aḥaronim* who were the authorities for Ashkenazic Jewry and who were not cited in *Bet Yosef.*[180] He also pointed to an additional important decision-making principle:

> Sometimes I have taken the more lenient view—in matters involving great financial loss, or for a poor man when something vital is at stake, or when something is needed for the suitable observance of the sabbath. The reason is that in those instances it is my opinion that technically, under the *Halakhah,* such a thing is completely permissible, except that the *aḥaronim* adopted the practice of forbidding it. I have therefore written that when it is impossible [to apply the stringent practice], the matter should be governed by the *Halakhah* [and not the practice instituted by the *aḥaronim*].

The view taken here by Rema is that if something is permitted by the *Halakhah* but the *aḥaronim* chose to be more stringent and prohibit it, it nevertheless should be held permissible in exceptional circumstances. The exceptional circumstances are: when the prohibition would cause great loss, or when the question affects a poor person and something vital is involved, or when the item is needed for the proper enjoyment of the sabbath.[181]

Rema's remarks in his Introduction to *Torat Ḥattat* as to his method of stating the views of other halakhic authorities are instructive. As previously observed, in Rema's Introduction to *Darkhei Moshe,* he emphasized the need for brevity, since prolixity tends to discourage study. In his Introduction to *Torat Ḥattat,* he stated that care must be taken not to be too cryptic, because of the danger of obscurity and misunderstanding, leading to erroneous decisions. This actually occurred, according to Rema, with the book *Sha'arei Dura,* which is so cryptic that "in these recent generations its statements are

180. *See* his Introduction to *Torat Ḥattat:*

There is a great need for this in order to arrive at the truth in every matter, for there are many laws as to which we do not follow the conclusion of the great rabbi, our teacher, Joseph Caro, of blessed memory, whose books have spread through all Jewry, so that if anyone follows his rulings, particularly in laws of *issur* and *hetter,* as he presents them in his *Shulḥan Arukh,* he will contravene all the customs that we follow in these lands.

181. Rema added at this point:

And thus we find that the early and later authorities also so ruled. Mahari Minz . . . wrote that a poor man on weekdays and a rich man on the eve of the sabbath are treated similarly, and the practice is to disclose to the people the reason [for the lenient rulings in each case]—that in the one case [that of the poor man], it is because of his poverty, and in the other case [that of the rich man], it is to permit the enjoyment of the sabbath. [The reason for the practice is] that people should not be surprised that sometimes the strict view and at other times the lenient view is followed.

See Resp. Mahari Minẓ u-Maharam mi-Padua #15, Fürth, 1766, p. 27a.

incomprehensible [lit. "closed"] and sealed, as though they did not exist"; and, although subsequent halakhic authorities composed glosses and commentaries on the book, its statements frequently appear to be contradictory and "many students have claimed it as authority for all sorts of nonsensical rulings, [with the result that] people use the book as they please, and who can stop them? . . . Whoever observes them [doing this] declares that all [these rulings] were given at Sinai and follows them. Thus people forbid and permit, contrary to the Torah and the *Halakhah;* and the 'improvements' of the authorities who intend to be constructive by condensing and clarifying turn out to be destructive." As a consequence, continued Rema:

> I thought it desirable to arrange matters correctly . . . briefly and without lengthy casuistic analysis or the arguments of Abbaye and Rava, so that all men, both great and small, will readily understand them. [And I decided] to include all the provisions of the laws found in the works of other authorities that are relevant to each subject referred to in *Sha'arei Dura.*

According to Rema, brevity and precision are desirable and even essential, so that "lengthy casuistic analysis" and "the arguments of Abbaye and Rava" should be omitted; but at the same time "all the provisions of the laws found in the works of other authorities that are relevant to each subject" should be included. Thus, Rema adopted the methodology of Jacob b. Asher who, in the *Turim,* also omitted the discussions found in the Talmudic sources, but presented the differing opinions of the halakhic authorities who preceded him.[182]

F. Glosses to the *Shulḥan Arukh*: The *Mappah*—Its Objectives and Methodology

Rema completed his landmark contribution to the field of codificatory literature with his third work—his glosses to the *Shulḥan Arukh* that he spread as a tablecloth (*mappah*) over the table (*shulḥan*) that Joseph Caro had set (*arukh*) for the *Halakhah.*[183] Had Caro written only *Bet Yosef,* Rema

182. *See supra* p. 1285. Jacob b. Asher in the *Turim* also accorded great weight to the principle of decision making that the law is in accordance with the views of the later authorities, and it was on the basis of this principle that he followed the opinions of his father Asheri.

183. *See* Rema's Introduction to his glosses to the *Shulḥan Arukh,* published in various recent editions of the *Shulḥan Arukh* and in facsimile editions of El ha-Mekorot and Pe'er ha-Torah; in the latter it appears in ḤM. Rema wrote: "The *gaon,* the author of *Bet Yosef* and the *Shulḥan Arukh* . . . I have come after him to spread a tablecloth [*mappah*] on his set table [*shulḥan arukh*]."

would very likely not have written this third work. His codificatory objectives had all been well realized in his *Darkhei Moshe* and *Torat Ḥattat.* He had never aspired to write a code as terse as the *Shulḥan Arukh,* and in fact, as has been noted, he was critical of such a code. However, the fact that Caro wrote two codificatory works—*Bet Yosef* and the *Shulḥan Arukh*—impelled Rema to deal with both of those works, each according to its own content and methodology.

As stated, two of the reasons why Rema continued to write his *Darkhei Moshe* even after *Bet Yosef* had reached him were: (1) Caro did not discuss a substantial portion of the opinions of the halakhic authorities, particularly the Ashkenazic authorities, and his conclusions were inconsistent with many of the accepted practices in Germany and Poland, and (2) Caro based his decisions on the majority opinion among Alfasi, Maimonides, and Asheri, and not on the principle that the views of the later authorities should prevail. If these two reasons were enough for Rema to continue his work on *Darkhei Moshe,* they were most certainly enough to induce him to write his glosses to the *Shulḥan Arukh.* Caro's main objective in the *Shulḥan Arukh* was to extract the normative conclusions from *Bet Yosef* and to present them in a separate book of *pesakim,* "briefly" and by "definitive statements of the applicable law, without discursive debate or argument."[184] That being so, Rema had no choice but to follow Caro's example and extract from his *Darkhei Moshe* his own halakhic conclusions arrived at by his own methodology, present them in the style of the *Shulḥan Arukh,* and append this work to the *Shulḥan Arukh.*[185]

In his glosses to the *Shulḥan Arukh,* Rema presented the conclusions derived from *Darkhei Moshe* in a "closed and sealed" form "using his [Caro's] method of stating the laws categorically," concisely, and without citation of sources.[186] In so doing, Rema deviated from his declared approach

184. Caro's Introduction to the *Shulḥan Arukh; see supra* pp. 1321–1322.

185. *See Resp. Rema* #35: " . . . and thus did I myself write in my work *Darkhei Moshe,* from which I composed [the glosses to] the *Shulḥan Arukh.*" In responsum #131, par. 3, he wrote: "It is true that I so ruled in the [gloss to the] newly reprinted *Shulḥan Arukh* at the end of OḤ ch. 263; I wrote the reason, with God's help, in my book [*Darkhei Moshe*], according to which I composed the laws in the [glosses to the] *Shulḥan Arukh.*"

186. The source references in Rema's glosses were not supplied by Rema himself. (The Cracow editions of the *Shulḥan Arukh* with Rema's glosses, 1583 and 1594, as well as ed. Venice, 1594, cite no sources.) The source references were added—for the first time in ed. Cracow 1607—by the printers, who took them from *Darkhei Moshe.* The title page of that edition explains that the references were added "because . . . many have said that the *gaon*'s [Rema's] words in the *Shulḥan Arukh* are 'closed and sealed' and the reader cannot understand them . . . inasmuch as he cannot fathom his [Rema's] intention [or] the correct meaning of the law." In the course of time, additional source references were added by others. The references were not always inserted with meticulous precision; and, consequently, there are instances where the source cited does not support the law as stated. The authors of *Shakh*

to codification as revealed by his Introduction to *Torat Ḥattat,* where he argued that the rulings in *Sha'arei Dura* were "closed and sealed" and led to misunderstandings and to erroneous decisions. However, this deviation by Rema was necessary in order for him to append his own normative conclusions to the *Shulḥan Arukh* in the style of the *Shulḥan Arukh* itself.

The substantive content of Rema's glosses to the *Shulḥan Arukh* is based on the same principles that underlay *Darkhei Moshe* and *Torat Ḥattat.* The glosses supplement the law presented in the *Shulḥan Arukh* with the conclusions derived from the views of the authorities of whom Caro did not take account, particularly those of Germany and France, "whose waters we drink and who are the eminent authorities of Ashkenazic Jewry and have always served as our eyes, and whose rulings have been followed from the earliest of times, namely, *Or Zaru'a,*[187] the *Mordekhai,* Asheri, *Semag, Semak,* and *Haggahot Maimuniyyot,* all of whom built on the *Tosafot* and the halakhic authorities of France, whose descendants we are."[188] Rema also supplemented the *Shulḥan Arukh* with the customs followed by Ashkenazic Jewry, "for there have been many differences between eastern and western Jews even in early generations, and how much more so in these latter generations."[189] Rema's glosses, of course, deprived the *Shulḥan Arukh* of its categorically authoritative quality and universal applicability throughout the Jewish world, but that was precisely what Rema intended:

---

and *Keneset ha-Gedolah,* as well as other commentators, have pointed out that many source references are actually misleading. *See Resp. Ḥayyim Sha'al* (by Ḥida), II, #38, sec. 51 (end); *Birkei Yosef,* OḤ #470, par. 3; *Sedei Ḥemed,* Kelalei ha-Posekim #14, Kelalei ha-Rema, subpar. 4 (vol. VI, p. 99). The Introduction of Joshua Falk to his *Bet Yisra'el* and to *Sema* (toward the end) states:

> The reader will understand and appreciate the great difference between the references inserted in the *Shulḥan Arukh* by the printers of the recent Cracow edition and the references and citations which I, with God's help, have provided. They supplied references only to statements by Rema and not to those of Rabbi Joseph Caro. . . . Even the source references for Rema's glosses are abridged and changed to the point where they are almost useless.

See Nissim, *supra* n. 176 at 34–37; Siev, *Resp. Rema,* Introduction, p. 18. Johanan b. Meir Kremnitzer, who printed the first edition of *Darkhei Moshe ha-Arokh,* wrote: "The master's [Rema's] statements in his glosses are unclear without arguments or proofs . . . , and although the source references given are sometimes helpful, they are often . . . worthless and they are also frequently . . . inaccurate." *See also* Nissim, *supra* at 37–39, as to additional glosses that were written in the course of time in the style of Rema, and which led to further mistakes and misunderstandings.

187. The observations in n. 146 *supra* apply to the authors and works referred to here.

188. Rema's Introduction to his glosses to the *Shulḥan Arukh.*

189. *Id.* For differences in customs in the earlier periods, *see* B.M. Lewin, *Oẓar Ḥilluf Minhagim bein Benei Ereẓ Yisra'el u-vein Benei Vavel* [Compendium of Differences in Customs between the Residents of the Land of Israel and the Residents of Babylonia], Jerusalem, 1942; M. Margaliot, *Ha-Ḥillukim she-bein Anshei Mizraḥ u-Venei Ereẓ Yisra'el* [The Differences

> I viewed all his [Caro's] statements in the *Shulḥan Arukh* as having been presented as though they were given by Moses at divine command so that students would come and drink his words without challenging them. . . . I therefore decided that, at those places where his [Caro's] statements do not seem to me to be correct, I would write down next to each such statement the opinions of the *aḥaronim*, in order to make the students aware of every instance where his statements are disputed.[190]

Rema believed that a judge should have available a book—even though it may be categorical in form and contain no source references—which presents as briefly as possible the different views of the halakhic authorities, so that in reaching his decision in each case, he can take into account the principle that the law is in accordance with the views of the later authorities, local custom and practice, and his own view as to what is appropriate in the particular circumstances of each case.[191] This basic approach to halakhic decision making had been developed by the spiritual founders of Polish Jewry, Jacob Pollack and Shalom Shakhna, to the extent that they opposed the writing of all codificatory works and would not even preserve copies of their own responsa. The essence of this approach was adopted by Rema even though he believed that the times demanded a code that contained the sources of the law.[192] He maintained this approach even when he followed in the footsteps of Caro and wrote a book of *pesakim*—alongside a book of *halakhot*—without citation of authority or sources. He believed that under no circumstances should a judge or other authority be deprived of all the relevant opinions; he regarded knowledge of the various opinions to be an indispensable requisite of the decision-making process.

Rema's glosses, in addition to presenting the various opinions and lo-

---

between the People of the East and the Residents of the Land of Israel], Jerusalem, 1938, and Margaliot's extensive Introduction. *See also supra* pp. 880ff. To corroborate the need to take custom into consideration, Rema cited Caro " . . . as the *gaon* himself wrote in his Introduction to his great book"—the reference being to Caro's statement in his Introduction to *Bet Yosef* on *Tur* OḤ to the effect that if a custom contrary to the rulings of Alfasi, Maimonides, and Asheri has been accepted, the custom should be followed, and if there is a custom to prohibit something which, according to law, is permitted, the custom is binding on those who have been following it. *See supra* p. 1318 and *infra* n. 191.

190. Rema's Introduction to his glosses to the *Shulḥan Arukh*.

191. *See id.*: "Whoever has a palate to taste will himself be able to distinguish between the 'sweetmeats' according to their flavors, and will not rely on others. Whoever has not attained this level should not deviate from the custom, as the *gaon* himself wrote in his Introduction to his great book." For a discussion of the last part of the quotation, *see supra* n. 189.

192. *Darkhei Moshe*, Introduction, p. 1b, 1st half of col. 1; *see also* our discussion *supra*.

cal customs, as well as reflecting his own different criteria for deciding the law, also emend the text of the *Shulḥan Arukh,* particularly where it was clear to Rema that the language of "the author" (*meḥabber,* as Caro is generally referred to in connection with the *Shulḥan Arukh)* had been corrupted by copyists and printers.[193] Sometimes, the glosses interpret and explain the text;[194] at other times, they point out where Caro's rulings are inconsistent.[195] Occasionally, a gloss was inserted by the printer in the wrong place.[196]

An interesting feature of Rema's glosses is that Rema sometimes added a law, not because it was disputed or because Caro did not accept it, but to enhance the *Shulḥan Arukh*'s comprehensiveness. An example appears at

193. This function of Rema's glosses was noted by *Sema* to Sh. Ar. ḤM 121:9. Rema stated in his gloss there: "If the lender said, 'I did not appoint him as an agent and I did not receive it [*i.e.,* the payment of the debt],' the agent may swear that he gave [the money] to the lender." *Sema* (subpar. 20) comments: "This whole passage is missing in the author's [Caro's] text, but Rema emended and corrected it in his glosses. And it is also in the *Turim,* par. 12." Similarly, in Sh. Ar. ḤM 129:14, Caro wrote: "If the lender stipulated with the surety, 'I will collect from whomever I wish,' he may collect in the first instance from the surety even if the borrower has [sufficient] assets [to pay]; but some authorities disagree with this. However, all agree that if the lender stated explicitly, 'I will collect from whomever I wish,' he can claim in the first instance from the surety even if the borrower has assets." The second sentence is impossible to fathom, since it contradicts the first sentence. The lender's stipulation in each instance is the same but the legal conclusions are inconsistent. Rema emended the text of the second sentence to make the stipulation read: "I will collect *in the first instance* from whomever I wish" (emphasis supplied), which must certainly have been the reading in Caro's original text, since *Tur* ḤM 129:14 and Maimonides, *MT,* Malveh ve-Loveh 25:3–4 both make the distinction between the form of stipulation that contains the italicized words and the form that does not. For further examples, *see* Nissim, *supra* n. 176 at 30, and Tchernowitz, *Toledot ha-Posekim,* III, pp. 47ff.

194. *See, e.g.,* Sh. Ar. ḤM 131:4 (end): "This law needs further consideration," to which Rema adds, "because some disagree"; *see also Sema* and *Shakh, ad loc.*, and *Bayit Ḥadash* to *Tur* ḤM ch. 131. For further examples, *see* Tchernowitz, *supra* n. 193.

195. *See* Tchernowitz, *supra* n. 193 at 55–56.

196. *See, e.g.,* Rema to Sh. Ar. ḤM 328:1: "And even if he did not so write, it is as though it was so written (Ha-Maggid [*Maggid Mishneh*] to ch. 18 of [*MT*], Sekhirut, and *Bet Yosef* citing *Tosafot* and Asheri)." Eds. Venice and Cracow, 1594, also attach this gloss, with a minor spelling difference, to par. 1. However, the gloss should be attached to par. 2 of Sh. Ar. ḤM ch. 328, which states: "If he [the sharecropper] did not work it [the field] but let it lie fallow, in whole or in part, an estimate is made of how much it could have yielded and he must pay [to the owner] his share of that amount." Both *Maggid Mishneh* to *MT,* Sekhirut 8:13 (not ch. 18 as cited in the gloss), and *Bet Yosef* to *Tur* ḤM 328:2, make the same comment on this law. Apparently the error was caused by the fact that Sh. Ar. ḤM 328:2 omits the clause "because he had so agreed in writing," which is contained in the Talmud, the *Mishneh Torah,* and the *Turim.* The printer therefore did not see its relevance to par. 2 and transferred the gloss to par. 1 where that phrase does appear. This error caused difficulties; *see Resp. Ḥavvot Ya'ir* #168 and *Pitḥei Teshuvah* to Sh. Ar., *ad loc.* For the differences between the *Shulḥan Arukh,* the *Mishneh Torah,* and the *Turim* in the formulation of this law, *see infra* Appendix B, example 2.

the beginning of *Hilkhot Sheluḥin* [The Laws of Agency] in *Shulḥan Arukh Ḥoshen Mishpat.*[197] In order to understand its significance, we first turn to the formulations of this law by Maimonides and the *Turim*.

Maimonides' *Hilkhot Sheluḥin ve-Shutafin* [Laws of Agency and Partnership] begins as follows:[198]

> If one says to his agent, "Go and sell land or chattels for me" or "Buy [land or chattels] for me," he [the agent] can sell or buy and carry out his agency, and all his acts are effective [to bind the principal].

In the *Turim,*[199] however, the formulation is:

> A person's agent is like himself for all matters [and binds the principal], except for the commission of wrongdoing, for the rule is, "There is no agency for wrongdoing."[200] Maimonides wrote, "If one says to his agent, 'Go and sell land or chattels for me' or 'Buy [land or chattels] for me,' he [the agent] can sell or buy and carry out his agency, and all his acts are effective."

The *Turim* thus preceded the concrete example of an agency to sell or buy with a statement of the basic principle of the law of agency that a person's agent is like himself except for an agency to commit wrongdoing, where the applicable principle is: "[When] the words of the teacher and the words of the disciple [conflict]—which should be obeyed?" In other words, the principal may assume that the agent will obey the words of God (the Teacher), who forbade the commission of the wrong, rather than carry out the words of the principal (the disciple).

In the beginning of Caro's treatment of *Hilkhot Sheluḥin*[201] he omitted the general principle that the *Turim* supplied and, following Maimonides, began with the concrete case of an agency to sell or buy. Clearly, the omission does not mean that Caro disagreed with the principle; rather, it reflects Caro's policy to be as brief as possible and to follow Maimonides' style.[202]

Rema added a gloss at the beginning of *Hilkhot Sheluḥin* in the *Shulḥan Arukh,* in which he set forth and elaborated on the principle stated in the *Turim:*

197. Sh. Ar. ḤM ch. 182.

198. *MT,* Sheluḥin ve-Shutafin 1:1. One of the Talmudic sources is TB Kiddushin 41a *et seq. See also supra* pp. 112–113.

199. *Tur* ḤM 182:4.

200. *See* TB Kiddushin 42b and parallels; Bava Meẓi'a 10b.

201. Sh. Ar. ḤM 182:1.

202. *See supra* pp. 1327–1341 and *infra* Appendix B.

> In all matters, a person's agent is like himself [and binds him], except for the commission of wrongdoing, for the rule is,[203] "There is no agency for wrongdoing." This applies only when the agent has the capacity to be liable [for the wrong], but if he does not have the capacity to be liable, he can be an agent even to commit wrongdoing.

Rema, following the *Turim,* thus introduced the laws of agency with the general principle that a person's agent is like himself except in regard to the commission of wrongdoing, and then added the qualification, also well established, that if the agent does not have the capacity to be responsible for his acts, the agency, even for wrongdoing, is effective, because the principal should have known that the agent would carry out the agency inasmuch as the agent would not thereby be committing any wrong himself.[204] Undoubtedly, a legal code, notwithstanding the desirability of brevity and conciseness, should begin the laws of agency with the basic principle governing that subject; in this gloss, Rema briefly and aptly filled this gap in the *Shulḥan Arukh.*

G. The *Shulḥan Arukh* as the Authoritative Code of Jewish Law

With his glosses to the *Shulḥan Arukh,* Rema concluded his own codificatory work[205] and also completed the authoritative code of the entire halakhic system. From this point, the "set table" of Jewish law included all of the law as followed in practice, with all its nuances and differences in customs and principles of decision making, as it developed in both eastern and western Jewry. Of course, since the completion of the *Shulḥan Arukh,* Jewish law has undergone further stages of development and generated a rich and wide-ranging literature of responsa, legislation, and customary law. Consequently, halakhic research and adjudication cannot stop with the *Shulḥan Arukh.* However, even today, the *Shulḥan Arukh* (in the generally accepted sense of the term, *i.e.,* the composite of Caro's work and Rema's glosses),[206] as explicated by its commentaries and the extensive halakhic

203. Eds. Venice and Cracow, 1594, read: "and the rule is."

204. *See Sema* to Sh. Ar. ḤM ch. 182, subpar. 2.

205. Rema apparently wrote *Torat Ḥattat* in 1568; the first edition appeared in 1569. *See supra* n. 177. He composed his glosses to Sh. Ar. OḤ afterward, and they were first printed in 1571. *See* Siev, *Resp. Rema,* p. 18 n. 12.

206. Both books collectively were referred to as the *Shulḥan Arukh* by Rema's contemporary, Mordecai Jaffe (1530–1612), in his Introduction to *Sefer ha-Levushim:* " . . . the *Shulḥan Arukh* of the two above-mentioned great authorities [Caro and Rema]"; *see also infra* pp. 1398–1399. Similarly, *Sema,* Introduction to Sh. Ar. ḤM, s.v. Ha-ḥamishit dife'amim: "I also took into consideration the work *Shulḥan Arukh,* written by the *geonim* our

literature written since Caro and Rema, remains the definitive and authoritative code of Jewish law.[207]

In concluding this chapter, it is instructive to compare the results of Rema's glosses to Caro's *Shulḥan Arukh* with Rabad's glosses to Maimonides' *Mishneh Torah.* Rabad severely criticized Maimonides' methodology; according to Rabad, "he [Maimonides] sought to improve, but he did not improve." Rabad's criticisms led to a strong movement opposed to the very notion of composing books of *pesakim,* as distinguished from books of *halakhot.* Over the course of time, this opposition led to the rejection of the *Mishneh Torah* as the definitive and authoritative code of Jewish law and deterred the composition of books of *pesakim* generally. On the other hand, Rema viewed Joseph Caro as "the light of Israel, the head of the Exile"[208] and viewed Caro's table (*shulḥan*) as set (*arukh*), needing only to be covered by a tablecloth (*mappah*) with "delicious fruits and delicacies"[209] and to be enhanced by the inclusion of additional laws, customs, and explanations. Far from impeding the success of Caro's code, Rema's glosses contributed to its acceptance and helped the *Shulḥan Arukh* to become the definitive and authoritative code for all Jews throughout the world.

Masters Rabbi Joseph Caro and Rabbi Moses [Isserles]." Maharam of Lublin also referred to both books collectively as the *Shulḥan Arukh; see infra* p. 1384 n. 52.

207. For detailed discussion of this point, *see infra* pp. 1417–1422.

208. *See supra* p. 1124.

209. Rema's Introduction to his glosses to the *Shulḥan Arukh.* Our reading (Hebrew *peri megadim u-mat'amim*) is that of ed. Cracow 1594; ed. Cracow 1584 has *peri megadim u-te'amim* (delicious fruits and tastes), which is the reading of El ha-Mekorot's facsimile ed., 1954.

Chapter 37

THE CODIFICATORY LITERATURE: REACTIONS TO THE *SHULḤAN ARUKH*, AND ITS FINAL ACCEPTANCE

I. Introduction
II. The Eastern Countries
  A. Joseph ibn Lev (Maharibal)
  B. The Agreement of Two Hundred Rabbis to Caro's Principle of Decision Making
  C. Critiques of Specific Laws in the *Shulḥan Arukh*
    1. Jacob Castro (Maharikash)
    2. Samuel Aboab
    3. Yom Tov Ẓahalon (Maharitaẓ)
  D. The Acceptance of the *Shulḥan Arukh*
III. The Western Countries
  A. Opposition to the *Shulḥan Arukh* without Proposing Any Alternative Type of Code
    1. Ḥayyim b. Beẓalel
    2. Judah Loew b. Beẓalel (Maharal of Prague)
    3. Samuel Eliezer Edels (Maharsha) and Meir b. Gedaliah (Maharam of Lublin)
  B. Opposition to the *Shulḥan Arukh* as Manifested by the Composition of Alternative Types of Codes
    1. Solomon Luria (Maharshal)
    2. Mordecai Jaffe
    3. Yom Tov Lipmann Heller
  C. Opposition to the *Shulḥan Arukh* as the Sole Basis for Legal Decisions; Commentaries on the *Shulḥan Arukh*
    1. Joshua Falk
    2. Joel Sirkes
IV. The Acceptance of the *Shulḥan Arukh* as the Definitive and Authoritative Code of Jewish Law
  A. The Completion of the Codificatory Structure of the *Shulḥan Arukh* by Its Commentaries
  B. Historical Circumstances as a Factor in the Acceptance of the *Shulḥan Arukh*

I. INTRODUCTION

Although the code of Joseph Caro and Moses Isserles (Rema) was generally well regarded and highly praised, many leading contemporaneous and subsequent halakhic authorities were critical of it. The doubts and reservations that had beset the codification of the *Halakhah* from its very beginning were again raised; and at the height of the debates and arguments, it seemed likely that the *Shulḥan Arukh,* too, would never become the authoritative code of Jewish law. However, in the course of time, historical circumstances as well as factors relating to codification of Jewish law worked together to tip the scales in favor of the acceptance of the *Shulḥan Arukh* and its accompanying literature as the definitive and binding halakhic code.[1]

Doubts and reservations with regard to the *Shulḥan Arukh* were expressed both in the eastern centers of Jewish life (such as Turkey, the Land of Israel, and Egypt) and in Poland and Germany. Some of the objectors questioned only the accuracy or language of particular rulings; others, the method used to arrive at the rulings. Still others, however, rejected Caro's and Isserles' basic approach to codification.

II. THE EASTERN COUNTRIES

Most criticisms in the eastern Jewish centers challenged the correctness and formulation of the legal conclusions in the *Shulḥan Arukh.* Some halakhic authorities objected to Caro's basic principle of decision making, *i.e.,* that whenever Alfasi, Maimonides, and Asheri disagree, the law follows the view of the majority of those three authorities. Immediately following the appearance of the *Shulḥan Arukh,* some halakhic authorities even rejected on principle the very idea of codifying Jewish law.

A. Joseph ibn Lev (Maharibal)

The initial opposition to the very idea of codifying the *Halakhah* was exemplified by Maharibal, a contemporary of Caro in Turkey, who is reported to have said when *Bet Yosef* was published "that the book would lead to a decrease in knowledge [of the sources]" and "he [Maharibal] forbade his

1. Such acceptance, however, was qualified by some reservations; *see infra.*

students to use it in their studies."[2] The same objection had been raised by Paltoi bar Abbaye, the *Gaon* of Pumbedita, at the very early stages of halakhic codification in the middle of the ninth century C.E., when he criticized students who preferred to study books that collected and summarized legal rules rather than study the basic Talmudic sources.[3] Maharibal thus expressed the concern that the relative ease of finding the law in a book such as *Bet Yosef* would lead to neglect of the study of the law through its sources, *i.e.*, Talmudic literature and commentaries, and the decisions of the halakhic authorities. However, an incident led Maharibal to change his mind, as Ḥayyim Joseph David Azulai (Ḥida) described:[4]

> They [the students] would study the *Turim* before him [Maharibal], and he would give the Talmudic source for each law. Because of his great erudition, it had never happened that Maharibal was unable to recall the sources. One day, after his above-mentioned order [forbidding the study of *Bet Yosef*], they were studying a certain law and the rabbi [Maharibal] became confused and forgot his learning; he made great efforts to find the source, but failed. Then Maharibal said, "Apparently, in heaven they want *Bet Yosef* to be accepted everywhere. Go and examine it [*i.e.*, see whether *Bet Yosef* supplies the source for the law stated in the *Turim*]." When they consulted the book they found the Talmudic source of the law.

As a result of this incident, Maharibal allowed his students to study *Bet Yosef*, "because he realized that he had known the Talmudic passage in question but it had escaped him, and he attributed this to the fact that Heaven favored our master [Caro], of blessed memory."

B. The Agreement of Two Hundred Rabbis to Caro's Principle of Decision Making

Although the halakhic authorities in the eastern Jewish communities ultimately accepted the idea that codification was needed, they had considerable concern about Caro's principle of decision making on the basis of the majority view among Alfasi, Maimonides, and Asheri. As has been pointed out in the previous discussion of the work of Rema, this principle contradicts the principle of decision making that the law is in accordance with the views of the later authorities;[5] and several Sephardic as well as Ashkenazic authorities—among them contemporaries of Caro—"attacked him and dif-

2. *Shem ha-Gedolim*, Books, Letter *bet*, #59.
3. *See supra* pp. 1157–1158.
4. *Shem ha-Gedolim*, *supra* n. 2.
5. *See supra* pp. 1354–1355.

fered with him face-to-face on the matter."[6] Even two centuries later, Ḥida wrote:[7]

> All our days we have been troubled by the position of our righteous master of blessed memory [Caro] regarding the compromise he adopted for arriving at a legal conclusion, namely (as is well known), to accept the opinions of Alfasi, Maimonides, and Asheri, or any two of them who agree on any point. Subsequent authorities disagreed with him and tried to abrogate that principle.

It seems that the hesitancy in accepting Caro's principle was overcome to some degree by an interesting tradition, also reported by Ḥida:

> Now, I will record a truth that I heard from holy rabbis who heard it from the great rabbi, . . . Ḥayyim Abulafia, of sainted memory, who heard it from the elders of his generation, [namely,] that nearly two hundred rabbis, contemporaries of Caro, accepted his principle. Therefore, he [Abulafia] used to say that whoever rules in accordance with Caro's decisions follows the authority of two hundred rabbis.[8]

Thus, the contradiction between Caro's principle and the principle that the law is in accordance with the views of the later authorities was to a large extent resolved, since two hundred halakhic authorities who were contemporaries of Caro accepted his principle. Consequently, it was "the later authorities" who agreed to rule according to the majority of the three earlier authorities, Alfasi, Maimonides, and Asheri.

C. Critiques of Specific Laws in the *Shulḥan Arukh*

As stated, the main criticism of the *Shulḥan Arukh* by the halakhic authorities in the eastern diaspora centered on the question of the substantive correctness of its statement of various laws. In particular, several of the leading halakhic authorities discovered apparent contradictions between *Bet Yosef* and the *Shulḥan Arukh* and, as a result, questioned the degree of authority that Caro himself intended the *Shulḥan Arukh* to have. The following are noteworthy among these critics.

6. *Resp. Reshakh,* I, #134 (ed. Salonika, 1586, p. 148, col. 1). *See also Birkei Yosef,* ḤM, #25, par. 29, stating, *inter alia:* "I have also seen a responsum in ms. of Rabbi Jehiel Kastilaẓ (the father of Maharam and Maharash Kastilaẓ), who was a contemporary of Caro and wrote at length with much vehemence on this subject."

7. *Birkei Yosef, supra* n. 6.

8. *Id.; Shem ha-Gedolim, supra* n. 2. On the basis of this tradition, an acrostic was created on the title *Maran* ("our master"), by which Caro is known: MaRaN = **M**atayim **R**abbanim **N**ismakh ("supported by two hundred rabbis").

1. JACOB CASTRO (MAHARIKASH)

Jacob Castro (Maharikash), the Chief Rabbi of Egypt, was a younger contemporary of Caro.[9] He attributed the contradictions between *Bet Yosef* and the *Shulḥan Arukh* to the fact that the *Shulḥan Arukh* "was written at the end of its author's life, and because of his weak condition, many such things [*i.e.*, errors] are to be found in it."[10] Maharikash, therefore, wrote glosses to the *Shulḥan Arukh*, and corrected the errors according to Caro's own *corrigenda*, which Caro had noted in his *Bedek ha-Bayit* on *Bet Yosef*.[11] Maharikash's glosses, which also cited many additional laws of both Sephardic and Ashkenazic authorities,[12] are very similar to those of Rema, and for a considerable period fulfilled the same function in the eastern countries (where they were widely distributed in manuscript form) as Rema's glosses did in Poland and Germany; and they too contributed to the spread and acceptance of the *Shulḥan Arukh*. However, when copies of the *Shulḥan Arukh* containing Rema's glosses reached the eastern communities, Maharikash's glosses were slowly displaced; and even when printed in the book *Erekh Leḥem* (1718), they did not regain their initial standing.[13]

2. SAMUEL ABOAB

Another attempt to explain contradictions between the *Shulḥan Arukh* and *Bet Yosef* was made by Samuel Aboab, a leading halakhic authority in Italy in the middle of the seventeenth century. He wrote:[14]

> I have heard it said that our teacher, Rabbi Joseph Caro, entrusted the abridgment of his great work, *Bet Yosef*, to his students; the result was the *Shulḥan Arukh*. Since both were not edited by the same person, there are some inconsistencies in substance as well as style, and it is very difficult to harmonize them without resorting to a tortured explanation that departs from the plain meaning of the text.

9. Maharikash was personally acquainted with Caro and had stayed at Caro's home in Safed. *See Kore ha-Dorot*, ed. Kassel, Berlin, 1846, p. 41a.

10. *Resp. Oholei Ya'akov* #20 (ed. Leghorn, p. 35b). *See also Yad Malakhi*, II, Kelalei ha-Shulḥan Arukh u-Rema [Principles of the *Shulḥan Arukh* and Rema], #2; *Shem ha-Gedolim*, Books, Letter *shin*, #75.

11. *See supra* p. 1343.

12. *See* I. Nissim, "Haggahoteihem Shel Rabbi Ya'akov Castro ve-Rabbi Ya'akov Ẓemaḥ al Shulḥan Arukh [The Glosses of Rabbi Jacob Castro and Rabbi Jacob Ẓemaḥ to the *Shulḥan Arukh*], *Sefunot*, II (1958), pp. 89ff.

13. *See id.* At *id.* p. 90 there appears a statement of Maharikash's great-grandson, Isaac b. Joseph Castro, who published *Erekh Leḥem* in Constantinople in 1718, noting the similarities and differences between the glosses of Rema and those of Maharikash. *See also id.* on the glosses of Jacob Ẓemaḥ and his comparisons of the glosses of Rema with those of Maharikash. (The articles on the glosses of Rema, Maharikash, and Jacob Ẓemaḥ were reprinted together in *Kovez R. Yosef Caro* [Joseph Caro Anthology], 1969, pp. 64–88.)

14. *Resp. Devar Shemu'el* #255. *See also Yad Malakhi* and *Shem ha-Gedolim*, *supra* n. 10.

3. YOM TOV ẒAHALON (MAHARITAẒ)

Yom Tov Ẓahalon (Maharitaẓ), a leading halakhic authority in Turkey and the Land of Israel at the end of the sixteenth and the beginning of the seventeenth centuries, was the most extreme of all the eastern critics. He held that the *Shulḥan Arukh* "was composed by Rabbi Joseph Caro, of blessed memory, for children and ignoramuses."[15]

However, such assumptions and speculations as to Caro's aim in writing the *Shulḥan Arukh* directly contradict Caro's own explicit statement of purpose in the Introduction to his book. There he stated: "I realized that it would be beneficial to gather the lilies and the sapphires [*i.e.*, the halakhic conclusions] of its [*Bet Yosef*'s] discussion, [and present them] briefly, clearly, and comprehensively, in an elegant and pleasant style." This indicates that Caro, and not any of his students, wrote the *Shulḥan Arukh*. Caro went on to describe his aims in the *Shulḥan Arukh*, one of which was that "when a scholar will be asked a matter of *Halakhah*, he will not need to hesitate. . . . The law to be applied in practice on any question that he will be asked will be clear to him because he will be fully familiar with this book, which is so excellently constructed." Although it is true that the *Shulḥan Arukh* was also intended to be a source for intensive study by beginners—as has always been the aim of every codifier for his work[16]—its primary purpose was to serve as a code that would be the basis for legal decisions, because "I trust that, by divine grace, the earth will be filled with the knowledge of God by virtue of this book—the small and the great, the student and the accomplished scholar."[17] Indeed, even those halakhic authorities who initially doubted the correctness and authoritativeness of the *Shulḥan Arukh* ultimately came to rely on it as an authoritative and binding code.[18]

15. *Resp. Maharitaẓ* #67. *See also Yad Malakhi* and *Shem ha-Gedolim, supra* n. 10.

16. *See supra* pp. 1153, 1185, 1265–1266, 1270.

17. Caro's Introduction to the *Shulḥan Arukh. See also Yad Malakhi, supra* n. 10, citing the *Keneset ha-Gedolah* (responsa).

18. *See, e.g., Resp. Maharitaẓ* #259: "We have also discovered that Joseph Caro in his concise book, *Shulḥan Arukh*, determined that this was the law. . . . Behold the elder and rabbi [*i.e.*, Caro] has already ruled, as we have written, that this was the practice." *See also Shem ha-Gedolim, supra* n. 10:

> It seems clear that our holy master [Caro] would not leave to his students, no matter how great they were, [the writing of] a work intended to be a code for all Israel, because that would lead to error. He certainly would not have divided the work among his students, or done anything similar, because the result would be enormous confusion. Furthermore, if, God forbid, he had done this, he would not have written that he wrote it, knowing that everyone will rely on it, while he himself would not know [what the book contained], but only his students [would know]. God forbid that he should be responsible for such a disaster.

D. The Acceptance of the *Shulḥan Arukh*

As stated, most Sephardic halakhic authorities accepted the rulings and decisions of *Bet Yosef* during the lifetime of its author. This is affirmed by Elijah b. Ḥayyim (Ranaḥ), one of the leading rabbis in Turkey in the second half of the sixteenth and the beginning of the seventeenth centuries.[19] Within a few years, *Bet Yosef*, together with the *Shulḥan Arukh*, became the authoritative and binding code of the *Halakhah* throughout the eastern diaspora except for Yemen, where the Jewish community generally followed the law as set forth by Maimonides.[20]

Ḥida proposed an interesting answer to the question of how there could be inconsistencies between *Bet Yosef* and the *Shulḥan Arukh*. He suggested that Caro in his *Bedek ha-Bayit* revised various rulings contained in *Bet Yosef* and that the *Shulḥan Arukh* reflects his later opinions. However, the manuscripts of parts of *Bedek ha-Bayit* were lost; and, as a result, some statements in the *Shulḥan Arukh* contradict not only *Bet Yosef* but also *Bedek ha-Bayit* as extant. *See Maḥazik Berakhah*, YD, #47, par. 4, s.v. Va-aḥashevah:

> It is possible that when our master wrote the *Shulḥan Arukh*, he changed his mind . . . and retracted what he wrote in *Bet Yosef*. . . . I believe it most likely that in *Bedek ha-Bayit* he explained everything, but that . . . several manuscripts were lost, as can be understood from his Introduction.

See also Birkei Yosef, OḤ, #188, end of par. 12, s.v. Ve-efshar lomar:

> There is reason to believe that he explained his statements in *Bedek ha-Bayit* and that this is one of the sections of *Bedek ha-Bayit* that were stolen or lost. As is known, he composed the *Shulḥan Arukh* after *Bedek ha-Bayit*.

See also Shem ha-Gedolim, Books, Letter *bet*, #31:

> From his son's Introduction, it is clear that several manuscripts [of *Bedek ha-Bayit*] were lost. Had we merited its publication *in toto*, it is possible that many criticisms made against our master would have been answered.

Here, Ḥida stated that it was Caro's son who confirmed that manuscripts of *Bedek ha-Bayit* were lost.

19. *See Resp. Ranaḥ* #109 (two responsa are numbered 109; our quotation is from the second): "The rabbi [Joseph Caro] has already been accepted as the rabbi [*i.e.*, halakhic authority] for our locality to follow his rulings" (p. 466b). *And see id.* #10 regarding a scholar who misunderstood a rule stated in the *Shulḥan Arukh; see* the question there and p. 69a, concerning "whether this person is to be regarded as only an unwitting transgressor because he relied on the apparent meaning of the *Shulḥan Arukh*, from which Torah goes forth."

20. *See Resp. Maharif* (by Jacob Faraji) #61; *Ta'alumot Lev* (by Elijah Ḥazzan), III, General Rules, p. 107b/c; *Mishpat u-Ẓedakah be-Ya'akov*, II, #5; *Yad Malakhi*, *supra* n. 10; I. Grunwald, *Ha-Rav R. Yosef Caro u-Zemano* [Rabbi Joseph Caro and His Times], pp. 174–177; I.M. Toledano, "Matai u-ve-eillu Mekomot Nitkabbel ha-Shulḥan Arukh le-Halakhah Pesukah" [When and Where the *Shulḥan Arukh* Was Accepted as the Authoritative Law], *Kovez R. Yosef Caro*, *supra* n. 13 at 184–188; I. Fauer ha-Levi, "Yaḥas Ḥakhmei ha-Sefardim le-Samkhut Maran ke-Posek" [The Attitude of the Sephardic Rabbis to Our Master's (Caro's) Authority as an Authoritative Decisionmaker], *Kovez R. Yosef Caro*, *supra* n. 13 at 189–197.

The Jews of Yemen generally adhered to the rulings of Maimonides until the eighteenth century, when a shift began. The Jews of South Yemen (the Shar'ab region) now

III. THE WESTERN COUNTRIES

In contrast to the eastern Jewish centers, the opposition to the codificatory work of Caro and Rema[21] in the west was much more fundamental. As stated previously, the founders of the Jewish spiritual center in Poland, Jacob Pollack and Shalom Shakhna, rejected the basic notion of codifying the *Halakhah,* because codification deprived the judge of the latitude he was entitled to exercise under the principles of decision making that the law accords with the views of the later authorities and that "a judge must be guided only by what his own eyes see."[22] Rema had succeeded in finding a middle course between this attitude of his teachers, on the one hand, and the need for codification, on the other;[23] but many of the leading authorities in Poland disagreed with his approach. For nearly a century after Rema, there were sharp and intense debates on the place of codification in Jewish law generally, on the legitimacy of recourse to codes, on methods of decision making, on how the law should be determined, and on many similar issues. This period—from the appearance of the *Shulḥan Arukh* with Rema's glosses until the middle of the seventeenth century—was one of the most

---

generally follow the *Shulḥan Arukh. See* R. Arusi, "Yiḥudo Shel Tarlal Mashta (le-Ḥeker ha-Olam ha-Ruḥani Shel Yahadut Shar'ab be-Me'ah ha-17)" [The Distinctiveness of Tarlal Mashta (A Study of the Spiritual World of the Jews of Shar'ab in the Seventeenth Century)], printed as the Introduction to *Tarlal Mashta Shabazi,* published in 1986 by Benjamin Japheth. However, the Jews of Central Yemen (the San'a region), the seat of the Jewish court for all Yemen, continued essentially to follow Maimonides.

During the eighteenth century, several Yemeni halakhic authorities attempted to adopt the *Shulḥan Arukh* as the binding code. The attempt failed, due largely to the opposition of Yehaiah b. Joseph Ẓalaḥ (Mahariẓ). However, the *Shulḥan Arukh* was not completely rejected, and today it is used along with the *Mishneh Torah.* For a detailed discussion of this subject, *see* R. Arusi, "Ha-Gorem ha-Edati bi-Fesikat ha-Halakhah (Kefiyyat Get be-Moredet "Ma'is Alai" Eẓel Yehudei Teiman)" [The Communal Factor in Halakhic Decision Making (The Practice of the Jews of Yemen to Compel Divorce in the Case of a *Moredet* for Incompatibility)], *Dine Israel,* X-XI (1981–1983), pp. 131–148; the article of Y.L. Nahum on the benediction over bread at public meals, in *Zohar le-Ḥasifat Ginzei Teiman* [Light on the Discovery of the Archives of Yemen], Tel Aviv, 1986, pp. 297–337, 338–360, and his articles: "Birkhat Hadlakat Ner Shel Yom Tov" [Benediction on Lighting the Festival Candles], *Sinai,* LXXXV (1979), pp. 55–91; "Keri'at Targum ha-Torah ve-Haftarah be-Ẓibbur" [Public Reading of the Torah and Haftarah in Aramaic Translation], *Sinai,* LXXXVIII (1981), pp. 219–238; "Avelut be-Furim" [Mourning on *Purim*], *Sinai,* XCII (1983), pp. 254–265. *See also* two unpublished theses, Bar-Ilan University: A. Gumaini, *Ḥadirat ha-Shulḥan le-Teiman* [The *Shulḥan Arukh*'s Penetration into Yemen], 1986; M. Gavra, *Le-Derekh Mahariẓ ba-Halakhah* [On Mahariẓ's Halakhic Methodology], 1986.

21. In the western countries, the focus of debate was the work of Caro and Rema collectively, since both books became known there simultaneously (*see infra* pp. 1384 and n. 52, 1398–1399). As pointed out *supra,* in the east at that time it was solely Caro's work that was the focus of the debate.

22. *See supra* pp. 1345–1348.

23. *See supra* pp. 1355–1356.

active and turbulent periods in the history of the codification of Jewish law. Indeed, had it not been for certain halakhic and historical circumstances at the end of that period, it is not at all certain that the codification of Jewish law would have eventuated as it did.

The halakhic authorities who opposed the *Shulḥan Arukh* can be divided into three principal categories: (1) those who rejected the *Shulḥan Arukh* without proposing any alternative type of code (some members of this group opposed codification on principle and others opposed the type of codification represented by the work of Caro and Rema); (2) those who rejected the methodology of Caro and Rema, and themselves composed codes that reflected their own approach or wrote commentaries on other codes that they found more compatible with their own codificatory principles; and (3) those who objected to relying solely on the *Shulḥan Arukh* for legal decisions, but did not reject the *Shulḥan Arukh* as a codificatory work; rather, they supplemented it with their own commentaries. Each category in turn is discussed here.

A. Opposition to the *Shulḥan Arukh* Without Proposing Any Alternative Type of Code

Two leading contemporaries of Caro and Rema, Ḥayyim b. Beẓalel and his brother, Judah Loew (known as Maharal of Prague), rejected halakhic codification in principle.

1. ḤAYYIM b. BEẒALEL

Ḥayyim b. Beẓalel (1520–1588) was the foremost opponent of the codification of Jewish law. Although less well known and certainly less influential than his illustrious brother, Judah Loew (Maharal), Ḥayyim b. Beẓalel was one of the leading rabbis in Germany in the sixteenth century. His opinions on the question of codification were not published until many years later,[24] but his acute and principled opposition to all codification is of great significance for an understanding of the nature of the *Halakhah* and the methodology of its study and decision making.

Ḥayyim b. Beẓalel was a disciple of Shalom Shakhna, with whom both he and Rema, whom he greatly respected and esteemed,[25] had studied.

24. *See* the title page of the first edition of his book *Vikku'aḥ Mayim Ḥayyim,* Amsterdam, 1712: "Indeed, for 137 years it [this ms.] was hidden and lost; no eye beheld it to publish it." The Introduction, in which Ḥayyim b. Beẓalel discussed codification of the *Halakhah,* was omitted in all subsequent editions. *See infra* n. 26.

25. *See* his Introduction to *Vikku'aḥ Mayim Ḥayyim,* which calls Rema "the wonderful rabbi," "the pious genius (*gaon*) of his generation," and "the pious sage" (sec. [*siman*] 2 of Introduction, *et al.*). *See* particularly the end of passage (*piskah*) 3 (p. 2b):

However, when a copy of Rema's *Torat Ḥattat* reached him, he wrote a critique of much of Rema's work in a book entitled *Vikku'aḥ Mayim Ḥayyim* [A Controversy over Living Water (*i.e.*, fresh, running water)]; the title is a word play on the author's name, Ḥayyim, which, as a noun, means "life," and as an adjective means "living." The book contains an extensive Introduction in which Ḥayyim b. Bezalel articulated his strong rejection in principle of Caro's and Rema's codificatory aims.[26] That rejection was largely based on the position of his teacher, Shalom Shakhna:

> When we [Ḥayyim b. Bezalel and Rema] studied together in the *yeshivah* of that outstanding luminary, our teacher, Rabbi [Shalom] Shakhna, of blessed memory, and heard his lectures on *Sha'arei Dura*,[27] we, his students, entreated him many times to compile all of the laws of *issur* and *hetter* in an appropriate order, but he responded that our request was in vain, doubtless for the reason I have written.[28]

I have decided to call this book [*Vikku'aḥ*] *Mayim Ḥayyim* [(A Controversy over) Living Water] because in the ceremony of purification [through the ashes of the red heifer, *see* Numbers ch. 19] a branch of cedar and a twig of hyssop were bound together and fresh, running water (*mayim ḥayyim*) was poured on them. Now, the author [Rema] is a rabbi who is like the stately cedar of Lebanon and I am a mere lowly hyssop growing in the wall.

26. As stated (*supra* n. 24), the Introduction appears only in the first edition, Amsterdam, 1712, and was omitted from later editions when the book was printed together with *Torat Ḥattat*. The full Introduction is printed in Tchernowitz, *Toledot ha-Posekim*, III, pp. 93–100. *Vikku'aḥ Mayim Ḥayyim* was printed together with *Torat Ḥattat* in ed. Zolkiew, 1859, ed. Piotrkow, 1904, and facsimile editions. Ed. Zolkiew, at the beginning of the book, contains "a strong letter" by Joseph Saul Nathanson, the Rabbi of Lemberg, stating that he had written a rebuttal against the sharp critiques of Rema in Ḥayyim b. Bezalel's Introduction: "In his Introduction he spoke disparagingly against our teacher and rabbi, Rema, without justification." Originally, Nathanson intended to publish his rebuttal, but later decided not to do so. His letter states: "I also wrote a rebuttal to defend our teacher Rema against his [Ḥayyim's] complaints, but I changed my mind and decided to print neither his Introduction nor mine." This apparently was the reason why Ḥayyim b. Bezalel's Introduction was not printed in ed. Zolkiew or in the subsequent editions.

Ḥayyim b. Bezalel was himself aware of the extreme acerbity of his criticism of Rema and, therefore, as he stated: "I did not consult with the great scholars of the country, the rabbinic leaders of the great community of Frankfurt, who are preeminent in the realm . . . for I was afraid that I would be a cause for laughter in their eyes, saying: How could a lowly ant like myself dare to attack the lion after his death?" However, he did not refrain from expressing his opinions, because "once I realized that this involved an element of profanation of God's name, I resolved that 'no wisdom, no prudence, and no counsel [can prevail against the Lord]' [Proverbs 21:30]." (*Vikku'aḥ Mayim Ḥayyim*, Introduction, near the end of sec. 3.) *See further supra* n. 24 and p. 1347 n. 138.

27. *Sefer Sha'arei Dura*, as to which *see supra* . pp. 1248–1249.

28. *Vikku'aḥ Mayim Ḥayyim*, Introduction, p. 1b–2a, end of sec. 2. *See supra* p. 1347 n. 138.

Although Ḥayyim b. Beẓalel offered many arguments against summarizing the *Halakhah* in a code, they can be reduced to two central points. The first is that codification negatively affects the intensive study of the *Halakhah*. Codes "lead to slackness in studying the ancient books";[29] "what has happened to the knowledge of Torah is that whenever its study was made easier, laziness increased . . . so that nowadays there are more ignoramuses than there were in former times."[30] The argument, so distressingly valid, is that making the material more convenient to use does not lead to more diligent and intensive study (as it should, because of the time it saves), but rather has the opposite effect—it leads to slothfulness and to neglect of study. Yet that is not the only or even the most severe adverse effect of codification on halakhic study. The main harm is that one who studies only codes believes that he understands the subject fully when in fact he does not. Ḥayyim b. Beẓalel aptly made this point in the following analogy:

> Anyone who seeks instruction only from the books of the later authors can be compared to a pauper who received much charity from many wealthy individuals. From one he received wheat; from another, wine; from yet another, fruit; from a fourth, clothing; and from a fifth, money. In all, he received what he needed. Another pauper came along and saw all these things the first pauper had received from the wealthy donors and thought the first pauper to be more wealthy than the benefactors, and so asked him for support. That fool [the second pauper] did not realize that it [the first pauper's "wealth"] was all the bread of poverty, because he [the first pauper] possessed only what the rich donors had given him. The same is generally true of contemporary knowledge. It is just a collection taken from earlier books—a little from here and a little from there[31]—and put together.[32]

29. *Vikku'aḥ Mayim Ḥayyim*, Introduction, p. 2b, beginning of sec. 4.

30. *Id.* at 3b, end of sec. 5.

31. The analogy can also be applied to Ḥayyim b. Beẓalel's second objection: that a judge should have all the divergent opinions available to him. Since he does not see the full original statements of the earlier authorities, but only "a little from here and a little from there," he is unable to study them properly in order to arrive at his own conclusion. The analogy appears after sec. 6, where Ḥayyim b. Beẓalel discusses the need to present the judge with a wide range of opinions (quoted *infra* n. 36).

32. Introduction, pp. 4b–5a, beginning of sec. 7. *See also id.*, the first half of sec. 6, for Ḥayyim b. Beẓalel's apt comparison of authors to minters of coins. Subsequently (*id.*, p. 4a/b; middle of sec. 6), he wrote that a book summarizing the law is legitimate and appropriate for one purpose only—the personal use of the author; and in this connection he compared such authors to coin collectors:

> There is another feasible alternative available. One may collect and compile every new thing that he finds in the works of earlier authorities and arrange them in proper order so as to avoid forgetfulness (which, because of the distractions of the times, is currently very prevalent). There can be no objection to this because such a person is like a collector of old coins who arranges them by putting each coin next to one like it, and

Ḥayyim b. Bezalel's second objection[33] to codification is rooted in his view of the very nature and methodology of the halakhic system. He argued that uniformity of the law, which is a central goal of codification, not only stifles spiritual creativity ("just as the nature of creation even today is that each person's face is different, so too one must believe that the wisdom in the heart of each man is different")[34] but is also inconsistent with the essential nature of Jewish law:

> Anyone who desires to render decisions should not rely solely on contemporary authors, but should merely make use of their books as an expression of their opinions because, in any case, they too are men amongst men [*i.e.*, are fallible human beings]. When he has studied all the differing opinions concerning the law in question, he should quickly turn to the sea of wisdom, the early authorities, and joyfully draw water from there, from the springs of salvation [*cf.* Isaiah 12:3], from which these [contemporary] authors also drew.[35]

> then keeps them as a treasured collection. In the same manner, this person collects for himself the statements of the earlier halakhic authorities, which are more valuable than silver or gold.
>
> Some sixteen years ago, I too decided to compile all the laws concerning matters of *issur* from the books of the *posekim,* one here and one there, and I arranged them in the proper order and formed them into an extremely concise digest. It is stored away and kept hidden. It happened that the students who were in my house stole it from me and secretly copied it. When I found out, I angrily took the copy from them, because I wrote it for myself only, as an aid to memory, and not for anyone else to rely on. Even the author of *Issur ve-Hetter ha-Arokh* wrote it only for himself and did not wish the book to be used by others to decide the law, as did that rabbinical author, of blessed memory [Rema].

33. Ḥayyim b. Bezalel also noted an additional interesting aspect of his first objection: a code that is comprehensible to everyone encourages ignorant laymen to use it as the basis for deciding the law for themselves because they think that they understand what is written in it; however, because they do not understand it correctly, they are bound to fall into error and mislead others. He described such an incident that had occurred in his community, and then commented (*id.*, p. 5b, end of sec. 7):

> The unintelligent believe that we are all wise enough to determine the law from what is found written in a book, without consulting any halakhic authority. . . . This is wrong! Even the simplest question requires the decision of a halakhic authority, because the slightest difference may affect the outcome, whether because the law itself is different or because of a difference in custom. A halakhic authority who makes legal rulings knows that the responsibility of decision making rests upon him, and it may be assumed that he is an expert in the law and is familiar with the variations in customs.

A similar fear was expressed by various authorities, such as Maharal of Prague and Maharshal, quoted *infra. See also Peri Megadim* (commentary to Sh. Ar. YD), Introduction.

34. *Vikku'aḥ Mayim Ḥayyim,* Introduction, near the end of sec. 4.

35. The passage continues:

> This had always been the practice among the Jewish people. Whenever an authority qualified to rule (*i.e.*, having reached the age of forty, the age of wisdom) was faced

> . . . And if a case that he had decided yesterday comes before him once again, he should rule in the second case as he did in the first, [but] with care, because the slightest change in circumstances can require a different legal result. . . . Furthermore, a person's opinion does not remain constant all the time, and perhaps he does not wish to give the same ruling he gave yesterday. Such a change is not a deficiency, nor does it imply that he has made the Torah into two Torahs, God forbid! On the contrary, such is the way of Torah, and both decisions are the words of the living God.[36]

Multiplicity of opinions is one of the characteristics of Jewish law and leads to a multiplicity of possibilities for deciding a case, depending on the viewpoint of the judge and the needs of the time. The composition of a code tends to confine legal research to that code alone and, in Ḥayyim b. Beẓalel's words, "Man shall live not solely by his book but also by all the utterances of the other books."[37]

2. JUDAH LOEW b. BEẒALEL (MAHARAL OF PRAGUE)

Whereas Ḥayyim b. Beẓalel dealt specifically with the methodology of decision making and offered a series of detailed arguments against codifying Jewish law, the opposition of his illustrious brother, Judah Loew b. Beẓalel (Maharal of Prague, 1525–1609), flowed from his general spiritual-educa-

---

> with a decision, he would open all the books of law and would read the opinions of those who forbid and those who permit. He would study them with great fear and trepidation; and if the matter seemed to call for a prohibition, he would immediately take the more strict view. If there was a custom that was permissive, he would follow it. If he could, he would gather all the scholars of his town and they would discuss the question until they reached a consensus.

36. *Id.* sec. 7. *See also id.*, at the end of sec. 6:

> Therefore they relied on the glosses [that had been written to existing books] that stated the law that should be followed. Glosses that would sometimes state two conflicting opinions that could not both be the law were considered by them to be preferable to glosses that would decide between the great "mountains" [*i.e.*, leading authorities] and thus in effect completely set aside the opinion of one of the earlier masters. They therefore saw fit to place both opinions before the rabbi who was making the ruling so that he might choose as Heaven would direct him, because the Torah vested in him the prerogative to make rulings and because no one can force him to accept another's opinion; for matters of *issur* (religious law) are not like other prohibitions, as I have written above.

Ḥayyim b. Beẓalel thus emphasized the need for pluralism in matters of *issur*—a view that is also apparent from the end of sec. 1 and his comments at the beginning of sec. 2, as well as from the beginning of sec. 10. It is possible that he accepted definitive and uniform rules in matters of *mamon* (civil law) in order to prevent the plea of *kim li* ("it is established for me that the law is in accordance with a particular authority who favors my position"), as to which *see supra* pp. 1281–1282 and *infra* p. 1386 n. 59. This question requires further study.

37. *Vikku'aḥ Mayim Ḥayyim*, Introduction, middle of sec. 6; *see supra* n. 36. *Cf.* Deuteronomy 8:3.

tional teachings. Maharal's rejection of books of *pesakim* in which the law is definitively set forth without sources and reasons was a corollary of his general views on the study and determination of the *Halakhah.* He strongly opposed the method of study that was widespread in his time among respected authorities:

> Any wise person who considers our custom [*i.e.,* the contemporary method of Torah study] cannot but be amazed. . . . For the early generations, the *tannaim, amoraim,* and *geonim,* and all the later authorities organized their studies in an orderly manner. First they studied Bible, then Mishnah, and then Talmud. Nowadays, however, they begin with Talmud. A child of six or seven already studies Talmud. Later, he turns to Mishnah [*i.e.,* the code book]—not to study it but only to seek out definitive laws. . . . Nowadays, there remain no Talmud, no laws, and no decisions except by way of [such] seeking. . . . The reason for this very unhappy situation . . . is that they start [their studies] with vain and incorrect hairsplitting discussions in *Halakhah* and arrive at wrong conclusions [which they justify by] saying that it [*i.e.,* this method] is meant to sharpen [the students'] minds.[38]

According to Maharal, the method of study known as *pilpul,* developed by Jacob Pollack and his disciples, had become, for a significant number of Talmud students, not a tool to discover the true meaning of Talmudic passages but an end in itself. Correct study—in the sequence of Bible, Mishnah, and Talmud—was put aside; and all the spiritual energy of the students was directed to devising novel and ingenious intellectual exercises for their own sake, even when it was clear that they did not arrive at the correct result. This method of study had become possible because finding the halakhic conclusion no longer required any effort:

> When we are required to render a decision or make a ruling . . . , a short way has now come into existence, to the extent that a set table [*shulḥan arukh*] is now available to everyone, concerning which they say, "This is the table before the Lord"; both the great and the small are invited to the table. There is no distinction between the wealthy [*i.e.,* the learned] and the poor [*i.e.,* the

38. *Derekh Ḥayyim,* Avot 6:6, the last passage (at the end of the commentary on the *mishnah* regarding the forty-eight methods by which knowledge of Torah is acquired). For a detailed discussion of Maharal's pedagogical theories and the method of study current in his time, *see* S. Assaf, *Mekorot le-Toledot ha-Ḥinnukh be-Yisra'el* [Sources for the History of Jewish Education], I, Introduction, pp. XVIIIff., 45ff.; A.P. Kleinberger, *Ha-Maḥashavah ha-Pedagogit Shel ha-Maharal mi-Prag* [The Educational Philosophy of Maharal of Prague], 1962, pp. 22–29, 130–134; J. Katz, Tradition and Crisis, 1961, pp. 194–195; H.H. Ben-Sasson, *Hagut ve-Hanhagah* [Concept and Conduct] (on the social concepts of Polish Jewry at the end of the Middle Ages), 1959, pp. 18ff.

> ignorant]; all partake of the Lord's table. Without knowing its rationale or logic, each of them proves the law from the Mishnah [*i.e.*, the code book].[39]

Furthermore, according to Maharal, rendering a decision on the basis of a code that presents only a final conclusion without the underlying reasoning is detrimental for more reasons than just the danger that without knowledge of the rationale of the law the decision may be wrong. That danger is generally agreed to have been alluded to in the *dictum* that "the *tannaim* wreak havoc in the world . . . because they decide the law on the basis of their Mishnah."[40] However, even when rulings made on the basis of a code are correct, exclusive reliance on the code still involves an element of "wreaking havoc in the world," because legal conclusions should be reached on the basis of understanding and as the result of study and the exercise of judgment. Maharal put it this way:

> It is more fitting and correct to decide on the basis of the Talmud. [This is true] even if there is a chance that [in this way] he [the judge] might not arrive at the truth and might not decide the law correctly according to the real meaning [of the Talmud]. In any case, all a halakhic authority has is what his own intelligence understands from the Talmud. Even if his intelligence and wisdom mislead him, he is nevertheless beloved of the Lord when he rules as his intelligence directs him, because a judge must be guided only by what his own eyes see. Such a judge is better than one who, like a blind traveler on a highway, decides on the basis of a code without understanding the underlying rationale at all.[41]

39. *Derekh Ḥayyim,* immediately preceding the quotation in the text, *supra* at n. 38. Ribash, in the fourteenth century, had already voiced the following sharp criticism of those "who pass an elephant through the eye of a needle" (*Resp. Ribash* #271, pp. 75d-76a):

> We have ourselves seen several scholars, clever and sharp in halakhic debate, who pass an elephant through the eye of a needle and pile up endless questions and answers on each and every point. Because of their cleverness, they never arrive at a conclusion that correctly reflects the *Halakhah,* and they permit what is forbidden and forbid what is permitted.

See also Ribash's further remarks, *id.*; H. Dimitrovsky, "Al Derekh ha-Pilpul" [On the Pilpulistic Method], *Jubilee Volume in Honor of Salo W. Baron,* Jerusalem, 1975, Hebrew sec., pp. 111–181.

40. TB Sotah 22a and Rashi, *ad loc.* The reference to *tannaim* here is to those whose function was to learn *mishnayot* and *baraitot* by heart and repeat them on request. *See supra* p. 1042. *See also Derekh Ḥayyim, supra* n. 38, and *Netivot Olam,* Netiv ha-Torah, ch. 15, last passage, s.v. Ve-od sham: ha-tannaim meval'ei olam.

41. *Netivot Olam, supra* n. 40. In an attempt to reconcile his opinion with the approach of previous codifiers, Maharal asserted:

> Although the early masters, such as Maimonides and the author of the *Turim,* also composed codes that contain no explanation of the laws, they only meant to present the final legal conclusions that flow from the Talmud. It never entered their minds

Maharal's position is diametrically opposed to that taken nearly five centuries earlier by Ri Migash, who had specifically encouraged decision making on the basis of code books.[42] Nowhere in the annals of Jewish law have the extremes in attitude toward codification ever stood in sharper relief than when the views of these two authorities are set side by side. As will be remembered, Ri Migash had written:

> It is rather those who presume to make authoritative legal pronouncements on the basis of their study of the *Halakhah* and on the basis of the strength of their Talmudic knowledge who ought to be restrained from doing so. . . . [They] believe . . . that the rightness of their decisions . . . [is] as clear as day, but . . . [they are] wrong; their decisions . . . [are] based on inapposite sources.

On the other hand, Ri Migash contended:

> One who makes rulings on the basis of the geonic responsa and finds support in them for his rulings is more suitable and praiseworthy, even though he does not understand the Talmud, than one who thinks that he knows his way through the Talmud and relies upon himself. For one who makes a ruling, even though flawed in reasoning, in reliance on what the *geonim* have said does not really err, for he at least acts on the basis of a decision of a distinguished and expert court.

Ri Migash, who was an enthusiastic supporter of codification, thus held that even an incorrect decision, if based on a clear and understandable code setting forth only the halakhic conclusions, is preferable to a decision reached on the basis of research into the Talmudic sources. At the other extreme, Maharal, the preeminent opponent of codes, preferred a possibly incorrect decision based on intensive study of the halakhic sources to a correct decision taken from a code by a judge who has no understanding of the underlying reasons for the ruling.[43]

> that anyone would rely on their books to reach a decision without knowing the source and rationale of the law. . . . Had those authors known that their works would lead to the complete abandonment of the Talmud and that decision making would be based [solely] on their works, those works would never have been written.

Maharal's disciple, Yom Tov Lipmann Heller (*see infra* pp. 1404–1406), and Joshua Falk (*see infra* pp. 1409–1410), as well as others, made the same point. Maharal wrote novellae to *Tur* YD, which were printed in 1775 and reprinted in *Tur,* ed. El ha-Mekorot, 1957–1959.

42. *Supra* pp. 1181–1184.

43. Maharal's influence on the method of studying the *Halakhah* was manifested in the spread of the study of the Mishnah, as attested to by his disciple, Yom Tov Lipmann Heller (*see supra* pp. 1108–1109 and *infra* p. 1404). However, neither his opposition in principle to codification nor the opposition of his brother ultimately prevailed. *See infra.*

3. SAMUEL ELIEZER EDELS (MAHARSHA) AND MEIR b. GEDALIAH (MAHARAM OF LUBLIN)

Many leading halakhic authorities in Poland in Caro's own time and immediately thereafter also rejected making decisions in reliance on a code rather than on study and clarification of the law on the basis of the Talmudic sources themselves; those authorities, too, did not propose any new approach as an alternative to codification. Two of the better known among these authorities were Samuel Eliezer Edels (Maharsha, 1555–1631) and Meir b. Gedaliah of Lublin (Maharam of Lublin, 1558–1616).

Maharsha, who served as rabbi in some of the largest Jewish communities in Poland at the end of the sixteenth and the beginning of the seventeenth centuries, recognized the importance of analyzing Talmudic passages in depth because "one cannot get to the roots and depths of a subject unless he has a teacher who instructs him in *pilpul.*"[44] He was, however, opposed to "vain *pilpul,*" in which "each one seeks to disprove the thesis of his fellow," because "such *pilpul* diverts a person from the truth and prevents him from achieving his desired goal."[45] Following his pattern of analysis to understand the meaning and plumb the depths of the Talmudic discussion, Maharsha composed his *Ḥiddushei Halakhot* [Halakhic Novellae], which is one of the best known and most widely accepted Talmudic commentaries, particularly for its discussion of Rashi's commentary and the novellae of the Tosafists.[46] Maharsha argued that analysis of the Talmud itself is the only valid method of arriving at halakhic decisions:

> In our times, there are those who make halakhic rulings on the basis of the *Shulḥan Arukh* without knowing the underlying reason for each matter. If

44. Maharsha, *Ḥiddushei Aggadot,* Bava Batra 73b, s.v. Ḥazinan, at the end.

45. Maharsha, *Ḥiddushei Aggadot,* Bava Meẓi'a 85a, s.v. De-lishtakaḥ. Maharsha specifically applied this description to "those who practice *pilpul* like the hair-splitting that goes on in the present generation." *See also* his *Ḥiddushei Aggadot,* Shabbat 31a, s.v. Pilpalta be-ḥokhmah; *id.,* Shabbat 63a, s.v. Al tikri.

46. *See* Maharsha, *Ḥiddushei Halakhot,* Introduction (in standard editions of the Talmud, it appears before *Ḥiddushei Halakhot va-Aggadot* to Tractate *Berakhot*):

> I decided to explore the plain meaning of [Talmudic] passages, both *Halakhah* and *Aggadah,* in accordance with the traditions I received from my teachers. . . . I beg acceptance of my apology by every scholar who reads this work and finds, because of his familiarity with the material, that it contains self-evident explanations of the plain meaning, and who will therefore ask, "Can he [the author] be considered a scholar?" I did not intend my work for those who surpass me in scholarship and understanding. I intended it only to serve as an aid to memory for myself and my colleagues who pay attention to what I say. However, it is possible that a careful examination of my work will give every reader some satisfaction, because, like other authors, I decided to present my thoughts briefly and I have not engaged in long-winded argumentation.

For a detailed discussion of Maharsha's approach to the writing of novellae, *see supra* p. 1128.

> they do not first examine the matter in the Talmud, which requires study under halakhic scholars, and if a decision they render is erroneous, they wreak havoc in the world and merit condemnation.[47]

Maharam of Lublin—one of the leading halakhic authorities of his time, who served as rabbi in Lvov (Lemberg) and Lublin and was the mentor of the outstanding Polish rabbis of the following generation[48]—was even more pointedly negative in his attitude toward the *Shulḥan Arukh.* He, too, composed commentaries and novellae on the entire Talmud; his work is called *Me'ir Einei Ḥakhamim* and has long been printed in almost all standard editions of the Talmud, along with Maharsha's commentary.[49]

Maharam of Lublin also wrote many responsa to questions sent from various European countries and even from the Ottoman Empire. He based his rulings on an analysis of the Talmudic sources and their commentaries, and he opposed decision making that relied on books that summarize the law. In one responsum,[50] he wrote:

> I see no need for any extended discussion of all the other lengthy arguments and proofs from the *Shulḥan Arukh* and the *Levushim*[51] advanced by the parties, for it is not my practice to place any reliance whatsoever on such books in arriving at a decision; they are like unenlightening chapter headings. Many are misled by their statements into permitting the forbidden or exonerating the liable—or vice versa.

Maharam of Lublin contended that erroneous decisions may result from reliance on the *Shulḥan Arukh* or the *Levushim* not only because the laws they contain are so cryptic that they are not fully understood, but also because their statements "are not the work of a single guide but are collections of statements compiled from separate sources that frequently should not be joined together [*i.e.*, are inconsistent]."[52] Although Maharam of Lublin recognized Joseph Caro as one of the leading halakhic authorities and occasionally explicitly relied on the rulings in Caro's *Bet Yosef* and *Shul-*

47. Maharsha, *Ḥiddushei Aggadot,* Sotah 22a, s.v. Yere et ha-shem beni. For a discussion of this comment of Maharsha, *see infra* p. 1422.

48. Such as Isaiah Horowitz, the author of *Shenei Luḥot ha-Berit;* Nathan Shapiro, the author of *Megalleh Amukkot;* and Joshua b. Joseph of Cracow, the author of *Meginei Shelomo* and *Resp. Penei Yehoshu'a.*

49. As to *Me'ir Einei Ḥakhamim, see supra* p. 1129 n. 104.

50. *Resp. Maharam of Lublin* #135, at the end of the question.

51. For a discussion of the *Levushim, see infra* pp. 1394–1403.

52. *Resp. Maharam of Lublin* #11 (at the end of the responsum). Maharam of Lublin was referring to "the statements of the authors of the *Shulḥan Arukh,*" meaning Caro and Rema (*see supra* p. 1365 and n. 206); *Resp. Maharam of Lublin* #94, #102, #126.

ḥan Arukh,[53] he refused to regard the *Shulḥan Arukh,* or any book that summarily stated only final legal conclusions, as the exclusive authoritative basis for legal decisions.

B. Opposition to the *Shulḥan Arukh* as Manifested by the Composition of Alternative Types of Codes

Three other important halakhic authorities who were contemporaries of Caro and Rema or lived soon after them also disagreed with their codificatory methodology.[54] Two—Solomon Luria (Maharshal) and Mordecai Jaffe—composed codes based on their own codificatory methodology, which differed from that of both Caro and Rema. The third, Yom Tov Lipmann Heller, wrote a detailed commentary on *Piskei ha-Rosh,* Asheri's summary of the laws of the Talmud, thus adopting Asheri's approach to codification, which was also entirely different from that of Caro and Rema.

1. SOLOMON LURIA (MAHARSHAL)

Solomon Luria (Maharshal, 1510–1574) was one of Poland's most profound and prolific authors.[55] He was sharply critical of the approach to codification in *Bet Yosef,*[56] and his own code is one of the largest and most important books of *halakhot.* Maharshal, like his contemporary, Rema, began his work independently, unaware that Caro had undertaken a similar task. Maharshal described in detail how he came to realize the need for a book that would summarize the law and decide disputed points. His main impetus for undertaking this task was the multiplicity of halakhic opinions: "From the days of the School of Shammai and [the School of] Hillel, the Torah has become like two Torahs."[57] As a consequence, books summarizing the law had been periodically written, such as the Mishnah of R. Judah Ha-Nasi, the Talmud edited by Ravina and Rav Ashi, the various books of *halakhot* of the geonic period, Maimonides' *Mishneh Torah,* and others.

53. *See, e.g., Resp. Maharam of Lublin* #118: "As to this, *Bet Yosef* stated . . . and he [Caro] similarly ruled in his *Shulhan Arukh,* and we relied on that [ruling] and arranged for the above-mentioned bill of divorcement."

54. In their comments, Mordecai Jaffe and Yom Tov Lipmann Heller discussed both Caro and Rema, but Maharshal referred only to Caro. *See infra* n. 56.

55. For details concerning Maharshal, *see* S.A. Horodezky, *Kerem Shelomo,* 1897; S. Assaf, "Mashehu le-Toledot Maharshal" [A Brief Biography of Maharshal], *Jubilee Volume in Honor of Louis Ginzberg,* Hebrew sec., pp. 45–63.

56. It is possible that Maharshal never saw the *Shulḥan Arukh,* since his comments are addressed entirely to *Bet Yosef.*

57. Maharshal, *Yam Shel Shelomo,* Bava Kamma, Introduction. The quotations that follow are also taken from that Introduction.

However, each of these works generated new halakhic material and raised new problems and doubts in determining the law. The result was

> an abundance of confusion, and the Torah has become not like two Torahs, but like 613 Torahs because of the proliferation of disagreement. Each one builds a rostrum for himself as though he is in charge of the scales of justice, and, using the sacred weight (*shekel*), he weighs (*shokel*) the opinions and decides in his own favor, and pronounces it [his decision] "blessed."

To these differences of opinion must be added others that stem from the variations among the different centers of Jewish life:

> The Sephardi says that an author is always right if he is a Sephardi—especially Maimonides, who was graced with all the superior attributes, both internal and external—and all the French [*i.e.*, Ashkenazic] authorities are of no value [lit. "like the peel of a garlic"] when compared to him. . . . But I found a responsum of Rosh [Asheri] in which he wrote . . . that he had a tradition that the French [Tosafists] Rabbenu Tam and Rabbenu Isaac were greater in wisdom and number than Maimonides.[58] Thus a party can always disagree [with the decision in his case] and say, "The law is established for me (*kim li*) by a particular one of them"; the Sephardi [can point] to the [decisions of the] Sephardic authorities and the Frenchman [*i.e.*, Ashkenazi] to [those of] the French authorities, each one choosing his own. Each group speaks its own language and believes the Torah to be its own estate. This is not the correct way, because since Ravina and Rav Ashi there is no tradition to follow the decisions of any particular *gaon* or later authority but only one whose decision is demonstrably correct and based on the [Babylonian] Talmud, or, when the [Babylonian] Talmud does not resolve the issue, on the Jerusalem Talmud or the *Tosefta*.[59]

58. The full quotation reads:

> But I found a responsum of Rosh [Asheri] in which he wrote that although Rabbi Moses b. Maimon was exceedingly great in all intellectual disciplines, nevertheless, whenever there is a conflict between him and Rabbenu Tam or Rabbenu Isaac the Elder, his [Maimonides'] opinion should not be followed, but one should follow the Tosafists, in view of the fact that he [Asheri] had a tradition that the French [Tosafists] Rabbenu Tam and Rabbenu Isaac were greater in wisdom and number than Maimonides.

See Resp. Asheri 94:5, *and see supra* p. 1227 n. 136.

59. Maharshal drew attention to the particular difficulties resulting from differences of opinion in civil law when a litigant asserts the plea of *kim li* (*see supra* n. 36). Jacob b. Asher, the author of the *Turim*, had previously noted the problem; *see supra* pp. 1281–1282. *See also Yam Shel Shelomo*, Bava Kamma, ch. 2, #5: "But once a judge makes a ruling—whether as a result of following the majority opinion or of agreeing for cogent reasons with a minority opinion—then however many there are who disagree with that minority view, the party in possession [of property that is the subject of the case] cannot argue '*kim li*,' and the judge can take [the property] away from him." *See also Resp. Maharshal* #35.

It was this lack of uniformity in the law, caused not only by differences of opinion as to the substance of the law but also by considerations of where halakhic authorities were born and studied, that motivated Maharshal to undertake the composition of a book of *halakhot,* which he called *Yam Shel Shelomo* [The Sea of Solomon], and which in scope and size is one of the largest books of *halakhot* ever written. Maharshal described his methodology as follows:[60]

> I decided to follow the course of wisdom and search out the roots of every subject, and, "by the Temple service" [this is a form of oath], I sometimes had to spend an entire week racking my brains until I discovered the root of a matter. Only then did I write it in the book. The following is my method: I include all the opinions—early, intermediate, and recent—codifiers, authors, and customs, law by law, authors of responsa, writers of epistles[?], collections and anthologies—so that no litigant will be able to argue: "Look how this author's laws and rulings have been written on the basis of his own imagination and doubtful proofs. If he had seen the book or the responsum of such-and-such a rabbi, he would never have dared to disagree and would most certainly have changed his mind."

Maharshal was not the first to set forth the various opinions on each legal issue; his independent spirit and originality manifested themselves in the manner in which he decided between the variant opinions. He showed no favor even to the greatest halakhic authorities; he investigated and examined every subject and decided solely according to his own conclusions based upon the Talmudic sources:

> I was therefore unyielding and said about them [the authorities he cited]: "They are all superior beings, but they will be examined as men" [*cf.* Psalms 82:6–7]. Therefore, I did not rely on any single author above his colleagues, even though whoever studies them thoroughly can discern great differences in quality between them; for, in any event, it is the Talmud that is determinative and supplies the proofs to justify an opinion. Occasionally, an author will state the legal rule correctly, but not for the right reasons. . . .
>
> Consequently, I closely examined and investigated, over and over again, every source and legal decision, with great effort and study (and little sleep), often consulting with my colleagues and especially my students. The reader will find in this book the origin of the law with clear proofs and will surely realize and understand that I did not neglect to study any author before I reached my conclusion.[61]

60. *Yam Shel Shelomo,* Ḥullin, First Introduction. The same passage in a somewhat briefer form appears in *Yam Shel Shelomo,* Bava Kamma, Introduction.

61. *See also* the passage preceding that quoted in the text:

I was not partial to any of them. . . . Since God has favored me and I have everything

Maharshal's method was thus to compile all the opinions on a specific subject and to determine on the basis of the Talmud alone which view was correct. As will be remembered, even Joseph Caro, although he realized that this method was the way to arrive at a correct determination of the law, declined to adopt it because he did not want to be in the position of judging between the early halakhic authorities, or, as he phrased it, "to put his head between the mountains—the mountains of God"—and because he saw it as "an exceedingly long journey" that was simply not feasible. Maharshal, however, was not daunted by this difficult challenge and undertook to determine the law on each and every issue according to his own understanding, with the Talmud as the sole criterion.[62] Occasionally, he spent days and even weeks on the clarification of a single subject.

Maharshal's methodology was thus the complete opposite of Caro's,

---

[*cf.* Genesis 33:11], blessed be the Omnipresent for His abundant grace, I delved to the depths of the *Halakhah*, and I deliberated on every law before I finalized it and committed it to writing. I wrote everything with clear explanation and excellent proofs. The present generation, because of its shortcomings, cannot imagine that a great author [of the past] could err, and they believe that anything written in an old book cannot be questioned. They seek only to tear down the opinions of their contemporaries; and whatever a contemporary scholar asserts, even if flawless and superlative, is greeted with the remark, "Is he better than anyone else? We are also scholars and know Talmud as well as he." But by the faith, I have proved many times that it is particularly the *aḥaronim* who have erred with regard to a number of Talmudic passages, just as if they were ordinary students who misunderstand the *Halakhah*.

62. However, Maharshal tended to accept the opinions and Talmudic interpretations of the Tosafists. *See* his Introduction, *supra* n. 60, opposing the "compromises" of Caro in *Bet Yosef* and stating that the decisions of *Bet Yosef* should not be accepted because "he [Caro] frequently decided against the Tosafists and the authorities whom we are accustomed to follow." In Maharshal's view, there is no compulsion to follow the opinions of the Babylonian *geonim*, since they too were post-Talmudic, as is clear from his statement quoted *supra:* "Since Ravina and Rav Ashi there is no tradition to follow the decisions of any particular *gaon* or later authority but only one whose decision is demonstrably correct . . . when the Talmud does not resolve the issue." This was also the view of Maimonides and Asheri (*see supra* pp. 1228–1229 and nn. 137, 138).

Tchernowitz's assertion (*Toledot ha-Posekim*, III, p. 82) that "he [Maharshal] did not recognize any authority after the completion of the Talmud except the *geonim*, whose opinions were based on tradition" is not precisely accurate.

Horodezky (*supra* n. 55 at 22) was closer to the truth when he wrote: "Nevertheless, he [Maharshal] was respectful of the *geonim* and was predisposed to their opinions." However, the proofs Horodezky offered for his statement must be closely examined (and the same is true for Tchernowitz), since the designation *gaon* does not necessarily refer to the Babylonian *geonim*. Horodezky's proof from *Yam Shel Shelomo*, Yevamot, ch. 4, #16, for example, is erroneous. The beginning of the passage there refers to one Shalom of Vienna, who, in one of his letters, interpreted a certain enactment. Maharshal went on to say: "However, far be it from me to disagree with the *gaon*, since he is an expert on legislation and all his statements are based on tradition, and Maharil . . . wrote of him. . . . " Here, *gaon* clearly refers to a Viennese authority and not to one of the Babylonian *geonim*.

which followed a majority of the three great codifiers (Alfasi, Maimonides, and Asheri)—a point that is addressed again below. Maharshal's methodology also differed from that of Rema, his contemporary and fellow countryman. Maharshal did not apply to the post-Talmudic period the rule that "the law is in accordance with the views of the later authorities"; his purpose in citing the opinions of prior authorities was not to rule according to the latest one, as did Rema, but to ensure that no one would be able to claim that he (Maharshal) was unaware of a particular opinion and that if he had known it, he would have followed it.

Using this method, Maharshal composed *Yam Shel Shelomo* on six tractates of the Talmud: *Bava Kamma, Bezah, Gittin, Yevamot, Kiddushin,* and *Ketubbot.*[63] His organization, unlike that of the *Mishneh Torah* and the *Turim,* was not topical, but followed the sequence of the Talmud. He adduced all the relevant material on each subject and determined the law according to his understanding of the Talmudic discussion. His treatment of each Talmud chapter is divided into sections (*simanim*), each preceded by a brief summary. Although the arrangement of the material according to the Talmudic sequence makes it extremely difficult to find any particular subject in the book,[64] he chose it to emphasize his reliance on the Talmud.

When Maharshal reached Tractate *Ḥullin,* he realized that if he continued with his method he would never succeed in completing his work on all the Talmudic tractates, and that no reader could assimilate the huge amount of material the work would contain.[65] He therefore decided to nar-

63. Only four chapters of *Yam Shel Shelomo* to Ketubbot have been printed. *See* the apology of the printer following these chapters. *See also infra* n. 67.

64. In order to locate a particular law in *Yam Shel Shelomo,* one must first know where the law is dealt with in the Talmud. Even then, it is not always initially obvious which Talmudic passage was selected as the locus of discussion of a particular subject. For example, *Yam Shel Shelomo,* Bava Kamma, ch. 8, #59, apropos of the discussion in the Talmud as to whether a person may intentionally wound himself, discusses at length the question whether a person may commit suicide rather than submit to forced apostasy. This is really a question of the law of martyrdom, which in the *Turim* is discussed in YD ch. 157 (and is also referred to in *Bedek ha-Bayit, ad loc.*). Similarly, *Yam Shel Shelomo,* Ḥullin, ch. 8, #14–42, discusses the laws of ritual washing of hands, which is treated in *Tur* OḤ chs. 158 *et seq.* In some tractates—*Bezah, Yevamot,* and *Ḥullin*—there is an index of the laws, but nevertheless it is difficult and tedious to locate laws in *Yam Shel Shelomo.*

65. As to this, Maharshal wrote (*Yam Shel Shelomo, Ḥullin,* Second Introduction):

> And now I am not ashamed to admit that I had not really understood what that wise man [King Solomon] meant when he said: "To the making of books there is no end" [Ecclesiastes 12:12]. His warning is plain. He was reproving those authors who want to solve all problems conclusively by means of elaborate proofs designed to make their opinions as impregnable as a wall of iron. It is indeed endless, and exhausting as well! [This is true] especially to a person like myself, who felt constrained to quote all the opinions, so that the commentary I wrote to Tractate *Bava Kamma* alone is as long as a whole book of one of the other authors. Then I started my commentary to Tractate *Yevamot,* and in two years I completed only one-half of the tractate. It took an entire

row its scope by discussing a subject in detail only where there was a particular need, such as when "confusion had developed concerning the matter." However, his methodology for determining the law did not change: he continued to rule on the basis of proofs from the Talmud, except that he was now content with only "a brief [exposition of the] proof."[66]

After Maharshal had decided to narrow the scope of the rest of his work—he had intended to cover all the tractates of the Talmud, even those in the Orders of *Kodashim* and *Tohorot,* although their laws had not been applicable since the time of the Second Temple[67]—a copy of Caro's *Bet Yosef* reached him. Maharshal's opinion of *Bet Yosef* was that in regard to scope, it "left virtually no room for significant improvement,"[68] but that its contents and methodology were deficient in three respects.

First, Caro "had made compromises in his rulings subjectively and arbitrarily [*mi-sevarat ha-keres,* lit. "by gut reasoning"] mostly in matters of *issur* . . . ; he made a compromise in regard to the three great authorities—Alfasi, Asheri, and Maimonides—by following any two of them when they agreed, and he paid no attention to all the other great authorities, as though he possessed the tradition from the days of the Elders."[69]

Thus, as already mentioned, Maharshal sharply opposed Caro's method of determining the law. Maharshal used the term "compromises" (*pesharot,* thenceforth adopted by many of Caro's opponents), because Caro did not seek out the truth by analytical study, but took the easy and perhaps more efficient way, notwithstanding that the conclusions to which it leads may be erroneous. Such "compromising," in Maharshal's words, was based on "gut reasoning"—an arbitrary numerical formula for determining the law according to any two of his "three pillars of instruction," leaving out of account "all the other great authorities." Maharshal also emphasized that

---

year's labor to finish the first two chapters of Tractate *Ketubbot* and I worked on [Tractate *Yevamot,*] chapter "Mizvat Ḥalizah" for more than six months. I warned myself, "'You will surely wear yourself out' [Exodus 18:18], and the reader as well. How long will you labor and be able to bear this great burden? It is impossible to bear the burden or to consummate the project for either of two reasons: either there will not be enough time to complete the whole work or, because of its length, the readers will become weary, the eyes of the scholars will glaze over it, and its weight will be beyond carrying because of its great length."

66. *Id.*

67. *Id.* In addition to the tractates listed *supra, Yam Shel Shelomo,* Ḥullin is also extant, making a total of only seven tractates. According to Maharshal's student, Eleazar Altshul (*see* the title page of *Yam Shel Shelomo,* Bava Kamma, ed. Prague, 1616), Maharshal completed his commentary on sixteen tractates.

68. *Yam Shel Shelomo,* Ḥullin, Second Introduction (near the end). This was the same reaction to *Bet Yosef* expressed by Rema in connection with his *Darkhei Moshe. See supra* p. 1351.

69. *Yam Shel Shelomo,* Ḥullin, Second Introduction (near the end).

Caro's approach to decision making often led to conclusions contrary to the *Halakhah* as practiced by Polish Jewry—"against the traditions we have received and practiced until now . . . inasmuch as he [Caro] frequently decided against the Tosafists and the authorities whom we are accustomed to follow."[70] However, Maharshal complained, the students did not realize this:

> The students follow his [Caro's] words and decisions without realizing the seriousness of the matter. . . . They are mistaken in this, but when they see it written in his book [*Bet Yosef*] that such is the law, they say "Caro so ruled explicitly!" That is their great deficiency—they believe whatever is written in a book. If a living person were to arise and proclaim that the law is otherwise and show unimpeachable proofs or even point to the traditional practice, they would pay no attention to him. . . . [71]
>
> Nowadays, because of our many sins, many are ordained but few study,[72] and consequently they latch onto the book, in which they [think they] can find all the wisdom. In this way, the ignorant become equal to the wise, and the young become equal to the old. I myself, because of our great sins, have seen all this.[73]

The second deficiency Maharshal found in *Bet Yosef* was that "in many places he [Caro] did not fully plumb the depths of the law, because of the

70. *See also* the succeeding passage, *id.*:

> Not only did our master, Rabbi Joseph Caro, make a compromise with regard to those three great authorities . . . , he also made other compromises, such as on the question of the permissibility of making a gift on the second day of festivals. *Halakhot Gedolot* and all the other authorities, including the recent ones, forbade this. Even Maharai wrote that it is prohibited, and the custom in our country has accepted this prohibition, but he [Caro] permitted it and followed a "majority" that is not a majority at all.

71. *Id.*

72. For further details on this point, *see Yam Shel Shelomo,* Bava Kamma, ch. 8, #58 (approximately in the middle):

> Because of our many sins, many are ordained but few are knowledgeable; those of shallow minds increase in number, and not one of them knows his place. As soon as a man is ordained, he becomes arrogant and spends a fortune to gather students around him, like the aristocrats who hire servants to run before them. These are the little foxes who damage the vineyard of the Lord, as Maimonides wrote. There are also elders . . . who do not fully understand the thrust of even a single Talmudic discussion and do not have a thorough understanding of the *Halakhah* at all. They are elders only in years and not in wisdom. . . . Even when occasionally there is one who is learned and erudite, his conduct is tainted; he does not study to increase knowledge or to be able to perform the commandments properly, but instead engages in lengthy casuistries to enhance his reputation. At present, all the students follow this path, and they even mock a scholar who fulfills the commandments conscientiously, engages in the study of Torah, does good deeds, observes even the minor commandments, and prays with concentration and great devotion. Such a scholar is a laughingstock in the eyes of the students.

73. *Yam Shel Shelomo,* Ḥullin, Second Introduction (near the end).

tremendous burden of his task."[74] Caro's third deficiency, according to Maharshal, was that Caro "did not have carefully edited texts of the various books and had copied them from printed editions that were erroneous, and so sometimes his entire structure was built on this faulty foundation."[75]

Because of these three deficiencies that Maharshal perceived in *Bet Yosef,* he decided to return to his original plan for his monumental work, *Yam Shel Shelomo.* His purpose was

> to discourage students from relying on his [Caro's] book and [to prevent them from] saying later that I was not acquainted with that book. Therefore, I shall return to my initial practice and discuss each law at length, citing all his [*i.e.,* Caro's] innovations, even on the occasions when there would be no need to take them into account except to demonstrate the exhaustiveness of my book; and I will express my opinion [on them].[76]

Maharshal found it inappropriate to link his *Yam Shel Shelomo* to Caro's *Bet Yosef,* as Rema had largely done with his book *Darkhei Moshe.* There were apparently two main reasons for Maharshal's attitude. First, the structure of *Yam Shel Shelomo* is very different from that of *Bet Yosef.* Caro had followed the topical arrangement of the *Turim,* whereas *Yam Shel Shelomo* follows the sequence of the Talmud; and such different structures could not possibly be merged. Second, the two works had different approaches to determining the law. For Maharshal, a consideration of each issue in the light of the sources contained in Talmudic literature was a prerequisite for codification and determination of the law, and much of *Yam Shel Shelomo* is dedicated to this task. On the other hand, although *Bet Yosef* quotes Tal-

74. *Id.*

75. Although Caro himself stated in his Introduction that he intended to correct the typographical errors in the *Turim* "according to carefully edited and correct copies that I have reviewed," this apparently did not satisfy Maharshal's critical sense and insistence on determining the correct text. Maharshal made emendations in many halakhic texts and particularly in the text of the Talmud. Printed editions of the Talmud first appeared in the generation preceding Maharshal, and the printers did not always work from manuscripts that had been carefully proofread and reviewed. In his book *Ḥokhmat Shelomo* [The Wisdom of Solomon], Maharshal restored a great number of correct readings. *Ḥokhmat Shelomo* is currently printed in all editions of the Talmud together with the commentaries of Maharsha and Maharam of Lublin. Originally, it was much more extensive, but in the course of time many of Maharshal's emendations were incorporated into the printed text of the Talmud itself.

Maharshal complained bitterly of the frivolous attitude and lack of care on the part of the printers: "Pay no attention to the books newly printed from erroneous manuscripts. For such is his [the printer's] way. He erases anything he does not understand and writes what he pleases, as I have demonstrated in several places" (*Ḥokhmat Shelomo,* Eruvin 61a, s.v. Kulei hai). Similarly: "Here the text has been corrupted in the new printing in Lublin" (*Ḥokhmat Shelomo,* Sanhedrin 38b, s.v. Gemara, u-le-mi-keẓeh ha-shamayim ad keẓeh ha-shamayim).

76. *Yam Shel Shelomo,* Ḥullin, Second Introduction (near the end).

mudic sources, it does so far less than *Yam Shel Shelomo*. Even more important, Caro did not share Maharshal's basic tenet that one must arrive at the correct interpretation of the Talmudic discussion in light of all the various opinions in order to be able to determine the law. For these two reasons,[77] it was impossible for the two works to be linked together.

This, however, was not the case with Rema's *Darkhei Moshe* and Caro's *Bet Yosef*; these works could easily be linked together. They were both planned from the beginning to follow the topical arrangement of the *Turim*. Therefore, when *Bet Yosef* appeared, all Rema had to do was to add to it the views of the more recent halakhic authorities, particularly those of Germany and France, as well as the customs of those centers, and to determine the law on the basis of these latter authorities and customs, in accordance with the principle that the law follows the views of the later authorities. Rema had begun his code independently, but then decided to merge it with Caro's. Notwithstanding their differences of opinion and divergent approaches to determining the law, they became partners in one great work of codification.

However, since Maharshal's methodology was completely different from Caro's, he had no choice but to compose an independent work—a work that became one of the great and illustrious works of Jewish law. However, Maharshal's rulings were not accepted when they conflicted with those of Rema.[78] Maharshal's *magnum opus* has been printed in only a few editions, and the later authorities do not cite him frequently.[79] One of the

77. Maharshal's originality and independence of mind were probably also factors in his decision not to link his book to Caro's work. In addition, *Bet Yosef* reached him while he was working on Tractate *Ḥullin, i.e.*, after he had already completed *Yam Shel Shelomo* to at least six tractates. Rema, however, heard of *Bet Yosef* while he was working on the laws of *Ḥallah, i.e.*, in YD, and thus had a very significant part of his work still ahead of him.

78. *See* the remarks of Isaiah Horowitz, the author of *Shenei Luḥot ha-Berit* and a disciple of Maharam of Lublin:

> Our great later masters [were] Rabbi Solomon Luria [Maharshal], of blessed memory, and Rabbi Moses Isserles [Rema], of blessed memory. . . . It has already become customary to follow Rema and determine the law according to his views, if only because he merited it from Heaven, just as the law was determined according to the views of the School of Hillel even though the School of Shammai had greater acuity [*see supra* p. 1067]. I must note that Maharshal is the later authority as to matters of *issur* . . . since his book was written after . . . *Torat Ḥattat*; . . . but I have already stated that it has become the accepted custom in the Jewish diaspora outside the Land of Israel [Horowitz was in the Land of Israel when he wrote these lines] in the kingdom of Poland, and in Bohemia, Moravia, and Germany, to follow the rulings of Rema.

Shenei Luḥot ha-Berit, Sha'ar ha-Otiyyot, Letter *kuf*, *Kedushah*, s.v. Od hineni modi'a etḥem, (ed. Amsterdam, 1698, p. 74b; ed. Warsaw, 1867, p. 54a). *See also* Ḥida, *Shem ha-Gedolim*, Persons, Letter *mem*, #98. *See further infra* pp. 1419–1422.

79. Maharshal is cited only by the principal commentators on the *Shulḥan Arukh*, such as *Shakh*.

reasons may be that it is difficult to find the law in *Yam Shel Shelomo* because it follows the sequence of the Talmud. Maharshal's independent approach to determining the law, which stood alone against the methodology generally accepted in those times in those centers, may also have been a factor in the failure of *Yam Shel Shelomo* to achieve greater authoritativeness and influence.

2. MORDECAI JAFFE

Another major book of *halakhot* that generated discussion of the correct approach to the study and codification of the *Halakhah* was *Levush Malkhut* by Mordecai b. Abraham Jaffe (1530–1612). Jaffe was a student of Maharshal and Rema, and served as rabbi in such important communities as Lublin, Prague, and Poznan. He was also a preeminent member of the Council of the Four Lands. Like Rema, his teacher, he made creative contributions to all areas of Jewish thought—*Halakhah* and *Aggadah*, philosophy and *Kabbalah*—as well as to astronomy. His literary output is contained in a work he described as being divided into eight books, although there are, in fact, ten;[80] the work is known as *Levush Malkhut* [Royal Robes] or, in short, the *Levushim* (the "Robes"—the title of each book being a particular *levush* or "robe").[81] The first five books constitute Jaffe's contribution to the codification of Jewish law. Like Maharal of Prague and other halakhic authorities of that period, his attitude to codification reflected his general approach to the study of the *Halakhah*. Both Maharal and Jaffe rejected outright the pilpulistic method of study that had been adopted by some of the students of the *yeshivot*, but this rejection led them to different conclusions with respect to codification. Maharal, as will be remembered, opposed the composition of codificatory books, whereas Jaffe, from the very same starting point, concluded that such works were desirable and their composition should be encouraged.

Like most of the other great codifiers, Jaffe wrote a detailed Introduction, stating his methodology and the considerations that led him to write

80. *See* Jaffe, *Sefer Levush Malkhut bi-Khelalo* [The Complete Book of Royal Robes], Introduction (printed at the beginning of *Levush ha-Tekhelet* [The Blue Robe] to *Tur* OḤ, I, ed. Venice), p. 4, beginning of col. 2. After listing the first five *Levushim* (to the four *Turim*, *see infra* pp. 1400–1401 as to the names of these books), he added: "The last three *Levushim* are *Levush Peshatei ha-Torah* [The Robe of the Plain Meanings of the Torah]; *Levush ha-Derashot* [The Robe of Exegesis]; and *Levush ha-Be'urim* [The Robe of the Explanations], which is made up of three books that treat the essential points of the three disciplines—philosophy, astronomy, and *Kabbalah*. . . . I have divided this *Levush* [*Levush ha-Be'urim*] into three books. . . . The first contains explanations of the *Moreh Nevukhim* [The Guide for the Perplexed]; the second, explanations of the calendar; and the third, explanations of *Kabbalah*. . . . The eight *Levushim* are thus divided into ten."

81. For the source of the book's title and the topical organization of the work, *see infra* pp. 1400–1401.

his code. In his Introduction, he first described the approach that had customarily been used by halakhic authorities "to determine each halakhic matter in its correct order and according to the accurate law."[82] He then described the entirely different method of halakhic study in his own time: it was no longer a search for the truth, but only a form of intellectual gymnastics.[83] "I too," said Jaffe, "used to be one of them, and part of the devastation,"[84] until he realized that he was on the wrong path:

> I became afraid lest, God forbid, the true Torah disappear and be forgotten. Only a handful of people are concerned . . . to fathom the true depths of the *Halakhah*. When they saw that no one disapproved of this perverse generation, they confined themselves to their own rooms, where they established houses of study for "the four cubits of the *Halakhah*." . . . When I too saw what was happening[85] . . . , I determined to fulfill my duty by means of this

82. *Sefer Levush Malkhut bi-Khelalo*, Introduction, p. 3, col. 1.

83. On this point, Jaffe wrote (*id.*):

> I will disclose the pain in my heart, for it is a gaping hole within me. It has sorely troubled me ever since I attained understanding . . . and I cannot refrain from stating it. I have seen God's people scattered over the high mountains like a flock without shepherds. Dressed in rags and torn clothing, they wander, "with great searchings of heart" [*see* Judges 5:15–16] and without aim, over the rugged mountains. When they realize that they are naked, ragged, and unkempt, they become ashamed and say to each other, "Let us go from here to Dothan [*see* Genesis 37:17] and build a city and a tower in the valleys and make a name for ourselves like the renowned great ones of the earth" [*see* Genesis 11:4]. They all speak one language and fabricate the same ideas, saying, "Let us conspire to create new rules," most of which are foolish and false. They have taught their tongues to speak falsehood and iniquity incessantly.
>
> Woe to ears that hear such things! They transform the good and pleasant words of the living God into low, corrupt, and evil words of vanity, at the sound of which all must flinch. Not one of them turns to the truth; it is as if they know only "the hollow of the sling" with which they shoot [*see* I Samuel 25:29]. They have torn the Torah, which is our apparel, into twelve rags. After pronouncing such vanities, each one goes out to seek his unjust gains.

Subsequently, Jaffe continued by comparing his own generation to the generation of the Tower of Babel "who said 'Let us make a name for ourselves'—which was their only purpose. Therefore, Scripture commanded the upright man in such a generation to separate from them and have no part of them; he should build a refuge for himself in his own workroom."

84. *Sefer Levush Malkhut bi-Khelalo*, Introduction, p. 3, col. 2.

85. In his further remarks, *id.*, Mordecai Jaffe described the attitude of most students of his time in a manner that recalls the statements of Maharal of Prague and Maharshal:

> When I too saw what was happening . . . [I said], "I will not be shamed by the scorners," and my spirit awakened me and proclaimed: "Why do you sleep like a person in shock, and why should you be the last to restore the crown of Truth, which has been thrown to the ground? 'Do not follow the young men, whether poor or rich' [*see* Ruth 3:10]." The others hear a "sound of the tune of defeat" [*see* Exodus 32:18], and their only intent and purpose is to deceive the people into giving them their daughters in marriage, bestowing on them a large dowry, and supporting them. If difficulties should arise, they then intend to throw off the yoke of the Torah of Moses.

> work, the purpose of which will be to demonstrate the correctness of the path I was commanded to follow in the face of present conditions. This [work] will also disseminate Torah for my contemporaries in my lifetime and after my death.[86]

Jaffe went on to describe some of the stages in the writing of his work. His first intention was to produce an abridged version of *Bet Yosef.* When that work "first arrived in these lands, all those who study Torah rejoiced in it, and it was received with favor, warmth, and great approbation by all who saw it."[87] However, the prolixity of its discussions made it difficult to study and to use as an authoritative source in deciding cases. Jaffe, therefore, decided to produce "a short summary of the laws according to his [Caro's] principle of reliance on the 'three pillars of instruction,' of blessed memory, but I will explain the reasons [for the laws] as briefly as possible."[88]

Jaffe's initial response to the method of study current in his time was to undertake the composition of a work that would briefly and clearly summarize each law together with its underlying rationale, so that the search for truth would again become the basic objective of halakhic study. This motive for the composition of a halakhic code had a novel and interesting aspect. Although several authors of codificatory works had previously stated that their books were intended for scholars as well as beginning students,[89] their statements were not meant to be critical of an existing method of study, but were simply expressions of the purpose and importance of their books. Jaffe's statement, however, began by describing the method of study current in his time, and stressed that he undertook to write his work to indicate his opposition to that method; he reiterated[90] that young students should study his work in order to acquire the ability to search for and understand the true meaning of the *Halakhah.* A further interesting aspect of Jaffe's work is that he was prepared—at least at that early stage—to accept Caro's principle of determining the law on the basis of the "three

86. *Sefer Levush Malkhut bi-Khelalo,* Introduction, p. 3, col. 2. This was Jaffe's justification for limiting his teaching in a *yeshivah.* He stated further (*id.*):

> I, therefore, decided to prepare for myself a small alcove as a study-room . . . and I said that it was best for me to separate from the ways of some of my contemporaries and to reduce the time I spend with the students that I referred to. . . . For I have not found any to my liking, inasmuch as they all choose to engage in vain bickering and argumentation; . . . few of them make the truth their objective.

Because of the students' attitude, Jaffe could not study with them, and his book was intended to substitute for the "dissemination of Torah" in a *yeshivah.*

87. *Id.*, p. 3, cols. 2–3.

88. *Id.*, p. 3, col. 3.

89. *See, e.g., supra* pp. 1153, 1185, 1265–1266, 1270.

90. *See infra,* in the description of the sections of the *Levushim.*

pillars of instruction"; he sought merely to abridge *Bet Yosef* by briefly presenting the final conclusions and their underlying reasons.

Due to various circumstances, the writing of Jaffe's work was delayed, and as a result it underwent a number of changes. The Jews were expelled from Prague in 1561, and Jaffe moved to Venice, Italy. There he learned that Caro was also preparing an abridged version of *Bet Yosef, i.e.,* the *Shulḥan Arukh.* Jaffe thereupon abandoned his own plan because "his [Caro's] abridgment will certainly achieve very great popularity, for he wrote the original work and knows it thoroughly."[91] However, when the *Shulḥan Arukh* reached Venice, Jaffe saw that it was not the abridgment that he had contemplated:

> He [Caro] has abbreviated it to the extreme, and it will be completely inadequate for those who will study it. It is like reading a closed book or [dreaming] a dream without knowing its interpretation—as if it all were "law given to Moses at Sinai," without statement of any reasons.[92]

Furthermore:

> He has persistently written most laws in conformity with the opinion of Maimonides . . . because this is the practice in Moslem lands where Caro . . . was the chief leader [of the Jewish community]. In these [western] lands, however, such is not the practice. I therefore decided to return to my task, to write and explain the laws practiced in these lands—Germany, Bohemia, Moravia, Poland, and Russia and their associated communities.[93]

According to Jaffe, two aspects of the *Shulḥan Arukh*'s methodology required correction. The first was its extreme brevity, which made it like a closed book, stripped of reasons and explanations. The second was its acceptance of Maimonides' view as to most laws, with no reference to the rules followed in Germany and Poland. Apparently, it was only after Jaffe reviewed the *Shulḥan Arukh* that he realized that a significant number of the rules followed by the Jews of Germany and Poland had been omitted by Caro; earlier, after his study of *Bet Yosef,* he had been prepared to follow Caro's decisions based on the majority opinion among Alfasi, Maimonides, and Asheri. In the meantime, Jaffe was informed that his teacher, Rema, "had undertaken, in the manner I had chosen for myself, to explain all the practices of the above-mentioned lands [*i.e.,* Ashkenazic Jewry]" and, therefore, "I once again abandoned this task, because he [Rema] is universally viewed as a great and outstanding rabbi, and I decided that I would

91. *Sefer Levush Malkhut bi-Khelalo,* Introduction, p. 3, col. 3.
92. *Id.*
93. *Id.*

not [be so presumptuous as to] stand in the place of great men."[94] Since Jaffe's teachers had anticipated him in all that he had proposed to do in the field of *Halakhah,* he turned to writing books of Bible commentary, philosophy, *Kabbalah,* and astronomy.[95]

With the growing popularity of the *Shulḥan Arukh* as well as Rema's glosses, Jaffe turned to the *Levushim* once again. He concluded that "the time has come for me to return to my original project, because my teachers have yet left me room to make a significant contribution of my own."[96] He felt that the two aspects of the *Shulḥan Arukh* that he had originally planned to correct still required correction despite Rema's glosses. First, Jaffe believed that Caro and Rema "had merely written chapter headings and cryptic rulings without any rationale, as though [all those laws] had been given to Moses at Sinai without any explanation. This [type of exposition] is adequate only for themselves and others of their [intellectual] stature."[97] In Jaffe's opinion, this extreme brevity raised three concerns:

> They [Caro and Rema] have set their table with all kinds of delicacies, but the dishes are tasteless without salt. When the wise eat them, each dish will have the taste that is familiar to them; but how will tasteless food without salt taste to us, the poor [*i.e.,* the unlearned]? Laws can no more be set forth without reasoning than food can be [served] without salt. Furthermore, when a law is accompanied by its rationale, it will be remembered more correctly . . . and we will also be able to analogize to it all similar future cases.[98]

Jaffe's first concern on account of the brevity of the *Shulḥan Arukh* was that, because a code is meant to be studied, it is extremely important that the rationale of each law be stated, so that the *Halakhah* will be more interesting and absorbing. Second, Jaffe believed, studying the underlying reasons as well as the laws themselves is essential to ensure that the laws will be fully understood. Third, Jaffe felt that it was necessary to provide the rationale of the laws in order to enable them to be used by way of analogy to solve new problems.[99]

94. *Id.*
95. *Id.*, p. 3, cols. 3–4.
96. *Id.*, p. 3, col. 4.
97. *Id.*
98. *Id.*
99. *See also id.*, p. 4. col. 1:

> When I saw that the above-mentioned authorities, of blessed memory, put only the delicacies on their table but held back the salt (which must be sprinkled on each sacrificial offering, and which heats up the food and warms the man), and have concealed it under their tongues [*see* Job 20:12] so that it is still hidden within them and others of their talents, I decided that the wool of my lamb will warm me and others like me from the outside.

The second aspect of the *Shulḥan Arukh* with Rema's glosses that Jaffe felt still required correction was:

> They have left out of their *Shulḥan Arukh* many laws contained in Rabbenu Jacob's *Turim* and in Caro's longer work, *Bet Yosef.* Perhaps this was because they considered them elementary, but I do not think that that is sufficient reason for omitting them. Certainly, if one reads their books [the *Shulḥan Arukh* and Rema's glosses] without reading the *Turim* or *Bet Yosef,* those [omitted] laws will in the course of time seem strange to him—he will be unfamiliar with them and will know nothing about them.[100]

Mordecai Jaffe therefore returned to his original plan of writing a book in accordance with the following guidelines:

> To write every law comprehensively and not to leave out anything that they [Caro and Rema] left out, and to complete [the laws], with the help of God, in all their details and with their reasons, as I had begun to do.[101]

Jaffe's examination of Caro's codificatory work also led him to the conclusion that dividing the code into two separate books—one lengthy and exceedingly detailed (*Bet Yosef*), and the other overly terse and cryptic (the *Shulḥan Arukh*)—prevents the code from achieving its purpose. It is burdensome to use the detailed book and not helpful to use the shorter volume. The correct approach to codification was the middle way:

> My book will be like the mean between two extremes. One extreme is the great work of . . . [Caro], of blessed memory, which he wrote on the *Turim,* and which is extremely lengthy. The other extreme is the *Shulḥan Arukh* of the two aforementioned masters, of blessed memory [Caro and Rema], which is very brief. My book will take the middle way between them: it will explain at length where there is a need for explanation; and it will be brief when brevity is appropriate, in order to make available to every reader a concise statement of all the reasons for the laws.[102]

Jaffe stressed that his work, which was intended to facilitate the study and knowledge of the *Halakhah,* would be useful to two types of readers. For those proficient in the *Halakhah* and familiar with its sources, the book would lighten "the burden of examining [the sources] continuously,"[103] and for beginners the book would be of exceedingly great value:

100. *Sefer Levush Malkhut bi-Khelalo,* Introduction, p. 3, col. 4.
101. *Id.*
102. *Id.*
103. *Id.*, p. 4, col. 1:
And you, my learned colleague, who can study the sources, do not complain against me, saying, "How have you benefited me?" I have greatly benefited you too . . . for I

> For those who are only beginning their studies and who desire to know everything in simple form, my presentation will be very helpful, because it will provide an apt explanation for all the very brief statements contained in the *Turim* and the *Shulḥan Arukh.* They [the students] will easily be able to understand them and to know them quickly and easily. [It will be] in very clear and intelligible language.[104]

Even in his choice of the name for his work, Jaffe emphasized that he intended not only to create a source for use in decision making, but also to facilitate the study and knowledge of the *Halakhah.* "Therefore, because of all the truth and justice [contained in it], I have called this book *Levush Malkhut* [Royal Robes]. For who are kings? The scholars. And this is clothing and raiment for the scholars. Even young students who are only beginning their studies should dress themselves in it in their youth, and it will become fluent on their tongues." The book is here compared to a garment; whoever studies it clothes himself with its contents.[105]

As previously stated, Jaffe divided *Levush Malkhut* into eight books, called *levushim* (robes),[106] the first five of which constitute a halakhic code. The first book covers those laws treated in the first part of *Tur Oraḥ Ḥayyim* (up to chapter 241): the rules pertaining to arising in the morning, to prayer, benedictions, and the like, or, as Jaffe called them, "the order of the day." This book is called *Levush ha-Tekhelet* [The Blue Robe] ("blue" is the

---

> have lightened for you the burden of examining [the sources] continuously; you will no longer have to delve deep for the reasons [for the laws]. My work will help you to remember what you already know.

This reason is directly contrary to the view of Maharal of Prague and his brother Ḥayyim, who believed that laborious and intensive study is a most important end in itself.

104. *Id.* At the end of this section, Jaffe reiterated his objective, which was "to fulfill my obligation to disseminate Torah among the Jewish people as best I can, with the help of Heaven." He further pointed out that he retained the chapter and paragraph numbers of the *Shulḥan Arukh*—even though it might have been better to further subdivide them on account of the large quantity of the material—"in order not to confuse the reader, who studies and is accustomed to . . . the codes already published. He will thus easily find what he is looking for in the *Levushim* and also find it in the correspondingly numbered paragraph."

105. Jaffe also gave another reason for his choice of title (*id.*):

> I relied on the verse in which my name [Mordecai] is mentioned (Esther 8:15–16): "Mordecai left the king's presence in royal robes of blue and white, with a magnificent crown of gold and a mantle of fine linen and purple wool. And the city of Shushan rang with joyous cries. The Jews enjoyed light and gladness, happiness and honor." Thus, there are eight [which is the number of books in his work, *see infra*], because "royal robes" includes them all.

106. "I divided it into eight robes like the number of priestly garments, because Torah scholars are also considered to be priests in that they serve the Most High. So the priestly crown and the royal crown will be in one place" (*id.*, before the passage quoted *supra* n. 105). *See supra* nn. 80 and 105.

first word following the words "royal robes" in the verse in the Book of Esther that was the source for the title of Jaffe's book).[107] The second book treats all the rest of the laws in *Tur Oraḥ Ḥayyim*—the laws of the sabbath and festivals and similar laws—and is called *Levush ha-Ḥur* [The White Robe].[108] The third book is devoted to the laws in *Tur Yoreh De'ah* and "includes all that is denoted by 'instruction' (*hora'ah*). . . . I have called it *Levush ha-Ateret Zahav Gedolah* [The Robe of the Magnificent Crown of Gold][109] because it contains the main part of the crown and diadem that adorn the heads of kings. And who are kings? The rabbis, who are called 'our teachers.'"[110]

The fourth book covers the laws in *Tur Even ha-Ezer, i.e.,* family law, and is called, following the sequence in the verse in the Book of Esther, *Levush Takhrikh Buẓ ve-Argaman* [The Robe of Fine Linen and Purple Wool].[111] The fifth and final book of Jaffe's halakhic code deals with the laws of *Tur Ḥoshen Mishpat* and is called *Levush Ir Shushan* [The Robe of the City of Shushan (Susa)], which, in the pattern of the names of the preceding books, is the phrase that follows next in the verse of the Book of Esther. Jaffe, however, added another reason for the name of the fifth book. Since it covers Jewish civil and public law, Jaffe wrote: "I called this *Levush Ir Shushan* because any city that conducts its business according to those laws certainly deserves to be called *Shushan,* for it is full of pleasant and beautiful lilies [*shoshanim,* a play on the name of the city—"Shushan"] and flowers."[112]

This was the path into which Mordecai Jaffe attempted to guide the codification of Jewish law: toward a work which, although presenting only the halakhic conclusion without the substance of the Talmudic discussion supporting it, yet provides a brief and lucid explanation of the underlying reasoning. He had two main objectives in this approach: (1) to prevent

107. *See supra* n. 105.

108. *Sefer Levush Malkhut bi-Khelalo,* Introduction, p. 4, col. 1. "White" appears in the source verse after "blue." The Introduction sets forth additional reasons for the choice of these two names.

109. These words come after "robes of blue and white" in the source verse.

110. Introduction, *supra* n. 108. The title "our teacher" (*morenu*) was used in Germany and other places in the second half of the fourteenth century as the honorific for a scholar who received ordination (*semikhah*) in the new sense of the term (which is not the same as ordination in the Biblical and Talmudic sense). The main significance of the new type of ordination is that it confers the right to rule on matters of *issur* ("religious" law), *i.e.,* those laws included in *Tur* YD. For details, *see* EJ, XIV, p. 1145, s.v. Semikhah, and bibliography listed there.

111. Another reason given by Mordecai Jaffe for the choice of the name for this book was: "Because it is the nature of women to take great pleasure in colorful clothes." Introduction, *supra* n. 108.

112. *Id.*

errors in determining the law, thereby facilitating the analogical use of existing law to solve new problems; and (2) to offer a convenient and correct method for the study of the *Halakhah.* In his Introduction, Jaffe described himself as "a tailor" who had undertaken the task of "sewing";[113] and, indeed, he succeeded in sewing a splendid royal robe for the halakhic system. For each law, his work presents very briefly and succinctly the reason, the Biblical source, and several apposite Talmudic *dicta;* and it also cites and explains opposing views.

Jaffe's work was widely distributed, even during his lifetime. As Jaffe himself wrote:

> I received a letter that the scholars of Jerusalem (may it be speedily rebuilt and re-established) join eagerly in regular study of my book, the *Levushim,* each day after the morning service when they leave the synagogue, so that they will be readily conversant with God's Torah.[114]

113. *See id.* (the beginning of the Introduction, "The tailor says . . . "); *see also Sefer Levush Malkhut bi-Khelalo,* after the Introduction, for Jaffe's remarks concerning the glosses to *Levush ha-Tekhelet* and *Levush ha-Ḥur* (which originated in a treatise by Joseph ha-Lavan who inquired of Jaffe regarding it, *see id.*), which also begin with the formula "The tailor says. . . . " Jaffe goes on to refer to "the reason why I sewed these ten royal robes."

114. This statement appears at the end of *Levush ha-Tekhelet* and *Levush ha-Ḥur* after the list of thirty-six customs. In a subsequent passage, Jaffe requested the various communities to set up a daily class to study the *Levushim* after the morning prayers; and he concluded: "These are the words of the one who beseeches, firm in his love of those who study God's Torah and are God-fearing. . . . This day, Friday, the 33rd day of the Omer [5]369 A.M." (= 1609 C.E.; the date is given in the form of the numerical value of the Hebrew letters of the name Mordecai Jaffe). The statement appears in *Levush Malkhut,* ed. Prague, 1609, which was published in the author's lifetime (as is indicated by the title page), but the statement was apparently omitted in all subsequent editions of the *Levushim.* The statement also appears in the Introduction to *Ḥagurat Shemu'el,* a commentary on the *Levushim* by Samuel b. Azriel of Lenzberg, in the following form:

> When the *Levushim* was printed, the scholars of Jerusalem made of it, within the lifetime of the author, belts for their garments with which they strongly girded themselves, joining together for regular study of his book the *Levushim* each day before they leave the synagogue, as the distinguished author himself wrote at the end of *Levush ha-Tekhelet ve-ha-Ḥur.*

David b. Judah, in the Introduction to his book *Migdal David,* commented (ed. Prague, 1616, p. 2a/b):

> Many of those who study the *Levushim* determine the law in accordance with the conclusions of its eminent author because he states the rationale [for those conclusions]. I have also frequently heard many attribute this practice [of following the *Levushim*] to the fact that the author of the *Levushim* lived after our master, Rabbi Joseph Caro, and Rabbi Moses Isserles [Rema], and since he is the later authority, his rulings supersede theirs.

David b. Judah went on to criticize the *Levushim* and asserted that the law should not follow Jaffe's rulings but those of Rema (*see infra* n. 161 for the full quotation). However, his comments provide additional important evidence of the great influence of the *Levushim* in his time (David b. Judah was an older contemporary of Isaiah Horowitz) and of the fact that

Similarly, Elijah Shapiro of Prague, who lived at the end of the seventeenth and the beginning of the eighteenth centuries, reported:

> As to *Sefer ha-Levush,* one's heart delights in it. It attracts the attention both of ordinary people and of students to study and teach it, to establish regular times [for its study] in their courtyards and towns, in the study halls and synagogues. . . . *Sefer ha-Levush* spreads its words like a cloak.[115]

However, the *Levushim* also aroused opposition. Toward the end of Jaffe's life, Joshua Falk, a younger contemporary, was critical of it;[116] and in the following generation there were many criticisms directed against it.[117] These were aimed to some extent at Jaffe's approach to codification, but in the main they questioned his specific rulings and decisions. The *Levushim* never succeeded in achieving the place in the codificatory literature of Jewish law to which its author had aspired.

3. YOM TOV LIPMANN HELLER

In the generation following Maharshal and Mordecai Jaffe, another attempt—apparently the last[118]—was made to return to the codificatory method exemplified by the books of *halakhot* of Alfasi and Asheri—a method that is the direct antithesis of the method developed by Caro and

---

there were many who followed Jaffe's rulings because he explained his decisions and was the more recent authority.

115. Elijah b. Benjamin Wolff Shapiro of Prague, *Sefer Eliyahu Zuta,* Introduction, printed together with the *Levushim* in ed. Prague, 1689, and subsequent editions. The book is a brief commentary on the *Levushim.* The same author wrote a lengthy commentary on the *Levushim* called *Eliyahu Rabba,* which was printed posthumously, together with Sh. Ar. OḤ (Sulzbach, 1757, and recently in facsimile ed.).

116. *See infra* nn. 137 and 142 for Joshua Falk's remarks regarding inaccuracies in the *Levushim.*

117. *See Resp. Penei Yehoshu'a* by Joshua b. Joseph of Cracow (who also wrote *Meginei Shelomo* and was the grandfather of the author of the *Penei Yehoshu'a* novellae on the Talmud), II, YD, #18:

> Regarding the difficulty you found in what Rabbi Mordecai Jaffe, of blessed memory, said, . . . my friend, I do not study his book at all, because I am a student of the author of *Sema* [Joshua Falk], of blessed memory, who taught me, for the sound reasons stated in the Introduction to *Sema,* not to follow his [Jaffe's] rulings. The Lord knows that I have hundreds of points of disagreements with him [Jaffe], but I do not want to respond to him.

See also Shem ha-Gedolim, Books, Letter *lamed,* #12, for a discussion of the *Levushim,* its critics, and its defenders.

118. To a certain degree, the balance had already been tipped some years earlier in favor of Caro's and Rema's method of codification as a result of the approach taken by Joshua Falk in *Sema* (which was printed in Prague in 1614; Heller's *Pilpula Ḥarifta—Ma'adannei Melekh* was printed in the same city five years later; *see* the discussion of *Sema, infra* p. 1411 n. 140, with regard to the date *Sema* was first printed).

Rema. This attempt was made by Yom Tov Lipmann Heller (1579–1654), a disciple of Maharal of Prague, and one of the outstanding halakhic authorities and communal leaders of Polish Jewry in the first half of the seventeenth century. In furtherance of Maharal's teaching that one should attain a thorough knowledge of the Mishnah before studying the Talmud and its commentaries, Heller composed his well-known commentary to the six Orders of the Mishnah, *Tosafot Yom Tov* [The Additional Glosses of Yom Tov]. His purpose was not only to explicate the text of the Mishnah, but also to interweave with the study of the Mishnah the halakhic conclusions on the points the Mishnah discusses.[119] After completing his commentary on the Mishnah, he remarked: "I turned my attention to the Talmud and what followed from it, *i.e.*, the halakhic authorities of every generation after it."[120] As part of this study, Heller surveyed the ongoing differences of opinion as to the proper method of codification of Jewish law and presented his own assessment.

Codificatory literature, according to Heller, can be divided into two categories:

> [In the first category] the author surveys the Talmud as it is and abridges the long passages and fine-spun discussions. The earliest extant book of this type is that of Alfasi, of blessed memory. After him came the great master, Maimonides, of blessed memory, who chose a [second and] different method of abridgment following the path of Rabbenu ha-Kadosh [R. Judah Ha-Nasi], the editor of the Mishnah. He [Maimonides] distilled all the rulings of the Mishnah and the Talmud and arranged them topically, one by one, so that any specific law and its details could be easily located. With lucid brevity, he presented to the people every law as it is, without explanation or statement of reasons—like one issuing decrees and saying "Do this!" and "Do not do that!"

In the course of time, continued Heller, "with the addition of the opinions of the halakhic authorities of France, Germany, and Spain, who searched the Talmud and discovered various new laws and interpretations on the basis of which many existing rules were revised and many new rules were introduced," two other works were written. One was *Piskei ha-Rosh* of Asheri, which follows the arrangement of *Sefer ha-Halakhot* of Alfasi, and the other was the *Turim* of Jacob b. Asher, which is organized in the same way as Maimonides' *Mishneh Torah.*[121]

In Heller's assessment of the two approaches to codification, he insisted that the law should not be determined on the basis of either the

119. *See supra* pp. 1108–1109.

120. Yom Tov Lipmann Heller, *Ma'adannei Yom Tov ve-Divrei Ḥamudot* on *Piskei ha-Rosh,* Introduction (printed in regular Talmud editions before *Piskei ha-Rosh,* Berakhot).

121. *Id.*

Mishneh Torah or the *Turim*. He conceded that Maimonides' work "is exceedingly meritorious because beyond doubt it vivifies a multitude of people who do not have the knowledge required to plumb the depths of each *halakhah* and swim in the great sea of the Talmud. . . . It cannot be praised too much, either as a whole or in its details, for the lucidity of its language and the beauty of its organization." However, for the same reason that the Sages of the Talmud said that those who decide the law solely on the basis of "their Mishnah" wreak havoc in the world,[122] so "it is inconceivable to decide the law on the basis of his [Maimonides'] Mishnah [*i.e.*, the *Mishneh Torah*], for there is no difference whatsoever between deciding from the Mishnah [of R. Judah Ha-Nasi] and deciding from his [Maimonides'] code."[123]

Heller thereupon arrived at the view—similar to that noted above,[124] which gained increasing support as a result of the prevailing attitude as to the proper function of books of *pesakim*—that Maimonides never intended his *Mishneh Torah* to be the exclusive halakhic code.

> And I say that Maimonides himself intended to write his work only for those who are expert in the Talmud and know its subject matter, but who grow weary trying to discover the final outcome of the Talmudic discussions of each law—whether the decision is "permitted" or "forbidden," "not liable" or "liable." [He] also [wrote his book] because not all matters are topically arranged in each Talmudic tractate, *e.g.*, many laws pertaining to the sabbath are to be found in other tractates [*i.e.*, other than Tractate *Shabbat*, which deals with the sabbath], and analogies are drawn from one tractate to another. Therefore, he wisely wrote his book for all those who have already studied the Talmud and know it—such persons may base rulings on his [Maimonides'] work.[125]

Heller held this view not only with regard to Maimonides:

122. TB Sotah 22a. *See supra* n. 40.
123. Introduction, *supra* n. 120, before the passage referred to in the text at n. 121.
124. *See, e.g.*, the passage from Maharal of Prague quoted *supra* n. 41.
125. Introduction, *supra* n. 120. Heller continued:

> I have found convincing proof for my view in the responsa of Maimonides, printed in a very small book. In thirty of them, he was asked what was the proper method of study, and he responded that it was [the study of] his work together with the book of Alfasi. From this it is clear that his benevolent intention was [not to be the exclusive authority,] exactly as I have said.

Heller was apparently referring to Maimonides' response to Phinehas, the judge (*dayyan*) of Alexandria, in which he wrote that he, Maimonides, had never intended that the books of his predecessors "should be burned," and that indeed he himself studied Alfasi's *Sefer ha-Halakhot* with his students (*see supra* pp. 1216–1217). However, that responsum in no way changed Maimonides' objective, which was that his *Mishneh Torah* should serve as the exclusive authoritative source from which the law should be determined. *See supra* pp. 1185–1186.

> I have no doubt that this was also the intention of the author of the *Turim:* that his book should be studied together with the book of his father, Rosh [Asheri], of blessed memory. . . . Even the great rabbi, Joseph Caro, of blessed memory, who contributed so much in his book *Bet Yosef,* from which he abstracted the work he called the *Shulḥan Arukh* (which follows the arrangement found in the *Turim,* always using Maimonides' style), never intended that his book should be the source for legal decisions. (May Heaven forfend such a thought!) [He intended] only that one who studies the *Turim* with the commentary of *Bet Yosef* but has difficulty in finding the halakhic conclusion would be able to comprehend it from the *Shulḥan Arukh.* That was his entirely proper intention.[126]

This hypothesis as to the intentions of the authors of books of *pesakim* is directly contrary to what we know of the factors that led to their composition, as well as contrary to the authors' own statements. Maimonides clearly underscored in his Introduction to the *Mishneh Torah* that "a person who first reads the Torah and then this work [*Mishneh Torah*] will know from it all of the Oral Law, and there will be no need to read any other book [written] between them." Both Jacob b. Asher and Joseph Caro explicitly declared that they intended their codes to be the source and basis of legal decisions, and not mere supplements to *Piskei ha-Rosh* or *Bet Yosef.* However, the general attitude as to the proper function of books of *pesakim* had changed so drastically that Heller could say "Heaven forfend" the thought that those great halakhic authorities had ever intended their works to be the sole source for legal decisions or to obviate the need to consult the underlying halakhic literature.

Notwithstanding the modesty of the codificatory intentions, as Heller saw them, of Maimonides, Jacob b. Asher, and Joseph Caro, Heller still rejected their codificatory methodology and preferred the approach of Alfasi and Asheri:

> It seems to me axiomatic that there can be no comparison between, on the one hand, studying a subject by examining the debate on the law and its implications, and on the other hand, studying [only] the conclusions that followed from the debate; for it is necessary . . . to investigate the source and the objective and identify the authors of the statements. . . . Yet even more important is the fact that studying the debate on the law enables one to know which points are sound and valid and which are illogical and invalid, and to learn the methodology of analogy and rebuttal. . . . The second method of study is of no value for this at all. This is clear to any open-minded and intelligent person.[127]

126. Introduction, *supra* n. 120.
127. *Id.*

Yom Tov Lipmann Heller thus clearly favored the format of a book of *halakhot,* since that format enables the reader to review the sources for each halakhic conclusion and thereby judge for himself the correctness of the opinions and the conclusions. Heller, therefore, concluded that Asheri's *Piskei ha-Rosh* represented the ideal code in both form and content, declaring: "Arise and take hold of it because it is the choicest to be studied and taught in Israel."[128] However, even *Piskei ha-Rosh* required a commentary to explain its meaning, to clear up difficulties and rebut objections, to correct errors that had crept into its text, and to add laws that had come into being after it was written; moreover, on occasion, rulings contrary to Asheri had to be made. In order to satisfy these needs, Heller wrote an extremely comprehensive commentary on *Piskei ha-Rosh* that thoroughly discusses every subject dealt with by Asheri to the extent that it almost transforms Asheri's work from a book of *halakhot* into a commentary on the Talmud.[129]

C. Opposition to the *Shulḥan Arukh* as the Sole Basis for Legal Decisions; Commentaries on the *Shulḥan Arukh*

Most leading halakhic authorities during Caro's and Rema's lifetimes and in the immediately following generation apparently held the same views of the *Shulḥan Arukh* as those discussed above.[130] It thus appeared that the joint codificatory creation of Caro and Rema, like all the preceding codes,

128. *Id.* The quotation in full is:

> Give honor and respect to books that follow this methodology, which we have demonstrated to be better. They are the books of Rif [Alfasi] and Rabbenu Asher [Asheri]. I have already told you truthfully that the book of Rabbenu Asher includes what Rif wrote and also supplements it—adding the opinions of authorities who preceded him [Asheri] and what he himself succeeded in teaching the people. Therefore, arise and take hold of it because it is the choicest to be studied and taught in Israel.

129. *See id.* A description of Heller's commentary and its organization then follows, as to which *see supra* p. 1254.

130. *See, e.g., Resp. Penei Yehoshu'a,* II, EH, #52:

> [Question:] When I find a ruling in the *Shulḥan Arukh* that an act is permitted, but on the basis of a serious objection [to the ruling], I believe it to be forbidden, must I declare it to be permitted or [if I declare it to be forbidden, must I] reimburse from my own pocket [the person to whom I cause a loss by my stringent ruling]?
>
> [Response:] May Heaven save us from such a thought! A judge must be guided only by what his own eyes see, and Jephthah in his generation [is equal to Samuel in his, although not as learned]. Thank God, I have already begun to compose [a work containing] important critiques of [decisions of] both early and later authorities, for in matters involving the words of the living God, no favor may be shown. I am also confident that the great and pious rabbi who wrote *Bet Yosef* would not have taken it amiss.

It appears that the main opponents of the *Shulḥan Arukh* were the leading halakhic authorities; however, many people followed its rulings even in this period. *See infra* pp. 1417–1418 and n. 161.

had failed to resolve the problem of the codification of Jewish law. However, there were other important halakhic authorities in this period, who, while also rejecting the *Shulḥan Arukh* as the sole source for legal decisions, adopted a different approach to obviate the errors that might ensue from such reliance on the *Shulḥan Arukh.* Far from impeding the acceptance of the *Shulḥan Arukh,* their approach was one of the major factors paving the way for the *Shulḥan Arukh's* acceptance (with certain limitations) as the preeminent code of Jewish law. Their method was to supplement the code by composing works that would comment upon it and become an integral part of it. First and foremost of those who adopted this method was Joshua Falk, the author of *Sefer Me'irat Einayim,* known by its acronym *Sema.*

1. JOSHUA FALK

Joshua b. Alexander ha-Kohen Falk (1555–1614) was the outstanding disciple of both Maharshal and Rema. In Falk's Introduction to his commentaries on the *Turim* and the *Shulḥan Arukh,*[131] he first presented a thorough history of the *Halakhah* from its beginnings until Caro's *Bet Yosef* and *Shulḥan Arukh* and Rema's *Darkhei Moshe* and *Mappah.*[132] He then provided a brief autobiographical sketch that relates that he initially had dedicated his energies chiefly to delving into "the depths of the sea of the Talmud" with his students. This study resulted in novellae to fourteen tractates of the Talmud, which had unfortunately been totally destroyed by fire. From that time, he concentrated on studying the Talmud together with the codificatory literature, beginning with Alfasi's *Sefer ha-Halakhot,* so as to be able "to clearly explain every difficult matter, as God has commanded us to do from His heavenly abode." Consequently, "I also directed my attention to the work *Bet Yosef* to see whether it met the needs of our own generation; and I discovered that it did not, due to our intellectual shortcomings, for several reasons."[133]

Falk enumerated five such reasons: (a) because of the great mass of material from the Mishnah, Talmud, codes, and responsa contained in *Bet Yosef,* "it is difficult for any reader to arrive at a clear understanding of the

131. *See* his Introduction to his books *Bet Yisra'el* and *Sefer Me'irat Einayim* at the beginning of Sh. Ar. ḤM. Our citations follow the pagination and columns of ed. Lemberg, 1876. In current editions, the Introduction is printed at the end of Sh. Ar. ḤM.

132. His survey has an abundance of material, particularly on codificatory literature from Alfasi until his own time.

133. Introduction, *supra* n. 131 at col. 4 (toward the bottom). Falk then went on to enumerate his reasons. Although earlier (in the first half of the column) he had noted that in *Bet Yosef* the legal determinations were made on the basis of the majority opinion among the three "renowned codifiers" and that the book does not contain sufficient references to the opinions of the Ashkenazic authorities, these complaints, which relate to Caro's methodology, were not included among Falk's criticisms of *Bet Yosef.*

law and to extract exactly what he needs out of the jumble of the material"; (b) many laws were not adequately explained "and he [Caro] was cryptic where he should have explained at length" (a particularly troublesome obstacle to deciding matters of civil law); (c) many of Caro's explanations are inconclusive; (d) many of Caro's queries can be resolved; and, (e) above all, *Bet Yosef* was not a careful and comprehensive commentary on the *Turim*. Thus, Falk's criticism of *Bet Yosef* did not concern its codificatory methodology, but centered on the correctness of particular statements in the book.[134]

Falk's attitude to Caro's *Shulḥan Arukh* and Rema's *Mappah* was quite different; he categorically rejected the notion that legal decisions could properly be based exclusively on them:

> I also directed my attention to the *Shulḥan Arukh,* written by the outstanding authorities, Rabbi Joseph Caro and Rabbi Moses Isserles, . . . and I concluded that while their intentions had been good, the book is an enigma to most readers. They had intended it to be used as a basis for decision only by those who had first studied the *Turim* with the *Bet Yosef* commentary and thereby acquired an understanding of each law and its rationale according to the Talmud and the great authors. The purpose of the *Shulḥan Arukh* was merely to refresh the recollection of such persons. But this is not the situation today . . . when many consider themselves to be intellectually gifted and insist on learning the Torah while standing on one foot [*i.e.,* without long and arduous study]. They prattle and make legal rulings [solely] on the basis of the *Shulḥan Arukh.* Such persons destroy our people, abrogate the covenant of our God's Torah, and do themselves great harm. Whoever, even if qualified to render halakhic decisions, relies on the *Shulḥan Arukh,* which is a "closed and sealed" book, will never fully understand the laws contained in that book; and he will certainly not be able to apply them by analogy to other cases. This is so because of the extremely cryptic style of the distinguished authors in that book.[135]

Joshua Falk, like other critics of the *Shulḥan Arukh,*[136] some of whom have been discussed above, believed that Caro and Rema themselves never intended that their work should be the sole basis for legal rulings, even though that belief, which became the accepted view among halakhic au-

134. *See supra* n. 133.

135. Introduction, *supra* n. 131 at cols. 4–5.

136. *See Yad Malakhi,* II, Kelalei ha-Shulḥan Arukh u-Rema [Principles of the *Shulḥan Arukh* and Rema], #1. *See also* Isaac Jesurun, *Panim Ḥadashot* (as to which, *see infra* pp. 1433–1434), Introduction: "It is well known that legal rulings should not be based on the *Shulḥan Arukh,* because its author intended it to be only a key [*i.e.,* index] to open the gates of the great house [*Bet Yosef*]."

thorities, is diametrically opposed to the express declarations of the two authors.

Falk undertook to remedy the deficiencies of *Bet Yosef* and transform the *Shulḥan Arukh* into a code that could properly be used as a source for legal rulings.[137] To this end, he composed a work consisting of four main sections (*roshim,* lit. "heads"). Three sections consisted of commentaries, novellae, and supplements to the *Turim:* the *Perishah* and the *Derishah* (two commentaries on the *Turim*) and *Haggahot* (Glosses), which was first intended as a supplement to the *Turim* but later became a collection of glosses incorporated into Rema's *Darkhei Moshe.* In these three sections, which have already been described in our discussion of the *Turim,*[138] Falk, on the basis of reasoned arguments and proofs, explained and interpreted the texts of the *Turim* and *Bet Yosef* and also added laws that had accumulated since the time of those two books. All of this, however, did not prevent decisions from being made solely on the basis of the *Shulḥan Arukh,* since, as Falk had himself pointed out, those who made their decisions on the basis of the *Shulḥan Arukh* did not usually consult either the *Turim* or *Bet Yosef* and would certainly not consult the commentaries and novellae he had added to them. The failure to consult these two books was due in no small measure to the difficulty and inconvenience of studying two separate books written in two different styles, and also to the vast bulk of the material quoted at length in *Bet Yosef.* In order to meet this problem Falk also composed a fourth section:

> a commentary on the *Shulḥan Arukh* . . . [of] our teachers, Rabbi Joseph Caro and Rabbi Moses [Isserles], . . . which because of its brevity requires an extensive commentary to explain it, to make it suitable, and to harmonize [difficulties in] it, so as to enlighten the eyes of the reader. . . .[139]

137. Falk subsequently noted that, although Mordecai Jaffe intended to remedy this deficiency in the *Shulḥan Arukh* by clarifying its obscure and cryptic statements and to that end "wrote the reasons for the laws and believed that he had thus prevented readers from erring and had done his duty to God and man," the reasons and explanations given by Jaffe did not correctly reflect the various sources. Falk attributed this to Jaffe's preoccupation with communal affairs and the administration of his *yeshivah,* which left him insufficient time to engage in research, and to the limitations of Jaffe's library. Falk also found fault with Jaffe's work in other respects; *see infra* n. 142.

138. *See supra* p. 1303.

139. *See also* Introduction, *supra* n. 131 at col. 5 (middle):

> Although the other authorities of this generation are far greater than I [lit. "their little finger is thicker than my loins"], and it is they who should have undertaken this task, nevertheless when I saw that they did not do this and that their goal was a different one—to educate students by way of *pilpul* and to create a "learned generation"—I decided that I would neither ignore nor delay this sacred duty.

Falk here hinted at the employment of the pilpulistic method by many students in the *yeshivot* and their failure to engage in study for the purpose of arriving at the correct halakhic

Falk's commentary was intended not only to explain the contents of the *Shulḥan Arukh*, but to become an integral part of it:

> I have called the fourth section, which is a commentary on the *Shulḥan Arukh*, *Sefer Me'irat Einayim* [The Book that Enlightens the Eyes, abbreviated as *Sema*] because it will truly enlighten the eyes of those who consult the obscure and cryptic statements of the *Shulḥan Arukh* and its glosses [of Rema]; without this commentary, it is forbidden to rely on it [the *Shulḥan Arukh*] for legal decisions.[140]

---

conclusions. However, it is only a slight innuendo. While it has a negative tone, it is not such sharp criticism as that of Maharal of Prague, Maharshal, Mordecai Jaffe, or even Joel Sirkes (*see infra*). A later passage in Falk's Introduction, however, raises questions still unanswered:

> I will speak, and I will not be ashamed [even] before kings. I will pay no heed to the band of frivolous idlers or to the bombastic tongue that has said to me, "You will build, and I will destroy"—even before reading a word. It is only arrogance that causes this. I know that all sincere readers [lit. "all whose hearts turn to the fear of Heaven"] will judge me as having proper intentions.

To what and to whom Falk was referring are questions requiring further research.

140. Introduction, *supra* n. 131 at cols. 5–6. There is a persistent error that should be noted regarding the date of the first printing of *Sema*. In two bibliographies of Hebrew books and treatises, namely, H.D. Friedberg, *Bet Eked Sefarim*, II, p. 533, and P.Y. Cohen, *Oẓar ha-Be'urim ve-ha-Perushim*, p. 386, *Sema* is listed as having been printed in Prague in 1606. Apparently, both authors copied the information from I. Benjacob, *Oẓar ha-Sefarim*, Letter *mem*, #98, pp. 278–279. However, Benjacob, in his note to the listing, expressed reservations as to the accuracy of the information, which was taken from *Siftei Yeshenim*. (He pointed out that *Siftei Yeshenim* makes no mention of any ed. 1614.) However, it is clear that the first edition of *Sema* was Prague, 1614. The title page of that edition reads as follows:

> *Shulḥan Arukh Ḥoshen Mishpat*, with the commentary *Me'irat Einayim* by . . . Joshua Falk b. Alexander Katz, of blessed memory, who sat in learned collegium with his students . . . in Lemberg [Lvov], and because of its utility, the scholars of Poland and Russia urged him to have it printed for the benefit of the public. And so he did. He sent it from his *yeshivah* in Lvov to Prague to be printed. However, before the printers began the printing, the learned author was called to the Academy on High.

The title page also relates that Joshua Falk on his deathbed directed his sons to use his entire estate for the printing of his books and the encouragement of their study. However, the estate did not cover even half of the printing costs; and therefore only some of his books were printed, in order to finance from the proceeds of their sale the printing of the rest. The date appears on the title page in the form of a Biblical verse (Leviticus 10:3), with bold print highlighting the letters whose numerical values add up to the year of publication. Their sum is 374 (= [5]374 A.M. = 1614 C.E.). Apparently, one of these letters (the letter *yod*, whose value is ten) was not recognized as such, and another (the letter *bet*, whose value is two) was erroneously read in its place; as a result, the author of *Siftei Yeshenim* read the date as 366 (=[5]366 A.M. = 1606 C.E.). He did not, therefore, refer to ed. 1614 because he believed it to have been printed in 1606. J.L. Maimon, "Shulḥan Arukh ve-Nos'ei Kelov" [The *Shulḥan Arukh* and Its Commentaries], *Koveẓ R. Yosef Caro*, 1969, pp. 50–51, was therefore in error when he wrote that Joshua Falk was very happy when he saw his *Sema* in print.

Joshua Falk's solution to the problem of codifying Jewish law was both novel and significant: in order to make it possible to decide questions of law on the basis of the *Shulḥan Arukh* and Rema's glosses,[141] while guarding against erroneous decisions resulting from misunderstanding its text, Falk wrote a commentary that was to be an essential and integral part of the *Shulḥan Arukh.* The *Shulḥan Arukh* would still be the preeminent code, but decisions relying upon it could be made only after an examination of the commentary printed in the margin of every paragraph. This would remedy the failure on the part of decisionmakers to consult the *Turim* and *Bet Yosef.* Annexed to the *Shulḥan Arukh* itself, at the margin of the text of each law, would be a brief discussion of the law's sources and rationale.

Falk did not go so far as to make the commentary a part of Caro's and Rema's text, as Mordecai Jaffe, the author of the *Levushim,* had done; he considered it improper to alter the original text of the *Shulḥan Arukh.* Falk's solution enabled a judge to examine the original text of the *Shulḥan Arukh,* study the commentary in the margin, and decide for himself whether the explanation offered was correct. If the judge believed that explanation to be incorrect, it was entirely proper for him to explain the text differently. By placing his commentary on the same page as the text of the *Shulḥan Arukh,* Falk sought only to ensure that the judge would examine it before rendering his decision and thus carefully consider the meaning of the terse texts of the *Shulḥan Arukh.* Once the judge did this, Falk continued, "I have never insisted that my opinion must be accepted; if it becomes clear that I did not correctly understand the views of the authors and that their intent was other [than what I wrote], the blame falls on me alone."[142]

141. In fact, judges and rabbis did base their decisions on the *Shulḥan Arukh,* but most of the leading halakhic authorities opposed this practice. *See infra* pp. 1417–1418 and n. 161.

142. This important principle that in order to preserve the full opportunity of others to make their own interpretations, no changes should be made in the text of the original source, was more fully stated by Falk as follows (Introduction, *supra* n. 131 at 2nd half of col. 6):

> I have placed my commentary alongside the text of the *Shulḥan Arukh* and its glosses, and indicated in it by means of the letters of the alphabet everything that requires explanation or clarification. [*I.e.,* the letters of the alphabet were placed in the text of the *Shulḥan Arukh* to indicate the points in the text to which Falk's comments relate, in the same way that footnote numbers would be used in current texts.] I did not integrate [my comments] into the texts of the eminent authors, because of the well-known statement by Judah ibn Tibbon in the Introduction to his Hebrew translation of the Arabic text of *Ḥovot ha-Levavot* . . . from which I drew a lesson with regard to my commentary on the *Shulḥan Arukh* of our masters, Rabbi Joseph Caro and Rabbi Moses [Isserles].
>
> These texts are obscure and cryptic in many places, being brief but pithy; but I decided not to rewrite their general and detailed statements as I understood them, and not to supplement them with rationales or [other] additions in order to compose out of them a separate book, as did that eminent rabbi, Mordecai Jaffe. For truly that was

Falk's commentary, as his Introduction states, presents new laws, harmonizes inconsistencies in the *Shulḥan Arukh,* and quotes from the *Mishneh Torah,* the *Turim,* and other codes "when it is necessary to quote them." The commentary gives the source references for the laws, and usually directs the reader to the codes and responsa from which a law was taken so that "if he desires . . . to go to the source of the law in order to draw analogies from it," he will be able to go back to the text of the source. Like the great codifiers before him, Falk sought to make it easier for the reader to find the law.[143] However, he went even further and sought to make it easier for the reader to find the source of the law: "In order to make the reader's search easier, I have put a source reference next to every law."[144] In this

---

> a serious error, for the reason given by Judah ibn Tibbon. I therefore followed the path of the early masters and left the statements of the eminent authors in their place, in their original language, making no changes [lit. "without raising my hand against the Lord's anointed or against their language"], because I feared for my soul lest I be burned by [touching] their fiery coals. All I did was place my commentary beside them. I have never insisted that my opinion must be accepted; if it becomes clear that I did not correctly understand the views of the authors and that their intent was other [than what I wrote], the blame falls on me alone.

143. *See* at the end of his Introduction:

> Since the text and glosses of the *Shulḥan Arukh* [are such that] . . . a person seeking a specific law may weary himself [in the search] yet not even find a hint of it . . . , I have therefore prepared new tables of contents, which list in detail the main laws and subjects [treated] in each chapter. . . . In this I have followed the practice of the early masters, namely, the tables of contents at the beginning of *Resp. Asheri* and *Sefer Adam ve-Ḥavvah* and [*Sefer*] *Meisharim* of Rabbenu Jeroham.

For other techniques adopted by Falk to facilitate the study of his commentary, *see id.*, Introduction, preceding s.v. Bet Yisra'el, and *infra* text accompanying n. 145; *cf.* also the detailed subject index of Sh. Ar. ḤM, called *Peri Megadim,* prepared by Samuel b. Alexander, who was active in Germany at the end of the seventeenth century. That index is extremely useful and has been attractively printed in Sh. Ar., ed. El ha-Mekorot, 1957.

144. Joshua Falk's remarks regarding his source references as compared to those previously provided for Rema's glosses are of interest (Introduction, *supra* n. 131 at col. 6 (toward the bottom)):

> The reader will appreciate the great difference between the source references that the printers in Cracow inserted into the *Shulḥan Arukh* recently printed there, and the references that, with the help of Heaven, I have provided. They gave references only for Rema's glosses, and none whatsoever for Caro's text, because they took the references from *Darkhei Moshe,* which Rema wrote. Perhaps they thought that everything that Caro wrote in his *Shulḥan Arukh* is to be found in the *Turim,* which is readily available to everyone, and that therefore there was no need for source references. They did not pay attention to the great number of new laws—not mentioned in the *Turim*—introduced by Caro in every chapter of his *Shulḥan Arukh.* Caro listed these laws in the tables of contents he prepared [for *Bet Yosef*] at the beginning of each *Tur,* and very few of them were omitted from the *Shulḥan Arukh.*
>
> Even those laws dealt with in the *Turim* are generally stated by Caro in the *Shulḥan Arukh* not in the language of the *Turim* but rather in the language of Maimonides. Caro followed the *Turim* only in its topical arrangement. It is well known

"twofold" assistance to the reader, Falk seemingly expressed the dual objectives that were becoming crystallized in the codification of Jewish law—determination and summarization of the law, and, at the same time, linking the law to its origins and sources.

Another innovation in *Sema* is of interest. Falk used special markings to highlight those laws as to which "I have disagreed with the great masters—Rabbi Joseph Caro, Rabbi Moses Isserles, or Rabbi Mordecai Jaffe—whether in regard to their interpretation, their statement of legal rules, or their innovations."[145] In writing his commentary, Falk did not proceed in the order of the *Shulḥan Arukh:* he did not begin with the first section, *Oraḥ Ḥayyim,* which concerns religious law, but rather with the last section, *Ḥoshen Mishpat,* which deals mainly with civil and public law. He put *Ḥoshen Mishpat* first because "it is the 'essence of Torah' and everyone looks to it to determine the law." This comment is instructive evidence of the importance of Jewish civil and public law in the practical affairs of the Jewish community at that time.

Falk had intended to write a commentary on the entire *Shulḥan Arukh,* but he was able to complete his commentary only on *Ḥoshen Mishpat.*[146] However, with his *Sema,* Falk made a significant contribution not only to the understanding of *Shulḥan Arukh Ḥoshen Mishpat* in particular, but also to the resolution of the overall problem of the codification of Jewish law. By writing a commentary that was intended to be—and did become—an integral part of the *Shulḥan Arukh,* he paved the way for the acceptance of the *Shulḥan Arukh* as the definitive and authoritative code of Jewish law and for the resolution of the problem of codification as well, as described below.

> that although Maimonides' Hebrew is pure, it is terse and cryptic because he stated the laws in the compressed style of the Mishnah and the Talmud; and since Caro copied them in the *Shulḥan Arukh* out of context, they are difficult to understand. I have, therefore, indicated all the sources [in the *Mishneh Torah*] by section and chapter and even by paragraph, because every chapter in Maimonides is divided into numbered paragraphs. I have done so to make it easier for the reader to find what he is seeking. Even the source references added by the printers to certain laws in Rema's glosses are truncated and inaccurate, and all but worthless.

See also supra p. 1360 and n. 186.

145. Introduction, *supra* n. 144.

146. *See id.*, preceding the passage quoted in the text accompanying nn. 144–145. At the end of the Introduction, Falk wrote: "Therefore my heart is ready, trusting that the Lord, who invigorates the weary like me and strengthens the weak, will grant me the privilege to begin this work and complete it on all four parts of the *Shulḥan Arukh,* without blunder or mistake."

2. JOEL SIRKES

Joel Sirkes (1561–1640), a younger contemporary of Joshua Falk and one of the outstanding scholars and leaders of Polish Jewry, adopted the same approach as Falk to ensure the acceptance of the *Shulḥan Arukh* as the authoritative code of Jewish law. He also complained bitterly against the extravagances of the pilpulistic method of Talmudic study and against those "whose eyes are closed and whose hearts are as stone to the truth of Torah. . . . Do not turn to the arrogant and the deceitful; their foolish methods will not help you,[147] . . . for they engage in hair-splitting exercises . . . and their utterances are fallacious."[148] However, Sirkes, like Maharsha, approved of in-depth study of the Talmud when the objective was to uncover its true meaning, like "the Tosafists and the other commentators who, filled with novellae as a pomegranate [is filled with seeds], descended to the depths of the sea of the Talmud and came to the surface with their hands full of glowing, brilliant, precious stones."[149]

Sirkes' insistence on intensive study of the *Halakhah* went hand in hand with his strong opposition to making legal rulings solely on the basis of the *Shulḥan Arukh:* "You surely already know that those who are drawn to making decisions in reliance on the *Shulḥan Arukh* do not rule in accordance with the *Halakhah,* because they do not know the origin or author of the law; they fabricate their own rationales and thus increase controversy among the Jewish people."[150] To the assertion that "the main subject of study should be Scripture, so that the student will be able to read from the scroll of the Torah according to its special cantillation and grammar, but the study of Talmud is unnecessary since everything is available in the *Shulḥan Arukh,*"[151] Sirkes reacted as follows:[152]

> I answered . . . calmly: It is impossible to decide most cases on the basis of the *Shulḥan Arukh* because most of its statements are cryptic, like those of Maimonides, particularly in the area of civil law.[153] In addition, we see that very many doubts have arisen with regard to laws that are applied every day; and the great halakhic authorities do not agree on most matters, so that one needs exceedingly great wisdom and erudition to be able to make adequately grounded decisions. Anyone unaccustomed to study the Talmud cannot render a correct decision, as is stated in the Talmud in chapter 3 of [Tractate]

147. *Cf.* TB Ketubbot 17a.
148. *Baḥ* on *Tur* ḤM, Introduction.
149. *Id.*
150. *Resp. Baḥ ha-Yeshanot* #80 (at the beginning of the response). *See also id.* #136.
151. *Resp. Baḥ ha-Ḥadashot* #42 (at the beginning of the response).
152. *Id.*
153. *See* Joshua Falk's statement, *supra,* to the effect that brevity is a problem that is most severe in regard to the area of the law covered by *Ḥoshen Mishpat.*

> *Sotah.*[154] It is very difficult to decide even on the basis of the other codes; how much more so on the basis of the *Shulḥan Arukh* alone.[155]

Like Joshua Falk, Joel Sirkes planned to write a commentary first on the *Turim* and then on the *Shulḥan Arukh,* apparently in order to facilitate the acceptance of the *Shulḥan Arukh.* Sirkes esteemed Caro's *Bet Yosef* very highly because of its broad scope, its explanations and final determinations of the law, and the fact that "as a result of its having been written, groups of scholars and students have been strengthened to gather together, glowing with enthusiasm [to study] halakhic rules that are well edited and set out."[156] That the publication of Joseph Caro's work had resulted in an increase in study with the purpose of clarification of the law is an interesting point that Joel Sirkes was the first to make. However, as to Caro's main purpose—to clarify and summarize the law—Sirkes felt *Bet Yosef* was an inadequate commentary on the *Turim.* Many matters had not been explained at all, and explanations that were given were vulnerable to "powerful objections":[157]

> [Therefore,] in order to satisfy the desire of the leading scholars and my outstanding students . . . who have encircled and pressed me to publish the thoughts and ideas that they heard from me in the course of halakhic discourse when I studied the *Turim* with them here in Cracow, a major Jewish community (may it so be until the Redeemer comes), I have decided to write an explanatory commentary on the *Turim* that will also explain the statements of other authors cited in the *Turim* when they need further explanation. All [my comments] will be based on the Talmudic discussions and the commentaries of Rashi, the Tosafists, and the other commentators and authorities. [I will] also resolve difficulties in its [the *Turim*'s] rulings and explain it with clear proof, as much as God will help me to do this. In some places, I will also quote and explain the statements of *Bet Yosef,* pointing out their difficulties, whether relating to [*Bet Yosef*'s] comments on the *Turim* or its explanations of statements made by Maimonides or other codifiers, and I will explain them [*Bet Yosef*'s statements] in a different, more acceptable way. . . . The culmination of [our] explanations and comments will be the determination of the law, with Heaven's help. [We will] also clarify obscurities resulting from the variant texts of the book.[158]

154. TB Sotah 22a: "The *tannaim* wreak havoc in the world . . . because they decide the law on the basis of their Mishnah." *See supra* n. 40.

155. *See also* later in the responsum, after s.v. Ve-ha-ta'am ha-sheni.

156. *Baḥ* on *Tur* ḤM, Introduction.

157. *Id.*

158. *Id.* For further information on Joel Sirkes, *see supra* pp. 1303–1304.

Joel Sirkes' commentary on the *Turim,* which he called *Bayit Ḥadash* [A New House], known by its acronym as *Baḥ,* was intended to be the first part of his codificatory work. This is clear from the latter part of his Introduction, where he remarks that in *Bayit Ḥadash* he will also discuss Joshua Falk's lengthy commentary on the *Shulḥan Arukh* (*Sema*), because Falk's "commentary and explanations give rise to laws that the early authorities had never contemplated. I, therefore, felt constrained to alert and warn the reader who wishes to draw conclusions for actual practice to rule correctly,"[159] when, in Sirkes' opinion, *Sema* was not correct. However, these comments on *Sema* were made only briefly in *Bayit Ḥadash,* since Sirkes intended to expand them in a separate commentary that he hoped to write on the *Shulḥan Arukh:* "If God will grant me life, I will treat [the matters] at length with clear proofs in the work I have begun to write on the *Shulḥan Arukh.*"[160] Sirkes thus sought to follow Joshua Falk's example and write a separate commentary on the *Shulḥan Arukh;* and it may be assumed that, like Falk, he considered that to be the way to ensure the acceptance of the *Shulḥan Arukh* as the code of Jewish law. Unfortunately, Sirkes was unable to continue his commentary on the *Shulḥan Arukh,* and even his initial effort has not survived.

IV. THE ACCEPTANCE OF THE *SHULḤAN ARUKH* AS THE DEFINITIVE AND AUTHORITATIVE CODE OF JEWISH LAW

A. The Completion of the Codificatory Structure of the *Shulḥan Arukh* by Its Commentaries

In composing his *Sefer Me'irat Einayim,* Joshua Falk not only created one of the greatest and most important commentaries on the *Shulḥan Arukh,* but also facilitated the halakhic authorities' acceptance of the *Shulḥan Arukh* as the binding and authoritative code of Jewish law.[161] By attaching to the text

159. *Baḥ* on *Tur* ḤM, Introduction.

160. *Id.*

161. There is a great deal of evidence that notwithstanding the opposition of the leading halakhic authorities, many rabbis and judges did render decisions on the basis of the *Shulḥan Arukh. See, e.g., Resp. Penei Yehoshu'a,* II, EH, #52, by Joshua b. Joseph of Cracow: "I well know that even if Joshua b. Nun had said it, you would not obey me, in line with the practice of the rabbis of our country, may the Lord preserve them, that a law printed in the *Shulḥan Arukh* may no more be changed, God forbid, than a law contained in the Torah of Moses." Subsequently, however, the responsum does state that one may disagree with the *Shulḥan Arukh* upon finding a serious objection to its statement of the law, because a judge can rule only in accordance with his own understanding. For more on this responsum, *see*

of the *Shulḥan Arukh* an authoritative commentary that a judge was required to consult before making a decision in reliance on the *Shulḥan Arukh,* Falk completed the codificatory structure of the *Shulḥan Arukh* and at long last solved the perennial problem that had beset every codifier of Jewish law: how to preserve the continuity of the law and its link to the sources, and present the full range of its variant legal opinions. The debates of many generations that had wrestled with this problem had clearly indicated that Jewish law was not prepared to accept a code that categorically stated the law and that was severed—even if only in form—from its sources.

Maimonides' *Mishneh Torah,* which had not maintained the connection with the sources, either in the text or in the margins, was not accepted as a definitive code; and even the *Shulḥan Arukh,* preceded and accompa-

---

supra n. 130. *See also supra* n. 78 for the view of Isaiah Horowitz that generally the rulings of Rema should be followed.

An opinion similar to that of Isaiah Horowitz, but also with regard to Joseph Caro, was expressed by David b. Judah, the author of *Migdal David.* He criticized Mordecai Jaffe's *Levushim* and rebutted Jaffe's criticisms of Caro and Rema. David b. Judah's Introduction states (ed. Prague, 1616, p. 2a/b):

> The consummate scholar, the eminent Rabbi Moses Isserles [Rema], . . . left after him no room for criticism. His decisions are accepted throughout all Jewry. . . . Many of those who study the *Levushim* determine the law in accordance with the conclusions of its eminent author because he states the rationale [for those conclusions]. I have also frequently heard many attribute this practice [of following the *Levushim*] to the fact that the author of the *Levushim* lived after our master, Rabbi Joseph Caro, and Rabbi Moses Isserles; and since he is the later authority, his rulings supersede theirs. However, many Torah scholars follow the rulings of Rabbi Moses Isserles; and the outstanding authorities in particular render decisions in accordance with his opinions, for they already know the sources from which these opinions were taken. . . . We are dependent on the words of Rabbi Joseph Caro and Rabbi Moses Isserles, and we must all follow in their paths because their rulings have been accepted throughout Jewry.

Migdal David was endorsed by Ephraim of Luntshits, the author of *Keli Yakar,* and by Isaiah Horowitz, the author of *Shenei Luḥot ha-Berit* (*see* the reverse side of the title page), who refer to the author of *Migdal David* as "the venerable elder, the exalted master, Rabbi David b. Judah, of blessed memory." It thus appears that David b. Judah lived not long after Caro and Rema. (His statements at the end of his Introduction and at the end of the book reveal that he was born in Russia. The Introduction also contains interesting material on Joshua Falk's methodology and decision-making process.) *See also infra* n. 168 for Ḥayyim b. Beẓalel's views. Maharshal (*supra* p. 1391), Joshua Falk (*supra* p. 1409), and Joel Sirkes (*supra* p. 1415) all indicate that it had become customary to decide the law on the basis of the *Shulḥan Arukh*—a practice to which they strongly objected. However, after Falk advanced the idea that the *Shulḥan Arukh* could be used as the basis for legal rulings so long as his commentary was first consulted, the leading halakhic authorities became reconciled to the use of the *Shulḥan Arukh,* provided that its accompanying commentaries were also examined before any decision was reached. Several of these authorities themselves composed commentaries on the *Shulḥan Arukh. See* the discussion *infra.*

nied as it was by *Bet Yosef,* in which the relevant sources were collected and preserved, did not meet the needs of the *Halakhah.* The sources had to be linked—in the literary structure itself—to the laws stated categorically in the code without reference to their authors; and the only way to do this was to attach to the text of the code an authoritative commentary that would be printed alongside each law and that a judge would be required to consult before reaching a decision.

Once the way was found, it was implemented very quickly. In the generation following the appearance of *Sema,* the leading halakhic authorities adorned all four parts of the *Shulḥan Arukh* with their commentaries: *Turei Zahav* (known as *Taz*) by David ha-Levi, *Siftei Kohen* (known as *Shakh*) by Shabbetai ha-Kohen, *Ḥelkat Meḥokek* by Moses Lima, *Bet Shemu'el* by Samuel b. Uri Shraga Phoebus, and *Magen Avraham* by Abraham Abele Gumbiner. These halakhic authorities also emphasized, as Joshua Falk had done[162]—but even more strongly than he—that it was perfectly legitimate for a reader to disagree with their comments and conclusions, and that they did not insist that their opinions be accepted, but merely that "truth will [have an opportunity to] show its way."[163] They sought only "to awaken the heart [*i.e.,* arouse the attention] of the reader; and the [opinion] that he, in his clear intelligence, chooses, he should adopt."[164]

The study of these commentaries became an integral and indispensable part of the process of decision making on the basis of the *Shulḥan Arukh,* and in the course of time their opinions were endowed with decisive authority.[165] The works listed above were—and still are—the classic and authoritative commentaries on the *Shulḥan Arukh;* and because of—and pursuant to—them, the laws of the *Shulḥan Arukh* achieved authoritative and binding effect.[166]

B. Historical Circumstances as a Factor in the Acceptance of the *Shulḥan Arukh*

It is possible, and even likely, that the problem of codification of Jewish law would not have been resolved as described above were it not for the calam-

162. *See supra* p. 1412.

163. From the author's Introduction to *Shakh* on Sh. Ar. YD, which *see* for further discussion.

164. From the author's Introduction to *Peri Megadim* on Sh. Ar. YD. For further discussion, *see id.,* s.v. Ani terem akhaleh. *See also* the author's Introduction to *Taz* on Sh. Ar. YD and the author's Introduction to *Bet Shemu'el* on Sh. Ar. EH.

165. *See* the comments of Jair Ḥayyim Bacharach quoted *infra* in text accompanying n. 169.

166. For further discussion of these and other commentaries, *see infra* ch. 38.

ities that befell the Jewish people at that point in history.[167] The generation of the commentators on the *Shulḥan Arukh* witnessed another great wave of persecution against the Jews of Europe. The decrees of 1648–1649, known in Hebrew as *gezerot taḥ ve-tat,* brought about the destruction of many European Jewish communities and of major centers of Jewish scholarship. In the past, calamity had intensified the trend toward codification, and this was also true of the seventeenth century. At that time, however, there already was a code at hand, and all that was necessary was its endorsement by the leading halakhic authorities—which is exactly what happened. Menahem Mendel Krochmal (1600–1661), one of the foremost halakhic authorities of the time, wrote:

> Now that the great work *Bet Yosef* and the same author's *Shulḥan Arukh* have appeared, followed by the glosses [of Rema], and these have been accepted throughout all Jewry, we have [*i.e.,* need, as sources for decision,] only their books.[168]

A short time later, Jair Ḥayyim Bacharach (1638–1701), a leading German halakhic authority, attested not only to the binding character of the views of Caro and Rema in the *Shulḥan Arukh,* but also to the authoritativeness of two of the important commentaries on the *Shulḥan Arukh:*[169]

> It is a rare occurrence nowadays to characterize [a decision] as an error in the judge's reasoning (*shikkul ha-da'at*), since the principle is that anything contained in a code is equivalent to a law stated in the Mishnah.[170] Similarly, a [party's] plea of *kim li* [*i.e.,* "it is established for me that the law is in accord-

167. There were also commentaries on Maimonides' *Mishneh Torah* and other codificatory works, but they did not overcome the opposition of the halakhic authorities to the acceptance of these codes as binding and authoritative.

168. *Resp. Ẓemaḥ Ẓedek* #9, at the end of the responsum. As we have seen (*supra* n. 161), even before this period, David b. Judah was of the opinion that Caro's and Rema's views should be accepted as law. As also previously noted, Ḥayyim b. Beẓalel refrained from submitting his criticisms of Rema to the rabbinic leaders of Frankfurt (*see* his *Vikku'aḥ Mayim Ḥayyim,* Introduction, and *supra* n. 26). It is thus clear that as early as 1575, the German halakhic authorities accepted Rema's rulings. *See also* Isaiah Horowitz's statement that the law should be determined in accordance with Rema's views (quoted *supra* n. 78).

169. *Resp. Ḥavvot Ya'ir,* ed. Frankfurt-am-Main, 1699, p. 262b, *errata* to p. 153b (#165). Beginning with ed. Lemberg, 1894, the *errata* were incorporated into the body of the text in #165, pp. 83d–84a. The statement of *Resp. Ḥavvot Ya'ir* is quoted in: *Urim ve-Thummim* to ḤM ch. 25, at the end, in the context of the discussion of the plea of *kim li* at the end of subpar. 125; *Netivot Mishpat* to ḤM ch. 25, in the context of laws of self-help, rule 20; and *Pitḥei Teshuvah* to ḤM ch. 25, par. 1, subpar. 2.

170. If a judge errs in his reasoning, the judgment is not set aside, but an error as to a law written in the Mishnah is ground for setting aside the judgment; *cf.* TB Sanhedrin 33a, and *see supra* pp. 982–985.

> ance with a particular authority who favors my position"][171] is not accepted when the issue has been determined in the *Shulḥan Arukh* to the contrary and the ruling in the *Shulḥan Arukh* has been accepted as binding and has not been contested by any subsequent halakhic authority. This is true even according to those who take the view that the plea of *kim li* is generally valid in matters of civil law. . . . Similarly, wherever he [Caro] stated a rule in the *Shulḥan Arukh,* and Rema in his gloss cited a contrary opinion with which he expressed agreement, Rema's ruling, too, is to be considered the equivalent of a law stated in the Mishnah in these countries where we have accepted his rulings.
>
> Where Rema wrote that "there are those who say," and did not himself decide between the opposing views, the rulings of *Sema* and *Shakh* are, in every instance, the equivalent of a law stated in the Mishnah. If *Sema* and *Shakh* disagree, the opinion of *Shakh* is binding, even [to the extent of relying on it to render judgment for a plaintiff] to take [money from a defendant]; it [the opinion of *Shakh*] is considered the equivalent of a law stated in the Mishnah because the principle is that the law is in accordance with the views of the later authorities. . . . [172] In the final analysis, I cannot understand how nowadays a case can arise in which there can be an error in the judge's reasoning.

Joseph Caro's rulings in the *Shulḥan Arukh,* Rema's in his glosses, *Sema*'s and *Shakh*'s when they agree and, at times, *Shakh*'s alone, were each accorded binding authority in particular circumstances; a judge's error in regard to their rulings is equivalent to an error with regard to a law stated in the Mishnah.[173] This authority is to be understood not only as a recog-

171. For a discussion of the plea of *kim li, see supra* pp. 1281–1282, 1386 and n. 59. The availability of this plea was an incentive for the composition of a binding code, particularly for the civil law.

172. The author of *Shakh* was a "later" authority than the author of *Sema,* so that the rulings in *Shakh* are more authoritative. *See* the further statement in *Resp. Ḥavvot Ya'ir, supra* n. 169:

> Although I have heard that it is very difficult to allow recovery against a defendant contrary to the view of *Sema,* and that at the very least we should say that if a judge follows the view of *Sema,* his error [is merely an error in his reasoning and] cannot be considered the equivalent of an error as to a law stated in the Mishnah, nevertheless, I still maintain my view [that the opinion of *Shakh* is binding and a judge who rules against *Shakh*'s opinion is considered as if he has erred as to a law stated in the Mishnah], unless the judge or judges have good reason to believe that the *Shakh* was wrong in disagreeing with *Sema.*

See further id. regarding cases where Rema cited differing opinions and the commentators do not arrive at any decision.

173. *See further* Jonathan Eybeschütz (1690–1764), *Urim ve-Thummim,* to ḤM, following ch. 25, subpars. 123, 124: "I have a tradition . . . that the halakhic authorities of the generation accepted as binding everything written in the brief formulations of the *Shulḥan Arukh* with the glosses of Rema. . . . It is entirely improper to plead *kim li* against a ruling of the author [Caro] and Rema."

nition of the prerogative of the *Shulḥan Arukh* and its commentaries to decide the law, but also as a legitimization of relying solely on them as a basis for decision.

What was the reason for this drastic change from the view held by the generation of Caro and Rema and the generation immediately thereafter? In the earlier period, most halakhic authorities had believed, as Samuel Edels (Maharsha) put it:

> In our times, there are those who make halakhic rulings on the basis of the *Shulḥan Arukh* without knowing the underlying reason for each matter. If they do not first examine the matter in the Talmud, which requires study under halakhic scholars, and if a decision they render is erroneous, they wreak havoc in the world and merit condemnation.[174]

Subsequently, however, it became acceptable to make legal rulings on the basis of the *Shulḥan Arukh.* The change in viewpoint is due to the commentaries on the *Shulḥan Arukh:*

> It is possible that [Maharsha adopted his position because] in Maharsha's time no glosses had yet been written to the *Shulḥan Arukh.* Nowadays, however, since *Taz, Shakh, Magen Avraham,* and other later commentaries have been written and the reason for each law is explained alongside it [*i.e.,* alongside the law itself], reliance on the *Shulḥan Arukh* and the later commentaries is appropriate.[175]

The *Shulḥan Arukh* was thus molded into its final structure. At its center is a book of *pesakim* containing a brief, monolithic, and consolidated statement of the law, arranged topically to satisfy the requirements of a legal code. Preceding it is *Bet Yosef,* a detailed and reasoned book of *halakhot,* and surrounding it are the authoritative commentaries that serve to ensure the continuity of the law, maintain the connection with its sources, and present the diverse opinions on each subject to guide judges in their legal rulings.[176] When all of this was in place, the *Shulḥan Arukh* assumed its position as *the* code of Jewish law among western Jews, having already been accepted as such by the Jews of the east.[177]

174. Maharsha, *Ḥiddushei Aggadot,* Sotah 22a, s.v. Yere et ha-shem beni. *See also supra* pp. 1383–1384.

175. Abraham Ẓevi Hirsch Eisenstadt (1813–1868, Horodno-Kovno; *see infra* p. 1414 concerning him), *Pitḥei Teshuvah,* Sh. Ar. YD ch. 242, subpar. 8. At the beginning of his comments, Eisenstadt quoted Maharsha (quoted *supra* in the text accompanying n. 174).

176. As to the finality of the rulings in the *Shulḥan Arukh, see also infra* pp. 1450–1451.

177. *See supra* p. 1373. As to the differences between eastern and western Jewry with regard to how the law is to be determined when Caro and Rema disagree, as well as in other similar situtions, *see* Toledano, *supra* n. 20; ET, IX, pp. 337–338, s.v. Halakhah, and sources cited there in nn. 392–394.

Chapter 38

THE CODIFICATORY LITERATURE: COMMENTARIES ON AND CODIFICATION AFTER THE *SHULḤAN ARUKH*

I. Introduction
II. Commentaries on *Ḥoshen Mishpat*
  A. *Sefer Me'irat Einayim* (*Sema*) by Joshua Falk
  B. *Turei Zahav* (*Taz*) by David b. Samuel ha-Levi
  C. *Siftei Kohen* (*Shakh*) by Shabbetai b. Meir ha-Kohen
  D. *Be'er ha-Golah* by Moses Rivkes
  E. *Urim ve-Thummim* by Jonathan Eybeschütz
  F. *Be'ur ha-Gra* by Elijah, Gaon of Vilna
  G. *Keẓot ha-Ḥoshen* by Aryeh Leib Heller
  H. *Netivot ha-Mishpat* by Jacob Lorbeerbaum
III. Commentaries on *Even ha-Ezer*
  A. *Turei Zahav* (*Taz*) by David b. Samuel ha-Levi
  B. *Ḥelkat Meḥokek* by Moses Lima
  C. *Bet Shemu'el* by Samuel Phoebus
  D. *Be'er ha-Golah* by Moses Rivkes
  E. *Be'ur ha-Gra* by Elijah, Gaon of Vilna
  F. *Avnei Millu'im* by Aryeh Leib Heller
IV. Commentaries on *Oraḥ Ḥayyim* and *Yoreh De'ah*
V. Responsa Compilations Arranged in the Topical Sequence of the *Shulḥan Arukh*
  A. *Panim Ḥadashot* by Isaac Jesurun
  B. *Keneset ha-Gedolah* by Ḥayyim Benveniste
  C. *Be'er Heitev* by Judah Ashkenazi and Zechariah Mendel b. Aryeh Leib
  D. *Leket ha-Kemaḥ* by Moses Ḥagiz
  E. *Yad Aharon* by Aaron Alfandari
  F. *Birkei Yosef* by Ḥayyim Joseph David Azulai (Ḥida)
  G. *Matteh Shim'on* by Simon Mordecai Bekemoharar
  H. *Sha'arei Teshuvah* by Ḥayyim Mordecai Margolioth
  I. *Pitḥei Teshuvah* by Abraham Eisenstadt
  J. *Oraḥ Mishpat* by Raḥamim Elijah Ḥazzan
  K. *Darkhei Teshuvah* by Ẓevi Hirsch Shapira and His Son Ḥayyim Eleazar Shapira
  L. *Oẓar ha-Posekim*
  M. *Halakhah Pesukah*
VI. Codificatory Literature after the *Shulḥan Arukh*
  A. In General
  B. Compilations of Tax Laws
    1. *Massa Melekh* by Joseph ibn Ezra
    2. *Avodat Massa* by Joshua Abraham Judah
    3. *Massa Ḥayyim* by Ḥayyim Palache
  C. Codificatory Literature Devoted Mainly to Religious Law

D. *Arukh ha-Shulḥan* by Jehiel Michal Epstein
E. Causes of the Decline of Codificatory Authority and Activity
F. The Problem of Codification at the Present Time

I. INTRODUCTION

As the previous chapter has shown, the *Shulḥan Arukh* became the focus of a developing literature of commentaries that became an integral part of the codificatory system. The commentary literature generated by the acceptance of the *Shulḥan Arukh* as the authoritative code of Jewish law was extremely ramified and, as is characteristic of such literature,[1] had a variety of purposes. Some commentaries explicated the text of the *Shulḥan Arukh* and supplemented it with additional views; some supplied source references; others criticized it or defended it against its critics; and still others used it as the starting point for purely theoretical discussions unrelated to the substance of the laws found in it. There was also an extensive literature of commentaries that classified many of the laws contained in responsa—particularly those after the *Shulḥan Arukh*—according to the topical arrangement of the *Shulḥan Arukh*. Many commentaries had more than one of these purposes.

Formally, some were composed as commentaries on the *Turim* and *Bet Yosef*. However, they are in fact commentaries on the *Shulḥan Arukh* as well, since the *Shulḥan Arukh* follows the topical order and classification scheme of the *Turim*.[2] This chapter describes some of the better-known commentaries, most of which are printed in the large editions of the *Shulḥan Arukh;* it focuses on the commentaries on *Even ha-Ezer* and *Ḥoshen Mishpat*, since they contain most of the material encompassed by *mishpat ivri*.[3]

II. COMMENTARIES ON *ḤOSHEN MISHPAT*

A. *Sefer Me'irat Einayim (Sema)* by Joshua Falk

Sefer Me'irat Einayim, known by its acronym as *Sema*, is one of the most important and authoritative commentaries on *Shulḥan Arukh Ḥoshen Mish-*

1. *See supra* pp. 1173–1176, 1231–1235, *et passim*.

2. After the publication of the *Turim* and the *Shulḥan Arukh*, their topical arrangement became the model for other types of halakhic literature. For example, the responsa written after the *Turim*, and especially after the *Shulḥan Arukh*, were generally compiled according to the topical arrangement of those two books. *See infra* p. 1524.

3. For the definition and nature of *mishpat ivri*, *see supra* p. 105.

pat.[4] As pointed out in the previous chapter,[5] Joshua Falk intended it to be an integral part of the *Shulḥan Arukh* qua code, *i.e.*, as an authoritative commentary on the law stated in the *Shulḥan Arukh* that was to be examined before rendering any decision made in reliance on the *Shulḥan Arukh.* The main aims of *Sema* were: (a) to correct printers' errors in the text of the *Shulḥan Arukh,* and particularly in Rema's glosses;[6] (b) to reconcile conflicts between Caro and Rema (even if the reconciliation was occasionally forced); (c) to add new laws introduced by halakhic authorities—including Falk himself—who lived after Caro and Rema; and (d) sometimes, to take issue with the views of Caro and Rema. *Sema* is clearly the leading commentary on the *Shulḥan Arukh.* Joshua Falk's general approach to codification, together with further details as to the nature of his commentary, has been discussed in the previous chapter.[7]

B. *Turei Zahav (Taz)* by David b. Samuel ha-Levi

David b. Samuel ha-Levi (1586–1667), known as "Taz" after the acronym for his commentary *Turei Zahav,* was the son-in-law of Joel Sirkes.[8] He served as rabbi in Poznan and later in Ostrog, Volhynia, where he headed an outstanding *yeshivah.* After the Chmielnicki pogroms (1648–1649), he served as Rabbi of Lemberg.

Turei Zahav covers all four parts of the *Shulḥan Arukh,* but the commentaries on *Oraḥ Ḥayyim* and *Yoreh De'ah* are particularly renowned. The commentaries on *Even ha-Ezer* and *Ḥoshen Mishpat* were not printed until many years after Taz's death and are more in the nature of notes on selected topics than comprehensive commentaries; they pass over many paragraphs and even whole chapters. *Turei Zahav* frequently criticizes the comments of *Sema.*

C. *Siftei Kohen (Shakh)* by Shabbetai b. Meir ha-Kohen

Shabbetai b. Meir ha-Kohen (1621–1662), known as "Shakh" after the acronym for his work *Siftei Kohen,* lived in Vilna, from which he fled during the pogroms of 1648–1649. Later, he was the Rabbi of Holesov, Moravia. He died at the early age of 41.

4. *See* the quotation from *Resp. Ḥavvot Ya'ir* concerning *Sema, supra* pp. 1420–1421.

5. *See supra* pp. 1408–1414.

6. Joshua Falk had been Rema's student and had a copy of the original manuscript of Rema's glosses.

7. *Supra* pp. 1408–1414.

8. As to Joel Sirkes, also known as Baḥ, after the acronym of his major work, *see supra* pp. 1415–1417.

Siftei Kohen is one of the most important and authoritative commentaries on *Ḥoshen Mishpat.*[9] The commentary also covers *Yoreh De'ah. Siftei Kohen* often supplements *Sema*'s explanation of the *Shulḥan Arukh;* but, in the main, it is a critique of the *Shulḥan Arukh* and of the authorities on whom Caro and Rema relied.[10] The work frequently refers to the multitude of opinions found in the responsa literature and other halakhic works; sometimes it merely refers the reader to the sources, and at other times it fully discusses the various opinions.[11]

D. *Be'er ha-Golah* by Moses Rivkes

Moses b. Naphtali Hertz Rivkes (died ca. 1671–1672) was born in Vilna, from which he fled during the pogroms of 1648–1649. He finally settled in Amsterdam, where he wrote *Be'er ha-Golah.* In the main, this work cites the sources of the laws contained in the *Shulḥan Arukh,* namely, the Talmud, the codificatory literature, Rashi's commentary, the Tosafists, and the responsa literature. Occasionally, it explains the *Shulḥan Arukh* or defines difficult terms, particularly in *Even ha-Ezer* and *Ḥoshen Mishpat.*[12] *Be'er ha-Golah* helped to establish a direct link between the *Shulḥan Arukh,* on the one hand, and the Talmud and the codificatory literature, on the other.

E. *Urim ve-Thummim* by Jonathan Eybeschütz

Jonathan b. Nathan Nata Eybeschütz (ca. 1690–1764) was head of the *yeshivah* and a *dayyan* in Prague. He later served as rabbi in Metz, France, and was subsequently elected to the rabbinate of the "Three Communities"—Altona, Hamburg, and Wandsbeck.[13]

Of his halakhic works, one of the best known is *Urim ve-Thummim,* a

9. *See* the quotation from *Resp. Ḥavvot Ya'ir, supra* pp. 1420–1421.

10. As to the objective of *Shakh*'s commentary in regard to decision making, *see supra* p. 1419.

11. Consequently, as compared to other commentaries, *Siftei Kohen* has a greater resemblance to the compilations of responsa that were arranged according to the topical order of the *Turim* and the *Shulḥan Arukh,* as to which *see infra* pp. 1432–1443.

12. The explanations and source references in *Be'er ha-Golah* to *Ḥoshen Mishpat* are longer and more detailed than those to the other three parts of the *Shulḥan Arukh; see* the author's Introduction. *See also* his comment, *id.:* "Because civil-law matters can be decided by any court, my commentary on *Ḥoshen Mishpat* is more comprehensive and expansive than [the commentary] on the first three parts."

13. About 1750, Jacob Emden accused Jonathan Eybeschütz of leanings toward Sabbateanism (belief in the messianic pretensions of Shabbetai Ẓevi), and the ensuing controversy had serious and intense repercussions throughout Ashkenazic Jewry.

commentary on *Ḥoshen Mishpat.* The book has two sections: *Urim* briefly explains the sources of the laws in the *Shulḥan Arukh,* cites the rulings of the early and later authorities, and summarizes the discussions contained in the other section, *Thummim. Thummim* consists of lengthy discussions of the Talmudic sources and commentaries and is really in the nature of novellae.

F. *Be'ur ha-Gra* by Elijah, Gaon of Vilna

Elijah b. Shelomo Zalman (1720–1797), best known by the title "Gaon of Vilna," or by his acronym, Gra (*G*aon, *R*abbi *E*lijah; the first letter of "Elijah" in Hebrew is *aleph,* which is generally transliterated "a"), was the outstanding Talmudic scholar of his age. His works deal with virtually all the sources of the *Halakhah:* the halakhic *midrashim,* the Mishnah, the Talmud, and the codes. He also wrote Biblical commentaries.

The Gaon of Vilna made a particularly important contribution in establishing the authentic texts of the sources by means of detailed comparison of parallel passages, and he wrote glosses on the Talmud and *Sifrei,* among other classic texts. His commentary on the four parts of the *Shulḥan Arukh,* known as *Be'ur ha-Gra,* is extraordinary for its innovative originality.[14] For each law, it presents the sources in the Babylonian and Jerusalem Talmuds, the halakhic *midrashim,* the *Tosefta,* and other Talmudic literature. It frequently reveals sources that the other commentators overlooked and even adduces support in Talmudic literature for post-Talmudic laws.[15] The commentary shows the direct connection between the *Shulḥan Arukh* and Talmudic literature, which is the primary source upon which the Gaon of Vilna based each law. Occasionally, on the basis of Talmudic sources and the opinions of other halakhic authorities, he even rejected rulings made by Caro and Rema.[16]

14. *Be'ur ha-Gra* on the *Shulḥan Arukh* is the only work of the Gaon of Vilna printed from his own manuscript. *See supra* p. 1136 n. 127.

15. *See, e.g.,* Rema's gloss to Sh. Ar. ḤM 163:6: "Communal undertakings do not require a *kinyan* [formal juristic act of acquisition]," on which *Be'ur ha-Gra, ad loc.,* subpar. 103, comments: "This is from TJ Megillah 3:2, 'Seven communal leaders. . . . '" The rule stated by Rema originated after the completion of the Talmud (for details, *see supra* pp. 704–707), but the Gaon of Vilna found support for it in TJ. The approach of many halakhic authorities was to find support in Talmudic sources for laws that they introduced. *See, e.g.,* the statements of Maharam of Rothenburg in regard to communal authority, *supra* pp. 704–705 and n. 99. The Gaon of Vilna used the same approach with regard to rulings in the *Shulḥan Arukh.*

16. *See, e.g., Be'ur ha-Gra* to Sh. Ar. YD 160:16, subpar. 35 (ed. El ha-Mekorot, subpar. 36). The Gaon of Vilna disputed Rema's view on a basic question involving the law of

G. *Kezot ha-Ḥoshen* by Aryeh Leib Heller

A study of the classic commentaries on *Shulḥan Arukh Ḥoshen Mishpat* clearly shows that the laws of *Ḥoshen Mishpat* were "living law" in the Jewish diaspora, including Poland and Germany, throughout the seventeenth and part of the eighteenth centuries. The commentators extensively discussed cases and judgments occurring in daily life and relied on customs and legislation—especially communal enactments—which were current in their communities. During this period, Jews in Poland, Lithuania, Moravia, and parts of Germany enjoyed broad juridical autonomy. Many cases were brought before the High Court that had jurisdiction over all the Jewish communities in Poland and sat at the major trade fairs in Lublin and Jaroslaw. These cases involved parties from different places, each of whom was subject to the judicial authority of a different community. The court also heard disputes between different communities and provinces.[17]

As a result of the gradual erosion of Jewish juridical autonomy, beginning in the second half of the eighteenth century, the practical application of *Ḥoshen Mishpat* progressively diminished. Although commentaries on it were still written, they were of a more academic and theoretical nature—study as an end in itself.[18] One of the most outstanding and best known commentaries of this later period is *Kezot ha-Ḥoshen* by Aryeh Leib b. Joseph Heller (ca. 1745–1813).

Aryeh Leib Heller served as rabbi in Rozhnyatov and then in Stry, both in Galicia, Austria-Hungary (later Poland). *Kezot ha-Ḥoshen,* which made him famous as a halakhic scholar, is a book of novellae on *Ḥoshen Mishpat* containing lengthy theoretical discussions of the Talmud and the writings of the *rishonim* and *aḥaronim* (early and later authorities). Its analyses are extremely profound and its legal distinctions are deft and comprehensive. The commentary is academic and theoretical, and was not designed to reach definitive legal conclusions. Its connection with the text of the *Shulḥan Arukh* is tenuous and only incidental. The book is very popular in the *yeshivot,* and its analyses and definitions are of great importance for the study of *mishpat ivri.*

---

interest. To support his position, he quoted from *Tosafot* and added that *Bet Yosef,* the *Levushim,* and *Taz* also differed with Rema on this point and that although *Baḥ* and *Shakh* supported Rema's view, "it does not appear correct; it is completely erroneous." Similarly, in *Be'ur ha-Gra* to Sh. Ar. YD 251:1, subpar. 1, the Gaon of Vilna held, contrary to the rule stated in the *Shulḥan Arukh,* that a transgressor must be given financial support if he is in need.

17. *See supra* p. 9 n. 20 and accompanying text.

18. This was the situation in European countries. Juridical autonomy continued in eastern countries for a much longer period (*see infra* pp. 1584–1586). In these countries, there was no change in the nature and subject matter of the commentaries on the *Shulḥan Arukh.*

H. *Netivot ha-Mishpat* by Jacob Lorbeerbaum

A second leading commentary in the later period is *Netivot ha-Mishpat* by Jacob Lorbeerbaum (ca. 1760–1832). Lorbeerbaum served as rabbi in various communities in Poland, including Lissa (Leszno). (He is also known as Jacob Lissa and Jacob Lisser.) He wrote many books and is recognized as an important halakhic authority.

Netivot ha-Mishpat is a commentary on *Ḥoshen Mishpat* and, like Eybeschütz's *Urim ve-Thummim*, is divided into two parts. One part, entitled *Be'urim* [Explanations], is also called *Mishpat ha-Urim* [The Law of the *Urim*]; and the other, *Ḥiddushim* [Novellae], is also called *Mishpat ha-Kohanim* [The Law of the Priests]. However, the titles of the two parts do not precisely reflect their contents. *Be'urim* contains mainly novellae and discussions of the Talmud and works of *rishonim* and *aḥaronim*, particularly *Urim ve-Thummim* and *Keẓot ha-Ḥoshen*. *Netivot ha-Mishpat* is particularly critical of *Keẓot ha-Ḥoshen;* Aryeh Leib Heller rebutted the criticisms in a publication called *Meshovev Netivot.*[19]

Keẓot ha-Ḥoshen and *Netivot ha-Mishpat* both contributed greatly to the continued study of *Shulḥan Arukh Ḥoshen Mishpat*, even though its laws were no longer applied to any great extent in practice. The two works have been, and are still today, regularly studied in the *yeshivot.*[20]

III. COMMENTARIES ON *EVEN HA-EZER*

A. *Turei Zahav (Taz)* by David b. Samuel ha-Levi

This work was discussed above in connection with the commentaries on *Ḥoshen Mishpat.*

B. *Ḥelkat Meḥokek* by Moses Lima

Moses Lima (ca. 1605–1658) served as rabbi in various Lithuanian communities, and is recognized as a leading halakhic authority. Lima's *Ḥelkat Meḥokek* was the first commentary to be written on *Even ha-Ezer.*[21] According to the author of *Bet Shemu'el* discussed next below, the *Ḥelkat Meḥokek*

19. *Meshovev Netivot* first appeared as an appendix to Heller's *Avnei Millu'im*, a commentary on Sh. Ar. EH; *see infra*. It was later printed together with *Netivot ha-Mishpat* or as an appendix to Sh. Ar. ḤM (as in ed. Pe'er ha-Torah), and was no longer included with *Avnei Millu'im.*

20. There are also two detailed indexes to Sh. Ar. ḤM. One, by Joshua Falk, is in the form of a detailed table of contents. The other, entitled *Peri Megadim*, by Samuel b. Alexander, is an alphabetical subject index. As to *Peri Megadim*, *see supra* p. 1412 and n. 143.

21. *Ḥelkat Meḥokek* is printed in most editions of Sh. Ar. EH together with *Bet Shemu'el* (*see infra*) under the joint title, *Apei Ravrevei.*

commentary made *Even ha-Ezer* readily accessible to the reader.[22] The commentary explains the text of this part of the *Shulḥan Arukh,* resolves inconsistencies, reconciles the various opinions cited, and analyzes the views of the *rishonim* and *aḥaronim,* particularly those upon whom the *Shulḥan Arukh* relies for its conclusions. The commentary was not finished and covers the material only as far as the middle of chapter 126. The manuscript was printed by Lima's son, who added explanations and source references of his own.

C. *Bet Shemu'el* by Samuel Phoebus

Samuel b. Uri Shraga Phoebus (middle of the seventeenth century) was born in Vadislav, Poland, studied in Cracow, and served as rabbi in various communities in Poland and Germany. His work *Bet Shemu'el* is considered to be one of the most important and authoritative commentaries on *Even ha-Ezer.*[23] In his Introduction, Phoebus stated that he decided to write on *Even ha-Ezer* because it had not yet been the subject of a comprehensive commentary. He respected *Ḥelkat Meḥokek,* but pointed out that its author, Moses Lima, had died before completing and editing it. Phoebus's commentary was originally brief and condensed. Later, when he became rabbi in Fürth, Germany, and reviewed *Even ha-Ezer* with his students, he rewrote his commentary and added a great deal of material. He also had the use of a manuscript of *Turei Zahav* on *Even ha-Ezer.*[24]

Bet Shemu'el explains the *Shulḥan Arukh* and discusses its sources. The explanations are not lengthy and are written in an easy and lucid style. Phoebus was independent in his judgments, sometimes disagreeing with Caro, Rema, and *Ḥelkat Meḥokek.*[25] *Bet Shemu'el* on *Even ha-Ezer* is very similar to *Sema* on *Ḥoshen Mishpat.*

D. *Be'er ha-Golah* by Moses Rivkes

This work was discussed above in connection with the commentaries on *Ḥoshen Mishpat.*

E. *Be'ur ha-Gra* by Elijah, Gaon of Vilna

This work was discussed above in connection with the commentaries on *Ḥoshen Mishpat.*

22. *See* Samuel Phoebus, *Bet Shemu'el,* Introduction.

23. *See also supra* n. 21.

24. *See Bet Shemu'el,* Introduction (near the end).

25. *See, e.g.,* Sh. Ar. EH 1:8, *Bet Shemu'el* subpar. 16; Sh. Ar. EH 1:9, *Bet Shemu'el* subpar. 22; Sh. Ar. EH 2:4, *Bet Shemu'el* subpar. 11, and many more examples.

F. *Avnei Millu'im* by Aryeh Leib Heller

This work was mentioned above (note 19) in connection with *Kezot ha-Ḥoshen* and *Meshovev Netivot.*

IV. COMMENTARIES ON *ORAḤ ḤAYYIM* AND *YOREH DE'AH*

An enormous commentary literature—in both quantity and scope—surrounds the *Oraḥ Ḥayyim* and *Yoreh De'ah* parts of the *Shulḥan Arukh.* The commentaries on these two parts and the commentaries on the commentaries proliferated, beginning with the eighteenth century. They far outnumber the commentaries on *Even ha-Ezer* and *Ḥoshen Mishpat.* One of the main reasons for the increase in the literature on *Oraḥ Ḥayyim* and *Yoreh De'ah* at that time was the abrogation of Jewish juridical autonomy. As a result, halakhic authorities turned their attention to those parts of the *Shulḥan Arukh* that deal with religious law still applied in practice—*Oraḥ Ḥayyim* and *Yoreh De'ah.*[26] The following are a few of the commentaries to those two parts of the *Shulḥan Arukh:*

Seventeenth Century: *Turei Zahav* (*Taz*) by David b. Samuel ha-Levi (*see* above), on *Oraḥ Ḥayyim* and *Yoreh De'ah; Magen Avraham* by Abraham Gumbiner, on *Oraḥ Ḥayyim; Siftei Kohen* (*Shakh*) by Shabbetai b. Meir ha-Kohen (*see* above), on *Yoreh De'ah; Be'er ha-Golah* by Moses Rivkes (*see* above), on *Oraḥ Ḥayyim* and *Yoreh De'ah.* In the same period, eastern Jewry produced an important commentary on the *Shulḥan Arukh—Peri Ḥadash* on *Oraḥ Ḥayyim, Yoreh De'ah,* and *Even ha-Ezer* (the laws of divorce) by Hezekiah Da Silva (1659–1695) of Jerusalem. This commentary aroused sharp controversy among the halakhic authorities because of the strong language Da Silva used against those who disagreed with him, as well as the marked independence of his conclusions. At the beginning of the eighteenth century, Ḥayyim b. Atar, another Jerusalemite, wrote a book, *Peri To'ar,* in which he disagreed with many of Da Silva's views. However, in the course of time, *Peri Ḥadash* became accepted as an authoritative work "and nowadays all the halakhic authorities thirstily drink its words."[27]

Eighteenth Century: Some commentaries were written directly on the *Shulḥan Arukh,* and other commentaries were written on previous

26. Of the subjects in Sh. Ar. EH, only laws concerning marriage, divorce, and *ḥaliẓah* (release from levirate marriage) were applied in practice. The laws relating to the financial relationships between husband and wife were not. *See also infra* pp. 1583–1584.

27. Ḥida, *Shem ha-Gedolim,* Persons, Letter *ḥet,* #3. *See also id.*, Books, Letter *pe,* #137.

commentaries. Of the direct commentaries, mention should be made of *Kreti u-Peleti* by Jonathan Eybeschütz (*see* above), on *Yoreh De'ah;* and *Be'ur ha-Gra* by Elijah, Gaon of Vilna (*see* above), on *Oraḥ Ḥayyim* and *Yoreh De'ah.* Of the commentaries on previous commentaries, the following is a partial list: *Peri Megadim* by Joseph Teomim (ca. 1727–1792), covering *Oraḥ Ḥayyim* and *Yoreh De'ah; Maḥaẓit ha-Shekel* by Samuel ha-Levi Kolin (1770–1806), on *Magen Avraham* (*see* above); *Levushei Serad* by David Solomon Eybeschütz, covering *Oraḥ Ḥayyim* and *Yoreh De'ah; Netiv Ḥayyim* by Nethanel Weil, on *Magen Avraham; Yad Ephraim* by Ephraim Zalman Margolioth of Brody, covering *Oraḥ Ḥayyim.* These latter commentaries, of course, also relate to and explain the *Shulḥan Arukh,* but they focus mainly on the commentaries on the *Shulḥan Arukh.*

In the eighteenth century, commentaries on the *Shulḥan Arukh* were written for the first time in Yemen. David Mashraki, a Yemenite halakhic authority of that period, wrote *Shetilei Zeitim* on *Oraḥ Ḥayyim* and *Roshei Besamim* on part of *Yoreh De'ah.* In addition to the usual reason for writing such commentaries, which is described above, there was an additional important purpose for writing these two commentaries. Yemenite Jews had always followed Maimonides' opinions, and Mashraki sought to induce the Yemenite community to follow the practice of the other communities of the diaspora, which relied on the *Shulḥan Arukh.*[28]

V. RESPONSA COMPILATIONS ARRANGED IN THE TOPICAL SEQUENCE OF THE *SHULḤAN ARUKH*

In addition to the various types of commentaries on the *Shulḥan Arukh* described above, it became apparent shortly after the *Shulḥan Arukh* was published that it would have to be linked to the responsa literature because responsa constituted the main source of continued halakhic creativity and development. Clearly, in order to draw analogies or make distinctions, a conscientious decisionmaker must study prior cases that are similar. The various types of commentaries on the *Shulḥan Arukh* already described discuss many decisions recorded in responsa.[29] Indeed, from the time that codificatory literature first began to appear, commentaries on codes have gen-

28. *See* R. Arusi, Introduction to *Shetilei Zeitim,* Jerusalem, 1966; *see also supra* p. 1373 n. 20.

29. Some commentaries, such as *Shakh,* are particularly noteworthy for the frequency with which they cite responsa; *see supra* pp. 1425–1426.

erally included material from the responsa literature. However, once the *Shulḥan Arukh* became the starting point for deliberation, the need arose for a new type of commentary on the *Shulḥan Arukh.* This new type of commentary would classify and systematize the material contained in the responsa literature according to the topical arrangement and the contents of the *Shulḥan Arukh,* so that anyone studying a specific subject in the *Shulḥan Arukh* would thereby be referred to the responsa on that subject. The need for such a commentary became especially urgent with the immense growth of the responsa literature following the publication of the *Shulḥan Arukh.* This literature contained many new decisions and rulings, and such a commentary would make them known to a judge using the *Shulḥan Arukh.*

To some degree, *Bet Yosef* had been a pioneer in this field;[30] and, with the passage of time, an entire literature came into being that compiled the material in the responsa relevant to each paragraph and subject in the *Shulḥan Arukh.* Some of these compilations also included material from other types of literature, such as novellae and commentaries on the codes; but this was incidental to the compilation of material from the responsa. A substantial number of these compilations did not, as a general rule, merely quote the responsa but also discussed and commented on them. Some books of this type were written on the *Turim* and *Bet Yosef* rather than directly on the *Shulḥan Arukh,* but in effect they related to the *Shulḥan Arukh,* since the topical arrangement of the *Shulḥan Arukh* is parallel to that of the *Turim.*

It should be pointed out that to some degree this type of commentary performed an additional important function: it classified, according to the arrangement of the *Shulḥan Arukh,* a large part of the previously uncatalogued material in the responsa literature. This made it much easier for students and judges to locate relevant decisions in that vast and uncharted sea. These compilations of responsa are still useful today. However, since they relate to only a minor portion of the vast material contained in the responsa literature, their utility is limited. The following is a partial list of this type of commentary.

A. *Panim Ḥadashot* by Isaac Jesurun

In the brief Introduction to his work *Panim Ḥadashot,* Isaac Jesurun (d. 1655), the Rabbi of the Portuguese Jewish Community in Hamburg, described the considerations that led to the composition of the Mishnah, the Talmud, and the *Shulḥan Arukh* with Rema's glosses. He then set forth his

30. *See supra* pp. 1313–1316.

aims in writing *Panim Ḥadashot,* which are also shared by the authors of all subsequent compilations:

> The work of the two above-mentioned rabbis [Caro and Rema]—"two are better . . . [than one]" [*see* Ecclesiastes 4:9]—is still not sufficient to satisfy the needs of every inquirer or to avoid error in decision in some matters . . . in view of the material that was in existence even at that time [Caro's and Rema's lifetimes] but had not been published; consequently, they [Caro and Rema] could not have considered those opinions in their work. It goes without saying [that this is true] with regard to the great rabbis who lived after them and wrote many responsa for practical application, some of which concur with their rulings [in the *Shulḥan Arukh*] and some of which do not. In addition, there is much excellent and cogent material contained in commentaries and novellae and the like in every generation; these are also fitting for the wise to know.[31]

Jesurun's objectives were thus: (1) to add the various opinions contained in responsa already written by the time of Caro and Rema but not cited by them because the responsa had not yet been published; (2) to add the responsa that were written later; and (3) to compile new material that had accumulated in other types of halakhic literature. Jesurun was most dramatic in describing the need he perceived for his book.[32] *Panim Ḥadashot* follows the arrangement of the *Turim* and briefly summarizes various rulings from thirty-three books, mostly responsa.[33] At the beginning of the book, there is a list of those works, and at the end there is an index listing the sources they cite.[34]

B. *Keneset ha-Gedolah* by Ḥayyim Benveniste

Ḥayyim Benveniste (1603–1673) was one of the outstanding halakhic authorities of the communities of Salonika, Constantinople, and Izmir. His

31. *Panim Ḥadashot,* ed. Venice, 1651, Introduction.

32. *Id.:* "For many times have I heard a heavenly voice thundering forth from the peak of the sacred mountains. I heard and saw it straining [to say], 'Who will give us a work that is brief and that collects the multitude of responsa that have been recently published?'"

33. *Panim Ḥadashot* to various parts of the *Shulḥan Arukh* has been printed by: Romm, Vilna; Pe'er ha-Torah, 1961; Makhon Ḥatam Sofer, 1966. In all these editions, it is printed together with *Leket ha-Kemaḥ,* as it is in the edition of *Leket ha-Kemaḥ* printed by Moses Ḥagiz. *See infra* pp. 1437–1438.

34. This index refers to every source in the thirty-three books, including the Mishnah, Talmud, *Mishneh Torah* and its commentaries, Rashba's books, and the *Turim,* among other works. *See Panim Ḥadashot,* Introduction: "This book is divided into two parts: The first [contains] the details of the laws and of prior cases (*ma'aseh*); the second, the sources from the Talmud and the halakhic authorities. It is good to have both." Many subsequent compilations contain similar indexes.

work *Keneset ha-Gedolah* is the largest and most sophisticated compilation of responsa keyed to the *Turim* and the *Shulḥan Arukh.*

In a long and detailed Introduction,[35] Benveniste surveyed the history of Jewish law (from the Mishnah and the Talmud through geonic literature, the works of Alfasi, Maimonides, and the *Turim,* and culminating with the works of Caro and Rema) and described the unique attributes of each work. Caro's work had been accepted throughout the Jewish world—"our eyes have seen that all students and judges use it constantly and continuously, and no one dares to make a ruling that is not based on it."[36] Benveniste, too, pointed to the many responsa relevant to matters discussed in the *Shulḥan Arukh* that were written in Caro's lifetime but not mentioned by Caro, as well as to responsa written after Caro's death. He pointed out that it was difficult to find these books; and even when one did succeed in doing so, it was extremely difficult to find the discussion of the subject at issue, because of the lack of an index or because the index was of very little practical use.[37]

Originally, Benveniste wrote down references to various responsa in his personal copy of the *Turim,* but later he decided that for the benefit of the public he would compose a work that

> would include all the details of the new laws that are found in the responsa of the foremost later authorities from the time of the Rabbi [Caro] . . . until the present. None of the responsa in my possession, whether in print or in manuscript, will be missing. [The work will also contain] some material from earlier authors that the Rabbi . . . omitted. Similarly, [it will include] every

35. *Keneset ha-Gedolah,* OḤ, Introduction, reprinted in ed. Jerusalem, 1966.

36. *Id.* at 2 (ed. Jerusalem).

37. Ḥayyim Benveniste's description of tables of contents in volumes of responsa extant in his time is of interest (*id.* at 4):

> If one can find [a book of responsa] and proceeds to examine its table of contents, that too will be an obstacle to gaining full knowledge of the subject matter. Into many books of responsa there is no entry whatsoever—no table of contents; and if there is a table of contents, it is not properly organized. Even those that are organized sometimes completely overlook some of the responsa [contained in the book] and make no reference to them. At times, the reader will believe that the law he is seeking belongs in a particular section, but when he looks for it there, he will not find it . . . [since], as is well known, in almost every instance, the table of contents refers only to the facts of each case. A responsum will sometimes discuss the intricacies of many different legal rules that are not directly relevant to the specific issue but are [only] collateral to it; and often a rule pertaining to religious law or to the subject of *agunah* will be discussed as incidental to an issue involving civil law, and vice versa. Even within the framework of a single subject, most discussions move from one point to another, whether or not they are all relevant. There is no mention of any of these things in the table of contents. To say that the reader should examine each responsum in detail is no solution, because that course may require days or weeks or months . . . to respond to a single question, depending on the nature of the subject.

See also infra pp. 1523–1528.

> source in which the authorities mentioned above, as well as other authorities, have discussed statements contained in the *Turim* and *Bet Yosef.*[38]

Benveniste called his book *Keneset ha-Gedolah* [The Great Assembly] because it is "a great assemblage of all the new laws found in the responsa of the foremost later halakhic authorities, and all the flocks will be gathered there" [*cf.* Genesis 29:3].[39] A supplement to the book, called *Sheyarei Keneset ha-Gedolah* [Remnants of the Great Assembly], contains the material that accumulated until close to the author's death. The entire work is printed in eight large volumes.[40] It follows the order of the *Turim* and *Bet Yosef,* and Benveniste's comments are presented in the form of glosses to those two works. Benveniste does not merely quote from his sources but often discusses them and expresses his own opinions and conclusions.[41]

Keneset ha-Gedolah is superior in scope, contents, and arrangement to *Panim Ḥadashot,* which reached Benveniste while he was engaged in the composition of his own work.[42] It was Benveniste's aspiration that

38. Introduction, *supra* n. 35 at 5. Benveniste emphasized (*id.* at 7) that he would refer only to the responsa literature in his compilation, "because my aim in this book is to make the burden of searching for the law in the books of responsa easier on the reader. I did not, therefore, collect the material from the other types of halakhic literature written by the later authorities, because it is easy for the reader to find the material in those works while he is engaged in studying that law." Benveniste was referring to the laws contained in the commentaries on the *Turim* and the *Shulḥan Arukh* and to the commentaries and novellae on the Talmud and similar works. To a certain degree, Benveniste changed his approach in his book on *Ḥoshen Mishpat,* where he did refer to the opinions of Rema, the *Levushim, Sema,* and *Baḥ,* as he pointed out in his Introduction to *Ḥoshen Mishpat,* Mahadura Kamma. Later in the Introduction to *Keneset ha-Gedolah,* he stated that occasionally he did quote from wherever he found material during his reading—including other types of halakhic literature (*id.* at 7) and even homiletical books (*id.* at 10).

39. Introduction, *supra* n. 35 at 6.

40. The following is the subject matter of each volume: *Vol. 1—Keneset ha-Gedolah,* OḤ, with discussions and texts taken from the early authorities, and principles of the Talmud and the codifiers and respondents (*i.e.,* the principles of Talmudic and codificatory methodology and decision making); *see infra* n. 45. *Vol. 2—Sheyarei Keneset ha-Gedolah,* OḤ, with discussions, texts, and rules. *Vol. 3—Keneset ha-Gedolah,* YD chs. 1–68. *Vol. 4—Keneset ha-Gedolah,* YD chs. 69–177. *Vol. 5—Sheyarei Keneset ha-Gedolah,* YD. *Vol. 6—Keneset ha-Gedolah,* ḤM chs. 1–156. *Vol. 7—Keneset ha-Gedolah,* Mahadura Batra, ḤM chs. 1–156, and *Keneset ha-Gedolah,* ḤM chs. 157–426. *Vol. 8—Keneset ha-Gedolah,* EH.

41. *See* Introduction, *supra* n. 35 at 7, which instructs the reader not to rely on the book for any determination of the law "unless I explicitly state that I am making a legal ruling or unless it is absolutely and indubitably clear that that is my intention." *See* Benveniste's further comments, *id.*

42. *Id.* at 7–10. Benveniste reported that he had received copies of *Panim Ḥadashot* and *Moreh Ẓedek.* The latter is on ḤM only, and is extremely terse. Although *Panim Ḥadashot* covers all four parts of the *Shulḥan Arukh,* Benveniste asserted that its author abstracted the law not from the texts of the responsa but from the questions submitted or from the concluding portions of the responsa or their tables of contents. He also criticized the arrangement of *Panim Ḥadashot. See id.*

> it will not be necessary for anyone who desires to know the basic thrust of a law, the halakhic conclusion, and the rulings of the later and early authorities, to consult all the books of responsa; he need only read *Bet Yosef* and this work [*Keneset ha-Gedolah*]. In them he will find everything he seeks that pertains to all the arguments and the laws, new and old; and he will have no need of any other work, for everything is explained and ready for use.[43]

Keneset ha-Gedolah undoubtedly fulfilled this aspiration at the time it was published. However, the hope that the reader "will have no need of any other work"—like the similarly expressed claim of Maimonides in regard to his *Mishneh Torah*[44]—could not possibly be realized by a compilation of responsa, since the law is not static but in a process of constant development. After *Keneset ha-Gedolah*, there were many other compilations of responsa; and the best of them used Ḥayyim Benveniste's work as a model.[45]

C. *Be'er Heitev* by Judah Ashkenazi and Zechariah Mendel b. Aryeh Leib

Judah b. Shimon Ashkenazi and Zechariah Mendel b. Aryeh Leib were halakhic authorities of the mid-eighteenth century. Judah Ashkenazi was a *dayyan* in the town of Tiktin, Lithuania. His *Be'er Heitev* is a digest of laws from various codes and responsa. To some degree, it also explains the *Shulḥan Arukh* and states legal rulings. Current editions of the *Shulḥan Arukh* contain Judah Ashkenazi's *Be'er Heitev* on *Oraḥ Ḥayyim* and *Even ha-Ezer*. Compilations on the *Shulḥan Arukh* called *Be'er Heitev* were also written by several other authors. The work of the same name on *Ḥoshen Mishpat* and *Yoreh De'ah* was written by Zechariah Mendel b. Aryeh Leib, who was the Rabbi of Belz, Poland; it follows the pattern of Ashkenazi's work.

D. *Leket ha-Kemaḥ* by Moses Ḥagiz

Moses b. Jacob Ḥagiz (1672–ca. 1751), known as Mani'aḥ, lived in Jerusalem. He traveled widely throughout the Jewish communities of Germany and France and then returned to the Land of Israel.

43. *Id.* at 10–11.

44. Maimonides, *MT*, Introduction; *see supra* p. 1185. *But see Sheyarei Keneset ha-Gedolah*, OḤ, Introduction, in which Benveniste stated that no author could possibly collect all the material available in his generation, "it being impossible not to leave gleanings."

45. Benveniste also appended to a part of his book an index of passages from the Talmud and the *rishonim*, and all the principles of the Talmud and the codifiers and respondents; *see supra* n. 40. *See also* Introduction, *supra* n. 35 at 5–6.

In *Leket ha-Kemaḥ* [The Collection of the Flour; the Hebrew for "the flour," *ha-kemaḥ,* is an acronym of **h***a*-**k***atan* **M***oshe* **Ḥ***agiz,* "the lowly one, Moses Ḥagiz"], Ḥagiz abstracted material from a number of books, most of them collections of responsa, and presented a summary of the halakhic rulings "in accordance with the opinion of each author, together with the main reasons for his conclusion, in lucid and brief language that scholars admire, so that my few words will convey all that the author set forth at length."[46] Ḥagiz included all the material that had been gathered in *Panim Ḥadashot;*[47] and in his own Introduction, he also quoted the Introduction to *Panim Ḥadashot.* Thus he avoided having to duplicate the research by the author of that book.

E. *Yad Aharon* by Aaron Alfandari

Aaron Alfandari (ca. 1690–1774) lived the major part of his life in Izmir, Turkey. In his old age, he settled in the Land of Israel and died in Hebron. His book *Yad Aharon* is a compilation from various volumes of responsa and other halakhic works. Its purpose was "that the reader, the scholar in search of the opinions of the later authorities, will easily be able to find them. . . . I have endeavored to make their path easier for them so that it should not be wearisome."[48] Alfandari also discussed the opinions in the responsa and stated his own rulings. Like *Keneset ha-Gedolah,* the book was arranged according to the *Turim* and *Bet Yosef,* following their subject matter in each chapter.

Yad Aharon was composed on *Oraḥ Ḥayyim* and *Even ha-Ezer.* In chapter 17 of *Even ha-Ezer,* Alfandari extensively discussed the laws relating to the *agunah* "because I realized that the laws of the *agunah* constitute an important subject; they have become extremely complex, this [authority]

46. *See Leket ha-Kemaḥ,* OḤ, Introduction. Near the end, the Introduction states: "I have gathered together all the material in the responsa of these later authorities; there is nothing I have overlooked or failed to put in its proper place." Ḥagiz collected material from books of responsa and from responsa quoted in other types of halakhic books (*see id.*). In the Introduction to his work on OḤ and YD and the Introduction to his work on EH, he presented a comprehensive list of the books from which material was culled for the various parts of his own book. In order to assist the reader, Ḥagiz published at the end of each part of his work an alphabetical index to the laws in the corresponding part of the *Shulḥan Arukh.* He took the index from a work previously published. It should be pointed out that *Leket ha-Kemaḥ* does not cover ḤM.

47. The material compiled in *Panim Ḥadashot* appears at the end of each paragraph in *Leket ha-Kemaḥ.* However, the second part of *Panim Ḥadashot, i.e.,* the source index (*see supra* n. 34), is not included in *Leket ha-Kemaḥ.* For various recent editions of the *Shulḥan Arukh* that include *Leket ha-Kemaḥ* together with *Panim Ḥadashot, see supra* n. 33.

48. *Yad Aharon,* OḤ, Introduction.

saying one thing and another [authority] saying something different."[49] Thirteen responsa treating various subjects in *Even ha-Ezer* are appended to the third volume.

F. *Birkei Yosef* by Ḥayyim Joseph David Azulai (Ḥida)

Ḥayyim Joseph David Azulai (Ḥida) (1724–1806) was active in the Land of Israel, Egypt, and elsewhere throughout the Jewish diaspora. He was extremely prolific in all areas of Jewish thought. *Birkei Yosef,* together with its supplements, *Shiyyurei Berakhah* and *Maḥazik Berakhah,* is one of Ḥida's most important halakhic works. The book covers all four parts of the *Shulḥan Arukh* and supplements each law with a wealth of material taken from all types of halakhic literature. Ḥida, who was also an important bibliographer, made extensive use of manuscript material he discovered on his various journeys.[50] He also recorded many customs he found in the literature as well as those he witnessed himself or of which he heard. He commented on the different opinions on particular issues and frequently rendered his own ruling. The book was widely accepted very quickly, and abridged versions of it have been printed.[51]

G. *Matteh Shim'on* by Simon Mordecai Bekemoharar[52]

Simon Mordecai b. Solomon Bekemoharar (died ca. 1814) served as rabbi in Adrianople, Turkey. *Matteh Shim'on* to *Tur Ḥoshen Mishpat* (in three parts) is very similar in form to *Keneset ha-Gedolah* in that it presents additional and supplementary material to the *Turim* and *Bet Yosef.* Its aim was "to compile and assemble the opinions of the various authors, in their details and branches, at the place of the main root [of the subject], each in its

49. *Yad Aharon,* EH, Introduction.

50. *See* Ḥida's brief Introduction to *Birkei Yosef,* OḤ.

51. For further details, *see* M. Benayahu, *Rabbi Ḥayyim Yosef David Azulai* (in Hebrew), pp. 107–109. *See also id.* at 187–188 as to the various editions of the above-mentioned works of Ḥida and the incorporation of *Shiyyurei Berakhah* into *Birkei Yosef. Birkei Yosef,* together with *Shiyyurei Berakhah,* covers the whole of OḤ and YD; but EH is covered only up to ch. 39 and ḤM only up to ch. 41.

52. The surname Bekemoharar is an acronym formed from the initial letters of the Hebrew phrase, **be**n **ke**v*od* **mo**r*enu* **ha**-**ra**v **R**. ("The son of his eminence, our teacher, Rabbi . . . "). Many of the members of this illustrious family served as rabbis in Adrianople. *See* S. Marcus, "Korot Shalshelet ha-Rabbanim le-Mishpaḥat Bekemoharar" [A History of the Rabbinic Dynasty of the Bekemoharar Family], *Mizraḥ u-Ma'arav,* V (1930), pp. 173–184, particularly at pp. 179–180.

proper place, to make it easy to find them."[53] The author's own responsa, entitled *Mira Dakhya,* are appended to volume 3.

H. *Sha'arei Teshuvah* by Ḥayyim Mordecai Margolioth

Ḥayyim Mordecai Margolioth (end of the eighteenth–beginning of the nineteenth centuries) was the Rabbi of Dubno, Poland. In his Introduction to his book *Sha'arei Teshuvah,*[54] he pointed out that since the composition of *Be'er Heitev,* which he was preparing to publish, a great deal of new material had accumulated in "all the books of responsa, in print and in manuscript, from then until now, from the luminaries of the times, the great halakhic authorities." He therefore resolved to compile the essence of this material to facilitate the work of judges and decisionmakers, who would thereby have access to all the material contained in the responsa literature—"perhaps they will see an analogous case, and derive one matter from another."

Ḥayyim Mordecai's brother, Ephraim Zalman Margolioth, the Rabbi of Brody, Galicia, wrote a comprehensive Introduction to *Sha'arei Teshuvah,*[55] in which he stressed the importance of compilations of halakhic material from the responsa literature.[56] He first reviewed the codificatory literature of the geonic period, Alfasi's work, Maimonides' *Mishneh Torah,* Rashba's *Torat ha-Bayit* (to which he gave special attention), the *Turim,* the work of Rabbenu Jeroham, *Bet Yosef,* and Rema's works. He then discussed the importance of the three compilations *Keneset ha-Gedolah, Panim Ḥadashot,* and *Leket ha-Kemaḥ.* He emphasized that, when rendering a decision, a judge does not have sufficient time to search through all the books of responsa to discover whether the particular issue involved has been previously dealt with. The compilations, arranged in the topical order of the *Shulḥan Arukh,* make it possible to locate any earlier treatment of an issue in a responsum. Ephraim Zalman Margolioth thereupon stressed the need to publish an additional compilation that would include the responsa not contained in previous compilations, particularly the responsa written since the prior compilations. He emphasized that knowledge of the material in the responsa

53. *Matteh Shim'on,* Author's Introduction.

54. *See* his statements in *Moda'ah Rabbah,* which has been printed in several editions of the *Shulḥan Arukh,* most recently in ed. Pe'er ha-Torah, Jerusalem, 1961 (at the beginning of OḤ, with the other Introductions).

55. The Introduction is printed in several editions of the *Shulḥan Arukh;* in ed. Pe'er ha-Torah, Jerusalem, 1961, it appears at the beginning of OḤ.

56. Ḥayyim Mordecai Margolioth also published, as a separate work, the glosses and commentaries of his brother, Ephraim Zalman, on Sh. Ar. OḤ, *Taz,* and *Magen Avraham,* under the title *Yad Ephraim; see supra* p. 1432.

literature is more important than acquaintance with the "new books that record laws in detail," because a law derived from a responsum is especially authoritative:

> As the Sages have said, "A *ma'aseh* [a case or event giving rise to a legal rule] is entitled to particular deference."[57] Halakhic authorities have also written that a responsum is more to be relied on than a code, since it is a ruling intended to be applied in practice and he [the respondent] is far more careful [in his ruling] than is a codifier, who writes the laws in solitude, perhaps for theoretical purposes only and not for practical application.[58]

The material in *Sha'arei Teshuvah*, which was composed on *Oraḥ Ḥayyim* only, is culled from more than two hundred books of responsa, particularly those written after the previous compilations had appeared.[59]

I. *Pitḥei Teshuvah* by Abraham Eisenstadt

Abraham Ẓevi Hirsch Eisenstadt (1813–1868) served as rabbi in various communities in Poland and Lithuania. In his detailed Introductions in his work *Pitḥei Teshuvah*,[60] he too emphasized the importance of knowing the laws contained in the responsa, the need to compile those laws, and the value of the earlier compilations, as well as of *Sha'arei Teshuvah*, which had just been published. Since Ḥayyim Mordecai Margolioth had written his *Sha'arei Teshuvah* only on *Oraḥ Ḥayyim*, Eisenstadt undertook to write a work "like *Sha'arei Teshuvah* . . . in the same form and style"[61] on the other three parts of the *Shulḥan Arukh*. His work is compiled from approximately one hundred eighty books.[62] Eisenstadt frequently commented on the responsa he quoted, and he also expressed his own opinions.[63]

57. TB Shabbat 21a; *see supra* p. 946.

58. For further discussion of this point, *see supra* pp. 975–978 and *infra* pp. 1457–1459.

59. *See* the Introduction of Ephraim Zalman Margolioth to *Sha'arei Teshuvah* (near the end). The book also contains some responsa written before the previous compilations, "because there are still responsa of *rishonim* not included in *Bet Yosef* that were also omitted from *Panim Ḥadashot* and *Leket ha-Kemaḥ*." *Id.*

60. *See* Eisenstadt's Introduction at the beginning of Sh. Ar. YD, and especially the Introduction to EH.

61. *Pitḥei Teshuvah*, YD, Introduction.

62. *Id.*

63. At the end of the Introduction to *Pitḥei Teshuvah* on EH, Eisenstadt stated that a few years later he added summaries of laws from other books, such as *Resp. Ḥatam Sofer.* As already seen *supra*, with the ongoing production of responsa, frequent updating is necessary. Thus, Ḥayyim Benveniste had to supplement *Keneset ha-Gedolah* with *Sheyarei Keneset ha-Gedolah* on OḤ and YD and a revised version of *Keneset ha-Gedolah* on ḤM.

J. *Oraḥ Mishpat* by Raḥamim Elijah Ḥazzan

Raḥamim Elijah Ḥazzan (d. 1840) was a *dayyan* in Izmir. *Oraḥ Mishpat*[64] is a comprehensive compilation of the responsa literature, the codificatory literature, and other halakhic (and even homiletical) literature arranged according to the topical order of the *Turim* and *Bet Yosef Ḥoshen Mishpat.* Ḥazzan not only discussed the material but also stated his own conclusions. *Oraḥ Mishpat* is particularly important because it is one of the last compilations of a substantial amount of material in the field of *mishpat ivri* from the halakhic literature of eastern Jewry in the relatively recent period.

K. *Darkhei Teshuvah* by Ẓevi Hirsch Shapira and His Son Ḥayyim Eleazar Shapira

Darkhei Teshuvah by Ẓevi Hirsch b. Solomon Shapira (1850–1913) and his son Ḥayyim Eleazar Shapira (1872–1932) summarizes the responsa pertaining to the subjects dealt with in *Shulḥan Arukh Yoreh De'ah.* The material is culled from a very large number of books of responsa—even larger than the number of sources for *Pitḥei Teshuvah.* The authors' own comments are also presented in the form of novellae.

L. *Oẓar ha-Posekim*

Oẓar ha-Posekim is a comprehensive and important but as yet uncompleted compilation on *Shulḥan Arukh Even ha-Ezer* by a group of Jerusalem rabbinic scholars originally headed by Chief Rabbi Isaac ha-Levi Herzog and Rabbi Isser Zalman Meltzer. The first volume appeared in 1947; by 1993, eighteen volumes, covering sixty-nine chapters of *Even ha-Ezer,* had been published.[65] The material is culled from a very large number of books of responsa, as well as other halakhic literature,[66] and is of great value in the day-to-day work of the Israeli rabbinical courts in the area of family law.

64. The word *Oraḥ* is a Hebrew acronym of Elijah Raḥamim Ḥazzan; *see* the book's Introduction written by the author's brother.

65. Six volumes are devoted solely to Sh. Ar. EH ch. 17, which treats the laws of the *agunah.*

66. *See* the list of books in vol. 1 (2nd ed., corrected and supplemented, 1955), pp. 368–371, and in subsequent volumes. *See also* vol. 1, pp. 375–402, for a bibliographical listing of the works of the codifiers and respondents.

M. *Halakhah Pesukah*

Halakhah Pesukah, published by the Harry Fischel Institute for Research in Jewish Law, is compiled and edited by a group of halakhic scholars headed by Jacob Meshullam Ginzburg. It abstracts from a very large number of books of responsa and other halakhic literature, by both early and later authorities, all the legal material pertaining to subjects treated in *Shulḥan Arukh Ḥoshen Mishpat.* It arranges the material according to the topical order of *Ḥoshen Mishpat,* contains brief supplementary notes and explanations, and briefly states its own determination of the law. To date, two volumes, covering the first twenty-seven chapters of *Ḥoshen Mishpat,* have been published. The first volume, which appeared in 1962, covers the first eight chapters, and the second, published in 1987, covers chapters 9–27.[67]

VI. CODIFICATORY LITERATURE AFTER THE *SHULḤAN ARUKH*

A. In General

As described in chapter 37, the negative reactions to the *Shulḥan Arukh* by contemporaneous and later halakhic authorities led to the writing of various books of *halakhot.* The two foremost examples, which were previously discussed, are *Yam Shel Shelomo* by Maharshal[68] and the *Levushim* by Mordecai Jaffe.[69] However, the addition of the classic commentaries on the *Shulḥan Arukh,* together with the particular historical circumstances already discussed, led to the acceptance of the *Shulḥan Arukh* as the authoritative code of Jewish law. Many books of *halakhot* were written after the *Shulḥan Arukh,* but most of them do not deal with matters within the scope of *mishpat ivri;* they are essentially different from the earlier codes, especially in the limited authority accorded them. For reasons meriting further analysis, from the time of the appearance of the *Shulḥan Arukh* some four centuries ago, no other work has achieved the status of an authoritative and binding code. However, before turning to that analysis, it should be noted that in various areas of *mishpat ivri* that were still applicable in practice, compila-

67. For further information, *see* the Preface to *Halakhah Pesukah,* vol. 1, pp. 25–34. At the end of the volume, there is a detailed and concise table of contents, to which detailed subject and source indexes are also appended. The second volume also contains subject and source indexes.

68. *See supra* pp. 1385–1394.

69. *See supra* pp. 1394–1403.

tions of laws continued to be published even after the *Shulḥan Arukh.* The compilations of tax laws provide an interesting example.

B. Compilations of Tax Laws

As has been extensively described elsewhere,[70] Jewish law includes a ramified and detailed system of tax law, covering numerous and varied aspects of the subject. The rudiments of tax law go back to the Bible, and the subject was developed and expanded in the Talmud; but the main creativity in the field began in the various Jewish centers in the twelfth century, and accelerated from the thirteenth century on. This process of development is also evident from the literary sources of Jewish law. Both Alfasi's *Sefer ha-Halakhot,* written in the eleventh century, and Maimonides' *Mishneh Torah,* in the twelfth century, contain extremely sparse material on tax law. The *Turim,* written in the fourteenth century, has a more extensive discussion of the subject;[71] and Caro's *Bet Yosef* and *Shulḥan Arukh* and Rema's *Darkhei Moshe* and glosses to the *Shulḥan Arukh,* written in the sixteenth century, deal with tax law much more comprehensively.[72] The subject is also abundantly discussed in the various compilations appended to the *Turim* and the *Shulḥan Arukh* and in the responsa literature. The responsa, particularly from the thirteenth century on, include sections devoted exclusively to tax law and contain a great deal of rich material on that subject. Tax laws are also treated in detail in the compilations of the legislative enactments of the various Jewish communities.

It is of interest that compilations of tax laws were also published separately. As early as the eleventh century, Joseph Tov Elem wrote a short work on the subject;[73] and in the fourteenth century, some fifty tax laws, in summary form, were set forth in the *Nimmukim* of Menahem of Merseburg.[74] However, large comprehensive compilations of tax laws did not appear until shortly after Caro's time. These large compilations were the product of eastern Jewry, where Jewish civil and public law continued to be applied in practice even after their practical application had begun to decline in western Jewish communities.[75] These compilations also deal with the binding nature and authority of custom, since that subject is closely bound up with tax law. The following are three examples of such compilations.

70. *See* M. Elon, EJ, XV, pp. 840–873, s.v. Taxation (reprinted in *Principles,* pp. 662–701), and *see supra* pp. 450–452, 745–751, 920–923.

71. *Tur* ḤM ch. 163.

72. Sh. Ar. ḤM ch. 163.

73. Published in *Resp. Maharam of Rothenburg,* ed. Prague, #940–941.

74. The collection is appended to *Resp. Mahari Weil.*

75. *See infra* pp. 1576–1577, 1584–1586

1. *MASSA MELEKH* BY JOSEPH ibn EZRA

Joseph b. Isaac ibn Ezra was a halakhic authority in Salonika in the sixteenth century. In the Introduction to his book *Massa Melekh,*[76] he wrote that until Joseph Caro published *Bet Yosef,* a "work whose equal in clarity and precise analysis has never been seen," judges and rabbis had faced great difficulties in making halakhic rulings on account of the proliferation of books and differences of opinion. Since the *Shulḥan Arukh,* however, "the world is at peace. When the wise men seek out the word of the Lord, they will find in it [the *Shulḥan Arukh*] all that they desire."[77] Nevertheless, Joseph ibn Ezra discovered that doubt and confusion still existed with respect to many laws, and he therefore began to compile a compendium of *halakhot* on *Tur Ḥoshen Mishpat,* following the topical sequence of the *Turim.*

When he reached chapter 163, he discovered that the *Turim* mentioned only a few laws concerning taxes, and that although *Bet Yosef* contained many additional references, it was still extremely difficult to find any particular tax law. Therefore, "I decided that it would be fitting to study and explore this subject, and I discovered that these laws are scattered over a large number of places. No one source contains them [all], and not even the many sources [fully cover the subject]. I [therefore] decided to compile all the laws on this subject and also include other pertinent novellae that I have expounded." Because of the large quantity of the material, ibn Ezra decided not to link his work to the *Turim,* "but to make it into a separate brief treatise that the reader will quickly apprehend, and that will be as frontlets before the eyes of the judge, who will thus know every matter thoroughly."

Massa Melekh is divided into seven sections according to a precise topical arrangement. Each section deals with a specific topic and is divided into chapters (*she'arim,* lit. "gates") that are further subdivided into paragraphs (*mishpatim,* lit. "laws"). The discussion of the laws is very detailed, and all the differing opinions are given on each point. Ibn Ezra also appended at the end of the book a "brief summary of all the laws, stated categorically, so that these laws should be familiar to all." He thus adopted a codificatory approach very similar to Caro's: first he expounded all the laws in detail, including all differences of opinion (like *Bet Yosef*), and then he presented a short, categorical statement of each law (like the *Shulḥan Arukh*).[78] Ibn

76. "I have called it *Massa Melekh* [The Burden of the King] because it deals with the burden the kings put upon us [*i.e.,* payment of taxes], by virtue of which our existence is secured." *See also supra* pp. 36–37, 745–746.

77. *Massa Melekh,* Introduction; subsequent quotations are also from this Introduction, ed. Salonika, 1601.

78. The seven sections begin on p. 7, col. 3 and end on p. 53, col. 2; the summary begins on p. 65, col. 1 and ends on p. 70, col. 2. Joseph ibn Ezra emphasized in his Intro-

Ezra believed that this dual arrangement would enable the reader and the judge to locate each law easily, together with all the different opinions with regard to it, "without needing any other book."[79]

A section of *Massa Melekh* is devoted to the laws relating to custom in Jewish law, because tax law "is dependent on custom, and the subject of custom also involves many details not found in any one book devoted to the subject. The laws are scattered and appear in many places. I therefore decided to collect them all and explain and clarify them."[80] He called this section of his work *Ne'ilat She'arim* [The Closing of the Gates]; and it, too, is arranged in the dual form of the rest of the book—a section of detailed treatment of the laws concerning the nature and force of custom, followed by a section summarizing the laws in categorical form.[81]

2. *AVODAT MASSA* BY JOSHUA ABRAHAM JUDAH

Joshua Abraham Judah was a halakhic authority in Izmir, in the nineteenth century. His book *Avodat Massa* [The Labor of the Burden] contains sixty-five chapters, which present a collection of enactments and customs and various responsa on tax law by Joseph Escapa (1570–1662), the Rabbi of Izmir, as well as responsa by later authorities.[82]

---

duction that in the final analysis it is the reader or judge who must determine what the law is, and that this determination must be made in accordance with the reader's own analysis: "Everyone, according to his own intelligence and opinion, will find in it something beneficial . . . so that the reader can easily determine, as to every law, whether it is universally accepted or is subject to dispute. He will thus be easily able to arrive at a judgment that is completely and truly correct [*din emet le-amito, see supra* pp. 159, 179–180] without having to consult any other book." The Afterword of the book states: "Everyone, according to his own intelligence, will find in it something beneficial, to the limits of his abilities." In his emphasis on the role of the judge's own analysis in reaching a legal conclusion, ibn Ezra's approach to decision making is evidently different from that of Caro, and closer to that of Asheri and other early authorities as well as to Jacob Pollack, Shalom Shakhna, Rema, and other Polish halakhic authorities. *See supra* pp. 1223–1229, 1346–1347, 1354–1356, 1378–1379, *et al.*

79. *See supra* n. 78. To this end, ibn Ezra added a detailed table of contents and detailed indexes of the sources on which he drew.

80. For a detailed discussion of the dependence of tax law on custom as a legal source, *see* M. Elon, EJ, XV, p. 845, s.v. Taxation (reprinted in *Principles*, pp. 668–669), and *supra* pp. 920–923.

81. The *Ne'ilat She'arim* section on the laws relating to custom begins on p. 53, col. 2 and ends on p. 65, col. 1; the summary begins on p. 70, col. 2 and ends on p. 72, col. 3. The book closes with a very short Afterword.

82. *Avodat Massa* is arranged as follows: the first twenty-five chapters are devoted to communal enactments; chs. 26–64 are apparently responsa regarding taxation; and ch. 65 is a short alphabetic collection of tax laws culled mainly from *Keneset ha-Gedolah*.

3. *MASSA ḤAYYIM* BY ḤAYYIM PALACHE

Ḥayyim Palache (1788–1869), one of the prolific nineteenth-century halakhic authorities in Izmir, wrote *Massa Ḥayyim* [The Burden of Life (*Ḥayyim*), *or* The Burden of Ḥayyim] shortly after *Avodat Massa* appeared. The work consists of three sections. The first contains a very large collection of enactments and customs largely relating to tax law. The second contains other laws relating to taxes, and the third deals with the subject of custom generally. The material in each section is arranged alphabetically.[83]

C. Codificatory Literature Devoted Mainly to Religious Law

The extensive literature of commentaries on the *Shulḥan Arukh* and the enormous growth of the responsa literature in the seventeenth and eighteenth centuries[84] gave rise to the need for new codes in the same way that the increase in halakhic literature had created a similar need in previous periods. However, the various codes written from the middle of the eighteenth century onward were vastly different from the earlier ones in both nature and scope. Most codificatory works written in this period deal mainly with the subjects treated in the *Oraḥ Ḥayyim* and *Yoreh De'ah* parts of the *Shulḥan Arukh, i.e.,* religious law; only a few discuss laws relating to *Even ha-Ezer* and even fewer deal with the subjects of *Ḥoshen Mishpat.*

Among the works written in this period are: *Tevu'at Shor* by Alexander Sender Schor (d. 1737), on *Shulḥan Arukh Yoreh De'ah;* the *Shulḥan Arukh* of Shneur Zalman of Lyady (1748–1813), the founder of the Ḥabad (Lubavitch) Hassidic movement;[85] *Ḥayyei Adam* [The Life of Man] by Abraham Danzig (1748–1820), on *Oraḥ Ḥayyim;* and *Ḥokhmat Adam* [The Wisdom of Man] by the same author, on *Yoreh De'ah.*[86]

The most popular and widely distributed work of this type is the *Kiẓẓur Shulḥan Arukh* [The Abridged *Shulḥan Arukh*] by Solomon Ganzfried (Hungary, 1804–1886), which covers all the laws pertinent to everyday life. Most

83. The choice of the titles *Avodat Massa* and *Massa Ḥayyim* was influenced by the title Joseph ibn Ezra gave to his book *Massa Melekh. See* Ḥayyim Palache, *Massa Ḥayyim,* Introduction.

84. As to the growth of the responsa literature, *see infra* pp. 1488–1491.

85. The book covers OḤ and part of YD. It also contains a section that treats "necessary [*i.e.,* applicable] laws compiled from *Tur* ḤM."

86. Abraham Danzig also wrote *Sha'arei Ẓedek,* which deals with the laws directly relating to the Land of Israel. He wrote the book in the hope that he would emigrate to the Holy Land, where he would need to know all these laws. It is interesting that whereas *Ḥayyei Adam* has been published in nearly sixty separate editions, and *Ḥokhmat Adam* in nearly twenty editions, *Sha'arei Ẓedek* was first published by the author in 1812 and was later printed twice in Jerusalem—in all only three editions.

of these laws are derived from *Oraḥ Ḥayyim,* some from *Yoreh De'ah,* and a few from *Even ha-Ezer* (marriage customs, the marriage ceremony, the *ketubbah*). Of the 221 chapters of the book, only eleven (179–189) deal with the laws relating to *Ḥoshen Mishpat* (loans, damage to persons and property, etc.), and even those have the character of behavioral norms rather than legal rules.[87]

Another popular work is *Mishnah Berurah* by Israel Meir ha-Kohen (known, after the name of another of his works, as "Ḥafeẓ Ḥayyim"; Lithuania, 1839–1933). This book is a commentary on *Shulḥan Arukh Oraḥ Ḥayyim* and is widely accepted as authoritative.

D. *Arukh ha-Shulḥan* by Jehiel Michal Epstein

An exceptional codificatory work written after the *Shulḥan Arukh* is *Arukh ha-Shulḥan* by Jehiel Michal b. Aharon Epstein (1829–1908), the Rabbi of Navardok, Poland. This work treats the material covered in all four parts of the *Shulḥan Arukh,* and additional material as well. Its purpose is to summarize the law as it had developed until the author's time and to decide between the different opinions held by the later halakhic authorities.

Epstein's instructive Introduction[88] first discusses the basis for the Oral Law, the nature and limits of halakhic disagreement, and the various codificatory works that preceded the *Shulḥan Arukh* and were intended to summarize and determine the law.[89] It then points out that many important books, some of which it names, had been written since the *Shulḥan Arukh,* and therefore "anxiety and confusion have reappeared, particularly in this lowly generation in which there are few students of Torah." Epstein therefore undertook to compose a work, arranged in the topical order of the *Shulḥan Arukh,* that would have as its main objectives: (1) to explain briefly

87. *Kiẓẓur Shulḥan Arukh* has been published in an extremely large number of editions, some of which have supplements and commentary. In Israel, editions have been published with vocalized Hebrew and with an appendix entitled *Kiẓẓur Dinei Ereẓ Yisra'el u-Minhageha* [A Summary of the Laws and Customs Applicable in the Land of Israel].

88. *Arukh ha-Shulḥan,* ḤM, part I, Introduction. Epstein began his work with ḤM "because it is a very deep subject, [requiring great efforts] to locate all the profound and extensive statements of the *aḥaronim.*"

89. Epstein, like many of his predecessors—among them Yom Tov Lipmann Heller (*see supra* pp. 1405–1406), whom he quoted—asserted that Caro and Rema never intended their "condensed" statement of the law to be the basis for legal rulings, and that to prevent this from occurring, "the great authority, Rabbi Mordecai Jaffe, composed his book, the *Levush,* in which he explained at somewhat greater length the [rationale of the] statements in the *Shulḥan Arukh.*" However, Epstein continued, since that time many great halakhic authorities had written books on the *Shulḥan Arukh*—such as *Sema, Baḥ,* and the other main commentators—thus causing anxiety and confusion to return. Epstein therefore wrote his work to correct this situation.

"with their underlying rationale" the rulings of the *Shulḥan Arukh;*[90] (2) to present the various opinions since the *Shulḥan Arukh* and decide between them (however, Epstein emphasized that the reader would be able to make his own final determination: "When there is a dispute between the later authorities, I have cited their opinions; where I felt that I could decide between them, I have done so, according to my humble opinion, but the final choice is up to the reader");[91] (3) to respond to the critics of Maimonides and Caro; and (4) to present laws culled from the *rishonim* that do not appear in existing codes, and also new laws introduced by the author himself.

Arukh ha-Shulḥan also includes laws that had been omitted from the *Shulḥan Arukh* because they no longer applied in practice. Some of these laws, such as the laws of ordination *(semikhah)*, laws relating to plotting witnesses (*hazzamah*), and laws of penalties, relate to general subject areas that are covered by the *Shulḥan Arukh.* As to such laws, *Arukh ha-Shulḥan* follows Maimonides—without attribution—with conflicting opinions introduced by the statement "there are those who say" and accompanied by the source reference.

Arukh ha-Shulḥan also codifies subjects that are outside the scope of the *Shulḥan Arukh,* such as the laws concerning the corners of the field in which gleanings must be left for the poor (*pe'ah*), and the priestly tithe (*terumah*)—both treated in the Mishnaic Order of *Zera'im*—as well as the laws of the Sanhedrin, the rebellious elder, and kings. This last part is entitled *Arukh ha-Shulḥan he-Atid* [The *Arukh ha-Shulḥan* of the Future].[92]

All parts of the work[93] bear the mark of a master craftsman. The discussions are brief, concise, and written in an easy and pleasant style; and

90. In *Arukh ha-Shulḥan,* statements from the *Shulḥan Arukh* are quoted without attribution. However, when opinions of other halakhic authorities are quoted, their sources are cited in brackets.

91. *Arukh ha-Shulḥan,* Introduction (near the end), subpar. 3. Thus, on this basic question of decision making, Epstein adopted the approach of Asheri and other *rishonim* and of the first major Polish authorities, Jacob Pollack and Shalom Shakhna, as well as Rema, Falk, and their successors. This approach requires a judge to consult the various opinions on the issue involved, to study the issue in the light of the discussion in the Talmud, and to decide in accordance with the opinion that seems to the judge to be correct. Consequently, Epstein took care to give the reasons for the laws, so as to enable judges and students to arrive at their own conclusions.

92. *See Arukh ha-Shulḥan he-Atid, Zera'im,* 1938, Introduction by the author's grandson, Meir Bar-Ilan (Berlin). *See also id.* for a detailed description of the book's organization. As far as *mishpat ivri* is concerned, mention should be made of the volume of *Arukh ha-Shulḥan he-Atid,* Jerusalem, 1962, which contains the laws of the Sanhedrin, the rebellious elder, kings, *shekalim* (the annual tax paid to the Temple), and the laws pertaining to the calendar.

93. *Arukh ha-Shulḥan* has eight volumes. As to *Arukh ha-Shulḥan he-Atid, see supra* n. 92.

the explanations are clear and lucid. However, notwithstanding its excellence, *Arukh ha-Shulḥan* has not been accorded the status of an authoritative and binding code; certainly it does not even begin to rival the unique authority of the *Shulḥan Arukh* of Caro and Rema.

E. Causes of the Decline of Codificatory Authority and Activity

Our study of the codification of Jewish law has revealed an interesting cyclical pattern with respect to codificatory activity. From the time that the first codes were composed by Babylonian *geonim* during the eighth and the ninth centuries C.E., new codificatory works have appeared at regular intervals of one to two hundred years. Each new code was written to satisfy the needs of its time: in the eleventh century, Alfasi's *Sefer ha-Halakhot;* in the twelfth century, Maimonides' *Mishneh Torah;* in the fourteenth century, Jacob b. Asher's *Turim;* and in the sixteenth century, Caro's and Rema's *Shulḥan Arukh.* However, since the *Shulḥan Arukh,* this historical pattern has been broken, and no new code has achieved recognition as authoritative.

It seems clear that this breach in the historical pattern is a result of the events commencing at the end of the eighteenth century with the advent of the Emancipation, which fundamentally changed the organization and nature of Jewish society. The abrogation of Jewish administrative autonomy, which led to the gradual abrogation of Jewish juridical autonomy and the division of Jewish society into traditional and nontraditional segments, led to a decline in halakhic authority and to a weakening of the dynamism of Jewish law. There was, consequently, less need for any additional code.

The area occupied by Jewish law and the influence of Jewish law in the daily life of the people steadily diminished. As a result, in the same way that the earlier codes, with rare exceptions, such as the *Mishneh Torah,*[94] did not concern themselves with the laws of sacrificial offerings and ritual purity because those laws were not then applicable in practice, so too the scope of codificatory literature from the middle of the eighteenth century became limited to areas of law relevant to the daily life of that time, *i.e.,* those subjects treated in the *Shulḥan Arukh* in *Oraḥ Ḥayyim, Yoreh De'ah,* and a portion of *Even ha-Ezer.* The laws of *Ḥoshen Mishpat* were virtually ignored in the codificatory literature; they were still the subject of academic study, but not for the purpose of determining the law for practical application.

Moreover, the codificatory works written after the *Shulḥan Arukh,* even as to the fields of law they covered, have been no challenge to the

94. Another exception is *Sefer Eẓ Ḥayyim* by Jacob Ḥazzan; *see supra* pp. 1255–1256.

Shulḥan Arukh as the authoritative code of Jewish law; in fact, they have become part of the vast literature of commentary surrounding that work. While it is certainly true that no judge applying Jewish law can reach a decision without first consulting the many commentaries on the *Shulḥan Arukh*—as well as the Talmudic commentaries, novellae, the responsa literature, and even the legislation and customs since the time of the *Shulḥan Arukh*—nevertheless Caro's and Rema's work has retained its supremacy as the authoritative and binding code of Jewish law.

F. The Problem of Codification at the Present Time

At the conclusion of this discussion of the history and nature of the codification of Jewish law, it is appropriate to address briefly the problem of codification in the contemporary period. This problem relates not merely to the "legal" part but to all facets of Jewish law. Our generation has witnessed some of the most far-reaching changes ever to occur in Jewish history; and it is evident that all the factors and conditions that in past generations impelled codification have reappeared—with even greater intensity—in our time. These factors and conditions include: conflicts of opinion among the halakhic authorities; difficulties in finding one's way through the enormous amount of halakhic literature (particularly the literature since the appearance of the *Shulḥan Arukh*); division of the Jewish people into traditional and nontraditional segments; and, above all, large numbers of problems arising from the social, economic, and technological conditions of the present time, which have become immeasurably more acute with the restoration of Jewish political sovereignty in the State of Israel. All these factors make it imperative that all the laws in the halakhic system—especially in those areas of Jewish law that apply in practice to life in a contemporary Jewish sovereign state—be compiled, and that in light of such a contemporary compilation, decisions on the new problems be arrived at, new enactments be adopted, and the law be perfected by the exercise of the broad power that Jewish law has always vested in the halakhic authorities.

This prerogative of the halakhic authorities includes not only the privilege of studying and expounding the law, but also the duty to produce practical solutions to problems, and to present contemporary society with a clear statement of the law relevant to the problems of the individual Jew and of the Jewish nation living in its own land. The call for a third code of Jewish law that should emerge from the Land of Israel—as did the other two great codes, the Mishnah and the *Shulḥan Arukh*—is thus entirely justified and indeed necessary to meet the needs of our time.

The code that is needed is not one that presents a single, uniform, and categorical statement of the law. Even if such a code could resolve all contemporary problems, it would be undesirable: not only would it by its very nature be controversial, but it would be alien to the nature of Jewish law and would even endanger the legitimacy and vitality of the halakhic system. Any summary must be faithful to the essential nature of Jewish law, which fosters multiplicity of opinions and approaches. We too, in our time, have the duty to make an additional and fundamentally important contribution to the body of codificatory literature: a code that will not replace, but will carry forward and blend with the *Shulḥan Arukh.* Jehiel Michal Epstein, the latest author of a book of *halakhot,* has described the *Halakhah* in the following felicitous metaphor:[95]

> All the different points of view among the *tannaim,* the *amoraim,* the *geonim,* and the later authorities are, for those who truly understand, the words of the living God. All have a place in the *Halakhah,* and this indeed is the glory of our holy and pure Torah. The entire Torah is described [in the Bible] as a song, and the beauty of a song is enhanced when the voices that sing it do not sound alike. This is the essence of its pleasantness. One who travels the "sea of the Talmud" will hear a variety of pleasant sounds from all of the different voices.

The *Halakhah* is a mighty symphony made up of many different notes; therein lies its greatness and beauty. In every generation, it needs a great conductor, blessed with inspiration and vision, who can find the interpretation of its many individual notes that will please the ear and respond to the needs of the contemporary audience.

95. *Arukh ha-Shulḥan,* ḤM, Introduction.

Chapter 39
THE RESPONSA LITERATURE

I. Introduction
II. Responsa in the Talmudic Literature
III. The Nature and Content of the Responsa Literature
    A. The Distinctiveness of the Responsa Literature as Compared with the Other Types of Post-Talmudic Halakhic Literature
    B. The Special Significance and Weight of the Rulings in the Responsa
    C. The Respondent as a Supreme Judicial Tribunal
    D. Responsa and the Development of Jewish Law
    E. Matters of *Mishpat Ivri* as the Major Subjects of the Responsa
    F. The Magnitude of the Responsa Literature
    G. Responsa as a Source for Knowledge of Enactments, Customs, Legal Documents, and Non-Jewish Law
    H. Responsa on Questions of Textual Interpretation, Philosophy, and Religious Beliefs
    I. Responsa as a Source for the History of Halakhic Literature
    J. Responsa as a Historical Source
    K. Responsa and Parallels in Other Legal Systems
IV. The Different Periods of the Responsa Literature
    A. The Geonic Period
    B. The Period of the *Rishonim* (Early Authorities)
        1. The Nature and Content of the Responsa in the Period of the *Rishonim*
        2. The Twelfth to Fourteenth Centuries
        3. The Fifteenth Century
        4. Summary
    C. The Period of the *Aḥaronim* (Later Authorities) up to the End of the Eighteenth Century
        1. The Nature and Content of the Responsa in the Period of the *Aḥaronim*
        2. The Sixteenth Century
        3. The Seventeenth Century
        4. The Eighteenth Century
    D. The Period of the Emancipation—the Nineteenth Century
        1. The Nature and Content of the Responsa in the Nineteenth Century and Thereafter
        2. The Responsa in Different Jewish Centers
    E. The Period of National Awakening, the Holocaust, and the Establishment of the Jewish State—the Twentieth Century
        1. The Responsa Literature until the 1940s
        2. The Responsa Literature in the 1940s and Thereafter
    F. Summary
V. General Overview of the Methodology, Structure, and Form of the Responsa
    A. The Questioners; Submission of Questions
    B. The Structure, Form, Style, Transmittal, and Copying of the Question and Response
    C. Fictitious Names of Persons and Places in the Responsa
    D. Hypothetical Responsa; *Terumat ha-Deshen*
VI. Compilations of Responsa—Redaction and Organization
VII. Research in the Responsa; Digest of the Responsa Literature

I. INTRODUCTION

The responsa literature is the third major type of literary source of Jewish law in the post-Talmudic period.[1] The term "responsa" includes all of the recorded rulings and decisions rendered by the halakhic authorities in response to questions submitted in writing. This literary source includes the preponderance—both quantitative and qualitative—of *mishpat ivri* in the post-Talmudic period.[2]

II. RESPONSA IN THE TALMUDIC LITERATURE

The practice of submitting questions and transmitting responsa from one place to another is noted as early as the tannaitic and amoraic literature. For example, the Talmud states:[3]

> R. Judah said in the name of Samuel: "The inhabitants of the 'region of the sea' [those residing overseas or outside of the Land of Israel] sent the following inquiry to Rabban Gamaliel: 'If a man comes from there to here [from the Land of Israel to a foreign land] whose name is Joseph but he is called Johanan, or his name is Johanan and he is called Joseph, how should he divorce his wife?' [*I.e.*, what name should be written in the bill of divorcement (*get*) to avoid subsequent problems?] Rabban Gamaliel thereupon enacted a *takkanah* that they should write: 'The man named So-and-so' and [then list] every other name by which he has been known, 'the woman named So-and-so' and [then list] every other name by which she has been known, in order to promote the public welfare."

In other words, Rabban Gamaliel the Elder promulgated an enactment to achieve an effective solution to the problem posed by the query put to him. Under his enactment, all of a person's names should be written in the *get*—both the present name or names and all previous names, thus precluding

1. In this chapter, several general topics pertaining to the responsa literature are discussed. A more detailed study of this literature is being prepared by the author.

2. *See infra* pp. 1462–1463. For further information on various aspects of the responsa literature, *see* I.Z. Kahane, *Meḥkarim be-Sifrut ha-Teshuvot* [Studies in the Responsa Literature], Jerusalem, 1973; S. Freehof, *The Responsa Literature*, JPS, Philadelphia, 1959.

3. TB Gittin 34b.

the possibility that after a woman remarries, the *get* in her possession could be said to be that of a different woman.[4]

During the amoraic period, there was a lively exchange of questions and responsa between Babylonia and the Land of Israel, as well as responsa from both Babylonia and Israel to all of the other centers of the diaspora: "Throughout the lifetime of Rav, R. Johanan wrote to him: 'To our esteemed teacher in Babylonia.'" When he [Rav] died, he [R. Johanan] wrote to Samuel: 'To our esteemed colleague in Babylonia.'"[5] These salutations reveal the relationship between R. Johanan, the leader of the second generation of *amoraim* in the Land of Israel, and Rav and Samuel, who were the leading *amoraim* at the beginning of the amoraic period in Babylonia. This correspondence took place "when R. Johanan wrote from the Land of Israel with a question or response."[6] Another source tells of an exchange of questions and responsa between Alexandria, Egypt, and the Land of Israel.[7] Many records of correspondence sent from the Land of Israel to Babylonia are extant.[8] Many questions and responsa were also sent from one city to another, and from one *yeshivah* (academy) to another, within Babylonia.[9]

The responsa during the Talmudic period were incorporated as an integral part of the Talmud where relevant to the subject matter discussed.[10]

4. As to this enactment, *see supra* pp. 563–564. Outside the scope of the present discussion are the sources that record questions that were asked orally and answered on the spot rather than transmitted from one place to another, such as M Beẓah 3:5: "It happened that they asked R. Tarfon about it. . . . He went into the study hall and asked, and they said to him. . . . "

5. TB Ḥullin 95b.

6. Rashi, *ad loc.*

7. TJ Kiddushin 3:12, 40b (3:14, 64d): "R. Tanḥum b. Papa sent a question to R. Yose [about] two cases in Alexandria, one involving an unmarried woman, and one involving a married woman. Regarding the married woman, he sent him in writing . . . ; regarding the unmarried woman, he sent him in writing. . . . He said to R. Maneh, 'Sit and sign' [*i.e.*, join in the responsum], and he signed. He said to R. Berakhiah, 'Sit and sign,' but he refused."

8. *E.g.*, by Ravin (TB Ketubbot 49b, Bava Meẓi'a 114a, Bava Batra 127a, Niddah 68a) and R. Dimmi (TB Temurah 14a/b); *see also* TB Bava Batra 41b, Sanhedrin 29a, *et al.*

9. TB Gittin 66b: "They sent from Rav's academy to Samuel"; TB Bava Batra 36b: "The residents of Pum Nahara sent to R. Naḥman b. R. Ḥisda"; *id.* 127a/b. *See also* Epstein, *Mavo*, pp. 699–700; Z. Frankel, *Entwurf Einer Geschichte d. Literatur d. Nachtalmudischen Responsen* [Outline of the History of the Post-Talmudic Responsa Literature], 1865, pp. 7–8; J. Müller, "Briefe und Responsen in der Vorgeonaischen Jüdischen Literatur" [Epistles and Responsa in Pre-Geonic Jewish Literature], *Vierter Bericht über die Lehranstalt fur die Wissenschaft des Judenthums in Berlin* [Fourth Report of the Berlin Institute for the Science of Judaism], 1886, pp. 3–36.

10. There were also exchanges between the Land of Israel and Babylonia in the savoraic period. *See, e.g.*, TB Ḥullin 59b ("They sent from there [*i.e.*, the Land of Israel]: 'The law follows the view of Samuel b. R. Abbahu [of the first generation of *savoraim*], but take care [in honoring] Rabbenu Aḥai [also of the first generation of *savoraim*], for he enlightens

They do not appear as a separate literary form; it is only from the geonic period that the responsa became a distinct literary source. The responsa from the geonic period onward also differ in scope, content, and style from those recorded in Talmudic literature. For these reasons, the responsa literature is not considered a separate genre of halakhic literature until the geonic period.

III. THE NATURE AND CONTENT OF THE RESPONSA LITERATURE

The responsa literature is distinctive in many respects: its essential character, which is unlike the other types of post-Talmudic halakhic literature; its subject matter; its importance for *mishpat ivri* in particular, as well as for Jewish law in general; its significant contribution to the history of the literary sources of the various periods of Jewish law; and the rich storehouse of information it provides about the history of the Jewish people in its different centers. The following sections discuss each of these aspects of the responsa literature.

A. The Distinctiveness of the Responsa Literature as Compared with the Other Types of Post-Talmudic Halakhic Literature

The basic purpose of the responsa literature is the same as that of the codificatory literature, *i.e.*, to determine the law and resolve legal problems. In this respect, responsa and codes differ from commentaries and novellae, which study the halakhic material so as to be able to understand and explain it, mainly for academic purposes rather than for practical application. Codes and responsa have a common goal; however, they differ greatly in the methods by which they attempt to reach it.

The author of a code arrives at a conclusion after examining the existing halakhic materials from a theoretical point of view. In contrast, the

---

the eyes of the exile.'"). *See also* N. Brüll, *Jahrbücher für Jüdische Geschichte und Literatur* [Jewish History and Literature Annual], II (1876), p. 27 n. 26; S. Assaf, "Bavel ve-Ereẓ Yisra'el bi-Tekufat ha-Geonim" [Babylonia and the Land of Israel in the Geonic Period], *Ha-Shilo'aḥ*, XXXIV, p. 228 and n. 7; Z. Yavetz, *Toledot Yisra'el* [History of the Jewish People], IX, pp. 215, 220; B.M. Lewin, *Rabbanan Savorai ve-Talmudam* [The Savoraic Rabbis and Their Teachings], 1937, pp. 14–15. *But see* H. Albeck, *Mavo la-Talmudim* [Introduction to the Talmuds], pp. 442–443 and n. 459, asserting that TB Ḥullin 59b refers to *amoraim* and not *savoraim*. The responsa of the *savoraim*, like their other supplementary material, were incorporated in the text of the Talmud.

reader of a responsum is in the midst of a real-life legal situation, listening to the facts and the arguments of the parties to an actual case and accompanying an authoritative halakhic decisionmaker during each stage of the progress to a final decision. The student and the researcher studying a responsum are participants in a creative process. They share in experimentation and creation. They participate in a comprehensive and penetrating legal analysis. They receive an objective description of the economic and social background as part of the legal discussion; and they can discern clues, some more apparent than others, to the arduous search of the halakhic authority for a legal solution that is anchored in the past, yet satisfies the manifold needs of his own generation.

B. The Special Significance and Weight of the Rulings in the Responsa

Because the legal principles derived from the responsa are the result of consideration of legal problems that have arisen out of practical life, those principles are accorded particular authoritative weight. Our discussion of *ma'aseh* as a legal source of Jewish law[11] took note of the special importance Jewish law attaches to a legal principle that is the outcome of a real-life situation. It was further noted that a rule introduced into Jewish law through a legal source other than *ma'aseh* is accorded special force and weight once it has been applied in practice and has been tested in the crucible of actual life, for "a *ma'aseh* is of great significance"[12] and "a *ma'aseh* is entitled to particular deference."[13] A decision that must be followed and is not open to argument comes about "if he [the student] asks and they tell him that the norm is intended to be applied in practice. [Then] he may go and apply it in practice [and it is unnecessary to ask for guidance in each such case that subsequently comes before him]."[14] This quality of living law applicable in real life, which is the essence of every responsum, endowed the legal rule derived from a responsum with special standing and force exceeding that of a rule resting on commentaries or novellae. Indeed, most halakhic authorities rank legal rules based on responsa even higher than those based on the books of the codifiers, to the point of resolving inconsistencies between codificatory literature and responsa literature in favor of the responsa literature.

At first blush—and this is the opinion of some halakhic authorities—

11. *See supra* pp. 945ff.
12. TB Shabbat 21a and Rashi, *ad loc.*
13. TB Bava Batra 83a.
14. *Id.* 130b; for detailed discussion, *see supra* pp. 963–964.

it would seem that a legal rule contained in a code should be preferred "since it was arrived at with a deeper analysis of the roots of the laws . . . , for sometimes one cannot be sufficiently thorough [in a responsum] because of the urgency in responding to the question";[15] therefore, when a conclusion is recorded in a code, "the halakhic scholar has achieved a clearer comprehension of the subject than that attained at a time when an actual problem is posed."[16] However, the majority of the halakhic authorities take the opposite view:

> As to what you wrote about not being able to rely on responsa, the contrary is true. Responsa embody decisions in actual cases, and we may learn more from them than from the statements of the codifiers, since they [the codifiers] did not write their conclusions in the process of determining the law for a concrete situation.[17]

The reason for this conclusion is that:

> It is possible that he [the codifier] wrote what he did because he thought it correct theoretically, but not for application in an actual case; however, in a responsum, [the author] takes great pains to state his reasoning meticulously in order to instruct the questioner how to act.[18]
>
> A more profound understanding of the subject is reached when responding for practical application than when engaging in theoretical study, and there is also greater divine guidance in an actual case. . . . Rulings arrived at in the course of a responsum in an actual case have greater force and are closer to the truth than conclusions reached as a result of theoretical study.[19]

15. Jonah Navon, *Resp. Neḥpah ba-Kesef,* II, EH #27 (beginning), s.v. Ra'iti. This statement was made by Navon in connection with a contradiction in the views of Ḥayyim Shabbetai (Maharḥash) between a ruling in his codificatory work, *Kunteres ha-Agunot,* and a decision contained in his responsa, *Resp. Torat Ḥayyim. See* Navon's further comment: "In the same way, we rely on the *Piskei ha-Rosh* [as to which *see supra* pp. 1251–1253.] rather than on his responsa in the event of any inconsistency, as is well known"; and *see infra* n. 19.

16. Moses Aryeh Bamberger, the Rabbi of Kitzingen, stating the explanation of his father, Isaac Dov Bamberger, for requesting that his responsa not be published. The statement is quoted by N.Z.J. Berlin (Neẓiv), *Resp. Meshiv Davar,* I, #24. *See further infra.*

17. *Resp. Maharil* #72. This responsum is quoted at greater length *supra* pp. 976–977.

18. Moses Benveniste, *Resp. Penei Moshe,* I, #12, s.v. Ve-hineh (p. 27b). *See also* his further statement: "Furthermore, it is possible that this responsum was written after his codificatory rulings, since many of his responsa cite those rulings"; and *see infra* n. 19. *See also* E.Z. Margolioth's Introduction to the compilation of responsa *Sha'arei Teshuvah* on OḤ: "A responsum is more to be relied on than a code, since it is a ruling intended to be applied in practice and he [the respondent] is far more careful [in his ruling] than is a codifier, who writes the laws in solitude, perhaps for theoretical purposes only and not for practical application." *See supra* pp. 1440–1441.

19. *Resp. Meshiv Davar,* I, #24. For further discussion of this responsum, *see supra* pp. 977–978. The inquirer had relied, *inter alia,* on "the agreement of the authorities that greater

The responsibility of rendering a judgment in an actual case submitted for decision stimulates analysis penetrating to the heart of a matter and is accompanied by divine guidance merited by the authority who takes upon himself the responsibility to solve real-life problems. The effect of all of this is that the decisions of such a person will be inspired by the search for truth and will correctly declare the law.[20]

---

reliance should be placed on Asheri's codificatory rulings (*pesakim*) than on his responsa." Neẓiv answered as follows:

> The authorities' agreement to rely on *Piskei ha-Rosh* when inconsistent with his responsa is not based on logic (*sevarah*) but on a tradition they received from his [Asheri's] son Rabbenu Judah, who presumably knew that the *pesakim* were written after the responsa and that Rabbenu ha-Rosh [Asheri] had retracted [what he had written earlier]. Take note that Ranaḥ [Elijah b. Ḥayyim] wrote in a responsum (I, #46) that if we know that he [Asheri] retracted in a responsum an opinion he had given in his *pesakim*, the responsum prevails. It follows, therefore, that the main reason [for generally preferring Asheri's *pesakim*] is that presumably the converse was true, and he retracted in his *pesakim* the opinion he had given in the responsa.

The statement of Judah, Asheri's son, referred to by Neẓiv, is found in *Resp. Zikhron Yehudah* #15: "When I discover a contradiction between the *pesakim* and the responsa, I follow the *pesakim* because they are later." This statement clearly supports Neẓiv's contention. Asheri's other son, Jacob, the author of the *Turim,* also explained his reliance on his father's ruling in the *pesakim* on a particular matter as against the view taken in one of his father's responsa by stating that the ruling in the *pesakim* "was later" (*Tur* ḤM ch. 72, end).

Some halakhic authorities concluded on the basis of these considerations that Asheri's *pesakim* should always prevail in case of inconsistency with his responsa; *see Bet Yosef* to *Tur* YD ch. 341, s.v. U-ve-inyan havdalah. *But see Perishah* to *Tur* ḤM 72:35. *See also Resp. Maharik* 161:7 (ed. Lemberg 1798; ed. Warsaw 1884 and facsimiles, #159 [2nd], p. 87a. #137 is missing in ed. Warsaw and #159 appears twice; thus, #160 and #161 both are numbered 159). Maharik indicated in his decision that he relied on Asheri's *pesakim* and not Asheri's responsa because Asheri's view in the *pesakim* on the specific issue followed that of Rabbenu Tam, and because several other authorities had agreed with Rabbenu Tam.

Elsewhere, however, Joseph Caro, in line with the view of most authorities, stated that Asheri's *pesakim* should not be relied on as against his responsa in every instance when the two are inconsistent because "he [Rabbenu Judah] did not lay down a general rule; it was only in regard to a particular responsum that he said that he knew that the ruling in the *pesakim* came later than the responsum. That case is no precedent for other cases." *Bet Yosef* to *Tur* YD chs. 168–169, s.v. Va-adoni avi z.l. katav bi-teshuvah (toward the end). *See Derishah, ad loc.*, subpar. 14, for an explanation of *Bet Yosef.* To the same effect, *see Bet Yosef* to *Tur* YD ch. 201, s.v. Aval rabbenu (in the middle, shortly before a large section containing a gloss of *Bedek ha-Bayit*). *See also Resp. Maharit,* II, ḤM #7: "During all those years when Rosh [Asheri] was occupied with his *pesakim,* did he post a gatekeeper at the entrance to the study hall to prevent people from asking him questions of *Halakhah*?" Most halakhic authorities are of the opinion that, as a general rule, even in the case of Asheri, rulings in responsa have greater weight than a statement of law in a code. *See* H. Michael, *Or ha-Ḥayyim,* s.v. Rabbenu Asher b. Jehiel, pp. 259–260. As to the general relationship of codes and responsa, *see* I.Z. Kahane, "Ha-Pesak ve-ha-Teshuvah" [The Codificatory Ruling and the Responsum], *Sefer ha-Shanah le-Madda'ei ha-Yahadut ve-ha-Ru'aḥ Shel Universitat Bar Ilan* [Bar Ilan University Annual for Judaic Studies and Humanities], I, pp. 270ff.

20. Although the essence of the common-law system is judicial decisions, and statutes constitute only "a gloss" (*see* Paton, *Jurisprudence,* 1964, 3rd ed., p. 219), a statute overrides

C. The Respondent as a Supreme Judicial Tribunal

In the Jewish legal system, there was always a supreme tribunal which dealt with problems the lower courts were unable to resolve, or to which certain types of legal issues or cases involving special circumstances were submitted in the first instance.[21] In the geonic period, such supreme tribunals existed in the Land of Israel and in Babylonia. The academy (*yeshivah*) in the Land of Israel considered itself to be "the court for the entire Jewish people."[22] The patriarch in the Land of Israel declared that his jurisdiction extended to the entire Jewish people, even to those residing in far-off places, and that judges everywhere were subject to his authority.[23] The Babylonian academies—in theory and in practice—regarded themselves as the successors to the High Court in Jerusalem, with all of the prerogatives that flowed from that status.[24]

With the decline in the authority and influence of these centers, the respondents—who were the legal and spiritual leaders of their generation—increasingly functioned as supreme tribunals. Complex problems that local courts could not resolve, and fundamental questions transcending the immediate parties and involving the wider public, ultimately reached one of the recognized respondents active in the various centers of the diaspora.[25] These respondents constituted an unofficial and informal supreme

---

a common-law judicial precedent to the extent of any inconsistency between them, because the statute is adopted by the superior authority—the legislature. In Jewish law, however, a codificatory work does not have the standing or the force of legislation, since it merely summarizes and restates the existing law. Even when a codificatory ruling makes a legal determination by choosing among different opinions, the source of the power to make such a ruling is precisely the same as the source of the power to reach a decision in a responsum, *i.e.*, the decision-making power of the halakhic authorities.

The counterpart in Jewish law of the statute in common-law jurisdictions is the legislative enactment—the *takkanah* and *gezerah; see supra* ch. 13 *et seq.* Indeed, a provision in a *takkanah* adopted by a competent authority overrides a contrary halakhic rule contained in a responsum or a codificatory work. *See also* B. Lifshitz, "Ma'amadah ha-Mishpati Shel Sifrut ha-She'elot ve-ha-Teshuvot" [The Legal Status of the Responsa Literature], *Shenaton,* IX–X (1982–1983), pp. 265ff., at p. 290.

21. *See* Deuteronomy 17:8–13; M Sanhedrin 1:5, 11:2; TB Sanhedrin 31b, 32b; Maimonides, *MT,* Sanhedrin 5:1, 6:6–9; Sh. Ar. ḤM 14:1–3. With regard to the question of appeals and appellate tribunals in Jewish law, *see supra* p. 801 n. 76 and accompanying text, pp. 824–826; *infra* pp. 1598–1599, 1809–1818.

22. *Sefer ha-Yishuv,* II (1944), Introduction, p. 36.

23. *Id.* at 32. *See id.* for a detailed discussion of the status of the leadership in the Land of Israel.

24. *See* L. Ginzberg, "Keta'im mi-Kitvei ha-Geonim min ha-Genizah she-be-Miẓrayim" [Fragments from the Geonic Writings from the *Genizah* in Egypt], *Ginzei Schechter,* II, pp. 47ff. and references there cited.

25. This transfer of authority, and particularly the halakhic basis for the respondent's authority, has yet to be adequately studied; *see infra* n. 43.

tribunal for Jewish law. In this role, the respondents also contributed to the preservation of a certain measure of uniformity of decision and to the maintenance of close ties among the different communities within each Jewish center and between one center and another.[26]

D. Responsa and the Development of Jewish Law

The responsa literature is extremely important for the development of Jewish law and for the study of the law's developmental process. Questions submitted to a respondent arose in the factual context of the time, and the responsum had to resolve the issues in a manner consonant with the contemporaneous circumstances. The subjects of the questions generally related to social, economic, technological, and moral conditions, which differed from period to period and from place to place. The social and economic circumstances of Babylonian Jewry in the eighth and ninth centuries C.E., for example, differed from those of Polish Jews in the sixteenth century; and the condition of Spanish Jewry in the thirteenth century bore no resemblance to that of the Jews of Salonika in the sixteenth and seventeenth centuries. The halakhic authorities in each generation were called upon to determine the position of Jewish law with regard to the questions that arose in their time; and if they could find no explicit solution in existing law or if, in their opinion, the existing legal rules did not satisfy the needs of the time, they sought and found a solution by means of one or more of the legal sources of Jewish law—interpretation, legislation, custom, *ma'aseh*, and legal reasoning (*sevarah*). The responsa literature thus reveals innumerable new problems that arose in the course of centuries and exemplifies how the methods for the development of Jewish law were utilized to find solutions.[27]

E. Matters of *Mishpat Ivri* as the Major Subjects of the Responsa

The responsa literature constitutes a treasury of information for all areas of Judaism.[28] However, its major concern and importance relate to the function for which it was created: the elucidation and practical application of Jewish law. It is a telling statistic that in the overwhelmingly greater part of

26. For further discussion of this point, *see infra* pp. 1468–1471, 1473–1476, 1482–1485.

27. Various examples are cited throughout this work. *See, e.g., Resp. Ribash* #484, discussed *supra* pp. 709–710; Elon, *Ḥerut*, pp. 140ff., 261ff.

28. Commentaries and novellae, as well as codificatory literature, also contain material on general history and the history of halakhic literature; but this material is of lesser quantity and importance than that contained in the responsa literature.

the thirteen hundred years during which the responsa literature has existed, the part of the law included in *mishpat ivri—i.e.*, all aspects of civil law and a large proportion of administrative, public, and criminal law—accounts for seventy to eighty percent of all the responsa, whereas only twenty to thirty percent deal with the laws of *Oraḥ Ḥayyim* and *Yoreh De'ah* (benedictions, prayers, festivals, permitted and forbidden foods, impurity, the ritual bath, relations with non-Jews on religious matters, mourning, etc.).

This distribution of subject matter in the responsa is a consequence of the juridical autonomy in all the Jewish centers until the onset of the Emancipation at the end of the eighteenth century.[29] The major problem areas that required halakhic solutions were in the "legal" part of the *Halakhah* and not its "religious" part. Although both segments of the *Halakhah* were applied in daily life, the overwhelming majority of the problems produced by changing conditions related to the "legal" segment. Jewish social life, commerce, and economy; Jewish public organization in the framework of the organized community and its governing institutions and elected officials; and the relation of the Jewish community to the surrounding non-Jewish population and to the general government—all these gave rise from time to time to problems for which there were sometimes no clear solutions in the existing Jewish law. Therefore, it was occasionally necessary to find new solutions that were different from those which Jewish law had reached in the past. The special, the difficult, and the novel in these problems—in addition to the usual clash of interests between the litigants (a factor that does not generally exist in connection with the religious laws of *Oraḥ Ḥayyim* and *Yoreh De'ah*)—caused these questions to be brought to the generally recognized central halakhic authority for final decision.[30]

F. The Magnitude of the Responsa Literature

As stated, the responsa literature contains the preponderance of the material on Jewish law produced in the post-Talmudic period. There were many more respondents than writers of books of commentaries, novellae, and codes; it is estimated that there are extant approximately 300,000 responsa—300,000 legal decisions—found in more than three thousand books by different authors.[31] This preponderance is understandable in light

29. *See supra* pp. 6–13.

30. Indeed, from the end of the eighteenth century, the proportions of these two parts of Jewish law in the responsa literature changed radically. *See infra* pp. 1491–1494.

31. A "book" of a single author may contain several volumes, *e.g.*, *Resp. Rashba*, *Resp. Tashbeẓ*, *Resp. Maharibal*, *Resp. Maharashdam*, *Resp. Ḥatam Sofer*, *Resp. Noda bi-Yehudah*, *Resp. Maharsham*, *Resp. Ḥikrei Lev*, *Resp. Sho'el u-Meshiv*, *Resp. Ḥikekei Lev*, and many others. *See also infra* Appendix C.

of the nature of Jewish law. As the discussion to this point has repeatedly noted, Jewish law requires that no legal ruling be made except after a study of the various relevant opinions and approaches and after an examination of the correctness of each opinion in the light of the Talmudic sources, and these requirements have given rise to a cautious and skeptical attitude toward any code that is not linked to the sources of the law.

The central function in Jewish law is performed by the halakhic authorities of each generation, who examine and probe the different opinions on any issue and decide, on the basis of the Talmudic sources and their own understanding of the needs of the time, which view should be followed. In this function, the respondent is primary; he performs this function in his responsum much more fully than does the commentator in his textual elucidations, the writer of novellae in his novel interpretations, or the codifier in his theoretical analysis. Because the halakhic authorities understood that their major task within the halakhic system was to decide practical questions in the manner described above, and because Jewish law has always grown and developed out of the confrontation with concrete problems arising out of practical life, the responsa literature has proliferated and has become—quantitatively as well as qualitatively—the major literary source of Jewish law in the post-Talmudic period.

G. Responsa as a Source for Knowledge of Enactments, Customs, Legal Documents, and Non-Jewish Law

The responsa literature contains still other important material bearing on the study and analysis of Jewish law. In addition to legal arguments, responsa contain many references not only to enactments adopted by the halakhic authorities or by the lay communities but also to customary practices. Indeed, responsa are often the only extant source for our knowledge of certain enactments and customs. The responsa literature is also the source for the text of a vast number of different types of legal documents such as bills of sale, marriage documents, wills, forms of witness subpoenas, and judgments of local courts, all of which are also of prime legal importance.[32] Provisions of non-Jewish law quoted in the questions or in the responsa are also of great interest and considerable importance both for the study of Jewish law and for research and understanding of the general law of the particular time and place.[33]

32. *See infra* pp. 1527, 1533–1535.

33. For details as to the historical significance of responsa, *see Mafte'aḥ ha-She'elot ve-ha-Teshuvot Shel Ḥakhmei Sefarad u-Ẓefon Afrikah* [Digest of the Responsa Literature of Spain and North Africa], ed. M. Elon, *Historical Digest,* I (1981), Introduction and Index; *Legal Digest,* I, II (1986), Introduction and Index. *See also supra* pp. 62–74 and *infra* pp. 1523–1528.

H. Responsa on Questions of Textual Interpretation, Philosophy, and Religious Beliefs

Like all of the Oral Law, the responsa literature is a blend of *Halakhah* and *Aggadah,* law and morals, and patterns of life and thought. It is not at all rare for a respondent to turn from a purely legal discussion to consideration of matters of *Aggadah* and ethics. There are even some responsa dealing not with a particular halakhic or legal issue, but with such matters as: the interpretation of a Biblical verse or a rule of the Mishnah or the Talmud; religious belief, philosophy, or ethics; the role of the Jewish people among the nations of the world; and angelology, demonology, and astrology. Certain periods are notable for the relative frequency of one or more of these matters in the responsa. The geonic period, for example, was notable for responsa dealing with the explanations of terms or passages in the Talmud, and with matters of religious belief and the like.[34]

I. Responsa as a Source for the History of Halakhic Literature

The respondents' detailed analyses and their efforts to decide the cases submitted to them led them to make extensive use of all the material in the

34. Occasionally, responsa contain discussions of scientific matters pertinent to questions arising out of the needs of the time. *See, e.g., Resp. Tashbeẓ,* I, #163, #164, #165, #166, #172, where various mathematical problems are discussed in connection with the measurement of the quantity of water required for the ritual bath. The author, Simeon b. Ẓemaḥ Duran (Rashbeẓ), referred the questions to Majorca, "to Anbalshum Ephraim, because he is expert in mathematics." Rashbeẓ turned to the mathematician because "the matter depends on that discipline and is not a subject mentioned in the Talmud, and books of that discipline [mathematics] are not at present available, and whatever I learned about it when I was younger I have almost completely forgotten as a result of the tribulations of my travels" (*Resp. Tashbeẓ,* I, #163).

From the Jewish center in Yemen, not many compilations of responsa are extant (*see infra* p. 1499 n. 131). Interestingly, however, two large and important compilations that have survived deal entirely with matters of faith and belief, as distinguished from the familiar compilations from other centers, which deal primarily with purely legal matters.

The first of these compilations from Yemen contains one hundred responsa by Ḥoter b. Solomon, a fifteenth-century Yemeni halakhic authority. All of the hundred questions and forty-five of the answers were published in Arabic and translated into Hebrew by J. Ḥubarah and published in Nahum, *Ḥasifat Genuzim mi-Teiman* [Laying Bare the Archives of Yemen], Ḥolon, 1981, pp. 244–285. Fifty-four responsa by the same author were published in Arabic and translated into Hebrew by J. Kafaḥ and published as an appendix to N. Fayyumi, *Gan ha-Sekhalim,* Halikhot Am Yisra'el, Kiryat Ono, 1984.

Another compilation of forty-four responsa on matters of philosophy by Peraḥiah b. Meshullam, a Yemeni halakhic authority of the late fourteenth and early fifteenth centuries, was published by J. Kafaḥ in Arabic, with a Hebrew translation, *Sefunot* [New Series], III (18), Ben-Zvi Institute, Jerusalem, 1985, pp. 111–192.

literary sources of Jewish law, *i.e.*, Scripture, halakhic *midrashim*, the Mishnah, *Tosefta*, the two Talmuds and the rest of Talmudic literature, aggadic *midrashim*, the codificatory literature, commentaries, and novellae. As a result, the responsa literature has preserved a vast number of textual variations in many Talmudic and post-Talmudic sources as well as in rabbinic texts that are extant only in manuscript form, if not completely lost.[35] The responsa literature also contains a considerable amount of material on oral traditions of decisions by halakhic authorities[36] and on how their books were composed and disseminated,[37] as well as much other literary-historical information.[38]

J. Responsa as a Historical Source

The responsa literature is an indispensable source for the history of Jewish law, for Jewish history in the different centers, and, to a certain extent, even for general history. A respondent—and, to some extent, his questioner—dealt with the particular facts of a concrete case, and in so doing transmitted, in a straightforward manner and without tendentiousness, descriptions of: diverse historical events relating to the political and legal status of the Jews (*e.g.*, the extent of their autonomy, their service in governmental and public offices, accusations made against them, and their expulsion from various centers); the locations of Jewish communities; the inhabitants and events in the various communities; the relationship between Jews and non-Jews with regard to economic and social matters and religious outlook; the Jewish communal institutions and their administrative processes; the social structure of the community; matters involving the judicial system; taxes; the family; education; language dialects (Yiddish, Ladino, etc.); folklore; extensive scientific information (diseases, vegetation, natural disasters); geography; the layout of cities, houses, and courtyards; weights and mea-

35. *See Mafte'aḥ She'elot u-Teshuvot ha-Rosh* [Digest of the Responsa of Asheri], ed. M. Elon, Introduction and pp. 427ff.

36. *See, e.g., Resp. Rashba,* I, #1206: "A case arose in our community and I so ruled in the presence of our rabbis, and my teacher, Rabbi Moses b. Naḥman [Naḥmanides], agreed with me." This is apparently the source for *Resp. Tashbeẓ,* II, #5: "We have also heard that Naḥmanides was asked about this matter orally, and he replied that all who marry do so subject to the conditions laid down by the Rabbis." *See also supra* pp. 853–854, 861.

37. *See, e.g.,* Maimonides (*Resp. Maimonides,* ed. Freimann, #152, p. 145) on "the first early version" of his *Mishneh Torah* and subsequent revisions of the text; as to Maimonides' statement regarding the dissemination of his work, *see supra* pp. 1222–1223. *See also* the statement of Asheri's son Judah, *Resp. Zikhron Yehudah* #15, quoted *supra* n. 19, concerning the sequence in which his father's codificatory work and responsa were written.

38. *See, e.g., Resp. Tashbeẓ,* I, #72, for a comprehensive and instructive responsum containing such information.

sures; coinage; utensils; basic materials; and similar matters. Responsa reveal innumerable details in all areas of the historiography of the community and the individual, on holidays, ordinary days, and somber days, in happy times and in times of mourning. It is difficult to exaggerate the importance and reliability of the responsa literature for the light it casts on significant historical periods.[39]

K. The Responsa and Parallels in Other Legal Systems

The form of the responsa is somewhat similar to the *responsa prudentium* of Roman law[40] and is particularly comparable, in its authoritative nature and its creative function, to the *Fatwa* (plural: *Fatwi*) of Moslem law.[41] The compilations of responsa in Jewish law are comparable to collections of judicial decisions in other legal systems, although there is a difference between them. Judicial decisions in other legal systems are rendered in cases that the parties have submitted to a court for determination, whereas a responsum is not handed down by a formal judicial tribunal. The respondent is an outstanding and recognized halakhic authority, and, generally speaking, it is not the parties, but the local judge before whom the parties have appeared, who submits the question to the respondent.[42]

39. *See* on this point *Mafte'aḥ ha-She'elot ve-ha-Teshuvot, supra* n. 33, *Historical Digest,* I (1981), Introduction; II (1987), Introduction. *See also infra* pp. 1525–1528. Clearly, caution must be exercised in drawing historical conclusions; there were textual changes and deletions because of both internal and external censorship (*see infra* pp. 1511, 1520–1521). Also, terms used by respondents sometimes had different meanings when the responsa were written than they had had in earlier periods or than they do today. Generalizations on the basis of one or more isolated instances should also be avoided. The fact that compilations of responsa were often edited not by the author but by his students or sons—at times long after the responsa were written—also calls for very careful deliberation in drawing conclusions. However, all these precautions must be taken in the critical examination of any text, and the need to take them in no way detracts from the particular reliability and importance of the responsa literature as a historical source.

40. *See* H.F. Jolowicz, *Historical Introduction to the Study of Roman Law,* Table of Contents and particularly pp. 369ff., concerning the procedures governing the respondents and the responsa in the imperial period.

41. As to the *Fatwa* in Islamic law as compared to the parallel institution in Roman law, and the *Fatwa*'s reduced importance with the advent of legislation in the Ottoman Empire, *see Encyclopedia of Islam,* II (1965), s.v. Fatwa (p. 866). *See also* S.D. Goitein and A. Ben Shemesh, *Ha-Mishpat ha-Muslemi bi-Medinat Yisra'el* [Moslem Law in the State of Israel], pp. 25ff., 29, 35.

42. *See further infra* p. 1501. Generally, neither the records nor judgments in court proceedings in the various periods of Jewish law have been preserved in halakhic literature, except for a few decisions in specific matters that are scattered throughout the Mishnah and Talmud (*see supra* pp. 950ff.), the responsa and other post-Talmudic halakhic literature (*see supra* pp. 973ff.), and other kinds of writings such as historical sources (*e.g.,* a court judgment in 1648 C.E. preserved in the records of the town scribe of Cracow; *see* Elon, *Ḥerut,* p.

However, this difference between responsa and judicial decisions is only superficial and formal. The common feature of both is that both contain a description of the facts, the parties' arguments, the evidence, and the legal analysis; both include a legal conclusion and a decision; and both are authoritative and definitive—the one by virtue of the judge's formal legal authority, and the other by virtue of the respondent's spiritual eminence as a halakhic authority.[43] The compilations of responsa are especially comparable to the Law Reports of English law and the law reporter systems of American law. The creativity of Jewish law lies mainly in its concrete decisions on practical questions, not in the formulation of general theoretical principles. This characteristic permitted the halakhic authorities a considerable amount of maneuverability and flexibility, because it made it possible for the decisionmaker to hold either that a prior legal decision controlled the case under consideration or that a distinction should be made between the cases.[44] This is also the method of the common law—which was created and evolved as case law and in which the art of distinguishing prior authoritative decisions plays an important and decisive role—in contrast to Continental law, which is based on and develops through codification. The largest and most substantial segment of the law in both the Jewish and the common-law systems is judge-made law—reported in the common law in the reports of judicial decisions and in post-Talmudic Jewish law in the compilations of responsa.[45]

---

188). It is only relatively recently—ca. eighteenth century—that judges' record books containing the judgments of various courts have been preserved. These judgments generally consist of only the legal conclusions and the final decision, with no detail or discussion of the arguments.

Transcripts of proceedings and full judicial opinions in cases in the rabbinical courts in the Land of Israel are available starting in the 1930s. In 1950, the first volume of the opinions of the Rabbinical Court of Appeals was published, covering opinions between 1943 and the establishment of the State of Israel in 1948. This volume contains about fifty edited and digested opinions (*see infra* p. 1601). Since 1956, reports of the opinions of the regional rabbinical courts and the Rabbinical Court of Appeals have regularly appeared; thirteen volumes have been published to date. Most of the opinions deal with family law; approximately thirty percent are concerned with issues in other areas of Jewish civil law. The opinions are published in their entirety; they contain a full statement of the facts, the evidence, the arguments, and the reasons for the decision. *See also infra* pp. 1818–1819.

43. Clearly, the authority of the respondent stemmed mainly from his expertise in the *Halakhah* and his spiritual stature. The writings of some authorities were viewed in many places, even in their own lifetime, as binding (*see supra* pp. 1222–1223, 1343–1344, *et al.*); such personages were accepted as authoritative respondents. However, as pointed out *supra* n. 25, the halakhic basis for the authority of a respondent still has not been completely clarified.

44. *See supra* pp. 960–968.

45. For the similarities and the differences between a responsum (and a *ma'aseh*) in Jewish law, on the one hand, and a judicial precedent in the common law on the other, *see*

In short, the nature and content of the responsa literature—with its unique qualitative and quantitative characteristics—and the fact that this literature, which has extended over a period of almost thirteen hundred years, encompasses the greater part of the structure and the process of development of Jewish law, make the examination and study of responsa central to the research of Jewish law.[46]

IV. THE DIFFERENT PERIODS OF THE RESPONSA LITERATURE

As stated, the responsa literature as a separate literary form originated in the beginning of the geonic period, and it continues to flourish to this very day. During this long period, the responsa literature—like other forms of halakhic literature—has reflected changes in content, style, and structure, corresponding to the era and sometimes even to the place in which it was written. At times, one can detect changes even within a single historical period,[47] such as between the beginning and the end of the period of the *rishonim*. However, for convenience of presentation, the following discussion examines the various periods as usually designated: the periods of the *geonim*, the *rishonim*, the *aḥaronim* up to the onset of the Emancipation, the Emancipation, the "National Awakening," and the establishment of the State of Israel.

A. The Geonic Period[48]

The writing of responsa on a large scale in the geonic period dates mainly from the middle of the eighth century C.E. At that time, the Babylonian academies (*yeshivot*) and the *geonim* who headed them still exercised spiri-

---

supra pp. 978–986. *See also* E. Shochetman, "Ḥovat ha-Hanmakah ba-Mishpat ha-Ivri" [The Obligation to State Reasons for Legal Decisions in Jewish Law], *Shenaton*, VI–VII (1979–1980), pp. 319ff., at pp. 338ff.

46. Responsa in Jewish law occupy a position similar to the central position of case law in the common-law system. As to the importance of responsa for research in *mishpat ivri, see supra* pp. 80–91.

47. *See supra* pp. 39–45.

48. On the literature of the geonic period, *see* Assaf, *Geonim*, pp. 211–220; B.Z. Dinur, *Yisra'el ba-Golah* [Israel in the Diaspora], I(2), pp. 120–126, and p. 149 n. 82; S. Abramson, *Ba-Merkazim u-va-Tefuẓot bi-Tekufat ha-Ge'onim* [In the Centers and the Diasporas in the Geonic Period], pp. 42, 94, 101; M. Margaliot, *Sefer Hilkhot ha-Nagid*, 1962, Introduction, pp. 3ff., *et al.* For further discussion of the geonic period and of the *geonim*, most of whom wrote responsa that are extant, *see supra* pp. 42–43.

tual hegemony over all the other Jewish centers of the diaspora.[49] The most common and frequent exchange of questions and responsa from the geonic period of which records are extant today was between Babylonia and the North African and Spanish Jewish communities. Many questions were received from the communities of Gabes, Fez, Kairouan, Tlemcen, Barcelona, and Lucena, and from communities in other centers, such as Egypt. The questions were generally assembled by the representatives of the *yeshivot* in the different centers and forwarded—sometimes tens in a parcel—by means of merchants and caravans. A central way station through which the caravans passed was Cairo, Egypt. Emissaries of the Babylonian *yeshivot*, usually outstanding scholars, resided in Kairouan and Cairo, where they occupied positions of honor; they sifted through the questions, polished their language, and, as far as possible, forestalled the transmission of questions that had been answered previously. Along with the questions, the inquirers sent donations of money for the support and maintenance of the *yeshivot*. It sometimes took a full year for the questions to reach their destination in Babylonia.

The answers of the *geonim* came back by the very same route; and as they passed through Cairo, they were copied by the *yeshivah*'s emissaries and by local scholars. Copies were kept there and also sent to other communities. As a result of this procedure, copies of many responsa were preserved in the storage chamber (*genizah*) of the Fostat (Old Cairo) synagogue, where they were discovered at the end of the nineteenth century. An invaluable treasure of geonic responsa that had been lost over the course of time was thus brought to light.[50]

The *gaon* was not the sole author of a geonic responsum; all the scholars of the *yeshivah* participated in its formulation. In this respect, geonic responsa differed substantially from those of the rabbinic period. Nathan ha-Bavli described the process as follows:[51]

> This was their [the geonic] practice in responding to questions: Each day in the month of Adar [one of the months of the *kallah*—the semiannual assembly when all of the scholars and students gathered together at the *yeshi-*

49. There was also at that time an active center in the Land of Israel, which, according to the little information available, was in contact with the diaspora, particularly with Italy; *see supra* p. 1460 and the references cited in nn. 22, 23. However, none of the responsa sent "from here to there" (from the Land of Israel to the diaspora) have yet been discovered, and the present work therefore does not deal with that subject. New responsa of the Babylonian *geonim* providing new information on geonic responsa literature continue to be discovered.

50. As to the Cairo *Genizah*, *see* S. Schechter, "A Hoard of Hebrew Manuscripts," *Studies in Judaism* (Second Series), JPS, 1908, pp. 1ff.; A.M. Haberman, *Ha-Genizah ve-ha-Genizot*, Jerusalem, 1971.

51. Neubauer, *Seder ha-Ḥakhamim*, II, p. 88.

> *vah*], he [the *gaon*] would present to them all the questions that he had received and give them leave to respond to them. They, out of respect for him, would reply: "We will not give a response in your presence," until he would prevail on them, and then each would give his answer in accordance with his knowledge and wisdom. They would ask questions, give answers, and debate each matter, examining it closely. The head of the *yeshivah* would hear what they said, consider their statements and queries to each other, and analyze their arguments until the truth was clear to him; he would then immediately [dictate the response and] direct the scribe to record [it]. This was their daily practice until they responded to all the questions that had reached them from the Jewish communities during the year. At the end of the month, the questions and answers would be read in the presence of the entire assembly and the head of the *yeshivah* would affix his seal on them, following which they would be sent to their recipients.

We learn from this description that each responsum was composed by the *gaon* only after deliberation and debate among the *yeshivah*'s scholars. Because all of the questions received over a period of time were answered during one of the two months (Adar and Elul) of the semiannual assembly, the *geonim* would dispatch parcels that sometimes included many tens of responsa. As can be seen from the dates recorded on certain responsa, they were sometimes also sent during the rest of the year when the question was urgent and means for delivering them were available. Copies were generally kept in the archives of the *yeshivot*.

The special authority over the other Jewish centers enjoyed by the Babylonian *yeshivot* and those who headed them was also expressed in the text of the responsa of this period. The language is generally categorical and imperative ("This is the *Halakhah*," "It may not be departed from," "It may not be modified," etc.); and the directive or decision in the responsum was accepted as binding in the community that had submitted the question. The responsa of the early *geonim* were, in the main, extremely brief. In the course of time they became longer, but even then they were fairly concise and focused on the question asked, citing only a few Talmudic sources.

The questions submitted to the *geonim* were extremely varied. Some requested the explanation of particular Talmudic terms or passages, and some the explanation even of entire chapters or tractates (Tractates *Shabbat* and *Avodah Zarah*; one responsum is an entire book—the *Siddur* [Prayer Book] of Amram Gaon).[52] Other questions related to matters of faith and belief, to which answers were needed for debates with Karaites or Moslems. Still others concerned medicine or science, or the validity of various customs. The famous epistle of Sherira Gaon was composed in response to a

52. *See supra* p. 1158 n. 31.

question on the history of the Oral Law.[53] Of course, many questions dealt with legal issues that arose out of daily life. The *geonim,* by basing their responsa on the Babylonian Talmud, greatly contributed to the dissemination and acceptance of that Talmud in all Jewish communities.[54]

The geonic responsa were collected in an early period—at the latest in the days of Hai Gaon—and grouped in compilations.[55] These compilations included responsa by different *geonim;* they were sometimes arranged according to subject matter, author, or sequence of the Talmudic tractates. As a result, responsa that had originally comprised a single unit were occasionally scattered among different compilations. Sometimes, the copyists or the editors of the compilations condensed and abridged the responsa, deleting the dates, the names and locations of the inquirers, and the opening and closing lines.[56] This editing makes it difficult to identify and to understand the meaning of many responsa. An interesting characteristic of the responsa literature appears as early as the geonic period: the use of fictitious names (generally, the names of the sons of Jacob and the names of the matriarchs—Reuben, Simeon, Sarah, Rebecca, etc.) rather than the actual names of the parties.[57]

53. *See infra* p. 1542.

54. *See supra* pp. 1099, 1131.

55. *See* Assaf, *Geonim,* p. 218; *see also Resp. Ri Migash* #114 (discussed in detail *supra* p. 977). Maimonides, *MT,* Introduction states: "Many requests were made to the *gaon* of the time by people from different cities to explain difficult passages in the Talmud, and he would answer them as he deemed wise. Those who made the requests collected the responsa and made books of responsa for study." It should be pointed out that Maimonides did not confine the title *gaon* to the Babylonian *geonim:* "All these *geonim* who arose in the Land of Israel, Babylonia, Spain, and France. . . . " Apparently, the compilations of responsa were edited outside Babylonia; and each compilation also contains responsa of European authorities who lived at the end of the geonic period or soon thereafter, such as Kalonymus and his son Meshullam, Moses the Captive and his son Enoch, and Alfasi. Some compilations of geonic responsa include responsa inserted by the editors from much later periods, such as responsa of Naḥmanides and Rabbenu Tam. *See* Assaf, *Geonim,* pp. 218–219, and Z. Grunner, "Le-Ẓuratan ha-Mekorit Shel Ḥamishah Kuntresei Teshuvot" [On the Original Form of Five Compilations of Responsa], *Alei Sefer,* II (1976), p. 5.

56. A question submitted to Ri Migash (beginning of the twelfth century) indicates an awareness of this problem: "You are surely aware that the responsa [of the *geonim*], particularly the earlier ones, have not all been accurately recorded; the copyists introduced errors and also attributed some of the responsa to the wrong authors. Furthermore, many *geonim* made rulings in responsa that [either] they later retracted, or others proved were erroneous" (*Resp. Ri Migash* #114). *See also* Rabad, *Temim De'im* (ed. Lemberg, 1812) #61, #62, particularly the beginning of #62 (p. 6d), as to mistakes in geonic responsa (in connection with the writing of an *orkhata*—a document assessing the value of a debtor's property for the purpose of enforcing the creditor's claim—on movable property). This responsum is published in *Teshuvot u-Fesakim le-Rabbenu Avraham b. David* (ed. J. Kafaḥ, 1964) #141, p. 193.

57. *See, e.g.,* Harkavy, *Teshuvot ha-Geonim* #594, p. 275: "We have issued a ruling and a responsum referring to Reuben, Simeon, and Levi, as is the custom in responsa."

The copyists or editors of the collections of geonic responsa also prepared tables of contents (or lists of the responsa) that very briefly indicated the subjects of the responsa in the compilations. These tables of contents were of great value in finding a particular matter in a compilation—not only to anyone who had a copy of the compilation, but also to anyone who could afford only a copy of the table of contents. Some of the tables were organized according to the sequence of the subject matter in the Talmudic tractates.[58]

The extant geonic responsa are only a small part of the total number written—a few thousand out of tens of thousands. A large proportion were lost when communities were destroyed or when other calamities occurred. Scholars are still engaged in deciphering and publishing many responsa buried in the Cairo *Genizah.* Many have been preserved in whole or in part in the writings of *rishonim,* such as *Sefer ha-Ittur, Or Zaru'a,* the *Mordekhai,* and the works of Isaac ibn Ghiyyat and Judah al-Bargeloni.[59] More than half of the extant geonic responsa were written in the last generations of the *geonim,* mostly by Sherira Gaon and his son Hai Gaon.

More than twenty compilations of geonic responsa are extant. The first appeared in print at the beginning of the sixteenth century;[60] however, most were not printed until the twentieth century, when they were published by various scholars specializing in the study of the geonic period and its literature.[61] The important work of Benjamin M. Lewin, *Ọzar ha-Geonim,* is extremely useful for knowledge of the geonic responsa. The work follows the sequence of the Talmudic tractates; and twelve volumes (from Tractate *Berakhot* to *Bava Kamma,* inclusive, and the beginning of tractate *Bava Mẹzi'a*) have been published.[62] Each volume contains geonic responsa arranged according to the subjects of the tractate. *Ọzar ha-Geonim* to Tractate *Sanhedrin,* edited by Ḥayyim Ẓevi Taubes, was published in 1967,[63] with the

58. Such tables of contents have been discovered in the Cairo *Genizah.* They contain references to many geonic responsa that have not yet come to light, they indicate the original order of the responsa in the compilation (which was frequently changed by the editors or copyists), and they give names of persons and places that were in the original but later omitted. *See* S. Abramson, *Inyanot be-Sifrut ha-Geonim* [Aspects of Geonic Literature], 1974, pp. 196ff.; *Ginzei Schechter,* II, pp. 416–420. *See infra* pp. 1512–1515, regarding the use of fictitious names in compilations of responsa of *rishonim.*

59. Judah al-Bargeloni included a great number of geonic responsa in his books; however, few of his works have survived. *See supra* pp. 1177–1178.

60. *Halakhot Pesukot min ha-Geonim* [Halakhic Rulings of the *Geonim*], Constantinople, 1516, reprinted by J. Müller, 1893.

61. For a list of the compilations, *see* Assaf, *Geonim,* pp. 219–220; M. Kasher, *Sarei ha-Elef,* pp. 246–248; *infra* Appendix C.

62. *Ọzar ha-Geonim,* 1928 and thereafter. *See supra* p. 1114 and n. 47.

63. *Ọzar ha-Geonim to Tractate Sanhedrin, Responsa and Commentaries,* ed. H.Z. Taubes, Jerusalem, 1967.

responsa arranged according to the same principle used by Lewin in *Oẓar ha-Geonim.*

B. The Period of the *Rishonim* (Early Authorities)

1. THE NATURE AND CONTENT OF THE RESPONSA IN THE PERIOD OF THE *RISHONIM*

Toward the end of the geonic period, the spiritual hegemony of the Babylonian center over the other Jewish communities came to an end; and from that time, different Jewish centers functioned side by side, and various centers flourished and declined. No single center was acknowledged to have binding authority over any other; essentially, the affairs of each center were conducted under the authority of its own leaders.[64] This historical and spiritual transformation strongly affected many aspects of the history of Jewish law,[65] including the nature of the responsa and the methodology of the respondents. After the geonic period, there is no longer the magisterial tone of the geonic responsa reflecting the authority of the respondents over the entire Jewish people. Instead, in increasingly greater measure, the tone is more modest: the responsa conclude with "in my humble opinion," or "may the Merciful One save us from the abyss of judgment," or some similar expression. In some instances, although rarely, the respondent even declares that his decision is only theoretical and not for practical application.[66] In addition, post-geonic responsa generally did not have the concurrence of all the scholars of the *yeshivah* but were the opinion of the respondent alone.[67] In most instances, the responsa were directed to the members of the community from which the question came or, at most, to all the communities in the same Jewish center. Unlike most geonic responsa, they were not intended to be binding on the entire Jewish people.

64. *See supra* pp. 43, 666–667, *et al.*

65. *E.g.*, legislation, custom, and decision making became local, and the scope of the halakhic authorities' legislative function became more limited; *see supra* pp. 666–667, 780ff., 936.

66. Even as great and strong an authority as Rashba occasionally stated in a responsum: "I say this in theory only, not for practical application" (*Resp. Rashba Attributed to Naḥmanides* #222), or, "So it appears to me in theory but not for practical application" (*id.* #112, at beginning of s.v. Ve-yesh mi-gedolei ha-morim). This was particularly true with regard to the authority to enact legislation to annul a marriage; *see, e.g., Resp. Tashbeẓ,* II, #5, *et al.;* for detailed discussion, *see supra* pp. 856ff.

67. However, when serious issues were involved—such as whether to declare a married woman to be no longer bound by marriage—the respondent would co-opt other halakhic authorities to his responsum, occasionally including even students in his own *yeshivah. See infra* pp. 1505–1506 and sources cited in n. 153.

Gradual changes also occurred with respect to the length and the content of the responsa. During most of the geonic period, responsa were brief and categorical. At the close of the geonic period, the discussion was often more extensive, and the *gaon* not only relied on Talmudic sources but also cited decisions of earlier *geonim,* either to support his opinion or to distinguish or disagree with them. (This was the case, for example, in many responsa by Sherira Gaon and Hai Gaon.) However, it is clear from the geonic responsa that the respondents were cognizant of their authoritative status and felt no need to persuade by means of detailed discussion.

After the geonic period, responsa became progressively longer and more detailed. Generally, the respondent relied not only on Talmudic sources but also on geonic decisions—which were considered to be almost as authoritative as the Talmud itself—and on the opinions of earlier *rishonim;* and he analyzed these sources at great length and in detail, not only to shed light on the issue involved but also to persuade and to demonstrate that his decision was correct. A more substantial change occurred in the last part of the period of the *rishonim:* the respondent no longer confined himself to citing the primary sources for his view but set forth all the sources that lent support to his conclusion.[68]

As the length of responsa increased, the scope of their subject matter narrowed. There were fewer questions seeking the explanation of Talmudic passages or dealing with matters such as faith and belief. The *geonim* had been the final authorities to whom all queries pertaining to Judaism were directed, including queries about the Talmud itself; but after the geonic period, the questions sent to respondents dealt mainly with halakhic issues. One reason for the change was that an extensive literature of commentaries on the Talmud had accumulated, such as those of Rabbenu Hananel, Ri Migash, and Rashi; and many specialized books had been written on matters of faith and belief, following Saadiah Gaon's *Sefer Emunot ve-De'ot* [The Book of Beliefs and Opinions].

An additional consequence of the historical differences between the periods of the *geonim* and the *rishonim* was the reduction of the time between the sending of the question and the receipt of the responsum. The far-off Spanish communities no longer turned to the Babylonian *geonim*—an extremely great distance in view of the methods of communication of those days. Instead, questions were generally sent from one community to another within the same center. Even when a question was sent from one

68. Apparently, this last development started mainly in *Resp. Tashbeẓ; see* H. Jaulus, "R. Simeon ben Zemach Duran," *MGWJ,* XXIV (1875), pp. 170–171. This question, however, still requires more thorough study.

center to another or to an eminent distant authority, the distance involved was generally less than in the geonic period.

All these differences, however, do not diminish the basic importance, the measure of authority, or the status of the post-geonic responsa in the halakhic system. To the contrary, the responsa of the period of the *rishonim* are of prime importance for the creativity and development that they engendered in Jewish law in general and in *mishpat ivri* in particular. The respondents in this period are among the leading post-Talmudic halakhic authorities. Their authority was uncontested, and the few occasions when they refrained from issuing a definitive ruling for practical application were exceptional and due to special circumstances.[69] In the overwhelming majority of the cases submitted to them, they rendered a clear and unequivocal judgment; and when the resolution of the problem before them compelled the development of new principles or the modification of existing law, they did not hesitate to employ all the creative methods of the halakhic system to resolve the matter within the framework of Jewish law.

As stated, the changes in the post-geonic period did not occur all at once, nor should their significance be exaggerated. That the exchange of questions and responsa after the geonic period was normally within each center does not mean that communication in the form of questions and responsa between the different centers ceased. Considerable information exists concerning questions and responsa that were sent—from and after the beginning of the post-geonic period—from one center to another. Questions and responsa were frequently exchanged between the Spanish halakhic authorities and Rabbenu Gershom Me'or Ha-Golah in Germany;

69. *Resp. Rashba Attributed to Naḥmanides* #222 (referred to *supra* n. 66) involved the complex question of lending out orphans' money at interest. There are major differences of opinion on this question. *See* M. Elon, EJ, VIII, pp. 282–283, s.v. Hekdesh (reprinted in *Principles*, pp. 704–705). Similarly, the problem of enacting legislation involving the annulment of marriage arose against the background of the contraction of the territorial scope of legislation and the effect of that contraction on the law of marriage and divorce. *See supra* pp. 867–869, 877–879. *See also Resp. Ran* #62 (near the end)—"In such cases [*i.e.*, whether to use compulsion in accordance with Maimonides' opinion to require the husband to give a divorce], I fear to give judgment"; *Resp. Ribash* #228 (at the end)—"This is my opinion and conclusion, not as a decisionmaker and determiner of the law, but only as a participant in the discussion," although Ribash had specifically declared (*id.* at the beginning), "Let judgment come forth." (The issue before Ribash involved the administration of the Jewish community of Barcelona, and the leaders of the community had a personal interest in the outcome.) *But see Resp. Tashbeẓ*, I, #85 (toward the end): "It appears to me in this case to be so in theory. However, as to practical application, I cannot disregard Naḥmanides' opinion . . . that one should not recite the *kiddush* over it." (The question related to the use of certain wine for the *kiddush* benediction.) This entire subject of abstention from rendering definitive rulings requires more thorough study.

there is extant an exchange of responsa, apparently dating from the middle of the eleventh century C.E., between "the people of Spain" and "our rabbis in France and Germany."[70] Questions were submitted from southern France, Germany, Italy, and England to Rabbenu Tam in northern France. There was extensive correspondence between Rashba in Spain and authorities in France and Germany; among those who submitted questions to Rashba were Asheri,[71] Ḥayyim Or Zaru'a,[72] Eliezer b. Joseph of Chinon,[73] and Maharam of Rothenburg.[74] Ribash sent a responsum to Isaiah b. Abba Mari in Germany; and there is also extant a well-known exchange of letters between Johanan b. Mattityahu of Paris (the Chief Rabbi of France) and Ribash and Ḥasdai Crescas concerning the opposition instigated by Isaiah b. Abba Mari against Johanan b. Mattityahu.[75] Later—especially from the sixteenth century on—there was a lively exchange of questions and responsa between the different centers.[76] Thus, the major difference between the geonic period and succeeding periods in regard to the flow of responsa was that in the geonic period the overwhelming majority of the questions came from every Jewish community to the Babylonian center,[77] whereas thereafter the bulk was within individual centers.

The style of the responsa also underwent gradual change. At the beginning of the period of the *rishonim,* a significant portion of the responsa—such as those of Ḥanokh and Moses, in the first generation of the rabbinic period in Spain,[78] those from North Africa in the middle of the tenth cen-

70. *See Shibbolei ha-Leket,* II, #75 (ed. Ḥasida, pp. 147–148). *See also Sefer ha-Yashar* of Rabbenu Tam, Responsa, 46:4 (p. 90), regarding the scholars of Narbonne and Spain who sent questions to Rabbenu Gershom. *See also* S. Assaf, *Mekorot u-Meḥkarim* [Sources and Studies], pp. 119, 123–129.

71. While Asheri was still in Germany, *see Resp. Rashba,* I, #366.

72. *Resp. Rashba,* I, #571.

73. *Id.,* III, #7; IV, #152.

74. The exchange of questions and responsa between Rashba and Maharam of Rothenburg concerned an informer whom Rashba had sentenced to death. Maharam agreed with this decision. The responsa were published by R.D. Kaufman in *JQR,* VIII (1896), pp. 228–238. The halakhic part of the exchange is quoted in *Bet Yosef* to *Tur* ḤM ch. 388, *Meḥudashot* sec. 8. The responsum is missing in later editions of the *Turim,* which were censored, but does appear in ed. Königsberg. *See also* Assaf, *Onshin,* pp. 65–67; Baer, *Spain,* pp. 168–170 and n. 56.

75. *Resp. Ribash* #193, #268–272.

76. The increased number of exiles and emigrants in the sixteenth century (*see infra*) gave rise to a lively exchange of questions and responsa between the various centers; and the respondents in the sixteenth century in particular, as well as later respondents, sent their responsa to most of the Jewish centers.

77. As to the exchanges of questions and responsa with the Jewish community in the Land of Israel, *see supra,* p. 1460 and the references cited in nn. 22, 23, *ad loc.*

78. Some of their responsa were published in *Teshuvot Ge'onei Mizraḥ u-Ma'arav* (ed. J. Müller, 1888), from #163 on; a more complete compilation was published by Müller (in German with Introduction) in "Die Responsa der spanischen Lehrer des 10 Jahrhunderts,

tury C.E. and thereafter,[79] and those of Alfasi and Ri Migash—are still relatively brief and to the point. Maimonides' responsa are especially noteworthy in this respect; their style is sometimes extremely terse and magisterial; his shortest responsum is a one-word reply to a lengthy and detailed question.[80] However, most of the responsa, even in the early period of the *rishonim*, including responsa of Maimonides, are more elaborate, as were those of the early respondents in Germany and France, such as Rabbenu Gershom,[81] Rashi, and other early French and German *rishonim*.[82]

2. THE TWELFTH TO FOURTEENTH CENTURIES

The twelfth to fourteenth centuries constitute one of the most prolific periods of the responsa literature. The expansion of commercial and economic life and the stabilization of many Jewish communities, on the one hand, and the persecutions and afflictions visited on various Jewish settlements, on the other, gave rise to a vast array of questions that were presented to the halakhic authorities in the different centers. The major legal problems concerned the structure and administration of the community, the selection of its governing bodies, and its taxes and maintenance. Many matters of private law were also dealt with, such as questions involving the law of acquisitions and obligations, numerous problems of family law and in-

---

R. Mose, R. Chanoch, R. Joseph ibn Abitur" [The Responsa of the Spanish Teachers of the Tenth Century, R. Moses, R. Ḥanokh, and R. Joseph ibn Abitur], *Siebenter Bericht uber die Lehranstalt für die Wissenschaft des Judenthums in Berlin* [Seventh Report of the Berlin Institute for the Science of Judaism], 1889, pp. 3–37. *See also* Margaliot, *supra* n. 48 at 7–9.

79. These responsa are found in various places, including collections of the Cairo *Genizah* fragments. *See infra* p. 1479 and n. 86.

80. *Resp. Maimonides* (ed. J. Blau), I, #14. The question was whether the sabbatical year cancels a debt arising from the *ketubbah*. Maimonides' answer was: "It cancels [which is one word in Hebrew]. Thus writes Moses [Maimonides]." In another responsum regarding the liability of a ritual slaughterer (*shoḥet*) for damages resulting from the slaughter of an animal in a manner that caused it to become unfit to eat, his answer was "He is liable to pay [which is two words in Hebrew]. Moses b. Maimon." The question to which this was the answer contains sixty-seven words (*id.*, II, #435). *See also id.*, II, #391, for Maimonides' responsum on the method of partitioning a dwelling owned concurrently by two or more people. For further examples, *see id.*, II, #364, #407. In one case, the questioner—Phinehas, the *dayyan*—included the lengthy and detailed text of a decision he had handed down and wrote to Maimonides, "This is the decision I have rendered, and I am sending it to you for you to inform me whether it is correct." The entire response was, "The decision is correct and requires no discussion—Moses b. Maimon ha-Dayyan" (*id.*, II, #412).

81. Further information concerning individual responsa and compilations of responsa of the respondents hereinafter referred to can be found in: Boaz Cohen, *Kunteres ha-Teshuvot* [A Bibliography of Responsa]; M. Kasher, *Sarei ha-Elef;* and Appendix C *infra*. Biographical details and examples of responsa by the various respondents appear throughout the present work. *See infra* General Index and Index of Sources.

82. For the major books of responsa of the eleventh century, *see* Appendix C.

heritance, and some aspects of criminal law. The many responsa from the twelfth to fourteenth centuries contributed to the substantial development of these areas of *mishpat ivri.* This chapter refers only to some of the more outstanding respondents in the different periods. A more detailed listing is found in Appendix C of the present work.[83]

Among the outstanding respondents in this period were: Jacob Tam (Rabbenu Tam) in northern France; Maimonides in Spain and Egypt; Naḥmanides and Rashba in Spain; Maharam of Rothenburg in Germany; and Maharam's disciple Asheri in Germany and Spain. Rashba in Spain (probably the leading respondent in the history of Jewish law) and Maharam of Rothenburg in Germany established the foundations and developed the structure of Jewish administrative law in the form in which it crystallized in this period.

The leading respondents in the twelfth to fourteenth centuries were concentrated during most of this period in France, Germany, and Spain. The Jews were expelled from France in 1306, and the volume of responsa declined in Germany in the fourteenth century. During that century, as a result of the deterioration of the political situation of Spanish Jewry, which reached its nadir in the persecutions of 1391, North Africa, once the home of leading respondents in the mid-tenth and eleventh centuries, again emerged as an important area for responsa literature.

This turning point was exemplified in the lives of two Spanish authorities. The first was Isaac b. Sheshet Perfet (Ribash), a leading Spanish respondent, who migrated in 1391 from Spain to North Africa, where he became Rabbi of Algiers. His responsa were the first to deal with a problem that became acute in his time: the status of the Jews who had been forced to become Christians, but who in their hearts remained loyal to Judaism. Various legal questions arose with regard to the Jewish *conversos;* especially acute was the problem of the validity of their marriages and other juristic acts not performed according to Jewish law. The second authority was Simeon b. Ẓemaḥ Duran (Rashbeẓ), who had also migrated from Spain to North Africa and was Ribash's younger contemporary and his successor as Rabbi of Algiers. Rashbeẓ produced an enormous output of responsa in all the areas of Jewish civil, public, and criminal law. His responsa (*Resp. Tashbeẓ*) are written with remarkable clarity; and in some of them, the discussion is fuller than that of prior respondents.[84]

83. Appendix C contains a more detailed chronological and geographical listing of some of the better known books of responsa. Readers wishing to know the main books of responsa of a particular period may refer to the appropriate chronological heading of that appendix.

84. *See supra* n. 68.

The reemergence of North Africa as a situs for the writing of responsa represented the return of a favor by one Jewish center to another. In the tenth and eleventh centuries, halakhic scholars had migrated from North Africa to Spain, where they established a renowned center for the study of Torah; at the end of the fourteenth century, Spanish Jewry reciprocated the favor to the Jews of North Africa when two of Spain's leading halakhic authorities settled in North Africa, where they inaugurated in the responsa literature a period of immense creativity extending over hundreds of years. The arrival of many Spanish Jewish exiles in North Africa also gave rise to friction and to many legal and halakhic disputes between the newcomers and the veteran settlers. New communities were founded in various cities, and sometimes a new community was organized in a city alongside an existing community.[85] This resulted in an increase in the number of local and communal customs and enactments. Many of the resulting problems are reflected in the responsa of the North African halakhic authorities in the fourteenth century and thereafter.[86]

3. THE FIFTEENTH CENTURY

During the fifteenth century, the North African center continued to produce a wide-ranging and comprehensive responsa literature. On the other hand, the Spanish center, which still existed during most of the fifteenth century, made no contribution to the responsa literature during this period. The constantly deteriorating political situation and the persecutions in Spain (which reached their climax with the extinction of this illustrious center in 1492) precluded the writing of responsa. The production of responsa in Germany had declined in the fourteenth century. The false accusations against the Jews in the wake of the Black Death midway through the century led to pogroms and persecutions, the major and most severe of which took place in Germany. However, there was a resurgence of creativity in the German center in the fifteenth century; among the leading respondents there were Jacob Moellin (Maharil) and Israel Isserlein (Maharai).

In the fifteenth century, the Italian Jewish center began to make its contribution to the responsa literature. At this time, there was a huge migration to Italy from Germany and Spain, which gave rise to many halakhic problems, as well as to the emergence of renowned respondents who struggled with those problems. One of the leading respondents in Italy in

85. *See supra* p. 672 and n. 27.

86. *See supra* pp. 804–809. For the major books of responsa of the twelfth to fourteenth centuries, *see* Appendix C.

this century was Joseph Colon (Maharik), whose responsa are considered classic.[87]

4. SUMMARY

The period of the *rishonim,* which ended in the fifteenth century, was the classic period of the responsa literature. This was the period when the responsum was given its basic form: a thorough and comprehensive decision that reviewed and determined the facts of the case at issue, analyzed the pertinent legal considerations, and set forth a final conclusion. The much greater detail contained in the responsa of most of this period, as compared to the geonic responsa, permits a better understanding of the methodology of the creative development of Jewish law. The period of the *rishonim* crystallized the essential distinction between the work of the codifier, whose main interest was in arriving at a final conclusion (which was also the major goal of the geonic responsum), and the post-geonic respondent, whose objective was not only to determine the law but also, and no less importantly, to explain how he reached his conclusion and to make a persuasive case for its correctness.

The discussion by the respondent was necessary not only for its own sake—to indicate the basis for his decision in Talmudic and post-Talmudic sources either by relying on or by distinguishing those sources—but also because the overwhelming majority of inquirers in this period were themselves judges and scholars whose questions often analyzed the halakhic sources and advanced one or more possible solutions to the problem, so that it was incumbent on the respondent to explain his decision to them and convince them of its correctness.[88] The detailed exposition contained in the responsum enables us to trace the respondent's method of resolving the problem—how he has analyzed and explained the sources, either rejecting or accepting them; how he has used restrictive or expansive methods of interpretation; and how he has made use of enactments or customs or availed himself of other judicial techniques in attempting to reach a solution. Such detailed discussion in a responsum is incomparably more significant than a theoretical halakhic discussion that is purely academic and not for practical application.

Although the extent of detail varied at different times during the period of the *rishonim,* and even at the same time between different respon-

87. For the major books of responsa of the fifteenth century, *see* Appendix C.

88. For further discussion of this point, *see infra* pp. 1508, 1510, *et al.* Requests made by those with little knowledge of the Talmud to explain Talmudic terms or passages were rare in the period of the *rishonim,* as compared to the geonic period.

dents, the discussion generally did not go beyond what was necessary for a thorough analysis directly relevant to the question at issue. This restriction of the discussion in a responsum to what is directly pertinent enhances the quality of the responsum and makes it easier to understand. (As will be seen below, there was a substantial change in this respect during the period of the *aḥaronim.*) The high quality of the responsa of the *rishonim* and the personalities and the standing of the respondents gave their responsa special force within the Jewish legal system as a whole and in the responsa literature in particular; responsa by the *rishonim* are highly authoritative and have become the starting point for the examination and resolution of questions that arose after their time.

Two additional features reflected in the responsa during the period of the *rishonim* are noteworthy. The first is that creative legal activity burgeoned in different centers at different times. Sometimes there was a great deal of literary productivity simultaneously in two or more centers, and sometimes one center seemed to be waiting its turn to succeed another whose creativity was declining. This ebb and flow was affected by various factors: the changing political and social conditions to which the Jews were subjected by the general government in one or another center; the number of halakhic and legal questions that arose as a result of internal and external circumstances (*e.g.*, migration from place to place and the emergence of groups of "newcomers" and "veteran settlers," the development of Jewish self-government, and the problem of the *conversos*); and, last but not least, the presence of outstanding leaders who were willing to confront the severe problems that faced their communities.

The second feature is the specialization that occurred in the writing of the different types of halakhic literature. A review of the names of the respondents[89] reveals that the major ones were not among the great codifiers. Although the leading codifier, Maimonides, wrote many responsa, these are not among the classic responsa of the period. We have no responsa whatsoever from Jacob b. Asher, the author of the *Turim.* Rashba did considerable work in the area of codification—his unique method was accepted, for the most part, by Joseph Caro[90]—but his activity and creativity as a respondent, both quantitatively and qualitatively, are incomparably greater than as a codifier. Maharam of Rothenburg, who did no codificatory work at all, was one of the leading respondents.

The transient nature of halakhic creativity is understandable against the background of the Jewish historical experience, and the specialization

89. *See* Appendix C.
90. *See supra* pp. 1273–1277.

in regard to different types of halakhic literature is a consequence of the different approaches of many of the foregoing halakhic authorities to halakhic creativity.[91] These two features also recur in later periods.

C. The Period of the *Aḥaronim* (Later Authorities) Up to the End of the Eighteenth Century

1. THE NATURE AND CONTENT OF THE RESPONSA IN THE PERIOD OF THE *AḤARONIM*

In the period of the *aḥaronim,* the responsa literature generally continued to develop in the form of detailed decisions. However, the responsa of the *aḥaronim* exhibit a number of important changes in both form and content.

At the end of the fifteenth century, with the Expulsion in 1492, the Spanish Jewish center ceased to exist. Spain was devoid of its Jews, who did not return for centuries. However, the great spiritual tradition of this remarkable Jewish community and the teachings of its scholars were transplanted to other Jewish centers, old and new. It is amazing how the Spanish Jewish exiles of 1492, after a century of physical and spiritual persecution, established and maintained a large number of new communities on a much larger scale than at the beginning of the fifteenth century, when Spanish exiles, headed by Ribash and Rashbeẓ, strengthened and invigorated Jewish spiritual life in North Africa. The exiles of 1492 were more widely dispersed; they went not only to North Africa but also, and principally, to the Balkans—which the scholars called "the Turkish lands" or "the Romanesque lands"—and to the Land of Israel and Egypt.[92] In some of these places, new centers were created; in others, new settlements or communities were established alongside existing communities; and in still others the new immigrants were integrated into the existing communities.

As had occurred a century earlier in North Africa, this situation gave rise to many problems in all the areas of the law. The previous inhabitants followed their own customs and enactments, and the newcomers brought with them the customs and life-style of their old communities. The establishment of new communities and the arrival of the new immigrants in places where Jewish communities already existed gave rise to disputes concerning the use of the power of taxation, the allocation of the tax burden

91. For example, Maimonides' main goal was to compose a code containing uniform and categorical legal rules. *See supra* pp. 1184–1186.

92. Some of the exiles from Spain and Portugal migrated to Poland and Western Europe. *See supra* pp. 1344–1345.

between the original inhabitants and the newcomers, the granting or withholding of the right to vote and to be elected to the communal institutions, etc. Many problems arose in connection with contracts and legal transactions entered into according to the circumstances existing at the exiles' former communities, but now challenged as invalid in their new homes. All these problems were brought before the Jewish courts, and the most significant and difficult issues reached the leading respondents. The responsa on all of these questions vastly enriched the responsa literature; and as a result of the increased creativity, all areas of Jewish law expanded in scope, including the conflict of laws—a very unlikely subject for Jewish law, given the personal character of that law.[93]

93. An interesting example of a problem of conflict of laws is contained in the decision of the Supreme Court of Israel in Miller v. Miller, 5 *P.D.* 1301 (1949). One of the issues in that case was, What law should govern the marriage of the parties, who were married in England and later emigrated to Israel? Justice Olshan relied on a similar English case, De Nicols v. Curlier, [1900] A.C. 21, which he summarized as follows (5 *P.D.* at 1318):

> A Frenchman and a Frenchwoman, domiciled in France, married in France in 1854 without a marital agreement. As a result, the community property provisions of the Napoleonic Code became applicable to them. . . . In 1863, they emigrated to England, and in 1865 they became British subjects. In England, the husband became very wealthy. He died in England in 1897, leaving a will. The widow claimed a portion of the estate pursuant to the community property provision of the French law. English internal law, however, did not give the same rights to the widow as French law. The House of Lords ruled in the widow's favor.

The applicable law was thus determined to be the law of the place of the marriage. In his opinion, Justice S. Assaf cited a sixteenth-century responsum that is remarkably similar to the *De Nicols* decision (5 *P.D.* at 1306):

> Incidentally, it is interesting to note that a case very similar to the *De Nicols* case cited by my learned colleague is found in our responsa literature from the mid-sixteenth century—the well-known dispute between the eminent lady, Gracia Mendes, and her younger sister and brother-in-law. The case was brought before the greatest halakhic authorities in Turkey and the Land of Israel; and the leading responsa were by the Chief Rabbi of Salonika, Samuel de Medina (Maharashdam) (*Resp. Maharashdam*, ḤM, #327), and the Rabbi of Safed, Moses b. Joseph Trani (Mabit) (quoted in Joseph Caro, *Resp. Avkat Rokhel* #80).
>
> Gracia Mendes and her husband were married in Portugal when they were both Marranos [Jews living as Christians but still secretly faithful to Judaism]; and there "it was the custom, by authority of the king and the kingdom from ancient times . . . , that when the husband dies, the widow takes half of all the property left by the husband." Later, Gracia Mendes, together with her late husband's heirs, arrived in Turkey "to find rest under the wings of the Divine Presence and observe the religion of Moses and Judaism" [*i.e.*, practice Judaism openly]. The question arose: Could the husband's heirs prevail over the widow as to the half of the estate [claimed by her] and leave her with only the dowry she had brought to the marriage?
>
> Maharashdam ruled in favor of Gracia Mendes on the ground "that is known even to infants, that all matters pertaining to marriage are governed by the customs of the place of the marriage." Mabit also decided in favor of Gracia Mendes but went even further and ruled that all provisions in contracts entered into by Marranos while

Enormous changes also took place at this time in Germany. The Jews of Germany were subject to severe persecutions and pogroms, and many of them turned eastward to Poland and Lithuania. From the sixteenth century, the Jewish center of Poland and Lithuania assumed a position of leadership in Jewish scholarship and in the spiritual life of the Jewish diaspora,[94] and made a very valuable contribution to the responsa literature. The problems resulting from the migration of Ashkenazic Jews to Eastern Europe differed from those resulting from the migration of the Spanish exiles into thriving Jewish centers. When the Ashkenazic Jews turned eastward, there were Jewish communities in Poland, but they were not well organized or established; and the new immigrants were often required to lay down firmer foundations for the community's structure, its methods of operation, the election of its leaders, and the maintenance of its institutions. Associations of a number of communities, and even associations of Jewish communities from different regions and countries, were also organized in these centers; and problems arose particularly with regard to such matters as maintenance of the communities, and the laws governing commercial activities. These

---

they were in Spain and Portugal were valid even after they came to other countries and returned to the practice of Judaism. This is so, even though the law now being applied [in their place of refuge] is Jewish law.

[Mabit pointed out that] if a non-Jew buys property from another non-Jew according to their own laws and modes of acquisition, and they then both convert to Judaism, the purchase remains valid and will not be set aside, even if Jewish law does not provide for such a mode of acquisition between two Jews. It is also beneficial for the Marranos that their previous transactions, entered into according to their [*i.e.*, non-Jewish] laws, be valid. The same applies to agreements at the time of marriage; they too remain valid. Furthermore, even if they have a second marriage ceremony in accordance with Jewish law and practice, so long as they do not expressly rescind the first agreement [which accompanied their marriage in the Christian religion], it is presumed that the second marriage is being entered into on the same understanding expressed in the original agreement.

As to the importance of the customs of the place of the marriage, *Resp. Rashba*, I, #662, is especially noteworthy. Rashba ruled that "if the husband entered into the marriage on the understanding that they would live in the place where the marriage was effected, he has also accepted the conditions [pertaining to marriage that are customary] in that place . . . , for anyone who writes a deed, marries, or takes possession of a field, etc., does so according to the customs of that place."

A fundamental question is involved here: What law should apply—the law of the place of the act or transaction, or the law of the forum (*i.e.*, where the case is being heard)? The problem arose because of geographical changes and the uprooting of Jewish communities from one place to another. Most of the leading halakhic authorities ruled that the applicable law is that of the place of the act or transaction. Thus, an important principle in the conflict of laws was established for Jewish law. For a detailed discussion, *see* M. Elon, EJ, V, pp. 882–890, s.v. Conflict of laws (reprinted in *Principles*, pp. 715–724); and *supra* pp. 78–79, 677.

94. *See supra* pp. 1345–1346.

problems required halakhic solutions, and consequently provided a broad opportunity for responsa to make a creative contribution in many areas of Jewish law.

As stated, beginning with this period there were a number of changes in the form and content of the responsa. By this time, an extensive responsa literature written by the *rishonim,* which dealt with many of the problems that faced the *aḥaronim,* had already been published. The standing and authority of the *rishonim* were such that a later respondent had to carefully consider the prior rulings on the subject at issue, and either follow them or—when the later respondent felt that the matter called for a different solution—distinguish the case before him from the previous rulings. Even if an entirely new question arose, the later respondent had to draw on the responsa of the *rishonim* to find an analogy or support for his decision. This need to discuss and distinguish earlier decisions caused responsa to become considerably longer. It also generated a more detailed consideration of the Talmudic sources and their commentaries, which in turn sometimes included long digressions having no direct bearing on the question at issue. The finespun dialectics (*pilpul*) and extremely subtle distinctions (*ḥillukim*) fashionable in the *yeshivot* of Poland in the sixteenth century[95] also had a strong influence on the respondents' approach and analysis, and resulted in the introduction into the responsa of theoretical discussions of the Talmud and the *rishonim* that were not directly relevant to the question posed.

For all these reasons, the responsa of the *aḥaronim* are far more lengthy and detailed than necessary for responding to the questions posed, and this sometimes makes them difficult for continuous study. The responsa literature of the Sephardic halakhic authorities in this period is simpler and easier to understand. Although their responsa, too, became much longer because of the need to consider the decisions of their predecessors, the Sephardic respondents tended to be more straightforward in their rulings, without the dialectics and distinctions unique to the Polish and German respondents.

Another change that took place in the period of the *aḥaronim* was a further decrease in the extent to which responsa dealt with matters of faith and belief. From this time forward, the responsa literature was confined almost exclusively to matters of *Halakhah.* Philosophy, ethics, the explanation of texts, and homiletics were dealt with in literary forms specifically devoted to those subjects.

There was also, beginning with this period, a noteworthy change in the titling of compilations of responsa. Increasingly, such compilations were not titled by the names of their authors—as had been the general practice

95. For detailed discussion, *see supra* pp. 1345–1346, 1380, 1394, *et al.*

until that time[96]—but their titles were based on Scriptural phrases or Talmudic expressions, which sometimes hinted at the names of the authors but often did not.

2. THE SIXTEENTH CENTURY

External and internal circumstances during the sixteenth century resulted in an enormous growth in the responsa literature in many Jewish centers. In the Land of Israel—and particularly in Safed, which again became a spiritual center for the entire diaspora—the important respondents included Jacob Berab (Ri Berab), Levi ibn Ḥabib (Ralbaḥ), and Joseph Caro. Caro's *Bet Yosef,* in addition to its great importance for the codification of Jewish law,[97] also made a significant contribution to the responsa literature by collecting the responsa of the leading respondents from the period of the *rishonim,* classifying them in the topical arrangement of the *Turim,* and bringing them to the attention of respondents in all the Jewish centers where copies of the *Bet Yosef* were obtainable. Among a number of respondents in Egypt, the most notable was David ibn Zimra (Radbaz), who wrote an enormous number of responsa, regarded as classic, in all areas of the law.[98]

In this period, an illustrious center for Jewish scholarship developed in the countries under Turkish rule; Constantinople and Salonika were

96. There were a few instances in the period of the *rishonim* where books of responsa had titles in which the authors' names did not appear, such as *Ẓofenat Pa'ne'aḥ* (responsa of Raban), *Sefer ha-Yashar* (responsa of Rabbenu Tam), and *Terumat ha-Deshen* (responsa of Israel Isserlein). However, in general, books of responsa were known by the names of their authors; *see infra* Appendix C. As to this practice, *see* M.M. Zlotkin, *Shemot ha-Seforim ha-Ivrim, Lefi Sugeihem ha-Shonim, Tekhunatam u-Te'udatam* [The Names of Hebrew Books, According to Their Respective Categories, Characteristics, and Purposes], Neufchatel (Switzerland), 1940.

97. *See supra* pp. 1313–1319.

98. Radbaz' attitude toward the Karaites is particularly noteworthy. Most halakhic authorities, such as Joseph Caro and Moses Trani in the Land of Israel, and Rema and Maharshal in Poland, forbade marriage to a Karaite even after the Karaite's return to rabbinic Judaism. They argued that the Karaites were Jews and their marriages while they were Karaites were thus valid. However, since their divorces were not halakhically valid, a woman remained married even after she had received a Karaite bill of divorcement. Thus, all the children she bore after she "remarried" were *mamzerim.* It follows that the whole Karaite community was tainted with the possibility of being *mamzerim.* Radbaz, however, permitted marriage with Karaites when they returned to rabbinic Judaism. He argued that Karaite marriages were invalid since the witnesses purporting to validate the marriages were Karaites and thus incompetent under Jewish law. Since the marriages were invalid, there was no need for divorce; and thus the subsequent children would not be *mamzerim.* A similar problem has re-emerged at the present time, and the opinions described above are the basis for the current deliberations; *see* Elon, *Ḥakikah,* pp. 178–181.

large Jewish communities led by halakhic authorities who were among the greatest of their generation; and in the sixteenth century and afterward, these communities produced respondents of the first rank such as Elijah Mizraḥi (Re'em) in Constantinople and Samuel de Medina (Maharashdam) in Salonika. Two additional leading respondents in this period should be counted as part of this center—David ha-Kohen (Mahardakh) of Corfu and Benjamin Ze'ev of Arta, Greece (generally, neither of these places appears on the map of Hebrew literature). During this century, responsa literature continued to be written in Italy, where an outstanding respondent was Meir Katzenellenbogen (Maharam of Padua).

The sixteenth century witnessed the beginning of a substantial and wide-ranging responsa literature in Poland. Jewish settlement in Poland had begun as early as the end of the tenth century C.E., and there is evidence of halakhic scholarship there from the thirteenth century onward, but the earliest literary output that has survived dates from the sixteenth century. In that century, the Jews of Poland attained a notable level of economic and social development; and they organized regional communal associations possessing administrative, juridical, and educational autonomy. All of the regions joined in establishing "The Council of the Four Lands" from which, after a while, "The Council of Lithuania" branched off. The two councils acted as the autonomous representative of Polish and Lithuanian Jews for about two hundred years.[99] The economic, social, and organizational changes gave rise, as usual, to a great many problems requiring halakhic solution. At the same time, Poland also became an important center of halakhic literature.

By the beginning of the sixteenth century, Jacob Pollack had migrated from Prague to Poland; and he, together with his disciple Shalom Shakhna, headed renowned *yeshivot* in different communities. They trained many students, spread halakhic scholarship throughout Poland and various other European countries, and paved the way for the new pilpulistic method of study that attracted many hundreds of students because of its intellectual challenges.[100] While, as has been noted in connection with the codificatory literature, Jacob Pollack and Shalom Shakhna opposed the writing of halakhic codes and even the recording of their own responsa,[101] their leading disciples, although generally accepting their teachers' views on the method of reaching decisions, did not agree with their teachers' opposition to codification and to the publication of responsa. These disciples left a rich legacy

99. *See supra* pp. 1345–1346.
100. For further discussion, *see id.*
101. *See supra* pp. 1346–1348.

of various forms of halakhic literature, including responsa. Among such leading respondents are Moses Isserles (Rema, author of the *Mappah,* the glosses to the *Shulḥan Arukh*), who took care to preserve copies of his responsa,[102] and Solomon Luria (Maharshal).

Two features stand out in the responsa literature of the sixteenth century.[103] One is the large number of places in which such literature was produced: the Land of Israel, Egypt, the Ottoman Empire, Italy, North Africa, and Poland (although in the sixteenth century virtually no responsa were written in Germany).[104] The second is that a very lively exchange of questions and responsa began to take place not only within each center but also between centers. To a certain extent, this had occurred in the previous centuries,[105] but from the sixteenth century onward, a considerable proportion of the questions and responsa were between different centers.[106]

3. THE SEVENTEENTH CENTURY

In the seventeenth and eighteenth centuries, the writing of responsa reached its peak. This productivity can be attributed first to the external and internal factors discussed above, which recurred in one form or another in the seventeenth century. These factors included the persecutions of 1648–1649, the pogroms, and the destruction of many communities in Poland, which caused a large number of Polish Jews to migrate to other European countries (mainly Moravia, Bohemia, and Germany) and gave rise to various halakhic problems requiring solution.

In addition to these "usual" factors, the publication of the *Shulḥan Arukh* (including Rema's glosses) throughout the entire Jewish diaspora, and its acceptance as authoritative,[107] had a bearing on the flourishing of responsa literature in the seventeenth century. Codification of Jewish law, especially when the code stated the law categorically, had always produced extended discussions concerning the sources as well as the accuracy of the rule as codified, in light of the Talmud and the writings of the *rishonim.* Such discussions markedly increased at this time when new problems arose for which there were no solutions in the *Shulḥan Arukh* or when the facts underlying the conclusion stated in the *Shulḥan Arukh* had to be distinguished from the new circumstances.

102. *See supra* p. 1349 and *infra* pp. 1511–1512.

103. *See infra* Appendix C.

104. In the sixteenth century, the main Jewish center moved from Germany to neighboring Poland.

105. *See supra* pp. 1475–1476.

106. For some of the more important books of responsa of the sixteenth century, *see infra* Appendix C.

107. *See supra* pp. 1419–1422.

The acceptance of the *Shulḥan Arukh* also influenced the organization of books of responsa. With the appearance of the *Turim* by Jacob b. Asher,[108] books of responsa began to be organized according to the topical arrangement of that work. After the *Shulḥan Arukh* followed the same topical arrangement, it became an almost universal practice to organize books of responsa according to that topical order, since the *Shulḥan Arukh* was the starting point for all halakhic study and research.[109]

In the seventeenth century, as noted above, responsa were again being written in Germany; occasionally, the same halakhic authorities served at different times in various Polish and German communities, and it is therefore appropriate, in studying the responsa literature, to view these two centers as one. Among the outstanding respondents in Poland and Germany were Joel Sirkes (Baḥ) and Jair Ḥayyim Bacharach.

The greatest centers for responsa literature in the seventeenth century remained the countries under Turkish rule and the Balkans. Constantinople, Izmir, and Salonika produced many outstanding respondents, including Joseph Trani (Maharit) in Constantinople and Ḥayyim Benveniste in Izmir. Benveniste greatly contributed to the dissemination of knowledge of the responsa literature through his book *Keneset ha-Gedolah,* which is the largest collection of responsa arranged according to the topical order of the *Turim.*[110] There were also a great many respondents in Salonika, among the outstanding of whom was Ḥayyim Shabbetai (Maharḥash).

The writing of responsa continued on a large scale in the Land of Israel, and among the most prominent respondents there was Moses ibn Ḥabib. Other leading respondents of the time were Mordecai ha-Levi in Egypt, Jacob Sasportas in North Africa, and Samuel Aboab in Italy.[111]

4. THE EIGHTEENTH CENTURY

A rich and ramified responsa literature continued to be written in the eighteenth century wherever responsa had been produced in the previous century. Some of the greatest respondents of the period of the *aḥaronim* were active in the eighteenth century in Germany and Poland; the most

108. *See supra* pp. 1277–1302.

109. Many books of responsa written after the *Turim* and before the *Shulḥan Arukh* were not arranged according to the topical order of the *Turim,* and it is difficult to identify any general pattern. After the *Shulḥan Arukh,* the vast majority of books of responsa were arranged according to its topical order. There were some exceptions, however, such as *Ḥavvot Ya'ir* of Jair Ḥayyim Bacharach. *See further infra* pp. 1523–1528.

110. *See supra* pp. 1434–1437.

111. For some of the more important books of responsa of the seventeenth century, *see infra* Appendix C.

outstanding were Jacob Emden (Ya'vez̩), son of Z̩evi Hirsch b. Jacob Ashkenazi (Ḥakham Z̩evi), and Ezekiel Landau. In Italy, David Pardo was a leading respondent.

During the eighteenth century, the Land of Israel and the Turkish and Balkan countries continued to maintain a leading position in the writing of responsa. This period also witnessed an increase in the volume of responsa in North Africa; and a new center, Babylonia, made its appearance. It is to be regretted that, on account of various historical factors, a considerable part of the responsa literature from these Sephardic centers was hardly known in the Ashkenazic countries of Germany, Poland, and Lithuania. This was especially true from the eighteenth century onward, although, to some extent, it was also true in the seventeenth century. The social and spiritual ties between these two segments of the Jewish people were weak and inadequate; consequently, halakhic deliberation and thought in each one of them was greatly impeded. The result was especially harmful in the areas of *mishpat ivri.* The existence of broad autonomy in the lands under Turkish rule and in North Africa in those centuries, as well as the exceptionally straightforward approach of the Sephardic respondents to decision making and to the judicial function, contributed greatly to the development of *mishpat ivri* in those places. Halakhic analysis and research in the Ashkenazic countries almost completely overlooked the rich halakhic literature of the Sephardic centers; and only recently has this literature once more become a subject of study and research.[112]

Among the prominent respondents in the Land of Israel were Moses Ḥagiz (Mani'aḥ), who also wrote *Leket ha-Kemaḥ* (a compilation of responsa arranged according to the topical order of the *Shulḥan Arukh,* which greatly helped to spread the knowledge and study of the responsa literature),[113] and Yom Tov Algazi. In this period, Ḥayyim Joseph David Azulai (Ḥida), a native of Jerusalem who traveled extensively to many other centers, was also active.[114]

There were also many notable respondents during the eighteenth century in the Ottoman Empire and the Balkans. Among the outstanding ones were Asher Shalem in Salonika, Ephraim Navon in Constantinople, and Raphael Joseph Ḥazzan in Izmir. In addition, the North African center produced many respondents in this period. Among the most prominent were Judah Iyash of Algiers and Jacob ibn Z̩ur of Morocco (Ya'vez̩ of North Af-

112. *See supra* p. 88 and n. 49.

113. *See supra* pp. 1437–1438.

114. *See supra* p. 1439 regarding Ḥida's *Birkei Yosef* on the *Shulḥan Arukh,* which also contains a large collection of responsa.

rica). Authorities who served as rabbis in Rhodes (such as Moses Israel and his son Elijah), in Babylonia (Ẓedakah Ḥuẓin of Baghdad), and in Yemen (Yehaiah b. Joseph Ẓalaḥ and David b. Solomon Mashraki) were also active respondents.[115]

D. The Period of the Emancipation—the Nineteenth Century

1. THE NATURE AND CONTENT OF THE RESPONSA IN THE NINETEENTH CENTURY AND THEREAFTER

The abrogation of Jewish juridical autonomy as a result of the Emancipation at the end of the eighteenth century, and the consequent decline in the application of Jewish law to practical life,[116] necessarily affected the content of the responsa literature. The nature and extent of that effect are most strikingly apparent from a comparison of the responsa of the Ashkenazic centers with the responsa of Turkey, the Land of Israel, Egypt, and North Africa. In Poland and Germany, the "legal" provisions of *Ḥoshen Mishpat* increasingly became the subject of academic and theoretical study only, and were no longer relevant to actual life, whereas in the countries under Turkish rule and in North Africa, these laws, like the "religious" laws in *Oraḥ Ḥayyim* and *Yoreh De'ah,* continued to be applied in practice.

This divergence was the product of the different historical conditions existing in each of these two geographical areas. Germany and Poland were entering upon the period of Emancipation which, on the one hand, offered freedom, equality, and the rights of citizenship for all, but, on the other hand, demanded the elimination of Jewish autonomy, the abrogation of major areas of Jewish adjudication—including civil, administrative, criminal, and a large portion of family law—and the overall lowering of the standing of Jewish courts. The laws of *Ḥoshen Mishpat* increasingly fell into the category of "laws that are not practiced at the present time," like the laws in the Orders of *Kodashim* and *Tohorot.* The problems in the area of *Ḥoshen Mishpat* that arose in the daily life of Jewish society were no longer submitted to the halakhic authorities for decision; solutions were sought in the legal and judicial systems of the countries in which the Jews resided. The situation in the Ottoman Empire and North Africa, which did not experience any decisive political or social changes, was quite different. The Jewish communities in those countries continued to enjoy autonomy, and

115. For some of the more important books of responsa of the eighteenth century, *see infra* Appendix C.

116. *See infra* pp. 1576–1588.

the Jewish courts there continued to adjudicate civil disputes between Jewish litigants.

The new age in Europe left its mark on many aspects of Judaism, including the subject matter of the responsa literature. Up to the eighteenth century, most of the responsa (between sixty and eighty percent) dealt with matters of *mishpat ivri.* However, beginning with the eighteenth century, the overwhelming majority of the questions considered in the responsa literature in Poland and Germany concerned "religious" matters covered by *Oraḥ Ḥayyim* and *Yoreh De'ah* and also some of the laws in *Even ha-Ezer* (marriage, divorce, levirate marriage, and *ḥaliẓah*). Responsa dealing with the laws of *Ḥoshen Mishpat,* especially from the second half of the nineteenth century and thereafter, were comparatively very few.

Even in the responsa on issues of civil law in this period in Poland and Germany, there is no sense of a living and practiced law; the goal of many of those responsa was to arrive at a compromise between the parties, in view of the lack of Jewish juridical authority and the absence of a system of regular adjudication. Other responsa concerned issues that arose as a consequence of litigation before non-Jewish courts (such as questions on the law of interest, which arose as the result of the judgments of non-Jewish courts and affected matters of *issur*), and there were also purely theoretical discussions cast in the form of responsa. At the same time, the laws of *Ḥoshen Mishpat* continued to play a prominent role in the responsa of the Ottoman Empire and North African countries; and the literature in those lands was as rich and as fruitful in those matters as it had been previously.

Nevertheless, there were many illustrious respondents in the Polish and German centers in the nineteenth century. External and internal factors gave rise to many new problems that required halakhic solutions. The far-reaching technological innovations in industry and commerce and in everyday life, the general social trends (such as the institution of civil marriage), and the rise of the Jewish Enlightenment (*Haskalah*) and the Reform Movement all produced an abundance of problems involving the laws of prayer, sabbath, festivals, medicine, ritual slaughter, etc. The halakhic authorities of the period, especially in Poland and Germany, responded meticulously to the inquiries submitted to them. Thus, there was created in Germany and Poland a voluminous and rich responsa literature on matters covered by *Oraḥ Ḥayyim* and *Yoreh De'ah* and on the laws of marriage and divorce contained in *Even ha-Ezer.*

One additional feature, which is also related to the spiritual condition of Jewish society from that time forward, stands out in the responsa literature of the nineteenth century. The Emancipation gave rise to a momentous historical development: the division of the Jewish people into two segments—one consisting of those who remained steadfast in their commitment to the *Halakhah,* and the other consisting of those who did not feel bound by the *Halakhah.* This division has had—and continues to have—a strong influence on innumerable aspects of Jewish society in general[117] and on the development of Jewish law in particular. One of the most deleterious results of this division has been that halakhic scholars have become increasingly reluctant to make rulings, even to the point of completely refusing to render decisions.

Diffidence in making legal pronouncements is not new to Jewish law. Indeed, it has always been considered desirable; a judge should possess both a sense of wisdom and trepidation, should be deliberate in judgment, and should consult with his colleagues, especially when a greater authority is available.[118] But such diffidence cannot justify abdicating the heavy responsibility of the judicial office; such abdication is even worse than decision making by an unworthy judge. As the Sages pointedly said in the following double-edged statement:[119] "'For many are those she has struck dead'[120]—this refers to the student who has not yet become competent to judge but does so; 'And numerous are her victims'—this refers to the scholar who has become competent to judge but does not do so."[121]

With the exception of a small number of cases involving special circumstances,[122] the halakhic authorities of all previous periods assumed their responsibilities, despite any misgivings they may have felt. However, from the nineteenth century on, and especially in the twentieth century, leading respondents have increasingly declared—and with regard to many important matters—that they fear the responsibility and will, therefore, refrain from rendering a clear and decisive judgment; or they have declared that they will render a judgment for theoretical purposes only and not for practical application. Occasionally, when a respondent rules that certain

117. One of the most serious consequences of this ideological split has been the founding of separate communities by certain groups of halakhically observant Jews. Other Jews, also halakhically observant, have opposed this development and have stressed the importance of maintaining the unity and integrity of the total Jewish community. This controversy was dealt with at length in nineteenth-century responsa; and from the perspective of *mishpat ivri,* the discussions contain material on Jewish public administrative law.

118. *See* M Avot 4:7; TB Yevamot 109b and Rashi, *ad loc.*, s.v. Ve-gamar halakhah; TB Sanhedrin 7b and Horayot 3b ("so that only the 'chip of the beam' should reach me," *i.e.,* that I take only part of the responsibility); TB Avodah Zarah 19b (*see infra* text at n. 119); Maimonides, *MT,* Sanhedrin 20:7–8; *Tur* ḤM 8:5–8, 10:2–6.

119. TB Avodah Zarah 19b.

120. Proverbs 7:26.

121. *See* Rashi, *ad loc.:* "Those who stand aloof and remain silent and refrain from judging destroy their generation." The Biblical quotation "and numerous are her victims" is also part of Proverbs 7:26.

122. *See supra* p. 1475 and n. 69.

conduct is permitted, he adds, "but he who follows a stricter view will be blessed."[123] Very often a respondent makes his decision conditional on the agreement of other authorities; such instances have steadily increased and are no longer exceptional. As stated, this phenomenon is the result of the split in the Jewish people in regard to observance of the *Halakhah;* and it has become stronger with the intensification of the trend in the halakhic system to become isolated, to withdraw into itself, to avoid innovaion, and to give preference to the principle of *shev ve-al ta'aseh* ("sit and do nothing"). This reluctance to make rulings began to spread in the nineteenth century, and has become a serious source of concern in the twentieth.[124]

123. Certainly, even in this period, there have been decisions by leading halakhic authorities that grappled with the needs of the time and with the problems of the specific cases submitted to them. In this respect, the following remarks of Ḥayyim Volozhiner (beginning of *Resp. Ḥut ha-Meshullash* #8) are instructive:

> Concerning the first part of your responsum transmitted to me by Rabbi H. Cohen with regard to the woman of Vilna who was not allowed to remarry ("the *agunah*"), I examined every statement and word and came to the conclusion that for the most part we are of the same mind. The only difference is that you incline toward stringency, since the responsibility for the matter is not yours. I, like you, did not turn to the more lenient aspects that emerge from the examination of the case until the yoke of decision was placed upon me. It seems that now, because of our many sins, the generation has become bereft of scholars in these regions, and the yoke of judging the whole region has been imposed upon me to the extent that they will never rule that anything is permissible without the concurrence of my humble opinion; hence I wrestled with my conscience [lit. "my Creator"] and felt myself duty bound to use my powers to the utmost to try to improve the plight of *agunot,* and may the One-Whose-Name-Is-To-Be-Blessed save me from errors.

Nevertheless, there was a demonstrable change in this period, as compared to previous periods, in the general approach to decision making.

124. This tendency is reflected in the introductory remarks of Isaac Halevi Herzog, the late Chief Rabbi of Israel, in his article "Haẓa'at Takkanot bi-Yerushot" [Proposed Enactments on Inheritance], *Talpiot,* VI (Nissan 1953), pp. 36–37, concerning the enactments (*takkanot*) on inheritance that he proposed to the Council of the Chief Rabbinate of Israel soon after the State of Israel was established:

> In 1949, I wrote a monograph, *Haẓa'at Takkanot bi-Yerushot,* which was submitted to the members of the Council of the Chief Rabbinate of Israel. I outlined the widest and most extreme perimeters for possible enactments, and the Council could have chosen to accept the proposal in whole or in part, or to reject it completely. The matter never came to a vote, but it was clear that most of the rabbis on the Council were not inclined to adopt any enactment. One who was the most extreme in his opposition argued that the proposal, even in its mildest form, would not satisfy the Government. The end was that the matter was shelved and the Government did what it did (there is no need for me to go into the sad details); and a law providing for total equality

2. THE RESPONSA IN DIFFERENT JEWISH CENTERS

Responsa literature in the nineteenth century continued to be published in almost all the centers in which it had appeared in the previous century. In the nineteenth century, additional geographical divisions were carved out of the German and Polish centers. Galicia and Hungary, because of their importance in the Jewish world and in the field of Jewish law, became recognized as separate centers.

An outstanding respondent in Germany was Akiva Eger; and one of the leading respondents of the age, Moses Sofer (Ḥatam Sofer), was active in Hungary. In Galicia, which was part of the Austrian empire after the partition of Poland, there were many distinguished respondents, among whom were Ephraim Zalman Margolioth, Joseph Saul Nathanson, Ẓevi Hirsch Chajes (Maharaẓ Chajes), and Shalom Mordecai Schwadron. Mention should also be made of Azriel Hildesheimer of Eisenstadt and Berlin. The prominent respondents in Russia and Lithuania were Naftali Ẓevi Judah Berlin (Neẓiv) (the head of the renowned *yeshivah* in Volozhin); Menahem Mendel Schneerson (the grandson of the author of the *Tanya,* who was the founder of Ḥabad [Lubavitch] Hasidism); and Isaac Elchanan Spektor.

In the Land of Israel, Turkey, the Balkan countries, Egypt, and North Africa, there were also many notable respondents in the nineteenth century. Some of the most outstanding were: Ḥayyim Palache and Ḥayyim David Ḥazzan in Izmir; Raphael Jacob Menasseh and Raphael Asher Kobo in Salonika; Jacob Saul Elishar, Moses Judah Leib Zilberberg,[125] and Meir Auerbach in the Land of Israel (Auerbach, who emigrated from Kalisz to Jerusalem, was the author of *Imrei Binah,* a book of novellae at the end of which were two sections of responsa); Elijah Ḥazzan in Egypt; Abraham Ankawa in Morocco and Algeria; and Isaac ibn Danan of Fez, Morocco.[126]

> was passed, contrary to Jewish law. . . . It may well be that some of the members of our Council now regret what happened. At the time, not one of them offered any halakhic objection to my proposals, except for one prominent rabbi whom I answered; the answer is reproduced here. At any rate, some record should remain for posterity of my efforts in this matter, which were truly for the sake of Heaven.

See the editor's note, *ad loc.* Although the quotation concerned the enactment of legislation, the background and the general tendency are the same as those noted *supra* in connection with rendering halakhic decisions.

125. Zilberberg emigrated from Kutno to Jerusalem, where he responded to many questions that arose at the time in the Land of Israel.

126. For some of the more important books of responsa of the nineteenth century, *see infra* Appendix C.

E. The Period of National Awakening, the Holocaust, and the Establishment of the Jewish State—the Twentieth Century

1. THE RESPONSA LITERATURE UNTIL THE 1940s

The twentieth century is marked by two events in Jewish history without counterpart at any time during all the years of the Jewish dispersion: the Holocaust, which destroyed most of European Jewry, and the realization of the great vision of the establishment of an independent Jewish state. These two events that occurred in the 1940s have had an impact on every aspect of Jewish life, including Jewish law.

Until the 1940s, most of the responsa literature was produced in the large Jewish centers of Eastern Europe and, to a certain extent, in Turkey, the Balkans, and North Africa. Among the foremost respondents in Galicia were Samuel Engel, Meir Arak, and Dov Berish Weidenfeld. The outstanding respondents in Poland, Lithuania, and Romania included: Ḥayyim Ozer Grodzinski, Joseph Rozin (the "Rogachover"), and Judah Leib Żirelson. Among the prominent respondents in Germany was David Żevi Hoffmann. The outstanding respondent in Turkey and the Balkans at the beginning of the twentieth century was David Pipano of Sofia and Salonika; and in North Africa, Raphael Ankawa of Morocco. In the great migration of the Jews of North Africa and the Arab countries to the State of Israel, the immigrants brought with them their local customs and halakhic approaches, all of which became an integral part of the pattern of Jewish law and life in the Land of Israel.[127]

---

127. It should be noted that prior to the mass immigration to Israel that occurred after the establishment of the Jewish state, the Jews living in the Land of Israel who had come from a particular community in the diaspora would sometimes turn to the halakhic authorities of their community who were still in the diaspora for answers to halakhic questions, particularly on those matters regarding which each community had its own customs.

Thus, in 1900, the Yemenite Jews in Jerusalem inquired of the halakhic authorities in San'a, Yemen, how they were to conduct the readings from the Torah in the synagogue, inasmuch as the customs of the Sephardic and Ashkenazic communities in the Land of Israel differed from their own. The responsa were published in *Resp. Anaf Ḥayyim* by Abraham Alandaf, Jerusalem, 1981, II, pp. 169–172. In 1910, the Yemenite Jews in Jerusalem asked the halakhic authorities in San'a whether they should continue the custom (which they had followed in Yemen) of baking *maẓẓah* not only before Passover but on the festival itself, in view of the custom of the Sephardic communities in the Land of Israel not to bake *maẓẓah* on Passover. The responsum by the halakhic authorities of Yemen was published by Professor Y. Ratzhabi, *Maḥanayim* (publication of the chaplaincy of the Israel Defense Forces) #80, 1963, pp. 130–133, and in Nahum, *Zohar le-Ḥasifat Ginzei Teiman* [Light on the Discovery of the Archives of Yemen], Tel Aviv, 1986, pp. 273–275. Similarly, in 1911, Abraham Isaac ha-Kohen Kook, then Rabbi of Jaffa, and later Chief Rabbi of the Land of Israel, wrote to the halakhic authorities in Yemen with regard to various customs of the Yemenite Jews. The

2. THE RESPONSA LITERATURE IN THE 1940s AND THEREAFTER

The great productivity of the Jewish centers of Eastern Europe came to a halt during the 1920s in the areas that fell under Communist rule, which prohibited the study and teaching of Judaism. During the 1940s, as a result of the Holocaust, such productivity completely disappeared in virtually all the remainder of Europe. In post-Holocaust Europe, there was once again a certain amount of activity by respondents in some Western European countries, one of the most notable being Jehiel Jacob Weinberg.

Part of post-Holocaust responsa literature deals with questions arising during the course of the Holocaust out of the terrible circumstances of Nazi rule and ghetto conditions. After being rescued, the respondents committed the questions and responsa to writing. Such responsa are found in most compilations of responsa published after the Holocaust; they constitute the major element in the work of some respondents, such as Simon Efrati and Ephraim Oshry.

The major centers of Jewish scholarship currently are: (1) first and foremost, the State of Israel, and (2) the United States. The Jewish migration to the United States, which began at the end of the nineteenth century and greatly increased at the beginning of the twentieth, was successful in establishing, in a comparatively short time, a large, active, and creative Jewish center. At first, American Jews transmitted their questions to the halakhic authorities of Eastern Europe, from which most of the immigrants to the United States had come; and a lively exchange of questions and responsa between these two centers developed. Over the course of time, and especially after World War II, when many halakhic authorities migrated to the United States, the writing of responsa in this new center greatly increased.

In addition to the questions that began to be raised in the nineteenth century in connection with technological innovations, and in addition to the problems created by the different religious movements within Jewish society—and which continued to arise with even greater intensity during the twentieth century—many new questions (such as the problem of *agunot*) arose as a result of the migration itself and the distance between the new home and the previous one. World War I, at the beginning of the twentieth century, and the turbulence and changes that came in its wake, also gave rise to numerous problems that were submitted to the respondents. Today, a wide-ranging halakhic literature, including responsa, is being produced in the United States. A foremost respondent was Moses

---

responsa were published in S. Yavne'eli, *Massa le-Teiman* [Journey to Yemen], Tel Aviv, 1952, pp. 185–200.

Feinstein, whose responsa reflect the spiritual and social life of a significant part of this large and flourishing Jewish society.

The national awakening at the end of the nineteenth century and the resulting increased migration to the Land of Israel also gave rise to a variety of halakhic problems. There were two major categories of such problems. The first involved the agricultural laws applicable in the Land of Israel, and the laws of the sabbatical year, in the context of the large-scale resettlement of the land. The second involved the relation between the different movements in Jewish society in connection with the settlement, redemption, and reconstruction of the Land of Israel. As a result, the volume of responsa literature written in the newly developing center in the Land of Israel increased. At the beginning of the twentieth century, as previously noted, these problems were, to a great extent, also dealt with in Eastern European responsa.

The responsa literature has steadily grown since the establishment of the State of Israel. The establishment of the State has given rise to many hundreds of problems in all areas of the law, *e.g.*, the sabbath and festivals, industry and agriculture, the postal system, transport and ports, defense and security, and many others. Many problems have also arisen pertaining to public affairs, such as the right of women to vote, the rules relating to the election and composition of the institutions of the Chief Rabbinate, the problem of satisfying religious requirements in the armed forces, the establishment of the National Independence Day, and the commemoration of the liberation of Jerusalem. All these problems require solutions so that a traditional Jewish mode of life can be maintained and yet a modern state can be administered in this technological age. There has been extensive discussion of such questions in many responsa by the halakhic authorities in the Land of Israel, and, to a certain extent, by halakhic authorities in the diaspora as well, both before and after the establishment of the State.

As a consequence of the jurisdiction of the Israeli rabbinical courts over matters of personal status, there is also a wide-ranging literature of responsa concerning the laws of *Even ha-Ezer* and the laws of inheritance. To a certain extent, the responsa literature has also begun to renew its consideration of the practical application of the laws of *Ḥoshen Mishpat* in consequence of the submission of such questions from time to time to the rabbinical courts.[128]

Not all of the questions receive answers; the fear of taking a stand sometimes results in abdication of responsibility, and abstention from rendering judgments. However, some halakhic authorities have dealt with a very large proportion of the questions extensively and with great delibera-

128. *See infra* pp. 1600–1605.

tion. Among the leading respondents in the Land of Israel in the modern era have been Abraham Isaac ha-Kohen Kook, the first Ashkenazic Chief Rabbi of Israel; Ẓevi Pesaḥ Frank, the Rabbi of Jerusalem; Ben-Zion Uziel, Sephardic Chief Rabbi of Israel; Isaac Halevi Herzog, Ashkenazic Chief Rabbi of Israel; Meshullam Rath; and Ovadiah Hadayah. Contemporary respondents include Eliezer Judah Waldenberg; Ovadiah Yosef, former Sephardic Chief Rabbi of Israel; and Joshua Menahem Ehrenberg.[129] Particular questions in connection with military matters involving the Israeli armed forces have been dealt with by Shlomo Goren, former Chief Chaplain of the Israel Defense Forces and former Ashkenazic Chief Rabbi of Israel; some of these responsa have been compiled and published by the Israel Defense Forces.[130]

F. Summary

Throughout its history, the responsa literature has been one of the most valuable and significant creations of the halakhic system in general and of *mishpat ivri* in particular. As a result of its link to the problems of daily life, the responsa literature in the post-Talmudic period, from both the literary and the legal-halakhic aspect, has been incomparably more extensive than the codificatory literature and the literature of commentaries and novellae. The quantity and the subject matter of the responsa have varied from time to time and from place to place, depending on various internal and external factors. However, in the final analysis, every center in the diaspora[131] has

129. For some of the more important books of responsa of the twentieth century, *see infra* Appendix C.

130. A few of these responsa have been published in various issues of *Maḥanayim*.

131. Only a few books of responsa are extant from the Jewish center in Yemen. The following reasons have been suggested:

1. Responsa by the Yemenite authorities were extremely brief. They were most often written on the margins of the small slips of paper containing the questions, and neither the originals nor any copies have survived. *See* J. Kafaḥ, *Halikhot Teiman* [The Practices of Yemen], 1961, pp. 75–76.
2. According to Kafaḥ, the halakhic authorities of Yemen did not want their decisions to bind later authorities; they believed that the courts of each generation should make their own decisions. *See* Maimonides, *MT*, Mamrim 2:1. As previously noted, the same view was taken in Poland in the fifteenth and sixteenth centuries by Jacob Pollack and Shalom Shakhna, who, for this reason, refrained from writing any codificatory works or preserving copies of their responsa; *see supra* pp. 1346–1348.
3. Kafaḥ is of the opinion that Maimonides held that the prohibition against committing the Oral Law to writing may be relaxed only in emergency situations because of special needs, but otherwise the prohibition stands; *see Sefer Mishneh Torah*, ed. Kafaḥ (on the basis of Yemenite mss. with a comprehensive commentary by the editor), Makhon Moshe, Jerusalem, 1984, I, Preface,

made a significant contribution to the development and flourishing of this type of halakhic literature in all areas of Jewish law.

---

pp. 23–24. It is possible that the Yemenite authorities were influenced by this view and therefore wrote down only what was absolutely necessary to put in writing, such as aggadic *midrashim* and ethical homilies, and—so far as *Halakhah* was concerned—the laws of *terefah* (concerning physical infirmities of animals that render them unfit for eating).

Yemenite rabbis customarily spoke at all public gatherings, especially at houses of mourning and at weddings, and therefore needed homiletic collections. The laws of *terefah* were put in writing inasmuch as meat customarily was eaten every day in Yemen even during public mourning periods and even on the day preceding the ninth day of Av (except for the meal directly preceding the fast), as was originally the law in the Talmud. *See* Kafaḥ, *Halikhot Teiman,* p. 44. Furthermore, the non-Jewish population of Yemen did not eat animals slaughtered by Jews, so that an animal found to be *terefah* could not be eaten by anyone. The halakhic authorities in Yemen therefore carefully studied the laws of *terefah* in order to be able to follow the most lenient authorities and avoid the monetary loss that would occur when a slaughtered animal was found to be *terefah. See id.* at 92.

4. The halakhic authorities in Yemen did not think it important to preserve their responsa, as is evident from the statements of one of the leading halakhic authorities in Yemen in the eighteenth century, Yehaiah b. Joseph Ẓalaḥ, who only at a late stage felt it important to collect and preserve his responsa. *See Resp. Pe'ullat Ẓaddik,* Tel Aviv, 1946, I, Introduction.

To these pertinent reasons, two more may be added: One is that many halakhic books were destroyed at the time of the Jewish expulsion from Mawza in 1679–1680. *See Resp. Pe'ullat Ẓaddik, supra,* Editor's Introduction. As to the tribulations of this expulsion, *see* the articles by Y. Ratzhabi in *Sefunot,* V (1961), pp. 339–395, and *Zion,* XXXVII (1972), pp. 196–215, and J. Tobi, *Iyyunim bi-Megillot Teiman* [Studies in Yemenite Documents], Jerusalem, 1986, under the entry *Galut Mawza.* The final reason for the sparseness of responsa from Yemen is the absence in Yemen of a publishing house, which first became available to the Yemenite Jews when they came to the Land of Israel.

Interestingly, certain compilations of responsa by halakhic authorities of Spain and Germany were preserved only in Yemen; these have now been published in Israel by J. Kafaḥ. Among these are compilations of the responsa of Rabbenu Tam, Ri Migash, Rabi (Abraham b. Isaac of Narbonne), Rabad, and Ritba. *See* Kafaḥ, "Kesharehah Shel Yahadut Teiman im Merkazei ha-Yahadut" [The Ties between the Jews of Yemen and the Centers of Jewish Life], *Yahadut Teiman—Pirkei Meḥkar ve-Iyyun* [Research Studies on the Jews of Yemen], Jerusalem, 1976, p. 43 and accompanying nn. In this essay, Kafaḥ proves that throughout the generations there always were strong ties between the Jews of Yemen and the Jews of the other centers of the diaspora, and that books by the halakhic authorities of the various centers reached Yemen soon after they were written. Thus, for example, in the period between Alfasi's and Maimonides' codes, Alfasi's code reached Yemen; and an unidentified Yemenite scholar composed at that time a commentary in Arabic on Alfasi's codification of the laws of Tractate *Ḥullin.* This book includes geonic responsa that are not found in Lewin's *Oẓar ha-Geonim* or anywhere else. It was published by Kafaḥ in 1960.

It should also be noted that Yemenite scholars are now engaged in compiling and publishing the remainder of the extant responsa by Yemenite halakhic authorities. Thus, for example, the responsum by the halakhic authorities in Yemen to the Yemenite community in the Land of Israel at the beginning of the twentieth century with regard to the baking of

V. GENERAL OVERVIEW OF THE METHODOLOGY, STRUCTURE, AND FORM OF THE RESPONSA

This section examines some of the main characteristics of the methodology, structure, and form of extant responsa, particularly those from the period of the *rishonim.*[132]

A. The Questioners; Submission of Questions

The questioners were ordinarily local rabbis who received inquiries by the members of their communities or were local judges who adjudicated legal disputes. When a question arose that they were unable to answer, or when a party requested that a difficult or novel case be given further consideration, the rabbi or judge referred the matter to the leading halakhic authority of that center,[133] or, occasionally, to a leading authority in a different center.[134] Certain matters—especially disputes between an individual and a community or any of its agencies,[135] and occasionally even ordinary

---

mazzah on Passover itself was published by Y. Ratzhabi, *supra* n. 127, and republished by Nahum, *supra* n. 127. The nineteenth-century responsum by the Yemenite halakhic authorities on the question of changing the distribution of the public charity fund is found in Kafaḥ, "Sheliḥim Niskharim le-Teiman" [Paid Solicitors for Charity in Yemen], in *Meḥkerei Erez Yisra'el,* Book 2/5, Jerusalem, 1956, pp. 297–300. The permissibility of conducting a eulogy for a scholar on the second day of a festival was the subject of a responsum by Yemenite halakhic authorities in the nineteenth century; *see id.* at 303–306. For a contrary view taken by other Yemenite authorities of that period, *see* S. ha-Levi, "Sippur Shevaḥav Shel Niftar Talmid Ḥakham be-Fanav be-Yom Tov Sheni" [Eulogizing a Deceased Halakhic Scholar on the Second Day of a Festival], *Kovez Har'el,* ed. Y. Ratzhabi and Y. Shavtiel, Tel Aviv, 1962, pp. 98–198. As to the difference of opinion among the halakhic authorities of Yemen in the nineteenth century with regard to the *ha-Mozi* blessing over bread at a public meal, and their responsa on that question, *see* A. Cohen, *Ozerot Teiman,* Bene-Berak, 1985, and the articles by R. Arusi in Nahum, *supra* n. 127 at 297–337, 338–340. For interesting information on the Jewish judicial system and decision making in the Jewish community of Yemen, *see* Kafaḥ, *Halikhot Teiman,* pp. 69–88.

132. For a discussion of the structure and form of geonic responsa, *see supra* pp. 1468–1473. Some of the characteristics described *infra* also apply to geonic responsa, as will be specifically pointed out.

133. *See, e.g., Resp. Asheri* 17:1, 85:5 (and *see* the end of the responsum, where Asheri invited the judges to turn to him again in case of doubt), and 97:1; *Resp. Ran* #72 (at the end); *Resp. Ribash* #5; *Terumat ha-Deshen,* Pesakim u-Khetavim, #89, #138; *Resp. Maharil* #70, #75, #77, #80; *Resp. Maharyu* #29, #80, #170; *Resp. Maharam of Padua* #40 (the enactment quoted there); and many other responsa.

Resp. Tashbez, II, #96–97 involve an interesting case. After Rashbez had issued a ruling on a case referred to him by a local judge, one of the parties, with the consent of the judge, submitted additional information, in light of which Rashbez reconsidered his opinion. *See further infra.*

134. *See supra* pp. 1474–1475, 1488.

135. *See, e.g., Terumat ha-Deshen,* Pesakim u-Khetavim, #128, #175, #214; *Resp. Maharyu* #151; *Resp. Zemah Zedek* #37 (by Menahem Mendel Krochmal, sitting as an ar-

cases[136]—were submitted in the first instance to a preeminent halakhic authority for a ruling. Sometimes, the general government or a non-Jewish court turned to a respondent to clarify the Jewish law relevant to a case involving Jewish litigants.[137] Some responsa did not reply to a question, but were written on the respondent's initiative, and sent to a community or to communal officials; these responsa conveyed the respondent's reaction to negative developments in the community and his instructions on the matter.[138]

There is evidence from an early period that the halakhic authorities were scrupulous to respond in litigated matters only to questions addressed to them by judges or by all the parties to a case. Rashi wrote:[139] "It is not our custom to behave like an advocate and give legal advice to one party. [This is] to avoid transgressing the injunction, 'You shall not utter a false report.'"[140] The halakhic authorities of all periods repeatedly emphasized that no responsum should be issued unless requested by a judge or by all the parties.[141] The reason was, as Rashi indicated, to prevent the respondent

---

bitrator); and many others. *See also Resp. Rashba,* V, #279, involving a dispute between individuals and a community, which had been decided by the local court, and was appealed to Rashba.

136. Particularly in those instances where they responded to a question submitted by only one of the parties; *see infra.* There were cases where the question was put by a woman; *see, e.g., Resp. Maharil* #70; *Terumat ha-Deshen,* Pesakim u-Khetavim, #261. In one case (*Resp. Tashbeẓ,* I, #124) the communal leaders of Tunis submitted a dispute between a husband and wife to Rashbeẓ when the local judge refused to continue to hear the case after being assaulted by the husband. Rashbeẓ issued a thorough responsum, at the end of which he chastised the local judge for withdrawing from the case and thereby violating the Torah's instruction to judges that they should "fear no man [Deuteronomy 1:17]."

137. *See* the sources cited *supra* n. 74 (which relate to an order to Rashba by King Pedro to judge a case involving an informer); *Resp. Asheri* 107:6(1) (p. 98a); *Resp. Ribash* #490, #510; *Resp. Tashbeẓ,* I, #152; *Resp. Rashba,* I, #1148 (to the effect that the royal court had agreed that the case should proceed in accordance with Jewish law, and it had been assigned to Rashba).

138. *See, e.g., Resp. Asheri* 78:3 (addressed to scribes and witnesses in Toledo regarding fraudulent conveyances and defaulting debtors); *Resp. Ribash* #79–80 (addressed to the Jewish community in Constantine regarding informers).

139. *Resp. Rashi,* ed. Elfenbein, #74 (p. 97); *see also* Elfenbein's hypothesis, *id.,* Introduction, pp. XXIV-XXV, as to why few of Rashi's responsa concern civil law, although it is certain that the Jewish community enjoyed full juridical autonomy.

140. *See Mekhilta* to Exodus 23:1 (ed. Horowitz-Rabin, pp. 321–322); and *see further infra.* The 1985 JPS *Tanakh* renders the verse: "You shall not carry false rumors." This does not convey the sense in which the verse is used here.

141. *See, e.g., Resp. Asheri* 17:10; *Resp. Ribash* #5, #175 (in the Introduction), #309 (at the end of the Introduction to the response), #473; *Resp. Maharil* #76; *Terumat ha-Deshen,* Pesakim u-Khetavim, #62 (as explicated by Maharam of Padua, *see infra* n. 147); *Resp. Avkat Rokhel* #81; *Resp. Maharam of Lublin* #100; *Resp. Ranaḥ* #93; *Resp. Noda bi-*

from becoming an advocate[142] supporting the claim of one side of the dispute. Other halakhic authorities elaborated on this reason: "From the responsum, the party will learn to put forward arguments that will be of help to him, thus turning the respondent into an advocate."[143]

However, it is clear that there was another and somewhat related reason for this policy. Ribash, who cited the danger of the respondent's becoming an advocate, had first given another reason: "To decide a dispute and issue a responsum before hearing all the arguments of both sides is both foolish and shameful because, after the first one is declared to be correct, his opponent will come and refute him; the respondent will have to reverse himself and he will become the laughingstock of the country."[144] The danger in not hearing both sides is that the judge may not learn all the pertinent facts, and his decision, not being based on the true facts, will be incorrect. Samuel de Medina (Maharashdam) was once involved in an incident that illustrates this danger. He bitterly deplored his having issued a responsum on one occasion at the request of only one of the parties to a dispute; his decision turned out to be erroneous because of his ignorance of all the facts:

> I was exceedingly angry that I responded to the questioner, and particularly to a question involving civil law, without first having the question written and signed by both parties. My affection [for a person] misled me, and I failed to heed what the *aḥaronim* had written, and because of that, what I am about to tell you occurred.

Maharashdam went on to describe how he made a wrong ruling on the basis of a question submitted to him by only one of the parties, and he concluded: "From now on, let no one expect a response from me" unless the question is submitted by both parties.[145]

Yehudah, Mahadura Kamma, ḤM, #20; and many more. As to writing a responsum or rendering a decision when the question is submitted by only one party, *see* Rema's gloss to Sh. Ar. ḤM 17:5: "No halakhic authority should write a decision to [only] one of the parties"; and *Pitḥei Teshuvah* to Sh. Ar. ḤM ch. 17, subpar. 11. *See also* Shochetman, *supra* n. 45 at 341ff. and Lifshitz, *supra* n. 20.

142. *See* M Avot 1:8; TB Ketubbot 52b; TJ Ketubbot 4:10, 30a (4:11, 29a); TJ Bava Batra 9:4, 28b (9:6, 17a); and *see infra*. *See also Tosafot Yom Tov* to M Avot 1:8 for Yom Tov Lipmann Heller's interpretation of *ke-orkhei ha-dayyanim* ("like advocates").

143. *Resp. Ribash* #179; *see also id.* #175 and other sources.

144. *Resp. Ribash* #179.

145. *Resp. Maharashdam*, ḤM, #109. Maharashdam's statement was: "From now on, let no one expect a response from me unless he meets the requirements." The requirements are stipulated at the beginning of the responsum, namely, that the question be in writing and signed by both parties.

An additional reason for the policy is indicated by Maharam of Padua:[146]

> Recently, my colleagues and I gathered to erect a safeguard for ourselves. We have undertaken not to respond to any dispute on a matter of civil law unless requested by both parties or by the judges chosen by both of them. For we have seen that much harm has been caused in this country by the following behavior: Each one of the parties cunningly puts a question [to an authority], and craftily deceives him. He [the party] thus acquires for himself a "rabbi" and a great authority to take his side, on whom he relies. He produces the decision [at the hearing] and proclaims "*kim li*" ("it [the law] is established for me"). This leads to great controversy between the rabbis and the laymen. Therefore, we decided to adopt this safeguard.[147]

This reason appears to be closely connected to the rationale that the respondent will probably not be given all the facts and will therefore render a decision favorable to one of the parties. However, Maharam of Padua's explanation points to an additional factor: A ruling by a halakhic authority in favor of one of the parties constitutes unfair influence on the local court that will hear the case; and the party who obtained the ruling is likely to assert the plea of *kim li,*[148] *i.e.,* that he follows the ruling in the responsum he received. Such behavior would almost certainly lead to "controversy between the rabbis and the laymen."

Notwithstanding all these considerations, however, respondents did occasionally issue responsa to questions put to them by only one of the parties. In such instances, the respondent usually began his responsum with an apology for departing from the accepted practice and an explanation of his action.[149] In some places, the general policy was not carried out

146. *Resp. Maharam of Padua* #40. *See also* M. Zena, "Le-Toledot Kehillat Bologna bi-Teḥillat ha-Me'ah ha-Shesh-Esreh" [Studies in the History of the Jewish Community of Bologna in the Early Sixteenth Century], *HUCA,* XVI (1941), Hebrew sec., pp. 35–98, at p. 75.

147. *See* Maharam of Padua's further discussion, where he relies on *Terumat ha-Deshen,* Pesakim u-Khetavim, #62 in refusing to respond on matters of civil law to a question posed by only one of the parties.

148. For a discussion of the plea of *kim li, see supra* pp. 1281–1282, 1386.

149. Various explanations were given for departing from the accepted practice:

1. A personal relationship existed between the respondent and the questioner (so that the respondent was confident that the questioner had not concealed any information and would not make improper use of the responsum); *see, e.g., Resp. Asheri* 17:10; *Resp. Maharil* #70.
2. The responsum was given as an interlocutory ruling in special circumstances (*Resp. Rashi,* ed. Elfenbein, #74), or as a temporary restraining order when it was feared that one of the parties would engage in conduct that would make a final judgment ineffective (*Terumat ha-Deshen,* Pesakim u-Khetavim, #260–261).

consistently, and other halakhic authorities remarked that this deviation should be corrected.[150]

Occasionally, the same question was submitted to more than one respondent. In such cases, the responsa were sometimes similar[151] and sometimes conflicting.[152] A respondent, particularly when faced with a serious

---

3. The respondent was at a great distance from the questioner, making communication difficult (*Resp. Ribash* #5; *Resp. Mabit,* III, #21).
4. An opinion had already been given by a different respondent, and a refusal to respond to the inquiry could be wrongly construed as agreement with that opinion (*Resp. Avkat Rokhel* #81, disagreeing with Mabit, quoted in *id.* #80).
5. There was a need for an opinion discussing basic principles.

Thus, *Resp. Rashbash* #230 states:

> A judge is prohibited from hearing [only] one party. . . . However, my father Rashbeẓ, as well as some of the rabbis who preceded him here, all responded to the questions posed by inquirers. They did not render a final judgment, but would say, "If the facts are such, the applicable law is thus," and the local judges would render judgment. If the question stated the facts correctly, they [the local judges] would render judgment according to the responsum, unless they found some flaw in it. If they found a flaw, they would resubmit the question until the correct law emerged. This was the practice of worthy Jewish judges whose intent was to arrive at a completely correct decision.

See also Terumat ha-Deshen, Pesakim u-Khetavim, #214 (at the end of the responsum): "I have written to you in the form of a responsum to your question, but not as a final judgment, since I have not heard the arguments of your adversary"; *Resp. Noda bi-Yehudah,* Mahadura Kamma, ḤM, #20; *Resp. Ranaḥ* #93. And *see* TB Ketubbot 52b and *Oẓar ha-Geonim, ad loc.;* TJ Ketubbot 4:10, 30a (4:10, 29a); TJ Bava Batra 9:4, 28b (9:6, 17a); and commentaries to TB Ketubbot 52b regarding the circumstances in which it is permissible for a judge to act as an advocate. *See also* B. Lipkin, "Arikhat Din be-Mishpat ha-Torah" [Advocacy under the Law of the Torah], *Sinai,* XXX, pp. 46ff.; XXXI, pp. 265ff.

150. *See Keneset ha-Gedolah,* ḤM, Mahadura Kamma, #17, Glosses to *Tur,* #19: "Nowadays it is a common practice that when an authority is asked a specific question, even by only one of the parties, he issues a responsum. Apparently, the justification is that the case will not be adjudicated by the respondent. However, Ribash indicates that even so, it is forbidden." From the conclusion in *Keneset ha-Gedolah,* it appears that its author, Ḥayyim Benveniste, opposed this practice. *See id.* for references to the subject in the responsa of the *aḥaronim,* and *see also supra* p. 791.

151. *See* the following examples:

1. *Resp. Ribash* #127 and *Resp. Tashbeẓ,* I, #1, regarding the validity of a divorce; the question was put to many other halakhic authorities—*see* the end of the question in the above responsa. (Although when the first decision validating the divorce was given there were still some who argued for the more stringent view, all the leading halakhic authorities that were consulted agreed to permit the woman to remarry; *see Resp. Tashbeẓ, id.*, at the end of the question.)
2. *Resp. Tashbeẓ,* I, #21, regarding immigration to the Land of Israel when the only means of travel was a caravan that traveled on the sabbath. *Resp. Ribash* #101 agreed with this ruling.
3. *Resp. Maharashdam,* ḤM, #218 and *Resp. Maharshakh,* I, #44, regarding suretyship for an invalid obligation.

152. The following are a few examples:

1. *Resp. Tashbeẓ,* I, #58 (end of s.v. Inyan, p. 31c): "I have been urged to render an opinion to the judges, and some of them [*i.e.*, the judges] sent it [their

question of family law involving marital status or other similar questions, would at times request that his responsum be reviewed by other halakhic authorities or would co-opt other authorities to his responsum, so that it would not be the ruling of only a single individual.[153]

---

request] to me because they were not satisfied with the rabbi's [Ribash's] responsum [*see Resp. Ribash* #46–52]; however, they did not feel themselves sufficiently competent to reject his ruling unless I agreed. To do the work of Heaven, I have dared to take issue with that rabbi who is outstanding in age and in wisdom." In this case, some of the local judges turned to Rashbeẓ because the ruling given by the previous respondent did not seem to them to be correct.

2. *Resp. Ribash* #120, #146 and *Resp. Tashbeẓ*, I, #50–51, regarding the validity of a Torah scroll in which the letter *kuf* was not written according to the Spanish custom but rather according to the custom "of these regions." Ribash ruled the scroll invalid; Rashbeẓ ruled it valid. *Resp. Tashbeẓ* #51 specifically alludes to Ribash's ruling.
3. *Resp. Maharibal*, II, #23; *Resp. Maharashdam*, ḤM, #327–332; *Resp. Avkat Rokhel* #80 (a responsum of Moses Trani), #81 (a responsum of Joseph Caro); *Resp. Naḥalah li-Yehoshu'a* (by Joshua Ẓonẓin) #12, regarding the right of inheritance of Gracia Mendes. *See supra* n. 93.
4. *Resp. Maharshakh*, III, #64, #65 (continuation of Maharshakh's ruling, decision by Solomon Gabizon, objections of Maharshakh), #66 (decision by Abraham Monzon); *Resp. Maharitaẓ* #129 (responsa by Maharitaẓ and Ḥayyim Kafusi); *Resp. Oholei Ya'akov* #45 (responsum of Maharikash). All the above responsa deal with the subject of an agent who deviates from his principal's instructions regarding the purchase of merchandise.
5. *Resp. Divrei Rivot* #216–218; *Resp. Maharashdam*, ḤM, #40 (responsa by Isaac Adarbi, Maharashdam, and Mordecai Matalon), regarding security for a loan. The sequence of these responsa is of interest. In a dispute between a debtor and a creditor, Isaac Adarbi decided in favor of the creditor (*Resp. Divrei Rivot* #216). The debtor turned to Mordecai Matalon and Maharashdam, both of whom ruled in his favor. *Resp. Divrei Rivot* #217 quotes their rulings, and in #218 Isaac Adarbi rebutted their objections to his decision and strongly defended his own original ruling. When *Resp. Divrei Rivot* was published, Maharashdam responded to it in detail, arguing that Adarbi's ruling was erroneous.
6. *Resp. Bet Yosef*, Dinei Kiddushin, #10 (responsa of Judah Ḥen le-Vet She'altiel, Shem Tov ibn Manhir, Abraham ibn Naḥmias, and Joseph Caro); *Resp. Maharam Alashkar* #83–85; *Resp. Zekan Aharon* #2–4 (Elijah ha-Levi, Elijah Capsali); and a responsum of Jacob Berab (from ms.; *see* Freimann, *Kiddushin ve-Nissu'in*, pp. 123–125)—all regarding the validity of the marriage of a young woman named Alona in Crete.

In the responsa literature of later periods, too, differences of opinion—often expressed in very sharp terms—are common, *e.g.*, the intense controversy over the famous bill of divorcement issued in Cleves in the eighteenth century. *See* the first thirty-three responsa in *Resp. Or Yisra'el* by Israel Lipschutz, who arranged for the divorce; *Resp. Or ha-Yashar*, in many parts of the book; *Resp. Matteh Levi* #19, *et al. See also* S. Tal, "Ha-Get mi-Klivah" [The Bill of Divorcement from Cleves], *Sinai*, XXIV, pp. 152ff., 214ff.; Freehof, *supra* n. 2 at 158ff.

153. *See, e.g., Resp. Raban*, EH, III, p. 47b (ed. Jerusalem) (the responsum is discussed in detail *supra* pp. 848–849); *Teshuvot Maimuniyyot* to *MT*, Hilkhot Ishut, #9 (at the end);

B. The Structure, Form, Style, Transmittal, and Copying of the Question and Response

It was extremely important for the questioner to submit the following information: a detailed and precise statement of the facts of the case; the text of any relevant enactments, legal instruments, or other documents; a summary of the arguments of the parties; and an accurate transcript of witnesses' testimony. Respondents would frequently state that they had thoroughly examined all the material submitted before reaching their decisions.[154] Responsa thus constitute a rich repository of texts of enactments, legal instruments, and other types of documents, as well as testimony and enlightening descriptions of the daily life of the people. The testimony and the arguments would occasionally be reported in the language in which they were given—Arabic, Ladino, Yiddish, and others—and the respondent would interpret the material according to its ordinary meaning in the language as commonly spoken.[155] Frequently, a respondent would point out a gap in the facts or a lack of clarity in the question.[156] In such cases, he would either refuse to respond until he received the additional information or the necessary clarification,[157] or he would discuss in prin-

---

Resp. Ribash #159 and *Resp. Tashbeẓ*, I, #100 (at the beginning of the response; *Resp. Ribash* #170 (at the end of the response) and *Resp. Tashbeẓ*, I, #23; *Resp. Ribash* #399 (toward the end of the response; and *cf. Resp. Maharam Alashkar* #48, *see supra* pp. 859, 867–869); *Terumat ha-Deshen*, Pesakim u-Khetavim, #47, #130, #161, #220, #222 (at the end of the responsa); *Resp. Maharil* #74 (at the end of the response); *Resp. Maharam Mintz* #21; *see also Resp. Ribash* #477, and other responsa. The notion of many authorities joining together and sharing responsibility for a decision is found in the Talmud (TB Sanhedrin 7b, Horayot 3b: "so that only a chip of the beam" [*i.e.*, part of the responsibility] should "reach" each one). *See also supra* p. 1493 and n. 118.

154. *See, e.g., Resp. Rashba*, III, #22, #213; IV, #57; V, #279; *Resp. Asheri* 5:6; *Resp. Ritba* #100; *Resp. Ribash* #475; *Terumat ha-Deshen*, Pesakim u-Khetavim, #55, #67, #83, #161. Maharil wrote that he reviewed only the facts and the arguments submitted to him by the judges, accepting no direct submissions from any of the parties (*Resp. Maharil* #76).

155. *See, e.g.*, for Yiddish, *Resp. Maharyu* #80, #124, #147; *Resp. Noda bi-Yehudah*, Mahadura Kamma, EH, #31. For a detailed discussion of the use of Yiddish in responsa, *see* Z. Rubashov (Shazar), "Yiddishe Gevi'us Eidus in die Shailes u-Teshuvos" [Testimony in Yiddish in the Responsa], *Yivo, Historishe Shriften* [Yivo, Historical Studies], I, pp. 116–195. For Ladino and Judeo-Arabic, *see Resp. Maharashdam*, ḤM, #327–332; *Resp. Avkat Rokhel* #80, #81; *Resp. Naḥalah li-Yehoshu'a* #12; and many other responsa. *See also* Rubashov, *supra*, Introduction, p. 124.

156. *See, e.g., Resp. Ramah* #255; *Resp. Rashba*, II, #182; III, #95; IV, #59, #172, #240, #320; V, #139, #168, #220, #284; *Resp. Asheri* 79:11(2), 80:4; *Resp. Ritba* #111, #156 (Ritba specifically criticized the failure to send him a diagram of the window that was the subject of the dispute); and others.

157. *See, e.g., Resp. Rashba*, II, #182; III, #95; IV, #172, #269; V, #139, #220, #284; *Resp. Ritba* #82. *See also Resp. Ribash* #475, in which Ribash wrote that because of insufficient evidence he should have refused to answer the question, but in order to save expense he was issuing a responsum stating the relevant legal principles.

ciple the basic point of law involved. At times, the respondent would fill in the missing facts from the material supplied to him or even give alternative answers to fit the possible factual situations.[158]

The questions frequently contained a discussion of the legal aspects of the case—sometimes in great detail—particularly when the question was posed by a judge. In such instances, the questioner would suggest one or more possible solutions to the problem and ask the respondent's opinion.[159]

Some responsa do not contain the text of the question as asked, and the question must be reconstructed from the answer. There were various reasons for this. Many of the questions were abridged or summarized by the copyists or the editors of the compilations of responsa, or, occasionally, by the respondent himself.[160] Apparently, neither the copyists nor the respondents thought it important to preserve the exact language of the question, since their main concern was with the respondent's legal discussion and decision. However, sometimes the respondent gave a different reason for having shortened the question.[161]

158. *See, e.g., Resp. Rashba,* II, #182; III, #138, #166. (In #166, the dispute concerned seating in a synagogue, and the questioner attached a diagram of the disputed seat and the adjacent seats. Rashba, however, stated that "the diagram of the seats in your question is quite confusing.") Other examples include *Resp. Rashba,* III, #426; IV, #258, #269; V, #139, #220, #284; *Resp. Rashba Attributed to Naḥmanides* #13; *Resp. Ritba* #182 (p. 220); *Resp. Tashbeẓ,* I, #93 (at the end), #94 (at the end); *see also* #62, s.v. Teshuvah (after s.v. Shenit); *Resp. Maharyu* #80. For further discussion, *see supra* pp. 458–459.

159. Such questions were numerous and very frequent. A notable example is Maimonides' very brief response (*supra* n. 80) to a detailed question sent to him by Phinehas of Alexandria. This is an extreme example. Generally, the respondent discussed the points raised by the questioner. Occasionally, a point raised by the questioner would be answered even though the respondent did not believe it to be relevant to the issues in the case; *see, e.g., Resp. Ribash* #175 (at the beginning of the response and toward the end of s.v. Teshuvah).

160. *See, e.g., Resp. Ramah* #251, #296; *Resp. Rashba,* VI, #1, #176; *Resp. Asheri* 97:1; *Resp. Ribash* #177 (in the question); and many others. Sometimes, a respondent would state that he had not summarized the question but had stated it "verbatim"; *see, e.g., Resp. Rashba,* IV, #215; V, #166, #168.

161. *See, e.g.,* Ezekiel Landau, *Resp. Noda bi-Yehudah,* Mahadura Kamma, Introduction:

> I also beg the rabbis who asked the questions to forgive me for not having stated their questions *verbatim,* with the cogent reasoning that they include. I have set forth only the gist of the questions . . . , because I did not want to glorify myself with the words of others and thereby inflate the size of my book by giving the questions in full. Moreover, the rabbis who have asked the questions are themselves leading halakhic authorities, and they may decide to publish their opinions in a book. . . . Why then should I precede them and publish their ideas and arguments? Only in a few instances, where it would otherwise have been impossible to understand the response fully, have I quoted the questions in full.

There are also responsa that do not state the question at all; the question in such cases must be reconstructed from the answer.

The respondents ordinarily confined their discussion to the arguments presented by the parties and to the specific question asked.[162] In order to avoid the appearance of being advocates, they were careful not to suggest additional arguments that could be raised by any of the parties. However, a respondent would touch on a subject not mentioned by the questioner if it was directly connected to the question submitted and was necessary for an adequate response.[163] When the parties put forward many arguments that were "groundless" or "insubstantial" or "burdensome and vexatious, and for the most part like mountains suspended on a hair and only wearying," the respondent ignored them "because it is very tiresome to answer all these frivolous arguments."[164]

The structure, style, and explicitness of a responsum largely depended on such factors as the personality and methodology of the respondent and the period in which the responsum was written. Some respondents prefaced their responsa with a brief introduction, summarized the arguments of the parties, and organized their responsa according to a particular system.[165] As has been noted, the early responsa were brief and to the point; but, in the course of time, responsa expanded to include numerous sup-

162. *See, e.g., Resp. Ramah* #273; *Resp. Naḥmanides* (in Assaf, *Sifran Shel Rishonim*) #75 (at the end of the response); *Resp. Rashba*, III, #98; *Resp. Ritba* #164. This was the practice of the *rishonim*. The *aḥaronim*, particularly in the later period, frequently discuss arguments that were not presented to them. *See supra* p. 1485.

163. *See Resp. Asheri* 64:3; *Resp. Ramah* #273. Occasionally, a respondent would extend his discussion to anticipate possible future questions. *See Resp. Ribash* #234 ("I will depart from the usual practice and answer what I was not asked, because I am obligated to do so by what the Sages said . . . : 'He must not remain silent, since Scripture says [Exodus 23:7]: "Keep far from falsehood."'"); *Resp. Tashbez*, I, #56 ("Although this discussion is not necessary [to my decision] to permit this wine [which was the issue raised by the question], I will deal with it at some length in order to draw implications from it"). *See also Resp. Ribash* #175.

164. *See, e.g., Resp. Rashba*, II, #96; *Resp. Asheri* 13:20 (at the end of the response), 19:6, 35:5 (at the end of the response); *Terumat ha-Deshen*, Pesakim u-Khetavim, #73; *Resp. Maharyu* #40, #89. Ribash in particular responded sharply when the questioner discussed at length issues not raised by the parties:

> I see that you have gone on at great length about irrelevant matters . . . and have written two superfluous pages that are completely beside the point. . . . But setting up straw men on your own initiative on behalf of the heir in order to knock them down is nothing but a waste of effort and paper.

(*Resp. Ribash* #168, beginning of response, pp. 36d-37a.) This was written to a questioner whom Ribash held in high esteem.

165. *See, e.g., Resp. Ramah* #242; *Resp. Asheri* 86:15; *Terumat ha-Deshen*, Pesakim u-Khetavim, #73. Occasionally, a respondent would provide a brief summary of the full discussion in his responsum; *see, e.g., Resp. Tashbez*, I, #73–80 (the question and the response), #81 (a summary of the extensive response: "We have thus reached the following conclusion from all this, briefly stated for the students . . . "); and *see* the rest of the responsa, *id.*, on the same subject.

portive sources, extensive reasoning, and greater detail.[166] It was often emphasized that when a communal body was involved in a dispute, an especially thorough and deliberate consideration of the issues was called for in order to safeguard the rights of the public.[167] Occasionally, when it helped to clarify the answer, a respondent would include a diagram in his responsum.[168] There were instances when the questioner was not satisfied with the response and posed another question on the same subject; the respondent would then give a more detailed answer and discuss the questioner's specific comments and objections.[169] Sometimes, one of the parties would request the respondent to reconsider his decision.[170] In many cases, respondents referred questioners to other responsa in which they had answered the same or similar questions.[171]

The responsa, like most halakhic literature since the Talmud, were customarily written in Hebrew interspersed with Aramaic; but some of the respondents used more Aramaic than Hebrew.[172] In certain periods, some responsa were written in other languages, particularly Arabic (geonic responsa and those of Alfasi and Maimonides, among others). The use of Arabic had two negative consequences: (1) a large number of these responsa were lost when the people migrated to non–Arabic-speaking countries and thus could not make use of these responsa, and (2) translations into Hebrew were frequently inadequate and obscured the true meaning.

The responsa generally began and ended with a few flowery sentences, which occasionally even rhymed, and with honorific titles and appellations

166. *See supra* p. 1474.

167. *See Resp. Mayim Amukkim* (section containing the responsa of Ranaḥ) #63 (at the beginning of the responsum): "The fact that rights of the public depend on it requires that whoever decides this case investigate and consider it thoroughly with a desire to benefit the public." *See also Resp. Ẓemaḥ Ẓedek* (by Menahem Mendel Krochmal) #37 (near the middle of the responsum). Krochmal states that he was not required to give the reasons for his decision, "since both parties have voluntarily agreed to submit the case to me" as an arbitrator. However, the case was a matter of public interest and affected all the members of the community, "some of . . . [whom] covet the property of others," and he felt that in such cases the reasons for the decision should be given.

168. *See, e.g., Resp. Asheri* 84:4.

169. *See, e.g., Resp. Tashbeẓ*, I, #94, #95, #96; *Resp. Maharil* #70, #100 (at the end); *Resp. Maharyu* #70; *Terumat ha-Deshen*, Pesakim u-Khetavim, #20, #221; responsum of Israel Isserlein quoted in *Resp. Mahari Bruna* #92. Sometimes the respondent would receive objections to his decision from another halakhic authority who had examined the responsum. The respondent would then reply and attempt to prove that his decision was correct. *See Terumat ha-Deshen*, Pesakim u-Khetavim, #19–21.

170. *See Resp. Mabit*, III, #228; the first decision on the point is *Resp. Mabit*, III, #188.

171. *See, e.g., Resp. Rashba*, IV, #61 (at the end), #330; VI, #62; *Resp. Ribash* #58 (at the end).

172. Such as Meir ha-Levi Abulafia; *see, e.g.,* his *Resp. Ramah* #271, #285, #290, #292, #305. He also used a great deal of Aramaic in his novellae; *see supra* p. 1124.

and similar types of address.[173] In regard to the language of the responsa, a great deal of care must be taken in interpreting various terms (such as *kutim, goyim,* and *yishme'elim*—all terms for non-Jews) that were changed because of outside censorship. Occasionally, entire sentences and paragraphs were deleted by the censor.[174]

The fact that throughout the centuries the halakhic authorities continued to write thousands of responsa in Hebrew—albeit interlaced with Aramaic—was a decisive factor in the preservation of Hebrew as a living language that, at least from a literary point of view, continued to develop and to find expression for the ongoing changes in law, natural science, technology, and other areas.[175]

The responsa were committed to writing by the respondents themselves, or dictated by them to their students or to members of their families.[176] Copies were made by the respondent, his students, the recipients,

173. This is a common feature in all responsa; *see* A. Aptowitzer, *Mavo le-Raviah* [Introduction to Raviah], pp. 421–435. Great care must be taken to properly understand and interpret the flowery language, especially when attempting to draw historical conclusions from it. For example, Gross (quoted by Aptowitzer, *supra* at 422) interpreted Raviah's statement, "I am the youngest of the poor thousands, despised and the cast-off of men, an orphan" as meaning that Raviah was bewailing the death of his father and that he was left a lonely orphan. Aptowitzer, however, demonstrates that Raviah was modestly referring to his own lack of knowledge—an orphan in learning—and that it was a figure of speech that he frequently used.

174. *See, e.g., Resp. Asheri* 17:1 (for particulars, *see supra* p. 802 n. 80). *Compare Resp. Asheri* 18:5, ed. Constantinople, 1522, *with Resp. Asheri* 18:4–5, ed. Venice, 1552, and ed. Vilna, 1885. There are many such examples; *see infra* pp. 1520–1521.

175. There has been scant research with regard to the influence of the responsa literature on the new expressions and technical terms that became part of the Hebrew language over the centuries. Eliezer Ben Yehuda's dictionary of the Hebrew language makes very little use of the enormous linguistic contributions made by the responsa literature. *See* S. Eidelberg, "Matbe'ot Lashon ba-Ivrit Shel Yehudei Ashkenaz be-Shilhei Yemei ha-Beinayim" [Hebrew Idioms and Expressions of the Jews of Germany at the End of the Middle Ages], *Sinai,* LXX (1972), p. 225, and *see* the note there referring to the author's other articles on the subject; N. Shapiro, "Ha-Lashon ha-Tekhnit ba-Sifrut ha-Rabbanit" [Technical Language in Rabbinic Literature], *Leshonenu,* XXVI (1962), pp. 209–216 (giving various examples of new technical terms). However, Shapiro (*id.* at 209) was inaccurate in stating that the innovations were confined to newly developed technology and that there was no need for other linguistic innovations because, except for new technology, Talmudic terminology was adequate for the needs of the responsa literature. An examination of the responsa literature in its various periods indicates that new terms were coined in connection with subjects other than technology. The matter merits thorough research. The following is one example of the coinage of a nonlegal term in a responsum: Jacob Weil (*Resp. Maharyu* #147, p. 99a) translates "Bürgermeister" as *rav iron,* the term *iron* being a new derivation of *ir* ("town") and meaning "town council." *Rav iron* means literally "the leader of the town council." The term is also used by Weil's contemporary, Israel Isserlein (*Terumat ha-Deshen,* Pesakim u-Khetavim, #161, p. 34).

176. *See, e.g., Resp. Asheri* 2:19 (written by Asheri to Rashba), 5:2, 43:9(2); *Terumat ha-Deshen,* Pesakim u-Khetavim, #124; *id.,* Pesakim u-Khetavim, #60 (= *Leket Yosher,*

and others.[177] There were frequently errors in the identification of the author of a responsum,[178] or inaccuracies in the responsum because of incorrect copying.[179] The responsa were sometimes sent to the questioners by special messenger; and their fate, as well as the timeliness of their arrival, often largely depended on the messenger, who was on occasion delayed because the respondent was ill or preoccupied with other matters. In such a case, the respondent would, at times, write a very brief responsum in order not to delay the messenger unduly.[180] In view of problems of communication in various periods, a group of questions were often sent together, and responses to them were also accumulated and sent in one bundle.[181]

C. Fictitious Names of Persons and Places in the Responsa

Unlike the law reports in other legal systems, the responsa do not generally record the actual names of the parties to the cases. The men are usually referred to by the names of the Biblical patriarchs (Abraham, Isaac, and Jacob) or the names of Jacob's sons (Reuben, Simeon, etc.) and the women by the names of the matriarchs (Sarah, Rebecca, Rachel, and Leah).[182] This

---

OḤ, pp. 63–64), reduced to writing by Petaḥiah, Israel Isserlein's son; *Leket Yosher,* YD, pp. 19–20, in Yiddish, reduced to writing by "Sheindel, the wife of Rabbi Israel, may God preserve him."

177. *See, e.g., Resp. Asheri* 23:9(2); 74:4(2); *Resp. Ribash* #262, #277 (at the end of the response); *Resp. Rema* #40, #81 (at the end of the response); and *cf. Resp. Mahari Bruna* #28; and many more. *See also* sources cited *supra* n. 160. Sometimes, responsa were copied without the author's permission; *see, e.g., Leket Yosher,* OḤ, p. 104.

178. *See, e.g., Resp. Ri Migash* #114, referring to copyists "who attribute some of their responsa [*i.e.*, responsa that they copy] to the wrong author." *See also Resp. Rashba,* I, #166: "Many responsa have been written and have been attributed to foremost halakhic authorities who, perhaps, never wrote them." *See also infra* n. 215.

179. *See, e.g., Leket Yosher,* OḤ, pp. 58, 105. Because of concern over such a possibility, some questioners requested that the responsum be in the respondent's own handwriting. *See, e.g., Resp. Asheri* 74:4, at the end of s.v. Teshuvah (the first one).

180. *See, e.g., Resp. Ramah* #259; *Resp. Asheri* 20:20, 100:1; *Resp. Maharaḥ Or Zaru'a* #222; *Resp. Ribash* #40 ("Your first letter, the long one, reached me by way of the horseman, and the second, the shorter one, by way of the runner"). *See also id.* #47 (opening remarks), #157 (at the beginning of the response), #194 (the reference there is apparently to responsum #193, which was sent to Germany; *see supra* p. 1476), #477 (at the end of the response); *Resp. Ran* #67; *Resp. Maharik* #186 (ed. Lemberg, 1798).

181. Such bundles of responsa were very frequent in all periods. As to the method of dispatching responsa in the geonic period, *see supra* pp. 1469–1470. Occasionally, responsa were lost because of the difficulties in communication; *see Resp. Ribash* #153 and *Resp. Maharil* #151. Ribash had to write a new responsum, since he had not retained a copy of the first one; *see Resp. Ribash* #153. The question and the first responsum are in #66.

182. There is, however, the possibility that a Biblical name in a responsum was the actual name of the party, so that caution is required before concluding that the name was

practice goes back to the geonic responsa[183] and has been followed ever since. From the historian's point of view, this practice is to be regretted, since references to real people and a knowledge of the names that Jews adopted in various periods can be of great historical value.[184]

According to some scholars, the editors of the compilations of responsa did not include the actual names of the parties to the cases for two reasons: (1) the editors were interested solely in publishing the halakhic discussion and the decision of the respondent, and considered the names of the parties to be of no significance; and (2) they believed that giving the actual names would constitute an unwarranted invasion of privacy and might damage the reputations of the parties—a matter of serious concern to the halakhic authorities.[185]

Although these may have been the reasons for omission of the actual names by the editors, some responsa indicate that the questioner himself had used fictitious names in his question.[186] Two reasons are given in these

---

fictitious. *See, e.g., Resp. Rabi Av Bet Din* (ed. Kafaḥ, Jerusalem, 1962) #149 (Assaf, *Sifran Shel Rishonim,* Jerusalem, 1935, *Teshuvot ha-Rabi* #41): "When Moses was drunk on Purim, he rose up against his fellow and killed him. What is his punishment? Response: He is not liable to the death penalty, because we do not know whether the drunkenness of this Moses reached the level of that of Lot." *See* later in the responsum for the various penalties imposed on this Moses as a deterrent. Here it may be fairly assumed that Moses was the real name of the defendant, since otherwise he should have been called Reuben (or some other Biblical name appropriate to the facts of the case, *see infra* n. 189).

It is sometimes difficult to determine whether a name is fictitious. *See, e.g., Resp. Ribash* #128: "Reuben went overseas on business and left his home and family here. He left his nephew Ḥeẓron to take care of his business here, and the above-mentioned Reuben used to send merchandise to Ḥeẓron by sea." In the Bible, Ḥeẓron is the name of Reuben's son (Exodus 6:14) and also of Judah's grandson (Genesis 46:12), whereas here he appears as Reuben's nephew. *See also infra* n. 189.

183. *See supra* p. 1471.

184. The actual names of the parties can sometimes be discovered from other responsa relating to the same parties. *E.g.,* in *Resp. Ribash* #46 the parties are, as usual, designated by Biblical names: Reuben, Simeon, Naphtali, etc. However, in a later discussion of the same case, *id.* #52, the real names are given in a copy of a document from the island of Majorca. Interestingly, *Resp. Tashbeẓ,* I, #58, which deals with the same case, gives the real names in full, although when Rashbeẓ quoted from *Resp. Ribash,* he used the fictitious names that Ribash had used. Generally, however, Rashbeẓ also disguised the identity of the parties.

Some responsa mention the name of a family member through whom the identity of the party can be deduced. *See, e.g., Resp. Maharam of Rothenburg,* ed. Prague, #927: "Reb Jeremiah has complained to us that his son-in-law frequently beats his daughter and shames her by removing her head-covering, thus violating Jewish religious practice [of keeping the head covered]; she was given [to him] to live and not to suffer."

185. *See* J. Mann, "The Responsa of the Babylonian *Geonim* as a Source of Jewish History," *JQR* (N.S.), VII (1916–1917), p. 460; Boaz Cohen, *Kunteres ha-Teshuvot,* p. 32 n. 2.

186. *See Terumat ha-Deshen,* Pesakim u-Khetavim, #257 (quoted *infra* n. 188); *Resp. Maharit,* I, #70 (quoted *infra* n. 187); *Resp. Maharam Mintz,* Introduction to the Table of

responsa for that practice: (1) to obviate the possibility that the respondent would be tempted to rule in favor of a party with whom he may have been personally acquainted;[187] and (2) so that the final judgment in the case would be given by the local court before whom the parties appeared, and not by the respondent, and the responsum could thus be characterized as only an advisory opinion.[188] Sometimes, names other than those of the pa-

---

Contents: "I will arrange into chapters the responses to the questions that I have been asked over a long period. Some of them were sent to me in the form of [questions involving] 'Reuben and Simeon,' and there were also disputes that came before me." *See also Resp. Mabit,* Introduction by the respondent's son, at the beginning of the book, first paragraph: " . . . like Reuben and Simeon . . . "; earlier in the same paragraph, however, the Introduction states: " . . . of Jews who are in dispute, who were called by their names to record them in the book." The author's exact meaning is unclear.

187. *See Resp. Maharit,* I, #70:

> This concerns a dispute between two prominent individuals, advisers to the government in Damascus. The case came to our attention and each of them submitted his argument in writing under the names of "Reuben and Simeon." Even though I know who they really are, they shall be to me as Reuben and Simeon, and I will show no favor to either of them. . . . Since the affair is public knowledge, it is proper to publish the names of the prominent personages involved. They are Eleazar Kuleif ha-Levi and David Gabizon, may the Lord preserve them.

Maharit thus made clear that although the question did not identify the disputants, he knew their real identities, since the affair had become well known, and he felt certain that he would nonetheless write his responsum impartially, as if he did not know who they were. Similarly, in *Resp. Maharitaz* #129 (referred to *supra* n. 152), the response begins as follows: "What makes it especially difficult for me is that the question was submitted with the real names of the parties, with no attempt to conceal their identities; and Jacob Riva is a close friend of mine and I would like him to be in the right. However, I love truth more." The fear of possible bias on the part of the respondent is somewhat surprising. After all, the respondent was a leading halakhic authority who generally did not live in the town where the dispute was being heard. Why then should there be greater concern with his possible bias than with that of the local judges who were acquainted with the parties who appeared before them?

188. *See Terumat ha-Deshen,* Pesakim u-Khetavim, #257:

> I will give my opinion because the case of that man called Baruch was not fully considered by the venerable Maharna, may the Lord preserve him. For I have noted that he [Maharna] always prefers that the parties not be identified to him except by [fictitious] names like "Reuben" and "Simeon," which give both parties equal status; and he expressed his opinion without having heard the parties personally. . . . However, if my teacher, Maharna, maintains his opinion after having read mine, then my opinion should be considered by him as a nullity.

Apparently, the intention of this passage is as we have suggested in the text. It should, however, be pointed out that this reason for anonymity, which significantly limits the authority of the respondent, is not easy to accept. In the overwhelming majority of responsa, the respondent determines and states the law by virtue of his own authority and does not merely give an advisory opinion. It is possible that the limited advisory status of certain responsa was connected with the particular conditions of a specific historical period. The matter requires further study.

triarchs or the sons of Jacob were given to the parties when this was more appropriate to the circumstances of the case.[189] The rabbinical courts in Israel today also follow this policy, and in their published opinions the parties are referred to as "A.," "B.," etc. Since most of the cases coming before the rabbinical courts are in the field of family law and personal status, the courts apparently wish to avoid invading the privacy of the parties.[190]

The names of places are also frequently fictitious, and we find European cities being designated in responsa as "Tiberias," "Sepphoris," or other cities that existed in the Land of Israel during Talmudic times.[191] The true identities of the towns involved in a dispute were disguised so that the attention of the general government would not be attracted when the cases concerned tax matters or other sensitive subjects. Copyists and editors often omitted place names altogether, apparently for the same reasons that personal names were omitted or changed.[192]

189. *See, e.g., Resp. Asheri* 32:11: "Reuben married a woman named Sarah and had ten children by her. Later, his heart led him astray and he began to behave licentiously. He attached himself to Shelomit, the daughter of Divri, who was married to Simeon." The fictitious name given to the woman suspected of adultery was Shelomit, the daughter of Divri. *Cf.* Rashi's commentary on Leviticus 24:11. Similarly, in *Resp. Asheri* 57:2: "Zimri killed Eliphaz." Since it was a murder case, the name Zimri was chosen; *cf.* I Kings 16:9–10 and II Kings 9:31. In addition, Eliphaz, according to the Midrash, pursued the patriarch Jacob to kill him (although in *Resp. Asheri* he is portrayed as the victim). Similarly, *Resp. Tashbeẓ,* I, #93: "Elkanah was married to Hannah but had no children by her. . . . He took an additional wife, Peninnah, and when Hannah saw her co-wife in the house of her husband . . . "; *cf.* I Samuel ch. 1.

It is sometimes difficult to fathom why a specific fictitious name was chosen. *See, e.g.,* Maimonides, *Commentary on the Mishnah,* M Makkot 1:5: "The matter is thus: Witnesses testified that Reuben killed Simeon and then Kehat and Ḥushim came and proved that those witnesses were liars, and then other witnesses came and gave the same testimony as the original witnesses, and Kehat and Ḥushim then proved that these latter witnesses were also liars." *See supra* p. 1307 n. 296 regarding the use of the name "Manasseh" in *Sefer Ḥukkot ha-Dayyanim.*

190. In rabbinical court opinions in other types of civil cases, the real names of the parties are usually given.

191. *See, e.g.,* the responsa of Joseph Tov Elem quoted in *Resp. Maharam of Rothenburg,* ed. Lemberg, #423. *Resp. Tashbeẓ,* III, #24 refers to the towns of "Hebron" and "Lydda," and *id.*, II, #117 uses "Caleb," "Jochebed daughter of Miriam," and "Hebron." *Resp. Ramah* #292 refers to an individual "who owned property in the Land of Judah, his birthplace, and he and his two sons moved to the Galilee." A similar sentence reappears in *id.* #293. *See also* S. Abramson, *supra* n. 58 at 236; E. Bashan, "Shemot Arei Ereẓ Yisra'el ke-Khinnuyim le-Arim be-Ḥuẓ la-Areẓ be-Sifrut ha-She'elot u-Teshuvot Shel ha-Tekufah ha-Ottomanit" [Names of Towns in the Land of Israel as Designations of Diaspora Towns in the Responsa Literature of the Ottoman Period], *Sefer ha-Shanah le-Madda'ei ha-Yahadut ve-ha-Ru'aḥ Shel Universitat Bar Ilan, supra* n. 19, XII (1974), pp. 137–165.

192. It should be noted that in some compilations, the names of the questioners and of the places where they live are given (generally in *Resp. Ribash,* and *Resp. Tashbeẓ,* I and

D. Hypothetical Responsa; *Terumat ha-Deshen*

The overwhelming majority of responsa were written in actual cases submitted to recognized halakhic authorities. However, some responsa treat legal questions of a purely theoretical nature.[193] Sometimes, the issue could have arisen in an actual case, but the questioner specifically stated, "This is not an actual case, but I wish to know the law."[194] Some hypothetical questions were posed because the point at issue was likely to come up later in an actual case.[195]

Leading *aḥaronim* have suggested that all the responsa in *Terumat ha-Deshen,* by Israel Isserlein, involve hypothetical cases. Shabbetai ha-Kohen, the author of *Siftei Kohen* on the *Shulḥan Arukh,* wrote:[196] "It is well known that the questions contained in *Terumat ha-Deshen* were made up by Israel Isserlein himself and were not asked by others, as they were in that part of his work called 'Pesakim u-Khetavim' [Legal Rulings and Writings]."[197] However, Samuel Phoebus, the author of *Bet Shemu'el* on *Shulḥan Arukh Even ha-Ezer,* argued that not all the responsa in *Terumat ha-Deshen* involved hypothetical questions. In discussing a specific responsum, he wrote: "Al-

---

II), while in others, the names of the questioners are generally omitted and only the place from which the question came is identified (as in a large proportion of *Resp. Rashba* and in *Resp. Tashbeẓ,* III).

193. *See, e.g., Terumat ha-Deshen,* Pesakim u-Khetavim, #102 ("Could the wife of the prophet Elijah . . . have remarried?"); *Resp. She'elat Ya'veẓ,* II, #82 ("Regarding the question raised by my father [Ḥakham Ẓevi] in [*Resp. Ḥakham Ẓevi*] #93: Can a person created by use of [the magical formulas in] *Sefer ha-Yeẓirah* be counted to make up a quorum for prayer?"). As to theoretical and academic discussions in responsa in which the main subject is an actual case, *see supra* p. 1508 and n. 159; *Resp. Tashbeẓ,* II, #119 (end), *et al.*

194. *Terumat ha-Deshen,* Pesakim u-Khetavim, #104.

195. *See, e.g., Resp. Maharil,* after #192 (before #193), s.v. Kankan: "It is my intention to gather, with your help, correct rulings to have as a record for my teachers and myself, because forgetfulness is very common and powerful. Do not make haste to answer me, but do so thoughtfully when you have time." The questioner submitted a group of eleven questions, and Maharil answered them in the subsequent responsa. A somewhat similar instance is found in *Resp. Tashbeẓ,* II, #292, where the enactments of the community of Algiers are quoted and interpreted. At the end of #292, s.v. U-lefi she-ani, Rashbeẓ wrote: "Therefore, in order to remove uncertainties on the part of the judges who will have to rule on the basis of these enactments, and in order to respond to some questions that have been submitted to me . . . , I have written all this to explain and clarify their [*i.e.,* the enactments'] intent." As to these enactments, *see supra* pp. 804–806.

196. *Shakh,* Sh. Ar. YD ch. 196, subpar. 20. The reference there was to the 354 responsa in *Terumat ha-Deshen,* and not to the 267 responsa in the part of the book called Pesakim u-Khetavim, which were rulings for practical application.

197. To the same effect, *see Taz,* Sh. Ar. YD ch. 328, subpar. 2; *Resp. Sha'ar Ephraim* #42; the decision-making principles for matters of *issur* in *Peri Megadim,* par. 9 (quoted in the Introduction to Sh. Ar. YD), in the name of *Tevu'at Shor;* Ḥida, *Shem ha-Gedolim,* Persons, Letter *yod,* #402.

though he [Isserlein] did not state that this responsum was based on an actual case, this ruling also appears in his *Pesakim,* where he indicated that it was based on an actual case, and we therefore conclude that the responsum in *Terumat ha-Deshen* involved an actual case."[198]

Later scholars have found many more parallels between *Terumat ha-Deshen* and other responsa by Isserlein, from which it may be deduced that these particular responsa in *Terumat ha-Deshen* dealt with questions that arose in actual cases.[199] It should also be noted that in more recent periods, purely theoretical works have sometimes been titled *She'elot u-Teshuvot* ("Responsa"). The question whether a particular responsum is hypothetical or based on an actual case is not only of literary interest; it significantly affects the weight to be given to the responsum[200] in the final determination of the law.[201]

VI. COMPILATIONS OF RESPONSA—REDACTION AND ORGANIZATION

The responsa of the *geonim* were assembled and organized in compilations at an early period.[202] Those of some of the *rishonim* were not printed in

198. *Bet Shemu'el,* Sh. Ar. EH ch. 130, subpar. 20.

199. For a discussion of the hypothetical nature of the responsa in *Terumat ha-Deshen, see* A. Berliner, "Rabbi Israel Isserlein," *MGWJ,* XVIII (1869), pp. 272–274; J. Freimann, *Leket Yosher le-Rabbenu Yosef b. R. Moshe, z.l.* [*Leket Yosher* by Rabbenu Joseph b. Moses, of Blessed Memory], Introduction (preceding the section on YD), XIV-XV. J. Dinari, *Ḥakhmei ha-Halakhah be-Ashkenaz be-Shilhei Yemai ha-Beinayim* [The Halakhic Authorities in Germany at the End of the Middle Ages], Jerusalem, 1987, pp. 302ff., arrives at some important conclusions in his discussion of this question.

200. Most halakhic authorities have taken the view that a legal conclusion in a responsum has greater weight than a statement of the law in a code because a responsum is written for practical application (*see supra* pp. 975–978 and pp. 1457–1459). Whether a responsum is "actual" or hypothetical may also have an additional significance. According to *Shakh,* Sh. Ar. YD ch. 196, subpar. 20, the principle that the opinion of a respondent can be deduced from his failure to deal with a particular point in the question applies only if the responsum is based on an actual case. *Baḥ* and *Taz,* however, both take the view that such deductions can also be made from the hypothetical responsa of *Terumat ha-Deshen; see Baḥ, Tur* YD ch. 196; *Taz,* Sh. Ar. YD ch. 328, subpar. 2. Similarly, in *Resp. Sha'ar Ephraim* #42 such deductions are made from *Terumat ha-Deshen,* specifically because the discussion there was not related to an actual case (*id.,* s.v. Ve-leka le-meidak ifkha). The argument supporting such a view is that when a question concerns an actual case it may contain irrelevant details, but when it is hypothetical, nothing in it will be irrelevant.

201. *See,* for earlier examples of hypothetical responsa, *She'elot u-Teshuvot min ha-Shamayim* [Responsa from Heaven], by the Tosafist Jacob of Marvege, republished by R. Margaliot, Jerusalem, 1957. For a discussion of the book, *see id.,* Introduction, pp. 20–24. For a discussion of the place of supernatural phenomena, such as voices from heaven, in deciding the law, *see id.* at 3ff. and 25ff. *See also supra* pp. 242–265.

202. *See supra* p. 1471.

separate compilations but were included in books containing their total halakhic-literary output. Thus, the responsa of Rabbenu Tam are found in his *Sefer ha-Yashar,* which also contains his novellae and his codificatory work; and similarly, the responsa of Eliezer b. Nathan (Raban) were published together with his other works. In contrast, the responsa of the Spanish *rishonim* such as Alfasi, Rashba, and Asheri, and the North African *rishonim* such as Ribash and Rashbeẓ, were printed in separate compilations.[203] In the course of time, this practice of the Spanish and North African *rishonim* became the practice generally followed.[204]

The overwhelming majority of the compilations prior to the period of the *aḥaronim,* and a large proportion of the compilations of responsa of the *aḥaronim,* were not redacted by the respondents themselves but by their sons, their students, or the students of their students,[205] after the death of the respondents.[206] Some compilations were not redacted until centuries

203. Compilations of responsa sometimes contain material from other types of halakhic literature. *See, e.g., Resp. Asheri* 4:10 and Principles (*Kelalim*) 14, 47, 48, and 49, which are codificatory in nature. However, almost the entire compilation is devoted to responsa, which is also the case with regard to most other collections of responsa.

204. There are also compilations that contain separate sections of responsa by different authors, such as *Mayim Amukkim, Ge'onei Vatra'ei, Asefat Geonim, Ḥut ha-Shani, Mishpatim Yesharim, Shenei ha-Me'orim ha-Gedolim, Zera Anashim,* and others.

205. There has been some research concerning how the compilations were redacted, the identity of the redactors, and similar questions. However, there is still room for much additional research. Biographies of various halakhic authorities (such as A. Hershman, *Rabbi Yiẓḥak bar Sheshet* [*ha-Ribash*], Jerusalem, 1955) supply a certain amount of information on the subject, as do the introductions to scientific editions of some of the compilations. Frequently, a close examination of the responsa contained in a compilation will reveal when and by whom the compilation was redacted. For example, in *Resp. Rashba,* IV, #61 (end), it is stated: "In the book of my responsa that you have, you will find a long discussion of this subject," which implies that in Rashba's lifetime there existed compilations of his responsa, which he knew of and approved. That *Resp. Tashbeẓ* was edited by its author, Rashbeẓ, is indicated by *Resp. Tashbeẓ,* III, #325 (end): "The question is discussed above in this work, #18. [signed] Your brother, Simeon b. Ẓemaḥ," which shows that Rashbeẓ himself edited the compilation and numbered his responsa. The middle of the same responsum states: "And so I wrote in a responsum to Moses Gabbai. It is written in my first volume of responsa, in #152"; thus, in Volume III of his responsa, Rashbeẓ referred to Volume I. Such internal cross-references can also be found in other places; *see further infra* n. 206.

206. This can frequently be discerned from the text of the responsa. *Resp. Asheri* and *Terumat ha-Deshen,* Pesakim u-Khetavim, are examples. *Resp. Asheri* 13:20 states: "These are the responsa of Asheri, of blessed memory." In *id.* 15:3, the question ends with: "Your son Jehiel, of blessed memory"; the words "of blessed memory" must have been added by a redactor. In *id.* 29:1, the redactor added a note at the beginning of the response; *id.* 32:14(2) contains a note by Asheri's son regarding his father's interpretation of a Talmudic passage; *id.* 51:2 (p. 49a) has: "A certain student came here to Toledo to study with my father, may the Lord preserve him, and copied the notes that my father, may the Lord preserve him, composed . . . and gave the information that herewith follows."

Two points emerge from these interpolations: (a) at least some of Asheri's responsa were redacted by his son; and (b) this redaction was done in Asheri's lifetime, as seen from

after the death of the respondents.[207] When not redacted soon after the lifetimes of the authors, a significant proportion of the responsa were often lost.[208] Like the copyists,[209] redactors of compilations took it upon themselves—and with even less restraint—to abridge, summarize, and even omit the questions;[210] to determine the correct text of the responsa by selecting from among the different copies they had; and to omit dates and the actual names of people, places, and the like. The redactors felt free to make such changes because their main interest lay in the clarification of the law and the decision rendered by the respondent; all other details had no particular significance to them. Occasionally, abridged versions of compilations of responsa were made and were helpful in locating the discussion of a particular subject in the responsa.[211]

---

his son's prayer for long life for his father. *Resp. Asheri* 104:5, however, states: "And my teacher, Asheri, ruled . . . ," which indicates that at least that responsum was redacted by one of Asheri's students. For a further discussion of this subject, *see* A.H. Freimann, "Ascher Ben Jechiel, Sein Leben und Wirken," *JJLG,* XII (1918), p. 306 nn. 1–4.

Terumat ha-Deshen, Pesakim u-Khetavim, is another example of this editorial pattern. Thus, #40 states, "I heard from my teacher, his eminence . . . ," and #42 and #61 refer to "My teacher, his eminence, of blessed memory"—indicating that the material was redacted by a student after the author's death. Other responsa also contain notes and additional editorial comments following the author's signature to the responsum. *See, e.g.,* #62 ("in a different place, he replied to his friend and not to someone else"); #161 ("And thus did they all agree to permit . . . "); #221 ("And that woman remarried near Marburg in accordance with the opinion of those who permitted it").

207. *E.g.,* the responsa of Maimonides began to appear in various compilations starting from 1517 C.E. In 1934, A.H. Freimann published a scientific edition of all Maimonides' responsa that were known at that time, with a comprehensive Introduction and notes. This Introduction lists six earlier compilations, as well as isolated responsa that appeared in other books or only in manuscript form. The most complete scientific edition of Maimonides' responsa, including translations of those written in Arabic (together with the original Arabic text), with notes and commentary, including Freimann's notes and Introduction, was prepared by J. Blau and appeared in three volumes in 1958–1961. Since then, more of Maimonides' responsa have been discovered.

208. Apparently this is why so few responsa of Naḥmanides, Meir ha-Levi Abulafia (Ramah), and other *rishonim* are extant. Also, relatively few compilations of the responsa of the halakhic authorities of Provence have survived.

209. *See supra* pp. 1511–1512.

210. Sometimes the redactor stated this explicitly. *See, e.g., Terumat ha-Deshen,* Pesakim u-Khetavim, #232 (end): "This was the question of Rabbi Pereẓ to Mahari Weil, which included lengthy proofs I decided not to record because they can be found in the responsum of Rabbi Isserlein and the responsum of Maharyu."

211. *Resp. Mabit,* II, #138 (p. 37, col. 2, at the top) describes the following experience:

> I looked for [*or:* I found] this statement of Rashbeẓ in the abridgment of his responsa that I made some years ago together with an abridgment of Ribash's responsa before they were printed, and I found the following text: [quotation omitted]. This is the end of the quotation from the abridgment of Rash[beẓ], which I made from his responsa in the possession of one of the Torah scholars here. That book contained nearly two

Another common occurrence in connection with the responsa literature is the publication of the same responsum in more than one place.[212] A compilation of the responsa of one respondent often contains responsa written by other respondents, sometimes under the name of their author, and sometimes without attribution.[213] An entire book of responsa has even been attributed to the wrong author.[214] Halakhic authorities have occasionally doubted that a particular responsum was in fact written by the author of the compilation in which the responsum is found.[215] Identification of the author of a responsum is particularly difficult when the names or acronyms of two respondents are almost identical.[216] Some compilations contain isolated responsa by authors who left no other halakhic writings.

The changes made in responsa because of censorship—both external

---

hundred responsa, and later I found more that I added to them. The responsum quoted above was the first and the longest of all his responsa.

As to compilations of geonic responsa, *see supra* n. 58 and accompanying text.

212. *See, e.g.*, the list of duplicated responsa in *Resp. Alfasi, Resp. Rashba,* and *Resp. Asheri* in *Mafte'aḥ ha-She'elot ve-ha-Teshuvot Shel Ḥakhmei Sefarad u-Ẓefon Afrikah* [Digest of the Responsa Literature of Spain and North Africa], ed. M. Elon, Institute for Research in Jewish Law, Hebrew University, *Index of Sources,* I (1981), pp. 320–328; *Legal Digest,* I (1986), pp. 36–44.

213. On the other hand, it has also happened that in a compilation of one author's responsa, a responsum whose heading attributed it to a different author turned out, upon investigation of its text, to have been actually written by the author of the other responsa in the compilation. *See, e.g., Resp. Avkat Rokhel* (which is a compilation of Joseph Caro's responsa) #201. The heading of the responsum attributes it to Maharashdam, and the responsum is not signed. However, it is clear that Caro was the author, since the responsum states: "And in my work *Bet Yosef* I wrote. . . . " There are also other indications that Caro wrote the responsum. For further discussion of this responsum, *see supra* p. 1317 n. 26.

214. The outstanding example of this is *Resp. Rashba Attributed to Naḥmanides.* Joseph Caro, in his Introduction to *Tur* OḤ, pointed out that Rashba was the author. *See supra* p. 1315 n. 22.

215. *See, e.g., Resp. Rashba,* I, #1166, as to a responsum by Rabbenu Hananel; *Resp. Ribash* #328, as to a responsum by Asheri; *Shakh,* Sh. Ar. ḤM ch. 46, subpar. 9, as to *Resp. Maharik* #74. *Resp. Maharik* #179 (in ed. Lemberg, the first responsum; in ed. Warsaw, #181—concerning a partnership between physicians) attempted to identify an unsigned responsum that is described as "an orphan": "Although this psalm [*i.e.*, responsum] is an orphan and does not give the name of its author, it is in fact the work of Rabad, who so wrote in [another of] his responsa." For a similar expression, *see Resp. Maharik* #94: "It lay before me like an orphaned psalm that did not tell who wrote it." *See also* H. Michael, *Or ha-Ḥayyim,* pp. 506–507, regarding the responsa of Alfasi.

216. A striking example of this difficulty is the problem of identifying the responsa of Rabbi Meir of Rothenburg, who is referred to by the acronyms Maharam, ha-Ram, and Moram, among others. These acronyms could also refer to Maimonides (**Ram**bam, **Ra**bbi **M**oshe), Moses Moellin, or other halakhic authorities. Also, the name Meir can refer to other respondents, *e.g.*, Meir ha-Levi Abulafia. For a full discussion of the problem, *see* I.Z. Kahane, *Maharam me-Rothenburg, Teshuvot, Pesakim u-Minhagim* [Maharam of Rothenburg, Responsa, Rulings, and Customs], I, Introduction, pp. 10ff.

and internal—also constitute a problem. It has been noted[217] that, on account of censorship, changes were made in the text, and complete sections were deleted. Entire responsa were even omitted from various compilations. Sometimes, such responsa were printed in the first edition, were then removed by the censor, and later reappeared in subsequent editions when censorship was no longer in force. There have also been cases when a particular responsum was never printed in the compilation of the author's responsa but is known from other sources.[218] Particular responsa have been omitted from compilations of responsa of Maharik,[219] Radbaz,[220] Israel Isserlein,[221] Rema,[222] Maharam of Lublin,[223] Ezekiel Landau,[224] and Moses Sofer,[225] among others.[226]

Finally, as to the organization of the responsa within the compilations,[227] it is very difficult to ascertain the system, if any, used by the redac-

217. *See supra* p. 1511 and n. 174.

218. For detailed discussion, *see* S. ha-Kohen Weingarten, "Teshuvot she-Nignezu" [Responsa That Were Suppressed], *Sinai,* XXIX (1951), pp. 90–99; I. Rivkind, review of *Le-Toledot ha-Defus ha-Ivri be-Folin* [Studies in the History of Hebrew Printing in Poland], *Kiryat Sefer,* XI (1934–1935), pp. 100ff. and n. 11.

219. *Resp. Maharik* #137; the responsum was omitted in ed. Warsaw, 1884, because of censorship. *See supra* n. 19.

220. *Resp. Radbaz,* II, #796 (his famous responsum regarding marriage between Jews and Karaites). In the current editions that follow ed. Warsaw, 1882, the responsum is printed at the end of the second part.

221. *Terumat ha-Deshen* #195, #196, *et al.* (discussing relations between Jews and gentiles). In current editions, these responsa are printed at the end of the book, after Pesakim u-Khetavim.

222. *Resp. Rema* #124, regarding the wine of gentiles. *See* A. Siev's note to this responsum in his edition of *Resp. Rema.*

223. *Resp. Maharam of Lublin* #138, concerning a case of murder by a Jew. *See also Resp. Baḥ ha-Yeshanot* #43. This responsum was printed in ed. Frankfurt, 1697, but was omitted in all the other editions.

224. *Resp. Noda bi-Yehudah,* Mahadura Kamma, EH, #72. At the beginning of the responsum, a section describing the facts of an incident of adultery was censored out, because its inclusion would have identified the family involved. The section is restored in current editions.

225. *See* Weingarten, *supra* n. 218 at 92–96. *See also id.* at 95, regarding the omission of Ẓevi Hirsch Chajes' name from a responsum addressed to him.

226. *See* Weingarten, *supra* n. 218. There are also examples of a type of self-censorship. *See, e.g., Resp. Tashbeẓ,* I, #162 (end), in regard to the controversy between Rashbeẓ and Ribash over Ribash's appointment as judge by the king (for discussion of which *see id.* #158 and *supra* pp. 132–137): "I also suppressed this and did not show it because of [his] honor and to promote peace." Rashbeẓ was referring to his refraining from publicizing his opinion criticizing Ribash. Similarly, *id.,* I, #123 (end): "I left out one point that I decided not to publicize in order to promote peace." This referred to a complex discussion regarding the voiding of a communal enactment. For a decision rendered on the basis of an erroneous reading of a section added by the censor, *see* Joshua Menahem Ehrenberg, *Resp. Devar Yehoshu'a,* II, #19.

227. It should be noted that in different editions of the same compilation the numbers given to the responsa are not always the same. *Resp. Maharik* is an example. In ed. Warsaw,

tors prior to the appearance of the *Turim* and the *Shulḥan Arukh*. These responsa were not arranged according to their topics; a responsum on torts would follow one on divorce, and a responsum concerning the ritual bath would be placed next to one on tax law. Sometimes, responsa addressed to the same questioner were grouped together even though they dealt with different subjects;[228] but even this technique was not followed consistently, as other responsa to the same questioner were sometimes put elsewhere in the compilation. The place from which the questions were sent was not the basis for organizing the compilations, nor were the compilations always organized according to the chronological order in which the responsa were written. The complete lack of system in the arrangement of the responsa makes it exceedingly difficult to locate the treatment of specific subjects.[229]

A small number of compilations prior to the appearance of the *Shulḥan Arukh* had a relatively topical organization. *Resp. Asheri,* for instance, is divided into 108 general "principles" (*kelalim*), which are subdivided into some 1050 chapters (*simanim*). Each *kelal* contains responsa on the same general subject.[230] Similarly, the first two sections of *Resp. Maharibal,* which was edited by its author, are each divided into ten *kelalim,* and the responsa in each *kelal* relate to the same subject.[231] Other compilations follow a similar arrangement.[232]

A substantial change for the better in the organization of compilations of responsa occurred after the *Turim* and the *Shulḥan Arukh* were published. From then on, collections of responsa were usually organized ac-

---

1884, responsum #137 was omitted; and, in addition, mistakes in numbering the responsa resulted in a different sequence than in previous editions. *See supra* nn. 19 and 219. Other examples are the different editions of *Resp. Asheri* and *Resp. Ran.* For a full listing of these instances, *see Mafte'aḥ ha-She'elot ve-ha-Teshuvot, supra* n. 212, *Historical Digest,* I (1981), pp. 276–279.

228. In such instances, responsa may have been grouped together in a compilation because a number of questions submitted to the respondent at the same time were answered together.

229. There are usually tables of contents in the compilations, either at the beginning or the end, but these are of very little value in researching specific points. *See infra* pp. 1523–1524.

230. There are, however, exceptions. Principle (*kelal*) #35, for example, which deals with family law, contains a responsum concerning the rental of houses (35:6(2)).

231. *See* the author's Introduction to the compilation. Another section of Maharibal's responsa is not organized in this way.

232. *E.g., Resp. Binyamin Ze'ev,* which is divided into twenty-eight sections, each of which contains a number of responsa on the same subject. The work contains 450 responsa, and was edited by its author. *See* his Introduction at the beginning of the compilation. Several other compilations of responsa are similarly divided into sections in a topical arrangement. *Resp. Ginat Veradim* is arranged according to the four sections of the *Turim,* and each topic is further divided into subtopics.

cording to the topical order of these two codes. Responsa concerning benedictions, prayer, and festivals were arranged according to the organization of *Oraḥ Ḥayyim*; the subjects of dietary laws, ritual slaughter, and other religious laws followed the sequence of *Yoreh De'ah*; questions on marriage, the *ketubbah*, divorce, and other aspects of family law were arranged in the sequence of *Even ha-Ezer*; and responsa treating civil, public, and criminal law followed the sequence of *Ḥoshen Mishpat*. This system greatly facilitates research in the responsa; once a law is located in the *Shulḥan Arukh*, the responsa on the same subject can easily be located in any compilation of responsa similarly organized.

VII. RESEARCH IN THE RESPONSA; DIGEST OF THE RESPONSA LITERATURE

The concentration of most post-Talmudic halakhic material in the responsa literature has created a major problem for research in Jewish law that has become even more pronounced as the number of responsa has increased: it is extremely difficult for a judge or scholar to find relevant responsa. The table of contents, ordinarily found in a compilation of responsa either at the beginning or the end of the book, is usually extremely general and unsystematic, and presents only a partial and inadequate statement of the facts and the issues involved in each responsum. The table of contents in compilations of responsa by Sephardic halakhic authorities is more detailed and sometimes also contains a table of citations to the Talmudic sources and the major codes cited in the responsa;[233] but even these are far from being sufficiently complete or precise to facilitate adequate research in the responsa literature. Ḥayyim Benveniste, the author of *Keneset ha-Gedolah*, the most important compilation of responsa organized according to the topical arrangement of the *Turim* and the *Shulḥan Arukh*,[234] made the following instructive comments regarding the usefulness to the researcher of the typical table of contents in a compilation of responsa:[235]

> If one . . . proceeds to examine its table of contents, that too will be an obstacle to gaining full knowledge of the subject matter. Into many books of responsa there is no entry whatsoever—no table of contents; and if there is a table of contents, it is not properly organized. Even those that are organized sometimes completely overlook some of the responsa [contained in the book]

233. Various compilations of geonic responsa also contain tables of citations to Talmudic sources; *see supra* p. 1472.

234. *See supra* pp. 1434–1437.

235. *Keneset ha-Gedolah*, OḤ, Introduction (ed. Jerusalem, p. 4).

> and make no reference to them. At times, the reader will believe that the law he is seeking belongs in a particular section, but when he looks for it there, he will not find it . . . [since,] as is well known, in almost every instance, the table of contents refers only to the facts of each case. A responsum will sometimes discuss the intricacies of many different legal rules that are not directly relevant to the specific issue but are [only] collateral to it; and often a rule pertaining to religious law or to the subject of *agunah* will be discussed as incidental to an issue involving civil law, and vice versa. Even within the framework of a single subject, most discussions move from one point to another, whether or not they are all relevant. There is no mention of any of these things in the table of contents. To say that the reader should examine each responsum in detail is no solution, because that course may require days or weeks or months . . . to respond to a single question, depending on the nature of the subject.

To some extent, these difficulties were alleviated by the compilations of responsa organized according to the topical order of the *Shulḥan Arukh*. Such compilations began to be published in the seventeenth century. The first was *Panim Ḥadashot*, followed soon after by the extremely valuable *Keneset ha-Gedolah;* and in the course of time many such helpful works have been and are still being produced.[236] However, these compilations, useful as they are, are only a partial solution to the problem, inasmuch as they do not encompass all the responsa literature, they usually summarize only the legal conclusion reached in each responsum, and they do not indicate all the legal rules deducible from the broader discussions in the responsa.

Another major problem is the lack of a complete and accurate list of the compilations of responsa. In 1930, Boaz Cohen published his *Kunteres ha-Teshuvot*, a bibliographical listing of compilations of responsa.[237] That list includes not only responsa but also other types of works, such as codes and novellae, that contain some responsa material. The list is tabulated according to countries, historical periods, and the places where the compilations were printed. *Kunteres ha-Teshuvot* was an important contribution to the study of responsa, but it is hardly exhaustive.[238]

236. For detailed discussion of such compilations, *see supra* pp. 1432–1433.

237. Boaz Cohen, *Kunteres ha-Teshuvot*, Budapest, 1930; facsimile ed., Jerusalem, 1970.

238. The list contains only a small portion of the responsa literature of the nineteenth and twentieth centuries (*see* Introduction, p. 2) and does not contain the compilations of responsa from earlier periods that have been published since 1930. A considerable number of books of responsa published since 1930 were listed in Solomon Freehof's supplements to Cohen's *Kunteres ha-Teshuvot. See Studies in Bibliography and Booklore*, V (1961), Cincinnati, pp. 30–41. Cohen's list also does not include all of the pre-nineteenth century responsa, particularly those from Turkey, the Balkans, and North Africa; and it is far from comprehensive with regard to the isolated responsa scattered throughout the other types of halakhic

The difficulty of finding relevant material in the responsa literature is especially severe for research in *mishpat ivri.* The major problem faced by the scholar or jurist when approaching the vast reservoir of material in Jewish law is that this material is not classified according to the accepted legal categories in other legal systems. The wide dispersion of the variegated material and the lack of any systematic index to any of the types of halakhic literature also add to the problem. These difficulties are especially acute with regard to the responsa literature, which has constituted, both quantitatively and qualitatively, the major component of Jewish law for the last thirteen centuries. Finally, there is yet another problem: the unique legal terminology of Jewish law and the need for its correct translation and transposition into the terminology currently used in other legal systems.[239]

In order to overcome these difficulties, the Institute for Research in Jewish Law of the Hebrew University in Jerusalem has undertaken the preparation of the *Digest of the Responsa Literature,* organized according to the geographical areas and historical periods of the respondents. The first period dealt with was that of the *rishonim, i.e.,* from the eleventh to the sixteenth centuries.[240] The Institute has completed the preparation of a digest of the responsa literature of the Spanish and North African authorities from the eleventh century until the expulsion of the Jews from Spain at the end of the fifteenth century, and it is now engaged in the preparation of a digest of the responsa originating in Germany, France, Italy, and the other centers of the Jewish diaspora.

The digest of the Spanish and North African responsa covers the material contained in the sixty compilations of the responsa written in those two centers in the period described[241] and will appear in seven volumes, of which five have been published. The digest has three parts: the *Legal Di-*

---

literature. *Kunteres ha-Teshuvot* lists some 2000 books of responsa, including the responsa that were printed in other types of halakhic literature (*see* pp. 41–107 = 1200 works; pp. 107–141 = 544 works; pp. 204–219 [additional notes to the list] = additional books and additional notes to material previously mentioned).

239. For a detailed discussion of this subject, *see supra* pp. 79–80.

240. From the standpoint of chronology, it would have been appropriate to begin with the geonic period. However, since much of the responsa literature of that period is still being published and is not yet sufficiently consolidated, it was decided to begin the project with the responsa of the *rishonim.* In addition, the geonic period is covered by B.M. Lewin, *Ozar ha-Geonim,* which organizes the geonic responsa according to the sequence of the Talmud and is therefore of some help to the researcher in that a responsum can be located through the relevant Talmudic passage; *see supra* pp. 1472–1473. A digest of the geonic responsa will be published at a later stage of the project.

241. For a detailed list of the responsa compilations covered in the digest, *see Mafte'aḥ ha-She'elot ve-ha-Teshuvot, supra* n. 212, *Historical Digest,* I (1981), pp. 31–32; II (1986), p. 10; *Index of Sources,* I (1981), pp. 30–31; *Legal Digest,* I (1986), pp. 32–33.

gest, which has already been published in two volumes; the *Historical Digest,* which will consist of three volumes, two of which have already appeared; and the *Index of Sources,* in two volumes, one of which has already appeared.[242]

The *Legal Digest* contains a detailed exposition of all the material of *mishpat ivri, i.e.,* civil, criminal, administrative, and public law, classified according to the Hebrew alphabet under a modern legal classification system.[243] Each topic is presented in great detail and is broken down into many subtopics, which are generally also arranged in alphabetical order.[244] When the modern Hebrew term for a particular topic is not the same as the original Talmudic term, the material appears under the Talmudic term and there is a cross-reference from the modern term.[245] The *Legal Digest* includes several appendixes, which contain additional important legal material found in the responsa literature, such as the contents of communal enactments,

242. As a preparatory step in the publication of the digests, a digest of the responsa of Asheri was published in 1965 to serve as a model; the main emphasis was on the legal digest and the index of sources. A model historical digest of the responsa of Ritba and those in Judah b. Asher, *Resp. Zikhron Yehudah,* was published in 1973; *see* the detailed Introductions to those two volumes. The final form of the *Digest of the Responsa Literature of Spain and North Africa* is patterned on those two volumes, albeit with important modifications.

243. The *Legal Digest* also contains a significant number of entries relevant not only to *mishpat ivri* but to all parts of Jewish law, *e.g.,* The Land of Israel; *Ḥazakah* (Legal Presumptions); *Ḥerem ve-Niddui* (Bans); *Yovel* (Jubilee Year); *Kelalei Pesikah* (Rules for Decision Making); *Minhag* (Custom); and many others. *See id., Legal Digest,* I (1986), Introduction, pp. 28–29.

244. For a detailed description of the contents of the *Legal Digest* and how it was prepared and edited, *see Legal Digest,* I (1986), Introduction, pp. 22–31. The *Legal Digest* is more detailed than an index in the usual sense of the term but not as detailed as the abstracts of cases found in *The English and Empire Digest* of the English law or the headnotes in the *American Digest* system. Because the bulk of the law in the common-law system is contained in innumerable court decisions, it has been necessary to create a wide-ranging literature of digests of those decisions, indexes to the material contained in the digests, and similar aids. The prime examples of this prodigious literature are *The English and Empire Digest* (which today also contains—in its approximately fifty volumes—the law of the member nations of the British Commonwealth) and the *American Digest* system of over four hundred volumes, covering all reported decisions in the United States.

In contrast to the English and the American digests, which are compilations of synopses of the statements of law found in the cases, the *Digest of the Responsa Literature of Spain and North Africa* does not give the legal conclusion on the issue involved but only states the issue; the reader must consult the responsum referred to in order to ascertain the position taken by the respondent on that issue. It is believed that this is a proper approach for the initial stage of the project. With the material developed in this manner, it will be possible, at a later stage, to present the ultimate position of Jewish law on each subject. *See further Legal Digest,* I (1986), Introduction, pp. 19, 22ff.

245. *E.g.,* the modern Hebrew term for unjust enrichment is *asiyyat osher ve-lo ve-mishpat.* The reader is referred from this term to the following Talmudic terms, all of which pertain to unjust enrichment: *zeh neheneh ve-zeh lo ḥaser, yored li-sedeh ḥavero, mavri'aḥ ari mi-nikhsei ḥavero, maẓẓil mamon ḥavero, pore'a ḥovo shel ḥavero she-lo mi-da'ato.*

regulations adopted by private associations, customs, and non-Jewish laws to which the responsa advert in the course of their discussion.

The *Historical Digest* includes all the historical material found in the responsa, classified according to topics and subtopics, such as: The Status of the Jews (Political, Legal, and Social) in the Various Centers of the Diaspora; The Community—Its Leadership and Institutions; Jewish Juridical Autonomy; Cultural, Economic, and Social Conditions; Faith and Belief; Daily Life and Experience; Biographies of Various Individuals; The Material World; Geography; and Medicine. The *Historical Digest* also includes topics pertaining to general history, which are also often referred to in the responsa. A separate appendix contains the text of all the legal instruments and documents quoted in the responsa,[246] as well as the formulas for oaths and vows and certain Hebrew expressions and terms.

The *Index of Sources* lists all the sources mentioned in the responsa: the Bible, the Mishnah, halakhic *midrashim*, Aramaic translations of the Bible, the *Tosefta*, the Jerusalem Talmud, the Babylonian Talmud, aggadic *midrashim*, the "minor" tractates, geonic literature, commentaries and novellae, codificatory literature, and all other literary halakhic sources.[247] The *Index of Sources* enables the reader to ascertain how Biblical verses, laws in the Mishnah and the *Tosefta*, Talmudic passages, laws in the codes of Alfasi and Maimonides, and the like, have been interpreted in the responsa literature.

The *Historical Digest* and the *Index of Sources* are also essential for researching and ascertaining Jewish law.[248] The *Historical Digest* contains a great deal of valuable material for the study of Jewish legal history. It includes data indicating the extent of Jewish juridical autonomy and the use by Jews of non-Jewish courts, as well as historical-factual information touching on various legal subjects such as the functioning of communal government, family law, taxes, interest, and credit. The *Index of Sources* is an additional tool for finding the material relevant to legal questions in the responsa literature when the researcher cannot find such material by means of the *Legal Digest*. For example, if the researcher knows where a point is discussed in the Talmud or in Maimonides' code, the *Index of Sources* will lead to every responsum that mentions that source and deals with that issue.

246. As to the importance of such a compilation of texts of legal instruments and documents, *see Legal Digest*, I (1986), Introduction, pp. 29–30.

247. The *Index of Sources* parallels the tables of statutes and cases, etc., contained in American and English volumes of reports of judicial decisions, digests, texts, and other aids to legal research that point to later discussions of a particular statute or decision.

248. For detailed discussion, *see Historical Digest*, I (1981), Introduction, pp. 16 and 26ff.; *Index of Sources*, I (1981), Introduction, pp. 24ff.

The *Historical Digest* and the *Index of Sources* are also invaluable for research into all aspects of Jewish history, for the explication of the various literary sources of the *Halakhah,* for the determination of the correct readings of many texts in Talmudic and post-Talmudic literature, and for a knowledge (through quotation or citation in the responsa) of writings that have not yet been printed or may no longer exist even in manuscript form.

In sum, the *Digest of the Responsa Literature,* by laying bare the hidden treasures of this vast, rich literary storehouse, is a major contribution to the research and study of Jewish law, as well as to a better understanding of Jewish history.[249]

249. Many scholars, starting with Zunz and Frankel, have noted the special importance of the responsa literature for the study of both Jewish history and the sources of Jewish law; *see* the bibliography listed in B. Cohen, *Kunteres ha-Teshuvot,* Introduction, and pp. 36–40, 202–204. *See also Historical Digest,* I (1981), Introduction, p. 26.

Chapter 40

LITERATURE FACILITATING RESEARCH IN JEWISH LAW: COMPILATIONS OF LEGAL DOCUMENTS, REFERENCE WORKS

I. Introduction
II. Compilations of Legal Documents
 A. Enactments
 B. Legal Instruments (*Shetarot*)
  1. *Sefer ha-Shetarot* [The Book of Legal Instruments] by Saadiah Gaon
  2. *Sefer ha-Shetarot* by Hai Gaon
  3. *Sefer ha-Shetarot* of Lucena, Spain
  4. *Sefer ha-Shetarot* by Judah al-Bargeloni
  5. Compilation of Legal Instruments in *Maḥzor Vitry*
  6. Compilations in *Sefer ha-Ittur* and *Yad Ramah*
  7. Compilations of Legal Instruments Used by English Jews in the Eleventh to Thirteenth Centuries
  8. Legal Instruments Used in Christian Spain in the Twelfth to Fifteenth Centuries
  9. *Tikkun Soferim* [The Scribe's Handbook] by Solomon b. Simeon Duran (Rashbash)
  10. *Tikkun Soferim* by Moses Almosnino and Samuel Jaffe
  11. *Tikkun Shetarot* by Eliezer Milli
  12. The Compilation in *Naḥalat Shiv'ah* by Samuel ha-Levi
  13. *Et Sofer* [The Scribe's Quill] by Jacob ibn Ẓur
  14. *Oẓar ha-Shetarot* [A Treasury of Legal Instruments] by Asher Gulak
  15. Legal Instruments Used in Spain and North Africa in the Eleventh to Fifteenth Centuries
III. Reference Works
 A. Guidebooks
  1. *Seder Tannaim va-Amoraim* [Chronicles of the *Tannaim* and *Amoraim*]
  2. *Iggeret Rav Sherira Gaon* [The Epistle of Rabbi Sherira Gaon]
  3. *Mevo ha-Talmud* [Introduction to the Talmud] by Samuel ha-Nagid of Egypt, Attributed to Samuel ha-Nagid of Spain
  4. Maimonides' Introduction to His *Commentary on the Mishnah;* The Introductions of Menahem Meiri to *Bet ha-Beḥirah*
  5. *Sefer Keritut* by Samson of Chinon
  6. *Halikhot Olam* by Joshua ha-Levi
  7. *She'erit Yosef* by Joseph ibn Verga
  8. *Kelalei ha-Gemara* [Principles of the *Gemara*] by Joseph Caro
  9. *Kelalei ha-Talmud* [Principles of the Talmud] by Beẓalel Ashkenazi
  10. *Yavin Shemu'ah* by Solomon Algazi

11. *Yad Malakhi* by Malachi ha-Kohen
12. Guidebooks from the Nineteenth Century and Thereafter

B. Encyclopedias
1. *Paḥad Yiẓḥak* by Isaac Lampronti
2. *Sedei Ḥemed* by Ḥayyim Hezekiah Medini
3. *Die Exegetische Terminologie der Jüdischen Traditionsliteratur* [The Exegetical Terminology of the Literature of the Jewish Tradition] by Wilhelm Bacher
4. *Mafte'aḥ ha-Talmud* [Key to the Talmud] by Jehiel Michal Guttmann
5. *Enẓiklopedyah Talmudit* [Talmudic Encyclopedia]
6. Halakhic Works Arranged Alphabetically
7. *Mishpat Ivri* Alphabetically Arranged by Subject

C. Biographies of Halakhic Authorities
1. Biographies According to Historical Periods
2. Biographies According to Geographical Areas
3. Biographies of Individual Authorities
4. Encyclopedias with Biographical Articles

D. Bibliographies
1. General Bibliographies
2. Bibliographies According to Type of Halakhic Literature
3. Bibliographies of Scholarly Literature on *Mishpat Ivri*

E. Lexicons
F. Books Explaining Abbreviations
G. Textual Variants
H. Concordances
I. Source References, Sayings, and Aphorisms
J. Scholarly Research in *Mishpat Ivri*
K. Journals and Periodicals on *Mishpat Ivri*

I. INTRODUCTION

Up to this point, our survey of the post-Talmudic literary sources of Jewish law has reviewed the three major categories of such sources: commentaries and novellae, codificatory works, and responsa. There are, however, also other types of post-Talmudic literary sources containing relevant material. Some of this additional material—like that contained in the three major categories—is recognized by the halakhic system as authoritative and binding; and the remainder, although not so recognized, is, nevertheless, of great value for researching and understanding Jewish law.[1] The material in these other literary sources is of two types: (1) compilations of legal documents (enactments and legal instruments), and (2) reference works. This

1. *See supra* p. 907 and nn. 9–11.

chapter briefly surveys these two types of literary sources and describes some of the main works of each type.

II. COMPILATIONS OF LEGAL DOCUMENTS

A. Enactments

The previous discussion of legislation as a legal source of Jewish law has noted that in addition to legislation by the halakhic authorities there was also wide-ranging communal legislative activity. Communal legislation, known as *takkanot ha-kahal* (communal enactments) or *haskamot ha-kahal* (communal agreements), began essentially in the tenth century C.E. Some communal enactments were adopted by only a single community, others by a number of communities, and still others by associations of communities from various countries or geographical areas. The halakhic authorities accorded communal legislation full halakhic force; they oversaw it and were its interpreters. Frequently, enactments were adopted as a result of the joint efforts of the halakhic authorities and the communal leaders.[2]

Many of these enactments are scattered throughout the massive and ramified halakhic literature of the post-Talmudic period. The responsa literature in particular contains much legislation, since the disputes that were referred to the respondents often turned on the interpretation of legislative enactments.[3] Some books of responsa contain compilations of enactments drafted by the author or in force during his lifetime.[4]

In many places, the communal scribes edited compilations of local enactments that served as codes of law governing many aspects of the social, spiritual, and legal life of the community. Some of these compilations yield a richer harvest of legal materials than others. Some covered all areas of Jewish law, while others covered essentially public law (such as laws relat-

2. For a detailed discussion of legislation after the tenth century C.E., *see supra* chs. 13, 18, 19, and 20.

3. *See supra* pp. 444ff., 780ff. The digests of the responsa literature being published by the Institute for Research in Jewish Law at the Hebrew University in Jerusalem collect the enactments recorded in the responsa literature; *see supra* p. 783 n. 7.

4. *E.g.*, the enactments of "Shum" (Speyer, Worms, and Mainz) in *Resp. Maharam of Rothenburg*, ed. Prague, #1022 (pp. 158b *et seq.*), *see supra* pp. 788–789 and n. 34; the enactments of Toledo and Molina in *Resp. Asheri* #55, *see supra* pp. 796–797 and nn. 63–64; the enactments of Algiers of 1394 in *Resp. Tashbeẓ*, II, #292, which were drafted by the author, Rashbeẓ, *see supra* pp. 804–806 and nn. 87 *et seq.*; the enactments of Fez from the end of the fifteenth century onward in *Kerem Ḥemer* by Abraham Ankawa, II, pp. 2–43 (setting forth the enactments and the pertinent responsa), *see supra* pp. 806–809 and nn. 100 *et seq. See also Resp. Ginat Veradim* by Abraham b. Mordecai ha-Levi, the Rabbi of Egypt, II, ḤM 6:1.

ing to communal government) or religious law or some other specific legal area. A significant number of compilations have been lost. Persecutions, pogroms, and the destruction of entire communities and the migrations of their inhabitants all resulted in the loss of many communal records and the text of many enactments. Several compilations, however, have survived; some are intact, while others have been reconstructed by scholars on the basis of manuscript fragments, various historical documents, and halakhic literary sources.[5]

The previous discussion of communal enactments and legislation referred to the major extant compilations of legislative enactments, which contain the legislation adopted in the following Jewish communities: Crete (from the thirteenth century onward);[6] Valladolid (1432);[7] Fez (from the end of the fifteenth century onward);[8] the Council of the Four Lands (from the second half of the sixteenth century onward);[9] Cracow (end of the sixteenth and beginning of the seventeenth centuries);[10] Lvov (Lemberg);[11] the Council of Lithuania (from the beginning of the seventeenth century onward);[12] Frankfurt-am-Main (1603);[13] Posen (Posnan);[14] Moravia;[15] Nikolsburg and other communities in Moravia;[16] and others.[17]

5. The record books (*pinkasim*) of various Jewish communities throughout the diaspora are being collected in the General Archive for Jewish History maintained by the Israel Historical Society at the Hebrew University of Jerusalem. Some of the communal record books have recently been published, *e.g.*, *Pinkas of the Community of Berlin*, 1723–1854, Jerusalem, 1962; *Pinkas of the Community of Padua*, 1578–1630, Jerusalem, 1974–1980.

A particularly important project is the publication of *Pinkas ha-Kehillot* [Record Book of the Communities] by the Yad va-Shem Institute. Six volumes have appeared; they contain a full description of various Jewish communities and their histories, together with a complete bibliography on each community.

6. *Supra* pp. 811–813 and n. 121.

7. *Supra* pp. 798–804 and n. 72.

8. *Supra* pp. 806–809 and n. 100.

9. *Supra* p. 818 and n. 142.

10. *Supra* pp. 821–822 and n. 153.

11. *Supra* p. 823 and n. 162.

12. *Supra* pp. 818–819 and n. 145.

13. *Supra* pp. 794–796 and n. 57.

14. *Supra* p. 820 and n. 151, and p. 823 n. 163.

15. *Supra* pp. 819–820 and n. 149.

16. *Supra* p. 823 and nn. 160, 161.

17. *See, e.g.*, M. Benayahu, "Sifrei Takkanot u-Minhagim Shel Yerushalayim" [Books of Enactments and Customs of Jerusalem], *Kiryat Sefer*, XXII (1945–1946), pp. 262–265; *id.*, "Takkanot Tiryah" [The Enactments of Tyre], *Kovez al Yad*, IV/XIV (1946), pp. 195–228. *See also* the bibliography at the end of the present work. Compilations of enactments of various craft guilds are also extant; *see supra* p. 823 and n. 164. Communal enactments are also quoted in articles and books by various scholars and historians, some of which have been cited *supra* in ch. 19, and particularly in ch. 20. Two such works merit mention here: Finkelstein, *Self-Government*, and Baer, *Die Juden in Christlichen Spanien, Urkunden und Re-*

B. Legal Instruments (*Shetarot*)

Another important source for the study of Jewish law in its various periods is the text of the legal instruments (*shetarot,* singular *shetar*) which create various types of legal relationships in such areas of the law as family and inheritance (*e.g., ketubbot* and wills), acquisitions and obligations (*e.g.,* bills of sale, deeds of gift, leases, suretyship agreements, etc.), public law (*e.g.,* tax documents), trial procedure and evidence (*e.g.,* authentication of documents, summonses, and affidavits) and enforcement of judgments (*e.g.,* appraisals, and warrants to seize property).

Legal instruments were utilized from the very beginning of Jewish law. Deuteronomy mentions a bill of divorcement,[18] and the Book of Jeremiah refers to a deed for the sale of a field.[19] Various legal instruments are mentioned in the Apocrypha,[20] and the text of legal instruments used in the Jewish colony at Elephantine, Egypt, is extant.[21] As early as the Mishnaic and Talmudic periods, a large number of instruments had become standardized, and there is reason to believe that "the scriveners of legal instruments had compilations of meticulously accurate standard forms from which they copied the instruments they penned."[22] However, except for fragments of such instruments scattered through the Mishnah, the *Tosefta,* the two Talmuds, and the other contemporaneous literary sources, no compilation of legal instruments, nor even the complete form of any such instrument of that period, has survived. The earliest extant compilation of legal instruments dates from the geonic period.

The text of a *shetar* consists of two parts. The first part is the *tofes* ("template"), which is the main body of the document containing its basic provisions and the principal clauses applicable to the particular type of legal transaction. This part is usually standard for all instruments pertaining to such transactions. The second part is the *toref,* or the "blank" section of the document to be completed by the parties, which identifies them and fills in the details of the transaction. The *toref* therefore is different in each transaction.

---

gesten, two volumes, Berlin, 1929–1936. The latter has not been translated into English. It is a source book for Baer, *Spain,* which has been translated.

18. Deuteronomy 24:1, and *see supra* p. 201.

19. Jeremiah 32:14, and *see supra* pp. 1022–1023.

20. *E.g.,* the Book of Tobit, which mentions a marriage contract, a promissory note, and a will; *see supra* p. 1034. *See also* A. Gulak, *Oẓar ha-Shetarot* [A Treasury of Legal Instruments], Introduction, pp. XXIIff.

21. *See supra* p. 1028.

22. Gulak, *supra* n. 20 at XXVI.

Each instrument also includes clauses called *shufra di-shetara* ("adornments of the *shetar*"). Their purpose is to enhance the document and make it more effective. An example of such a clause is the "trustworthiness (*ne'emanut*) clause," a waiver of defenses whereby the obligor undertakes not to challenge the efficacy of the instrument and relieves the obligee of the oath that the law would otherwise require.[23] The parties may even include clauses that conflict with the law that would otherwise be applicable, since in monetary matters the parties may effectively "contract out" of a Biblical law.[24] Such a clause is void only when it violates a basic principle of Jewish law, as, *e.g.*, when it would permit imprisonment for nonpayment of a debt[25] or permit the creditor to levy on the debtor's assets without a court order.[26] Most of the clauses inserted as "adornments of the *shetar*" deal with matters concerning which the parties have full freedom of contract; over the course of time, many of these clauses were incorporated into the standard forms. Some of these "adornment" clauses were redundant and added nothing to the legal effectiveness of the instrument—a characteristic not infrequently shared by documents in many legal systems.

It is important to distinguish between the "positive" and "negative" provisions in the body of the instrument. The positive part describes the transaction—*e.g.*, "My field is hereby sold to you"—and states the purchase price and the other conditions of the sale. The negative part states what is excluded from the sale, may waive all objections, and may declare void *ab initio* any attempts to deny the efficacy of the transaction.[27]

Legal instruments were usually written by professional scribes. In the Mishnaic, Talmudic, and geonic periods, they were generally in Aramaic. Beginning with the period of the *rishonim*, they were written for the most part in Hebrew, although some Aramaic expressions and phrases continued to be used.

The legal instruments that have survived not only supply much information about various areas of the law, but also frequently shed light on the incorporation at various times of new legal principles into the Jewish legal system in the wake of changes in social and economic conditions and in the moral climate. This is particularly true of the provisions introduced into the *shetar* as "adornment" clauses:

> When laws became obsolete and commercial conditions made changes necessary, the scribes, who were involved in practical affairs, would "enhance"

23. *See* Gulak, *Yesodei*, II, pp. 123–127.

24. *See supra* pp. 123–127.

25. *See Resp. Rashba*, I, #1069; *Resp. Ribash* #484. *See also* Elon, *Ḥerut*, pp. 122ff., 140ff.

26. *See Tur* ḤM 61:9–13. *See also supra* pp. 123–127.

27. *See* Gulak, *supra* n. 20 at XXXV.

> and "improve" the text of the *shetar* by adding special clauses to adapt the instrument to the new requirements of commercial practice. These "adornment" clauses were gradually accepted and incorporated into the standard forms, thereby making significant improvements in the civil law.[28]

This avenue for the development of Jewish law to meet emergent needs was sometimes extremely significant:

> In times of trial and tribulation and in the course of wanderings in exile, the Jewish courts did not always have the ability to change the laws and enact legislation to meet the needs of everyday life. It was then that the people themselves made the necessary changes in the law by means of the very practical expedient of changing the wording of their legal instruments. They improved and strengthened these instruments to such an extent that many obstacles to trade and commerce were overcome.[29]

The following are some of the more important extant compilations of legal instruments.

1. *SEFER HA-SHETAROT* [THE BOOK OF LEGAL INSTRUMENTS] BY SAADIAH GAON

In 1986, M. Ben-Sasson published "Seridim mi-Sefer ha-Edut ve-ha-Shetarot le-Rav Saadiah Gaon" [Surviving Fragments of the Book of Evidence and Legal Instruments by Rabbi Saadiah Gaon],[30] which contains excerpts found in the Cairo *Genizah,* some of which had previously been published.[31] It is to be hoped that additional parts of *Sefer ha-Shetarot* will be revealed from the *Genizah* and will fill in the present gaps.

Saadiah Gaon wrote *Sefer ha-Shetarot* before all his other halakhic works. He explained: "I have become aware of the great need of the people for it, and I know that it will be a great help to them." The book was composed before he was appointed as *gaon,* while he was still head of the *yeshivah* at Pumbedita. Many writings of the *rishonim* dealing with legal instruments make reference to this work.

The book is divided into three parts.[32] The first is a general introduction, the second consists of eight sections that discuss the law relating to

28. Gulak, *Yesodei,* II, p. 124. Similarly, *see* Elon, *Ḥerut,* pp. 122ff. *See also* Fuss, EJ, XIV, pp. 1385–1390, s.v. Shetar (reprinted in *Principles,* pp. 183–190); and sources cited *infra* n. 41.

29. Gulak, *Yesodei,* II, p. 127.

30. *Shenaton,* XI–XII (1984–1986), pp. 135–280.

31. S. Assaf, "Sefer ha-Shetarot Shel Rav Saadiah," published in *Kovez̤ Rav Saadiah Gaon—Kovez̤ Torani-Madda'i,* Jerusalem, 1943, pp. 65–93; *id., Sefer ha-Shetarot le-Rav Hai b. Sherira Gaon,* Introduction, pp. 6–7.

32. Saadiah Gaon's Introduction to Part III of his book so indicates.

legal instruments; and the third contains fifty-four forms of *shetarot*, divided into three categories, on the basis of the relative frequency of their use. Ten additional instruments relating to communal administration are appended to the third part.

The instruments in the book are presented in a standard form. There is a full treatment, in Arabic, of the laws relating to each *shetar*, based on the Talmudic sources. Excerpts from those portions unique to each instrument are quoted in Aramaic, together with the necessary explanatory comments with regard to the text, the signatures, and other such matters.[33]

2. *SEFER HA-SHETAROT* BY HAI GAON

Sefer ha-Shetarot by Hai Gaon[34] contains forms of twenty-eight legal instruments[35] in various areas of the law. Many commonly used instruments are missing, such as those pertaining to family matters and enforcement of judgments. Some scholars believe that the book in its present form is not Hai Gaon's version but the result of a copyist's editing.[36]

3. *SEFER HA-SHETAROT* OF LUCENA, SPAIN

Early in the eleventh century, in 1021, a book of legal forms, *Sefer ha-Shetarot*, was compiled in Lucena, Spain. The surviving fragments of this compilation include forms for sales, sharecropping, divorce, etc.[37]

4. *SEFER HA-SHETAROT* BY JUDAH al-BARGELONI

This *Sefer ha-Shetarot* is part of a more comprehensive book, called *Hilkhot Tikkun Shetarot* [The Laws Relating to the Preparation of Legal Instruments], written by Judah al-Bargeloni at the beginning of the twelfth century.[38] The author drew on the compilation of Saadiah Gaon and perhaps on earlier compilations that had been extant in Spain.[39]

33. For detailed discussion, *see* the Introduction to Ben-Sasson's article in *Shenaton*, *supra* n. 30.

34. This compilation was published, with Introduction and notes, by S. Assaf, *Sefer ha-Shetarot le-Rav Hai b. Sherira Gaon*, Supplement to *Tarbiẓ*, I (1930). For a description of the compilation, *see* Assaf's Introduction, pp. 5–11.

35. Form #26 and the beginning of Form #27 are missing from the ms. *See* Assaf, *supra* n. 34 at 52 n. 2.

36. *See id.*, Introduction. In an appendix, the editor added a number of forms from various mss.

37. Fragments of this compilation were published in S. Assaf, "Le-Toledot ha-Yehudim bi-Sefarad" [On the History of the Jews in Spain], *Mekorot u-Meḥkarim* [Sources and Studies], 1946, pp. 100–103.

38. *See* the Introduction of the copyist and *Resp. Tashbeẓ*, I, #15. *See also supra* p. 974. This book was published with an Introduction and notes by S.Z.H. Halberstam in 1899; facsimile ed., Jerusalem, 1967.

39. *See* Al-Bargeloni's Introduction to his *Sefer ha-Shetarot*. *See also* Assaf, *supra* n. 37 at 100.

Al-Bargeloni's compilation contains seventy-three forms, arranged in alphabetical order, covering most legal areas.[40] The language is Hebrew, and the forms were apparently translated from Aramaic. The forms pertaining to family law, such as the *ketubbah* and the bill of divorcement, are in the original Aramaic.

5. COMPILATION OF LEGAL INSTRUMENTS IN *MAḤZOR VITRY*

Maḥzor Vitry was composed by Simḥah b. Samuel of Vitry, France, a student of Rashi. The work is essentially a book of prayers, together with commentaries, relevant customs, and laws based on the rulings of Rashi and other authorities.

The book is supplemented by a collection of legal forms, some of which are accompanied by an exposition of the relevant laws.[41] The forms include: bills of divorcement, *ḥaliẓah* (release from levirate marriage), and *me'un* (declaration by an adult daughter, given in marriage by her mother or brothers when she was a minor, that she no longer wishes to be married to her husband); and other forms relating to family law, acquisitions, obligations, and administrative law (communal enactments; the *ḥerem*, or ban). The forms are in Hebrew with some Aramaic.

6. COMPILATIONS IN *SEFER HA-ITTUR* AND *YAD RAMAH*

Some books of novellae, and some codes, of the twelfth and thirteenth centuries include compilations of various legal instruments and the full texts of other selected forms. Both *Sefer ha-Ittur* by Isaac b. Abba Mari of Marseilles, France,[42] and *Yad Ramah* by Meir ha-Levi Abulafia of Spain,[43] contain such a compilation.

7. COMPILATIONS OF LEGAL INSTRUMENTS USED BY ENGLISH JEWS IN THE ELEVENTH TO THIRTEENTH CENTURIES

Various scholars have published compilations of legal forms used by the Jews of England in the eleventh to thirteenth centuries. The forms are

40. A number of forms pertaining to public law, which are the province of "halakhic authorities, elders, and communal leaders" (p. 138), are added at the end of the book (pp. 131–138).

41. *Maḥzor Vitry le-Rabbenu Simḥah, Eḥad mi-Talmidei Rashi, Zal* [*Maḥzor Vitry* by Rabbenu Simḥah, a Student of Rashi, of Blessed Memory] by Simeon ha-Levi Ish Hurwitz, Nuremberg, 1923, II, pp. 778–799.

42. *See supra* p. 1267. Generally, the relevant legal instrument follows at the end of the treatment of each subject.

43. *Yad Ramah*, Bava Batra, ch. 10, #89 (Abulafia's commentary to TB Bava Batra 169a). The compilation covers the various proceedings in connection with the enforcement of judgments. *See also* Gulak, *supra* n. 20 at XXVII–XXVIII.

written in Hebrew interlaced with Aramaic and have been translated into English, with notes and copious explanations.[44]

8. LEGAL INSTRUMENTS USED IN CHRISTIAN SPAIN IN THE TWELFTH TO FIFTEENTH CENTURIES

Many forms of the legal instruments used by the Jews in Christian Spain from the twelfth to fifteenth centuries are found in the book of sources to *A History of the Jews in Christian Spain* by Y. Baer.[45]

9. *TIKKUN SOFERIM* [THE SCRIBE'S HANDBOOK] BY SOLOMON b. SIMEON DURAN (RASHBASH)

This book treats the laws of *shetarot.* Its author, Solomon b. Simeon Duran (Rashbash), succeeded his father, Rashbeẓ, as Rabbi of Algiers, North Africa, in the fifteenth century.[46]

10. *TIKKUN SOFERIM* BY MOSES ALMOSNINO AND SAMUEL JAFFE

This *Tikkun Soferim* by Moses Almosnino, one of the outstanding halakhic authorities of Salonika in the sixteenth century, is a compilation of legal instruments. It was copied in the second half of the sixteenth century by Samuel Jaffe, a halakhic authority in Constantinople, who was a disciple of Maharibal. Jaffe added notes and described the customs of the Jews of Constantinople. From chapter 80 to the end of the book, he also added forms of legal instruments used in Constantinople and Adrianople.[47] The compilation thus includes the *shetarot* used by the Jews of Salonika and Constantinople in the sixteenth century.

11. *TIKKUN SHETAROT* BY ELIEZER MILLI

This compilation[48] was published in Venice in 1552 and contains the instruments then in use there. The forms provide important information about the legal and economic life of the Jews of Italy in the sixteenth century.

44. *See* I. Abrahams and H.P. Stokes, *Starrs and Jewish Charters Preserved in the British Museum,* three volumes, London, 1930–1932; M.D. David, *Hebrew Deeds of English Jews before 1290,* London, 1888.

45. *See supra* n. 17. The forms can be located through the indexes at the end of the two volumes.

46. The book was printed together with Rashbeẓ's *Yavin Shemu'ah,* a work on the laws of ritual slaughter of animals.

47. *See* S. Assaf, "Al Kitvei Yad Shonim" [On Various Manuscripts], *Kiryat Sefer,* XI (1934–1935), pp. 497–498.

48. The full title of this compilation is *Le-Khol Ḥefeẓ ve-hu Tikkun Shetarot ha-Nehugim bi-Venei Yisra'el ke-Dat Moshe u-khe-Halakhah* [For Every Need, Being the Forms of Legal Instruments Used by Jews According to the Law of Moses and the *Halakhah*].

12. THE COMPILATION IN *NAḤALAT SHIV'AH* BY SAMUEL HA-LEVI

Samuel ha-Levi was a disciple of David ha-Levi, author of the *Taz,* and served as rabbi in several German communities in the seventeenth century. The compilation of legal instruments in *Naḥalat Shiv'ah* is one of the most important of its kind. It contains more than forty forms, together with explanations of the laws pertaining to their wording. The book was very popular in Germany and Poland, and was used there by judges and scribes, who drafted most of their instruments in accordance with its forms.[49]

13. *ET SOFER* [THE SCRIBE'S QUILL] BY JACOB ibn ẒUR

Jacob ibn Ẓur ("Ya'veẓ of North Africa," 1673–1752) was a leading halakhic authority in North Africa in the eighteenth century. He served as the head of the court in Fez, was a prominent respondent (*Resp. Mishpat u-Ẓedakah be-Ya'akov*), and was also knowledgeable in *Kabbalah.* He was a noted author of liturgical poetry, an expert draftsman, and an accomplished linguist.[50] His work *Et Sofer* includes a compilation of various legal forms.[51] The work was published by Abraham Ankawa, a judge in the Jewish community of Morocco in the middle of the nineteenth century, in the second part of his book *Kerem Ḥemer.*[52]

14. *OẒAR HA-SHETAROT* [A TREASURY OF LEGAL INSTRUMENTS] BY ASHER GULAK

Asher Gulak's *Oẓar ha-Shetarot*[53] contains 403 legal forms taken from some of the books described above and from other types of halakhic literature; seventy-seven were taken from manuscripts. The forms are divided into five subject areas:

a. Family law (engagement, marriage, divorce, wills and inheritance, guardianship, support and maintenance, etc.)

49. In the eighteenth century, several compilations of legal instruments were printed in Germany and Poland, such as *Tikkun Shetarot* by Ḥayyim the Communal Scribe in Berlin, and *Tikkunei Shetarot bi-Leshon ha-Kodesh u-ve-Yiddish* [Legal Forms in Hebrew and Yiddish] by Samuel Flekeles. The forms in these compilations are nearly identical with those in *Naḥalat Shiv'ah. See* Gulak, *supra* n. 20 at XXVIII–XXIX.

50. *See* Elon, *Yiḥudah Shel Halakhah,* pp. 23–25.

51. *See* I.M. Toledano, *Ner ha-Ma'arav, Toledot Yisra'el be-Morokko* [The Light of the West: A History of the Jews of Morocco], Jerusalem, 1911, p. 142; *Resp. Mishpat u-Ẓedakah be-Ya'akov,* Introduction by M. Amar.

52. Pp. 43c–63d. This part of *Kerem Ḥemer* also contains the enactments of Fez from the end of the fifteenth century and thereafter. *See supra* n. 4 and Elon, *Yiḥudah Shel Halakhah,* pp. 19–21.

53. The full title is *Oẓar ha-Shetarot ha-Nehugim be-Yisra'el* [A Treasury of the Legal Instruments Used by Jews], Jerusalem, 1926.

b. Commercial law (sales, gifts, obligations, suretyship, pledges, powers of attorney, etc.)
c. Judicial procedure (authentication and copying of documents, summonses, affidavits, judgments, etc.)
d. Public law (taxes, etc.)
e. Miscellaneous

The book contains a brief introduction to each category, together with brief notes and explanations for each form. A comprehensive general introduction contains a historical survey of the legal instruments used by Jews and a discussion of the nature and characteristics of the instruments, as well as of the various compilations in print and in manuscript.[54]

15. LEGAL INSTRUMENTS USED IN SPAIN AND NORTH AFRICA IN THE ELEVENTH TO FIFTEENTH CENTURIES

Many legal forms in all areas of the law are contained in whole or in part in the responsa literature. The *Digest of the Responsa Literature of Spain and North Africa, Historical Digest,*[55] includes an appendix containing a compilation of the legal instruments in the responsa literature of Spain and North Africa from the eleventh to fifteenth centuries.

III. REFERENCE WORKS

After the completion of the Talmud, various additional literary genres were created to help judges, scholars, and students in researching, studying, and understanding the vast amount of material in Jewish law. These additional genres were also occasionally the source of new legal rules; and some of these types of works were recognized as authoritative, although they were written not for that purpose but as reference works for the study of the

54. As to additional compilations of legal instruments, *see* A. Eisenstadt, *Ein Mishpat,* pp. 32–38 and p. 390. For a discussion of legal instruments in Jewish law in its various historical periods as compared with legal instruments in other legal systems, *see* A. Gulak, *Das Urkundenwesen im Talmud* [The Nature of Legal Instruments in the Talmud], Jerusalem, 1935; J.J. Rabinowitz, *Jewish Law: Its Influence on the Development of Legal Institutions,* New York, 1956; R. Yaron, *Gifts in Contemplation of Death in Jewish and Roman Law,* Oxford, 1960; *id., Ha-Mishpat Shel Mismekhei Yev* [Law in the Elephantine Papyri], Jerusalem, 1962; L. Auerbach, *Das Jüdische Obligationenrecht* [The Jewish Law of Obligations], ed. A.M. Fuss, 1976, in Fuss's Introduction, p. 14.

55. *See Mafte'aḥ ha-She'elot ve-ha-Teshuvot Shel Ḥakhmei Sefarad u-Ẓefon Afrikah* [Digest of the Responsa Literature of Spain and North Africa], ed. M. Elon, Institute for Research in Jewish Law, Hebrew University, *Historical Digest,* I (1981), pp. 37–41, 103–106, 124–126, 259–272; II (1986), pp. 283–302. For a description of the digest, *see supra* pp. 1525–1528.

history and methodology of the *Halakhah*. The reference works include: guidebooks; encyclopedias; biographies of halakhic authorities; bibliographies; lexicons; books explaining abbreviations; textual variants; concordances; source references, sayings, and aphorisms; and scholarly research in *mishpat ivri*.

A. Guidebooks

Guidebooks to the Talmud, and to Jewish law generally, deal with the methodology of the Mishnah and the Talmud—how the Talmudic literature was composed, definitions of terms and expressions used in the Talmud and in other tannaitic and amoraic literature, methods and canons of interpretation, and the like. They also collect and arrange the rules for decision making and for determining the law when there are differences of opinion between *tannaim* or *amoraim*. The methodology and the rules for decision making are called in the guidebooks *kelalei ha-Talmud* (lit. "the principles of the Talmud"). Some guidebooks, particularly the early ones, also include chronologies and biographies of halakhic authorities, but in the course of time entire books were devoted to such chronologies and biographies. These books are discussed below under the heading "Biographies of Halakhic Authorities."

There are many guidebooks to the Talmud and to Jewish law.[56] The following are some of the major ones.

1. *SEDER TANNAIM VA-AMORAIM* [CHRONICLES OF THE *TANNAIM* AND *AMORAIM*]

Seder Tannaim va-Amoraim is the earliest guidebook to the Talmud. Its author is unknown, although he was apparently one of the halakhic authorities of the academy of Sura in Babylonia. It is believed that the book was written at the end of the ninth century C.E., but some scholars date it later, to the time of Hai Gaon.[57]

The work is extremely brief and contains only a few folios. It has survived in several versions, and many corruptions have crept into the text.[58] The book includes a chronology of the leading personalities of each gener-

56. A. Jellinek published *Kunteres ha-Kelalim* (Vienna, 1878; facsimile ed., Jerusalem, 1970), which contains a listing of more than two hundred books of general principles and guidebooks to the Talmud. For a more limited listing, *see* P.I. ha-Kohen, *Oẓar ha-Be'urim ve-ha-Perushim* [A Treasury of Explications and Commentaries], 1952, pp. 448–462.

57. *See* Assaf, *Geonim*, p. 147; I.H. Weiss, *Bet Talmud*, Year I, p. 27.

58. *Seder Tannaim va-Amoraim* has been published in several editions; it also appears at the end of *Sefer Yuḥasin ha-Shalem*, ed. Filipowski (*see infra* p. 1557). A scientific edition was published by Kalman Kahana, Frankfurt, 1935.

ation from the time of Moses: the Biblical judges, the prophets, the *Zugot* ("pairs"), the patriarchs (*nesi'im*), the *tannaim*, the *amoraim*, and the *savoraim* through the last generation. The father and the teachers of each *tanna* and *amora* are listed, and occasionally, Sages referred to in the Talmud without being explicitly named are identified. *Seder Tannaim va-Amoraim* also contains a systematic presentation of the "principles of the Talmud," both those recorded in the Talmud itself and those that were transmitted by the *savoraim* and the *geonim*.

The book is not mentioned in geonic literature, but is widely quoted in the works of the *rishonim*. It is an important source, particularly for biographical information about the *amoraim* and the *savoraim*.[59]

2. *IGGERET RAV SHERIRA GAON* [THE EPISTLE OF RABBI SHERIRA GAON]

Sherira was *gaon* in Pumbedita from 968 to 998 C.E. His work *Iggeret Rav Sherira Gaon* is called "Epistle" because it was written in response to a question by Jacob b. Nissim and a group of halakhic authorities in Kairouan, North Africa. They asked Sherira Gaon how the Mishnah, the *baraitot*, and the Talmud had been written and edited, when the *Tosefta* was written, and what was the chain of tradition of the *Halakhah* from the *savoraim* until his own time. The epistle answers all these questions in detail.

The first part describes the history of the *Halakhah* and the composition and redaction of the classical texts of the period of the *tannaim* and the *amoraim*. The second part details the chronology of the halakhic authorities from the time of Ezra and Nehemiah through the *Zugot*, the *tannaim* and *amoraim*, and particularly the *savoraim* and *geonim* until Sherira's time. The chronicles in the archives of the Babylonian *yeshivot* were the source for the epistle, which was written in Aramaic in the style of the geonic responsa. The epistle is one of the most important and reliable sources for the history of the *Halakhah* generally and for Jewish history, including the history of the *geonim*, in Babylonia in the geonic period.

The epistle has survived in two main versions, one known as the Spanish recension and the other as the French.[60] The two versions are printed alongside each other in the edition by B. M. Lewin, with the variant readings indicated.[61]

59. Other guidebooks to the Talmud were written in the geonic period, such as *Mevo ha-Talmud* [Introduction to the Talmud] by Saadiah Gaon (which has not survived, except for quotations from it in other books) and a book with the same title by Samuel b. Ḥophni Gaon; *see* Assaf, *Geonim*, p. 147.

60. As to the two versions, *see further* Assaf, *Geonim*, p. 153.

61. *Iggeret Rav Sherira Gaon*, ed. B.M. Lewin, Haifa, 1921, with an extensive Preface and Introduction, notes and text of other epistles. For the various editions of the *Iggeret* and

3. *MEVO HA-TALMUD* [INTRODUCTION TO THE TALMUD] BY SAMUEL HA-NAGID OF EGYPT, ATTRIBUTED TO SAMUEL HA-NAGID OF SPAIN

Mevo ha-Talmud is a very brief work mainly devoted to the definition of various Talmudic terms. The author divides the Talmud into Mishnah, and commentary on the Mishnah (*i.e.*, *Gemara*). The discussion of the *Gemara* is subdivided into twenty-one *peratim* (lit. "details"), *i.e.*, terms, each of which is discussed separately. The end of the book contains a list of rules for decision making.[62]

The book has been attributed to Samuel ha-Nagid, who lived in Spain at the end of the tenth and the first half of the eleventh centuries. However, the accuracy of this attribution of authorship is doubtful. Joseph Sambari, a seventeenth-century halakhic authority in Egypt, wrote: "Samuel ibn Hananiah ha-Nagid, the head of the *yeshivah* in Egypt, [is] the author of the guidebook to the Talmud that is attributed to Samuel ha-Nagid [of Spain]."[63] Samuel ibn Hananiah ha-Nagid of Egypt lived more than a century after the death of Samuel b. Joseph ha-Levi ha-Nagid of Spain.[64]

4. MAIMONIDES' INTRODUCTION TO HIS *COMMENTARY ON THE MISHNAH;* THE INTRODUCTIONS OF MENAHEM MEIRI TO *BET HA-BEḤIRAH*

The introductions by various authors to their own works should also be included in any list of guides to the Talmud. The outstanding introductions of this nature are Maimonides' Introduction to his *Commentary on the Mishnah* and Menahem Meiri's various introductions to his work on the tractates of the Talmud, and to his commentary on Tractate *Avot*. These introductions discuss in detail the history of Jewish law and its literature; they constitute important sources on many aspects of the history and methodology of Jewish law.[65]

---

a discussion of their correctness, *see* Lewin's Introduction. The edition by Aaron Hyman (London, 1911) contains a commentary, *Patshegen ha-Ketav*. In that edition, the epistle is divided into sections and chapters and prefaced by two indexes—an index of names of the halakhic authorities and an index of names of the towns. The indexes add to the practical usefulness of Hyman's edition. *See also* Epstein, *Amoraim*, Appendix on *Iggeret Rav Sherira Gaon*, pp. 610–615.

62. This work was printed at the end of Tractate *Berakhot* in the Vilna edition of the Talmud, and in all the later editions based on or photocopied from the Vilna edition.

63. The statement by Sambari is quoted from Sambari's *Divrei Yosef* as published in Neubauer, *Seder ha-Ḥakhamim*, I, p. 156.

64. For detailed discussion, *see* M. Margaliot, *Sefer Hilkhot ha-Nagid* [The Book of Laws of the Nagid], 1962, pp. 68–73. According to Margaliot, Sambari's identification of the author as Samuel ha-Nagid of Egypt is correct.

65. These introductions have frequently been relied upon throughout this work. *See* the Index of Sources *infra* for pages referring to them.

5. *SEFER KERITUT* BY SAMSON OF CHINON

Samson of Chinon, France, was one of the outstanding halakhic authorities in France at the end of the thirteenth and the beginning of the fourteenth centuries. He was a contemporary of Rashba, with whom he corresponded. His main literary creation was *Sefer Keritut,* a comprehensive guidebook to the Mishnah and Talmud. The book is divided into five parts:

a. *Battei Middot* [The Chambers of the Canons] is an explanation of R. Ishmael's thirteen canons of Biblical interpretation. It is arranged in thirteen "chambers"—one for each canon.[66]
b. *Bet ha-Mikdash* [The Temple] discusses the special canons of interpretation applied to matters relating to the Temple.
c. *Netivot Olam* [Eternal Paths] explains why R. Ishmael listed only thirteen canons whereas R. Eliezer b. R. Yose the Galilean listed thirty-two.[67]
d. *Yemot Olam* [The Days of Yore] presents the chronology of the *tannaim* and *amoraim* and the rules for determining the law on questions in dispute among them. The sources for this part include *Seder Tannaim va-Amoraim* and *Iggeret Rav Sherira Gaon.*
e. *Leshon Limmudim* [The Language of Study] is arranged in three sections. The first discusses modes of Biblical interpretation not included in the thirteen canons of R. Ishmael or the thirty-two of R. Eliezer. The second deals with the methodology of the Mishnah and *baraitot;* and the third deals with the methodology of the *Gemara,* including definitions of Talmudic terms and expressions. The end of the third section extensively discusses the laws of *migo* and some of the laws relating to the general principle of *kavu'a ke-meḥeẓah al meḥeẓah* (lit. "things with a fixed location are like half-and-half").[68]

Sefer Keritut is the earliest extant comprehensive and systematic treatment of Talmudic methodology. Its arrangement and its comprehensive and

66. *See supra* pp. 318–319.
67. *See supra* pp. 317–319.
68. For a discussion of *migo, see supra* pp. 993–995 and n. 27. An example of the application of *kavu'a ke-meḥeẓah al meḥeẓah* is the following: If nine of ten butcher shops in a town sell kosher meat, and a person buys from one and does not remember which, the fact that a majority of the shops are kosher does not justify treating the meat as kosher, since whichever shop sold the meat has a fixed location, and the purchaser went there to buy; the probabilities are treated as evenly balanced ("half and half"). On the other hand, if one found a piece of meat that is by happenstance lying on the street, it is assumed to be kosher because the majority of the shops from which the meat could have come are kosher. *See,* for a further example, TB Ketubbot 15a.

systematic discussion blazed a new trail for guidebooks to the Talmud. "It constituted the foundation upon which all the later writers on Talmudic principles constructed their works; all of them pored over its statements again and again."[69]

6. *HALIKHOT OLAM* BY JOSHUA HA-LEVI

Joshua ha-Levi lived in the fifteenth century. Due to persecutions, he was forced to leave his native Tlemcen in Algeria; and he settled in Toledo, Spain, where he wrote *Halikhot Olam.* The book discusses the methodology of interpretation and the methodology of the Mishnah and, particularly, of the *Gemara.* Although following upon *Sefer Keritut* and commenting on the views expressed in it, *Halikhot Olam* differs from *Sefer Keritut* in both form and content. The first section is a general introduction to the Oral Law and includes a chronological listing of *tannaim* and *amoraim.* The second section treats the methodology of the *Gemara;* the third, the methodology of the Mishnah; the fourth, the methodology of interpretation. The fifth is a compilation of rules for decision making. Two outstanding halakhic authorities wrote commentaries on this book, entitled *Kelalei ha-Gemara* and *Yavin Shemu'ah* (*see* below), which are printed in current editions of *Halikhot Olam.* The book also has indexes that are of great value in locating desired material.

7. *SHE'ERIT YOSEF* BY JOSEPH ibn VERGA

She'erit Yosef by Joseph ibn Verga, a Spanish exile, discusses the principles of the Talmud. The book is divided into eight "paths," which deal with the methods of interpreting the Mishnah and the *Gemara.* Subjects addressed include whether interpretation should be expansive or restrictive, what are the aims of the questioner in the Talmud, what is a sufficient response, and similar matters. The last "path," the "Path of the *Halakhah,*" sets forth the rules for decision making.

8. *KELALEI HA-GEMARA* [PRINCIPLES OF THE GEMARA] BY JOSEPH CARO

Joseph Caro, the author of *Bet Yosef* and the *Shulḥan Arukh,* wrote his *Kelalei ha-Gemara* as a commentary on Joshua ha-Levi's *Halikhot Olam.* In a brief introduction, Caro explained that he chose to write his work as a commentary on an existing book in order to avoid repeating things already

69. I.H. Weiss, *Bet Talmud,* Year II, p. 7. For discussion of *Sefer Keritut,* its author, and its methodology, *see* Urbach, *Tosafot,* pp. 556ff.

written. As noted previously, this was one of the reasons why he wrote his *Bet Yosef* as an extension of the *Turim.*[70] At the end of *Kelalei ha-Gemara,* Caro added many principles of Talmudic methodology that he had discovered in various halakhic works but were not included in *Halikhot Olam.*[71]

There is an interesting difference of opinion as to the date when *Kelalei ha-Gemara* was written. The issue arose in connection with the question as to how the law should be determined when there is a contradiction between *Kelalei ha-Gemara* and the *Shulḥan Arukh.* The opinions expressed on this question also throw light on the attitudes of various halakhic authorities to halakhic guidebooks. According to one opinion:

> It appears that Joseph Caro wrote his *Kelalei ha-Gemara* at an advanced age after he composed his *Bet Yosef,* since in his youth he would not have spent his time on "principles" but rather on the substance of the law. Only after God allowed him to complete his table [the *Shulḥan Arukh*—the "Set Table"] did he turn his attention to "principles." The result is that if he is inconsistent, what he states in the "principles" is accepted [since they were written later].[72]

In contrast, Malachi ha-Kohen, the author of *Yad Malakhi* (*see* below), strongly took issue with the assumption upon which this conclusion is premised:

> In my humble opinion, if that is the basis for the conclusion, it is unfounded. Is spending time on "principles" an unimportant matter? We have seen that the most renowned authorities, such as Maimonides, Rabbenu Baruch, Rabbenu Beẓalel, Rabbenu Samson, and many other rabbis devoted their time to composing books of "principles," for there is no more important task in the study of Torah. Thus, it is entirely possible that he [Caro], following in the footsteps of his predecessors, first wrote the "principles" and then later decided to write his code.[73]

70. *See supra* p. 1314.

71. The principles are not arranged topically and are therefore difficult to locate. At the end of his commentary, Caro wrote that because of ill health he was unable to compose an index to his book.

72. Quoted in *Yad Malakhi,* II, Kelalei ha-Ribah u-Moharika [Principles of the *Turim* and Caro], #42, in the name of *Bet David* on *Tur* YD ch. 133.

73. *Id.* It is interesting that the solution to the question of the order in which Caro wrote the two works turned on the degree of respect in which books of principles were held. It was thus the degree of such respect that was crucial to the determination of the law when *Kelalei ha-Gemara* and the *Shulḥan Arukh* do not agree. As to *Yad Malakhi, see infra.*

9. *KELALEI HA-TALMUD* [PRINCIPLES OF THE TALMUD] BY BEẒALEL ASHKENAZI

Beẓalel Ashkenazi, a halakhic authority of the sixteenth century, was active in Egypt and the Land of Israel.[74] Part of his book *Kelalei ha-Talmud* was published by A. Marx[75] and the balance by E. Shochetman.[76] It appears that Ashkenazi used *Sefer Keritut* by Samson of Chinon[77] as the basis for his own book. His plan for *Kelalei ha-Talmud* was the same as the one he used for his work *Shittah Mekubbeẓet*, in which he collected the novellae and the commentaries of the *rishonim* to various tractates of the Talmud. In *Kelalei ha-Talmud*, he collected the statements of the *rishonim* concerning Talmudic "principles," his aim being to provide a supplement to Samson of Chinon's *Sefer Keritut*.[78]

10. *YAVIN SHEMU'AH* BY SOLOMON ALGAZI

Solomon Algazi lived in the seventeenth century and was active in Jerusalem and in Izmir, Turkey. He was a leader of the opposition to the false messiah, Shabbetai Ẓevi. As a consequence of harassment by the Sabbateans in Izmir, he moved to Jerusalem, where he served as head of the rabbinical court for a short period.

Algazi wrote three books on Talmudic methodology: *Yavin Shemu'ah*, a commentary on Joshua ha-Levi's *Halikhot Olam; Halikhot Eli*, arranged in alphabetical order; and *Gufei Halakhot*. In *Yavin Shemu'ah*, he explained and commented on *Halikhot Olam* as well as on some of the passages in *Sefer Keritut* and *Kelalei ha-Gemara*. At the conclusion of his book, he added many principles that he asserted were omitted by his predecessors. The sections of the book are numbered, and there is a helpful index at the end.

11. *YAD MALAKHI* BY MALACHI HA-KOHEN

Malachi ha-Kohen was Rabbi of Leghorn, Italy, in the eighteenth century and was a leading halakhic authority of his time. *Yad Malakhi* is an extremely important work in that it summarizes the principles of Talmudic methodology and the rules of decision making and also discusses, briefly and succinctly, the substance of specific laws. The book makes extensive use

74. *See supra* pp. 1126–1127.

75. *Jubilee Volume in Honor of Rabbi David Hoffmann*, Berlin, 1914, Hebrew section, pp. 179–217; German section, pp. 369–382.

76. *Shenaton*, VIII (1981), pp. 248–308.

77. As to *Sefer Keritut*, *see supra* pp. 1544–1545.

78. *See Shenaton*, *supra* n. 76 at 258.

of all the existing literature on Talmudic methodology and adds its own contribution; there is hardly a principle that it does not treat.

The arrangement of the book differs from that of all previous guidebooks. It is divided into three sections: "The Principles of the *Gemara*," "The Principles of the *Posekim*,"[79] and "The Principles of the Laws." The material in the first and third sections is not arranged in logical or topical order but alphabetically according to the first word of the principle under discussion. Occasionally, a great deal of ingenuity is needed to locate a particular principle. The contents of the three sections are as follows:

a. "The Principles of the *Gemara*" is a comprehensive explanation and discussion of Talmudic terms and expressions and of the rules of decision making in cases where *tannaim* or *amoraim* disagree. At the end of this section, there is an alphabetical index of the principles.
b. "The Principles of the *Posekim*" lists the principles pertaining to the methodologies and approaches of the post-Talmudic halakhic authorities and the rules of decision making when they disagree. The methodology of each authority is discussed separately—Alfasi, Maimonides, *Tosafot*, Asheri, the *Turim*, and the *Shulḥan Arukh*, among others.
c. "The Principles of the Laws" lists alphabetically various principles pertaining to the *Halakhah*.[80]

12. GUIDEBOOKS FROM THE NINETEENTH CENTURY AND THEREAFTER

The movement for the scientific study of Judaism (*ḥokhmat Yisra'el, jüdische Wissenschaft*) began in the nineteenth century. Its scholars and researchers undertook to apply to Judaic studies—including the history and literature of Jewish law—the principles of scientific-historical research. Their scholarship concentrated in the main on the Talmudic period and gave scant attention to post-Talmudic developments. The movement pro-

79. The term *posekim* is used here in its wider sense as meaning all those acknowledged to be entitled to make authoritative rulings, including the *geonim* as well as post-geonic codifiers, respondents, and other acknowledged halakhic decisionmakers; *see Yad Malakhi*, immediately following the principles of the two Talmuds. It should be noted that the first chapter of this section of *Yad Malakhi* covers the principles of both the Babylonian and Jerusalem Talmuds, and discusses the rules of decision making when there is a conflict between the Babylonian Talmud and the Jerusalem Talmud, or between the Babylonian Talmud and the *Tosefta*, the "Minor" Tractates, or the *midrashim*.

80. It is difficult to discern why the author chose to discuss the laws included in this section of *Yad Malakhi* or why he discussed any substantive laws, in view of the fact that the book is a guidebook to halakhic literature and not a work of substantive *Halakhah*. However, this tendency is apparent in the earlier work, *Sefer Keritut*; *see supra* pp. 1544–1545.

duced a wide-ranging literature consisting of books and articles in many diverse learned journals and anthologies.[81]

Foremost among such scholars was Ẓevi Hirsch Chajes (1805–1855), who lived in the province of Galicia in Poland and served as Rabbi of Zolkiew. Chajes was a recognized halakhic authority and wrote many responsa.[82] In several of his works, he adopted a scientific-historical approach in describing the history of Jewish law and its legal and literary sources; and he maintained contact with some of the leading members of the "Jewish Enlightenment" (*Haskalah*) in Galicia and Italy, particularly Nachman Krochmal (Ranak). Of his many books, three are especially noteworthy: *Torat Nevi'im* [The Law of the Prophets], a study of Talmudic methodology (Zolkiew, 1836); *Darkhei Hora'ah* [The Methodology of Decision Making] (Zolkiew, 1843); and *Mevo ha-Talmud* [Introduction to the Talmud] (Zolkiew, 1845).[83] Chajes's works served as the foundation for many other guidebooks to halakhic literature as well as for research studies in the history and literature of Jewish law.

The following is a partial list, in chronological order, of comprehensive guidebooks to the literature of the *tannaim,* the *amoraim,* the *geonim,* and the *rishonim,* as well as some of the basic studies of the history of Jewish law and the halakhic authorities:

a. N. Krochmal, *Moreh Nevukhei ha-Zeman* [A Guide for the Perplexed of the Time] (Lemberg, 1851), reprinted in Krochmal's collected works (ed. Simon Rawidowicz, 1924).
b. Z. Frankel, *Darkhei ha-Mishnah* [Methodology of the Mishnah] (Leipzig, 1869), reprinted many times, and *Mevo ha-Yerushalmi* [Introduction to the Jerusalem Talmud] (Breslau, 1870; facsimile ed., Jerusalem, 1967).
c. J. Brüll, *Mevo ha-Mishnah* [Introduction to the Mishnah], two parts (Frankfurt, 1876–1885; facsimile ed., Jerusalem, 1970).
d. H. L. Strack, *Einleitung in Talmud und Midrash* (first ed., 1887; fifth ed. by the author, 1921). A Hebrew translation entitled *Mevo ha-Talmud* was also published (Vilna, 1913; facsimile ed., Jerusalem, 1971). An English translation, entitled *Introduction to the Talmud and Midrash,* was pub-

81. In various places throughout this present work, reference has been made to a considerable part of this literature; *see also* the bibliography at the end of this work.

82. *Resp. Moharaẓ,* 1849–1850; reprinted in *Kol Kitvei Maharaẓ Ḥayyot* [The Collected Works of Z.H. Chajes], 1958, II.

83. These three books have been reprinted in *Kol Kitvei Maharaẓ Ḥayyot,* two vols., 1958. Chajes's monograph, *Mishpat ha-Hora'ah* [The Law of Decision Making] (*Collected Works,* p. 361), which is part of his book *Ateret Ẓevi,* is also very significant in this area. Chajes's *Mevo ha-Talmud* has been translated into English as *The Student's Guide through the Talmud,* London, 1952; 2nd ed., New York, 1960.

lished in 1931 (JPS, Philadelphia) and has since been reprinted several times.

e. I. H. Weiss, *Dor Dor ve-Doreshav* [The Generations and Their Interpreters—a history of the Oral Law], five parts (Vilna, 1893; reprinted many times, *e.g.*, Tel Aviv, 1944).

f. I. I. Halevy, *Dorot ha-Rishonim* [The Early Generations—a history of the Oral Law to the *geonim*], several sections and volumes from 1897 on; published in three parts (Berlin–Vienna, 1923).[84]

g. Ch. Tchernowitz (Rav Ẓa'ir), *Toledot ha-Halakhah* [History of the *Halakhah*], four parts (New York, 1945), and *Toledot ha-Posekim* [History of the *Posekim*], three parts (New York, 1946).

h. J. N. Epstein, *Mavo le-Nusaḥ ha-Mishnah* [Introduction to the Text of the Mishnah], two parts (Jerusalem, 1948); a second edition with more detailed indexes was published by E. Z. Melamed in 1964. Also, *Mevo'ot le-Sifrut ha-Tannaim* [Introductions to Tannaitic Literature] (Jerusalem, 1957) and *Mevo'ot le-Sifrut ha-Amoraim* [Introductions to Amoraic Literature] (Jerusalem, 1962).

i. S. Assaf, *Tekufat ha-Geonim ve-Sifrutah* [The Geonic Period and Its Literature] (Jerusalem, 1956).

j. E. E. Urbach, *Ba'alei ha-Tosafot, Toledoteihem, Ḥibbureihem ve-Shittatam* [The Tosafists: Their History, Writings, and Methodology] (Jerusalem, 1956; 4th enlarged edition, 1980).

k. H. Albeck, *Mavo la-Mishnah* [Introduction to the Mishnah] (Jerusalem, 1959); *Mavo la-Talmudim* [Introduction to the Talmuds (Babylonian and Jerusalem)] (Jerusalem, 1969); *Meḥkarim be-Varaita ve-Tosefta ve-Yaḥasan la-Talmud* [Studies in the *Baraita* and the *Tosefta* and Their Relation to the Talmud] (Jerusalem, 1970).

l. Adin Steinsaltz, *The Talmud, A Reference Guide,* Random House (New York, 1989).

Most of the guidebooks listed above deal with Jewish law only up to the completion of the Talmud; a few discuss various post-Talmudic periods. I. H. Weiss's *Dor Dor ve-Doreshav* treats the history of Jewish law up to the sixteenth century.[85] None of these works deals with the subject from the point of view of juristic thought. To some degree, the studies in *mishpat ivri*

84. An additional section, "The Biblical Period," was published in Jerusalem in 1939; a further addition dealing with the end of the Second Temple period was published in *Sefer Zikkaron le-Rabbi Yiẓhak Isaac ha-Levi* [Isaac ha-Levi Memorial Volume], ed. M. Auerbach, Bene Berak, 1964. *See also infra* n. 85.

85. Halevy's *Dorot ha-Rishonim* extends through the geonic period. In *Toledot ha-Halakhah,* Tchernowitz treated only the early periods in the development of Jewish law; and in *Toledot ha-Posekim,* he dealt with the post-Talmudic codificatory literature.

that have been discussed elsewhere in this present work[86] do include treatment of the material from such a point of view.

B. Encyclopedias

Encyclopedias, an entirely new genre of halakhic literature, did not appear until the eighteenth century. These works present the various topics of Jewish law in articles arranged alphabetically. They define and expound the topics and provide source references to all the types of Talmudic and post-Talmudic halakhic literature. Most of these works also contain a summary of the pertinent decisions and novellae. Encyclopedias are designed to facilitate research into the source material on each topic and are of great practical value as an important research tool for judges, students, and scholars.[87] However, the terminology generally used is Talmudic-halakhic, and often the word that determines the alphabetical listing of an entry is peripheral to the basic issue or simply the first word of a halakhic phrase or sentence. This makes it difficult to find the desired discussion of the subject being researched.

The following is a chronological review of the major comprehensive encyclopedic works.

1. *PAḤAD YIẒḤAK* BY ISAAC LAMPRONTI

Isaac Lampronti (1679–1756) was rabbi and head of the *yeshivah* of Ferrara, Italy. His main halakhic work was *Paḥad Yiẓḥak,* an encyclopedia of Jewish law containing "hundreds and thousands of entries on even the smallest point, heaps upon heaps of laws, all completely set out in good order. It contains everything: Mishnah, *baraita,* Talmud, Alfasi, and [the other] codes. Everything with all its details."[88]

The book presents a vast number of references to all areas of Talmudic literature—including codes, novellae, commentaries, and responsa—and particularly the responsa of Italian halakhic authorities.[89] There are references to material in books and manuscripts that have not survived. Some-

86. *See supra* pp. 80–91.

87. The purpose of encyclopedias is similar to that of the compilations of responsa that were arranged according to the topical order of the *Turim* and the *Shulḥan Arukh; see supra* pp. 1442–1433. However, the two types of literature are substantially different in the organization and presentation of their material.

88. This description appears on the title page of the book.

89. Boaz Cohen, "Mazkeret Meḥabberei ha-Teshuvot be-Sefer Paḥad Yiẓḥak" [A Record of the Authors of the Responsa in *Paḥad Yiẓḥak*], *Alexander Marx Jubilee Volume,* ed. D. Frankel, New York, 1943, pp. 47–57, lists the authors of the responsa included in *Paḥad Yiẓḥak.* The list does not include responsa from compilations that have survived intact. For a list of the sources of *Paḥad Yiẓḥak, see Paḥad Yiẓḥak,* ed. Mosad ha-Rav Kook, I, pp. 7ff.

times, entire passages from books are quoted, and some entries contain Lampronti's own analysis. Responsa of Lampronti's contemporaries, as well as his own responsa, are also quoted.

Paḥad Yiẓḥak was Lampronti's life's work, but he saw only a small part of it in print. The printing began in his lifetime, but took 138 years to complete. The first parts, until the letter *mem,* were printed in Italy between 1750 and 1840, and the rest, from letter *nun* on, were published in Germany between 1864 and 1885 by the Mekiẓei Nirdamim Society. More recently, various sections of *Paḥad Yiẓḥak* have been published in a scientific edition.[90]

2. *SEDEI ḤEMED* BY ḤAYYIM HEZEKIAH MEDINI

Ḥayyim Hezekiah Medini (1832–1904) was born in Jerusalem. He served as a *dayyan* in Constantinople and was later a rabbi in Crimea. At the end of the nineteenth century, he returned to Jerusalem, where he lived until he was appointed the rabbi of the Jewish community in Hebron, in which capacity he served until his death.

His life's work was *Sedei Ḥemed* [The Pleasant Fields], a comprehensive encyclopedia of the entire halakhic literature, with emphasis on the responsa. The relevant sources are cited and also frequently summarized.

The book is divided into two parts. The first contains general rules (*kelalim*) arranged alphabetically, with each letter of the alphabet having its own table of contents. The second part, *Asefat Dinim* [Compilation of Laws], is composed of main titles, also arranged alphabetically, with each title containing the laws pertinent to its subject. For example, the main title *Ishut* [Family Law] includes all the laws falling under that heading. Each of the letters of the alphabet in this part also has its own table of contents, as does each main title. After the book was published, Medini added supplements that he entitled *Pe'at ha-Sadeh* [The Corner of the Field]; and he then added a supplement to the supplements, which he called *Sheyarei Pe'at ha-Sadeh* [The Remnants of the Corner of the Field]. Notwithstanding its great importance, the book is difficult to use, mainly because of its unclear termi-

90. *Paḥad Yiẓḥak ha-Shalem* [The Complete *Paḥad Yiẓḥak*], published by Ẓevi Kanel, 1936–1942, reached only the letter *ḥet* (*Ḥazeret*). That edition included, for the first time, Lampronti's second version, which contains supplements to the original text. The work on this edition was supervised by Jacob Freimann and his son, Abraham Ḥayyim Freimann; *see* their Introduction to the edition. In 1962, work was begun on a new edition of *Paḥad Yiẓḥak* (first and second versions), with notes and supplements, under the auspices of Mosad ha-Rav Kook, Jerusalem. Up to the present, five volumes of this edition, through the letter *gimmel* (Gat), have appeared. For a list of articles on Lampronti, *see* ed. Mosad ha-Rav Kook, I, Introduction and p. 5 n. 1. A facsimile edition of the entire *Paḥad Yiẓḥak* was published by Makor, Jerusalem, 1970–1971.

nology and its lack of precise criteria for classifying the material. The existence of separate supplements also adds to the difficulties.[91] The two most recent editions of *Sedei Ḥemed* include new features, which, to some degree, make the book easier to use.[92]

3. *DIE EXEGETISCHE TERMINOLOGIE DER JÜDISCHEN TRADITIONSLITERATUR* [THE EXEGETICAL TERMINOLOGY OF THE LITERATURE OF THE JEWISH TRADITION] BY WILHELM BACHER

Wilhelm Bacher (1850–1913) was one of the outstanding scholars in Judaic studies and semitic philology. For a short period, he served as Rabbi of Szeged, Hungary, and then joined the faculty of the Rabbinical Seminary of Budapest, of which he later became head.

Bacher's work was published in two volumes in 1899 and 1905. It was translated into Hebrew by A. Z. Rabinowitz under the title *Erkhei Midrash* [Midrashic Terminology], Tel Aviv, 1923. It contains, in alphabetical order, the terms and expressions (which are scattered throughout Talmudic literature) used in interpreting Biblical passages. Each term is concisely explained, with citations to the places where it appears. The book is divided into two parts: *Erkhei Midrash Tanna'im,* which presents the exegetical terms used in tannaitic literature, and *Erkhei Midrash Amora'im,* which covers the Hebrew and Aramaic terminology of the *amoraim* of the Land of Israel and Babylonia.

4. *MAFTE'AḤ HA-TALMUD* [KEY TO THE TALMUD] BY JEHIEL MICHAL GUTTMANN

Jehiel Michal Guttmann (1872–1942) was a scholar who taught Talmud in Budapest and Breslau. His work *Mafte'aḥ ha-Talmud,* in four volumes, covers only the letter *alef,* the first letter of the Hebrew alphabet.[93]

91. *E.g.*, the problem of the status of the Karaites under Jewish law is treated both in the main work in the section on general rules (under the letter *bet* in an entry entitled *Benei Mikra*) and in the *Pe'at ha-Sadeh* supplement. The principles applicable to the *posekim* are contained in a separate entry between the section entitled *Kelalim* and the section entitled *Asefat Dinim*.

92. *Sedei Ḥemed,* ten vols., New York, 1959, includes in its last volume indexes of entries, books, and authors, which, to some degree, make it easier to use the work. *Sedei Ḥemed,* ten vols., Bene Berak, 1963–1964, adds the various supplements at the end of the respective volumes to which they relate, and each volume has its own subject index. Volume 9 contains a general subject index of the whole work (Volume 10 is devoted to Medini's responsa). The entries in the index are "in the style of the entries in the work" and it, therefore, is useful only to the extent that the terminological difficulties are overcome.

93. Budapest-Breslau, 1906–1930. Guttmann had completed the work through the whole alphabet, but the rest of the ms. was lost during the German occupation. *See Ha-Enẓiklopedyah ha-Ivrit,* X, p. 341, s.v. Guttmann.

The work consists of quotations from Talmudic literature, excerpts from the commentaries and the codes, occasional explications of the substance of an entry, and discussions of various related subjects.

5. *ENẒIKLOPEDYAH TALMUDIT* [TALMUDIC ENCYCLOPEDIA]

The *Enẓiklopedyah Talmudit* is a major contemporary project of a team of rabbinic scholars in Jerusalem. Its editor-in-chief was Solomon Joseph Zevin (1890–1978). As of 1991, twenty volumes had been published, up to the entry "Tirpa" (writ of execution), together with a complete index of the titles and subjects in the first seventeen volumes. The purpose of the encyclopedia is "to encompass in brief form, and in alphabetical order, the basic principles and detailed rules of all halakhic subjects, . . . and to present the essence and substance of the laws, concepts, terms, and principles of Talmudic-Torah literature, with their sources, rationales, legal reasoning, and differing opinions."[94] Four volumes of the encyclopedia have appeared in English.

6. HALAKHIC WORKS ARRANGED ALPHABETICALLY

In addition to the books already mentioned, many halakhic works, especially those written from the eighteenth century on, have been organized alphabetically. Such books can sometimes be of value in locating halakhic material on particular subjects, and can illuminate the halakhic discussions current in their authors' times and places.[95]

7. *MISHPAT IVRI* ALPHABETICALLY ARRANGED BY SUBJECT

The *Encyclopaedia Judaica,* an English-language encyclopedia of Jewish culture, history, and religion, which appeared in sixteen volumes in 1971, was the first work to contain an exposition of the entire system of *mishpat ivri,* with the topics arranged alphabetically according to subject matter. The relevant laws in each article are discussed conformably with scientific legal methodology, the relevant sources in halakhic literature are cited, and each article concludes with a bibliography of the pertinent scholarly research.

The central article on Jewish law in the *Encyclopaedia Judaica* is entitled

94. *See* the Introduction by Meir Berlin (Bar-Ilan) in Volume I. Bar-Ilan was co-editor-in-chief of the first two volumes.

95. Boaz Cohen, *supra* n. 89, lists chronologically forty halakhic books arranged alphabetically (*see id.*, p. 46 n. 3). They include: *Ar'a de-Rabbanan* by Jacob Algazi; *Zekhor le-Avraham* by Abraham Samuel Alkalai; *Kehillat Ya'akov* by Israel Jacob Algazi; *Mishkenot ha-Ro'im* by Uzziel Laḥayikh; *Zera Avraham* by Ẓevi Ze'ev b. Abraham Issachar; *Bet ha-Oẓar* by Joseph Engel. The following should be added to Boaz Cohen's list: *Melo ha-Ro'im* by Jacob Ẓevi Jallisch; *Kesef Nivḥar* by Baruch Benedict Goitein; *Divrei Geonim* by Ḥayyim Aryeh ha-Kohen.

"*Mishpat Ivri.*"[96] The following is a list of the articles pertaining to *mishpat ivri,* arranged according to subject matter:[97]

THE SOURCES OF LAW: Authority, Rabbinical; Codification of Law; Interpretation; *Ma'aseh; Minhag; Mishpat Ivri; Sevarah; Takkanot; Takkanot ha-Kahal.*

GENERAL: Agency, Laws of; *Asmakhta;* Conditions; *Ḥazakah* (in part); Law and Morals; Legal Person; Majority Rule; Maxims, Legal; Mistake; Noachide Laws; *Ones; Shetar;* Slavery.

THE LAWS OF PROPERTY: Acquisition; Gifts; *Ḥazakah; Hefker; Hekdesh;* Lost Property, Finder of; *Maẓranut; Ona'ah;* Ownership; Property; Sale; Servitude; Slavery; *Ye'ush.*

THE LAWS OF OBLIGATION: Antichresis; Assignment; Contract; Gifts; *Ha'anakah; Hassagat Gevul;* Labor Law; Lease and Hire; Lien; Loans; Maritime Law; *Meḥilah;* Obligation, Law of; Partnership; Pledge; Sale; *Shalish; Shi'buda de-Rabbi Nathan; Shomerim;* Surety; Unjust Enrichment; Usury.

THE LAWS OF TORT: *Avot Nezikin;* Damages; *Gerama;* Nuisance; Theft and Robbery (civil aspects); Torts.

FAMILY LAW AND INHERITANCE: Adoption; *Agunah;* Apostate (Family Law); *Apotropos;* Betrothal; Bigamy; Child Marriage; Civil Marriage; Concubine; Divorce; Dowry; Embryo; Firstborn (Legal Aspects); Husband and Wife; *Ketubbah;* Levirate Marriage and *Ḥaliẓah;* Maintenance; *Mamzer;* Marriage; Marriage, Prohibited; Mixed Marriage (Legal Aspects); Orphan; Parent and Child (Legal Aspects); Succession; Widow; Wills; *Yuḥasin.*

CRIMINAL LAW: Abduction; Abortion; Adultery; Assault; Blood Avenger; Bribery; Capital Punishment; City of Refuge; Compounding Offenses; Confiscation; Crucifixion; Expropriation and Forfeiture; Contempt of Court; Divine Punishment; Extraordinary Remedies; Fine; Flogging; Forgery; Fraud; Gambling; *Hafka'at She'arim; Ḥerem;* Homicide; Imprisonment; Incest; Informer (Legal Aspects); Oppression; Ordeal; Penal Law; Perjury; Police Offenses; Punishment; Rape; Rebellious Son; Sexual Of-

96. EJ, XII, pp. 109–151 (reprinted in *Principles* as the Introduction, pp. 5–46). The same article in a shorter version also appears in *Ha-Enẓiklopedyah ha-Ivrit,* XXIV, pp. 679–694.

97. This list of articles is contained in EJ, XII, s.v. Mishpat ivri, at p. 135. The general editor of the Jewish law division of EJ was M. Elon, and the editors for the different subject areas were M. Elon, H. Cohn, S. Albeck, and B. Schereschewsky. *See* in detail EJ, I, p. 21. Various other scholars participated in writing the articles. Articles on different areas of *mishpat ivri* are also included in *Enẓiklopedyah Mikra'it* [Biblical Encyclopedia], 1950–1984, and *Ha-Enẓiklopedyah ha-Ivrit.*

fenses; Slander; Sorcery; Suicide; Talion; Theft and Robbery (Criminal Aspects); Usury; Weights and Measures (Criminal Aspects).

THE LAWS OF PROCEDURE AND EVIDENCE: Admission; Arbitration; Attorney; *Bet Din;* Compromise; Confession; Evidence; Execution (Civil); Extraordinary Remedies; *Ḥerem;* Imprisonment for Debt; Limitation of Actions; Oath; Pleas; Practice and Procedure (Civil and Penal Law); *Shetar;* Witness.

MERCANTILE LAW:[98] Acquisition; Agency, Laws of; Contract; *Hafka'at She'arim; Hassagat Gevul;* Imprisonment for Debt; Labor Law; Lease and Hire; Legal Person; Loans; Maritime Law; *Minhag;* Obligation, Law of; *Ona'ah;* Partnership; Sale; *Shalish; Shetar; Shomerim; Takkanot; Takkanot ha-Kahal;* Taxation; Usury.

PUBLIC AND ADMINISTRATIVE LAW: Confiscation; Expropriation and Forfeiture; *Dina de-Malkhuta Dina; Hekdesh;* Public Authority; *Takkanot ha-Kahal;* Taxation.

CONFLICT OF LAWS: Conflict of Laws; *Dina de-Malkhuta Dina;* Domicile.

All these articles have been collected and published in a separate volume—*The Principles of Jewish Law* (ed. M. Elon, Keter Publishing House, Jerusalem, 1975)—which is organized according to the following subjects: The Sources of Law; General Legal Institutions; Law of Property; Law of Obligations; Law of Torts; Family Law and Inheritance; Criminal Law; Jurisdiction, Procedure, Evidence and Execution; Public and Administrative Law; Conflict of Laws. There is a detailed subject index at the end of the book. *The Principles of Jewish Law* constitutes an important complement (Volume V as it were) to Volumes I through IV of the present work.[99]

C. Biographies of Halakhic Authorities

In order to understand any halakhic subject thoroughly, one must know something about the life and background of each halakhic authority involved, the circumstances of the period in which he lived, and his work in Jewish law as well as in other areas. Such information is widely scattered throughout all of the different types of Talmudic and post-Talmudic literature. Some of it can also be found in the works on Jewish history by such authors as Graetz, Jawitz, and Dubnow, and in the books and articles of many scholars and historians who concentrated on specific periods and

98. The articles on mercantile law are listed under other headings, but they are also listed together here because of their relevance to mercantile law.

99. *See Principles,* Preface.

centers of Jewish life. Much important material of this type is also available in the guidebooks previously discussed. In addition, an extensive biographical literature, entirely devoted to describing the lives and activities of the halakhic authorities of different periods, is available to facilitate research and study.

The biographical works are organized in various ways: some according to historical periods; others according to cities, countries, and Jewish centers; still others according to the names, in alphabetical order, of the halakhic authorities—the most common form of organization of the most recent biographical literature. Many of the guidebooks previously discussed (such as *Seder Tannaim va-Amoraim, Iggeret Rav Sherira Gaon,* and most guidebooks written in the nineteenth century and thereafter) contain sections devoted to biographies of halakhic authorities.

1. BIOGRAPHIES ACCORDING TO HISTORICAL PERIODS

The following is a list of some of the more important works mainly devoted to biographies of the halakhic authorities[100] in the different historical periods:[101]

a. *Sefer ha-Kabbalah* by Rabad I (Abraham b. David ha-Levi of Spain), twelfth century, published by A. Neubauer as part of *Seder ha-Ḥakhamim ve-Korot ha-Yamim* [Medieval Jewish Chronicles], I, pp. 47–84.[102] There is an edition of *Sefer ha-Kabbalah* in English: *The Book of Tradition* (*Sefer Ha-Qabbalah*), ed. G. Cohen, JPS, Philadelphia, 1967.
b. *Yiḥusei Tannaim va-Amoraim* [Genealogies of *Tannaim* and *Amoraim*] by Judah b. Kalonymus of Speyer, twelfth century; ed. J. L. Fishman (Maimon), Jerusalem, 1942.[103]
c. *Sefer Yuḥasin ha-Shalem* [The Complete Book of Genealogy] by Abraham Zacuth, fifteenth century; ed. Ẓevi Hirsch Filipowski, 1857.[104]

100. Some of the books listed here (*e.g.*, Rabad's *Sefer ha-Kabbalah*) are both historical chronicles and biographies of halakhic authorities; others are entirely biographical.

101. The works are listed chronologically. Some contain biographies of all the halakhic authorities up to the time they were written; others are limited to halakhic authorities of a specific period or place.

102. Both parts of Neubauer's *Seder ha-Ḥakhamim* contain much important material on Jewish history and on the biographical literature relating to the halakhic authorities. *See, e.g.*, part I, "Likkutim mi-Divrei Yosef le-R. Yosef b. Yiẓḥak Sambari" [Selections from *Divrei Yosef* by Joseph b. Isaac Sambari], pp. 115–162 (*see supra* p. 1543—this text served to identify the real author of *Mevo ha-Talmud* attributed to Samuel ha-Nagid of Spain); "Seder Olam," etc. The same is also true of part II. A facsimile edition of Neubauer's book was published, Jerusalem, 1967.

103. Only part of the book (from letter *bet* to letter *tet*) has been published.

104. A second edition of *Sefer Yuḥasin ha-Shalem,* with an Introduction and index by A.H. Freimann, was published in Frankfurt in 1925. That edition was reprinted in 1963

d. *Korei ha-Dorot* [Chronicles] by David Conforte, seventeenth century; ed. Kassel, Berlin, 1846, and facsimile eds.
e. *Seder ha-Dorot* [The Order of the Generations] by Jehiel Heilprin, Warsaw, 1876, and other editions.
f. *Shem ha-Gedolim, Va'ad la-Ḥakhamim* by Ḥayyim Joseph David Azulai (Ḥida), eighteenth century. The book is divided into two parts: *Ma'arekhet Gedolim* [Persons], an alphabetical biographical listing of halakhic authorities; and *Ma'arekhet Sefarim* [Books], an alphabetical listing of halakhic books.[105]
g. *Toledot* [Biographies] by Solomon Judah Loeb Rapaport (Shir), published in *Bikkurei ha-Ittim,* from 1829 on; reprinted in two volumes, Warsaw, 1913.[106]
h. *Toledot Tannaim va-Amoraim* [Biographies of *Tannaim* and *Amoraim*] by A. H. Hyman, London, 1910 (three volumes); reprinted, Jerusalem, 1964.
i. *Ḥakhmei ha-Talmud* [The Sages of the Talmud] by Joseph Omansky (Babylonian Talmud, Jerusalem, 1949; Jerusalem Talmud, Jerusalem, 1952).

2. BIOGRAPHIES ACCORDING TO GEOGRAPHICAL AREAS

Many works containing biographies of halakhic authorities are organized according to geographical areas. The following is a partial listing:

a. *Toledot Gedolei Yisra'el u-Ge'onei Italyah* [Biographies of the Leading Jewish Authorities and Scholars of Italy] by Mordecai Samuel Gerondi, Trieste, 1853; facsimile ed., Jerusalem, 1965.
b. *Anshei Shem, Toledot Rabbanei Lvov* [Men of Renown: Biographies of Lemberg's Rabbis] by Solomon Buber, Cracow, 1895; facsimile ed., Jerusalem, 1968.[107]

(with supplementary material), together with other shorter books such as *Seder Tannaim va-Amoraim* and *Iggeret Rav Sherira Gaon.*

105. A new, well-organized edition of *Shem ha-Gedolim,* with some notes, was published by Isaac Benjacob (the author of *Ozar ha-Sefarim, see infra* p. 1561) in Vilna, 1852. Supplements have been published to *Shem ha-Gedolim: Shem ha-Gedolim he-Ḥadash* by Aaron Walden, Warsaw, 1865, and *Shem ha-Gedolim ha-Shalem* by Menahem Mendel Krengel (reprinted with additions, New York, 1958).

106. *Toledot* contains detailed biographies of the *geonim* and the leading *rishonim* such as Eleazar ha-Kallir, Saadiah Gaon, Hai Gaon, Nathan b. Jehiel, Rabbenu Hananel, Rabbenu Nissim, and Ḥefeẓ b. Yaẓli'aḥ. A facsimile edition has recently been published.

107. Biographies of the rabbis of Lvov (Lemberg) are also contained in *Kelilat Yofi* by Ḥayyim Nathan Dembitzer. Biographies of halakhic authorities who served in particular cities also appear in more general historical literature. *See, e.g.,* with regard to Vilna: *Ir Vilna, Zikhronot Adat Yisra'el ve-Toledot Ḥayyei Gedolehah* [Vilna, A History of the Jewish Community and Biographies of Its Leading Halakhic Authorities] by Hillel Noah Steinschneider,

c. *Shalshelet Rabbanei Salonik* [The Rabbis of Salonika] and *Shalshelet ha-Rabbanim me-Ir Sofiyah* [The Rabbis of Sofia] by David Pipano, appended to *Ḥagor ha-Efod*, Sofia, 1925.
d. *Rabbanei Frankfurt* [The Rabbis of Frankfurt] by Mordecai ha-Levi Horowitz, completed by Joseph Unna. The book was originally written in German and translated into Hebrew by Joshua Amir, Jerusalem, 1972.
e. *Sefer Ḥakhmei Ahu* [The Book of the Halakhic Authorities of "Ahu" (***A***ltona, ***H***amburg, and ***W***andsbeck)] by Yeḥezkel Dukas, Hamburg, 1908.
f. *Toledot Ḥakhmei Yerushalayim* [Biographies of the Halakhic Authorities of Jerusalem] by Aryeh Leib Frumkin, Jerusalem, 1928–1930; facsimile ed., Jerusalem, 1969.
g. *Malkhei Rabbanan* [Biographies of the Rabbis of Morocco] by Joseph Ben Na'im, Jerusalem, 1931.
h. *Fas ve-Ḥakhameha* [Fez and Its Halakhic Authorities] by David Ovadiah, Jerusalem, 1979.
i. *Toledot ha-Rabbanim le-Mishpaḥat Yisra'el mi-Rodos* [Biographies of the Rabbis of the Israel Family in Rhodes] by Simon Marcus, Jerusalem, 1935.
j. *Gedolei Saloniki le-Dorotam* [The Rabbis of Salonika Through the Ages] by I. S. Immanuel, Tel Aviv, 1936.
k. *Divrei Yemei Yisra'el be-Togarma* [History of the Jews in Turkey], I (2nd ed. 1930); *Korot ha-Yehudim be-Turkiyah u-ve-Arẓot ha-Kedem* [History of the Jews in Turkey and the Eastern Countries], II–VI (1936–1945), by Solomon Abraham Rosanes. This is a historical work, but a large part is devoted to biographies of halakhic authorities.
l. *Tuv Miẓrayim* [The Best of Egypt] by Raphael Aharon Ben Shimon, Jerusalem, 1908.
m. *Ḥakhmei Yisra'el be-Djerba u-ve-Tunis* [Halakhic Authorities in Djerba and Tunis] by Boaz Hadad, Jerusalem, 1982.
n. *Me'orei Galiẓiah, Enẓiklopedyah le-Ḥakhmei Galiẓiah* [The Lights of Galicia, Encyclopedia of the Scholars of Galicia] by Meir Wunder. Four volumes have been published, Jerusalem, 1978, 1982, 1986, and 1990.
o. *Atlas Eẓ Ḥayyim* by Raphael Halpern, Hekdesh Ru'aḥ Ya'akov, Tel Aviv, 1978–1985, fourteen volumes.

3. BIOGRAPHIES OF INDIVIDUAL AUTHORITIES

Another type of biographical literature consists of books describing the character, work, and teachings of a particular halakhic authority. There are

Vilna, 1900; *Kiryah Ne'emanah* [The Faithful City], a history of the Jewish community of Vilna, with biographies of its scholars, sages, authors, and philanthropists, by Samuel Joseph Finn, Vilna, 1915; and many more.

many such biographies from the Talmudic period up to our own times. These biographies are important for an accurate understanding of the contribution of their subjects to the development of Jewish law.

4. ENCYCLOPEDIAS WITH BIOGRAPHICAL ARTICLES

Some encyclopedias contain biographies of halakhic authorities or include articles on leading halakhic authorities. Examples include:

a. *Enẓiklopedyah le-Ḥakhmei ha-Talmud ve-ha-Geonim* [Encyclopedia of the Talmudic Sages and the *Geonim*], ed. M. Margaliot, two volumes (reprinted frequently).[108]
b. *Enẓiklopedyah le-Toledot Gedolei Yisra'el (mi-Sof Tekufat ha-Geonim ad ha-Me'ah ha-Tesha-Esreh)* [Biographical Encyclopedia of the Leading Halakhic Authorities (from the Geonic Period to the Nineteenth Century)], ed. M. Margaliot, four volumes (reprinted frequently).
c. *Ha-Enẓiklopedyah ha-Ivrit* [Hebrew Encyclopedia], Jerusalem–Tel Aviv, 1949–1981, thirty-two volumes. An index volume to the entire encyclopedia was published in 1985.[109]
d. *The Jewish Encyclopedia* (English), New York–London, 1901–1906, twelve volumes (also in facsimile ed., undated, Ktav, New York).
e. *Encyclopaedia Judaica* (German), only to the letter "L," Berlin, 1927–1936, ten volumes.
f. *Encyclopaedia Judaica* (English), Jerusalem, 1971, sixteen volumes. A general index is contained in Volume I.

A considerable amount of biographical information can also be found in bibliographical works that describe and identify halakhic books;[110] these are discussed in the following section.

D. Bibliographies

Sometimes it is difficult to identify the particular authors or the halakhic works intended to be described by source references. In addition, it is important to establish the correct text of a halakhic work, particularly when

108. This encyclopedia does not provide a bibliography for each article, and other sources should therefore be consulted.

109. This encyclopedia has two supplementary volumes: the first, which appeared in 1967, covers the first sixteen volumes, and the second, published in 1983, covers all thirty-two volumes.

110. Some books combine biographies of halakhic authorities with bibliographies of their works. The outstanding example of this dual function is *Shem ha-Gedolim* by Ḥida, which is divided into two parts: (1) Persons and (2) Books.

its meaning is not clear or when there is reason to believe that the text has been changed because of external or internal censorship.[111] It is therefore necessary to ascertain whether there were different editions or manuscripts of a work, and if so, to determine what they contain and when they appeared. For this purpose, there is a bibliographical literature that lists the books alphabetically and identifies and describes them and their various editions. Some bibliographies cover the entire field of halakhic literature, while others deal with the literature of a specific historical period (such as post-Talmudic halakhic books, or books written only until the *Shulḥan Arukh*). An additional function of bibliographical literature is to list in one place all the books belonging to a specific type of halakhic literature (such as the responsa literature or the commentaries) or all the books that have been written on a particular subject.

1. GENERAL BIBLIOGRAPHIES

The following are some of the more important general bibliographical works:

a. *Shem ha-Gedolim, Va'ad la-Ḥakhamim* by Ḥayyim Joseph David Azulai (Ḥida), *Ma'arekhet Sefarim* [Books].[112] As previously noted in this chapter under the section "Biographies of Halakhic Authorities," various supplements have been added to the work.
b. *Or ha-Ḥayyim* by Ḥayyim Michael, Hamburg, 1891; 2nd revised ed., Mosad ha-Rav Kook, Jerusalem, 1965.
c. *Oẓar ha-Sefarim* [A Treasury of Books] by Isaac Benjacob of Vilna, 1877–1880. Part II, by Menahem Mendel Zlotkin, containing notes and supplements to Benjacob's work, was published in Jerusalem, 1965.
d. *Toledot ha-Posekim* [History of the *Posekim*] by Simon Moses Hannes, Warsaw, 1911.
e. *Bet Eked Sefarim,* a bibliographical lexicon by Ḥayyim Dov Friedberg, assisted by Baruch Friedberg; 2nd enlarged and revised ed., Tel Aviv, 1951, four volumes;[113] facsimile ed., 1970.
f. *Sarei ha-Elef* by Menahem M. Kasher and Jacob Dov Mandelbaum, New York, 1959; revised ed., Jerusalem, 1979, two volumes. This book is

111. *See supra* pp. 1520–1521.

112. An earlier work of the same type is *Siftei Yeshenim* by Shabbetai Meshorer Bass, of Prague (published, Amsterdam, 1680). That work, however, is no longer used, and whatever it contains is found in subsequent bibliographies. It contains inaccuracies that were frequently copied in later works. *See, e.g., supra* p. 1411 n. 140.

113. There are two indexes at the end of volume 4: an index of book titles arranged according to subject matter and an index of authors. These two indexes facilitate the use of the work.

organized according to subject areas (Bible, Bible translations, midrashic literature, commentaries, responsa, codes, etc.). The books in each area are listed alphabetically.

2. BIBLIOGRAPHIES ACCORDING TO TYPE OF HALAKHIC LITERATURE

Of the bibliographies that list books by the type of halakhic literature to which the books belong, the following two are noteworthy:

a. *Kunteres ha-Teshuvot* by Boaz Cohen, Budapest, 1930 (facsimile ed., Jerusalem, 1970). This book is a substantial bibliography of the responsa literature, but it is not exhaustive.[114] It is divided into sections: geonic responsa; post-geonic responsa; compilations of responsa listed alphabetically by name; other works that contain or quote responsa; and books and articles treating the responsa literature. It also contains an index of the respondents and the places where the books were printed.
b. *Ozar ha-Be'urim ve-ha-Perushim* [A Treasury of Explications and Commentaries] by Pinḥas Jacob ha-Kohen, London, 1952. This book lists the commentaries and novellae composed on the various categories of literary sources of Jewish law. It is unique in that it is arranged according to the literary works on which the commentaries and novellae were written: the Mishnah; the *Tosefta;* the Babylonian Talmud (this category is subdivided into novellae and commentaries covering all the tractates of the Talmud, and those on only particular tractates); the Jerusalem Talmud; etc. The books in each category are listed by title in alphabetical order. The work also lists, in the manner described, commentaries and novellae on Maimonides' *Mishneh Torah,* the *Turim,* and the *Shulḥan Arukh,* as well as guidebooks, indexes, and books of source references to the Talmud, etc.[115]

3. BIBLIOGRAPHIES OF SCHOLARLY LITERATURE ON *MISHPAT IVRI*

The following is a list of bibliographical references to scholarly literature on *mishpat ivri:*

a. *Ein Mishpat* by S. Eisenstadt, Jerusalem, 1931. *Ein Mishpat* is a very comprehensive bibliography of scholarly literature in all areas of *mishpat ivri.*

114. *See supra* p. 1524. A considerable number of responsa published after 1930 are included in the listing of Solomon Freehof; *see supra* p. 1534 n. 238.

115. The lists of the commentaries and novellae of the *rishonim* that had been compiled earlier by Aaron Jellinek and Aron Freimann are included in *Ozar ha-Be'urim ve-ha-Perushim; see* the author's Introduction.

It is organized on the basis of generally accepted modern legal categories, and it is both useful and easy to use.

b. *Kiryat Sefer.* This publication is the bibliographical quarterly of the National and University Library in Jerusalem. The first issue was published in 1924–1925, and as of 1992, sixty-three volumes had appeared. *Kiryat Sefer* lists all the newspapers, books, and articles published in the State of Israel and throughout the world on Hebrew literature and Judaic studies. Articles appearing in journals are listed by title. Each category is subdivided by subject: Biblical studies, Talmud, Midrash, Rabbinic literature, Religion, Jewish philosophy, Contemporary Jewry, The Land of Israel, History of Zionism, and many more. It is difficult to use *Kiryat Sefer* to keep abreast of published materials relevant to *mishpat ivri,* since such materials are generally scattered throughout various other subject areas such as Biblical studies, Talmud, midrash, rabbinic literature, and the Land of Israel.

c. *Reshimat Ma'amarim be-Madda'ei ha-Yahadut* [Bibliography of Articles in Judaic Studies] by Issachar Joel. This publication first appeared in 1969 and listed the various articles on Judaic studies that had been published in 1966 in anthologies and journals in Hebrew and other languages. The listing is by subject, and articles on *mishpat ivri* are listed under Bible, *Halakhah,* and The Land of Israel. Beginning with the issue of 1970, which listed all the relevant articles that had appeared in 1967, a separate heading of *Mishpat Ivri* was added. This heading is subdivided into: General, Public law, Civil law, Family law and Inheritance, Criminal law, Procedure and Evidence, and Jewish law in the State of Israel. This bibliography is published with some regularity, and as of 1992, thirty issues had appeared.

d. *Me'ir Einayim* by Meir Wunder. *Me'ir Einayim* is an index of selected articles in the areas of Torah and religion, Jewish law, and contemporary Jewish problems. Three issues were published in Jerusalem, 1970–1972, covering, respectively, 1967, 1968, and 1969. Beginning with the second issue, the bibliography was arranged according to subjects, and there is a separate listing for matters pertaining to *mishpat ivri* that are treated in the rulings of the rabbinical and general courts of Israel. Two volumes appeared in 1973–1979 under the title *Me'ir Ẓiyyon;* and beginning in 1980, the bibliography by Meir Wunder has been published in the periodical *Teḥumin* starting with Volume III.

e. *Oẓar ha-Mishpat* [A Treasury of Law], a bibliographical index of *mishpat ivri* by N. Rakover, Jerusalem, 1975. This index lists Hebrew books, monographs, articles and entries in journals, anthologies, *Festschriften,* memorial volumes, and encyclopedias in all areas of *mishpat ivri* and also to some extent in associated fields. The material is divided into sections and subsections according to topic, and each section is arranged alphabetically according to the author's name. The bibliography is comprehensive, helpful, and easy to use. A second volume, covering the years 1975–1990, appeared in 1990.

f. A bibliography of Jewish law in English was published in the first two volumes of *Shenaton le-Mishpat Ivri u-le-Dinei Mishpaḥah be-Yisra'el* [Annual of Jewish Law and Israeli Family Law], eds. Z. Falk and A. Kirschenbaum, 1970 and 1971 (English section).

g. "A Bibliographic Guide to Mishpat Ivri: Books and Articles in English" by R. F. Warburg appeared in the first volume of the *National Jewish Law Review,* published by the National Jewish Law Students Network, U.S.A., in 1986, pp. 61–135.

h. Each issue of *The Jewish Law Annual,* ed. B. S. Jackson, contains a bibliography in English under the title, "Survey of Recent Literature." Up to 1990, nine volumes have been published.

i. *Jewish Law: Bibliography of Sources and Scholarship in English* by Phyllis H. Weisbard and David Schonberg, Fred B. Rothman & Co., 1989, is topically organized and contains various appendixes and a subject and author index.

j. N. Rakover, *The Multi-Language Bibliography of Jewish Law,* Jerusalem, 1990, contains almost 15,000 entries, listing books, monographs, journals, *Festschriften,* encyclopedias, and unpublished doctoral dissertations, written in languages other than Hebrew.

E. Lexicons

Many halakhic authorities and scholars have composed works explaining Talmudic terms and expressions. The first of such works appeared in the geonic period soon after the completion of the Talmud, when it became necessary to explain difficult terms found in the Babylonian Talmud for the benefit of those who lived outside Babylonia and did not speak Aramaic as their everyday language.[116] As time passed, the difficulty of understanding Talmudic terminology increased, and a lexicographical literature developed, of which the following are the major examples:

1. *He-Arukh* by Nathan b. Jehiel (1035–ca. 1110), the head of the *yeshivah* in Rome, is an alphabetical lexicon of words and expressions found mainly in the Babylonian Talmud and, to a lesser extent, in the Jerusalem Talmud, the *Tosefta,* and the halakhic and aggadic *midrashim.*[117]

116. *See supra* pp. 1113–1114.

117. For a discussion of the composition, methodology, and sources of the *Arukh, see* Alexander Kohut's Introduction to *Arukh ha-Shalem* at the beginning of Volume I. Solomon

Each entry explains a term, translates it into other languages (including Greek, Latin, Arabic, and Persian), and discusses the subject matter to which the term pertains. The main sources of the work were the commentaries on the Talmud by Rabbenu Hananel and Rabbenu Gershom, as well as by *geonim*, particularly Hai Gaon. Some scholars believe that another source was the *Arukh* of Ẓemaḥ b. Paltoi (Gaon of Pumbedita ca. 872–ca. 890), which may have even served as a model. Ẓemaḥ b. Paltoi Gaon's book has not survived. From a certain perspective, the *Arukh* can be classified as a commentary on the Talmud and, indeed, many *rishonim* refer to it in their commentaries and novellae.

Beginning in the twelfth century, many supplements, corrections, and comments were written on the *Arukh*. Among them are: *Musaf he-Arukh* [Additions to the *Arukh*] by Benjamin Musafia (1606–1675), Hamburg–Amsterdam, who added various new entries and clarified those insufficiently explained in the original, and *Hafla'ah she-ba-Arakhin* (two volumes) by Isaiah Berlin (also known as Isaiah Pick, 1725–1799, Berlin–Breslau), which contains explanations, glosses, and additions to the *Arukh*.

Especially noteworthy is the *Arukh ha-Shalem* [The Complete *Arukh*] by Alexander Kohut (1842–1894, Hungary and New York). This book is a scientific edition of the *Arukh* based on various manuscripts. Kohut supplemented and corrected existing entries, and added translations into German, new entries, discussion of the sources, and various notes. The results of modern philological research and new sources that Nathan b. Jehiel was discovered to have used were added in *Tosafot he-Arukh ha-Shalem* [Additions to *Arukh ha-Shalem*] by S. Krauss *et al.*, Vienna, 1937. *Arukh ha-Shalem* is in eight volumes, to which *Tosafot he-Arukh ha-Shalem* was added as the ninth.[118]

The *Arukh*, with its various supplements, remains a basic work used for understanding Talmudic terminology.

2. *Chaldäisches Wörterbuch Über die Targumim* [Chaldean Dictionary of the *Targumim*] by Jacob Levy, two volumes, Leipzig, 1867. This dictionary translates the terms of the *Targumim* into German and is very valuable for an understanding of the terminology of the Jerusalem Talmud and the Aramaic translations of the Bible.
3. *Wörterbuch Über die Talmudim und Midraschim* [Dictionary of the Talmuds and *Midrashim*] by Jacob Levy, four volumes, 2nd revised and expanded

---

Judah Rapoport (Shir) wrote a comprehensive monograph on Nathan b. Jehiel: *Toledot Rabbenu Natan Ish Romi* [The Life of Rabbenu Nathan of Rome], published in *Toledot*, I, first article, until p. 127 (*see supra* p. 1558).

118. A number of valuable indexes are at the end of Volume 8.

ed. published by E. Goldschmidt, Berlin–Vienna, 1924. This dictionary also translates Talmudic and midrashic terms into German, and contributes greatly to the understanding of Talmudic terminology.

4. *Dictionary of Talmud Babli, Yerushalmi, Midrashic Literature and Targumim* by Marcus Jastrow, two volumes, Philadelphia, 1903; New York, 1950. This English dictionary provides useful explanations of Talmudic terms.
5. *Dictionary of Jewish-Palestinian Aramaic* by M. Sokoloff, Bar-Ilan University Press, 1990.
6. *Dictionary of Greek and Latin Legal Terms in Rabbinic Literature* by D. Sperber, Bar-Ilan University Press, 1984.

The lexicographical works listed above are of a scholarly nature.[119] Useful dictionaries of a more popular nature have also been written. An example is *Millon Shimushi la-Talmud, la-Midrash ve-la-Targum* [Practical Dictionary of the Talmud, Midrash, and Targum] by Baruch Krupnik, two volumes, London, 1927; reprinted, Tel Aviv, 1970.[120]

F. Books Explaining Abbreviations

Lexicographical literature is connected with another type of reference book, which explains abbreviations such as *notarikon* (a type of shorthand in which words are shortened or only one letter of a word is used) and similar devices. Abbreviations are very widely used in halakhic literature and in Jewish legal documents such as the *ketubbah* and wills. Care must be exercised in using these reference works on abbreviations, since an abbreviation can have more than one meaning, depending on the context.[121] Recent works alphabetically list a great number of abbreviations and explain their meanings. The following are two such works:

1. *Sefer Notarikon, Simanim ve-Khinuyim* [The Book of *Notarikon*, Symbols, and Appellations] by Meir Heilprin, Vilna, 1912; 2nd ed. by M. Rabinowitz, Jerusalem, 1930.

119. Some of the works described *supra* as encyclopedias (*e.g.*, Bacher's *Erkhei Midrash*) are very similar to the lexicons. Some of the guidebooks also contain a great deal of lexicographical material.

120. Many of the literary sources of Jewish law have been translated into other languages, *e.g.*, the Mishnah (*see supra* p. 1110 n. 29), the halakhic *midrashim* (*see supra* p. 1111 n. 36), and the Babylonian Talmud (*see supra* p. 1129 n. 105). Parts of Maimonides' *Mishneh Torah* have also been translated into English by J.J. Rabinowitz, A.M. Hershman, I. Klein, and others, under the title *The Code of Maimonides*, in the Yale Judaica Series of the Yale University Press.

121. For a discussion of abbreviations, *notarikon*, and similar devices, and of how to decipher and use them, as well as a discussion of the relevant literature, *see* Meir Heilprin's extensive Introduction to *Sefer Notarikon* (described *infra*), pp. V–XLIX.

2. *Ozar Roshei Teivot be-Lashon u-ve-Sifrut mi-Mei Kedem ad Yameinu* [A Treasury of Linguistic and Literary Abbreviations from Ancient Times until the Present] by Samuel Ashkenazi and Dov Yarden, Jerusalem, 1965. A supplement by Samuel Ashkenazi appeared in 1969, containing additional explanations of *notarikon* that had not been included in the original edition.

G. Textual Variants

The correct understanding of a Talmudic discussion and the different opinions there expressed often depends on a comparison of the variant readings of the text, which helps to ensure that the legal conclusion reached is the correct one. The following are reference works for textual variants:

1. *Dikdukei Soferim* by Raphael Nathan Nata Rabbinovicz. This work compares the printed text of the Babylonian Talmud with the text of ms. Munich. The notes contain readings from other manuscripts, as well as variant readings of Talmudic texts as they appear in books by many *rishonim*. The work is prefaced by a valuable survey of the history of the printing of the Talmud.[122] *Dikdukei Soferim* consists of sixteen volumes (1868–1897) and covers the tractates in the Orders of *Zera'im, Mo'ed, Nezikin,* and part of *Kodashim* (Tractates *Zevaḥim, Menaḥot,* and *Ḥullin*).[123] In the Order of *Nashim,* which Rabbinovicz did not cover, *Dikdukei Soferim* has been published on three tractates: *Nedarim* and *Nazir* by Mordecai Heimann (Chicago, 1943) and *Gittin* by Meir Simḥah ha-Kohen Feldblum (New York, 1966). *Dikdukei Soferim* is indispensable for researching legal-halakhic questions.
2. *Dikdukei Soferim ha-Shalem* [The Complete *Dikdukei Soferim*] is being published by Mekhon ha-Talmud ha-Yisra'eli ha-Shalem (Yad ha-Rav Herzog), Jerusalem, in its edition of the Babylonian Talmud. To date, there have appeared: Tractate *Yevamot,* three volumes, 1983–1989; Tractate *Ketubbot,* two volumes, 1972–1977; Tractate *Sotah,* two volumes, 1977–1979; Tractate *Nedarim,* one volume, 1985.[124]

122. This Preface has been published separately, with supplements, by A.M. Haberman, Jerusalem, 1952. Noteworthy among Haberman's additions is a list of the printings of the Jerusalem Talmud (*id.* at 203ff.).

123. *Dikdukei Soferim* on Tractate *Ḥullin* was completed and published by Heinrich Ehrentreu, after Rabbinovicz's death.

124. Currently, as more and more photocopy reproductions of manuscripts and early editions are becoming available, the researcher is able more easily to examine and compare variant readings. Such facsimile editions have been frequently noted throughout this present work.

H. Concordances

Concordances of various works of Talmudic literature[125] are now being written. These concordances were initiated by Chayim Yehoshua Kasovsky and are being carried forward by his sons, Benjamin and Moses. The concordances are extremely valuable in that they make possible a full examination of particular terms or subjects, wherever they appear throughout Talmudic literature. As of the present time, the following concordances have been published:

1. *Ozar Leshon ha-Mishnah,* on the Mishnah, two volumes, Jerusalem, 1927; reprinted, Jerusalem, 1957.
2. *Ozar Leshon ha-Tosefta,* on the *Tosefta,* six volumes, Jerusalem, 1933–1961.
3. *Ozar ha-Targum,* on the Aramaic translation of the Bible by Onkelos, two volumes, Jerusalem, 1933–1940.
4. *Ozar Leshon ha-Talmud,* on the Babylonian Talmud, forty-one volumes, Jerusalem, 1954–1982. This was supplemented by *Ozar ha-Shemot le-Talmud ha-Bavli,* on the names in the Babylonian Talmud, five volumes, Jerusalem, 1976–1983.
5. *Ozar Leshon Talmud Yerushalmi,* on the Jerusalem Talmud. As of 1992, four volumes had been published, up to the letter *kaf* (Jerusalem, commencing 1980), with the supplement *Ozar ha-Shemot,* Jerusalem, 1985.
6. *Ozar Leshon ha-Tannaim,* on *Mekhilta de-R. Ishmael,* four volumes, Jerusalem, 1965–1966.
7. *Ozar Leshon ha-Tannaim,* on *Sifra–Torat Kohanim,* four volumes, Jerusalem, 1967–1969.
8. *Ozar Leshon ha-Tannaim,* on *Sifrei* (to Numbers and Deuteronomy), five volumes, Jerusalem, 1971–1975.

I. Source References, Sayings, and Aphorisms

Various other reference works contain source references for all the Biblical verses quoted in Talmudic literature, and also alphabetical listings of sayings and aphorisms of the Sages throughout the halakhic and aggadic parts of the Talmudic literature. Among these works are the following:

1. *Torah ha-Ketuvah ve-ha-Mesurah* [The Written and Transmitted Torah] by Aaron Hyman, 1st ed., 1936; 2nd revised and enlarged ed. by the author's son, Dov Hyman, Tel Aviv, 1979. A supplementary volume by Dov Hyman was published in Jerusalem in 1985. The three parts of this

125. On the Bible, there is, in addition to others, the well-known concordance by Solomon Mandelkern.

work cover the Pentateuch, the Prophets, and the Hagiographa, respectively. Next to each verse is a listing of all the places in Talmudic literature, and, to some extent, in the works of the *rishonim* in the post-Talmudic period, where the verse is cited and discussed.

2. *Ozar Divrei Ḥakhamim u-Fitgameihem* [A Treasury of the Sayings and Aphorisms of the Sages] by Aaron Hyman, 1934. This work lists, in alphabetical order, approximately 30,000 sayings and aphorisms that are scattered throughout Talmudic literature.
3. *Oẓar Imrei Avot* [A Treasury of the Sayings of the Sages] by Ẓevi Larinman, five volumes, 1959–1969. This work lists in alphabetical order some 70,000 halakhic and aggadic sayings and aphorisms from the Talmud, *midrashim, Sefer Ḥasidim,* and *Ḥovot ha-Levavot,* among others. Brief explanatory notes taken from the commentaries of the *rishonim* are sometimes included.
4. *Mikhlol ha-Ma'amarim ve-ha-Pitgamim* [An Anthology of Sayings and Aphorisms] by Moses Savar, edited by Abraham Darom, three volumes, Jerusalem, 1961–1962. This work contains an alphabetical listing of approximately 100,000 sayings. In addition to the sources from which Hyman took his material, Savar's work covers the *Zohar,* various books on ethics, medieval Hebrew poetry, and several other sources. His work also has more halakhic maxims than Hyman's.
5. *Oẓar Ma'amarei Halakhah* [A Treasury of Halakhic Maxims] by Israel Isaac Ḥasida, two volumes, Jerusalem, 1960. This book is an alphabetical listing of approximately 35,000 halakhic maxims taken from the two Talmuds, the *midrashim,* and the *Zohar.* It contains a very useful, comprehensive, and detailed index, arranged according to topics and subtopics.
6. *Oẓar ha-Aggadah* [A Treasury of the Aggadah] by Moses David Gross, three volumes, Jerusalem, 1961. This work contains aggadic sayings from the Mishnah, the *Tosefta,* the Talmuds, the *midrashim,* and the *Zohar,* arranged according to an alphabetical listing of the subject matter.

J. Scholarly Research in *Mishpat Ivri*

The various types of works described up to this point in this chapter are reference works intended to facilitate research in any subject relevant to Jewish law.[126] They provide access to the primary literary sources of the law, which may then be directly and thoroughly probed.

126. The present work has also referred to other reference works such as indexes to the Talmud and to various codes. *See, e.g., supra* p. 1129 n. 105; p. 1172 n. 84; p. 1250 n. 63; p. 1413 n. 143.

Since the inception of research into *mishpat ivri,* which progressively increased in the wake of the movement at the beginning of the twentieth century for the reestablishment of Jewish national independence, a large number of valuable books and articles have been written in all areas of *mishpat ivri.*

K. Journals and Periodicals on *Mishpat Ivri*

Research into *mishpat ivri* is published in Hebrew, English, and other languages not only in legal periodicals but also in periodicals devoted to Judaic studies generally. The leading periodicals dealing exclusively with *mishpat ivri* in all its aspects are the following:

1. *Shenaton ha-Mishpat ha-Ivri* [Jewish Law Annual], an annual of the Institute for the Research in Jewish Law of the Hebrew University of Jerusalem. The first volume appeared in 1974, and through 1992 seventeen volumes were published. The first ten were edited by Menachem Elon; others were under the editorship of Alfredo Mordechai Rabello, Shmuel Shilo, and Eliav Shochetman. An index to the first ten volumes (Jerusalem, 1988) is a helpful guide to the material covered in those volumes. The index includes a listing of the articles, the sources cited, and the statutes and cases (both Israeli and foreign) discussed.

   Some of the volumes contain bibliographies of scholars in the field of *mishpat ivri,* and a number of volumes have been dedicated to major contributors to the field: Justice Haim Cohn (Volumes 6–7, 1979–1980), Professor Asher Gulak (Volumes 9–10, 1982–1983), and Justice Menachem Elon (Volume 13, 1987).

   A number of volumes deal with a specific topic, *e.g.,* Volumes 9–10 (Agency), Volumes 11–12 (Geonic Literature), Volume 13 (Obligations), Volumes 14–15 (Maimonides). The articles on the Foundations of Law Act, 1980 (which is discussed in chapters 44 and 45 of the present work) have been particularly useful; they discuss various aspects and implications of the statute and how to apply it in the Israeli legal system (Volume 13). The articles are in Hebrew, but there is a table of contents in English as well as in Hebrew.
2. *Dine Israel,* an annual of the Faculty of Law of Tel Aviv University. From 1970–1992, fifteen volumes were published under the editorship of Aaron Kirschenbaum, Ze'ev Falk, and others. Each year, a section is devoted to critical reviews of books and articles dealing with *mishpat ivri.* Another section reviews the decisions of the Israeli courts that are based on Jewish law or deal with it for comparative purposes. From time to time, there are listings of research projects of various academic institu-

tions. A number of the volumes deal with a specific topic, *e.g.*, Volumes 10–11 (the Israeli rabbinical courts and the status of Jewish marriage and divorce in various countries), and Volume 12 (*Halakhah* and Economics). The articles are generally in Hebrew, with a few in English; a table of contents in English lists all the articles, including those in Hebrew.

3. *The Jewish Law Annual,* published in English by the Institute of Jewish Law of the Boston University School of Law. From 1978–1992, ten volumes were published under the editorship of B.S. Jackson. Most of the volumes include a section dealing with a specific topic of *mishpat ivri.* Among the topics have been: Maimonides' *Mishneh Torah* (Volume 1); Codification and Restatement (Volume 2); Unjust Enrichment (Volume 3); The Wife's Right to Divorce (Volume 4); Jewish Law in Israel (Volume 5); The Philosophy of Jewish Law (Volumes 6–7); Criminal Law, Husband and Wife (Volume 9); Parent and Child (Volume 10).

   In addition to articles, the periodical includes a listing of studies in Jewish law in various languages, as well as a summary of judicial decisions in Israel and elsewhere relating to *mishpat ivri.* In 1980, two supplementary volumes were published, one on Modern Research in Jewish Law, and the second on Jewish Law in Legal History and the Modern World.

4. *National Jewish Law Review,* From 1986–1992, five volumes were published by the U.S. National Jewish Law Students Network. The first volume contains a valuable bibliography of books and articles in English on *mishpat ivri.* The articles deal with the entire range of *mishpat ivri* and include historical, analytical, comparative, and philosophical discussions of personalities, doctrines, and movements in Jewish law.

5. *Ha-Mishpat Ha-Ivri.* This was the earliest periodical exclusively devoted to *mishpat ivri,* and although it was published only for a relatively short time, it deserves mention for the important historical role it played in the scholarly research of *mishpat ivri.* The first volume was published in 1918, in Moscow, Russia. Five additional volumes appeared in the Land of Israel from 1926 to 1937 under the aegis of the Ha-Mishpat Ha-Ivri (Jewish Law) Society. The editors were Paltiel Dikstein (Dykan) and Mordechai Eliash.

   These volumes, written in Hebrew, mark the beginnings of the movement to revitalize Jewish law in the renascent Jewish community in Palestine under the British Mandate. The Introduction to the first issue was addressed to "the Jewish leaders, writers, and scholars in the Land [of Israel] and the diaspora" and called on the Jewish community of the Land of Israel to participate in the creative renewal of Jewish law. The motto of the periodical, "Zion shall be redeemed with justice" (Isaiah 1:27), also reflects the aspiration of the members of the Ha-Mishpat Ha-Ivri Society to establish an independent Jewish state founded upon Jewish law.

The volumes contain much valuable material for the scientific study of Jewish law, including summaries of dozens of lectures sponsored by the Ha-Mishpat Ha-Ivri Society, reviews of literature bearing on *mishpat ivri,* and summaries of decisions rendered by Mishpat Ha-Shalom Ha-Ivri (the Jewish Court of Arbitration), a judicial system that functioned for a period of time under the British Mandate. (A detailed discussion of the Ha-Mishpat Ha-Ivri Society and Mishpat Ha-Shalom Ha-Ivri is contained in chapter 41 of the present work.) At the end of the third volume (1928), there is an index to the first three volumes.

Chapter 3 of the present work has extensively discussed the product and the methodology of the research into *mishpat ivri* and has outlined a suggested approach for the future.[127] The results of this research are of great value to scholars and jurists alike; and, indeed, careful review of that scholarly literature is a prerequisite for reaching sound conclusions on issues of *mishpat ivri.*

Earlier Hebrew editions of the present work concluded at this point with the following statement:

> The reader of this work—together with its author—has completed a long journey, examining the history, the fundamental principles, and the legal and literary sources of Jewish law as all of these have manifested themselves throughout a long and momentous course, both in the sovereign Jewish state and in the diaspora.
>
> We have attempted to review this noble record of achievement and creativity in the prayerful hope that it will lead to the study of Jewish law through examination of its own sources. Would that such study help enable the present generation of the Jewish people, which has seen the restoration of sovereignty in its homeland, to accomplish the great and long-cherished objective of incorporating Jewish law into the legal system of the State of Israel, and making Jewish law operative there once again.

The time is now ripe, with the preparation of the present edition of this work, to ascertain whether this hope has been realized, and if so, how and to what extent. To this end, Volume IV, consisting of five new chapters, discusses the subject of Jewish law in the State of Israel.

127. *See supra* pp. 80–91.

GLOSSARY

aggadah ("telling") the non-halakhic, non-normative portion of the *Torah she-be-al peh* consisting of historical, philosophical, allegorical, and ethical rabbinic teachings

aginut the state of being an *agunah*

agoria, ***pl.*** **agoriot** non-Jewish court

agunah ("anchored" or "bound") a woman unable to remarry because she is "bound," *e.g.,* to a husband who has disappeared and cannot be legally proved dead or who has abandoned her or who refuses to divorce her

aḥarei rabbim le-hattot "follow the majority" of a court or of legislative representatives

aḥaronim ("later ones") later halakhic authorities, generally referring to those from the sixteenth century onward. *See also rishonim*

am ha'areẓ ("people of the land") (1) national council; (2) hoi polloi; (3) ignorant, unlearned person; (4) a person not punctilious in observance, opposite of *ḥaver* and *ḥasid;* (5) the assembled public

amora, ***pl.*** **amoraim** (1) rabbis of the Talmudic period (220 C.E. to end of the fifth century C.E.); (2) *meturgeman,* which *see*

Anshei Keneset ha-Gedolah ("Men of the Great Assembly") Ezra, Nehemiah, and those who entered with them into the covenant to observe the laws of the Torah after the return of the Babylonian exiles. The Great Assembly was the supreme institution of the Jewish people during the time it was active, from the latter half of the fifth century B.C.E.

arba'ah shomerim ("four bailees") the four types of bailees in Jewish law—the unpaid bailee (*shomer ḥinam),* the borrower (*sho'el*), the paid bailee (*shomer sakhar*) and the hirer (*sokher*)

arev kabbelan one who has undertaken to be a surety by a declaration that entitles the creditor to look to him for payment without first pursuing a claim against the principal debtor

arka'ot (shel goyim) non-Jewish courts

arvit evening prayer

asharta judicial "certification" that a legal document has been properly authenticated

asmakhta ("something to lean on," "supportive device") (1) an action or transaction without an unqualified and deliberate intention to take the action or enter into the transaction; (2) a transaction involving a penalty or forfeiture; (3) exegesis identified by the Sages as integrative, not creative; (4) according to some, a strained and far-fetched (symbolic and figurative) exegesis that is necessarily only integrative

avak ribbit ("dust of interest") any form of benefit (other than actual stipulated interest) received by a lender that exceeds the value of the money or property lent; it is not expressly prohibited by the Torah, but is rabbinically proscribed because it partakes of the nature of interest

av bet din ("father of the court") (1) one of the two national leaders during the period of the Zugot; (2) presiding judge

avot nezikin ("fathers of damages") primary categories of causes of damage, namely, "ox" "pit," "grazing animal," and "fire." *See bor, mav'eh,* and *shor*

Bagaẓ acronym for *Bet Din Gavo'ah le-Ẓedek,* which *see*

bal tigra ("you shall not take away") the prohibition (Deut. 4:2, 13:1) against taking away from any commandments (*miẓvot*) set forth in the Torah; antonym of *bal tosif*

bal tosif ("you shall not add") the prohibition (Deut. 4:2, 13:1) against adding to the commandments (*miẓvot*) set forth in the Torah

baraita, ***pl.*** **baraitot** tannaitic *dictum* not included in the Mishnah (capitalized if referred to collectively)

be-di-avad ("after the fact," ***ex post*****)** usually employed in connection with the question whether an act in violation of a prohibition is not only a transgression but also without legal effect. *See also le-khateḥillah*

bein adam la-Makom ("between man and God") (1) involving human relationships with God; (2) pertaining to "religious" law as distinguished from civil law; (3) pertaining to matters of private conscience

bein adam le-ḥavero ("between a person and his fellow") (1) involving relationships between people; (2) pertaining to civil as distinguished from "religious" law

berurim ("selected ones," "arbiters") (1) members of the community council; (2) representatives for enacting legislation; (3) arbitrators selected by the parties; (4) lay judges; (5) communal leaders

bet din, ***pl.*** **battei din ("house of law")** (1) a court or panel of judges who adjudicate in accordance with the *Halakhah;* (2) a Jewish arbitral tribunal

Bet Din Gavo'ah le-Ẓedek "The High Court of Justice," the capacity in which the Supreme Court of Israel sits as a court of original jurisdiction to review administrative or governmental action claimed to be arbitrary or in excess of jurisdiction

bet din shel hedyotot ("a court of ordinary people") (1) a court lacking a rabbinic judge who is ordained; (2) a court composed entirely of laymen not knowledgeable in the law

Corpus Juris (Civile) ("Body of the [Civil] Law") (1) The Code of Justinian; (2) a comprehensive legal code that has achieved ultimate authoritative status

corpus juris the total body of law in a given legal system

darkhei shalom ("the ways of peace") the social and religious interest in peace and tranquillity

darshan (1) "exegete"; (2) preacher, homilist

dat (1) religious faith; (2) law, particularly law based on custom; (3) established practice

dayyan ("judge") a judge according to the *Halakhah;* a judge of a rabbinical court

de-oraita "Biblical"; the precise contours of this concept cannot be indicated in a glossary. *See* vol. 1, pp. 207ff.

de-rabbanan "rabbinic"; for the precise contours of this concept, *see* vol. 1, pp. 207ff.

derishah va-ḥakirah ("inquiry and examination") thorough interrogation of witnesses by the *dayyanim* of a *bet din*

din, *pl.* **dinim ("law")** (1) law generally; (2) "interpretation," particularly analogical or syllogistic interpretation or *a fortiori* reasoning; (3) sometimes, law included in the Order of *Nezikin;* (4) law based on a source other than custom or legislation

din Torah (1) Jewish law generally; (2) a case before a rabbinical court

dinei issur ve-hetter ("laws of prohibition and permissibility") laws governing religious and ritual matters, *i.e.*, matters involving relationships with God

dinei kenasot ("law of fines") (1) laws in civil cases pursuant to which the prescribed payment is not equivalent to actual loss suffered; (2) in modern usage, also a criminal fine or civil penalty

dinei malkot or **makkot ("laws of flogging")** laws relating to offenses punishable by flogging

dinei mamonot ("monetary laws") the body of Jewish law generally, but not completely, corresponding to civil law in contemporary legal systems

dinei nefashot ("law of souls") the body of Jewish law involving (a) capital crimes, (b) crimes punishable by corporal punishment, or (c) criminal law

din emet le-amito ("a judgment that is completely and truly correct") a judgment that combines principled decisionmaking with individualized fairness and equity based on thorough understanding of the particular circumstances as well as the law and the general background

divrei kabbalah ("matters of tradition") (1) the writings of the Prophets and the Hagiographa; (2) teaching transmitted orally by teacher to disciple, from one generation to the next; (3) Jewish mysticism (a much later meaning)

divrei soferim ("words of the Scribes") (1) equivalent to *de-rabbanan;* (2) matters essentially rooted in the written Torah but explained by the Oral Law; (3) enactments of the Scribes

divrei Torah ("words of the Torah") equivalent to *de-oraita* ("Biblical")

ed sheker "false witness"

edim zomemim ("scheming witnesses") witnesses who conspire to testify falsely

ein li ("I have nothing") an oath by a debtor attesting inability to pay the debt and undertaking to fulfill certain stringent requirements as to future earnings

erusin ("betrothal") (1) synonym for *kiddushin;* creates the personal status of husband and wife *vis-à-vis* the whole world, but marital rights between the couple do not arise until after *nissu'in, i.e.,* entry under the *ḥuppah* (marital canopy); (2) (in modern Hebrew) engagement

eruv ("merging") a method or device to (a) extend the boundaries within which one may walk or carry on the sabbath, or (b) permit food to be cooked on a festival for consumption on the sabbath immediately following

Even ha-Ezer one of the four principal divisions of the *Sefer ha-Turim* and the *Shulḥan Arukh,* dealing mainly with family law

exilarch the head of the internal Jewish government in the Babylonian diaspora

gabbai, *pl.* **gabba'im** (1) collector of dues, charitable contributions, or assessments; (2) director of a craft guild; (3) manager or director of a synagogue, with particular reference to the religious service

gaon, *pl.* **geonim** *see geonim*

garmi (geramei, gerama) (1) indirect causation; (2) harm other than by direct physical impact

GeFeT Hebrew acronym for "Gemara, Ferush, and Tosafot," *i.e.,* Talmud, Rashi, and Tosafot

Gemara ("completion" or "study" or "tradition") that part of the Talmud that contains discussion of the Mishnah

gematria a method of reaching or supporting conclusions on the basis of the numerical equivalents of letters of key words

gemirut da'at serious, deliberate, and final intent, without reservation, to enter into a legal transaction or perform a juristic act

geonic pertaining to the *geonim* or the gaonate

geonim heads of Talmudical academies (*yeshivot*), (the most famous being Sura and Pumbedita in Babylonia), from the end of the sixth or middle of the seventh century C.E. to the middle of the eleventh century C.E. in the west and the thirteenth century in the east

get bill of divorcement

get me'usseh ("a compelled divorce") a divorce that is invalid because given not voluntarily but rather as a result of improper compulsion

gezel mi-divreihem ("robbery by their words") theft under rabbinic law, *i.e.,* acts designated by the Rabbis as theft, although they do not constitute theft under Biblical law and were not prohibited by the Bible at all

gezerah ("decree") legislative enactment by the halakhic authorities; in the technical sense, as used by some authorities, limited to an enactment that extends or adds prohibitions beyond preexisting *Halakhah,* as distinguished from *takkanah,* an enactment prescribing performance of designated acts

gezerah shavah ("[comparison with] similar matter") inference from similarity of words or phrases. One of the thirteen canons of Biblical interpretation

guda ("wall") a ban

ha'anakah ("bonus," or "gratuity") a sum given to a Hebrew slave upon attaining freedom after six or more years of service; *see* Deuteronomy 15:11–18

haftarah, *pl.* **haftarot** prophetic reading that supplements the weekly Torah portions read during the synagogue service on sabbaths and other holy days

ḥakham, ***pl.*** **ḥakhamim ("sage")** (1) through the Talmudic period, rabbinic Sage; (2) in subsequent periods, halakhic authority, Talmudic scholar

halakhah le-ma'aseh a legal norm intended to be applied in practice, as distinguished from a theoretical or academic statement

Halakhah the generic term for the entire body of Jewish law, religious as well as civil

halakhah, ***pl.*** **halakhot ("the law")** (1) a binding decision or ruling on a contested legal issue; (2) a statement of a legal rule not expressly based on a Biblical verse, made in a prescriptive form; (3) in the plural, a collection of any particular category of rules

halakhah le-Moshe mi-Sinai ("law given to Moses at Sinai") (1) a law specifically given to Moses at Sinai, not indicated by or deducible from the Biblical text; (2) a law unanimously accepted by the Sages, having a tenuous connection with the Biblical text, given the designation to emphasize the law's authority; (3) a law so well settled that it is as authoritative as if it had explicitly been given to Moses at Sinai

halanat ha-din ("deferring judgment") deliberation in judgment

ḥaliẓah ("removal," "pulling off") release from levirate marriage by a rite whose central feature is removal of a sandal from a foot of the *levir. See* Deuteronomy 25:7–10. *See also levir*

ḥasid (1) pious; (2) equitable, more generous than the law requires; (3) punctilious in observance; synonym for *ḥaver*

haskamah, ***pl.*** **haskamot** (1) "agreement"; (2) (as the term was used by Spanish halakhic authorities) enactment

hassagat gevul (1) "removing a landmark" [*i.e.*, boundary marker]; (2) copyright infringement; (3) unfair competition; (4) unfair interference with contract or economic advantage

ḥaver (1) "friend," "comrade, "fellow"; (2) one punctilious in observance of the laws of ritual purity, (3) generally a halakhic scholar

ḥazakah (from ***ḥazak,*** **"strong")** (1) a mode of acquisition of property; (2) a legal presumption; (3) possession; (4) the rule that possession of real property for three years under claim of right is equivalent to a deed as proof of ownership; (5) an act of dominion such as putting up a fence or locking the premises

hedyot ("ordinary") (1) pertaining to mundane affairs, as distinguished from matters of Torah; (2) layman; (3) one untutored in the law

hefker bet din hefker ("ownerless [declared by] a ***bet din*** **is ownerless")** a halakhic court has the authority to expropriate property; the principle was later used as authority to legislate

hefker ẓibbur hefker ("ownerless" [declared by] the community is ownerless") the community has the authority to expropriate property and legislate

hekkesh ("analogy") analogical reasoning, a method of Biblical interpretation

hekkesh ha-katuv ("Scriptural analogy") analogy made by the Bible itself

henpek same as *asharta,* which *see*

ḥerem, ***pl.*** **ḥaramim ("ban")** (1) a ban as a sanction for transgression; (2) in its most severe form, total excommunication, an enforced exclusion from communal Jewish religious, social, and civic life; (3) oath; (4) sanctification

ḥerem ha-yishuv ("ban with respect to settlement") an enactment prohibiting settlement in a town without the consent of the townspeople, and providing penalties for violation

ḥezkat kashrut "presumption of propriety," *i.e.*, the presumption that persons behave correctly and that what should have been done has been properly done

ḥezkat shanim "possession for [a specified number of] years," which may serve as a substitute for proof of ownership

ḥiddushim, *sing.* **hiddush ("innovations")** novellae, *i.e.*, new legal interpretations and insights

hilkheta Aramaic for *halakhah*

hilkheta gemiri (1) "a determined [settled and accepted] rule"; (2) a rule handed down by tradition; (3) equivalent of *halakhah le-Moshe mi-Sinai*

hilkheta ke-vatra'ei "the law is in accordance with [the view of] the later authorities"

ḥiyyuv (1) contract; (2) obligation; (3) debt

ḥok (1) law; (2) statute; (3) regulation

hora'at sha'ah ("a directive for the hour") a temporary legislative measure permitting conduct forbidden by the Torah when such legislation is a necessary precaution to restore people to the observance of the faith; some legislation originally adopted or justified as a temporary measure has become an established part of Jewish law

Ḥoshen Mishpat one of the four principal divisions of the *Sefer ha-Turim* and the *Shulḥan Arukh*, dealing mainly with matters of *mishpat ivri*

ḥuppah the nuptial "canopy," under which bride and groom join in the concluding phase (*nissu'in*) of the marriage rite

innuy ha-din ("torture of the law") delay of justice, the law's delays

issur, also **issura ("prohibition")** and **issur ve-hetter ("prohibition and permission")** "religious" or ritual law; laws other than *dinei mamonot*

Jerusalem Talmud the Talmud of the *amoraim* of the Land of Israel

jus cogens ("compelling law") a mandatory legal norm not subject to variance or modification by agreement of the parties affected

jus dispositivum ("displaceable law") a legal rule that can be varied by agreement, as distinguished from *jus cogens*, which may not be varied by agreement

jus naturale ("natural law") law whose source is "in nature" and which is therefore common to all humanity; sometimes called "higher law," superior to law pronounced or enacted by human agency. *Cf.* Noahide laws

jus non scriptum ("unwritten law") in Roman law, law not reduced to writing, *e.g.*, custom. Not synonymous with the Jewish Oral Law

jus scriptum ("written law") in Roman law, law that has been reduced to writing. Not synonymous with the Jewish Written Law

kabbalah ("tradition") *See divrei kabbalah*

kabbalat kinyan assumption of an obligation made binding by exchange of a symbolic object (*sudar*) as "consideration" for the obligation

kallah (1) semiannual assembly of scholars and teachers at a *yeshivah*; (2) bride; (3) daughter-in-law

kal va-ḥomer ("easy and hard," "minor and major") inference *a fortiori* (one of the thirteen canons of Biblical interpretation)

karet, *pl.* **keritot** or **keretot ("extirpation"** or **"excision")** premature death by divine action as punishment for sin

kasher ("fit") (1) kosher; (2) competent (as applied to a witness)

kashrut ("fitness") dietary laws as to permissible and forbidden foods and food preparation. *See also ḥezkat kashrut*

kehillah the organized Jewish community, especially when possessed of juridical autonomy

kelalei ha-Talmud ("principles of the Talmud") methodology and rules of halakhic decision making

kerem be-Yavneh ("the vineyard in Yavneh") the academy of the Sages in Yavneh (also called Jabneh and Jamnia)

ketubbah, *pl.* **ketubbot ("writing")** marriage contract prescribing a wife's economic entitlements during the marriage and in the event of divorce or the husband's death, in addition to such other provisions as may be agreed by the parties

Ketuvim ("writings") the Hagiographa; *i.e.*, the third division of the Hebrew Bible, the other two being the Torah (Pentateuch) and the Prophets

kim li ("it is established for me") a plea that the defendant's position is supported by a halakhic authority, and that therefore the defendant is not liable. The plea lost its effectiveness with the acceptance of the *Shulḥan Arukh* as the authoritative code of Jewish law

king's law (*mishpat ha-melekh*) the legal authority of the Jewish king (later extended to other forms of Jewish governance), which includes the power to temper the *Halakhah* to meet social needs

kinyan ("acquisition") (1) a formal mode of acquiring or conveying property or creating an obligation; (2) ownership; (3) contract; (4) abbreviation of *kinyan sudar*

kinyan agav karka ("acquisition incident to land"); also **kinyan agav** a conveyance of land in which chattels are incidentally transferred without limitation as to quantity, kind, location, or value

kinyan ha-guf ownership or acquisition of property as distinguished from the right to income

kinyan ḥalifin ("acquisition by barter") exchange of one chattel for another, in which each party acquires the other's chattel

kinyan meshikhah ("acquisition by pulling") a mode of acquisition created by an enactment pursuant to which ownership is not acquired upon payment of the purchase money (which is sufficient under Biblical law to transfer ownership to the buyer) but is acquired only when actual possession is taken

kinyan perot (1) the right to income; (2) acquisition of the right to income

kinyan sudar ("acquisition by kerchief") symbolic barter. The transferee gives the transferor a symbolic object such as a *sudar* (kerchief) in exchange for the object that is the subject of the transaction. The *sudar* is returned to the transferee upon completion of the transaction. This mode of acquisition is also used to create a contractual obligation

kiyyum shetarot ("validation of legal instruments") judicial authentication and certification of legal instruments

Knesset the Israeli parliament

kohen "priest," a member of the tribe of Levi descended from the branch of the tribe authorized to perform the Temple service and other sacred duties

kol de-alim gaver ("whoever is the stronger [of claimants to property] prevails") whoever obtains possession by self-help when self-help is permissible may retain the property

kol di-mekaddesh ada'ata de-rabbanan mekaddesh ("all who marry do so subject to the conditions laid down by the Rabbis") a principle upon which the Rabbis were empowered to annul marriages

kum va-aseh ("arise and do") a category of legislation permitting the performance of an act prohibited by the Torah

laẓeit yedei shamayim ("to fulfill a duty in the sight of Heaven") fulfilling a moral, but not legal, obligation

le-hatnot al mah she-katuv ba-Torah ("to contract out of a law contained in the Torah") by agreement between the parties, varying or rendering inapplicable a rule of the Torah

le-khateḥillah ("in the beginning") *ex ante,* in the first instance. *See also be-di-avad*

le-ma'aseh ("for action") in actual practice, or for practical application as distinguished from *"le-halakhah"* ("for law," *i.e.,* as theoretical doctrine, not practical application)

le-migdar milta ("to safeguard the matter") the principle that authorizes the halakhic authorities, as a protective measure, to adopt enactments in the field of criminal law that prescribe action the Torah prohibits

lefi sha'ah ("temporarily") a principle authorizing legislation permitting conduct contrary to the Torah as a temporary measure under exigent circumstances

leshon benei adam ("colloquial usage of the people") (1) the principle that terms in a legal document should be construed according to their colloquial meaning, not in the sense used in Scripture or by the Sages; (2) according to R. Ishmael, the principle that the Torah speaks as people speak, and therefore there are redundancies in the Torah and not every word has midrashic significance

letakken olam ("to improve [or mend] the world") to promote the public welfare

levir brother-in-law of the widow of a man who has died leaving no children; he must marry the widow unless the rite of ḥaliẓah is performed (Deut. 25:5–10). *See also ḥaliẓah*

lifnim mi-shurat ha-din ("on the inside of the line of the law") acting more generously than the law requires

ma'amad sheloshtan ("a meeting of the three") a method of assignment of property rights or obligations: the creditor-assignor, in the presence of the debtor and the assignee, states that the ownership of the property or obligation is assigned to the assignee

ma'aseh, ***pl.*** **ma'asim** "act," "incident," "event," or "case" that is the source of a new halakhic norm or declarative of a preexisting norm

ma'aseh adif ("a *ma'aseh* takes precedence") a *ma'aseh* is entitled to particular deference

ma'aseh ha-ba ba-averah a transaction involving illegality

ma'aseh rav "a *ma'aseh* is [of] great [significance]"

ma'aseh yadeha "her [a wife's] handiwork," *i.e.*, the domestic services to which a husband is entitled from his wife in consideration of his obligation to support her

mah lo leshakker ("why should he lie") *see migo*

makkot mardut disciplinary flogging

malkot flogging; stripes

malshinut (1) "slander"; (2) informing, betrayal, *i.e.*, a slanderous accusation against a Jew of a kind that, if heard by a non-Jew, would likely cause harm to the person accused

mamon; also **mamona** "money" matters, *i.e.*, civil-law matters, as distinguished from religious-law matters

mamzer ("misbegotten") offspring of an incestuous or adulterous union that is subject to capital punishment by a court or extirpation (*karet*) by God; often mistranslated as "bastard," in the sense of one born out of wedlock

Mappah ("Tablecloth") the title of the commentary by Moses Isserles (Rema) on Joseph Caro's *Shulḥan Arukh* ("Set Table")

mattenat bari ("gift of a healthy person") a form of disposition of property essentially equivalent to a will, whereby the donor "gives" property to his beneficiaries but retains possession and control during his lifetime

mattenat shekhiv me-ra ("gift of one facing imminent death") gift in contemplation of death made by a *shekhiv me-ra*, or the last will and testament of a *shekhiv me-ra*, for which the usual formal requirements are relaxed

me-aḥar ("since") *see migo*

Megillah "scroll," usually referring to the Book of Esther

meḥusar amanah ("lacking in trustworthiness") a description applied by a court as a sanction to a person who reneges on a transaction as to which there is only an unenforceable oral agreement

me'ilah ("sacrilege") unlawful use of consecrated property

Mejelle the Ottoman code of civil law, based on Mohammedan principles and formally repealed in the State of Israel in 1984

melog, also **nikhsei melog ("plucked [usufruct] property")** property belonging to a wife, of which the income belongs to the husband and the principal remains the wife's; the husband is not responsible for loss or diminution in value of *melog* property as he is for *ẓon barzel* property

memrah, ***pl.*** **memrot ("statement")** a law originated by the *amoraim*

meshikhah ("pulling") *see kinyan meshikhah*

meturgeman (1) spokesman; (2) one who repeated aloud the words of a speaker to a large audience for whom it would be difficult to hear the speaker directly; (3) interpreter

me'un ("refusal") disaffirmance by a woman of a marriage entered into when she was a minor

meẓavveh meḥamat mitah "a testator on the brink of death," for whose will the usual formal requirements are relaxed

mezuzah (1) parchment scroll containing Deuteronomy 6:4–9 and 11:13–21, affixed to the right doorpost in a wooden, metal, or other case; (2) doorpost

mi-de-oraita *see de-oraita*

mi-de-rabbanan *see de-rabbanan*

middah, *pl.* **middot** (1) canon of interpretation; (2) desirable quality of character

middat ḥasidut ("the quality of piety or benevolence") pious or altruistic behavior

mi-divrei soferim ("from the words of the Scribes") *see divrei soferim*

midrash (1) interpretation of Scripture and *Halakhah;* (2) exegesis; (3) a particular midrashic text (when used in this sense in this work, *midrash* is italicized)

midrash ha-Halakhah interpretation of *Halakhah*

midrash mekayyem ("confirming exegesis") integrative exegesis, by which existing law is "integrated" or connected with a Biblical text

midrash yoẓer ("creative exegesis") exegesis that is the legal source of new law

migo ("since," "because" [Aramaic]) a procedural rule to the effect that a claim, despite insufficiency of proof, is deemed valid "since" (or "because") if the claimant had desired to lie, he could have stated a more plausible case that would have been accepted as true, and therefore the weaker claim actually made should also be accepted; also called *me-aḥar* and *mah lo leshakker*

mikveh ("collection of water") ritual bath

minhag (1) "custom" (in modern Hebrew, custom operating as an independent legal norm), *cf. nohag;* (2) legislative enactment (*takkanah*); (3) prescribed practice, *i.e.*, a legal rule for which the Torah itself is the source

minhag garu'a ("bad custom") custom deemed undesirable, which some halakhic authorities held for that reason legally ineffective

minhag ha-medinah ("custom of the region") local custom

minhag le-dorot ("a prescribed practice for the generations") a law for all time

minhag mevattel halakhah ("custom overrides the law") the principle that in monetary matters, custom controls even if contrary to the *Halakhah*

minḥah afternoon prayer

minyan ("number") a quorum of ten, the minimum number for public congregational prayer

mi she-para ("He Who punished . . .") an imprecation by the court addressed to a party who has violated a moral obligation for which there is no legal sanction

Mishnah the code of R. Judah Ha-Nasi, redacted about 200 C.E., which is the basis of the Gemara

mishnah, *pl.* **mishnayot** the smallest division of the Mishnah; the Mishnah is divided into Orders, tractates, chapters, and mishnayot (paragraphs)

mishnat ḥasidim ("standard of the pious") a higher ethical and personal standard than the law requires

Mishneh Torah Maimonides' Code, also called *Yad ha-Ḥazakah*

mishpat (1) adjudication, the act of judging; (2) decision; (3) justice; (4) a system of laws; (5) a legal right; (6) custom, usage, or practice

mishpat ivri ("Jewish law") that part of the *Halakhah* corresponding to what generally is included in the *corpus juris* of other contemporary legal systems, namely, laws that govern relationships in human society

mishpat ha-melekh *see* "king's law"

mishum eivah ("because of enmity") a principle of legislation to the effect that laws should be designed to prevent strife and enmity

miẓvah, *pl.* **miẓvot ("commandment")** (1) religious obligation; (2) good deed

miẓvah ha-teluyah ba-areẓ ("precept dependent upon the land") a precept directly relating to the Land of Israel, *e.g.*, the sabbatical year and the law of the firstfruits

mored a "rebellious" husband who refuses to cohabit with his wife

moredet a "rebellious" wife who refuses to cohabit with her husband

mu'ad ("forewarned") having given notice of propensity for causing harm. Opposite of *tam;* if the cause of harm is *mu'ad*, damages are higher than if the cause is *tam*

na'arah ("girl") a female minor, *i.e.*, a girl who is more than twelve years and one day old but has not reached the age of twelve years, six months, and one day

na'arut ("girlhood") the legal status of a *na'arah*

nasi, *pl.* **nesi'im ("patriarch")** president of the Sanhedrin

naval bi-reshut ha-Torah ("scoundrel within the bounds of the Torah") one who keeps within the letter but violates the spirit of the Torah

nekhasim benei ḥorin ("free [*i.e.*, unencumbered] property") property fully subject to execution of a judgment against the owner

nekhasim meshu'badim ("encumbered property"); nekhasim she-yesh lahem aḥarayut ("property bearing responsibility") real estate, which is responsible for and secures the owner's contractual obligations by virtue of an automatic lien created by entry into the contract

nekhasim she-ein lahem aḥarayut ("property bearing no responsibility") personal property, as to which no lien arises upon the creation of a contractual obligation

Nevi'im the Prophets, *i.e.*, the second division of the Hebrew Bible, the other two being the Torah and the Ketuvim (Hagiographa)

nezikin (1) damages; (2) torts; (3) injuries

niddui ("banning") semi-ostracism, a less severe ban than total excommunication

nikhsei melog *see melog*

niksei ẓon barzel *see ẓon barzel*

nissu'in ("marriage") joinder under the *ḥuppah* (wedding canopy). *See also erusin*

nohag (1) "usage," "conventional custom"; (2) in modern Hebrew, custom given operative effect not as an independent legal norm but because parties are presumed to have acted pursuant to it. *Cf. minhag*

nos'ei kelim ("armor bearers") commentaries and glosses to a legal code

novellae *see ḥiddushim*

ona'ah ("overreaching") taking unfair advantage, as by fraud or deception, in a legal transaction (Lev. 25:14)

ones, pronounced **o-nes ("force")** (1) coercion; (2) duress; (3) act of God (*vis major*); (4) rape

Oraḥ Ḥayyim ("The Way of Life") one of the four principal divisions of the *Sefer ha-Turim* and the *Shulḥan Arukh,* generally dealing with ritual and religious matters outside the scope of *mishpat ivri*

Oral Law (Torah she-be-al peh) all of Jewish law except the part explicitly written in Scripture

parshanut ("explanation") (1) commentary; (2) synonym for midrash

pasul unfit; opposite of *kasher*

pe'ah, *pl.* **pe'ot** "corner" of a field, where a portion of the crop must be left for the poor by the reapers

perat u-khelal ("specification and generalization," "particular and general") inference from a specification followed by a generalization. One of the thirteen canons of Biblical interpretation

peri eẓ hadar ("product of hadar trees") the *etrog* (citron)

perushim "commentaries"

pesak, *pl.* **pesakim** (1) legal ruling; (2) judgment in a litigated case

pesharah "compromise," "settlement"

peshat "plain meaning," as distinguished from midrash

pilpul a method of halakhic study characterized by subtle dialectics and finespun distinctions

piskei ba'alei battim ("judgments of householders") lay judgments

posek, *pl.* **posekim** (1) authoritative decisionmaker, decisor; (2) codifier

praesumptio juris a legal presumption whereby the law assumes the existence of a fact or condition unless the presumption is rebutted by proof to the contrary

prosbul a legal formula authorized by an enactment of Hillel whereby a debt would not be released by the sabbatical year, notwithstanding Deuteronomy 15:1–12, which prescribes such release

rabbinic period the period following the *geonim* to the present time. There are three subperiods: (a) the period of the *rishonim* (eleventh to sixteenth century C.E.), (b) the period of the *aḥaronim* (sixteenth century to the beginnings of the Jewish Emancipation in the late eighteenth century), and (c) the post-Emancipation period

regi'ah ("rest," "allocation of time [rega]" an agreement in restraint of trade allocating time for work and rest (*margo'a*)

resh galuta exilarch

rishonim (1) in prior historical periods, "earlier" halakhic authorities who lived longer ago than in the then recent past; (2) in contemporary usage, halakhic authorities from the eleventh to the sixteenth century. *See also aḥaronim*

rosh yeshivah head of a talmudical academy

Sanhedrin (1) the assembly of 71 ordained scholars constituting the supreme legislative and judicial authority of the Jews during the period of the Second Temple and some time thereafter; (2) the name of a tractate of the Talmud

savoraim ("reasoners") rabbinic Sages from the end of the fifth to the beginning of the sixth or middle of the seventh century C.E.

seder, *pl.*, **sedarim ("order")** (1) one of the six major divisions of the Mishnah; (2) the ritual meal on the first night of Passover

sefer halakhot a code that includes a discussion of the range of views of the various authorities

Sefer ha-Turim the code of Jewish law written by Jacob b. Asher

sefer keritut "bill of divorcement"; *see also get*

sefer pesakim a code written in prescriptive terms, without discussion of legal theory or conflicting opinions

semikhah ("laying on of hands") rabbinic ordination

sevarah "legal reasoning"

shali'aḥ "agent"

she'elot u-teshuvot ("questions and answers") responsa

Shekhinah Divine Presence, the "immanent" or "indwelling" aspect of God

shekhiv me-ra one who is dangerously ill and faces or otherwise reasonably apprehends imminent death

Shema three Biblical passages recited twice daily, beginning with "Hear (shema) O Israel" (Deut. 6:4), constituting the confession of the Jewish faith

shetar, *pl.* **shetarot** (1) legal document; (2) contract; (3) deed

shev ve-al ta'aseh ("sit and do not do") a category of legislation directing that an affirmative precept, obligatory according to Biblical law, not be performed

shevi'it ("seventh [year]") the sabbatical year

shevu'at ha-edut ("witness's oath") an oath by one formally called upon to bear witness, to the effect that the affiant has no knowledge of the matter about which he is called to testify

shevut ("[sabbath] rest") (1) work rabbinically forbidden on the sabbath; (2) the rabbinical prohibition of such work

shi'bud nekhasim ("encumbrance of property") (1) lien, security interest; (2) the general lien on the real estate of an obligor that arises automatically upon creation of the obligation

shi'buda de-oraita "Biblical lien"

shiddukhin an agreement to enter into marriage

shikkul ha-da'at (1) [judicial] "discretion"; (2) decision on a moot point of law; (3) the zone of permissible latitude of a *dayyan* to disagree with other authorities

shimmush (1) "service" to the Torah; (2) attendance upon a halakhic scholar; (3) apprenticeship to a halakhic authority

shi'ur (1) prescribed measure; (2) "lesson," talmudic lecture

sho'el ("borrower") a bailee in possession of property as a result of borrowing it from another

shofet (1) "judge"; (2) magistrate, ruler

shomer ḥinam "an unpaid bailee," *i.e.*, one who undertakes without compensation to preserve property of another

shomer sakhar a "paid bailee" who is compensated for his service in connection with the bailment

shufra de-shetara ("adornment of the *shetar*") clauses designed to enhance the effectiveness of a legal document, *e.g.*, waiver of certain defenses otherwise available

Shulḥan Arukh (the "Set Table") the code of Jewish law written by Joseph Caro in the sixteenth century; the most authoritative of the Jewish legal codes

sitomta ("seal") mark placed on a barrel or other large container identifying the owner; placing the mark was recognized as a mode of acquisition

sofer, *pl.* **soferim ("counter," "scribe")** (1) a halakhic authority of the period of Ezra the Scribe; (2) a scholar of the Talmudic period. *See divrei soferim*

sof hora'ah ("the end of instruction") the completion of the Talmud

sokher ("hirer") a bailee or lessee who pays for the right to possession of the bailed or leased property

sudar ("kerchief") the instrument used in the most widespread mode of acquisition in Jewish law. *See kinyan sudar*

sugyah, *pl.* **sugyot** (1) passage; (2) discussion; (3) issue; a Talmudic subject or area

sukkah "booth" or "tabernacle" erected for the festival of *Sukkot*

supercommentary a commentary on a commentary

takkanah, *pl.* **takkanot ("improvement," "repair")** legislative enactment by halakhic or communal authorities. *See also gezerah*

takkanah kevu'ah ("established enactment") legislation permanently in effect, as distinguished from a temporary measure. *See also hora'at sha'ah*

takkanat ha-kahal "communal enactment"

takkanat ha-shavim ("enactment for the encouragement of penitents") a category of enactments to encourage penitence and rehabilitation, *e.g.*, an enactment providing that a thief may be relieved of the obligation to return stolen property and may pay its value instead, when the property has been incorporated into a building and would be very expensive to retrieve

takkanat ha-shuk ("enactment for the market") an enactment to promote the security of transactions in the open market ("market overt") by protecting the purchaser from a thief at such a market against claims by the owner of the stolen property

takkanat medinah "a regional enactment," intended to be applicable to many Jewish communities (*kehillot*)

talmid ḥakham ("wise scholar") (1) halakhic scholar; (2) learned and pious person

Talmud the Mishnah and the discussion of the Mishnah by the *amoraim* of Babylonia (comprising the Babylonian Talmud) and the *amoraim* of the Land of Israel (comprising the Jerusalem Talmud)

talmud ("learning") (1) academic study; (2) midrash; (3) the colloquy between *tannaim* on a specific law

Talmud Bavli Babylonian Talmud

talmud lomar ("the text teaches") a statement introducing a conclusion derived by implication through exegesis

Talmud Yerushalmi Jerusalem Talmud

tam ("innocuous") not chargeable with notice of propensity to cause harm (opposite of *mu'ad*); if the cause of harm is *tam*, damages are less than if the cause is *mu'ad*

tanna, *pl.* tannaim rabbi of the Mishnaic period (first century to approximately 220 C.E.)

tanna kamma ("the first *tanna*") a *tanna* whose opinion is stated first, without attribution, in a *mishnah*

tenai, *pl.* tena'im (1) "condition"; (2) legislative enactment (*takkanah*); (3) in plural, (a) marriage contract, (b) formal betrothal contract

tenai bet din ("stipulation [or requirement] imposed by the court") a legislative enactment (*takkanah*); the term indicates that the legislation is based on prior private agreements that have become more or less standard

terumah ("contribution") (1) priestly tithe, which only priests and their families are permitted to eat; (2) in modern Hebrew, a donation

teshuvah (1) responsum; (2) "return," or repentance; (3) refutation

tikkun (ha-)olam ("improvement [or mending] of the world") promotion of the public welfare; the verb form, "to promote the public welfare," is *letakken olam*

tofes ("template") the main body of a legal document, containing basic and generally standard provisions relating to the type of transaction involved

tom lev ("purity of heart") (1) good faith; (2) wholeheartedness; (3) integrity; (4) sincerity

Torah ("teaching") (1) the five books of Moses (Pentateuch); (2) the entire Hebrew Bible; (3) doctrine; (4) custom; (5) the prescribed procedure; (6) divine revelation; (7) all Jewish study, the entire religious and ethical and cultural literature of Judaism

Torah min ha-shamayim ("Torah from Heaven") divine revelation, the article of Jewish faith that the Torah was given by God to the Jewish people

Torah she-be-al-peh ("Oral Law") (1) all Jewish law that is not set forth in Scripture; (2) the entire Teaching of Judaism, including aggadah

Torah she-bi-khetav "Written Law," *i.e.*, the law explicitly set forth in the text of the Torah

toref ("blank") the parts of a legal document relating to the individual aspects of the transaction, filled in as to the details of the particular transaction

Tosafot ("additions") critical and explanatory glosses on the Babylonian Talmud written by a school of scholars in France and Germany in the twelfth and thirteenth centuries

tosefet ketubbah ("addition to the *ketubbah*") an optional supplement to the mandatory minimum amount of the *ketubbah*

Tosefta ("additions") a collection of tannaitic statements supplementing the Mishnah

tovei ha-ir ("the good citizens of the town") lay judges or communal officials. Sometimes called "the seven *tovei ha-ir;*" they were the political and economic heads of the community

uvda Aramaic for *ma'aseh*—an act, incident, event, or case that gives rise to new law or is declarative of an existing norm

Va'ad Arba (ha-)Araẓot ("Council of the Four Lands") the central institution of Jewish self-government in Poland and Lithuania from the sixteenth to the eighteenth century

Written Law law explicitly set forth in Scripture

Yad ha-Ḥazakah the *Mishneh Torah,* Maimonides' Code

Yavneh (Jabneh, Jamnia) a town in Judea where R. Johanan b. Zakkai established an academy for teaching and studying the law after the destruction of the Temple in 70 C.E. *See kerem be-Yavneh*

yeshivah ("a place of sitting") academy for Talmudic study

yeẓe din ẓedek le-ẓidko ("let a righteous judgment justly issue") a judgment must do justice, let justice be done

Yom Tov ("good day") festival, holiday

Yoreh De'ah ("it will teach knowledge") one of the four principal divisions of *Sefer ha-Turim* and the *Shulḥan Arukh*

zaken mamre ("rebellious elder") a rabbi who adjudicates contrary to the ruling of the Sanhedrin

zav, *pl.* **zavim ("bodily issue")** *Zavim* is the title of a tractate of the Talmud in the Order of *Tohorot*

ẓavva'at shekhiv me-ra a deathbed will, or a will of one who apprehends imminent death. *See shekhiv me-ra*

ẓon barzel ("iron flock") assets of a wife over which a husband has almost complete dominion; he is responsible for any loss or diminution in value of these assets, as distinguished from *melog* property, since he has undertaken to preserve "like iron" the value of the *ẓon barzel* property at the time of the marriage

Zug, *pl.* **Zugot ("pair")** the *Zugot* consisted of the *nasi* and the *Av Bet Din,* who were the acknowledged leaders of the Jewish people from 160 B.C.E. to the beginning of the common era